PUBLICATION

West Bengal TET

Paper 2 : Social Studies

Latest Edition
Practice Kit

10 Tests
10 Practice Test

Based On Real Exam Pattern

✓ Thoroughly Revised and Updated

✓ Detailed Analysis of all MCQs

<table>
<tr><td>Title</td><td>: West Bengal TET Paper 2 : Social Studies</td></tr>
<tr><td>Author Name</td><td>: Mr. Rohit Manglik</td></tr>
<tr><td>Published By</td><td>: EduGorilla Community Pvt. Ltd.</td></tr>
<tr><td>Publishers Address</td><td>: 12/651, First Floor Opp. Arvindo Park, Near Jama Masjid,
Indira Nagar, Lucknow, Uttar Pradesh-226016, India</td></tr>
</table>

Copyright EduGorilla

Disclaimer EduGorilla

TABLE OF CONTENTS

Child Development and Pedagogy

1. **Which one of the following statements best sums up the relationship between development and learning?**
   (a) Learning and development are synonymous terms.
   (b) Learning and development are inter-related in a complex manner.
   (c) Development is independent of learning.
   (d) Learning trails behind development.

2. **Which one of these is not a principle of development?**
   (a) Development is Life-Long
   (b) Development is influenced by both heredity and environment
   (c) Development is modifiable
   (d) Development is governed and determined by culture alone

3. **For optimum development of an individual:**
   (a) Only heredity is essential
   (b) Both heredity and environment are essential
   (c) Only environment is essential
   (d) Neither heredity nor environment is essential

4. **Process of primary socialisation begins from ______.**
   (a) infancy   (b) childhood
   (c) adolescence (d) adulthood

5. **According to Piaget the child is able to apply logical thoughts to all classes of problems, this development occurs in which of the following periods?**
   (a) The sensory motor period
   (b) The pre-operational period
   (c) The formal operational period
   (d) The concrete operational period

6. **Which of the following is a sub-stage in Kohlberg's 'conventional state's of Moral Development?**
   (a) Instrumental purpose and exchange
   (b) Universal ethical principles
   (c) Morality of contract, rights and law
   (d) Social concern and conscience

7. **Child centered system of education lays major emphasis on:**
   (a) Learning without burden
   (b) Incidental learning and self expression
   (c) Activity based learning
   (d) Learning under free environment

8. **Gardner's Multiple Intelligences Theory support the idea that:**
   (a) Most students can be considered "intelligent" in some way
   (b) Intelligence changes multiple times across the life span
   (c) Creative individuals are considered to be more intelligent
   (d) Intelligence can be multiplied through academic and non-academic tasks

9. **Shorya is a renowned dancer. So he must posses with ________.**
   (a) Linguisitc Intelligence
   (b) Body-kinesthetic Intelligence
   (c) Musical Intelligence
   (d) Inter-personal Intelligence

10. **The cause of downfall of a particular language is:**
    (a) Acceptance of language other than the native language
    (b) Narrow thinking
    (c) Intolerance
    (d) Both (B) and (C)

11. **Gender is a/an:**
    (a) Social Construct
    (b) Biological Determinant
    (c) Economic Concept
    (d) Psychological Entity

12. **Which of the following is NOT an effective strategy to cater to individual differences in the class?**
    (a) Reflect on one's verbal and non-verbal communication
    (b) Recognize and respect differences
    (c) Use diverse pedagogical strategies
    (d) Identify deficits in students and correct them

13. **Which one of the following is not a social-personal quality assessed under Continuous and Comprehensive Evaluation (CCE)?**
    (a) Cleanliness   (b) Painting
    (c) Co-operation   (d) Discipline

14. **In absolute grading, the reference point for an assessment of students performance happens to be a:**
    (a) Pre-determined standard
    (b) Standard determined on the basis of a normal probability curve
    (c) Standard determined on the basis, of dividing the equal percentage of cases from top to bottom
    (d) Standard determined on the basis of arbitrarily chosen percentages of cases for various grading groups

15. **A teacher has to enhance the readiness level of his students. Which will be the best way to do so?**
    (a) By organizing a creational activity in the classroom related to the particular topic
    (b) By organizing an indoor game in classroom
    (c) By story telling method
    (d) By giving monitoring to one of the student of the class

16. **Hearing impaired children exhibit:**
    (a) Barriers in communication by language
    (b) Barriers in moving around
    (c) Barriers in individuals self-care skills
    (d) Barriers in tactile skills

17. **In inclusive term, exceptional children means ______.**
    (a) the children with mental disabilities
    (b) the children with low IQ
    (c) the children with maladjustment problem
    (d) the gifted, intelligent, backward, mentally retarded childrens

18. **Children with special needs should be:**
    (a) Given no education at all.
    (b) Given only vocational training.
    (c) Segregated and put in separate institutions.
    (d) Included in 'regular' set-ups with special provisions.

19. **A creative learner refers to one who is:**
    (a) Capable of scoring consistently good marks in tests
    (b) Good at lateral thinking and problem-solving
    (c) Very talented in drawing and painting
    (d) Highly intelligent

20. **The gifted children:**

(a) Are always calm and quiet

(b) Always behave extraordinarily

(c) Solve the problem quickly

(d) Perform any task quickly

21. Which one of the following is the last stage of learning?

(a) Acquisition (b) Adaptation

(c) Fluency (d) Maintenance

22. Rohini, a newly admitted student, is unable to adjust to the classroom, as a teacher you will:

(a) Give her small group work and supervise.

(b) Will try to find out the reason.

(c) Will leave her on time.

(d) Will call the guardians

23. Which one of the following statements about teaching is not correct?

(a) Teaching is an interactive process.

(b) Teaching is a tripolar process.

(c) Teaching is an effect - directed process.

(d) Teaching is a process confined only to the classrooms.

24. Children's misconceptions and errors:

(a) Are a hindrance and obstacle to the teaching-learning process.

(b) Should be ignored in the teaching-learning process.

(c) Signify that children's capabilities are far inferior to that of adults.

(d) Are a significant step in the teaching-learning process.

25. Errors made by children are indicative of:

(a) Poor intelligence

(b) Low ability

(c) Their inability to reproduce knowledge

(d) Children's thinking process which is qualitatively different from that of adults

26. What is the definition of cognition?

(a) The process of acquiring and understanding knowledge through our thoughts, experience and sense

(b) The process of biological and psychological changes

(c) Developing attitude and interest

(d) Structural and physiological changes

27. Motivation and learning are inter-related. Which among the following is not true about the principle of motivation?

(a) Depends on curiosity

(b) It provides a purpose for learning

(c) Helps to get a higher position

(d) Skills and knowledge

28. Which of the following is an environmental factor which impact learning?

(a) Attitude

(b) Motivation

(c) Personality traits

(d) School

29. Learning is influenced by:
i. Psychological factors
ii. Socio-Cultural factors
iii. School-related factors
iv. Teacher related factors
Choose the correct option.

(a) i (b) i, ii

(c) i, ii, iii (d) i, ii, iii, iv

30. How should teachers promote motivation to learn among their students?

(a) Use incentives to help students learn.

(b) Give the students things to study that will be tested rather than things that won't.

(c) Give easier tests.

(d) Let the students make the test.

Language - I: English

Ques (31-39): Direction : Read the passage carefully and answer the questions that follow.

The Indus Waters Treaty is a water-distribution treaty between India and Pakistan, brokered by the World Bank, then the International Bank for Reconstruction and Development. The treaty was signed in Karachi on September 19, 1960, by Prime Minister of India Jawaharlal Nehru and President of Pakistan Ayub Khan.

According to this agreement, control over the three "eastern" rivers — the Beas, the Ravi, and the Sutlej — was given to India, while control over the three "western" rivers — the Indus, the Chenab, and the Jhelum — to Pakistan. In aftermath of the 2016 Uri attack, India reviewed the treaty and its provisions and proposed several changes. The treaty was reviewed by India to explore possible ways to use its share of water from rivers, including the Jhelum, flowing into Pakistan.

According to the IWT, India is permitted to construct water storage on western rivers -Indus, Jhelum, and Chenab -up to 3.6 million acre-feet for various purposes, including domestic use.

India is currently building 3 hydro projects on the rivers that flow to Pakistan in their course. One of this projects is the 1000 MW Pakul Dul dam on Chenab. Another one includes a 120 MW on Miyar, which would be located across Miyar Nalla, a right-bank tributary of the river Chenab and a 43 MW hydro project on the Lower Kalnai Nalla; another tributary of Chenab. Pakistan objected to these projects stating that these projects are in violation of the Indus Water Treaty of 1960.

India refused to countenance any change of design of the Miyar dam in J&K, as asked by Pakistan and plans to continue utilization of its allocation under the Indus Waters Treaty.

31. Which of the following river is not included according to IWT for the construction of water storage for India?

(a) Indus (b) Beas

(c) Jhelum (d) Chenab

32. Which of the following is not a correct pair of the eastern and western rivers according to the passage?

(a) Beas, Jhelum

(b) Ravi, Chenab

(c) Sutlej, Indus

(d) Chenab, Jhelum

33. Which of the following is refused by India as asked by Pakistan?

(a) 1000 MW Pakul Dul dam construction on Chenab.

(b) Permit to construct the water storage in eastern rivers.

(c) To allow the access to all the three eastern rivers.

(d) To countenance any change of design of the Miyar dam in J&K.

34. Choose the word which is most nearly the OPPOSITE in meaning to the word 'permit'.

(a) Allow (b) Back

(c) Ban (d) Authorize

35. Choose the word which is most nearly the SAME in meaning to the word 'explore'.

(a) Initiate (b) Investigate

(c) Intimate (d) Neglect

36. In <u>aftermath</u> of the 2016 Uri attack, India reviewed the treaty and its provisions and proposed several changes.
The part of speech 'aftermath' is a/ an:

(a) Adverb (b) Adjective

(c) Noun (d) Preposition

37. What is the theme of the passage?
(a) Rivalry between India and Pakistan
(b) River issues in both the countries
(c) Indus Waters Treaty
(d) Construction issues of Dam

38. Find an error in a part of the sentence and mark the corresponding option.
One of this/ projects is /the 1000 MW/ Pakul Dul dam on Chenab.
(a) One of this
(b) projects is
(c) the 1000 MW
(d) Pakul Dul dam on Chenab.

39. Which of the following river is included which is reviewed by India to use its share of water from rivers?
(a) Beas
(b) Sutlej
(c) Ravi
(d) Jhelum

Ques (40-45): Direction: Read the following poem and answer the question by choosing the correct/most appropriate option.
I love to rise in a summer morn,
When the birds sing on every tree;
The distant huntsman winds his horn,
And the skylark sings with me.
O! what sweet company.
But to go to school in a summer morn,
O! it drives all joy away;
Under a cruel eye outworn,
The little ones spend the day,
In sighing and dismay.
Ah! then at times I drooping sit,
And spend many an anxious hour.
Nor in my book can I take delight,
Nor sit in learning's bower,
Worn thro' with the dreary shower.
How can the bird that is born for joy,
Sit in a cage and sing.
How can a child when fears annoy,
But droop his tender wing,
And forget his youthful spring.

40. How does the school boy feel when he goes to school?
(a) Very happy
(b) Cheerful
(c) Romantic
(d) Unhappy

41. Whom is the school boy compared to?
(a) A bird
(b) Summer
(c) Winds
(d) Dreary shower

42. Which figure of speech has been used in the line?
sky-lark sings
(a) Apostrophe
(b) Alliteration
(c) Assonance
(d) Simile

43. Which figure of speech has been used in the line?
Under a cruel eye outworn.
(a) Anaphora
(b) Apostrophe
(c) Alliteration
(d) Metaphor

44. What does the sweet company refer to in the first stanza?
(a) Skylark
(b) Summer morning
(c) Huntsman horn
(d) Both (A) and (C)

45. What takes away all the happiness of the child?
(a) Going to the school in the winter morning
(b) Getup early in the morning
(c) Going to the school in the summer morning
(d) When skylark sings with him

46. A child learns his/her first language in a:
(a) Friendly setting
(b) Tutored setting
(c) Formal setting
(d) Natural setting

47. Language learning is _____.
(a) Not a conscious attempt by the learner.
(b) Conscious attempt by the learner.
(c) An act which occurs naturally.
(d) Conscious attempt by the teacher.

48. Teaching a lesson, through a number of language activities connected with the topic, refers to which principle of second language teaching?
(a) Structural Approach
(b) Multiple Line of Approach
(c) Circular Approach
(d) Bilingual approach

49. "From small utterances, the students can easily pass on to longer sentences." Which principle of second language teaching could be associated with this statement?
(a) Give Priority to Sounds
(b) Language Habit through Language Using
(c) Present Language in Basic Sentence Patterns
(d) Individual Differences

50. 'Decorum' in spoken language pertains to:
(a) Correct grammatical usage
(b) Voice quality or loudness
(c) Clarity and purity of style
(d) Appropriate gestures

51. Teaching of grammar will help the learners to:
(a) Differentiate the phoneme
(b) Have a basic knowledge of phonetics
(c) Have a good conversational skill
(d) Know the structure of the language

52. The principle of which of the following method is to memorize the rules of grammar?
(a) Structural Approach
(b) Direct Method
(c) Grammar Translation Method
(d) Natural Approach

53. What is the main challenge of teaching language in a diverse classroom?
(a) Challenge of a mixed-ability group of learners.
(b) Challenge of teaching-learning materials.
(c) Challenges to curriculum design.
(d) All of the above

54. Language skills can be learnt better:
(a) If they are taught in an integrated manner
(b) With the help of challenging drills
(c) Through written tests and practices
(d) If taught in isolation

55. Which of the following skills comes under the productive category of language skills?
(a) Speaking and Listening
(b) Listening and Reading
(c) Reading and Writing
(d) Writing and Speaking

56. Evaluation of speaking consists of:
(a) Evaluation of pronunciation
(b) Evaluation of intonation
(c) Evaluation of stress
(d) All of the above

57. Which of the following is not a useful activity of evaluating listening skills?
(a) Dictations
(b) Oral presentations
(c) Vocabulary assessment task
(d) Listen and Draw

58. Flannel board is useful for:
  (a) Teaching picture composition
  (b) Developing reading skill
  (c) Developing acting skill
  (d) Improving thinking skill

59. What can be used as props for dialogues to teach new lexical or structural items?
  (a) Textbook
  (b) Reference book
  (c) Realia
  (d) Dictionary

60. Remedial teaching is a:
  (a) Preparation of teaching
  (b) Systematic process
  (c) Pre-teaching program
  (d) Random process

Social Studies

61. The Vaishnav Bhakti saints in South India were called:
  (a) Alvars (b) Nayanars
  (c) Saguna (d) Nirguna

62. Name King Ashoka's son whom King Ashoka sent to other places to carry out duties of Buddhist missionary ______.
  (a) Kunala (b) Mahendra
  (c) Tivala (d) Jaluka

63. Who elects the Chairman of the Municipality?
  (a) Educated citizens of the town
  (b) Tax-payers of the town
  (c) Elected ward members
  (d) Members of the Legislative Assembly

64. The Chairman of the Drafting Committee of the Constituent Assembly of India was ______.
  (a) K. M. Munshi
  (b) D. P. Khaitan
  (c) Dr. B.R. Ambedkar
  (d) T. T. Krishnamachari

65. Which Article ensures Abolition of Untouchability?
  (a) Article 16 (b) Article 17
  (c) Article 18 (d) Article 19

66. Which of the following earthquake waves is first recorded on the Seismograph?
  (a) P-waves
  (b) Rayleigh waves
  (c) S-waves
  (d) Love waves

67. Direction : Match List - I with List-II

and select the correct answer using the codes given below:

List-I (Economic Activity/Agriculture region)	List-II (Country)
1. Commercial dairy farming	(a) Argentina
2. Commercial grain farming	(b) France
3. Commercial plantation farming	(c) Denmark
4. Commercial fruits production	(d) Malaysia

  (a) 1 - c, 2 - a, 3 - d, 4 - b
  (b) 1 - a, 2 - b, 3 - c, 4 - d
  (c) 1 - d, 2 - c, 3 - b, 4 - a
  (d) 1 - b, 2 - d, 3 - a, 4 - c

68. Which among the following volcanoes is not a part of the Circum Pacific Belt?
  (a) Mt. Stromboli
  (b) Cotopaxi
  (c) Fujiyama
  (d) Mt. Mayon

69. In the eight fold noble paths given by Budha, which of the following is the basis of 'Right Knowledge'?
  (a) Right speech and Right Action
  (b) Right Action and Right Living
  (c) Right Thought and Right Concentration
  (d) Right Faith and Right Resolve

70. Who destroyed Vikramasila in 1202 and Nalanda Universities in 1203A.D.?
  (a) Mahmud Ghazni
  (b) Mohmmad Gauri
  (c) Qutubudin Abek
  (d) Muhammad-bin-Baktiyar Khilji

71. Who abolished "Dual Government" in Bengal?
  (a) Sir John Shore
  (b) Warren Hastings
  (c) Lord Hastings
  (d) Lord Cornwallis

72. The Ryotwari System was introduced by:
  (a) Warren Hastings
  (b) Lord Cornwallis
  (c) Thomas Munro
  (d) Lord Ripon

73. Moving from tropopause to mesopause in the atmosphere, the temperature:
  (a) First increases then decreases.
  (b) First decreases then increases.

  (c) Remain constant.
  (d) Increases only.

74. Air moves from the region where the air ______.
  (a) Humidity is high to the region where the humidity is low
  (b) Pressure is low to the region where the pressure is high
  (c) Pressure is high to the region where the pressure is low
  (d) Humidity is low to the region where the humidity is high

75. Which of the following is FALSE in the context of Secularism in India?
  (a) The Indian state works in various ways to prevent domination of a particular religion.
  (b) The Indian state does not intervene in religious affairs.
  (c) The Indian state is not ruled by a religious group.
  (d) The Indian state adopts a strategy of non-interference to prevent domination a religious group over the other.

76. ________ of the Indian Constitution talks about the fundamental rights.
  (a) Part I (b) Part III
  (c) Part IV (d) Part VI

77. Under the Pradhan Mantri Shram Yogi Manthan Yojana, the minimum monthly pension for each subscriber is:
  (a) Rs. 3,000 (b) Rs. 2,500
  (c) Rs. 2,000 (d) Rs. 1,500

78. Nai Manzil Yojana is related to ________.
  (a) Pension to old women
  (b) Skill India
  (c) Relating to farmers
  (d) Skills to Minority Youth

79. Which of the following statements is true?
  (a) Social science deals with the history of man.
  (b) Social science prepares students for a holistic social life.
  (c) Social science is the study of human development.
  (d) Social Science is an extra-curricular course and not a core course.

80. Field work provides students:
  (a) First-hand book
  (b) A lot of home-work
  (c) First-hand knowledge
  (d) Short answer type test

81. The branch of science that deals with the institutions and activities of human society and studies the interactions of individuals as members of society is known as.
(a) Social science
(b) Educational Sociology
(c) Social studies
(d) Civics

82. The Social Studies teacher must be conversant with different methods of teaching mainly because:
(a) A teacher can encourage students' participation
(b) It helps the teacher to avoid unnecessary repetition
(c) There is no royal road to successful learning
(d) It helps the teacher in having control over the classroom

83. While teaching the means of production, the teacher can take students to a nearby factory. Which method of teaching social science is followed by the teacher?
(a) Role-play
(b) Demostration
(c) Field-work
(d) Questioning

84. Which one of the following is the correct sequence of Hebartian's five step approach of lesson plan?
(a) Preparation - Presentation - Application - Generalization - Association
(b) Preparation - Application - Association - Presentation - Generalization
(c) Preparation - Association - Presentation - Generalization - Application
(d) Preparation - Presentation - Association- Generalization - Application

85. Teacher needs to aim at achieving instructional objectives continuously by using:
(a) Formal or informal assessment
(b) Teaching-learning strategies
(c) Both (A) and (B)
(d) None of the above

86. How many stages involved in the development of critical thinking?
(a) 2　　　　(b) 4
(c) 5　　　　(d) 6

87. In Social Science, the recent NCF position paper on examination reform emphasizes on:
(a) Open-book exams
(b) Flexible sitting arrangement while testing
(c) Test performane
(d) Continuous assessment

88. Formal and Informal group plans are the forms of which teaching method ?
(a) Problem solving
(b) Brain storming
(c) Project
(d) Social Recitation

89. Which of the following misperception does a social science teacher face while teaching?
(a) Students consider it redundant as it does not teach daily life skills
(b) Some consider it is merely encyclopedia
(c) Subjects like history is emphasize on retention of information
(d) All of them

90. Which of the following question asked by a social studies teacher is based on a type of application suggested by Bloom's classification?
(a) What are the main features of the Indian Constitution?
(b) What was the impact of British rule on independent India?
(c) When the time in New Delhi is 12 noon, what time will it be in Paris?
(d) Are you in favor of parliamentary government and why?

91. How can we develop reasoning and support skills through social studies?
(a) By organizing field trips
(b) Through map notation exercises
(c) By conducting a quiz
(d) By holding a debate

92. The subject _____ encompass diverse concerns of society and includes a wide a range of content, drawn from the disciplines of history, geography, political science, economics and sociology.
(a) Social work
(b) Socially useful productive work
(c) Social sciences
(d) Sociology

93. What is the main reason for the plight of primary education in present times?
(a) Relying on guide books
(b) Nuclear family
(c) Students spend more time in doordarshan
(d) Teacher-student inappropriate ratio

94. Which of the following is termed as the Magna Carta of English Education in India?
(a) Elphinstone's minute
(b) Macaulay's minute
(c) Wardha education scheme
(d) Wood's Despatch

95. Which of the following laboratory resources is not generally used in geography teaching?
(a) Globe　　　(b) Model
(c) Rain gauge　(d) Timeline

96. Project work given to the students develops in them :
(a) Leadership
(b) Creativity
(c) Understanding of basic concepts
(d) All of above

97. Structured, unstructured and semi structured are the types of which of the following evaluation technique?
(a) Case study
(b) Interview
(c) Rating scale
(d) Questionnaire

98. Which of the following type of question is difficult and time consuming to prepare but relatively easy for evaluation?
(a) Objective
(b) Objective based
(c) Very short answer type
(d) Short answer type

99. Consider the following pairs:

Organization	Associated Leader
1. Indian League	Sisir Kumar Ghosh
2. Poona Sarvajanik Sabha	Badruddin Tyabji
3. Bombay Presidency Association	Pherozshah Mehta
4. Madras Mahajan Sabha	P. Anandacharlu

Which of the pairs given above is/are correct?
(a) 1 and 2 only
(b) 1 and 4 only
(c) 1, 3 and 4 only

(d) 2, 3 and 4 only

100. Consider the following pairs:

Center of revolt	Leaders
1. Delhi	Bahadur Shah
2. Kanpur	Khan Bahadur
3. Lucknow	Begum Hazrat Mahal
4. Bareily	Nana Saheb
5. Bihar	Kunwar Singh

Which of the pairs given above is/are correct?

(a) 1, 2 and 5 only
(b) 1, 2, 3 and 5 only
(c) 1, 3 and 5 only
(d) 2, 3, 4 and 5 only

101. Consider the following statements about, the Aruvippuram movement:
1. It was a movement born out of a conflict between the depressed classes and upper castes.
2. It was started by E.V. Ramaswamy Naicker.
3. The movement drew the famous poet, Kumaran Asan as a disciple of Narayana Guru.
Which of the statements given above is/are correct?

(a) 1 and 2 only (b) 2 and 3 only
(c) 1, 2 and 3 (d) 1 and 3 only

102. With reference to the Ramakrishna movement, consider the following statements:
1. One of the objectives of the mission is to bring together a band of monks dedicated to a life of renunciation and practical spirituality.
2. Swami Vivekananda founded Ramakrishna Math to promote this objective of building a band of monks.
Which of the statement given above is/are correct?

(a) 1 only
(b) 2 only
(c) Both 1 and 2
(d) Neither 1 nor 2

103. Consider the following statements:
1. Prithviraj III a Chahamana ruler defeated an Afghan ruler named Sultan Muhammad Ghori in 1191.
2. Sultan Mahmud of Ghazni was a contemporary of the Chola King Rajendra I.
Which of the statements given above is/are correct?

(a) 1 only

(b) 2 only
(c) Both 1 and 2
(d) Neither 1 nor 2

104. With reference to Mughal literature, consider the following pairs:

King	Writers/Poets
1. Akbar	Abul Faizi
2. Jahangir	Ghiyas Beg
3. Shah Jahan	Abdul Hamid Lahori

Which of the pairs given above is/are correct?

(a) 1 and 2 only (b) 2 and 3 only
(c) 1, 2 and 3 (d) 1and 3 only

105. With reference to Mughal India, what is/are the difference between 'jaat' and 'savar'?
1. 'Jaat' indicates the individual rank of an officer, while 'sawar' denotes the size of the army maintained by the mansabdar.
2. Even if the rank of sawar was higher than the rank of jaat, the rank of mansabdar was not affected in the official hierarchy as it was determined by the rank of caste.
Select the correct answer using the code given below :

(a) Only 1
(b) Only 2
(c) Both 1 and 2
(d) Neither 1 nor 2

106. With reference to the creation of Legislative Councils in a state, consider the following statements:
1. For the creation or abolition of the Legislative Council in a state, a simple majority is required in the Parliament.
2. A simple majority is also required in the state assembly for the proposal for the creation of a Legislative Council in the state.
Which of the above statements is/are correct?

(a) Only 1
(b) Only 2
(c) Both 1 and 2
(d) Neither 1 nor 2

107. Consider the following statements with respect to Family Courts Act, 1984:
1. It makes it obligatory for the state governments to set up a Family Court in every city with a population exceeding one million.
2. It provides for only one right of appeal which shall lie to the

District Court.
Which of the statements given above is/are correct?

(a) 1 only
(b) 2 only
(c) Both 1 and 2
(d) Neither 1 nor 2

108. Which of the following functions were performed by Constituent Assembly?
1. It ratified India's membership of the United Nations.
2. It abolished the privy purses.
Select the correct answer using the code given below:

(a) 1 only
(b) 2 only
(c) Both 1 and 2
(d) Neither 1 nor 2

109. Consider the following statements with reference to the Central Council of Ministers:
1. A nominated member can be appointed as a minister, but within six months he must become an elected member of either House of Parliament.
2. The salaries and allowances of ministers are given in the Second Schedule of the Indian Constitution.
Which of the statements given above is/are correct?

(a) 1 only
(b) 2 only
(c) Both 1 and 2
(d) Neither 1 nor 2

110. Which of the following statement(s) is/are correct about different ocean systems?
1. The mesopelagic zone is called the twilight zone because of the low amount of sunlight.
2. The bathypelagic zone is called the midnight zone in which no light enters.
Select the correct answer using the code given below :

(a) Only 1
(b) Only 2
(c) Both 1 and 2
(d) Neither 1 nor 2

111. With reference to frontal reproduction, consider the following statements:-
1. If a warm air mass moves towards a cold air mass, the contact area changes to a cold front.
2. The wind fronts bring about a sudden change in temperature and due to the rising of the air

clouds are formed and cause rain. Which of the above statements is/are correct?
(a) Only 1
(b) Only 2
(c) Both 1 and 2
(d) Neither 1 nor 2

112. Consider the following rivers:
1. Raidak
2. Rind
3. Sengar
Which of the above is/are the tributaries of Yamuna?
(a) 1, 2 and 3
(b) 2 and 3 only
(c) 1 and 2 only
(d) 1 and 3 only

113. Consider the followings:
1. Price of the commodity
2. Income of the consumer
3. Prices of related goods
4. Taste and preferences of the consume
Which of the above factors affects an individual's demand for a commodity?
(a) 1 and 4 only
(b) 2, 3 and 4 only
(c) 1, 2 and 3 only
(d) 1, 2, 3 and 4

114. With reference to Monetary Policy Committee, consider the following statements:
1. It is a constitutional and institutional framework under the Reserve Bank of India Act, 1934.
2. The Deputy Governor of RBI is the ex-officio chairman of the committee.
3. In 2014, a committee appointed by RBI under the then Deputy Governor Urjit Patel recommended setting up of Monetary Policy Committee.
Which of the above statement(s) is/are correct?
(a) 1 and 2 only
(b) Only 1
(c) Only 3
(d) 1, 2 and 3

115. Which of the following are the true functions of the electoral process in a democracy like India?
1. To keep the government responsive to the popular will
2. To bring together citizens to choose public decision-makers
3. To change the government periodically or if necessary
4. To support a competitive party system
Select the correct answer from the codes given below:
(a) 1 and 2
(b) 1, 2 and 3
(c) 1, 3 and 4
(d) 2, 3 and 4

116. Direction:
The following item consists of two statements, a statement I and statement II. Examine these two statements carefully and select the correct answer from the code given below.
Statement I:
Not content with merely laying down the fundamental principles of governance, the framers of the Indian Constitution followed the Government of India Act, 1919 in providing matters of administrative details.
Statement II:
The framers of the Indian Constitution had the apprehension that in the prevailing conditions of the country at that time, the Constitution might be subverted unless the form of administration was also included.
(a) Both Statements I and Statement II are individually true and Statement II is the correct explanation of Statement I.
(b) Both Statements I and Statement II are individually true but Statement II is not the correct explanation of Statement I
(c) Statement I is true but Statement II is false
(d) Statement I is false but Statement II is true

117. The principle of 'collective responsibility' under parliamentary democracy implies that
1. A motion of no confidence can be moved in the Council of Ministers as a whole as well as in an individual minister.
2. No person shall be retained as a member of the Council of Ministers if the Prime Minister says that he shall be dismissed.
Select the correct answer using the options given below.
(a) Only 1
(b) Only 2
(c) Both 1 and 2
(d) Neither 1 nor 2

118. With reference to the Circle of Illumination, consider the following statements:
1. It is the hypothetical line that divides the earth into two equal halves.
2. Location of the line on earth is independent of the season.
Which of the statements given above is/are correct:
(a) 1 only
(b) 2 only
(c) Both 1 and 2
(d) Neither 1 nor 2

119. In order to measure accurately the position of any place on the surface of the earth, knowledge of which of the following is required?
1. Latitude
2. Distance from the sea
3. Longitude
Choose the correct answer from the options given below:
(a) 1 and 2 only
(b) 2 and 3 only
(c) 1 and 3 only
(d) All of the above

120. With reference to Daylight Saving Time (DST), consider the following statements:
1. It is customary to set the clocks one hour ahead of standard time during the summer months.
2. Countries located in the Southern Hemisphere usually start DST in the month of March-April.
Which of the above statements is/are correct?
(a) Only 1
(b) Only 2
(c) Both 1 and 2
(d) Neither 1 nor 2

// Hints and Solutions //

1(B). Development and learning are inter-related and inter-dependent and contribute to each other.
- Development is a product of maturity and learning.
- Learning and development are inter-related in a complex manner.
- Maturity is more or less automatic, unfolding biological potential which is an irreversible sequence and entails biological changes.
- Such changes are relatively independent of environmental factors as long as environmental factors remain normal.
- There is a more or less permanent change in human behaviour from the individual's experience in the environment.
- Learning occurs across the entire life span, which differs from maturity.
- However, learning depends on the process of maturing i.e. individual readiness (mental and physical) for certain activities.

So, we conclude that learning and development are inter-related in a complex manner.

2(D). Principles of development include:
- Development is Life-Long/Principle of continuity: This principle defines that development is a life-long process as it does not stop at maturation and continues gradually until reaching its maximum growth.
- Development is modifiable: Development may be explained as the series of overall changes in an individual due to the emergence of modified structures and functions that are the outcome of the interactions and exchanges between the organism and its environment.
- Development follows a pattern: Prenatal (before birth) and postnatal (after birth) development of human beings follow a pattern or a predictable sequence. Physical development, motor or language development and intellectual development take place in definite sequences.
- Product of hereditary and environment: Hereditary and environment play a vital role in determining the development of an individual as all the mental and social traits depend on the environment and all the inborn traits, instincts, potentials, and I. Q. depends on heredity.

So, it could be concluded that development is governed and determined by culture alone is not a principle of development.

3(B). Heredity and environment are the elements that play a vital role in determining the personality development of an individual. How a person will develop depends on the environment but how far a person can develop depends on heredity.
- Heredity and environment play an important role in the development of the personality and other qualities in the individual.
- From the earliest moments of life, the interaction of heredity and the environment works to shape who children are and who they will become.
- While the genetic instructions a child inherits from his parents may set out a road map for development, the environment can impact how these directions are expressed, shaped or event silenced.
- In order to understand child development, it is important to look at the biological influences that help shape child development, how experiences interact with genetics and some of the genetic disorders that can have an impact on child psychology and development.
- The complex interaction of Heredity and the environment does not just occur at certain moments or at certain periods instead it is persistent and lifelong.

Thus, it can be concluded that for optimum development of an individual both heredity and environment are essential.

4(A). Primary socialization: Inculcation of norms and values within the family is called primary socialization. Here children want to know themselves and try to find their identity and learn the daily routine tasks of humans.

Characteristics of primary socialization:
- Primary socialization begins from the age of infancy.
- Self-identity formed.
- Children start to go familiar with their innate abilities and disabilities.
- Children start learning their daily needs, such as toilet training.

So, it is concluded that process of primary socialisation begins from infancy.

5(C). According to Piaget, in the 'Formal Operational Period', the child is able to apply logical thoughts to all classes of problems as in this period:
- Mental capabilities develop to the maximum level.
- Metacognition and problem-solving skills develop in children.
- Children understand world through abstract & scientific thinking.
- Children become capable of hypothetical and deductive reasoning.

So, it could be concluded that according to Piaget the child is able to apply logical thoughts to all classes of problems, this development occurs in 'Formal Operational Period'.

6(D). Stages of Moral Development: Kohlberg's theory is broken down into three primary levels. At each level of moral development, there are two stages.

Level 1. Preconventional Morality (4 to 10 years): Preconventional morality is the earliest period of moral development. At this age, children's decisions are primarily shaped by the expectations of adults and the consequences of breaking the rules. There are two stages within this level:
- Stage 1 (Obedience and Punishment): Children at this stage see "rules as fixed and absolute". Obeying the rules is important because it is a way to avoid punishment. In this children ignore the intention of others and instead focus on the fear of authority and negative consequences.
- Stage 2 (Instrumental purpose and exchange): At the individualism and exchange stage of moral development, children account for individual points of view and judge actions based on how they serve individual needs.

Level 2. Conventional Morality (10 to 13 years): The next period of moral development is marked by the acceptance of social rules regarding what is good and moral. During this time, adolescents and adults internalize the moral standards they have learned from their role models and from society.
- Stage 3 (Good-Boy Good-girl orientation): This stage of the interpersonal relationship of moral development is focused on living up to social expectations and roles. There is an emphasis on conformity, being "nice" and consideration of how choices influence relationships.
- Stage 4 (Social concern and conscience): This stage is focused on ensuring that social order is maintained. The focus is on maintaining law and order by following the rules, doing one's duty, and respecting authority.

Level 3. Postconventional Morality (13 to 16 years): At this level of moral development, people develop an understanding of abstract principles of morality. The two stages at this level are:
- Stage 5 (Social Contract and Individual Rights): At this stage, the people believe that rules of law are important for maintaining a society, but members of society should agree upon these standards.
- Stage 6 (Universal Ethical Principles): Kohlberg's final level of moral reasoning is based on universal ethical principles and abstract reasoning. At this stage, people follow these internalized principles of justice, even if they conflict with laws and rules.

So, we can conclude that social concern and conscience is a sub-stage in Kohlberg's 'conventional state's of Moral Development.

7(C). A child-centered system of education is designed to develop the individual and social qualities of a student rather than providing generalized information or training by way of the prescribed subject matter.

Characteristics of the child-centered education system:
- More focus is being placed on the holistic development of a child.
- To help the child become independent, responsible, and confident.
- Child-centered teachers engage in an 'active learning' process.
- Students actively engaged in their own learning.
- They have opportunities to investigate and discover.
- Continuous evaluation.
- Gives respect to the individuality of the child.

Thus, it can be concluded that the child-centered system of education lays major emphasis on activity-based learning.

8(A). Gardner's Multiple Intelligences Theory supports the idea that", Most students can be considered Intelligent" in some way.

For example: as all individuals have some different strengths, so the Intelligence. Fish is not a good climber as that of a monkey but has strength in swimming, so we cannot expect the fish to be good climbers instead we should recognize the natural potential otherwise they may lose their essence.

- The Teachers should be aware that every class has different learners, and they learn in different ways, including their own intelligence profile.
- Should practice content using several points of entry and various strategies.
- Knowing the learners in your current teaching context, what intelligences do they have and what activities can you implement to maximize their learning potential
- Students should be encouraged to practice their strengths and opposed to practicing one universal strength.

9(B).

Bodily-Kinesthetic Intelligence	Persons who said to be good at body movement, performing actions, and physical control. People have excellent hand-eye coordination, Physical movement, and motor control.	• Dancer • Builder • Sculptor • Actor

So, we can conclude that Shorya is a renowned dancer. So he must possess Body-kinesthetic Intelligence.

10(D). Our attitude towards diversity in languages influences the existence of linguistic diversity or multiline quality.

- If we have a positive attitude to linguistic diversity, we help in the existence and growth of all the languages spoken in the environment.
- On the contrary, intolerance and narrow thinking towards languages other than one's own may result in discord and disagreement.
- For example, there are 21 sub-castes in the Naga community and about the same numbers of languages are spoken in the community. People of a particular sub-group speak to the other members of their sub-group in their mother tongue. When people of one sub-group need to talk to people of the other sub-group they use Nagameez language and when they have to speak to people outside

their community (i.e. people outside Nagaland and Manipur) they use Hindi and English. This is an example of the positive attitude that Naga people have towards linguistic diversity and this is what makes them multilingual.

- On the other hand, residents of Goa keep fighting over the existence of Marathi and Konkani. Similarly, residents of Belgaon in Karnataka are arguing over the existence of Kannada and Marathi.

So, we conclude that the cause of the downfall of a particular language is intolerance and narrow.

11(A). Gender refers to the socially constructed differences between men and women. It refers to the masculine and feminine qualities, behavior, roles, and responsibilities that society upholds. Gender can be changed / re-oriented.

- Gender is such a familiar part of life that it usually takes a deliberate disruption of our expectations of how women and men are supposed to act to pay attention to how it is produced.
- Transvestites and transsexuals construct their gender status of dressing, speaking, walking, gesturing in the way of prescribed for women or men whichever they want to be taken for and so does any normal person.
- Gendering is legitimated by religion, law, science, and society's entire set of values.

So, from the above-mentioned points, it becomes clear that Gender is a social construct.

12(D). Individual differences are characteristic of all living organisms. It refers to the difference which distinguishes an individual from another on the basis of psychological characteristics.

Effective strategies to cater to individual differences in the class:

- Recognize and respect differences: Teachers should recognize individual differences in their classroom, fulfill students' needs and respect the diversity and individual differences of learners.
- Use diverse pedagogical strategies: Teachers should use diverse pedagogical strategies to teach students because every student learns in their style, some learn by reading, some learn by doing, etc.
- Reflect on one's verbal and non-verbal communication: While communicating with students teachers should pay attention to their verbal and non-verbal communication to provide required guidance.

So, we can conclude that identifying deficits in students and correcting them is not an effective strategy to cater to individual differences in the class.

13(B). Continuous and Comprehensive Evaluation (CCE) has been introduced as a school-based system of evaluation by the CBSE in 2009 with the enactment of the 'Right to Education Act.

- CCE refers to all-around development including both scholastic and co-scholastic aspects of a child's growth.
- It never assesses students according to their economic status rather it emphasizes the continuity of assessment.

The list of personal-social qualities (PSQ) that are assessed under Continuous and Comprehensive Evaluation:-

- Regularity and Punctuality
- Neatness (cleanliness)
- Discipline, Co-operation, and Responsibility
- Physical health
- Emotional stability and leadership qualities
- Consciousness with a spirit of social service
- Positive attitude towards school, teachers, peers, studies, and society
- Entrepreneurship, etc.

So, it becomes clear that painting is not a social-personal quality assessed under CCE.

14(A). In absolute grading, the reference point for an assessment of a student's performance is a pre-determined standard.

- Each point value is assigned a grade represented by a letter with each grade assigned based on a predetermined or predefined standard that corresponds to the level of performance by a student
- The grades are associated with that fixed standard irrespective of the distribution of grades in the class
- For example, all students who score 95% and above are collectively grouped under outstanding category and awarded an A grade the categories like outstanding, excellent, very good etc are predetermined and each grade specifically assigned are associated only with that predetermined standard
- This system is used to evaluate students under scholastic areas.

So, we can conclude that in absolute grading, the reference point for an assessment of students' performance happens to be a pre-determined standard.

15(A). A teacher can enhance the readiness level of his students by organizing a creational activity in the classroom related to the particular topic as:

- Inclusion of purposeful creational activities makes learning meaningful and fruitful. It is best for teaching students of class three.
- Creative expressions in learning ensure the active involvement of the child and develop the ability to assimilate the concept efficiently by building creative thinking skills.

Form of Creational Activities in Teaching-learning Process:
- Writing: Poetry, songs, dramas, etc.
- Graphic Arts: Designing posters, banners, etc.
- Music: Songs related to environmental messages.
- Movement and dance: Performing non-verbal arts.
- Puppetry: Transmitting environmental messages.

So, it could be concluded that organizing a creational activity in the classroom related to a particular topic will be the best way to enhance the readiness level of his students.

16(A). Hearing impairment refers to hearing loss that prevents a person from totally receiving sounds through the ear. If the loss is mild, the person has difficulty hearing faint or distant speech.

Language and Speech Development Barrier in Children with Hearing Impairment:
- Hearing impairment is a great barrier to the normal development of language; the child with such impairment is at a severe disadvantage in virtually all aspects of language development.
- A considerable number of educators of deaf individuals believe that many of the problems of people who are hearing-impaired related to social and intellectual development are primarily due to their deficiencies in language.
- When the child meets other hearing-impaired children and realizes other people face similar challenges and manage fine, regardless of language or level of hearing, it supports identity development and increases confidence.

So, we can conclude that Hearing-impaired children exhibit barriers in communication by language.

17(D). Exceptional Children refer to deviated children as they are the ones:
- who deviate significantly from the normal children in respect to social, mental, physical, and emotional characteristics.
- who show deviations falling far above or extremely below from the average which limits their participation in normal activities.

Exceptional types of children include:
- Gifted children: It refers to the children who perform tasks extraordinarily when compared with others of their peer group. They are independent in their judgments as they possess advanced logical and creative thinking.
- Intelligent children: These categories of children have divergent thinking, curious in nature, and are able to find solutions for different problems on their own.
- Backward children: These are those children who are low in achieving academic skills. Backward learners not

only lag behind other students in academics but in areas of social, emotional, and psychological well-being.
- Mentally Retarded children: The mentally retarded are those whose normal intellectual growth is arrested before birth, during the birth process, or in the early years of development.
- Physically handicapped learner: These categories of children can not participate in educational, social, and vocational activities on fairly equal terms with their peers due to physical disabilities.
- Disabled child: Disabled children are again divided into different groups based on types of disabilities. They can be learning, cognitive, developmental, intellectual, mental, physical, sensory, or some combination of these.

So, it could be concluded that in inclusive term, exceptional children means the gifted, intelligent, backward, mentally retarded children.

18(D). Children with special need are disabled ns any restriction or lack (resulting from an impairment) of ability to perform an activity in a manner or within the range considered normal for a human being.
- Special education is individualized education for children with special needs. Special education means, "Specially designed instruction, to meet the unique needs of a child with special needs including instructions conducted in the classrooms.
- Inclusive education, as an approach, seeks to address the learning needs of all children (disabled and non-disabled) with a specific focus on those who are vulnerable to marginalization and exclusion.
- Inclusion emerged as a result of the social justice movement in the field of disability which emphasizes that schools should create an environment in which students with special needs are seen as valuable members of the social community.

Thus from above-mentioned points, it is clear that children with special needs should be included in 'regular' set-ups with special provisions.

19(B). Characteristics of Creative learner:
- A creative learner can make unusual associations or connections between seemingly unrelated or remote ideas They can rearrange elements of thought to create new ideas or products.
- Also, they pose many ideas or solutions to problems.
- They display intellectual playfulness, fantasize, imagine, and daydream. Also, a creative learner doesn't need to have a high IQ.
- They are good at lateral thinking and

problem-solving. Creativity is associated with lateral thinking for the generation of new ideas.
- These children have divergent thinking and are very curious in nature that's why sometimes the classroom seems monotonous to them because they grab things fastly than their age-peers.
- Divergent thinking in creativity leads to a broadening of the definition and criteria of the problem to generate a wide variety of possible solutions.
- The creative learner has personality traits such as sensitivity to problems, fluency, flexibility, originality, ability to transform meaning, and ability to elaborate.

So, we can conclude that a creative learner refers to one who is good at lateral thinking and problem-solving.

20(C). Gifted children are those who show consistently remarkable performance in educational endeavours. They possess superior intellectual ability within the range of the upper two to three per cent of the population. Characteristics of Gifted Children:
- Learning commensurate with that expected of older students, often reading at an earlier than average age.
- Gifted child solve the problem quickly
- Knowing about things of which other students are unaware.
- They have a high ability for abstract and symbolic thinking.
- Curiosity indicated by asking serious questions.
- They have a large vocabulary and mature, expressive ability.
- They require limited exposure and fewer repetitions to learn. They have extra-ordinary memory.
- They can apply knowledge to unfamiliar situations.

So, from the above explanation, it can be concluded that gifted children solve the problem quickly.

21(B). 'Learning' means a relatively permanent change in behaviour that occurs as a result of experience with the environment.

Learning, in the case of all persons, proceeds through five stages. These are as follows :
1. Acquisition: During this stage, the person learns a new task.
2. Fluency/Proficiency: During this stage, the person learns to perform the new task to a higher degree of accuracy.
3. Maintenance: During this stage, the person is able to perform the task independently, even after teaching has ended.
4. Generalization: During this stage, the person learns to generalize the learned skills/tasks to other situations or environments; in ' other words, he is

able to perform the task in situations other than the ones in which he had learnt it.

5. Adaptation: During this stage, the learner applies a previously learnt skill in a new area of application without direct instruction or guidance.

So, we can conclude that the fifth and last stage is "Adaptation".

22(B). The teacher is a friend, philosopher, and guide to the students.

- If a new student is unable to adjust in the classroom, the teacher will make the classroom environment comfortable.
- The teacher will try to find out the reason by talking to her and try to resolve it.
- The teacher can introduce the new student to old students to make her comfortable.
- The teacher tells the other students to help her with all the work.

Thus, it is concluded that Rohini, a newly admitted student, is unable to adjust to the classroom, as a teacher, will try to find out the reason.

23(D). Teaching is a process related to the effective transmission of knowledge and skills in an individual. It limits or enhances the ways the learners learn and assimilate concepts and ideas.

- Teaching becomes much more effective when 'Learner-centered instruction' and 'Interactive methods' are used which provides autonomy to students to control their own work.
- In these approaches, students work in flexible, cooperative groupings to solve problems and analyze texts to demonstrate an understanding of a task.

Characteristics of teaching:

- Teaching is a tripolar process. This process of education considers that the development of the child takes place in and through the society, in which the teacher and the child live together.
- Active engagement and student participation are fostered by the teachers through a series of interactive processes in the form of debate, group tasks, projects, etc.
- Teaching is a purposeful and effect-directed process that ends at desired changes of learners' behavior. When the desires and goals are fulfilled teaching is effective.

So, we can conclude that teaching is a process confined only to the classroom's statements about teaching is not correct.

24(D). Error: When a learner can't master a topic, he/she is vulnerable to make errors. Errors are nothing but incorrectness made by a child during learning.

Misconceptions: It takes place due to the mismatch in previously assimilated and the newly accommodated knowledge.

Children's errors and misconceptions:

- Are a significant step in the teaching-learning process.
- Are necessary in the learning process to give insight into children's thinking.
- Help the teacher to be aware of learners' learning styles, to cater them according to their needs.
- Are considered as a part of the teaching-learning process as it helps to understand the child.

So, it could be concluded that children's errors and misconceptions are a significant step in the teaching-learning process.

25(D). All learners make mistakes. As someone has said: "You can't learn without goofing". Whether you are learning how to ride a bicycle, how to fly a kite or learn a language, everyone does make mistakes.

- An error is an incorrect form and a sure indication that the learner has not mastered the core of the selective topic in a learning process.
- The qualitative difference in children's thinking as compared to adults is reflected in the type of errors made by the children.
- Errors can occur in adults as well as children. The qualitative effect of errors can be observed through the type of error.
- Adults tend to make silly mistakes that may not be serious as they tend to overlook minor details and focus on bigger things.
- Whereas children may make a significantly big error as they may not have the experience of the concept.

Thus, it is concluded that errors made by children are indicative of children's thinking process which is qualitatively different from that of adults.

26(A). The term 'cognition' refers to all processes by which the sensory input is transformed, reduced, elaborated, stored, recovered, and used. Cognitive development refers to the development of the ability to think and reason.

- Cognition develops in the learners through the interaction of innate power (heredity), environment and maturation.
- Cognition is the process of acquiring and understanding knowledge through our thoughts, experiences, and senses.
- Cognition embraces all those aspects of human intelligence that we use to adapt to and make sense of the world and the emotional environment around him has an impact on his cognitive thinking.
- Cognitive skills are used to comprehend, process, remember, and apply incoming information.
- Cognition describes how mental processes i.e. learning, remembering, problem-solving, and thinking develop from birth until adulthood.

Understanding cognitive development is useful in determining the kind of thinking children are capable of at different age levels.

- It develops the ability to solve problems, learn from experiences, and apply knowledge to deal with new situations. It is a mental process that facilitates obtaining, transform, store, retrieve, and use information.

So, it becomes clear that cognition is a process of acquiring and understanding knowledge through our thoughts, experience, and sense.

27(C). Motivation is something that makes the person to action and continues him in the course of action already initiated. There are two identifiable components of motivation. These are needed and drive.

Important principles of motivation in learning are as follows:

- All learning must have a purpose.
- Students need skills and knowledge.
- Specific directions empower students.
- Students want to have fun while they learn/work.
- Curiosity
- A blend of praise and Encouragement
- A combination of intrinsic and extrinsic rewards.
- Involvement in collaborative activities.

Thus from the above-mentioned points, it is clear that helps to get a higher position is not true about the principle of motivation.

28(D). Learning is the process by which skills, attitudes, knowledge, and concepts are acquired, understood, applied, and extended. All human beings, whether grown-ups or children engage in the process of learning, either consciously, or subconsciously.

Environmental factors that impact learning:

- Environmental factors refer to the combination of all external and environmental factors that affect the learning process.
- Some schools operate in dilapidated buildings with leaking roofs. They may not have a lab, library, toilets, or drinking water facilities which creates a barrier in the path of learning.
- On the other hand, a well-designed school environment fosters positive peer relationships, promotes pleasant interactions between teachers and children, and allows teachers to assist children in achieving their objectives.

So, school is an environmental factor that impacts learning.

29(D). Learning is a process by which behavior is either modified or changed through experience or training. Learning is thus a relatively permanent change in response potentiality which occurs as a function of reinforced practice. There are many factors that influence learning.

Learning is influenced by:

Psychological factors:

- Psychological aspects are the elements of one's personality that limit or enhance the ways that one learns and thinks.
- Several psychological factors such as intelligence, personality, attitude, interest, and aptitude have considerable influence on the learning of a child.

Socio-Cultural factors:

- Socio-cultural factors refer to the combination of social and cultural factors. These factors play a vital role in shaping the abilities and behaviors of a child.
- The immediate environmental structure of social culture is where an individual has direct interaction with their significant others such as parents, siblings, teachers, and peers.

School-related factors:

- Overcrowding classrooms is another contributing factor. In some big cities, houses are converted into English medium schools. In small rooms, sixty to seventy children are made to sit and are unable to benefit from highly verbal instruction.
- The condition of the setting where the learning process takes place can also enhance or interfere with the intake of information.

Teacher-related factors:

- Learning problems may occur because of inadequate or inappropriate teaching. The child may have difficulty in learning because the teacher does not provide adequate or appropriate instruction.
- If the teacher is a poor communicator or uses monotonous and uninteresting methods, the children are put at a disadvantage.

So, it is clear that learning is influenced by all Psychological, Socio-Cultural, School-related, and Teacher related factors.

30(A). One of the major approaches to understand motivation is the behavioural approach.

- The behavioural approach considers the role of external rewards and punishment in motivation in the classroom. According to this approach, the role of positive and negative stimuli as incentives is very important in encouraging or discouraging a particular behaviour. The role of reinforcement is also considered important in teaching and learning. This approach promotes the use of grades, stars, rewards, certification, appreciation, etc., for enhancing the motivation of learners.
- Incentives motivate students to be more productive, as they create a sense of pride among students.
- The incentive is an amazing way to ensure that students stay motivated to do their work and learning.

Thus from the above-mentioned points, it is clear that teachers should promote motivation to learn among their students by using incentives to help students learn.

31(B). According to the passage, "According to the IWT, India is permitted to construct water storage on western rivers -Indus, Jhelum, and Chenab -up to 3.6 million acre-feet for various purposes, including domestic use."

So, it is concluded that Beas is not included according to the Indus Water Treaty for the construction of water storage for India.

32(D). According to the passage, "According to this agreement, control over the three "eastern" rivers — the Beas, the Ravi, and the Sutlej — was given to India, while control over the three "western" rivers — the Indus, the Chenab, and the Jhelum — to Pakistan. In aftermath of the 2016 Uri attack, India reviewed the treaty and its provisions and proposed several changes. The treaty was reviewed by India to explore possible ways to use its share of water from rivers, including the Jhelum, flowing into Pakistan."

So, it can be concluded that Chenab, Jhelum is not the correct pair of the eastern and western rivers.

33(D). According to the passage, "India refused to countenance any change of design of the Miyar dam in J&K, as asked by Pakistan, and plans to continue utilization of its allocation under the Indus Waters Treaty."

So, to countenance any change of design of the Miyar dam in J&K is refused by India as asked by Pakistan.

34(C). The meaning of the given words:

- Permit: to allow somebody to do something or something to happen, authorize, sanction, grant, license, and power.
- Ban: to officially say that something is not allowed, often by law, prohibition, forbid, veto, proscribe, outlaw, and embargo.

From the above meaning, it is evident that Ban is the opposite meaning of the word Permit.

35(B). The meaning of the given words:

- Explore: to travel around a place, etc, in order to learn about it, traverse, survey, inspect, scout, reconnoiter, prospect and recce.
- Investigate: trying to find out all facts about something, probe, scrutinize, look into, and explore.

From the above meaning, it is evident that Investigate is the same meaning as the word Explore.

36(C). 'Aftermath' is a noun.

- A noun is a part of speech that is a name of a thing, a place, or a person. Example:

Slovakia.

- Here, "in" is the preposition that is used before the noun "aftermath" to show the time of happening of the Uri attack.
- Aftermath means the consequences or after-effects of a significant unpleasant event.

37(C). According to the passage, "The Indus Waters Treaty is a water-distribution treaty between India and Pakistan, brokered by the World Bank, then the International Bank for Reconstruction and Development. The treaty was signed in Karachi on September 19, 1960, by Prime Minister of India Jawaharlal Nehru and President of Pakistan Ayub Khan."

So, it can be concluded that the only option Indus Waters Treaty is the correct theme of the passage as it is mentioned in the passage and is also signed between the two countries in order to solve the issues related to water distribution and also the construction of the Dam and also the complete story of the passage revolves around the treaty between these two countries.

38(A). "One of" refers to a single entity of a group or subject.

A noun or pronoun or subject of such phrase will be in the plural form and the verb in such cases will always be singular as it refers to only a single subject.

The rule for such sentences:

- One/Every/Each/Neither/Either + of + Noun (Plural) + Verb (Singular).
- Example: One of the best students in the class is Manish.

Here, the error lies in "One of this" as the noun "projects" is in the plural form we need demonstrative adjectives "these" instead of "this" to define the plural noun "projects".

39(D). According to the passage, "The treaty was reviewed by India to explore possible ways to use its share of water from rivers, including the Jhelum, flowing into Pakistan."

So, it is concluded that Jhelum is included which is reviewed by India to use its share of water from rivers.

40(D). According to the given lines, "O! what sweet company.

But to go to school in a summer morn,

O! it drives all joy away;

Under a cruel eye outworn,"

So, it is concluded that the school boy feels unhappy when he goes to school.

41(A). According to the given lines, "How can the bird that is born for joy,

Sit in a cage and sing.

How can a child when fears annoy,

But droop his tender wing,"

So, it is concluded that the school boy is compared to a bird.

42(B). Alliteration: The repetition of an

initial consonant sound in words that are in close proximity to each other.

Alliteration does not refer to the repetition of consonant letters that begin words, but rather the repetition of the consonant sound at the beginning of words. Ex: Piper picked a peck

Here, sky-lark sings. The sound of s represents Alliteration figure of speech in the above line.

43(D). Metaphor: An expression, often found in literature, that describes a person or object by referring to something that is considered to have similar characteristics to that person or object. Ex: I'm feeling red. Here, 'Under a cruel eye outworn' represents the teacher who keeps a close eye on students. The child hates to be under scrutiny. He dislikes the fact that he had to spend his day in the supervision of an inconsiderate person.

44(D). According to the given lines,
"I love to rise in a summer morn,
When the birds sing on every tree;
The distant huntsman winds his horn,
And the skylark sings with me.
O! what sweet company."
So, it is concluded that sweet company refer skylark and huntsman horn.

45(C). According to the given lines,
"But to go to school in a summer morn,
O! it drives all joy away;"
So, it is concluded that going to school in the summer morning takes away all the happiness of the child.

46(D). Language acquisition: It refers to the subconscious process of learning a native or second language because of the innate capacity of the human brain.
- It is a natural process whereby children acquire language by observing and repeating what they hear in the natural setting of their native environment.
- Language acquisition does not require any formal instruction, children acquire the language without being taught. It is a natural process so, one does not forget one's native language.

So, it could be concluded that a child learns his/her first language in a natural setting.

47(B). Language learning: When a child learns a language as a second or third language, it is assumed as language learning.
- It refers to having a basic knowledge of grammatical rules and their use in communication.
- It is effectively done by providing comprehensible inputs to make the learners actively involved in real communication.
- It refers to the result of deliberate and conscious effort in a formal environment, for a better understanding of foundational skills of language

learning.

So, it could be concluded that language learning is a conscious attempt by the learner.

48(B). Multiple Line of Approach:
- The term "multiple line" implies that one is to proceed simultaneously from many different points towards the one and the same end. In teaching a language, it implies attacking the problem from all fronts.
- It means a lesson that is to be taught by the teacher should be tackled from many sides. So, it reflects that the Multi-line approach consists of reaching the same target from different directions and means.
- For example, there is a lesson on 'Holidays' in the textbook. The teacher can have a number of language activities connected with the topic such as oral drill, reading, sentence writing, composition, grammar, translation, language exercises, etc.

So, we can conclude that Teaching a lesson, through a number of language activities connected with the topic, refers to Multiple Line of Approach.

49(C). Present Language in Basic Sentence Patterns:
- Present, and have the students' memories, basic sentence patterns used in day-to-day conversation. From small utterances, the students can easily pass on to longer sentences.
- In the case of learning mother-tongue, the student's memory span can retain much longer sentences than those of a foreign language.
- The facility thus gained in a foreign language enables the learners to expand the grasp of the language material in respect of sounds and vocabulary items.

So, we can conclude that the 'Present Language in Basic Sentence Patterns' principle of second language could be associated with the above-mentioned statement.

50(D). 'Decorum' in spoken language pertains to appropriate gestures.

Decorum was a principle of classical rhetoric, poetry and theatrical theory that was about fitness or otherwise of a style to a theatrical subject. The concept of decorum is also applied to prescribed limits of appropriate social behavior within set situations.

51(C). The teaching of grammar will help the learners to have good conversational skills as the ultimate aim of every language learner is to acquire the ability to speak and write the language correctly.
- In order to do this, he/she requires knowledge of grammar in some form or the other.
- So, any course in language teaching

assigns an important role to grammar.
- The more we are aware of how it works, the more we can monitor the meaning and effectiveness of the way we and others use language.

From the above, we can conclude that Teaching of grammar will help the learners to have good conversational skills.

52(C). Grammar-translation method:
- The Grammar-Translation method of learning a language is through the detailed study of its grammar.
- In this method, the learner first learns grammatical rules and then applies those rules in translating sentences from the target language into the mother tongue.
- Primarily, the mother tongue or native language is used to teach the rule of grammar to the learners so that translations become easier.
- Vocabulary is built using bilingual word lists i.e., to teach the meaning of words in the mother tongue and in the target language.
- Rote learning or memorization plays a vital role when it comes to learning the rules of grammar.

So, the principle of the grammar-translation method is to memorize the rules of grammar.

53(D). The Main Challenges of Teaching Language in a Diverse Classroom are:
- Issues and challenges to curriculum design.
- Challenge and issues of the teaching-learning process.
- Challenge of teaching-learning materials.
- Challenge of a mixed-ability group of learners.
- Challenge maintaining justice and democracy in the classroom.

So, we can conclude that all of the above are the main challenges of teaching language in a diverse classroom.

54(A). Language skills can be learned better in an integrated manner since it exploits all the skills. For example, when we speak, we also listen simultaneously, when we write we are also reading.

This engagement with language enables us to internalize the underlying grammaticality of the language. This leads to language learning.

So, from the above-mentioned points, it becomes clear that language skills can be learned better if they are taught in an integrated manner.

55(D). Listening and Reading comes under the receptive category while speaking and writing comes under the productive category of language skills.
- Speaking and writing come under the productive category of language skills because these generate output in form

of oral and written. This why these are known as productive skills.

- Listening and Reading comes under the receptive category because the learner receives the inputs given by the teacher. That is why these are known as receptive skills.

So, we can conclude that speaking and writing comes under the productive category of language skills.

56(D). Components in the evaluation of speaking:

- Articulation: While evaluating the speaking of students, the teacher must pay attention to their articulation of words i.e., how they join words including their way of speaking.
- Intonation, stress, and voice quality: The power of persuasion often depends on convincing voice quality. Intonations (Ups and downs in the voice), stressing on important words, and voice quality (change in sound as per the mood and requirement) are an important part of speaking. So, it is important for a teacher to assess the intonations and voice quality of students while they are speaking during their evaluation of speaking skills.
- Vocabulary and Pronunciation: While evaluating the speaking skills, it is important to note down the kind of vocabulary used by the speaker and how he is pronouncing the words. It reflects the proficiency of the speaker in the target language.
- Body language: Using hand and body movements while speaking helps the speaker to connect with the audience and to gain attention. Thus, the body language of students should also be evaluated along with the evaluation of speaking skills.
- Concentration: Children need to know that clear thought in an organized manner keeps the attention of the listener. So, they should speak by organizing their thoughts by concentrating on the main idea of the topic.

Thus, it is clear that evaluation of speaking consists of the evaluation of pronunciation, intonation, and stress.

57(C). Followings are some great activities in which teachers can evaluate students listening skills:

- Listen and Draw: this particular activity can be used with students who struggle to express themselves in English, Listen and Draw isolates listening from speaking. Simply have your students take out a blank piece of paper and give them instructions on what to draw.
- Dictations: with this activity, the teacher can easily evaluate students listening skills. The teacher just needs to select a couple of words and then call the words

one by one and repeat at least once after calling the words. After calling all the words which the students have to write on a separate piece of paper. The teacher collects the papers and from there he can start evaluating each student based on their listening comprehension.

- Oral Presentations: It is more viewed in academic courses where the test takers have to talk about a given or selected topic, nevertheless, that doesn't mean that it cannot be used to assess other learners. Scoring is also easy because the test-taker speaks about a specific topic.

So, we can conclude that the vocabulary assessment task is not the activity of evaluating listening skills.

58(A). Flannel boards can be used in classrooms in a variety of situations.

- The advantage of using a flannel board is that it provides the flexibility of using a material to teach students.
- Flannel boards are used to display pictures, messages.
- In the English Language classroom, it can be used to teach picture composition.
- It allows children to explore stories, apply their imagination, boost fine motor skills, and enhance their creativity.
- The flannel board increases the child's learning abilities.

From the above, we can conclude that the flannel board is useful for teaching picture composition.

59(C). Realia refers to the objects associated with everyday life to be used in the classroom. Realia can be used as props for dialogues to teach new lexical or structural items as it is a tangible teaching-learning object.

- It includes coin, newspaper, map, tickets, fruits, vegetables, etc.
- It makes learning more interesting and enliven by bringing the class to life.
- It ensures the use of accurate and realistic materials in the teaching-learning process.
- It encourages healthy classroom interaction and helps in meeting individual differences.

So, we conclude that realia can be used as props for dialogues to teach new lexical or structural items.

60(B). Remedial teaching: During learning, a child makes mistakes willingly-unwillingly or due to some alternative conceptions. It is the job of a teacher to help students to correct those mistakes after diagnosing them. The method so followed is known as remedial teaching. The following are its characteristics:

- It can be used for improving language skills

- To rectify a particular problem area, it can be used. For example, a student is confused among the pronunciation of 'no' and 'know', he can be taught the concept of silent letters.
- It is carried out after the identification of problems and challenges faced by students.
- A teacher should be well aware of students' strengths and weaknesses to apply this method.
- It is a systematic process as the teacher first diagnoses the problem of students and then applies appropriate remedial methods.

So, we conclude that remedial teaching is a systematic process.

61(A). The Vaishnav Bhakti saints in South India were called Alvars.

Sagun Bhakti refers to devotion and prayer to god having some form and with attributes whereas Nirguna Bhakti refers to devotion and prayer to formlessness god without any attributes.

The Nayanars and Alvars were the Tamil poet-saints who played a key role in propagating the Bhakti Movement in Southern India.

Nayanars were the group of saints devoted to Lord Shiva while Alvars were the group of saints devoted to Lord Vishnu, Vaishnav Bhakti.

62(B). Name King Ashoka's son whom King Ashoka sent to other places to carry out duties of Buddhist missionary Mahendra .

- After the Kalinga war, the Mauryan emperor Ashoka converted to Buddhism from Hinduism, to propagate Buddhism he sent his son Mahendra and his daughter Sanghmitra as missionaries to Ceylon about 251 BC .
- They converted the royal family of Ceylon, who helped them in propagating Buddhism across the state.
- Mahendra's name has not been found in any of the inscriptions of Ashoka, but his existence had been found in the famous Ceylonese chronicles Dipavaṃsa and Mahavaṃ sa written in Pali language .

63(C). The bill relating to Urban Local Bodies was passed in MP State Assembly on 30th December 1993. The government of Madhya Pradesh had passed the Municipality Act 1994 to enforce the 74th Constitutional Amendment Act 1992.

The 3-tier system has been implemented in the state for Urban local bodies. It includes:

- Nagar Panchayat
- Nagar Palika
- Nagar Nigam

64(C). The Chairman of the Drafting Committee of the Constituent Assembly of India was Dr. B.R. Ambedkar.

On 29 August 1947, the Constituent Assembly set up a Drafting Committee under the Chairmanship of Dr. B.R. Ambedkar to prepare a Draft Constitution for India.

There were 7 members in the drafting committee and, a Drafting Committee was headed by B.R Ambedkar.
- Dr. B R Ambedkar (Chairman)
- N Gopalaswami Ayyangar
- Alladi Krishnaswamy Ayyar
- Dr. K M Munshi
- Syed Mohammad Saadullah
- N Madhava Rau (He replaced B L Mitter who resigned due to ill-health.)
- T T Krishnamachari (He replaced D P Khaitan who died in 1948.)

65(B). Article 17 ensures 'Abolition of Untouchability'.
- Article 17 of the Indian Constitution eliminates the practice of untouchability.
- 'Untouchability' is abolished and its practice in any form is forbidden.
- The enforcement of any disability arising out of 'Untouchability' shall be an offense punishable in accordance with the law.

66(A). Primary Waves (P-waves): Primary waves are the fastest body waves (twice the speed of S-waves) and arrive first during an earthquake. They are similar to sound waves, that is, they are longitudinal waves, in that the particle motion is in the same direction of wave propagation. They move through solid, liquid and gaseous substances.
- There are basically two types of earthquake waves - body waves and surface waves.
- There are two types of waves in the system. They are called P and S-waves.

67(A). The correct match is:

List-I (Economic Activity/Agriculture region)	List-II (Country)
1. Commercial dairy farming	(c) Denmark
2. Commercial grain farming	(a) Argentina
3. Commercial plantation farming	(d) Malaysia
4. Commercial fruits production	(b) France

68(A). Mt. Stromboli is a part of the Mediterranean Belt.
The Circum Pacific belt extends to the margins of the pacific ocean. Almost 80% of the volcanoes are situated here.

69(D). The Truth of the Path is generally described as the noble eightfold path . Some books divide them into three groups . They are wisdom (prajna) , morality (sila) , and meditation (samadhi) . Among the eight first two are classified in the group of wisdom , the next three are in the group of morality and the last three are in the group of meditation. They are:
1. Right Faith (samyak drsti)
2. Right Resolve (samyak Sankalpa)
3. Right Speech (samyak vak)
4. Right Conduct (samyak karmanta)
5. Right Livelihood (samyak ajiva)
6. Right Effort (samyak Vayama)
7. Right Mindfulness (samyak smriti)
8. Right Concentration (samyak samadhi)
The first two of the eight-fold path, namely, right faith and right resolve, are together called Prajna, because they are related to consciousness and knowledge.
The third, fourth, and fifth, namely, right speech, right conduct, and right livelihood, are collectively known as Sila because they deal with the correct and morally right way of living.
The last three, namely, right effort, right awareness, and right concentration are collectively known as Samadhi, because they deal with meditation and contemplation.
So, i n the eightfold noble paths given by Budha, Right Faith and Right Resolve is the basis of 'Right Knowledge'.

70(D). Muhammad-bin-Baktiyar Khilji destroyed Vikramshila in 1202 and Nalanda University in 1203 AD.
About Vikramshila:-
- It was established (783 to 820 AD) by Pala emperor Dharmapala.
- It is one of the three most important Buddhist monasteries in India.
- Around 1200 it was destroyed by the forces of Muhammad-bin-Baktiyar Khilji.

71(B). Duplex (dual) government was introduced by Robert Clive and Warren Hastings abolished "dual (dual) government" in Bengal in 1772. Warren Hastings was the first Governor-General of Bengal.
Under the Duplex (dual) Government, the administration of Bengal was divided into two parts: the Diwani, and the Nizamat.

72(C). Thomas Munro introduced the Ryotwari system in Bombay and Madras in 1820. The Ryotwari system was a land revenue system introduced during the British Raj.
- Warren Hastings served as the Governor-General of Bengal from 1772 to 1785.
- Lord Cornwallis is known as the 'Father of Civil Services in India'.
- Lord Ripon is known as the 'Father of Local Self Government' in India.

73(A). Moving from the troposphere to the mid-range in the atmosphere, the temperature first increases and then decreases. On the basis of temperature, there are five layers in the composition of the atmosphere. These layers are:
1. Troposphere
2. Stratosphere
3. Mesosphere
4. Outer atmosphere
5. Exosphere
Troposphere -
- It is considered to be the lowest layer of the Earth's atmosphere.
- All kinds of weather changes take place within this layer.
- The temperature decreases with the increasing altitude of the atmosphere at the rate of 1°C for every 165 m of altitude. This is called the normal lapse rate.

74(C). Air moves from high-pressure (low temperature) to low-pressure (high temperature) areas. Wind speed changes due to variations in temperature and pressure.
These differences in temperature and pressure are experienced in the form of air. When the temperature of an area is high due to the heat of the sun, the vertical temperature difference causes air to rise because warmer air is lighter than colder air. Now because the hot air rises up, an empty space is created which is filled with cold air.

75(B). The Indian state intervenes in the religious affairs of the country. For example, when the issue of discrimination on the basis of caste was noticed in the country, the Government of India banned untouchability. Therefore, the Indian state intervenes so that:
- Eliminate discrimination;
- To ensure that the fundamental rights of every individual are protected.

76(B). Fundamental rights in India are the rights guaranteed under Part III (Articles 12-35) of the Constitution of India.
There are six fundamental rights recognized by the Indian constitution:
1. The right to equality (Articles 14-18)
2. The right to freedom (Articles 19-22)
3. The right against exploitation (Articles 23-24)
4. The right to freedom of religion (Articles 25-28)
5. Cultural and educational rights (Articles 29-30)
6. The right to constitutional remedies (Article 32 and 226)

77(A). In PM Shram Yogi Maandhan Yojana (PM Shram Yogi Maandhan Yojana) beneficiaries will get Rs 3000 or Rs 36 thousand annually pension scheme after 60 years of age.
The main objective of Pradhan Mantri Shram Yogi Maandhan Yojana 2022 is to provide facilities to the labor citizens working in the unorganized sectors. It has been started to provide social security pension scheme to labor citizens in old age life.

78(D). The 'Nai Manzil Yojana' was

launched by the Ministry of Minority Affairs in 2015. The main objective of this scheme is to equip minority youth with employable skills.

The scheme mainly focuses on minority youth in the age group of 17 to 35 years. They are school dropouts and educated youth in community education institutions like madrassas. Skill training along with certification is also provided to the selected youth under the 'Nai Manzil Yojana'. This scheme helps the youth to find better employment in the organized sector. In this scheme 30% seats are reserved for minority girls.

79(B). "Social science prepares students for a holistic social life." This statement is completely true.

Social science is the branch of science devoted to the study of societies and the relationships between individuals within those societies. The term was formerly used to refer to the original "science of society" field of sociology established in the 19th century. It is a field that deals with human behaviour, relationships, resources and institutions.

80(C). Fieldwork provides students first-hand knowledge.
- Fieldwork is an important learner-centred instructional method in social sciences. It means taking the class into the "real" world.
- It is conducted in real-life situations where they observe a phenomenon, collect the relevant data, process and analyse the data and arrive at conclusions.
- Fieldwork should be related to an ongoing unit of work. For example, while teaching the means of production, the teacher can take students to a nearby factory where students observe the various processes involved in the production of goods.
- Fieldwork provides students with first-hand knowledge and enables them to see how a number of skills and processes are integrated.
- The experiences which students get from fieldwork contribute towards effective and permanent learning.

81(A). The branch of science that deals with the institutions and activities of human society and studies the interactions of individuals as members of society is known as social science.
- Social science constitutes a broad field of knowledge and deals with human beings in relation to their social behavior.
- Social science studies concepts or issues such as culture, tradition, lifestyle, place and environment, power and authority, governance, economy, civic sense, etc., which have social implications.

- Social sciences are basically concerned with human relations. The study of the nature of human society is the ultimate goal of all social sciences.
- Social sciences have their own/specific subject areas and methods for acquiring and understanding knowledge. Some of the common methods used in social sciences to understand knowledge are historical, thematic, participatory, non-invasive, quasi-experimental, etc.

82(A). The social studies teacher should interact primarily with the various methods of teaching as a teacher can encourage student participation.
- Social studies studies social relations in the context of history, geography, civics, economics, sociology, art and culture. Therefore, social studies is the study of the social environment.
- As it studies the different areas of our life in an integrated manner, the teacher should interact in different ways to make teaching interesting and provide learning friendly environment.
- The teacher must be flexible when using teaching methods to encourage student participation in the teaching process. Teaching methods help teachers to plan and present lessons in a coherent manner.

83(C). Teacher is using field work method in teaching social science.

Field work:
- Field work is an important learner-centred instructional method in the social sciences. This means taking the orbit into the "real" world. It is conducted in real-life situations where they observe an event, collect relevant data, analyze the data and reach conclusions.
- Field work must be related to an ongoing unit of work. For example, when teaching the workings of the means of production, teachers may take students to a nearby factory, where students observe the various processes involved in the production of goods.
- Field work provides students with hands-on knowledge and enables them to see how skills and processes are integrated.
- The experiences students gain from fieldwork contribute to effective and sustainable learning.

84(D). The steps to be followed in the Herbartian method of lesson plans are preparation - presentation - associative - generalization - application.
- Preparation: Linking new content to previous knowledge.
- Presentation: introducing students to new information by stating the objectives of the lesson.
- Associative: New ideas or knowledge

related to situations in daily life.
- Generalization: The learning material leads to some generalizations and conclusions.
- Application: The knowledge gained is applied to certain situations.

85(C). The teacher should aim to achieve instructional objectives consistently by using formal or informal assessment and teaching-learning strategies.
- An instructional objective describes the specific learning outcome, the behavior required to perform it, and determines the means to measure or evaluate it.
- This type of assessment is based on directional statements that identify expected learner outcomes, establish objectives and determine levels of achievement.
- Instructional objectives are specific and arc practical in nature. These are mainly based on specific observable or measurable goals in a stude.

86(D). The development of deep thinking involves 6 stages.

The 6 stages involved in the development of intensive thinking are as follows:
- Step one: irreversible thinker (individual is unaware of important problems in thinking)
- Step 2: Challenge Thinker (Person is aware of problems in thinking)
- Step Three: Initial Thinkers (Attempted to make personal reforms but without regular practice)
- Step Four: Practicing Thinker (identifying the need for regular practice individually)
- Step Five: Advanced Thinker (Personal advance according to practice)
- Step Six: A skillful thinker

87(D). In the social sciences, the recent NCF position paper on exam reform emphasizes continuous evaluation.

National Curriculum Framework (NCF) 2005 is one of the four NCF published in India by NCERT. It seeks to provide a framework for the betterment of educational purposes and experiences.

Social Science According to NCF 2005:
- The objective of teaching the social sciences is to develop an understanding of the earth as the habitat of humankind and other forms of life.
- It helps to initiate the learner into a study of her/ his own region, state, and country in the global context.
- NCF position paper on examination reform emphasizes on continuous assessment.

88(B). Formal and informal group planning are forms of brain stimulation teaching method.

Brain stimulation is a technique that helps humans to mobilize their creative powers to form ideas. Brain stimulation is a

teaching-learning technique that can be used in groups in two different ways:
- **Formal Group Plans** - It is a group made by the teacher and has a specific objective or topic to discuss. It follows a top-down approach.
- **Informal Group Plans** - It is an informal discussion among the students based on their common interests and proximity in sharing ideas. It follows a bottom-up approach.

89(D). There are some popular beliefs about social science that social science is nothing but an encyclopedia of events and places.
- Students also feel that the social science textbook transmits information that only needs to be memorized.
- There is a general belief that since the subject does not develop any particular skills required for the job market, social science students are generally denied jobs in the market. Therefore, people sometimes consider social science as a redundant subject.
- There is a common belief among people that social science emphasizes the retention of information without understanding.
- Since textbooks in the social sciences often do not incorporate local content and realities, social science textbooks lack interest and relevance due to the absence of local content and realities among students, teachers, and the community.

Therefore, we conclude that all the above points are misconceptions about social science.

90(C). What will be the time in Paris when the time in New Delhi will be at 12 noon? The question asked by a social studies teacher is a type of application-based question as suggested by Bloom's classification.

Benjamin Bloom's classification is a set of three hierarchical models that refer to the classification of educational learning objectives. In the classification, Bloom identified three areas of learning which include cognitive, affective and psychomotor.

91(D). The teacher should holding debates to develop reasoning and support skills through social studies teaching.
- The teaching of social studies aims to help learners develop a greater awareness of themselves, clarify and examine their values, and establish a sense of self-identity.
- Teaching of social studies helps to promote the learner's thinking for developing understanding and acceptance of others having different values and lifestyles.

Hence, the correct option is (B).

92(C). Social science covers the diverse concerns of society and includes a wide range of subject matter drawn from the disciplines of history, geography, political science, economics and sociology.
- The disciplines of social sciences are mainly interdisciplinary and interdependent in nature, as they have functional relationships among themselves.
- Social science as a field of study includes a large number of subjects like political science, anthropology, law, economics, geography etc.
- Various social science subjects like history, political science, anthropology, law etc. are taught as independent/ optional subjects at higher education/ high school level.
- At the basic school level, social science is taught under an integrated field of study, designated as a 'social studies curriculum' or a 'social science curriculum'.

93(D). Education is very important to lead a good life. Primary education is compulsory and forms the basis of the individual. There are many reasons for the plight of primary education in today's time.

Answer	Statement	Conclusion
Most appropriate	teacher-student inappropriate ratio	This is the most appropriate option. In today's time, the teacher-student ratio is not appropriate for providing them with proper education.
Appropriate	relying on guidebooks	This is the second most appropriate option. Students rely on guidebooks to learn, by this students would not be able to gain knowledge.
Less considerable	students spend more time in Doordarshan	This is a less considerable option. Spending time on TV affects their education.
Inappropriate	nuclear family	This is an inappropriate option. A nuclear family does not affect primary education.

94(D). Wood's manifesto is called the Magna Carta of English Education in India.
- Charles Wood was president of the English East India Company's Board of Control.
- In 1854, he sent a despatch to Lord Dalhousie then Governor-General of India.
- It was laid down to set the groundwork for the modern educational system.
- According to Wood's dispatch, In primary schools, vernacular languages should become the medium of instruction.
- He also advised in the despatch that anglo-vernacular be used in high schools and that English be used for college-level education.
- As a result, Wood's Despatch is regarded as India's "Magna Carta" of English Education.

95(D). Timelines are not commonly used in the teaching of geography.

Timeline: It provides the chronological orders of the events and incidents that happened earlier. It starts from the earliest event and moves forward to the next through time. It is effective in teaching history to make the learning of historical events easier.

The teaching method is a way to put theory into practice. It generally describes the pedagogy of children, general principles, and management strategies that are to be used through the whole teaching-learning process.

96(D). The project work given to the students helps in developing their leadership qualities, creativity and understanding of basic concepts.

Using project work a teacher can develop:
- It lets the teacher have multiple assessment opportunities.
- It allows a child to demonstrate their creativity and capabilities while working independently.
- It enhace the child's ability to apply desired skills such as doing research and using their understanding of the basic concepts.
- It develops the child's ability to work with his or her peers , building teamwork and group skills and seeing their leadership skills.
- It allows the teacher to learn more about the child as a person.
- It helps the teacher communicate in progressive and meaningful ways with the child.
- Students become engaged builders of a new knowledge base and become active, lifelong learners.

97(B). There are types of interviews structured, unstructured and semi-structured.
Structured:

- Pre-formatted queries cannot be changed.
- It includes both open ended and closed ended questions.

Unstructured:

- The interviewer exercises autonomy in asking questions.
- The format of any question is not fixed.

Semi-transmitted:

- It collects open ended qualitative data in a predetermined framework.
- It is conducted to find out the thoughts and feelings of the interviewer.

98(A). Objective type questions are difficult and time consuming to prepare for evaluation but relatively easy.

Objective type questions: Objective questions are those based on fact, where a respondent's answer can be determined as right, wrong, true, or false. An example of an objective question would be to ask where someone lives or what they bought from your store. The forms vary questions of fact, sentence completion, true-false, analogy, multiple-choice, and matching.

99(C). The Indian League was started in 1875 by Sisir Kumar Ghosh. Hence, pair 1 is correct.

- It was started with the object of "stimulating the sense of nationalism amongst the people" and of encouraging political education.
- Poona Sarvajanik Sabha was founded in 1867 by Mahadeo Govind Ranade and others. Hence, pair 2 is incorrect.
- Started with the objective of serving as a bridge between the government and the people.
- Ganesh Vasudeo Joshi was a prominent leader of the Sabha.
- It started as an elected body of 95 members elected by 6000 persons.
- The organization was a precursor to the Indian National Congress which started with its first session from Maharashtra itself.
- The first President of the Pune Sarvajanik Sabha was the Shrimant Shrinivasrao Pant Pratinidhi.
- Rao Bahadur Vizirungum Aya Mudliar was appointed as Chairman of the Managing Committee.
- Many eminent personalities such as Bal Gangadhar Tilak, Gopal Hari Deshmukh, Maharshi Annasaheb Patwardhan, etc. served as the Presidents of the organization.

100(C). The 1857 revolt had gained immense momentum in a short period of time.

Within a month of the capture of Delhi by the rebels, the Revolt spread to different parts of the country.

Leaders of the revolt of 1857:

- At Delhi, the nominal and symbolic leadership belonged to the Mughal emperor Bahadur Shah though the real command was laid in the court of soldiers headed by General Bakht Khan. Hence, pair 1 is correct.
- Begum Hazrat Mahal took over the reins at Lucknow where the rebellion broke out on 4 June 1857 and popular sympathy was overwhelmingly in favour of the deposed Nawab. Hence, pair 3 is correct.
- In Bihar, the revolt was led by Kunwar Singh. Hence, pair 5 is correct.
- Maulvi Ahmadullah of Faizabad was another outstanding leader of the revolt.

101(D). The Sree Narayana Guru Dharma Paripalana (SNDP) movement or Aruvippuram movement was an example of a religious movement born out of the conflict between the depressed classes and upper caste. Hence, statement 1 is correct.

- It was started by Sree Narayana Guru among the Ezhavas of Kerala. Hence, statement 2 is incorrect.
- The Aruvippuram movement drew the famous poet Kumaran Asan as a disciple of Narayana Guru. Hence, statement 3 is correct.
- In 1889 the Aruvippuram Kshetra Yogam was formed which was decided to expand into a big organisation to help the Ezhavas to progress materially as well as spiritually.

102(A). The objectives of the Ramakrishna movement were:

- To bring into existence a band of monks dedicated to a life of renunciation and spirituality from among whom teachers and workers would be sent out to spread the universal message of Vedanta as illustrated in the life of Ramakrishna. Hence, statement 1 is correct.
- In conjunction with the lay disciples to carry on preaching, philanthropic and charitable works look upon all men, women and children irrespective of caste, creed or colour as veritable manifestations of the divine.
- The Ramakrishna Math was founded by Sri Ramakrishna's chief disciple, Swami Vivekananda (1863–1902), who is considered one of the main molds of the modern world. Ramakrishna Math was registered as a trust in 1901 by Swami Vivekananda himself. So, statement 2 is false.
- The second objective was taken up by Swami Vivekananda after Ramakrishna's death when he founded the Ramakrishna Mission in 1897.

103(C). The most famous ruler was Prithviraj III (1168–1192), Sultan Rebellion would be a kingdom in 1191, as is the present state in 1192. Hence, there is 1 sentence.

- After joining control in the war, the fan was posted in Vayu Shakti, to be known as Pathan.
- Tried to test the control of his controls in the west and east, where the maneuvers of the aircraft and the defenses of western Uttar Pradesh were resistant.

Sultan Mahmud of Ghazni was a contemporary of Rajendra I. Hence, statement 2 is correct.

- Rajendra Chola I, the king of the Great Chola of India, Rajaraja Chola I, remained as her husband to 1014 as Chola emperor.
- This Gangaikonda Cholapuram trial has been done to build a new capital.

104(C). Language and Literature under the Mughals:

Akbar:

- By the time of Akbar's reign, the Persian language had become widespread in the Mughal Empire.
- Many historical works were written during this period.
- These include Ain-e-Akhbari and Akbarnama written by Abul Fazl.
- The prominent poet of this period was his brother Abul Faizi. Hence pair 1 is correct.

Jahangir:

- Jahangir's autobiography Tuzuki-i-Jahangiri was famous for its style.
- He also patronized many scholars like Yas Beg, Naqib Khan and Niyamatullah. Hence pair 2 is correct.
- Shah Jahan also patronized many writers and historians.
- Padshahnama is authored by Abdul Hameed Lahori. Hence pair 3 is correct.

Shah Jahan:

- Shah Jahan also patronized many writers and historians.
- Padshahnama is authored by Abdul Hameed Lahori. Hence pair 3 is correct.
- Inayat Khan, who wrote Shah Jahannama.

105(C). Jaat denotes the individual rank of an officer and sawar denotes the size of the military force formed by the mansabdars. Hence statement 1 is correct.

On the basis of the strength of the party, the mansabdars were divided into three categories. Let us take the example of a mansabdar whose rank was 7000 jaat and 7000 sawar (7000/7000).

The position of the mansabdar in the government hierarchy was not affected even if the position of the sawar was high. It was decided by caste rank. Hence statement 2 is correct.

For example, the rank of a mansabdar of 4000 jaat and 2000 sawar was higher than the mansabdar of 3000 jaat and 3000 sawar.

106(A). According to the Constitution, Parliament can pass a resolution for the creation or abolition of a Legislative Council in a State, provided the State Legislature concerned passes a resolution to this effect. Parliament then passes an Act to this effect by a simple majority, like any ordinary law, outside the purview of Article 368. Hence statement 1 is correct.

The legislature of the state concerned is required to pass a resolution to this effect by a special majority i.e. a majority of the total number of the House and a two-thirds majority of the members present and voting.

107(A). The Family Courts Act, 1984 was enacted to promote the conciliation of disputes relating to marriage and family matters and to establish Family Courts to ensure speedy settlement.

- It provides for the establishment of Family Courts by the State Governments in consultation with the High Courts.
- It makes it mandatory for state governments to set up a family court in every city or town with a population of more than one million. Hence statement 1 is correct.
- This makes it mandatory for the Family Court to attempt, in the first instance, to reach a conciliation or settlement between the parties to a family dispute. It provides for the cooperation of social welfare agencies, counselors, etc. during the stage of conciliation.
- It provides only one right of appeal which will be in the High Court. Hence statement 2 is wrong.

108(D). India ratified its membership of the United Nations on 26 June 1945 during the British period. Hence statement 1 is not correct.

The Constituent Assembly held its last session on 24 January 1950.

However, it did not end, and continued as the Provisional Parliament of India from 26 January 1950 until the formation of the new Parliament after the first general elections in 1951–52.

Privy purses continued to be paid to royal families until the 26th Amendment in 1971, by which all their privileges and allowances from the central government were abolished, which was enforced after a two-year legal battle. Hence statement 2 is not correct.

In India, a privy purse was a payment made to ruling families of erstwhile princely states after India's independence as part of their agreements to first integrate with India in 1947 and later merge their states in 1949, Due to which their ruling rights ended.

109(D). A person who is not a member of either house of the Parliament can also be appointed as a minister.

But, within six months, he has to become a member of either House of Parliament (either by election or nomination), otherwise, he will cease to be a minister.

Hence statement 1 is not correct. The salaries and allowances of ministers are determined by the Parliament from time to time. A minister gets the salary and allowances that are payable to a member of parliament.

In addition to this, he gets an assistant allowance (according to his rank), free accommodation, traveling allowance, medical facilities etc.

There is no mention of the Council of Ministers in the Second Schedule. Hence statement 2 is not correct.

110(C). This area is often referred to as the Twilight Zone due to the insufficient amount of light. Hence statement 1 is correct.

- Temperatures range from 5 to 4 °C (41 to 39 °F) in the mesopelagic zone.
- There is high pressure here; It can weigh up to 1,470 pounds per square inch (10,100,000 Pa) and grows with depth.
- 90% of the ocean lies in the bathypelagic (aphotic) zone in which no light penetrates. Hence statement 2 is correct.
- It is also called the midnight zone.
- Here the water pressure is very high and the temperature is close to freezing (range 0 to 6 °C (32 to 43 °F).

111(B). When cold air moves towards a warm air mass, its contact area is called a cold front, while if warm air mass moves towards a cold air mass, the contact area is a warm front. Hence statement 1 is wrong. The fronts occur in mid-latitudes and are characterized by a sharp gradient in temperature and pressure. They bring sudden changes in temperature and lift the air to form clouds and cause precipitation. Hence statement 2 is correct.

There are four types of fronts:
- Cold
- Hot
- Permanent
- Occupant

112(B). Among the given rivers Rind and Sengar are tributaries of Yamuna. Raidak River is a tributary of Brahmaputra. Hence option B is correct.

Yamuna River System:
- Origin: Yamunotri Glacier on the south-western slopes or Bandarpunch peak in the Mussoorie range of the lower Himalayas.
- Flows Through: Enters Uttarakhand, Himachal Pradesh, Haryana, Delhi and merges with the Ganges near Triveni Sangam, Allahabad (Prayagraj).
- It is the largest tributary of the Ganges in the northern plains.

113(D). Price of given item:
- The price of a commodity is the most important determinant of demand.
- When the price of a commodity falls, its demand increases and when its price rises, its demand falls.

Hence statement 1 is correct.
Related goods price:
- When the price of substitute goods rises, the demand for the given commodity also increases and vice versa.
- When the price of complementary goods rises, the demand for the given good falls and vice versa.

Hence statement 3 is correct.
Consumer Income:
In order to examine the effect of changes in the income of households on their demand, commodities are divided into two categories:
- General items
- Substandard goods
- Requirements

Hence statement 2 is correct.
Consumer tastes and preferences:
- The demand for a commodity is also influenced by tastes and preferences. It increases if there is a favorable change in consumer tastes and preferences and vice versa.

Thus, statement 4 is correct.

114(C). The MPC sets the policy interest rate (repo rate) required to achieve the inflation target (4%).

The RBI-appointed committee headed by the then Deputy Governor Urjit Patel in 2014 recommended setting up of the Monetary Policy Committee. Hence statement 3 is correct.

It is a statutory and institutional framework under the Reserve Bank of India Act, 1934 to maintain price stability keeping in view the objective of development. Hence statement 1 is not correct.

Further, Section 45ZB states that "the Monetary Policy Committee shall determine the policy rate necessary to achieve the inflation target".

The decision of the Monetary Policy Committee will be binding on the bank. Section 45ZB says that the MPC shall consist of 6 members.

RBI governor as its ex-officio chairman, therefore, statement 2 is not correct.

115(B). Elections are the most powerful indirect democracy tools because they motivate individuals to elect representatives who later pass laws on their behalf.

So it holds the government responsible for the majority as they can replace them. Hence statement 1 is correct.

People will choose those who will influence the administration and take important decisions. So indirectly citizens are involved in decision making. Hence statement 2 is correct.

Elections ensure that no government is elected for eternity, resulting in tyranny. Hence statement 3 is correct.

Political parties are at the center of election of office bearers.

The selection and nomination of

candidates, an important first stage of the electoral process, is usually in the hands of political parties; An election serves only as the final process in recruitment to political office. Hence statement 4 is not correct.

116(D). Statement I is false but statement II is true.

Government of India Act, 1935:

- The structural part of the Constitution is largely derived from the Government of India Act 1935.
- More than half of the provisions of the Constitution are similar or identical to the 1935 Act.
- Federal planning, judiciary, governor, emergency powers, public service commission and most of the administrative details are taken from this act. Hence statement 1 is false.
- The framers of the constitution also included rules and regulations regarding the form of administration to avoid any confusion.
- The framers of the Indian Constitution were apprehensive that in the prevailing circumstances of the country at that time, the Constitution could be distorted unless the form of administration was also included. Thus, statement 2 is correct.

117(B). Article 75 clearly states that the Council of Ministers is collectively responsible to the Lok Sabha.

This means that all the ministers take joint responsibility towards the Lok Sabha for all their lapses and commissions.

No-confidence motion is moved against the council of ministers as a whole, not as a minister alone. Hence statement 1 is wrong.

In this system of government, the prime minister plays a leadership role. He is the leader of the Council of Ministers, the leader of the parliament and the leader of the party in power.

No person shall be retained as a member of the Council of Ministers if the Prime Minister states that he shall be dismissed. Thus, statement 2 is correct.

118(A). The circle of illumination is the imaginary line that separates the parts of the Earth from day and night.

It divides the earth into two equal parts. Hence, statement 1 is correct.

- It separates the light from the darkness and the day from the evening.
- The Earth's axis is an imaginary line running from top to bottom from the center of the Earth. Thus, while the circle of illumination divides light from darkness and day from night, the axis is a line along which the Earth rotates.

The exact location of the circle of illumination depends on different seasons. This is because the Earth rotates on its axis, and the circle of illumination remains in the same general position. Thus, statement 2 is wrong.

119(C). Knowledge of latitude and longitude is essential to accurately measure the position of any place on the Earth's surface.

- They are components of the geographic grid system.
- Longitude represents the east-west location of a place.
- This is shown on a map or globe by a series of north-south lines that all come together at the North Pole and South Pole and are widest at the equator. These lines of longitude are called "longitude lines".
- Latitude represents the north-south location of a place.
- This is shown on a map or globe by a series of lines running east-west that are parallel to the equator, which marks the midpoint between the two poles around the circumference of the Earth. These lines of latitude are called "parallel lines".

Every place on Earth lies at the intersection of a particular parallel line (latitude) and a particular longitude line (longitude). Thus knowledge of latitude and longitude is essential to accurately measure the position of any place on the earth's surface.

120(A). Daylight Saving Time (DST) is the practice of setting clocks one hour ahead of standard time during the summer months. Hence, statement 1 is correct.

- It is practiced because the duration of a day on Earth is unequal. Places near the equator experience days and nights of almost equal length, ie: 12 hours.
- Whereas other places on Earth experience more daylight in summer than in winter.
- The main purpose of daylight saving time is to make better use of daylight.
- Southern Hemisphere countries like Australia, New Zealand, most of South America etc usually start DST period in September-November and end DST in March-April. Hence, statement 2 is wrong.
- Many countries in the Northern Hemisphere (North America, Europe, Asia) use DST in the summer.

Child Development and Pedagogy

1. Which of the following principle of development is incorrect one?
(a) There are individual differences in development.
(b) Development is the result of coincidences.
(c) It is a continuous process.
(d) It is predictable.

2. Which of the following human relationships comes under tertiary relationship?
(a) Nephew   (b) Uncle
(c) Mother   (d) Friend

3. While working on a jig-saw puzzle, 5 years old Najma says to herself, "Where is the blue piece? No, not this one, darker one that would go here and make this shoe".
This kind of talk is referred to by Vygotsky as:
(a) Private speech
(b) Talk aloud
(c) Scaffolding
(d) Egocentric speech

4. Giving cues to children and offering support as and when needed is an example of __________.
(a) reinforcement
(b) conditioning
(c) modelling
(d) scaffolding

5. Instruction at the primary stage need to be:
(a) Teacher centered
(b) Textbook centred
(c) Student centered
(d) Teacher and Textbook centrered

6. An educational psychologist works:
(a) only within the classroom, focusing on children's behaviour.
(b) at multiple levels, with individual children, groups of children, parents and at the organizational level.
(c) exclusively with individual children with special education need.
(d) only at administration level

7. Which of the following Psychologist viewed that cognitive development of children as a socially mediated process in which children depend on assistance from adults and more expert peers?
(a) Bronfen Brenner
(b) Freud
(c) Vygotsky
(d) Jean Piaget

8. A positive or negative evaluative reaction towards a stimulus, such as a person, action, object or concept is known as:
(a) Attitude   (b) Aptitude
(c) Interest   (d) Appreciation

9. In Indian context (According to RPWD Act, 2016) a person can be considered as 'Deaf' if:
(a) He has 70 dB or more hearing loss in speech frequency on both ears.
(b) He has 60 dB to 70 dB hearing loss in both ears.
(c) He has 60 dB to 50 dB hearing loss in both ears.
(d) He has 50 dB or less hearing loss in both ears.

10. Which of the following can not be considered as a characteristic of an activity-based classroom?
(I) Children are totally involved in doing their work by collaborating with their peers.
(II) If children are asked what they are doing they could not state the objectives of that activity.
(a) Only I
(b) Only II
(c) Both I & II
(d) None of these

11. What are the critical role played by a teacher
I. Observer and diagnostician of learner
II. Provider of the environment for learning
II. Facilitator of learning
(a) Only I   (b) I and II
(c) II and III   (d) I, II, and III

12. Which of these is a planned performance of an occupational skill, scientific principle or an experiment?
(a) Jigsaw method
(b) Problem solving
(c) Synthetic method
(d) Demonstration

13. Which of the following is incorrect about Autistic Spectrum Disorder?
(a) It affects the child's ability to communicate.
(b) Frequently associated with repetitive behaviour.
(c) It appears after first 3 years of life.
(d) It affects the ability to develop inter-individual relationship.

14. The test should be reliable, valid and standardized. Here the term validity refers to:
(a) if it measures something consistently
(b) the degree to which it measures what it intends to measure
(c) comparison of a score of a person with those of others in a defined group
(d) the procedure of administration of a test to all persons in the same way under the same condition

15. If you are unable to get a job of teacher, then you will:
(a) start giving tuition at home
(b) remain at home till you get a job
(c) take some another job
(d) continue applying for teaching

16. Which of the following is the approximate age range related to Erickson's psychological stage termed as "Initiative versus Guilt"?
(a) 3-6 years   (b) 6-11 years
(c) 1-3 years   (d) 13-18 years

17. Students should be involved in keeping their school clean to create a sense of responsibility and pride in their school environment. What can be the result of this statement.
(a) School campus will be clean and hygienic
(b) Teachers and staff have less burden to clean the school
(c) Students will keep their home clean
(d) Skills learnt in school may be carried into other environments, hopefully for many years.

18. According to Bronfenbrenner's Bio-Ecological model, 'War' can be included in which of the following system?
(a) Individual system
(b) Micro system
(c) Meso system
(d) Chrono system

19. Which of the following things a teacher should consider while creating individual learning situation in the classroom?

I. Communication of assignments clearly
II. Monitor students' work
III. Provide appropriate feedback

(a) I and II   (b) I, II and III
(c) I and III   (d) II and III

20. _____ education is life oriented.
(a) Formal
(b) Non-formal
(c) Informal
(d) All of the above

21. Which of the following factor influences personality development of a child?
(a) Hereditary
(b) Physical environment
(c) Social environment
(d) All of the above

22. Which one of the following is an example of intrinsic motivation?
(a) Competition
(b) Praise
(c) Rewards
(d) Level of aspiration

23. In the context of education, socialization means:
(a) creating one's own social norms
(b) respecting elders in society
(c) adapting and adjusting to social environment
(d) always following social norms

24. What should a teacher do to develop spirit of labour in students?
(a) Give example of people who put in labour
(b) Teacher should indulge in labour
(c) Give detailed lectures on importance of labour
(d) Give opportunities to students to do labour often

25. Which of the following is NOT a factor that is essential for the success of work education?
(a) Positive relationship between community and school
(b) Broadmindedness
(c) Dignity of labour and pessimistic attitude
(d) Feelings of co-operation

26. As Freud observed 'Electra Complex' develops at a particular age of child. The age of developing an electra complex falls under which of the following Piagetian stage?
(a) Sensory Motor stage
(b) Pre-operational stage
(c) Concrete operational stage
(d) Formal operational stage

27. Which of the following step shall be taken to transform the assessment for school development ?
(a) The progress card of all students for school-based assessment will be completely redesigned by States/UTS.
(b) The progress card will be a holistic, 360 degree, multidimensional report that reflects in great detail the progress.
(c) Both 1 and 2
(d) Only 2

28. Which of the following are those teaching learning materials that are prepared by teachers and students in most of the schools?
I. Graphs
II. Number and alphabet cards
III. Flash cards on different themes

(a) I and IV   (b) I and II
(c) I, II and III   (d) II and III

29. Which of the following is not the step of social learning theory of Albert Bandura?
(a) Attending to and perceiving the behaviour
(b) Remembering the behaviour
(c) Converting the memory into action
(d) Generalization of the Imitated Behaviour

30. In which principle of development, the child develops in sequence and follows two tends?
(a) Learning and Maturation
(b) Development is correlated
(c) Development is flexible
(d) Cephalo-caudal and Proximodistal

Language - I: English

Ques (31-39): Direction : Read the passage given below and answer the following questions.

Gender inequality is the main social issue in India. There is a need to accelerate women empowerment to bring men and women on par. The upliftment of women in all fields should be included in the national priority. The disparity between men and women gives rise to many problems which can pose as major obstacles in the development of the nation. It is the birthright of women that they should get equal importance to men in society. To really bring empowerment, women should be aware of their rights. Not only domestic and family responsibilities but also women should play an active and positive role in every field. They should also know the happenings around them and in the country.

Women empowerment has this power to change a lot in society and the country. She can deal with any problem in society better than men. She can understand well the loss of overpopulation for the country and the family. With good family planning, she is fully capable of managing the economic condition of the country and the family. Women are more capable of handling any effective violence than men, whether it is family or social.

Through women empowerment, it is possible that a country with female-male equality of a strong economy can be replaced with a country with male influence. With the help of women empowerment, every member of the family can develop easily without much effort. A woman is considered very responsible for everything in the family, so she can solve all problems well. With the empowerment of women, the whole society will automatically become strong.

Women empowerment is a better solution to any small or major problem related to human, economic or environmental. In the last few years, we are getting the benefit of women empowerment. Women are more conscious about their health, education, job, and responsibility towards family, country and society. She participates prominently in every field and shows her interest. Finally, after many years of struggle, they are getting their right to follow the right path.

31. What attribute of a women can bring the real empowerment?
(a) Women should know her responsibility towards family, country and society.
(b) Women should help in improvising economic condition of the country
(c) Women should be aware of their rights
(d) All of the above

32. What has the power to change a lot in society?
(a) Women health
(b) Economic condition
(c) Male influence
(d) Women empowerment

33. Choose the word which is opposite in meaning to 'influence'.
(a) Impotence   (b) Powerful
(c) Efficacy   (d) Impact

34. Find the error.

A women (a)/ can deal (b)/ with any problem in the society (c)/ in best way.(d)

(a) a   (b) b
(c) c   (d) d

35. Read the following statements:
A. A country with female-male equality forms a strong economy.
B. Human, economic or environmental problems can not be dealt with by Woman empowerment.

(a) A is true
(b) B is true
(c) Both A and B are true
(d) Both A and B are false

36. Identify the part of speech of the underlined word:
The disparity between men and women gives <u>rise</u> to many problems.

(a) Preposition   (b) Adjective
(c) Pronoun   (d) Conjunction

37. Which of the following is NOT true?
(a) The disparity between men and women gives rise to many problems
(b) No one in the country can understand the loss of overpopulation for the country and the family
(c) Women are active participants in every field
(d) Women are more conscious about their health, education, job, and responsibility

38. Identify the part of speech of the underlined word:
The disparity <u>between</u> men and women gives rise to many problems.

(a) Adverb   (b) Preposition
(c) Conjunction   (d) Verb

39. Disparity in the line, "The disparity between men and women gives rise to many problems which can pose as major obstacles in the development of the nation." means
(a) Equality   (b) Similarity
(c) Difference   (d) Unity

Ques (40-45): Directions : Read the extract given below and answer the questions that follow by selecting the most appropriate options:
I have a little shadow
that goes in and out with me.
And what can be that use of him
is more than I can see.
He is very, very like me
from the heels upto the head;

And I see him jump before me
When I jump into my bed.
The funniest thing about him
is the way he likes to grow-
Not at all like proper children,
Which is always very slow;
For he sometimes shoots up taller
like an India rubber ball,
And he sometimes gets so little that
There's none of him at all.

40. The expression 'that goes in and out with me' refers to:
(a) The shadow
(b) Child
(c) The poet
(d) A rubber ball

41. Which of the following statement is not true?
(a) The shadow's appearance is just like the poet from toe to head.
(b) The shadow does not become taller than him.
(c) The poet finds his shadow funny.
(d) The poet observes that his shadows goes before him.

42. Which of the following adjectives do not apply to the shadow?
(a) Funny
(b) Slow
(c) Tall
(d) None of these

43. What is the meaning of the word 'coward'?
(a) Wimp   (b) Daredevil
(c) Valiant   (d) Stalwart

44. Which literary device is used in the expression 'He is very, very like me'?
(a) Assonance
(b) Alliteration
(c) Simile
(d) Personification

45. Name the figure of speech used in 'He stays so close beside me'.
(a) Metaphor
(b) Alliteration
(c) Simile
(d) Personification

46. The primary objective of teaching new words is:
(a) To enable the students to become better readers
(b) To enable the students to become better writers
(c) To enable the students to translate words into another language
(d) To enable the students to coin new words

47. In a constructive classroom, language learning should be based on:
(a) the transaction of the prescribed textbook by the teacher
(b) learners' previous knowledge in constructing their new knowledge using authentic tasks
(c) the assumption that the English language can only be learned if the teacher transmits it to the learners
(d) drill and practice of grammatical items

48. Which of the following is not the aim of language pedagogy?
(a) To develop learners' communicative skills
(b) To encourage the learners to express their ideas in an organized and systematic way.
(c) To enable them to use appropriate vocabulary in writing various forms of composition.
(d) To prepare them for good handwriting

49. Which of the following statements is not true about teaching?
(a) Teaching is modifiable
(b) Teaching is formal and informal
(c) Teaching is a science as well as art
(d) Teaching is instruction

50. A language teacher is planning to teach grammar. Which one of the following might be a good strategy for teaching grammar?
(a) Providing the chance to practice grammar in context
(b) Emphasizing students to note down the rules clearly
(c) Teaching grammar using a standard book
(d) Asking students to practice questions only to learn rules

51. What does 'comprehensible input' means in language learning?
(a) Engagement with language which is comprehensible to all learners.
(b) Engagement with written and formal language below the level current level of master of the learner.
(c) Exposure to high level of written and spoken language above the learner's current level of mastery.

(d) Exposure to meaningful oral and written language somewhat above the learners' current level of mastery.

52. **TBLT in second language teaching is:**
    (a) Tool Based Language Teaching
    (b) Task Book Language Teaching
    (c) Task Based Language Teaching
    (d) None of the above

53. **A teacher "teaching again" the content that students previously failed to learn. Here, the teacher is using:**
    (a) measurement process
    (b) remediation process
    (c) evaluation process
    (d) observation process

54. **A teacher brings a newspaper to her class VIII students and asks them to find some advertisements. She then asks them to list out how advertisements are designed and what an advertisement contains. What is the newspaper have?**
    (a) For reading.
    (b) An instrument of language learning.
    (c) A technique of language learning.
    (d) Materials for language learning.

55. **Students are asked to read a short text and make points for discussion. What skills of the learners are assessed?**
    (a) Study skills
    (b) Listening skills
    (c) Speaking skills
    (d) Writing skills

56. **What is the status of English in India? It is:**
    (a) an associate official language.
    (b) the official language
    (c) a regional language
    (d) a foreign language

57. **A class VII student makes mistakes in spelling. As a teacher would you:**
    (a) allow the student to use a mobile dictionary?
    (b) ask the student to re-pronounce the word?
    (c) show him his mistakes and ask him to re-pronounce them?
    (d) gnore the mistakes?

58. **How can a language teacher help a student in learning English whose exposure to the target language (English) is limited?**

(a) By giving him extra remedial classes.
(b) Being extra sensitive towards his needs.
(c) By giving him supplementary reading materials.
(d) By enrolling him in language library.

59. **A teacher one of his students about "what was it to study in your previous school?" This type of question is:**
    (a) Lower-Order Question
    (b) Higher-Order Question
    (c) Close Ended Question
    (d) None of the above

60. **Which of the following is most helpful in presenting the needs of a multilingual classroom?**
    (a) Miscellaneous written exams
    (b) More than once, linguistic assessment
    (c) More than one textbook
    (d) Miscellaneous text material

Social Studies

61. **Match the List - I with List - II and choose the correct answer from the code given below :**

	List - I		List - II
(a)	Harappa	(i)	Dancing girl statue
(b)	Mohenjo Daro	(ii)	Early Dentistry
(c)	Kalibangan	(iii)	Zebu
(d)	Mehrgarh	(iv)	Ploughed fields

(a) (a) - (iv), (b) - (iii), (c) -(i), (d) - (ii)
(b) (a) - (i), (b) - (ii), (c) - (iv), (d) - (iii)
(c) (a) - (iii), (b) - (i), (c) - (ii), (d) - (iv)
(d) (a) - (iii), (b) - (i), (c) - (iv), (d) - (ii)

62. **Which of the following pairs (of dynasties and their founders) is NOT correctly matched?**

Dynasties	Founder
A. Slave Dynasty	Balban
B. Tughlaq Dynasty	Ghiyasuddin
C. Khilji Dynasty	Jalaluddin
D. Second Afghan Empire	Sher Shah Suri

(a) Only A　　　　(b) Only C
(c) A and D　　　(d) B and C

63. **Consider the following statements with respect to Megasthenes :**
    1. He was a Greek ambassador in the court of Bindusara.
    2. He wrote a book named Indica.
    Which of the statements given above is/are correct?
    (a) 1 only
    (b) 2 only
    (c) Both 1 and 2
    (d) Neither 1 nor 2

64. **Which of the following statements about Gupta coinages are true?**
    i. Gupta rulers issued well-minted gold coins.
    ii. The obverse of coins depicts the reigning king in various poses.
    iii. The reverse of the coins has religious symbols.
    iv. Chandragupta-II Vikramadita issued Lion-Slayer type coins.
    Choose the right code :
    (a) i, iii & iv　　(b) ii & iv
    (c) i & iv　　　　(d) i, ii, iii & iv

65. **Who conducts municipal and panchayat elections?**
    (a) State government
    (b) State Election Commission
    (c) Central government
    (d) Central Election Commission

66. **The state leading in manganese production is:**
    (a) Odisha
    (b) Karnataka
    (c) Andhra Pradesh
    (d) None of these

67. **Indian Constitution presents three list for the distribution of power between Centre and States. Which two Articles regulate that distribution?**
    (a) Article 4 and 5
    (b) Article 56 and 57
    (c) Article 141 and 142
    (d) Article 245 and 246

68. **Read the following statements.**
    Statement (A): There is considerable socio-cultural diversity in India.
    Statement (B): Diversity necessarily leads to equal opportunity.
    Choose the correct option.
    (a) Both (A) and (B) are true and (B) is the correct explanation of (A).
    (b) Both (A) and (B) are true but (B) is not the correct explanation of (A).
    (c) (A) is true but (B) is false.

(d)   (A) is true but (B) is false.

69. Indian society is _______ in nature.
    (a) tribal   (b) pluralistic
    (c) rural   (d) urban

70. Consider the following statements for Government in India and choose the correct option.
    A) Measuring land and keeping land records is the main work of the Patwari.
    B) Each Patwari is responsible for a group of urban blocks.
    (a) Only A is correct
    (b) Only B is correct
    (c) A and B both are correct
    (d) A and B both are incorrect

71. Who among the following were the members of the drafting committee of the Constitution?
    (i) N. Gopalswami
    (ii) Jawaharlal Nehru
    (iii) Alladi Krishnaswami Ayyar
    (iv) Sardar Patel
    Select the correct answer using the code given below:
    (a) (i) and (iii)
    (b) (i) and (iv)
    (c) (i), (iii) and (iv)
    (d) (ii), (iii) and (iv)

72. In which of the following rivers is the Majuli River Island situated?
    (a) Ganga
    (b) Brahmaputra
    (c) Godavari
    (d) Indus

73. Consider the following statements about Motion of the earth:
    1)Revolution is the movement of the earth on its axis.
    2)Rotation is the movement of the earth around the sun in a fixed path or orbit.
    3)Days and nights occur due to rotation of the earth.
    Which of the following statement is/are correct?
    (a) 1 only   (b) 1 and 2 only
    (c) 1 and 3 only   (d) 3 only

74. Which of the following statement is true regarding the Opposition party?
    A) elected representatives who are not members of the ruling party
    B) play the role of questioning government decisions and actions
    C) raise new issues for consideration in the Parliament.
    (a) Only A and C is true

(b) Only B and C is true
(c) Only A and B is true
(d) All A, B, and C is true

75. Famous companies like HCL, Barclay's, Samsung, Agilent, CSC are contribution to the increasing economy of the state of UP. These are located in:
    (a) Moradabad   (b) Mirzapur
    (c) Agra   (d) Noida

76. The combustion of coal, petrol and diesel etc is the basic source of:
    (a) Water pollution
    (b) Air pollution
    (c) Land pollution
    (d) Noise pollution

77. Ozone holes are more pronounced at the:
    (a) Equator
    (b) Tropic of Cancer
    (c) Tropic of Capricorn
    (d) Poles

78. With reference to the Plate Tectonics Theory, consider the following statements:
    1. The divergent motion of plates results in the formation of a new crust or submarine mountains.
    2. When two continental plates converge, the subduction at the Benioff zone gives rise to Volcanoes.
    3. Highly seismic zones are found along the parallel boundaries of plates.
    Which of the statements given above is/are correct?
    (a) 1 and 2 only   (b) 1 and 3 only
    (c) 2 and 3 only   (d) 1, 2 and 3

79. Which of the following curriculum approaches of social studies emphasize organizing the concepts in layers in several classes to fill in more complexity and depth?
    (a) Unit approach
    (b) Concentric approach
    (c) Tropical approach
    (d) None of these

80. The suggestive measures for gender friendly classroom environment is:
    (a) Allocation of classroom duties
    (b) Sharing of examples of gender neutrality
    (c) Boys and girls should participate equally
    (d) Encourage the participation of boys

81. Teaching, conduct of examination, evaluation of learner performance are the examples of:
    (a) Co-curricular activities
    (b) Curricular Activities
    (c) Both (A) and (B)
    (d) None of these

82. The collection of weather information from the local newspaper is an example of which type of source?
    (a) Primary
    (b) Secondary
    (c) Tertiary
    (d) Both primary and tertiary

83. From which monument, Gautama Buddha propagated his divine knowledge of Buddhism to the world?
    (a) Humayun's Tomb
    (b) Mahabodhi Temple Complex
    (c) Qutub Minar
    (d) Red Fort Complex

84. Direction: Answer the following questions by selecting the correct / most appropriate options.
    Statement A): Seals may have been used to stamp bags or packets containing goods that were sent from one place to another.
    Statement B): If the sealing was intact, one could be sure that the goods had arrived safely.
    (a) Both A) and B) are true and B) is the correct explanation of A)
    (b) Both A) and B) are true, but B) is not the correct explanation of A)
    (c) A) is true, but B) is false
    (d) A) is false, but B) is true

85. As per Asoka's inscriptions, which among the following place was declared tax free and proclaimed only 1/8th part as taxable?
    (a) Kushinagar   (b) Lumbini
    (c) Kathmandu   (d) Sarnath

86. In which year was the Widow Remarriage Act passed?
    (a) 1897   (b) 1856
    (c) 1899   (d) 1857

87. Which organisation was established by Swami Vivekananda?
    (a) Brahmo Samaj
    (b) Arya Samaj
    (c) SGPC
    (d) Ramakrishna Mission

88. Identify the crop on the basis of the following characteristics:

1. India is the seventh-largest producer worldwide.
2. It is used both as food and fodder.
3. The top Producing State in India is Karnataka.
Select the correct answer using the code given below:

(a) Rice
(b) Wheat
(c) Maize
(d) Pulses

89. Cocos plate lies between:

(a) Central America and Pacific Plate
(b) North America and Pacific Plate
(c) South America and Pacific Plate
(d) None of these

90. Match List-I with List-II and select the correct answer using the codes given below the lists:

List – I (Mountain Pass)	List – II (State)
(A) Manaa	(i) Sikkim
(B) Nathula	(ii) Jammu & Kashmir
(C) Zozila	(iii) Himachal Pradesh
(D) Sipki La	(iv) Uttarakhand

(a) (A) - (2), (B) - (3), (C) - (1), (D) - (4)
(b) (A) - (4), (B) - (3), (C) - (2), (D) - (1)
(c) (A) - (4), (B) - (1), (C) - (2), (D) - (3)
(d) (A) - (4), (B) - (1), (C) - (3), (D) - (2)

91. Consider the following statements about Salinity of Water
1. It influences the composition and movement of the sea: water and the distribution of fish and other marine resources
2. Salinity affects seawater density, which in turn governs ocean circulation and climate
Which of the above statements is/are correct?

(a) 1 only
(b) 2 only
(c) Both 1 and 2
(d) Neither 1 or 2

92. Statement A: India has an independent judiciary system.
Statement B: The independence of the judiciary allows the courts to play a central role in ensuring that there is no misuse of power by the legislature and the executive.
Statement C: It protect the Fundamental Rights of citizens because anyone can approach the courts.

Choose the correct option.
(a) Only A
(b) Only B and C
(c) Only A and C
(d) A. B, and C

93. Group project work helps in developing

(a) Strong intra-group competition
(b) Individual sense of achievement
(c) Collaboration and problem solving skills
(d) All of the above

94. Students at the upper primary level can be asked to go for a field visit as part of Social Science projects so that:

(a) it is participative and fun for students.
(b) it enables comparison of realities with the ideas and concepts.
(c) it frees the teacher to do other activities while students are busy.
(d) it fulfils the mandatory requirement of project completion.

95. Which of the following social science questions provides opportunity to develop students' critical thinking?
A. Explain your views on installing solar power panels on a building.
B. Do you think that electric vehicles can help in reducing air pollution? Discuss.
C. How did the conflict between Russia and Ukraine started?
Choose the correct option

(a) A, B, and C
(b) A and B
(c) B and C
(d) A and C

96. A teacher uses a research article with rich data, as a resource to teach students about India's relations with other nations. However, during the class, the teacher and students come across a paragraph that paints a neighbouring country in a strongly negative light.
Which of the following is the most responsible approach for the Social Science teacher?

(a) Tell students that you were not aware of these paragraphs and they should only use their textbook for learning various topics.
(b) Switch to another, less useful, source instead, to continue the class. Discussing the controversy would only waste time.
(c) Analyse the paragraph along with students, where they can discuss and debate the assumptions made or data given about the country.
(d) Continue reading the article as-is, since the students in your class are all from India and it should not hurt their sentiments.

97. ____ is a type of teaching that encourages students to play a more active role in their learning process by solving problems designed to answer a general concept or answering a series of questions.

(a) Exploration approach
(b) Inquiry approach
(c) Lecture method
(d) Expository approach

98. Arrange the name of the following Pallava rulers according to their reign in correct chronological order and select the correct answer from the codes given below:
1. Parameshvaravarman I
2. Narsinghvarman I
3. Nandivarman II
4. Mahendravarman I

(a) 4, 2, 1, 3
(b) 4, 3, 1, 2
(c) 1, 3, 2, 4
(d) 3, 2, 1, 4

99. Activity based questions make Social Science lessons:

(a) lengthy
(b) comprehensive
(c) joyful
(d) debatable

100. Which of the following statements about a 'diverse society' is correct?

(a) It would have differences and inequalities in language, religion and culture.
(b) It would have differences in culture and power.
(c) It would have similarities of language, religion and culture.
(d) It would have differences and similarities in language, culture and religion.

101. Which of the following is an effective activity when teaching political science through a conversation strategy in the classroom?

(a) Asking students to play the role of a panchayat president who is addressing members of the gram sabha
(b) Asking students to prepare a play based on any current political issue

(c) Asking students to write a play on the subject of political science

(d) Asking students to watch a dramatized drama based on politics

102. The main problem of Social Science teaching is

(a) Conventional teaching practices

(b) Lack of library facilities

(c) Untrained teachers

(d) All of these

103. While teaching controversial issues in Social Science class, you should:

(a) Take them up occasionally and conduct brief discussions.

(b) Take them up with proper planning to initiate a dignified discussion

(c) Keep in mind students' background and discuss only non-hurtful aspects.

(d) Completely avoid confrontations.

104. You observe that students exhibit prejudices in a Social Science class. What would be your most appropriate response?

(a) Bring the chapter to a close

(b) Organize a discussion on dimensions of social reality.

(c) Ignore these comments.

(d) Reprimand students.

105. Which of the following is not an aim of teaching social studies?

(a) Good citizenship

(b) Character building

(c) Scoring well

(d) Proper use of leisure

106. Which of the following statements is/are correct about the social science nature?
I. Social science as a subject of study includes a large number of subjects like political science, anthropology, law, economics, geography etc.?
II. Social science is predominantly interdisciplinary and interdependent in nature.
III. It should be integrated with various disciplines while conducting social science curriculum.

(a) I and III   (b) I and III

(c) I, II and III   (d) I and II

107. Social Studies is supposed to study
(i) Economical relations of man
(ii) Political relations of man
(iii) Social relations of man
(iv) Social geographical relations of man

(a) (i), (ii), (iii)

(b) (ii), (iii), (iv)

(c) (i), (iii), (iv)

(d) (i), (ii), (iii), (iv)

108. Which criteria is not correct for a good evaluation?

(a) Validity   (b) Reliability

(c) Objectivity   (d) Subjectivity

109. What is the main purpose of an Open-Book Evaluation?

(a) Teachers need not undergo extra pressure to frame new questions.

(b) Students need not read extra books.

(c) Students can answer exactly according to the textbook.

(d) Students need not feel the burden to rote memorise all facts and details

110. Consider the following pairs regarding the governors of Muhammad Ghori and the territories where they ruled almost independently after the death of Muhammad Ghori.

Governors of Muhammad Ghori	Territories
1. Yaldoz	Indus
2. Kubacha	Bengal
3. Muhammad-ibn-Bakhtyar	Ghazni
4. Aibak	Delhi

How many pairs given above is/are correctly matched?

(a) Only one pair

(b) Only two pairs

(c) Only three pairs

(d) All four pairs

111. Read the statements and choose the correct option.
Assertion (A) : Sangam texts have been composed and compiled in assemblies of poets that were held in the city of Madurai.
Reasoning (R) : The Sangam poets and the unknown Greeks were contemporaries.

(a) Both (A) and (R) are true and (R) is the correct explanation of (A).

(b) Both (A) and (R) are true but (R) is not the correct explanation of (A).

(c) (A) is true but (R) is false.

(d) Both (A) and (R) are false.

112. Given below are two statements: One is labelled as Assertion A and the other is labelled as Reason R.
Assertion (A) : The Gupta period saw the ascendency of Hinduism, especially Bhagavatism or vaishnavism
Reason (R) : Fahsien given the impression that Buddhism was flourishing during this period. It may be said first that four Buddha images were added at the four entrances of the great stupa of Sanchi. Nalanda also became a centre of Buddhist education during this period.
In the light of the above statements, choose the most appropriate answer from the options given below:

(a) Both (A) and (R) are true and (R) is the correct explanation of (A)

(b) Both (A) and (R) are true but (R) is NOT the correct explanation of (A)

(c) (A) is true but (R) is false

(d) (A) is false but (R) is true

113. Which Article of the Constitution deals with Urban Local Bodies?

(a) Article 243 P - Article 243 ZG

(b) Article 243 A - Article 243 O

(c) Article 243 P - Article 243 ZJ

(d) Article 243 A - Article 243 P

114. Statment A: Public Interest Litigation or PIL to increase access to justice.
Statement B: It allowed any individual or organization to file a PIL in the High Court.
Statement C: The Supreme Court has nothing to do with PIL.
Which of the above statemet is/are is not correct.

(a) A and B   (b) B and C

(c) Only B   (d) Only C

115. In the month of June 2022 who has launched the scheme known as "SHRESHTA" for residential education for students in High school?

(a) Virendra Kumar

(b) Amit Shah

(c) Narendra Modi

(d) Rajnath Singh

116. Which State/ Union territory has recently launched Super-75 scholarship scheme?

(a) Delhi

   (b) Kerala

   (c) Jammu and Kashmir

   (d) Karnataka

117. In India, which of the following is constitutionally empowered to act as the final interpreter of the Constitution?

   (a) President of India

   (b) Union Council of Ministers

   (c) Parliament

   (d) Supreme Court

118. Which of the following are secondary agencies of socialization?
(i) Family
(ii) Media
(iii) Religious institutions
(iv) School

   (a) (i), (ii), (iv)

   (b) (i), (iii), (iv)

   (c) (ii), (iii), (iv)

   (d) (i), (ii), (iii), (iv)

119. The last Tirthankara of Jainism was __________.

   (a) Parshvanath

   (b) Mahavira

   (c) Ajitnath

   (d) None of them

120. What is the meaning of Production in terms of Economics?

   (a) Forming

   (b) Making

   (c) Manufacturing

   (d) Creating Utility

// Hints and Solutions //

1(B). Development is a continuous process from the womb to the tomb and continues gradually until reaching its maximum growth.

The rate of development is not uniform and everyone has their own particular rate of development.

It is a wide and complex process, thus there are some principles that need to be followed for a better understanding of the concept.

Principles of development include:

- Development is cumulative.
- Development is predictable.
- Development is the process of interaction.
- Development follows uniformity of pattern.
- Development is predictable and sequential.
- Development proceeds from general to specific.
- Development rate varies from person to person.

Therefore, it could be concluded that 'Development is the result of coincidences' is not a principle of development.

2(D). We conclude that friend comes under tertiary relationship.

Society is a 'web of relationship' and these relations are fundamental for understanding human behaviour and different institutions of society. Different forms of relations in family, community and society are:

Within the family, there are relations like mother, father, son, daughter, husband, wife, brother, sister which we put under primary relations

uncle, aunt, nephew, niece are called secondary relatives.

There are also tertiary relatives like friends, neighbourhood relations and many other similar relations.

3(A). Lev Vygotsky introduced the term 'Private speech' in his Sociocultural theory, which refers to when children 'think out loud'. It illustrates that children use speech to guide their own actions.

Concept of private speech:

- Private speech refers to the speech produced aloud by young children which seems to be addressed either to the self or to others, which sometimes cannot be easily conceived by a listener.
- It has a major role in the augmentation of the self and self-consciousness.
- For example, Najma says to herself, "Where is the blue piece? No, not this one, darker one that would go here and make this shoe". This is a kind of self-talk by Najma, so it can be considered as private speech.
- This phenomenon starts in the early years of life and proceeds to the end of adolescence and even later.

4(D). Scaffolding is a teaching method that enables a student to solve a problem, carry out a task, or achieve a goal through a gradual shedding of outside assistance. Scaffolding literally means the structure which is made to support the work crew while a building is constructed or repaired.

- Scaffolding is a technique that is linked to the concept of the Zone of Proximal Development (ZPD), which refers to a range of tasks that a child can achieve only with assistance from a more skilled adult or peer.
- This concept was developed by the Russian psychologist, Lev Vygotsky in his "Sociocultural Theory of Learning".
- Scaffolding refers to a technique that provides the right kind of support in the right amount at the right time to increase a child's competence.
- In other words, it is a means by which a child's 'zone width' (or potential for new learning) can be assessed, i.e. scaffolding

helps with providing support to learners in their initial phase of learning, which is in the right amount and gradually decreases as the learner progresses.

- As children are given assistance or shown how to perform certain tasks, they use this information as a guide on how to perform these tasks and eventually learn to perform them independently.
- It helps a learner to move from a Zone of Actual Development to a Zone of Proximal Development and finally reach to Zone of Desired Development, with the help of a more experienced person like peers, elders in the family, or teachers.
- For example, a teacher gives a lesson on vocabulary before making the child read a difficult passage and provides necessary cues and prompts when the child faces difficulty.

5(C). At primary stage covers the children of class I-V. At this stage, the child is very curious to learn new things. In this age group, children are not able to comprehend the learning. Therefore, at the primary stage when children have to learn basic concepts they should be taught through play and activities arid not through the 'chalk and talk' method.

Learner-Centered Instruction at the primary stage: There are demands for learner-centered methods so that learning is meaningful to learners.

- It should basically have a child-centered approach involving the interaction of children. The activities .should be interesting, relevant, based on the daily life experiences of the child.
- The age. mental level. aptitude, interest, and abilities of the child should be the main criteria for selecting the activities.
- It should enhance the natural curiosity of the child; It should help the child in developing attitudes and qualities such as self-confidence, the spirit of inquiry, initiative, courage to ask questions.
- It should encourage the child to think of solutions to problems in higher day-to-day life.
- It should develop the desired skills in children; It should help a child to develop logical thinking; It should help a child to take an active interest and participate in solving some simple problems in a limited way.

6(B). Education Psychology is a part of your course on Behavioural Sciences.

- Educational psychology by its very nature is dynamic and constantly evolving from childhood till death. Man learns by his intelligence, ability and motivation.
- It helps the teacher to foster harmonious overall development of the student.

7(C). Cognitive development is the process in which cognition (thinking) develops. It is the orderly development of mental and intellectual processes, like logical thinking, making sense of new ideas, solving problem and the like, that takes place over a period of time.
- Even the process of concept formation is a part of cognition.

Lev Vygotsky:
- The cultural theory of Vygotsky attempts to explicate this relationship between individual cognitive processes and the historical, cultural, and social settings in which it occurs.
- It sees psychological processes as culturally mediated, historically developing, and socially engendered.
- He stresses the impact of culture and language on the cognitive development. According to him, without culture, our intellectual functioning is limited to apelike, elementary mental functions. With intensive interaction with the elements of culture and a healthy language development, we become capable of higher mental functions involved in thinking, reasoning, remembering and so on.

Therefore, Lev Vygotsky ,the famous Russian psychologist viewed that cognitive development of children as a socially mediated process in which children depend on assistance from adults and more expert peers.

8(A). Attitude: Allport (1935) defined attitude as "a mental and neural state of readiness, organised through experience, and exerting a directive or dynamic influence upon the individual's response to all objects and situations with which it is related" .

9(A). Disability: A disability is defined as any restriction or lack (resulting from an impairment) of ability to perform an activity in the manner or within the range considered normal for a human being.
Hearing impairment :
- "deaf" means persons having 70 DB hearing loss in speech frequencies in both ears;
- "hard of hearing" means person having 60 DB to 70 DB hearing loss in speech frequencies in both ears.

10(B). Activity-based learning is a "learner-centered" approach in the teaching-learning process. In this approach, the 'learner' or 'child' is the main focus of the educational program. It emphasizes learning rather than teaching.
- During activity-based learning, the learners use their multiple senses to understand the concepts and enhance learning.

11(D). The learner is at the centre of all activities in learner-centred approach. The teacher plays the role of a facilitator of the learning process and an organizer of the learning situation to "stimulate curiosity and independent thinking, develop problem-solving skills, promote planning and execution of projects and develop self-learning involving acquisition of knowledge through observation of phenomena, creative thinking and activities." (National Curriculum for Elementary and Secondary Education-A Framework,1987). In the learner-centred approach, as a teacher, you have the following three critical roles to play:
- Observer and diagnostician of learner: You must constantly watch the behaviour and activities of learners in and out of the classroom so as to estimate and diagnose strengths, weaknesses, learning needs, and learning dispositions. This would help you in shaping and providing appropriate learning environments and learning activities for the learners.
- Provider of the environment for learning: Once you diagnose the various learning needs of the learners, it becomes your primary duty to plan a learning environment that is conducive so that each learner would find enough scope and opportunity to fulfil his/ her needs.
- Facilitator of learning: You always need to look out for occasions to help the learners while they are engaged in learning. This is more challenging than directly teaching. As we know that each learner has a distinct learning style, variations in learning dispositions, we have to provide support at the appropriate situations during their period of learning. Further, you need to encourage the learners to be engaged in learning activities whenever you find them remaining inactive.

12(D). Demonstration means any planned performance of an occupation skill, scientific principle or experiment.
- The most effective way to teach an occupational skill is to demonstrate it. demonstrate it. one of the two most essential teaching skills is the ability to demonstrate; the other is the ability to explain. Both are vital to the success of either an operation lesson or an information lesson.
- The demonstration is defined as a method of teaching by exhibition and explanation. It implies the presence of an organized series of events or equipment to a group of students for their observation.
- It is a combination of lecture and laboratory work. The teacher makes the use of classroom and demonstration table area in the classroom to teach and demonstrate.
- Some part of the teaching is done before the demonstration, some during the demonstration, and some after demonstration to explain the purposes, articles used, underlying principles, and termination of the procedure, etc.

13(C). Autism: It is a developmental disorder that is characterised by impaired development in communication, social interaction, and behaviour.
- Autism is classified as a pervasive developmental disorder (PDD), a category of disorders that is often described interchangeably with the broad spectrum of developmental disorders affecting young children and adults called the autistic spectrum disorders (ASD).
- The behavioral symptoms of autism spectrum disorder (ASD) often appear early in development. Many children show symptoms of autism by 12 months to 18 months of age or earlier.

14(B). A psychological test is a structured technique used to generate a carefully selected sample of behavior.

15(D). If you are unable to get the job of a teacher, then you will continue applying for teaching. A person who is dedicated and passionate about teaching will continue applying for the teacher job by upgrading skills and attitude. This dedication and towards teaching will help in getting the job of the teacher. Characteristics of a Teaching Profession:
- It essentially involves an intellectual operation.
- It draws material from science.
- It transforms raw material for a practical and definite end.
- It possesses an educationally communicable technique.
- It tends towards self-organization.
- It essentially performs a social service.
- It involves a lengthy period of study and training.
- It has a high degree of autonomy.
- It is based upon a systematic body of knowledge.
- It has a common code of ethics.
- It generates in service growth.

16(A). Psychosocial development reflects an interrelationship between psychological developments, emotional needs and the way individuals interact with their environment.
Initiative vs Guilt - 3 to 6 years
- The child continues to be more accepting and take more initiative, but may become too forceful, which can lead to feelings of guilt.
- Children who are successful at this stage feel capable of leading others.
- People who fail to acquire these skills are left with a sense of guilt, self-doubt, and a lack of initiative.

17(D). Habits that are learned at a young age tend to sustain for many years. Many students learn to be obedient, sincere, and punctual. If you teach a kid, a habit of playing football, he or she may continue to pursue football, even at older ages, and may even represent the nation someday in the sport.
- Keeping the school clean also yields the same results. The habit of keeping the environment clean sustains throughout the life and tend to keep their surroundings clean whether it is a workplace or their home.

18(D). Urie Bronfenbrenner's Ecological Theory: The seminal work on ecological systems theory in 1979 asserts the role of environmental systems in human development.
- His theory described the child's ecology as comprising of levels of environmental contexts, from most proximal to the most distal systems.
- With the individual in the centre and other systems forming concentric layers, the structure is akin to the Russian nesting dolls, one level opening into another.

19(B). The aim of education is to enable every individual child to become an able learner and as such individualized learning is the ultimate goal of all teaching-learning processes used in the classroom so that each learner becomes self-reliant in acquiring learning experiences. Individualized learning, also known as self-paced learning, requires individual efforts and interest to perform a task. The teacher gives clear instruction to every learner on the carefully designed set of learning activities to be successfully completed, at his/her own pace. The following guidelines may be considered while creating an individual learning situation in the classroom:
- Communicate assignments/activity clearly, so that each student can have a full understanding of what he/she is supposed to do. If necessary, give example to illustrate your point.
- Monitor student's work: While the activity is going on, you should move around the class and provide help whenever necessary. Do not interfere else they may feel discouraged.
- Checking students' assignments: Students will work at a different speed, so the class will not finish the task at the same time. In a large class size, checking student's work is a challenging task. Sometimes, this can be accomplished by getting students' to check each other's work. This is particularly appropriate for assignment involving fixed / specific answers. But certain assignments require your careful reading.
- Provide appropriate feedback: Learning

occurs when students receive feedback on the performance of their assignments. All assignments need to be corrected and feedback should be given. This should occur as soon as possible after the assignments have been handed over.

20(B). Learning is a sequence of events that we can recall for a long period, and hence, it offers experience and the behavioural changes through learning are relatively permanent.
NON-FORMAL: Non-formal Education (NFE) is any organized educational activity that takes place outside the formal educational system.
Usually, it is flexible, learner-centred, contextualized, and uses a participatory approach.
There is no specific target group for NFE; it could be kids, youth, or adults.
It is life-oriented as it is not limited to schooling.

21(D). Personality is all that a person is. It is the totality of one's behavior towards one's own self as well as others.
- Personality includes everything about the person, his/her physical, emotional, social, mental, and spiritual make-up.
- It refers to the different aspects of a person's character such as his/her interest, behavior, cognition, etc.

22(D). Motivation is usually defined as an internal state that arouses, directs, and maintains behavior.
Intrinsic motivation
- Intrinsic motivation is the natural human tendency to seek out and conquer challenges as we pursue personal interests and exercise our capabilities.
- When we are intrinsically motivated, we do not need incentives or punishments, because the activity itself is satisfying and rewarding. This is also known as the level of aspiration.
- Satisfied Spenser studies chemistry outside school simply because he loves learning about chemistry; no one makes him do it.
- Intrinsic motivation is associated with many positive outcomes in school such as academic achievement, creativity, reading comprehension and enjoyment, and using deep learning strategies.

23(C). Socialization is a process by which an individual becomes a member of a society through a mechanism of interaction. Its purpose is to prepare individuals for future roles.
- Socialization is a process of acquiring values, beliefs, and expectations.
- Socialization is a combination of personality development and cultural development.
- Socialization is a life-long process that

continues throughout life from birth to adulthood.

24(D). A teacher do to develop spirit of labour in students ,Give opportunities to students to do labour often. In the present study, teachers have been asked what their goals are with regard to the development of values related to labour in their students. It shows which values related to labour teachers wish to develop in their students: which labour identity they want to construct in their students. The study focuses on the role of teachers in education: on their opinion about the pedagogical task of education.

25(C). Work education is considered purposeful and meaningful physical labor, which is organized as the inherent part of the educational process. It is deemed as the production of meaningful material and community service, in which the children share the experience of contentment and pleasure. Work education emphasizes including knowledge, understanding, practical skills in educational activities.

26(B). Electra Complex is defined as when a girl, aged between 3 -6 years, becoming subconscious sexually attached to her father but increasingly hostile toward her mother. It is first introduced by Carl Jung.

27(C). National Education Policy-
"National Education Policy is an ambitious and futuristic policy that ensures opportunities for children to hone their talents by fixing the lacunae in the education system".
- National Education Policy 10+2 system is to be replaced by a four-stage 5+3+3+4 structure.
- NEP 2020 is the third education in the history of independent India after the policy of 1968 and the second policy of 1986.
- The main goal of the school education regulatory system is to improve educational outcomes so that children can learn to implement the acquired knowledge and skills in their practical life.
- National Education Policy emphasis on a skill like analysis, critical thinking, and vocational subjects will diversify their learning.
- Students will be given increased flexibility and choice of subjects to study.

28(C). Aids used by the teacher to facilitate the teaching-learning process is known as teaching material/teaching-learning materials or teaching aids.
- It can be made and used by both students and teachers.
- The appropriate use of teaching material in a classroom makes the learning relatively permanent.
- It should be noted that teaching material

should be used by the teachers based on the objectives of the lesson.
- The most commonly used teaching-learning materials in the classrooms are graphs, models, charts, flashcards, number cards and alphabet cards.
- Teaching materials can be classified into audio -aids, visual aids and audio-visual aids.
- Thus, we can conclude that graphs, numbers and alphabet cards and flashcards are those teaching-learning materials that are prepared by teachers and students in most schools.

29(D). Social cognitive theory is basically a social leaning theory based on the ideas that people learn by watching what others do and that human thought processes are central to understanding personality.

30(D). The term 'development' refers to qualitative changes in an individual such as a change in personality or other mental and emotional aspects. However, very often growth and development are used interchangeably. The process of development continues even after the individual has attained physical maturity (growth). The individual is continuously changing as he/she interacts with the environment.
Development is governed by certain principles which apply to all individuals. Let us learn about these principles in this section. The various principles of development are:
The development follows a fixed pattern/ sequence: Each child may have a different rate of development. However, the development of all human beings follows a similar pattern, similar sequence, or direction. Sequential pattern of development can be seen in two directions:
- Cephalo-caudal sequence: means that development spreads over the body from head to foot i.e. individual begins to grow from head region downwards. Sufi first gained control of her head, then she could catch hold of objects, sit, crawl and later she could stand and walk.
- Proximodistal sequence: means that the development proceeds from the central part of the body towards the peripheries. In this sequence, the spinal cord of the individual develops first and then outward.
Hence, we can conclude that in the cephalo-caudal and the proximodistal principle of development, the child develops in sequence and follows two tends.

31(C). To really bring empowerment, women should be aware of their rights. Not only domestic and family responsibilities but also women should play an active and positive role in every field. They should also know the happenings around them and in the country.

32(D). Women empowerment has this power to change a lot in society and the country. She can deal with any problem in society better than men. She can understand well the loss of overpopulation for the country and the family.

33(A). Influence: The power to have an effect on people or things, or a person or thing that is able to do this
Impotence: Lack of power to change or improve a situation

34(D). "The" is missing before the superlative adjective "best" in part d of the sentence.

35(A). Through women empowerment, it is possible that a country with female-male equality of a strong economy can be replaced with a country with male influence.

36(B). The marked option is adjective which is used to qualify a noun or a pronoun.

37(B). Women empowerment has this power to change a lot in society and the country. She can deal with any problem in society better than men. She can understand well the loss of overpopulation for the country and the family.

38(B). Prepositions are commonly used to show a relationship in space or time or a logical relationship between two or more people, places or things.
They are most commonly followed by a noun phrase or pronoun

39(C). Disparity means a noticeable and usually significant difference or dissimilarity; lack of similarity or equality.
There is great disparity between the amount of work that I do and what I get paid for it.

40(A). In the above lines, the poet says that he has a little shadow that keeps following him whenever he goes. At the same time, the poet also wonders what is the use of shadow.

41(B). In the above line, the poet is curious to observe how the shadow keeps changing his shape. The poet observes that sometimes, the shadow becomes taller than him like a huge rubber ball.
According to the above lines it can be deduced that the shadow becomes taller than him.

42(B). According to the above lines it can be deduced that adjective 'slow' does not apply to the shadow. It applies to the children.

43(A). 'Coward' means a person who is not brave and is too eager to avoid danger, difficulty, or pain, a person who is easily frightened.
'Wimp' means a person who is not strong, brave, or confident.

44(C). 'Simile' is a comparison between two unlike things using the words "like" or "as". It is used to compare an object or a person with something else to make the description more vivid and clear.
Similarly in the given expression ' He is very, very like me', 'Simile' is the figure of speech used as a child is comparing his shadow with himself using the word 'like'.

45(B). 'Alliteration' is the series of words which commence with the same letter. Alliteration consists of the repetition of a sound or of a letter at the beginning of two or more words.

46(A). All of the skills, such as reading, writing, speaking, and listening, are built on vocabulary. This demonstrates the importance of learning new vocabulary. Knowing a word's meaning as well as how the word blends into different contexts are referred to as vocabulary awareness. Vocabulary is learned inadvertently by indirect word experience and consciously through explicit instruction in specific topics.

47(B). Constructivism is a view of learning based on the belief that knowledge isn't a thing that can be simply given by the teacher. Constructivism is a theory based on observation and scientific study about how people learn. It says that people construct their understanding and knowledge of the world, through experiencing things and reflecting on those experiences.
Constructivist classrooms are structured in such a way that learners are immersed in experiences within which they may engage in action, imagination, invention, interaction, and personal reflection.
In language learning, constructivism is a language theory to help the students in constructing something based on their understanding. It emphasizes students' role than the teacher'.
It is one of the language theories that give a contribution to the education field. So, for the constructive classroom, language learning should be based on the learners' previous knowledge.

48(D). Pedagogy refers to the set of principles that influence the approaches to the teaching-learning process. It consists of a learning environment, teaching-learning arrangements, methods, general educational principles, etc.
- In Language pedagogy, a learner learns about various methods and approaches to learning language, tools, and techniques. It lets the learner know about skills required to learn a language, that is, listening, speaking, reading, and writing.

49(D). Teaching is a methodology in which pupils are made learned a skill, theory and application. The following are the characteristics of teaching:

- It is flexible because teaching should take place according to pupils' understanding levels
- Teaching at schools and colleges is formal while teaching by parents is informal.
- Teaching is called science because various techniques are devised to make students understand better, on the other hand, choosing the right technique at the right time is an art
- It provides guidance and training.
- It is helpful for students since it makes students adjusting to the environment and society.

50(A). Grammar is the backbone of any language. It is the womb that gives birth to sentences. These sentences are fertilized using grammar to form correct and appropriate speech.

- Grammar is defined as a theory of language. We consider language as rule-governed behavior, relating to sounds, word formation, and structure. Here grammar constitutes a subset of rules relating to morphology and syntax.

51(D). Comprehensible input' refers to using language that children are capable of understanding, and at the same time holds challenges for them. An important part of making this language comprehensible is providing it in natural, communicative situations that are meaningful to children and this will help children in meeting the challenge.

52(C). According to Willis, who supported the idea that TBLT is a learner-centred approach, "A Task can be defined as an activity where the target language is used by the learner for a communicative purpose in order to achieve an outcome".

- Task-based language teaching (TBLT), also known as task-based instruction (TBI), focuses on the use of authentic language and on asking students to do meaningful tasks using the target language.

53(B). During the teaching-learning process, you have to locate and identify the areas where the learner commits mistakes. It is the crucial stage of the teaching-learning process where you have to Diagnose and prepare instructional material for Remedial teaching to ensure the desired quality of learning.

54(D). Teaching Learning Material (TLM), also known as instructional aids, facilitate a teacher in achieving the learning objectives formulated by her/him before teaching-learning activities start. For example, newspaper, dictionary, sticker, etc. Accurate and realistic teaching-learning material is the one which:

- Facilitates the learning process in a meaningful and productive way.
- Makes learning more interesting and enliven by bringing the class to real-life.
- Encourages healthy classroom interaction and helps in meeting individual differences.

55(C). Speaking skills have two major components. First, there are motor perceptive skills. These are the means of perceiving, recalling, and articulating in the correct order the sounds and structure of a language. Generally, these are developed at the primary level where learners are put through the various look and say exercises, or pattern practice.

Ways of Assessing Speaking Skills: Assessing speaking skills is a complex task for a teacher. The teacher has to be more creative and vigilant in assessing speaking skills. The ways of assessing speaking skills as follows:

- Discussion: Students are asked to read a short text and make points for discussion. This would offer the students to get a deep understanding of the text which is helpful in speaking.
- The teacher can make the groups of learners and learners are asked to read the text by taking turns.
- Read aloud Task: The teacher can record the speaking of the learner and listen to a recording and evaluate the students in a series of phonological factors and fluency.
- Interactive Speaking Strategy: The Teacher can use an interactive speaking strategy, in which the student and teacher having the face to face conversation,
- Role-Play is also another way to assess the speaking skills of students while he/she producing dialogues in play.
- Story-Telling: Students are asked to tell a story of a new of something they heard or read.
- Oral Presentation: The teacher can use oral presentations for assessing the speaking skills of students.

56(A). English in India: It's Status: The English language is used in satisfying our practical need for social mobility, opportunity, power, and communication on the other hand.

57(C). If the students make mistakes in spelling, the teacher has to show him his mistakes and ask him to re-pronounce them. It will help the learner to know about where he put errors in the spelling and can correct them while re-pronouncing the same spelling.

Ways to Overcome committing mistakes in spelling:

- The teacher should provide the etymology of each word.
- Teacher should compare the written reproduction vocabulary with the recognition vocabulary.
- Teachers should compare recognition and reproduction vocabulary to find out the common words.
- Use mnemonics to learn the spelling.
- Students should divide the words into chunks and re-pronounce it and combined it, to make a proper spell out.

58(B). India is a multi-lingual country with numerous languages and dialects. There are approximately 1652 languages and dialects that belong to the five different language families in the country. Around 40 languages are used as a medium of instruction in schools and universities and the English language is one of them.

59(B). A question is a sentence that seeks an answer for information collection, tests, and research. Right questions produce accurate responses and aids in collecting actionable quantitative and qualitative data.

Higher-Order Questions:

Higher-order questions are those that the students cannot answer just by simple recollection or by reading the information "verbatim" from the text.

Higher-order questions put advanced cognitive demand on students. For example, asking students about their previous school, its atmosphere, its strength and weaknesses etc.

They encourage students to think beyond literal questions. Higher-order questions promote critical thinking skills because these types of questions expect students to apply, analyze, synthesize, and evaluate information instead of simply recalling facts.

Lower-Order Questions:

Lower order questions are those that require "brief thought" and a basic amount of understanding of an already learned subject or area.

These kinds of questions are meant to encourage students to recall or remember basic information.

60(D). A multilingual classroom is a classroom with learners having more than one language including learners from different backgrounds.

61(D). The Harappan civilization was located in the Indus River valley. Its two large cities, Harappa and Mohenjo-Daro, were located in present-day Pakistan's Punjab and Sindh provinces, respectively.

- Its extent reached as far south as the Gulf of Khambhat and as far east as the Yamuna (Jumna) River.

Dancing Girl is a prehistoric bronze sculpture made in lost-wax casting about c. 2300–1750 BC in the Indus Valley Civilisation city of Mohenjo-Daro in modern-day Pakistan.

The majestic zebu bull, with its heavy

dewlap and wide curving horns, is perhaps the most impressive motif found on the Indus seals was found in Harappa.

Kalibangan excavations in the present western Rajasthan show a ploughed field, the first site of this nature in the world.

Early dentistry was found in the city of Mehrgarh. This belongs to the Indus valley civilization period.

Hence, Dancing girl statues, Early dentistry, zebu and ploughed fields are found in Mohenjodaro, Mehrgarh, Harappa and kalibangan Respectively.

62(A). The establishment of the Delhi Sultanate began with the invasion of Muhammad Ghori.

- He had brought a large number of slaves and appointment them as officers.
- When he died in AD 1206 resulted in a scramble for supremacy among his three generals- Qutub-ud-din Aibek (Commander of his army), Tajuddin Yalduz (ruled Karman and Sankuran between Afghanistan and Sind), and Nasiruddin Qubacha.

Timeline of Delhi Sultanate in chronological order and their founder:

Dynasties	Founder
Slave dynasty or Ilbary dynasty	Qutub-Ud-din A ibek
Khilji Dynasty	Jalal-ud-din Khi lji
Tughlaq Dynasty	Ghiyasuddin Tu ghlaq

The Second Afghan Empire was established by Sher Shah Suri after defeating the Mughal emperor Humayun in the Battle of Chausa and the Battle of Kanauj. He occupied the throne of Delhi in 1540 AD. After Humayun's defeat, he conquered Malwa, Rajputana, Multan, Sind, and Punjab.

Thus, we can conclude that Slave Dynasty was not founded by Balban .

63(B). Megasthenes :
- Megasthenes was the Greek ambassador in the court of Chandragupta Maurya.
  - Hence statement 1 is incorrect.
- He was sent by the Hellenistic king Seleucus I.
- His book Indica has survived only in fragments.
  - Hence statement 2 is correct.
- Yet, his account gives details about the Mauryan administration, particularly the administration of the capital city of Pataliputra and also the military organization.
- His picture of contemporary social life is notable.
- He gave the most complete account of India then known to the Greek world and was the source for work by the later historians Diodorus, Strabo, Pliny, and Arrian.

- The major faults of Megasthenes' work were mistakes in details, an uncritical acceptance of Indian folklore, and a tendency to idealize Indian culture by the standards of Greek philosophy.

64(A). The Gupta coinage started with a remarkable series in gold issued by Chandragupta I, the third ruler of the dynasty.

- The reverse of the coin bears the wheel, which is symbolic of the chakravartin or the universal monarch . It is also a symbol of Vishnu.
- Chandragupta - II . Chandragupta - II issued the lion slayer type of coins. Chandragupta did not continue the types of coins issued by his father and added two new to them.
- Skandagupta issued five types of gold coins:
  1. Archer type,
  2. King and queen type,
  3. Chhatra type,
  4. Lion-slayer type and
  5. Horseman type.
- His silver coins are of four types: Garuda type, Bull type, Altar type, and Madhyadesha type.
- The obverse (heads) is the front of the coin and the reverse (tails) in the back.
- Edge is the outer surface, which can have lettering, reeding, or be plain.
- On the reverse, the king and the queen are sitting on a couch facing each other .
- The king is offering to the queen an object with a curved handle and a thick knob.

65(B). The State Election Commission constituted under the Constitution (Seventy-third and Seventy-fourth) Amendments Act, 1992 for each State / Union Territory are vested with the powers of conduct of elections to the Corporations, Municipalities, Zilla Parishads, District Panchayats, Panchayat Samitis, Gram Panchayats, and other local bodies. It is independent of the Election Commission of India.

- The SEC is a single-member Commission headed by the State Election Commissioner. It has a Secretary who is also the Chief Electoral Officer for the State.
- The Commission discharges its Constitutional duty by way of preparing electoral rolls and holding elections for Panchayati Raj Institutions as well as for Municipal bodies.

Thus, it is correct to say that State Election Commission conducts municipal and panchayat elections.

66(A). The state leading in manganese production is Odisha. Odisha tops the total reserves/ resources with 44% share followed by Karnataka (22%), Madhya Pradesh (12%), Maharashtra & Goa (7%)

each, Andhra Pradesh (4%) and Jharkhand (2%).

India ranks third in the production of manganese ore in the world, next only to Russia and South Africa. It is a hard brittle silvery metal, often found in minerals in combination with iron.

Manganese is a transition metal with a multifaceted array of industrial alloy uses, particularly in stainless steel.

67(D). The Constitution of India is the supreme law governing the country. The seventh schedule under Article 246 of the constitution deals with the division of powers between the union and the states. The constitutional provisions in India on the subject of the distribution of legislative powers between the Union and the States are defined under several articles; the most important in this regard being specifically under articles 245 and 246 of the Constitution of India . It contains three lists; i.e. Union List, State List, and Concurrent List.

Article 245 extent of laws made by Parliament and by the Legislatures of States:

- Subject to the provisions of this Constitution, Parliament may make laws for the whole or any part of the territory of India, and the Legislature of a State may make laws for the whole or any part of the State.
- No law made by Parliament shall be deemed to be invalid on the ground that it would have extra territorial operation.

Thus, it is clear that Article 245 and 246 regulate the distribution of power between Centre and States.

68(A). Socio-cultural diversity concerns aspects of culture that can influence an individual's interactions with others of different backgrounds.

- There is considerable socio-cultural diversity in India.
- Diversity leads to equal opportunity.
- There is no equality in opportunity if diversity is not recognized and valued.
- Diversity refers to recognising and respecting and valuing differences in people.

Thus, we can say that both Statement (A) and Statement (B) are true and Statement (B) is the correct explanation of Statement (A).

69(B). Indian society is pluralistic in nature. Pluralism refers to the existence within a nation or society of groups distinctive in ethnic origin, cultural patterns, language, religion, etc. The Indian culture followed the concept of "Vasudhaiva Kutumbakam" (The world is one family) resulting in a great cultural heritage.

70(C). The role of patwari in rural administration is of utmost importance.
- The term patwari is a standard term

across the Northern and Central parts of India.

- The patwari is the government official whose primary role is to keep records of all the land in the villages that are overseen by him. The patwari is also known as the village accountant.
- The patwari acts as a liaison between the government and the farmers. The patwari is the first person or contact point for people if they wish to know any details about their land.

Hence, Patwari is an official who kept the land records of rural areas and also known as lethal in some parts of India.

71(A). The drafting committee of the constitution:

The Drafting Committee had seven members:

1. Alladi Krishnaswami Ayyar
2. N. Gopalaswami
3. B.R. Ambedkar
4. K.M Munshi
5. Mohammad Saadulla
6. B.L. Mitter
7. D.P. Khaitan.

- At its first meeting on 30th August 1947, the Drafting Committee elected B.R Ambedkar as its Chairman.
- Towards the end of October 1947, the Drafting Committee began to scrutinize the Draft Constitution prepared by the B.N Rau, the Constitutional Advisor.
- It made various changes and submitted the Draft Constitution to the President of the Constituent Assembly on 21 February 1948.
- The Drafting Committee and its members were very influential in Indian constitution-making during the Committee stages and the deliberations of the Constituent Assembly.
- The majority of the debates in the Constituent Assembly revolved around the Draft Constitution(s) prepared by the Drafting Committee.
- Out of 166 sittings of the Constituent Assembly, 114 were spent debating the Draft Constitution(s).

72(B). Majuli is a large river island situated in the middle of the Brahmaputra River in Assam.

- Majuli is depicted as the largest river island in the world.
- This island has been formed over a period of time due to the change of direction and area of the Brahmaputra river and its tributaries especially the Lohit river.
- Majuli can also be called the 'cultural capital of Assam'.
- Majuli is located in the northern part of the Jorhat district and is separated from the mainland by the Brahmaputra river.

Brahmaputra River flows through Tibet, India and Bangladesh.

- The Brahmaputra rises in the north of the Himalayas near Lake Mansarovar in the Purang district of Tibet, where it is known as the Yarlung Tsangpo.
- Flowing in Tibet, this river enters the Indian state of Arunachal Pradesh.
- Flowing in the valley of Assam, it is called the Brahmaputra, and then it is called Jamuna as soon as it enters Bangladesh.

73(D). There are primarily two motions: Rotation and Revolution .

- Rotation : It is the movement of the earth on its axis. Hence statement 1 is incorrect .
- Earth rotates along its axis from west to east.
- It takes approximately 24 hrs to complete one rotation .
- Days and nights occur due to the rotation of the earth. Hence statement 3 is correct.
- Revolution : It is the movement of the earth around the sun in a fixed path or orbit. Hence statement 2 is incorrect.
- It takes 365¼ days (one year) to revolve around the sun.

74(D). Parliamentary opposition is a form of political opposition to a designated government,

- The Opposition is the largest non-government party or coalition of parties in the Legislative Assembly or the parliament.
- The Opposition party leaders are the elected representatives but they are not the part of the ruling party
- .The opposition party questions the ruling government and its actions. The Opposition's main role is to question the government of the day and hold them accountable.
- Opposition party leaders raise new issues of people's welfare in the parliament.

Hence, The Opposition party is representative only but not part of the ruling party, and the question the government holds them accountable.

75(D). Noida Software and Mobile companies:

- Noida has also become a hub for software and mobile app development companies like HCL, Barclay's, Samsung, Agilent, CSC.
- These companies are contributing a lot to the increasing economy of state of UP.

76(B). A chemical process in which a substance reacts with oxygen to give off heat is called combustion .

- Combustion of most fuels releases carbon dioxide into the environment . Thus, causing air pollution .
- Increased concentration of carbon dioxide in the air is believed to cause global warming .
  - Global warming is the rise in the temperature of the atmosphere of the earth.
  - This results, among other things, in the melting of polar glaciers, which leads to a rise in the sea level, causing floods in the coastal areas.
  - Low lying coastal areas may even be permanently submerged underwater
- The burning of coal and diesel releases sulphur dioxide gas.
- It is an extremely suffocating and corrosive gas .
- Moreover, petrol engines give off gaseous oxides of nitrogen.

So, we can say that the combustion of coal, petrol and diesel etc is the basic source of Air Pollution .

77(D). Ozone Hole:

- It refers to a region in the stratosphere where the concentration of ozone becomes extremely low in certain months.
- Ozone (chemically, a molecule of three oxygen atoms) is found mainly in the upper atmosphere, an area called the stratosphere, between 10 and 50 km from the earth's surface.
- Ozone absorbs the harmful UltraViolet (UV) radiations from the sun eliminating a big threat to life forms on earth.
- UV rays can cause skin cancer and other diseases and deformities in plants and animals.
- The ozone holes most commonly refer to the depletion over Antarctica, forming each year in September, October, and November, due to a set of special meteorological and chemical conditions that arise at the South Pole, and can reach sizes of around 20 to 25 million sq km.
- Hence, we can say that Ozone holes are more pronounced at the poles. Hence, Option 4 is correct.

78(B). The term Plate was first coined by JT Wilson in 1965.

- The Plate tectonics theory explains the large scale motion of the earth's lithosphere.

Three types of plate boundary:

Divergent Plate Boundary:

- When two plates move away from each other, a crack develops between them.
  - The molten lava of the asthenosphere comes out from these cracks to the surface continuously & after solidification forms a new crust.
  - It causes two changes:
    - Formation of new crust.
    - Formation of submarine mountains or ridges.
    - Hence, statement 1 is correct.

Convergent Plate Boundary:

- When two plates collide with each other, the denser one is subducted below the lighter one.
- The region where the subduction takes

place is called the Benioff zone.
- When two continental plates converge, the subduction at the Benioff zone is not so effective that it can give rise to Volcanoes.
  - Hence, statement 2 is incorrect.

Transform fault Boundary :
- Parallel plates do not create new crust or destroy the old as they pass each other along a common boundary.
- They push each other & produce transform faults.
- Highly seismic earthquake zones are found along these boundaries .
  - Hence, statement 3 is correct.

79(B). The Concentric approach is a design or pattern of organization used in making decisions about the various aspects of curriculum development and transaction.
- The curriculum approach is thus a plan that the teachers follow in providing learning activities (or experiences) to the students in school.
- The pattern or design of the curriculum to a large extent determines the nature of the outcomes that will be achieved after transacting the curriculum.

80(C). The classroom environment can facilitate students learning and remove gender bias and stereotype. In fact, a gender-friendly environment can easily be created by a teacher in any context. It just requires sensitivity and positive intent. A gender friendly classroom environment and its overall management can build harmonious relations between boys and girls at different stages of education.

81(B). Curricular activities include teaching, the conduct of examination, evaluation of learner performance, adoption of remedial teaching and the like that facilitate students' intellectual development.
- The activities, like the teaching of subjects of study (Language, Mathematics, Science and Social Science), the conduct of examinations/ tests at different points of time in a year/ session, evaluation of learner performance, preparation of progress card of the students are called curricular activities or scholastic activities.
- These activities are strict as per the prescribed curriculum and hence are compulsory for all students of the class.
- A formal timetable is followed to conduct these activities which are mostly confined to classroom lessons.

Thus from the above-mentioned points, it is clear that teaching, the conduct of examination, evaluation of learner performance are examples of curricular activities.

82(B). An Information Source is a source of information for somebody, i.e. anything that might inform a person about something on providing knowledge to somebody. Information sources may be observations, people speeches, documents, pictures, organizations etc

Primary Information Sources: It contains first-hand information, meaning that you are reading the author's own account on a specific topic or event that s/he participated in. Examples of primary resources include scholarly research articles and diaries.

Secondary Information Sources:
- Secondary sources of information are those which are either compiled from or refer to primary sources of information.
- The original information having been casually modified selected or reorganized so as to serve a definite purpose for a group of users.
- Such sources contain information arranged and organized on the basis of some definite plan. Manuals, Tables, Handbooks, newspapers , dictionaries are examples of Secondary information sources.

Tertiary Information Sources: Tertiary sources summarize or synthesize the research in secondary sources. For example, textbooks and reference books are tertiary sources. Tertiary sources are usually not credited to a particular author. Hence, it becomes clear that The collection of weather information from the local newspaper is an example of Secondary type of source.

83(B). Gautama Buddha propagated his divine knowledge of Buddhism to the world from the Mahabodhi Temple Complex monument.
- This Temple is located at Bodhgaya , Bihar.
- It is famous as Buddha propagated his divine knowledge of Buddhism from this Temple.
- For this, it is known as the ' Great Enlightenment Temple '.
- It was declared UNESCO World Heritage Site in 2002 .

84(B). The correct answer is Both A) and B) are true, but B) is not the correct explanation of A).
Indus Valley Civilisation produced a lot of artifacts and art forms.
Indus Valley art form emerged during the second half of the third millennium BCE (i.e. from 2500 BC onwards).
- Thousands of seals have been discovered by archaeologists from the Harappan sites.
- Most of the seals were made of steatite , which is a kind of soft stone.
- A few of them were also made of terracotta, gold, agate, chert, ivory, and faience .
- It is believed that the seals were used for commercial purposes .

- Seals may have been used to stamp bags or packets containing goods that were sent from one place to another .
- After a bag was closed or tied, a layer of wet clay was applied to the knot, and the seal was pressed on it.
- The impression of the seal is known as sealing.
- If the sealing was intact, one could be sure that the goods had arrived safely .

Thus, we can say that both statements A and B are true, but B is not the correct explanation of A.

85(B). As per Asoka's inscriptions, Lumbini was declared tax free and proclaimed only 1/8th part as taxable.
At the 20th anniversary of his enthronement, Asoka announced Lumbini as tax-free and proclaimed only 1/8th part as taxable. Description of this fact is found in the inscriptions of Nigliva and Rumindei.

86(B). The Hindu Widows' Remarriage Act 1856, also Act XV, 1856, passed on 16 July 1856, legalised the remarriage of widows in all jurisdictions of India under East India Company rule. The act was enacted on 26 July 1856. It was drafted by Lord Dalhousie and passed by Lord Canning before the Indian Rebellion of 1857. It was the first major social reform legislation after the abolition of sati pratha in 1829 by Lord William Bentinck.

87(D). Ramakrishna Mission organisation was established by Swami Vivekananda.
Ramakrishna Mission (RKM) is a Hindu religious and spiritual organisation which forms the core of a worldwide spiritual movement known as the Ramakrishna Movement or the Vedanta Movement. The mission is named after and inspired by the Indian spiritual Guru Ramakrishna Paramahamsa and founded by Ramakrishna's chief disciple Swami Vivekananda on 1 May 1897. The organisation mainly propagates the Hindu philosophy of Vedanta–Advaita Vedanta and four yogic ideals– Jnana, Bhakti, Karma, and Raja yoga.

88(C). Maize
- Temperature: Between 21-27°C
- Rainfall: High rainfall.
- Soil Type: Old alluvial soil.
- Top Maize Producing States: Karnataka> Tamil Nadu > Utter Pradesh
- India is the seventh-largest producer worldwide.
- It is used both as food and fodder.
- The use of modern inputs such as High-Yielding Variety seeds, fertilizers, and irrigation have contributed to the increasing production of maize.
- Technology Mission on Maize is one of the government's initiatives for maize.

89(A). The Cocos Plate is a young oceanic tectonic plate beneath the Pacific Ocean off the west coast of Central America, named for Cocos Island, which rides upon it. The Cocos Plate was created approximately 23 million years ago when the Farallon Plate broke into two pieces, which also created the Nazca Plate. The Cocos Plate also broke into two pieces, creating the small Rivera Plate. The Cocos Plate is bounded by several different plates. To the northeast it is bounded by the North American Plate and the Caribbean Plate. To the west it is bounded by the Pacific Plate and to the south by the Nazca Plate.

90(C). The correct answer is (A) - (4), (B) - (1), (C) - (2), (D) - (3)

Mana Pass -
- It is located in Uttarakhand.
- It connects Uttarakhand and Tibet region.
- It is mainly located in Greater Himalayas.

Nathu La -
- It is located in Sikkim.
- It is located near the India-China border.

Zozi La -
- It is located in Kashmir.
- It connects Srinagar with Kargil-Leh.

Shipki La -
- It is located in Himachal Pradesh.
- It connects Himachal Pardesh and Tibet.
- It is a trade route between China and India.

91(C).

Salinity refers to the total content of dissolved salts in seawater.
- It is calculated as the amount of salt (in gm) dissolved in 1,000 gm (1 kg) of seawater.
- The salinity of ocean water is usually around 35 parts per thousand on an average at zero degrees Celsius.
- This implies that in the total weight of ocean water, dissolved salts amount to 3.5 percent.
- Sodium chloride or the common salt is the most common among all the dissolved salts in the sea.

Impact of Salinity in Water
- Salinity determines compressibility, thermal expansion, temperature, density, absorption of insolation, evaporation and humidity. Hence, Statement 1 is correct.
- It also influences the composition and movement of the sea: water and the distribution of fish and other marine resources. Hence, Statement 2 is correct.

92(D). According to the Constitution, the powers and functions of the government are divided into three organs - the legislature, the executive and the judiciary.
- As an organ of government, the judiciary plays a crucial role in the functioning of India's democracy. It can play this role only because it is independent .
- It is the independence of the judiciary that allows the courts to play a central role in ensuring that there is no misuse of power by the legislature and the executive .
- It also plays a crucial role in protecting the Fundamental Rights of citizens because anyone can approach the courts if they believe that their rights have been violated.

Therefore, the correct answer is - A,B and C

93(D). Project-based learning gives a thorough practical exposure to a problem upon which the project is based. Projects are developed generally in groups where students can learn various things such as working together, problem-solving, decision making, and investigating activities. So it can be known as group project-based learning.
- The Principle of Purpose: Knowledge of purpose is a great stimulus that motivates the child to realize his/her goal. The student must have a purpose. 'Why is he doing certain things?' Purpose motivates learning. Interest cannot be aroused by aimless and meaningless activities. Due to motivation, the student develops an Individual sense of achievement.
- The Principle of Activity: Opportunities should be provided to students that make them active and learn things by doing. Physical, as well as mental activities, is to be provided to them. They are to be allowed to 'do' and to 'live through doing'.
- The Principle of Experience : Experience is the best teacher. What is learned must be experienced. The children learn new facts and information through experience.
- The Principle of Social Experience : The child is a social being and we have to prepare the student for social life. Training for a corporate life must be given to him. In the project method, the students work in groups to develop the strong intra-group competition, collaboration and problem-solving skills.
- The Principle of Reality: Life is real and education to be meaningful must be real. The project method is a method of educating the child and therefore, it must also be real. Real-life situations should be presented in the life of the school.

Group project work helps in developing all of the above-mentioned points.

94(B). Social Science as a discipline has the unique capability of being able to look at both developmental and normative issues of the society. It includes disciplines of History, Geography, Political Science, Economics, and Sociology.

Co-curricular activities in Social Science are usually organized outside the classroom to provide opportunities for students to develop their special talents and to creatively express themselves through various forms. For example, participation in social science activities, field visits , involvement in science dramas, social welfare activities, etc.

Field visits for students are like an educational experience that they never could have had in the classroom. Field visits are considered fun, but the children learn as well, whether they realize it or not because they require significant planning and coordination for teachers and administrators to make a great combination of learning and fun together.

Hence, students at the upper primary level can be asked to go for a field visit as part of Social Science projects so that enables comparison of realities with the ideas and concepts.

95(A). Social science is a collection of academic disciplines that study human behavior, specifically how people interact with one another, act, evolve as a culture, and influence things. This wide and diverse field of science includes disciplines like anthropology, economics, political science, psychology, and sociology.
- Explain your views on installing solar power panels on a building . Here, in this question, the student will do analyses, evaluations, and innovative findings and then will give a creative solution. This provides an opportunity to develop students' critical thinking.
- Do you think that electric vehicles can help in reducing air pollution? Discuss. Here, in this question, the student will do critical thinking in finding an innovative and creative solution. This provides an opportunity to develop students' critical thinking.
- How did the conflict between Russia and Ukraine start? Here, in this question, the student will do an analysis and evaluation. This provides an opportunity to develop students' critical thinking.

Hence, we can conclude that A, B, and C are correct.

96(C). There are different approaches of teaching social sciences. While some approaches to teaching are subject-oriented and teacher-centered, others are learner-centric in nature.

Here, the teacher and students come across a paragraph that paints a neighboring country in a strongly negative light.
- So, for this, the most responsible of the teacher is to discuss and debate about the issue that is highlighted in the paragraph.
- By discussing the issue, students would be able to understand the negative points and can conclude their topic well.

Thus, it is concluded that Analyse the paragraph along with students, where they can discuss and debate the assumptions made or data given about the country is the most responsible approach for the Social Science teacher.

97(B). An inquiry-based approach emphasizes to connect the child with their own experiences by posing questions and making decisions in the search of new understanding.

It is based on heuristic reasoning which is also a self-discovery approach proposed by 'H.E. Armstrong' . It makes the process of problem-solving and decision making quick and efficient by:

- promoting the use of critical and imaginative thinking.
- raising problems before students to activate their thinking power.
- emphasizing active involvement of learners to boost their understanding.
- enabling students to acquire knowledge by discovering the facts themselves.

Hence, we conclude that the above statement is about inquiry approach.

98(A). Mahendravarman I (600 AD – 630 AD):

- Succeeded by Simhavishnu.
- Composed Vichitrachita and Mahavilasa Prahasana.
- Introduced rock-cut temple architecture.
- Was a Jain who converted to Saivism.
- Died in battle with the Chalukyas.

Narsinghvarman I (630 AD – 668 AD):

- Also known as Mamallan (great wrestler), and Mamallapuram (Mahabalipuram) was named after him.
- Defeated and killed Pulakesin II in 642 AD.
- Sent a naval expedition to Sri Lanka.
- Hiuen Tsang visited the Pallava kingdom during his reign.

Paramesvaravarman I (670 – 695 AD):

- He was killed by the Chalukya king Vikramaditya II.
- He was the last ruler of the Simhavishnu line of Pallavas.

Nandivarman II (731 – 796 AD):

- He built the Vaikuntha-Perumal Temple.

So, the correct chronological order is 4, 2, 1, 3.

99(C). Social Science is a branch of science that deals with human behaviour and social relationships, which rely primarily on empirical approaches. Social science includes disciplines of History, Geography, Political Science, Economics, and Sociology.

Activity-Based Questions in Social Science Lessons:

- It indulges students in activities by stimulating their senses, such as sight, smell, vision, or feeling, and getting them involved in the subject.
- In activity-based learning, students are involved in learning activities more than listening, and less emphasis is placed on transmitting information and more on developing student's skills.
- Activity-based questions make social Science lesson joyful, interesting for the students.
- Students are involved in higher-order thinking such as analysis, synthesis, and evaluation.

Hence, from the above-mentioned points, it becomes clear that Activity-based questions make Social Science lessons joyful.

100(D). Diversity refers to the phenomenon where there are groups of people hailing from different races, religions, and cultures .

- It fosters a feeling of oneness and a sense of belongingness in each of the members of the society.
- Diverse society refers to the co-existence of the different social groups within a given geopolitical setting or differentiation of society in groups.
- The main sources of a diverse society are ethnic origins, religions, and languages.
- A diverse society would have differences and similarities in:
  - race
  - culture
  - religion
  - language
  - occupation
  - gender, etc.

Hence, it could be concluded that the statement 'social diversity would have differences and similarities in language, religion, and culture' is correct in the context of social diversity.

101(A). Political Science is a social science discipline concerned with the study of the state, nation, government and politics, and policies of the government. It deals extensively with the theory and practice of politics, and the analysis of political systems, political behaviour, and political culture. It intersects with other fields, including economics, law, sociology, history, anthropology, public administration, public policy, national politics, international relations, comparative politics, psychology, political organization, and political theory.

Dramatization/Role Play: It is a useful activity in teaching political science to help learners' understand different viewpoints . Appropriate topics are generally easy for teachers to identify and they can research for the background information that is needed.

For example, while dealing with a chapter on the Panchayati Raj system , a group of students may play the role of a panchayat president who is addressing members of the gram sabha . In this activity, the students conversate with each other or dialoguing with each other to sensitize their own learning.

Hence, it can be concluded that in the above situation the effective activity is asking students to play the role of a panchayat president who is addressing members of the gram sabha.

102(D). Social Science is a branch of science that deals with human behaviour and social relationships, which rely primarily on empirical approaches

Social Science occupies an important place in the school curriculum, nevertheless, Social Science teaching faces several problems which includes:

- Untrained teachers.
- Lack of library facilities.
- Less use of Audio Visual aid.
- Traditional examination system.
- Conventional teaching practices.
- Lack of inadequate training facilities.

So, it could be interpreted that the all mentioned problems are related to Social Science teaching.

103(B). Social Science is a branch of Science that deals with human behavior and social relationships , which rely primarily on empirical approaches .

The teaching method or strategy is a way to put theory in practice with the help of principles, pedagogy, and management strategies. It helps the teachers to plan and present the lesson coherently .

Proper planning should be done to initiate a dignified discussion to teach a controversial issue in Social Science class as discussion is a teaching methodology which facilitates meaningful learning by emphasizing upon:

- sharing ideas and experiences with peers and teachers.
- learning through meaningful interaction in group settings.
- looking at any issues from different angles and points of view.
- developing a democratic way of thinking and the spirit of tolerance.
- increasing the maximum participation of students in the learning process.

Hence, it could be concluded that while teaching controversial issues in Social Science class a teacher should take them up with proper planning to initiate a dignified discussion .

104(B). Prejudice refers to a negative attitude or unreasonable opinion for a specific group of people. It is a preconceived opinion which is not based on concrete experience or reality.

Prejudices in the classroom could be avoided by o rganizing a discussion on dimensions of social reality as discussing different dimensions of social realities will make learners:

- understand the different aspects of society and life.
- assimilate lifelong learning skills through social interaction.

- respect other's perspectives, culture, religion, language, etc.
- understand how prejudice leads to bullying and discrimination which is unlawful.

Hence, it could be concluded that o rganizing a discussion on dimensions of social reality would be the most appropriate response in the context of the question.

105(C). The term "social studies" is used to describe a broad range of academic fields that focus on human interaction. History, psychology, sociology, economics, political science, and occasionally philosophy and religion are among the popular social studies fields

- The aim of teaching social studies is to provide students an awareness of how social life develops in the framework of time, space, economics, and political will in order to create social peace, advance, and use reason when making decisions. This is accomplished by interacting with the community and the environment in a balanced manner to promote the well-being of the country and the world.

Hence, we can conclude that scoring well is not an aim of teaching social studies.

106(C). Social Sciences is one of the school subjects and it encompasses diverse concerns of the society, and includes a wide range of content drawn from the disciplines of History, Geography, Political science, Economics, Sociology and Anthropology . Knowledge of social sciences is indispensable for building a just and peaceful society .

- Social science subjects are mainly interdisciplinary and interdependent in nature, since, they have functional relationship among themselves.
- Social sciences as a field of study includes the large number of subjects like political science, anthropology, law, economics, geography, etc.
- At the higher education/high school level, different social science subjects like history, political science, anthropology, law, etc. are taught as independent/optional subjects.
- At the basic school level, social sciences are taught under a single unified area of study designating itself as 'social studies curriculum' or 'social sciences curriculum'.

Hence, we conclude that all the above points are in the context of nature of social science.

107(D). Social Science is the study of people and their interactions with one another. Social Studies are carried out about man's historical, geographical, social, economic, and political environments. The nature of social studies ranges from a study of human beings favouring a separate subject approach to an integrated one in which the subject matter is indistinguishable as history, geography, civics, and so on

Social Studies is the-

- Study of man's progress about his environments, his interactions with various environments, and his geographical relations .
- Study of political and economical relations of man.
- It covers the study of communities at all levels, local, regional, national, and international with a focus on man and his social environment.
- Study of how people live and work together at the local, national, or international level.
- Study to enhance the understanding of the past to interpret the present or current trends to develop skills.

Hence, it becomes clear that social studies are supposed to study of economical, social, political and social relations of man.

108(D). Evaluation is a goal-oriented process. According to the concept of evaluation, the whole process of learning is responsible for the success and failure of students.

- It gives guidance to teachers.
- It clarifies the objective of teaching.
- It is both qualitative and quantitative.
- It is a child-centered method.
- It helps the teachers to identify the difficulties, problems, and weaknesses of the students.

Validity	◦	The extent to which a te st is measured.
	◦	It is an external correlat ion.
	◦	Purpsiveness of the test.
Reliabilit y	◦	It is a consistency of sco res.
	◦	It is an internal correlati on.
	◦	Reliability and validity b oth are related to each o ther.
Objectivi ty	◦	Elimination of personal judgment.
	◦	It affects reliability and validity.
Usability	◦	The good test must be n icely made and attractiv e.
Compre hensiven ess	◦	Give equal importance t o tests.
	◦	Includes all topics and s ubjects in a test.
Diagnost ic	◦	Diagnose the weakness and strengths of studen ts.

Thus, it is concluded that subjectivity is not included in the criteria of a good evaluation test.

109(D). Evaluation is a systematic way to assess learner's abilities, analyze performance, provide appropriate feedback to each learner and help them to progress.

- High-quality evaluation required in teaching for successful learning.
- Evaluation needs to be integrated with the process of teaching and learning.

Open Book Evaluation:

- It refers to an exam that a llows students to bring their books or notebooks in the exam and to consult their books while answering questions.
- Open book evaluation tests the skills of problem-solving and critical thinking rather than memorizing the given facts of textbooks
- The main purpose of this type of evaluation is to reduce and eliminate the burden of rote memorization and to teach students how to take information and apply it in a thoughtful, deep manner.

Hence, it becomes clear that the main purpose of an Open-Book Evaluation is that students need not feel the burden to rote memorize all facts and details.

110(A). Ghori first invaded Multan in 1175 AD. At this time, Karamati, the followers of the Shiites was ruled. These Karamati were Buddhists before becoming Muslims. Ghori won the Multan.

- Ghori did the second invasion of Gujarat in 1178 AD , but Moolraj II defeated him in the foothills of the Abu Mountains. This was the first defeat of Muhammad Ghori in India. this war was conducted by Nayika Devi, the wife of Moolraj.
- After Ghori's death, his kingdom was divided into three of his main slaves.
  - Qutubuddin Aibak – made Delhi the center of the Islamic Empire. -- Pair 4 is correctly matched.
  - Tajuddin Yaldoz – Ghazni area -- Pair 1 is incorrectly matched.
  - Nasiruddin Kubacha – Uchchh and Sindh (Pakistan) -- Pair 3 is incorrectly matched.
  - Muhammad ibn Bakhtyar - Bengal -- Pair 2 is incorrectly matched.

111(B). Some of the earliest works in Tamil, known as Sangam literature, were composed around 2300 years ago.

- These texts were called Sangam because they were supposed to have been composed and compiled in assemblies (known as sangams) of poets that were held in the city of Madurai.
- Sangam literature is one of the main sources used for documenting the early history of the ancient Tamil country, be it the kings, rulers, poets, etc.
- The Sangam poets and the unknown Greeks were contemporaries.
- For example, o ne of the most detailed accounts of that time that has been found was by an unknown Greek sailor.

- He described all the ports that he visited in his accounts.

Based on the above discussion, we can conclude that b oth (A) and (R) are true but (R) is not the correct explanation of (A).

112(B). The Gupta Empire was one of the most prosperous during its time.
- Hinduism was widely practised during the Gupta Empire. The ideas and features of Hinduism have aided the religion in surviving over time. .
- Those who practised Hinduism to a serious extent eventually broke into two sects came into existence- -Vaishnavism and Shaivism.
- Vaishnavism was mostly prevalent in Northern India while the Shaivism in southern India. At this time the tantric (liberation of consciousness) beliefs had left their mark on Hindu religion.
- An important feature of Vaishnavism in the Gupta period is the conception of Lakshmi or Sri as Vishnu's wife . A second wife of Vishnu was supposed to be the Earth, called Vaishnavi in some epigraphs.
- Therefore, this was also the beginning of the worship of wives/consorts of Indian Gods such as Lakshmi, Parvati, Durga, Kali and other goddesses
- Hinduism also underwent some important changes during these times. The sacrifice was replaced by worship (pooja) and mediation of the Brahmins was somewhat replaced by Devotion and Bhakti.

Hence, the statement is given in Assertion (A) is true.
- Chinese pilgrims visiting India between 400 and 700 CE discerned a decline in the Buddhist community and the beginning of the absorption of Indian Buddhism by Hinduism. Among these pilgrims was Faxian, who left China in 399, crossed the Gobi , visited various holy places in India, and returned to China with numerous Buddhist scriptures and statues.
- During this period Buddhist monastic centres proliferated, and there developed diverse schools of interpretation, distinctively Mahayana tendencies began to take shape.
- One of the oldest surviving stone structures in India and a specimen of Buddhist architecture, the Great Stupa at Sanchi.
- One of the best conserved Stupas, the Great Stupa at Sanchi with its four ornamental toranas or gateways lures visitors from all over the world to this day who spend hours at the site marvelling at this Buddhist architectural masterpiece and the richness of its sculptures.
- The great Maurya ruler, Ashoka, who reigned over the entire subcontinent between 268 and 232 BCE , can be

credited for laying the foundation of a typical Vihara (Buddhist monastery) architecture as evident in Sanchi.
- Nalanda , ancient university and Buddhist monastic centre southwest of Bihar Sharif in central Bihar state, northeastern India. Nalanda's traditional history dates to the time of the Buddha (6th–5th centuries BCE).

Here statement of the Reason (R) is also true.

113(A). The 74th Constitutional Amendment Act, 1992 relates to the Urban Local Government.
- It has added Part- IX-A of the constitution which deals with the administration of Urban local bodies i.e. Municipalities and Nagar Palika.
- It consists of Article 243 P to Article 243 ZG.
- It is included in the 12th Schedule of the Indian Constitution which contains 18 Subjects.

114(D). Public Interest Litigation or PIL is a mechanism to increase access to justice. It allowed any individual or organisation to file a PIL in the High Court or the Supreme Court on behalf of those whose rights were being violated. Hence statement A is correct.
- PIL can be filed in both the Supreme Court and the High Court but strictly for public interest only. Hence statement B is correct and statement C is incorrect.
- Justice Bhagwati and Justice V R Krishna Iye r were among the first judges in the country to file PILs.

115(A). Union Minister of Social Justice and empowerment Dr. Virendra Kumar has launched the Scheme "SHRESHTA"-Scheme for residential education for students in High school in Targeted Areas on June 3,2022 . The Scheme for Residential Education for Students in Targeted Areas (SHRESHTA) has been formulated with the objective to provide quality education and opportunities for even the poorest.

116(C). Jammu and Kashmir have launched the Super-75 scholarship scheme. It was launched on the occasion of International Women's Day.

Super-75 scholarship scheme

It will support the education of meritorious girls from poor families.

This scholarship scheme aims to facilitate the education and entrepreneurship of women.

Jammu and Kashmir launched another scheme on the same day titled Tejaswini.

Under this scheme, financial assistance of Rs 5 lakhs will be provided to the girls between the age group of 18 to 35 years to start their business.

117(D). The President of India:
- Has the duty to preserve, protect, and

defend the constitution.
- But, he is no authority to interpret the constitution. So, option A is NOT correct.

The Council of Ministers:
- Must function as per the constitutional interpretations of the Judiciary (Supreme Court and High Courts). So, option B is NOT correct.

Parliament:
- May disagree with the Supreme Court on the interpretation of the constitution.
- It is also empowered to amend the constitution in case of such disagreement.
- However, the Supreme Court gives the final word on the validity of such an amendment and can even strike it down. So, option C is NOT correct.
- This tussle between the judiciary and Parliament over constitutional interpretation is best seen in the recent NJAC case. So, option D is correct.

118(D). Types of Socialization: There are mainly two types of socialization including primary and secondary socialization.

Secondary Socialization:

It occurs once the infant passes into the childhood phase and continues into maturity.

It refers to the process that begins in the later years through agencies such as Schools, Peer groups, Media, Religious institutions, etc.

During this phase more than the family, some other agents of socialization begin to play a role in socializing the child.

119(B). In Jainism, there were twenty-four Tirthankaras.

Lord Rishabha was the first Tirthankara and Lord Mahavira was the last Tirthankara.

Mahavira wandered for twelve years to attain perfect knowledge later he was known as Jina(conqueror) and the followers of Mahavira were called Jains.

In Jainism, there are three jewels- right belief, right knowledge, and right action to achieve salvation.

Jain monks followed non-violence very strictly and they opposed the caste system.

120(C). Manufacturing. is the meaning of Production in terms of Economics.

Manufacturing is the creation or production of goods with the help of equipment, labor, machines, tools, and chemical or biological processing or formulation. It is the essence of secondary sector of the economy.
- Economic production is an activity carried out under the control and responsibility of an institutional unit that uses inputs of labor, capital, and goods and services to produce outputs of goods or services.
- According to Bates and Parkinson:
  - "Production is the organized activity of transforming resources into

finished products in the form of goods and services; the objective of production is to satisfy the demand for such transformed resources".

Child Development and Pedagogy

1. Jean Piaget has presented his thoughts about the preoperation stage, how the child starts doing his own work like wearing clothes, eating food, keeping a copybook, etc. Which of the following is not a limitation of pre-operative thought?
   (a) Development of symbolic thought
   (b) Conservation
   (c) Decentralization
   (d) Seriation

2. In context of progressive education the appropriate statement among the given below is:
   (a) Knowledge is generated through direct experience and collaboration.
   (b) Examination is norm centered and external.
   (c) Teachers are the originator of information and authority.
   (d) Education is teacher centered.

3. If Rachna learns from her family about how to be a good daughter, sister, friend, wife and mother. This learning results from the process of:
   (a) Adaptability (b) Change
   (c) Maturity (d) Socialisation

4. There are lot of debates all around whether girls and boys have specific set of abilities due to their genetic materials. In this context which among below option is most agreeable?
   (a) All girls have inherent talent for arts, while boys genetically programmed to be better at aggressive sports.
   (b) Girls are socialised to be caring, while boys are discouraged to show emotions such as crying.
   (c) Boys cannot be caring since they are born this way.
   (d) After puberty, boys and girls cannot play with each other since their interest are completely opposite.

5. In a class individual learners differ from each other in terms of:
   (a) Sequence of development
   (b) Principles of growth and development
   (c) General capacity for development
   (d) Rate of development

6. Which among the following are the parameters for measuring the validity of a test?
   (A) Construct
   (B) Stability
   (C) Criterion
   (D) Content
   (a) A, B only
   (b) A, B, C
   (c) A, C, D
   (d) All of the above

7. According to Piaget's cognitive theory of learning, identify the process among the following by which the cognitive structure is modified.
   (a) Perception
   (b) Assimilation
   (c) Schema
   (d) Accommodation

8. According to Vygotsky, 'the relationship between development and learning' summarizes best by which among the following option given below:
   (a) Development is synonymous with learning
   (b) Development is independent of learning
   (c) Development process lags behind learning process
   (d) Learning and development are parallel process

9. Which among the following is correct regarding ability grouping?
   (a) Ability grouping of student should be encouraged as it promotes competition among students.
   (b) Ability grouping of students should be discouraged as it gives the message that ability is valued more than effort.
   (c) Ability grouping of student should be encouraged as it maximizes learning using special methods.
   (d) Both (A) and (C)

10. If a child fails to perform well in the class test leads us to believe that-
    (a) There is no need to reflect upon the syllabus, pedagogy and assessment process
    (b) Children are born with certain capabilities and deficits
    (c) There is a need to reflect upon the syllabus, pedagogy and assessment processes
    (d) Some children are deemed to fail irrespective of how hard the system tries

11. In which factor children's language development is depended?
    (a) Freedom of expression
    (b) Better schooling
    (c) Co-education
    (d) Technical education

12. According to Piaget's stages of cognitive development, with whom the 'sensory-motor state' is related?
    (a) Concerned with social issues
    (b) Simulation, memory and mental representation
    (c) Logically problem-solving ability
    (d) Ability to interpret and analyze options

13. The best measure of identifying mildly mentally retarded is:
    (a) Administration of standardized intelligence test
    (b) Administration of behavior test
    (c) Administration of adjustment test
    (d) A combination of all

14. A child in school is called a problem child when:
    (a) He is able to solve the problems of other children
    (b) He suggests useful approaches to teachers when they are explaining any problem
    (c) He behaves in such a way that becomes a problem for the teacher to understand him
    (d) He is very resourceful in suggesting good problems for the class to workout

15. Visual-spatial dysfunction is a _______ disability.
    (a) mental (b) learning
    (c) physical (d) social

16. In a heterogeneous and mixed ability class, a teacher should:
    (a) employ one type of teaching for all
    (b) use a variety of teaching-learning methods
    (c) conduct many tests
    (d) employ teacher-directed teaching

17. What does SEN mean?
(a) Social Education Standard
(b) Special Education Needs
(c) Social Education Needs
(d) Social Exception Needs

18. Special education is a branch of education that deals with ______.
(a) Educating children in special schools
(b) To provide opportunity of special education to students
(c) Instructions designing for students with special needs
(d) Education for preparation of students for special jobs

19. Repeatedly asking children to engage in learning activities either to avoid punishment or to gain a reward:
(a) decreases extrinsic motivation
(b) increases intrinsic motivation
(c) would encourage children to focus on mastery rather than performance goals
(d) decreases children's natural interest and curiosity involved in learning

20. Learner-centred teaching means that:
(a) learners are considered passive recipients and teacher has the 'right' knowledge.
(b) learners are slow in learning and teacher stresses completion of syllabus.
(c) learners are given an opportunity to construct knowledge and teacher is a guide in the learning process.
(d) learners know little and teaching involves transmission of facts to them.

21. In most schools today the primary consideration for homogeneous grouping is based on:
(a) grade levels
(b) age levels
(c) ability levels
(d) pupil preferences

22. Psychosocial theory emphasises on which of the following?
(a) Stimuli and Response
(b) Ophallic and Latency stages
(c) Industry versus Inferiority stage
(d) Operant Conditioning

23. Micro-teaching is:
(a) Scaled down teaching
(b) Effective teaching
(c) Evaluation teaching
(d) Real teaching

24. According to Aristotle Emotional catharsis is:
(a) Feeling highly depressed
(b) Bringing out emotional repression
(c) Increasing the ability to tolerate emotional repression
(d) Suppression of emotions

25. How a teacher can enhance the learning as per the context of motivation theories?
(a) By setting uniform standards of expectation
(b) By not having any expectation from students
(c) By setting extremely high expectation from students
(d) By setting realistic expectations from students

26. Which among the following is not a personal factor influencing learning?
(a) Sensation or perception
(b) Needs
(c) Cultural demands
(d) Emotional conditions

27. Which among the following is an autocratic strategy of teaching?
(a) Heuristic method
(b) Discovery method
(c) Brain storming method
(d) Demonstration method

28. Errors made by children are indicative of-
(a) poor intelligence
(b) low ability
(c) their inability to reproduce knowledge
(d) children's thinking process which is qualitatively different from that of adults

29. The cephalocaudal principle of development explains how development proceeds from:
(a) General to specific functions
(b) Differentiated to integrated functions
(c) Head to toe
(d) Rural to urban areas

30. According to Piaget, which one of the following factors plays an important role in influencing development?
(a) Reinforcement
(b) Language
(c) Experience with the physical world
(d) Imitation

Ques (31-39): Direction: Read the passage given below and then answer the questions given below the passage. Some words may be highlighted for your attention. Pay careful attention.

In the UK, roughly a third of the food grown in the field never actually makes into anybody's mouth. For every three pigs raised on a farm, the equivalent of one will ultimately be sent to landfill. A third of all apples, perfectly good for consumption, will somehow be discarded. The message is simple: we waste food, and we waste a lot of it.

Food waste is a global problem, but in the developed world, where our farming and manufacturing practices are efficient, the food waste that occurs at these early stages is largely unavoidable (meat bones, eggshells, banana peel, and the like).

Conversely, in UK homes – where 7m of the 13m tonnes of food waste comes from each year – 77% of waste is either avoidable (at some point, it has been perfectly good food) or possibly avoidable (food that some people eat, but others don't, such as potato skins and meat fat). This is akin to throwing away one shopping bag in five as you leave the supermarket – with an annual cost to a family of four of more than £740.

Clearly, not all food waste is equal. The cost and environmental impact of a kilo of beef are much higher than that of a kilo of potatoes, as would be expected. And so with short **shelf-life** food categories. Fresh produce, bakery, meats, and dairy top the most wasted list – and have the largest energy, CO_2, and water footprints – and so should be the main focus for reducing waste.

It seems too easy to say that it is the responsibility of consumers to reduce these **ridiculous** levels of waste. And it is too easy. A couple of years ago, Professor Tim Lang wrote here about food waste being a symptom of a much bigger problem, explaining that the relatively low cost of food almost forces a consumer society to buy more food than it can eat. It is arguably the economic powerhouses (in this case, the food giants) that drive this through brand advertising, store layouts, and clever pricing strategies. So the question is now: isn't it the food providers' responsibility to reduce food waste?

Well, the answer is that both providers and consumers have a part to play. For the consumers, the argument for this is easy: wasting less food equals saving more money, and you feel good for doing less harm to the environment. For the providers (manufacturers and retailers), the drive is less clear: selling less food equals less profit.

So how can food providers help consumers reduce food waste, but still remain profitable? There are a few options, but some of them are not easy to **swallow**. The price of food seems a pretty obvious place to start. Consumers currently spend around 11% of their income on food and drink. Five decades ago, the proportion was three times higher, so naturally, people wasted less. In sub-Saharan Africa, where consumers spend half of their income on food, it would be difficult to envisage high levels of waste. But increasing the price of food such that consumers "value" it more is likely to be very unpopular – and such a move would fly in the face of the modern food industry and its apparently eternal price wars.

Looking at the statistics, it appears that a large proportion of food waste is due to products with short shelf-lives not being used in time. Consequently, there is potential for improvements in food processing or packaging and storage to increase the useable life of such products and reduce the potential for spoilage before use.

But given that leading supermarkets demand 90% of product life at the point of store entry, and goods already have extended lifetimes due to already excessive packaging and protective atmospheres, significant increases in shelf-life are unlikely.

A brave move might be to abolish "use-by" and "best-before" dates (we didn't have them before the 1970s), but this would open up a legislative **can of worms.** Until somebody invents a device that can reliably tell whether a leg of lamb has gone off, I suspect these dates are likely to stay. You could just make sure you eat the food before it goes bad, but the nation's already bulging waistline might struggle with this extra consumption. Food waste via overconsumption is yet another issue.

Perhaps the greatest improvement would be to completely change the food provision market. Consumers are like micro-manufacturers: they buy stock (ingredients) and use processes (cook) to meet demand (their family's hunger). But unlike manufacturers, consumers aren't very good at managing their inventory, using their processes efficiently, or predicting demand accurately. This leads to food waste.

There is therefore an argument for food providers to help consumers meet their families' needs by selling meals, not food. It's not inconceivable to imagine in the future people planning meals and then ordering them off the internet for home delivery – it might build better relationships between providers and consumers, too. Even if consumers pay more for food which is delivered when wanted and actually gets eaten, it would be more convenient and could well end up being cheaper overall.

31. Which of the following is a correct inference that can be drawn from the facts given in the passage?

(a) Wastage of left over food only contributes to what is called food wastage

(b) Only households contribute to food wastage

(c) There are other factors besides wastage of left over food that contribute to 'wastage of food

(d) Agriculture based industries are the real culprits when it comes to food wastage

32. Which of the following top the list of wasted food products in the UK?

(a) Fresh produce, bakery, meats and dairy

(b) Vegetables, agriculture produce and dairy

(c) Bakery, fruits and dairy

(d) Perishable goods and food grains

33. Which of the following is most similar in meaning to term 'shelf life' as used in the passage?

(a) The life a product after preservatives have been added

(b) The life of a product when kept in the worst kind of environment

(c) The length of time for which an item remains fit for consumption without the addition of preservatives

(d) The length of time for which an item remains fit for consumption with or without the addition of preservatives

34. What role does the market play in food wastage in the UK?

(a) The agriculture industry in the US is so prosperous that the markets gets flooded with food products which are wasted as the demand is not as much

(b) Relatively lower food prices encourage people to buy more food products than they require and the extra food ultimately ends up getting wasted

(c) The price of food being exceptionally high leads to wastage of food as people are incapable of buying them

(d) The online shopping websites in the race of providing the best end up wasting a lot of food

35. Which of the following is most similar in meaning to the word 'ridiculous' as used in the passage?

(a) Reasonable　(b) Amusing

(c) Evil　(d) High

36. What is the major roadblock in the face of the food providers to control wastage of food?

(a) They cannot compromise with the supply as they never want to run short in case of sudden excessive demands

(b) The idea of selling less food products is not congrous to the profit they intend to make

(c) The providers cannot control the supply as in any way the food would be wasted in the farms if they do not reach the manufacturers and retailers

(d) All the above

37. Which of the following is most similar in meaning to the word 'swallow' as used in the passage?

(a) Eat　(b) Understand

(c) Believe　(d) Memorise

38. Which of the following comes closest in meaning to the phrase (to)'open a can of worms' as given in the passage?

(a) A dark secret

(b) To reveal a secret

(c) To make obvious while trying to hide something

(d) To make things even more complicated while attempting to solve a problem.

39. Which one of the following constitute the possible solutions to reduce food wastage from the end of 'providers' as mentioned in the passage?

(a) Increase the price of the food products

(b) To do away with the approximate expiry dates mentioned in packaged products

(c) To keep consuming edible items even after the mentioned expiry dates have passedA

(d) Both (A) and (B)

Ques (40-45): Direction: Read the following poem and answer the questions by choosing the correct/most appropriate options:

A thing of beauty is a joy for ever:
Its loveliness increases; it will never
Pass into nothingness; but still will keep
A bower quiet for us, and a sleep

Full of sweet dreams, and health, and quiet breathing.
Therefore, on every morrow, are we wreathing
A flowery band to bind us to the earth,
Spite of despondence, of the inhuman dearth
Of noble natures, of the gloomy days,
Of all the unhealthy and o'er-darkened ways
Made for our searching: yes, in spite of all,
Some shape of beauty moves away the pall
From our dark spirits. Such the sun, the moon,
Trees old and young, sprouting a shady boon
For simple sheep; and such are daffodils
With the green world they live in; and clear rills
That for themselves a cooling covert make
'Gainst the hot season; the mid forest brake,
Rich with a sprinkling of fair musk-rose blooms:
And such too is the grandeur of the dooms
We have imagined for the mighty dead;
All lovely tales that we have heard or read:
An endless fountain of immortal drink,
Pouring unto us from the heaven's brink.

40. The overall tone of the poem is:
- (a) Optimistic
- (b) Gloomy
- (c) Bitter
- (d) Challenging

41. Which figure of speech has been used in the line?
"For simple sheep; and such are daffodils"
- (a) Metaphor
- (b) Simile
- (c) Alliteration
- (d) Personification

42. The poem underlines that:
- (a) We need not preserve things of beauty as they wane some day.
- (b) We should preserve and take care of the things of beauty.
- (c) We should preserve only beautiful things.
- (d) Beauty diminishes with the time and disappeared.

43. The poem tells us about:
- (a) Beauty is mortal
- (b) Love with nature wanes with time
- (c) The beauty of nature degrades with time
- (d) Beauty never diminishes or fades

44. Which figure of speech has been used in the line 'we wreathing, A flowery band to bind us to the earth'?
- (a) Alliteration
- (b) Metaphor
- (c) Personification
- (d) Simile

45. Identify the part of speech of the underlined word in the following line:
A flowery band to bind us to the earth
- (a) Noun
- (b) Pronoun
- (c) Adjective
- (d) Conjunction

46. Language Acquisition stands for:
- (a) learning a language with a deliberate and conscious effort.
- (b) learning a language without making any deliberate or conscious effort.
- (c) learning a language through some specific language methodology.
- (d) acquiring a language by taking recourse to one's mother tongue.

47. Grammar-Translation method is:
- (a) costly method
- (b) economical method
- (c) consume more time
- (d) None of the above

48. While evaluating writing skill of a learner which of these will be the most important criteria?
- (a) The Learner is able to take dictation
- (b) The Learner is able to express ideas coherently and systematically
- (c) The Learner is able to write about a character
- (d) The Learner is able to comprehend the questions and write their answers.

49. The teacher informs the children about the 'adjective' and asks them to give at least one feature and definition of the adjective. What is such a method called?
- (a) Inductive Method
- (b) Deductive Method
- (c) TPR
- (d) Immersion Method

50. Which of the following are receptive skills ?
- (a) Writing and reading
- (b) Speaking and listening
- (c) Speaking and writing
- (d) Listening and reading

51. A good language textbook should include:
- (a) extracts from British and American literature
- (b) more grammar exercises
- (c) interesting stories
- (d) attractive fonts, illustrations and learner-friendly texts

52. Which is an effective way of teaching-learning grammar?
- (a) Teaching the rules first followed by examples.
- (b) Presenting grammar form in a natural discourse, then explaining how the form is made and used.
- (c) Presenting single sentence examples in plenty of ways and then explaining the form.
- (d) Teaching through a typical grammar book

53. Causes of poor reading skills
- (a) Lack of concentration
- (b) Lack of graded materials
- (c) Deficiency in associating phoneme and grapheme
- (d) All of the above

54. Remedial teaching in language learning is____
- (a) one to one approach
- (b) group approach
- (c) multiple approach
- (d) Both 1 & 2

55. Which one of the following is not a language component?
- (a) Structure
- (b) Script
- (c) Vocabulary
- (d) Sound

56. Complete the following statement: Language tests are designed to measure ______ at a particular moment in the teaching programme.
- (a) the learner's liking for the language
- (b) the learner's knowledge of the language
- (c) the teacher's knowledge of the language
- (d) the learner's attitude towards the language

57. Teena, a 5 years old girl, begins to speak language structures that she has not heard before because when children are exposed to speech, certain general principles for discovering or structuring language automatically begin to operate. This function of the human brain is called:
- (a) Innate ability

(b) Generative grammar

(c) Language Acquisition Device

(d) Universal grammar

58. **When we want to test speaking skills, we test the ability of the students :**
    (a) to use proper punctuation marks
    (b) to narrate incidents or events
    (c) to make conclusions from the given extract
    (d) to understand the main thought

59. **Deficiency in the ability to write associated with impaired handwriting is a symptom of**
    (a) Dyscalculia   (b) Dysgraphia
    (c) Dysphasia   (d) Aphasia

60. **A good teaching-learning material (TLM) can best:**
    (a) Help the teachers to learn a language
    (b) Help the learners acquire a language
    (c) Facilitate the teaching-learning process
    (d) Be a source of entertainment

Social Studies

61. **Which of the following Veda depicts the information about the most ancient Vedic age culture?**
    (a) Rig Veda   (b) Yajurveda
    (c) Atharvaveda   (d) Samaveda

62. **The dynasty of Delhi Sultanate ruled for the shortest time is:**
    (a) Khalji dynasty
    (b) Tughlaq dynasty
    (c) Sayyid dynasty
    (d) Lodi dynasty

63. **Which of the following straits connects the Mediterranean Sea to the Atlantic Ocean?**
    (a) Strait of Hormuz
    (b) Bosporus Strait
    (c) Strait of Gibraltar
    (d) Dover Strait

64. **The innermost layer of the Earth is mainly made up of:**
    (a) Silica and Iron
    (b) Nickel and Alumina
    (c) Silica and Alumina
    (d) Nickel and Iron

65. **Asteroids are found between the orbits of ________.**
    (a) Saturn and Jupiter

(b) Mars and Jupiter

(c) The Earth and Mars

(d) Saturn and Uranus

66. **When was the battle of Chausa fought?**
    (a) 1560   (b) 1539
    (c) 1545   (d) 1535

67. **Which town was not related with Revolt of 1857?**
    (a) Meerut   (b) Delhi
    (c) Amritsar   (d) Lucknow

68. **Who led the 1857 Revolt in Bihar?**
    (a) Babu Amar Singh
    (b) Hare Krishna Singh
    (c) Babu Kunwar Singh
    (d) Raja Shahzada Singh

69. **The oldest mountain range of India is:**
    (a) Vindhya   (b) Aravalli
    (c) Nilgiri   (d) Himalaya

70. **Which is the largest tributary of the river Indus?**
    (a) Jhelum   (b) Chenab
    (c) Sutlej   (d) Beas

71. **Who coined the phrase Unity in Diversity?**
    (a) Mahatma Gandhi
    (b) Jawahar Lal Nehru
    (c) Rabindra Nath Tagore
    (d) Sardar Vallabh Bhai Patel

72. **A system of government in which power is divided between a central authority and various constituent units is called a ________.**
    (a) Democratic state
    (b) Federal state
    (c) Unitary state
    (d) Communist state

73. **Which of the following articles provide protection to persons arrested or detained under preventive detention law?**
    (a) Article 17   (b) Article 21
    (c) Article 22   (d) Article 25

74. **When a community is forced to live on the fringes of social and economic development, this is known as ____.**
    (a) malnourishment
    (b) displacement
    (c) marginalisation
    (d) communalisation

75. **What is NOT true in regard to Ayushman Bharat Scheme?**

(a) Sectoral and segmented approach of health service delivery

(b) Creation of Health and Wellness Centres

(c) Vision is 'Healthy India, Prosperous India

(d) Comprehensive need-based health care service

76. **The Human trafficking and forced labour are prohibited under ______.**
    (a) Culture and Educational Rights
    (b) Right against Exploitation
    (c) Right to freedom of Religion
    (d) Right to Property

77. **Which is an important way to control the executive in Parliament?**
    (a) Adjournment motion
    (b) Zero hour
    (c) Question hour
    (d) None of the above

78. **Assertion (A): Social sciences possess distinct nature, which is different from nature of physical sciences and many other sciences. Reasoning (R): Social sciences are concerned with studying social issues like community living, state, administration, government, culture, tradition, ritual, social wellbeing and welfare, economic system, religious systems, etc.**
    (a) Both (A) and (R) are true and (R) is the correct explanation of (A).
    (b) Both (A) and (R) are true and (R) is the incorrect explanation of (A).
    (c) (A) is true but (R) is false.
    (d) (A) is false but (R) is true.

79. **The teacher of social studies has different roles to play such as:**
    (a) Developing personality values
    (b) Attitudes and civic responsibility to live together
    (c) Only A
    (d) Both A and B

80. **Essential qualities of the social studies teacher are:**
    (a) Knowledgeable, an imperative mind and curios
    (b) Unprofessional and Rigid
    (c) Both A and B
    (d) None of these

81. **They represent real things in all respects except size and shape. Large objects are reduced to small size so that they could be observed by students with greater precision.**

(a) Cartoons
(b) Audio Aids
(c) Models
(d) All of the above

82. Which of these relate to classroom activity?
(a) Principles   (b) Methods
(c) Philosophy   (d) Techniques

83. Biases, discrimination and prejudices in the classroom could be avoided by:
(a) Organising a lecture on humanity.
(b) Ignoring them, as children will grow out of them one day.
(c) Discussing different dimensions of social realities.
(d) Handing out the Preamble of the Constitution.

84. Social Studies help the learners to:
(a) Think locally and act globally
(b) Think globally and act locally
(c) Build intelligent autocratic citizenship
(d) Judge issues subjectively

85. How a social science teacher can connect literature of a language with social sciences in a classroom teaching learning process?
(a) Asking the students to conclude a concept of social sciences in their own words
(b) Assigning literature based tasks like writing poetry on social science based content
(c) Asking the students to recall their previously learned concepts of social studies
(d) Encouraging the students to read the literature based social science content

86. While teaching a topic, a History teacher comes across a particular paragraph which paints a famous historical figure in a bad light.
Which of the following is the responsible approach for the History teacher?
(a) Analyse the paragraph along with students and discuss the assumptions made in the book.
(b) Continue reading the paragraphs since the particular figure is not important in her view.
(c) Tell students more about why the particular figure has been painted in a negative light.
(d) Ask students to ignore the negative part since history should focus on positive aspects

of leaders and continue to work on the topic.

87. Which activity uses the inquiry/ investigation-based approach?
(a) View a Power Point or slide display
(b) Visit the community to collect data
(c) Listening to lectures
(d) Write an essay on the topic

88. On which of the following part does Social Studies lay emphasis ?
(a) On the theory part of human affairs
(b) On the functional part of knowledge
(c) On the part of cultural knowledge
(d) On the advanced studies of human affairs

89. The objective of discussing 'gender' in a social science classroom is to :
(a) Expected action from a man and women.
(b) Male superiority over women.
(c) Biological difference between man and women.
(d) None of these

90. The teacher of Social Studies is expected to keep in mind the following fact is natural:
(a) Clear vision in the relation of specific facts and things
(b) Concept of general fact or qualities
(c) Establishment of fact, rule, definition, knowledge, and method
(d) All of the above

91. Which method is most useful for teaching History and Geography at primary level?
(a) Observation
(b) Field visit
(c) Story-telling
(d) Project and demonstration

92. On which one of the following Tarachand Committee provided recommendations?
(a) Student unrest
(b) Religious and moral education
(c) Vocationalization education
(d) Secondary education

93. Who was the Chairman of Secondary Education Commission set up in 1952?
(a) Dr. B.R. Ambedkar

(b) Sh. K.C. Pant
(c) Dr. A.L. Mudaliar
(d) Dr. S. Radhakrishnan

94. Which of the following is/are type(s) of charts used as learning resource in social science?
I. Relationship charts
II. Tabulation charts
III. Flow charts
IV. Organisation charts
V. Pedigree charts
(a) I, II, III and V
(b) I, II, III, IV and V
(c) I, II, III and IV
(d) I, II and III

95. Which of the following is not included within map study?
(a) Map interpretation
(b) Map preservation
(c) Map symbols
(d) Map reading

96. To understand the ability, interest, and capabilities of learner, teacher uses:
(a) Summative evaluation
(b) Formative evaluation
(c) Placement evaluation
(d) None of these

97. The type of evaluation which gives feed-back to students as well as teachers is:
(a) Placement evaluation
(b) Formative evaluation
(c) Summative evaluation
(d) Diagnostic evaluation

98. Which of the following statements regarding Democracy is/are correct?
1. It is a form of government that guarantees economic development.
2. It seeks to promote and accommodate social diversity.
Select the correct answer using the code given below:
(a) only 1
(b) Only 2
(c) Both 1 and 2
(d) Neither 1 nor 2

99. Consider the following pairs:

(Historical Place)	(Well known for)
1. Koldihwa and Mahagara	Circular huts along with crude hand made pottery
2. Mehrgarh	The earliest Neolithic site
3. Gufkral	The neolithic men used tools and weapons

made of bones.

Which of the pairs given above is/are correctly matched?

(a) 1 and 2 only   (b) 2 and 3 only
(c) 1 and 3 only   (d) 1, 2, and 3

100. With reference to the Individual Satyagraha, consider the following statements:
1. Individual Satyagraha was the direct result of the Simmon Commission offered.
2. Vinobha Bhave was first and Nehru was second to offer Satyagraha.
3. Though the aim of Satyagraha was limited, it was successful in displaying unity and patience in the masses of India.

Which of the above statement is/are correct?

(a) 1 only   (b) 2 and 3 only
(c) 1 and 2 only   (d) 1, 2, and 3

101. Consider the following pairs:

1. Debendranath Tagore	Secretary of British Indian Association
2. Dwarkanath Tagore	Founder of Bengal British India Society
3. Lala Lajpat Rai	Founder of Servants of People Society

Which of the above pairs is/are correctly matched?

(a) 1 only   (b) 1 and 3 only
(c) 2 and 3 only   (d) 1, 2 and 3

102. Consider the following pairs:

Major energy pipelines	Countries involved
1. Keystone pipeline	USA-Mexico
2. Power of Siberia	Russia-China
3. Nordstream-I	Germany-Norway

Which of the following pairs is/are correctly matched?

(a) 1, 2 and 3   (b) 1 and 3 only
(c) 1 and 2 only   (d) 2 only

103. Consider the following statements regarding Mission Antyodaya :
1. The Ministry of Social Justice and Empowerment is the nodal agency to take this mission forward.
2. The main objective is to ensure optimum use of resources by making gram panchayat the hub of a development plan.

Which of the statements given above is/are correct?

(a) 1 only
(b) 2 only
(c) Both 1 and 2
(d) Neither 1 nor 2

104. Consider the following regarding India's Coal Reserves :
1. India holds fifth-largest coal reserves in the world.
2. India's total coal supply comes from the states of Jharkhand, Chhattisgarh, Odisha, West Bengal and Madhya Pradesh.
3. Coal can help the country meet its energy needs without depending on imports as it is abundantly available domestically.

Which of the statements given above is/are correct?

(a) 1 and 2   (b) 2 and 3
(c) 1 and 3   (d) 1, 2 and 3

105. Consider the following statements :
1. India currently ranks fifth after China, U.S., Japan and Germany in terms of installed solar power capacity.
2. Lack of consumer awareness is one of the reasons behind struggling India's rooftop solar market.

Which of the statements given above is/are correct?

(a) 1 only
(b) 2 only
(c) Both 1 and 2
(d) Neither 1 nor 2

106. Consider the following Statements:
1. Sacred groves are forest fragments having significant religious values.
2. The Ganges Shark is listed as a Vulnerable on IUCN Red List.

Which of the statements given above is/are correct?

(a) 1 only
(b) 2 only
(c) Both 1 and 2
(d) Neither 1 nor 2

107. Consider the following pairs:

Oceanic Trenches	Region
1. Mariana trench	Pacific ocean
2. Puerto Rico trench	Atlantic ocean
3. Eurasia basin	Indian ocean
4. Java trench	Arctic ocean

Which of the pairs given above are correctly matched?

(a) 1, 2 and 4 only
(b) 1 and 2 only
(c) 3 and 4 only
(d) 1, 2, 3 and 4

108. Consider the followings:
1. High levels of inflation
2. High unemployment
3. Very slow growth

Which of the above is/are characteristic of Stagflation?

(a) Only 1 and 3   (b) Only 1
(c) All 1, 2 and 3 (d) Only 2 and 3

109. If the RBI decides to adopt a contractionary monetary policy, which of the following would it do?
1. Increase Statutory Liquidity Ratio
2. Increase the Marginal Standing Facility Rate
3. Sells government securities

Select the correct answer using the code given below:

(a) 1 and 2 only   (b) 2 and 3 only
(c) 1 and 3 only   (d) 1, 2 and 3

110. Consider the following pairs:

Congress Session	Significance
1. Faizpur Session (1936)	National Planning Committee was set up.
2. Haripura Session (1938)	First session in a village.
3. Karachi Session (1931)	Resolution on National Economic Programme

Which of the pairs given above is/are correct?

(a) 2 only   (b) 3 only
(c) 1 and 3 only   (d) 1, 2 and 3

111. Consider the following events in the history of India:
1. Chuar uprisings
2. Santhal rebellion
3. Munda uprisings
4. Kol rebellion

What is the correct chronological order of the above events, starting from the earliest time?

(a) 1-4-2-3   (b) 1-2-3-4
(c) 4-3-2-1   (d) 4-1-3-2

112. With reference to India, consider the following statement:
1. The Preamble as of 26 January 1950, defines India as a secular nation.

2. Unlike the strict separation between religion and the State in western secularism, in Indian secularism the State maintains a principled distance vis-à-vis religion.

3. Government schools can promote any, one or all religions either in their morning prayers or through religious celebrations.

4. Indian State recognises that wearing a pugri (turban) is central to a Sikh's religious practice.

Which of the statements given above is/are correct?

(a) 1. 2 and 3 Only

(b) 2 and 4 only

(c) 1, 2, 3 and 4

(d) 2 and 3 Only

113. Consider the following statements:

1. The ward councillors are elected officials who take complicated decisions that affect the entire city.

2. The Commissioner is an appointed official who oversees the implementation of the decisions taken by the councillors.

Which of the statement given above is/are correct?

(a) 1 only

(b) 2 only

(c) Both 1 and 2

(d) Neither 1 nor 2

114. Which one of the following statements defines the Oligarchy form of government?

1. Government in which a collection of individuals rules over a nation.

2. Government in which a nation extends its sovereignty over other territories.

3. Government in which a specific religious ideology determines the leadership, laws, and customs.

4. Government in which the ruling party recognizes no limitations.

Select the appropriate option.

(a) 1 only   (b) 2 only

(c) Both 1 and 2 (d) 1, 2 and 4

115. Consider the following statements:

1. A government refers to a political institution that represents sovereign people who occupy a definite territory.

2. The head of the government is the real executive in India.

Which of the statements given above is/are correct?

(a) 1 only

(b) 2 only

(c) Both 1 and 2

(d) Neither 1 nor 2

116. With reference to village administration, consider the following statements:

1. Patwari is responsible to maintain and update land records of the village.

2. The Patwari is also responsible for informing and educating the farmers about the crops to be grown in the area.

Which of the statements given above is/ are correct?

(a) 1 only   (b) 2 only

(c) Both 1 and 2 (d) Both 1 and 2

117. With reference to the history of India, consider the following statements:

1. Nizam-ul-Mulk Asaf Jah established the state of Hyderabad.

2. He never openly declared his independence from the Mughal emperor.

Which of the statements given above is/are correct?

(a) Only 1

(b) Only 2

(c) Both 1 and 2

(d) Neither 1 nor 2

118. Consider the following pairs:

Book	Author
1. Amukthamalyada	Krishnadevaraya
2. Gangadevi	Maduravijayam
3. Allasani Pedanna	Manucharitam

Which of the pairs given above is/ are correct?

(a) 1 and 2 only (b) 2 and 3 only

(c) 1 and 3 only (d) 1, 2 and 3

119. Consider the following pairs:

Philosophy	Saint
1. Visishtadvaita	Ramanuja
2. Advaita	Sankara
3. Dvaita	Nimbarka
4. Dvaitadvaita	Madhava
5. Suddhadvaita	Vallabhacharya

Which of the pairs given above is/ are correct?

(a) 1 and 2 only

(b) 2, 4 and 5 only

(c) 1, 3 and 4 only

(d) 1, 2 and 5 only

120. Shah Jahan effected treaties in 1636 with which of the following states to expand Mughal suzerainty over the Indian subcontinent:

1. Golconda

2. Bidar

3. Bijapur

Select the correct answer using the code given below.

(a) 1 and 3 only (b) 2 and 3 only

(c) 1, 2 and 3 (d) 1 and 2 only

// Hints and Solutions //

1(A). Jean Piaget, a Swiss psychologist, has made a systematic study of cognitive development in his theory that is categorized into four stages.

Preoperational stage:

- The preoperational stage is the second stage in Piaget's theory of cognitive development.
- This stage begins around age 2, as children start to talk, and lasts until approximately age 7.
- During this stage, children begin to engage in symbolic play and learn to manipulate symbols.
- Three main characteristics of pre-operational thinking are centration, static reasoning, and irreversibility.
- In this stage, children can verbalize thoughts but think intuitively rather than logically.
- The key development of this stage is learning to form internal representations.
- During this period, children are thinking at a symbolic level but are not yet using cognitive operations.

Limitation of Pre-operational stage:

- Inability to decenter, conserve, understand seriation (the inability to understand that objects can be organized into a logical series or order) and to carry out inclusion tasks.
- Children in the preoperational stage are able to focus on only one aspect or dimension of problems.

Thus, it can be concluded that the Development of symbolic thought is not the limitation of the pre-operational stage.

2(A). Progressive education focuses on learning that is both experiential and collaborative.

Some of the progressive educations qualities are:-

- Emphasis on learning by doing
- Integrated curriculum focused on thematic units
- Strong emphasis on problem solving and critical thinking
- Group work and development of social skills

- Collaborative and cooperative learning projects
- Education for social responsibility and democracy
- Emphasis of lifelong process and social skills

3(D). If Rachna learns from her family about how to be a good daughter, sister, friend, wife and mother. This learning results from the process of socialisation. Socialisation is a life long process of inheriting norms, customs and philosophies from prevailing environment. It provides an individual with the necessary skills and habits that help him/her get accustomed to the given social environment.

4(B). Girls are socialised to be caring while boys are discouraged to show emotions such as crying, is a gender-biased thought of the society. Girls are considered to be more caring as they are quick in showing emotions than boys who are not expected to act emotionally in front of others.

5(D). In a class individual learners differ from each other in terms of rate of development.
The rate of development of an individual child is different from that of another child. This principle is known as the 'principle of individual differences'. For instance, some children may learn to walk in 8 months, while some may take more than a year to start walking.
It is important for teachers to know variables such as physical characteristics, intelligence, perception, gender, ability, learning styles, which are individual differences of learners. An effective and productive learning-teaching process can be planned by considering these individual differences of students.

6(C). To have confidence that a test is valid, and thus the inferences we make based on the test scores are valid, three kinds of validity evidence are:
Construct - It is the extent to which the content of the test matches the instructional objectives.
Criterion - It is the extent to which scores on the test are in agreement with or predict an external criterion.
Content - It is the extent to which an assessment corresponds to other variables, as predicted by some rationale or theory.

7(D). According to Piaget's cognitive theory of learning, identify the process among the following by "Accommodation" the cognitive structure is modified.
There is accommodation when a child either modifies an existing schema or forms an entirely new schema to deal with a new object or event. This concept was developed by Jean Piaget, a Swiss developmental psychologist who is best known for this theory of cognitive development in children.

8(C). "Development process lags behind learning process" best summarizes the relationship between development and learning as proposed by Vygotsky.
According to Vygotsky, learning is a process that occurs anytime in everyday life and that isn't just an external phenomenon. His theory of Zone of Proximal Development (ZPD) expanded learning and development, which posits that learning precedes development processes.
- Development: It refers to a progressive and systematic series of changes that occur in the life of an individual he/she grows from infancy to old age.
- Learning: The process by which a person alters his responses and behavior in order to adjust himself to the changing environment is called learning.

9(B). Sorting of students according to their talents in a classroom is ability grouping. It should be discouraged as it gives the message that ability is of more value than effort.
Ability grouping is the practice of placing student of similar academic ability level within the same age group for instruction as opposed to placement on age and grade level. Ability grouping can be implemented in regular and special education classrooms. Groups are typically small, consisting of ten and fewer students.

10(C). If a child fails to perform well in the class test leads us to believe that there is a need to reflect upon the syllabus, pedagogy and assessment processes.
The failure of a child is also the failure of the syllabus pedagogy and assessment. So we need to reflect upon all these points before making any judgment about the students. To avoid failure or to tackle it when it looks likely, both parents and teachers must get involved. They can do this by involvement of parents, skill development, increase in the motivation.

11(A). Language development is even more impressive when we consider the nature of what is learned. It may seem that children merely need to remember what they hear and repeat it at some later time. But as Chomsky pointed out so many years ago, if this were the essence of language learning, we would not be successful communicators. Verbal communication requires productivity, i.e. the ability to create an infinite number of utterances we have never heard before. Therefore Freedom of expression is a must for children's language development.

12(B). According to Piaget's theory of cognitive development, our thoughts and logic are part of adaptation. Cognitive development takes place in a certain order of steps. Sensory motivational state is simulation. It is based on memory and mental representation.
Hence, the correct option is (B)

13(D). The following are good ways to identify a mentally retarded person:
- The Management document of the standardized intelligence test presents intellectual performance significantly.
- Management of behavior and adjustment testing should document deficits in at least two adaptive behavioral areas.
- Management document of emotion that mental retardation affects school performance.
Following are the symptoms of mentally retarded person:
- IQ (IQ) score of 50-69.
- cannot be easily diagnosed.
- More likely to be guilty than easily.
Therefore, it can be concluded that a combination of standardized intelligence tests, behavioral and management of adjustment tests is the best approach to identify people with low mental retardation.

14(C). A child in school is called a problem child when he behaves in such a way that becomes a problem for the teacher to understand him.
A child in school is called a problem child who:
- Demonstrate aggressiveness.
- Dominate the discussion and demands attention.
- Are inattentive and unprepared.
- Behaves in such a way that becomes a problem for a teacher.
- Make excuses.

15(B). Visual-spatial disability is a non-verbal learning disability. The children have problems with visual-spatial information. It includes:
- Difficulties with visual-spatial orientation.
- Difficulties in interpreting graphs, charts, maps.
- Difficulties in judging rotate figures because of the direction and position concepts.
- Difficulties with a sense of direction, estimation of size, shape, distance, time.
Thus, it is concluded that Visual-spatial dysfunction is a learning disability.

16(B). To deal with a mixed-ability class a teacher should use a variety of teaching-learning methods.
- Make sure that there is a variation in the content i.e., using different types of content to develop contextual understanding.
- In addition to a common supply of learning materials and learning activities that contains the basic

learning material, provide opportunities for students to obtain additional explanation and revision, or more in-depth analysis and extension. Make it clear to the students what the core of the material is and what involves extension or broadening.

- Give examples from different settings. This way, students with different interests and prior knowledge feel included. Teachers can also ask students to present their own case studies or examples from their own experience or reference framework.
- Provide sufficient variety in teaching methods and teaching strategies during your teaching-learning process.
- Teachers can create variety by asking questions, creating interaction, providing room for discussion, in addition to theory also paying attention to applications and exercises, telling a small anecdote, or giving examples.

Therefore, to make sure that the teacher is effectively dealing with heterogeneous and mixed classrooms, they should use a variety of teaching-learning methods.

17(B). Special education needs(SEN) mean specially designed instruction for children with the above-mentioned challenges in all settings such as classrooms, homes, workplaces, public places, the street, and rehabilitation homes. Special Educational Needs (SEN) refer to learners with learning, physical, and developmental disabilities; behavioural, emotional, and communication disorders; and learning deficiencies. Children's Special Educational Needs (SEN) are met through certain methodologies of special education.

18(C). Special education is the practice of educating students in a way that provides accommodations that address their individual differences, disabilities, and special needs. Ideally, this process involves the individually planned and systematically monitored arrangement of teaching procedures, adapted equipment and materials, and accessible settings. Special education refers to a range of educational and social services provided by the public school system and other educational institutions to individuals with disabilities who are between three and 21 years of age. Special education is designed to ensure that students with disabilities are provided with an environment that allows them to be educated effectively.

19(D). Repeatedly asking children to engage in learning activities either to avoid punishment or to gain a reward decreases children's natural interest and curiosity involved in learning.

Tips to Encourage Curiosity in Children:
- Be a good role model: Your child does everything he or she sees you doing. So

take advantage of this behaviour to increase their curiosity.
- Encourage your child's interest: Your child's curiosity will lead him or her naturally towards subjects and topics that are of interest to them.
- Give your child curiosity tools: Give your kids the ability to pursue their curiosity on their own. Try to build a good stock of books at your home as well as getting them membership in the local library.
- Let your child make mistakes: As parents, our tendency is to prevent our kids from feeling disappointed, hurt, discouraged, or rejected. But making mistakes and pulling themselves up again keeps your child curious and resilient.
- Fight boredom: Your child learns from you. When you label any activity or situation as "boring" they too will learn that only.
- Teach them how to observe: When you are with them encourage them to look around themselves and notice things that seem interesting, mysterious, exciting, etc. Teach them to look for the small details also and not just the big picture.
- Talk to your child about the impact of curiosity: Explain to your child how so many of the things that are staples in our lives are born out of someone's curiosity about that subject.
- Give open-ended materials to play: Along with toys that have specific ways to be played with give your child open-ended materials like sand, arts and craft supplies, empty boxes, blocks that can be used in any way they want.

20(C). The learner-centred approach of teaching puts learners in the centre and gives primacy to children's experiences and needs. It strongly believes that when children are given the freedom to work at their own pace, they develop the ability to assimilate the concepts efficiently.

21(C). Grouping based on Ability: Grouping based on ability levels alone is attempted if the primary learning goal is the enhancement of students' attainments. In the context of ability levels, the groups can be homogeneous and heterogeneous.

22(C). Erikson's theory describes the impact of social experience across the whole lifespan. He felt the course of development is determined by the interaction of the body (genetic biological programming), mind (psychological), and cultural (ethos) influences. the psychosocial theory basically asserts that people experience eight 'psychosocial crisis stages' which significantly affect each person's development and personality. Each crisis stage relates to a corresponding life stage and its inherent challenges.

Erikson used the words 'syntonic' for the first listed 'positive' disposition in each crisis (example trust) and 'dystonic' for the second listed 'negative' disposition (example, Mistrust).

23(A). As the term itself indicates, microteaching is scaled-down teaching in which the teacher teaches a short lesson to a small group of students for a short period. One teaching skill is practiced at a time. Thus microteaching is a miniature form of teaching in which teaching is scaled down in terms of class size, time, complexity, and activities with a focus on developing a specific teaching skill.

"Microteaching is a real teaching" this is an assumption in microteaching because it has nothing to do with students' learning. It totally focuses on teachers' teaching skills.

24(B). According to Aristotle Emotional catharsis is bringing out emotional repression.

Aristotle describes the catharsis as the purging of the emotions of pity and fear that are aroused in the viewer of a tragedy. The concept is linked to the positive social function of tragedy by Aristotle. Catharsis is the process of venting aggression as a way to release or get rid of emotions in general terms.

25(D). According to the theories of motivation, a teacher can enhance learning by setting realistic expectation from students. This is because a teacher's expectation have a strong effect on the performance of his/her students. The expectation of a teacher from his/her students works as a motivational force for them which in turns results of better performance.

26(C). Cultural demand is an environmental factor influencing the learning.

Learning-centred education focuses on the learning process. Although its primary concern is on the learning of the students, all those involved in the education of students such as teachers are also co-learners with the students in the learning-centred education. It is basically learner-centred but includes teachers in the process of learning in a classroom situation.

Learner-related factors affecting learning are:

Following are the factors affecting individual learning:
- Physical health
- Sensation or perception
- Needs
- Emotional conditions
- Mental health
- Willingness to learn
- Learning time
- Readiness to learn
- Student's basic ability
- Intelligence level

- Interest
- Motivation level

27(D). Demonstration method- it is the autocratic strategy of teaching. Teacher shows all the activities given in a lesson to the students as an action and explains the important points before them during demonstration. It is a teaching method used in technical and training colleges and in teacher education. This strategy focuses to achieve psychomotor and cognitive objectives.

Heuristic method- it is a democratic strategy of teaching. Students learn themselves as teachers raise problem before the students and ask them to discover the answer.

Discovery method- this method is used in social science to clarify the facts and concepts. This is democratic style of teaching.

Brain storming- a problem is given to the students and they are asked to put forward their views one by one, conclusion is drawn after evaluating their jumbled ideas.

28(D). An error is an incorrect form and a sure indication that the learner has not mastered the core of the selective topic in a learning process. The qualitative difference in children's thinking as compared to adults is reflected in the type of errors made by the children.

Errors can occur in adults as well as children. The qualitative effect of errors can be observed through the type of error. Adults tend to make silly mistakes that may not be serious as they tend to overlook minor details and focus on bigger things. Whereas children may make a significantly big error as they may not have the experience of the concept.

Thus, it is concluded that errors made by children are indicative of children's thinking process which is qualitatively different from that of adults.

29(C). The cephalocaudal principle states that development proceeds from head to toe. According to this principle, a child will gain physical control of their head first. After this, physical control will move downward to the arms and lastly to the legs.
- The Head region starts growth at first and followed by other organs.
- The child gains control of the head first, then the arms and the legs.
- Infancy develops control of the head and face movements at the first two months. In the next few months, they are able to lift themselves up by using their arms and then gain control over the toe and able to crawl, walk, jump, climb, day by day.
- The cephalocaudal principle applies to both physical and functional development.
- Development is seen in the earliest years

of post-natal development specifically ranging from infancy into toddlerhood.

A child develops in an orderly sequence which is almost similar in all children. The rate and speed of development may vary in individual cases but the sequence of development patterns is almost the same in all children.

30(C). **Swiss psychologist Jean Piaget** was the most well known and influential theorist for cognitive development. Piaget was interested in how children reacted to their **environments**.
- He envisioned a child's knowledge as composed of schemas, the basic unit of knowledge used to organize past experiences and serve as a basis for understanding new ones.
- Development is influence the most when a child's experiences interact with his physical environment.
- These processes are influenced by the child's experience and activity, social interactions, and biological process of becoming mature (maturation).
- They perform all activities and think within the framework of their socio-cultural environment. Therefore, their developmental processes can be only understood by studying children's (or people's) interactions with their culture.
- Interaction of physical factors such as temperature, humidity, pollution, and natural disasters on human behavior. The influence of the physical arrangement of the workplace on health, the emotional state, and interpersonal relations are also investigated.

Thus from the above-mentioned points, it is clear that according to Piaget, experience with the physical world plays an important role in influencing development.

31(C). The very first paragraph of the passage mentions that in the UK, roughly a third of the food grown in the field never actually makes into anybody's mouth. This means that food is wasted in the farms itself. Later the passage mentions that not only the consumers but also the providers have a hand in wasting a lot of food. So there are other factors besides wastage of leftover food that contribute to 'wastage of food'.

32(A). According to the fourth paragraph of the passage, 'Fresh produce, bakery, meats and dairy top the most wasted list'.

33(D). The term shelf life refers to 'the length of time that a commodity may be stored without becoming unfit for use, consumption, or sale.' This is independent of the fact whether preservatives are added or not.

Hence, the correct option is (D)

34(B). According to the fifth paragraph of the passage, 'the relatively low cost of food

almost forces a consumer society to buy more food than it can eat.' This is the effect of the prevailing market dynamics.

The other options are irrelevant with reference to the passage.

35(D). According to the passage the ridiculous levels of waste need to reduced. 'Ridiculous' means 'laughable' or 'funny' but in the given context it means that the exceptionally high rate of food wastage must be reduced.

36(B). The passage discusses how both providers and consumers have a part to play in food wastage and only their combined effort can solve the problem. The consumers can be encouraged not to waste food as it would help them save more money and in this way, they can also do less harm to the environment. However, the incentive is not as strong for the food providers as selling less food will yield less profit. Thus major roadblock for the providers is that selling less (in order to reduce food wastage) is inversely proportional to the profit they make.

37(C). The passage mentions the statement: 'There are a few options, but some of them are not easy to swallow'.

The phrase 'not easy/ hard to swallow' means that a particular thing is hard to believe or accept.

38(D). 'Opening a can of worms' is an idiom which means 'to examine or attempt to solve some problem, only to complicate it and create even more trouble'.

39(D). The passage mentions both options (A) and (B) as possible solutions to reduce food wastage from the end of 'providers'.

Thus both the options are correct.

Note that the passage also suggests that the "use-by" and "best-before" dates must be abolished to reduce food wastage, but it nowhere says that edible items should be continued to be consumed even after the mentioned expiry dates have passed.

40(A). To find out the tone of the poem, we should focus on the words and devices used by the poet.
- From reading the poem we can clearly see that the tone of this poem is full of loving, peaceful and optimistic.
- In the second line "loveliness increases", These words just create a gentle yet vivid image in the reader's mind.
- "a bower quiet for us", "sweet dreams" these words describe pleasant mood of the poet.
- "Some shape of beauty moves away the pall, From our dark spirits" define that Some beautiful shapes or a thing of beauty removes the pall of sadness from our hearts or spirits.
- "An endless fountain of immortal drink" these lines tells us about that beautiful

bounty of the earth, has bestowed us with sun, moon, flowers, rivers, greenery.

"inhuman dearth", "gloomy days", "unhealthy and o'er-darkened ways" in these lines the poet says that beauty fills us with the feeling of being alive. Without beauty the earth would be full of cruel people and sad moments and It is beauty that brings happiness to our hearts'.

Thus, we can clearly see that the tone of the poem is full of love, peaceful and optimistic.

41(C). Alteration figure of speech has been used in these word in the above line: simple sheep such.

Alliteration: a literary device that reflects repetition in two or more nearby words of initial consonant sounds. Alliteration does not refer to the repetition of consonant letters that begin words, but rather the repetition of the consonant sound at the beginning of words.

42(B). Beautiful things are a source of endless joy. It is the eternal beauty that never goes away.

A beautiful thing is like a shady shelter that gives us sweet dreams, good health and good sleep.

If there are no beautiful things in life, then we will go on getting attached to materialistic things and will get away from eternal happiness. Because this earth is full of hatred, greed and negativity. And because of this negativity we will be surrounded by sadness all around and get carried away with positive thoughts of beautiful things. That's why it is necessary that we should preserve and take care of beautiful things.

43(D). The poet describes that beauty is everywhere and it lies in the eye of the beholder.

In the first stanza 'The poet says that beauty lasts forever. It never ends but keeps on increasing with time'.

In the second stanza 'The poet says that beauty fills us with the feeling of being alive. Without beauty the earth would be full of cruel people and sad moments and It is beauty that brings happiness to our hearts'.

In the third stanza 'According to the poet, worldly things and material things keep us away from eternal happiness.

In the fourth stanza 'These are those beautiful things that are immortal and give us a reason to live on earth despite having so much suffering in our lives'.

Thus from all the points given above, we can conclude that the poem is about 'Beauty never diminishes or fades'.

44(B). Metaphor figure of speech has been used in the above lines: wreathing, A flowery band. The poet has used the phrase wreathing a flowery band to show how beautiful things bind humans to Earth.

Metaphor: An expression, often found in literature, that describes a person or object by referring to something that is considered to have similar characteristics to that person or object.

45(C). "Flowery" is an adjective.

Adjectives are words that describe the qualities or states of being of nouns. Here, band is a noun and flowery describes what kind of band the poet is talking about. A noun is always qualified by an adjective.

46(B). Language acquisition is the process by which humans acquire the capacity to perceive and comprehend language as well as to produce and use words and sentences to communicate.

- The acquisition is the process by which humans acquire the capacity to perceive and comprehend knowledge as well as to produce and use words and sentences to communicate.
- The major difference between language acquisition and learning is that language acquisition is natural and language learning is deliberate/instructed.
- As regards language acquisition, the procedure is selecting appropriate vocabulary, grammatical rules and pragmatic conventions governing language use.

Hence, from the above-mentioned points, it becomes clear that Language Acquisition stands for learning a language without making any deliberate or conscious effort.

47(B). Principles of Grammar-Translation method: This method has its own basic principles that would justify the measures it advocates for the teaching of English. Apparently, the rules of the conduct of the method have their justification in their own way:

- It is easier to teach the foreign language through the medium of the mother tongue than through the foreign language itself as the former would smoothen all the complexities at a single stroke.
- Teaching through translation is a quick and economical process. A teaching procedure should economies on time, energy, and labor and should aim at quick results.
- Translation allows comparison and contrast between the language patterns of the mother tongue and those of English.
- Such a comparative study quickens the pace of learning and makes it firm in the minds of the learners.
- The liberal use of the mother tongue conforms with the well-known maxim of learning that going from the known to the unknown elements of knowledge.

Hence, we can conclude that the Grammar-Translation method is an economical method.

48(B). While evaluating writing skills it is most important to evaluate whether the learner is able to express their ideas systematically and coherently because:

- if the ideas are systematically expressed then we can conclude that the thoughts are clear in the mind of the learner.
- it ensures that they are able to express their experiences and thoughts beautifully and can convey the information in the best way.
- it encourages learners to exercise their creative minds by using their imaginations. It improves their ability to come up with alternatives.

Thus, it is concluded that the most important criteria of evaluating writing skills is that the learner is able to express ideas coherently and systematically.

49(B). In this question, the teacher is teaching Adjectives and then asks to give them at least one feature and definition. This method is called Deductive method of teaching.

Deductive method:-

- In this method, teachers start teaching by giving rules, then examples, then practice.
- It is a teacher-centered approach.
- This method is used mostly to teach grammar structures.
- For example- The teacher has taught the concept of adjectives and asked them to describe one feature.

Thus, it is concluded that The teacher informs the children about the 'adjective' and asks them to give at least one feature and definition of the adjective. This method is called deductive method.

50(D). Language skills are necessary for effective communication in any environment and to interact with others. It allows an individual to comprehend and produce language for proper and effective interpersonal communication. These foundational skills of language are divided into two categories which are receptive and productive skills.

Receptive skills:

- The receptive skills of language are listening and reading because these skills don't require the production of language.
- These skills focus on an individual's ability of understanding and comprehending language.

51(D). A textbook is a tool to be used in the teaching process to facilitate effective learning. Language textbooks primarily provide comprehensible inputs to develop a good understanding of the concept for better academic outcomes. A good language textbook should include:

- child-centered material,
- teacher-friendly instruction,
- content-related materials which have

more syntactical items in its content,
* attractive fonts, illustrations, and learner-friendly texts.

52(B). Inductive method is a method which makes grammar learning an effective and productive process by:
* presenting grammar form in a natural discourse, then explaining how the form is made and used.
* promoting divergent and critical thinking and leading learners from known to unknown or example to formula.
* giving illustration in sentences or paragraph to help students to learn grammatical rules in context and integrated manner.

Hence, we conclude that presenting grammar form in a natural discourse, then explaining how the form is made and used is an effective way of teaching-learning grammar.

53(D). Problems Students often Encounter with Reading
* **Lack of concentration** is another mentionable reason for students' poor reading because concentration is an important factor for good and effective reading. Comprehension of a text results from reading with concentration. But students, in most cases, cannot or do not concentrate properly while reading, or they cannot hold their attention for a long time due to their lack of practice and patience.
* **The long and complex structure of sentences** often causes a reading barrier for most of the students. They cannot understand the proper subject-verb relationship in a long or complex sentence, which creates constant difficulties. Eventually, these difficulties result in poor and insufficient reading.
* **Lack of graded materials** is another important reason for the failure of reading. This inadequacy of proper texts or textual materials affects students' reading much. Sometimes students are not supplied with their texts according to their linguistic level.
* **Deficiency in associating phoneme and grapheme** is another reason for students' poor reading. Sometimes poor reading results from students' "inability to relate symbols, to associate the proper phoneme with the proper shape, or to match a visual sequence with an auditory sequence. The pupil has great difficulty acquiring phonic skills." And obviously, this lack of phonic skills results in their inability to associate experiences and meanings with symbols.

Hence, we can conclude that all of the above are the causes of poor reading skills.

54(A). **Remedial Teaching** is an integral part of the teaching-learning program, also known as compensatory or corrective teaching.
* The objective of remedial teaching is to give additional help to learners who have fallen behind the rest of the class in any topic or subject.
* It is one to one approach, in which teacher gives remedial measures as per the learning difficulties faced by a particular child.
* It is the process of identifying slow learners and providing them with the necessary help and guidance to overcome their problems.

Hence, we can conclude that remedial teaching in language learning is one to one approach.

55(B). **Language** is a medium through which one can express one's ideas, thoughts, and feelings. The script is not a part of the language component.
* **The script** is related to the return part of language every language can be written in many steps as well as the Hindi language written in Devnagri script.
* Structure, Vocabulary, and Sound are important parts of the language.

Structure of language contains five major points are:-
1. Phonemes
2. Morphemes
3. Lexemes
4. Syntax
5. Context

Hence, from the above-mentioned points, it becomes clear that the Script is not a language component.

56(B). Language tests are tests that play a significant role in the teaching-learning process of language. Language tests measure the learning, skills learnt by learners and also help in finding mistakes and weak areas of the ner in any subject.

Language Tests are designed to:
* Diagnose learners' strength and weakness in language learning
* Measure learner's knowledge of the language
* Test the level of learner's language skills to make them proficient in communication
* Evaluate how well an individual uses a particular language to communicate in daily life

There are many types of language tests which include proficiency test, achievement test, diagnostic test, placement test, etc.

Hence, it becomes clear that language tests are designed to measure the learner's knowledge of the language at a particular moment in the teaching programme.

57(C). The above-mentioned function of the human brain is called **Language Acquisition Device** as according to Chomsky, Language acquisition device is a **hypothetical tool** in a child's brain that makes learners able to:
* acquire and produce language.
* learn and assimilate language easily.
* analyze language and extract basic rules.
* encode the grammatical structure of language.

Hence, it could be included that the above-mentioned function of the human brain is called Language Acquisition Device.

58(B). Before speaking we plan in our minds, as to what we should speak about such that the listener understands what we are saying.

We also make up our minds about 'what' and 'how' to speak depending upon who we are speaking to.

When a teacher wants to test the speaking skills of students, he needs to check how they speak which includes their way of pronouncing words and how correctly they are able to words in a well-structured form. And it can be best done by asking them to narrate incidents or events. As when the students will narrate incidents they will use language in the natural form i.e., how they use a language to communicate with others. The teacher can spot the error and later correct them by giving remediation.

Thus, it is clear that to test the speaking ability of the students, a teacher should ask them to narrate incidents or events.

59(B). **Dysgraphia** refers to a learning disability which:
* affects learners' ability to write coherently.
* hinders in organizing letters, numbers, or words on papers.
* leads to problems with poor spelling, impaired handwriting, etc.

R emedies useful for treating students with **Dysgraphia** :
* giving extra time for writing assessment, will reduce the copying activity and will emphasize the importance of writing original answers.
* dividing tasks into small steps will enable the learners to assimilate the idea easily and will help them in putting their thoughts on paper.
* providing low-stress opportunities will allow the learners to learn and write at their own pace and to foster their own strategy of learning and writing.

Hence, we can conclude that deficiency in the ability to write associated with impaired handwriting is a symptom of dysgraphia .

60(C). A good teaching-learning material is very necessary for effective teaching and facilitates the teaching-learning process in a proper way.
* Advantages of TLM are as follows:
* Facilitates learning and teaching
* Helps students to grasp concepts easily

- Makes classroom activities interesting

When these points are integrated, it can be rightly said as the teaching-learning process as it includes all above pints.

Accurate and realistic teaching-learning materials encourage healthy classroom interaction and are helpful in meeting individual differences.

61(A). Rig Veda depicts the information about the most ancient Vedic age culture.

The Rig-Veda is the oldest of the four collections of hymns and other sacred texts known as the Vedas. It contains most of the information about the religious and social life of the early Vedic period. These works are considered the "sacred knowledge" of the Aryans. The Rig-Veda also contains ideas that served as the basis for India's system of castes(Varna).

62(A). The dynasty of Delhi Sultanate ruled for the shortest time is Khalji dynasty. The Khalji dynasty was of Turko-Afghan heritage. The Khaljis ruled only for 30 years from 1290-1320. They had long been settled in present-day Afghanistan before proceeding to Delhi in India. The first ruler of the Khalji dynasty was Jalal ud-Din Firuz Khalji(1290-96). The last Khalji ruler was Ala ud-Din Khalji's 18-year-old son Qutb ud-Din Mubarak Shah Khalji, who ruled for four years before he was killed by Khusro Khan.

63(C). The Strait of Gibraltar connects the Mediterranean Sea to the Atlantic Ocean.

The Strait of Gibraltar is a narrow waterway connects the Atlantic Ocean from the Mediterranean Sea. This 13-kilometer-wide waterway also separates Europe and Africa, with Spain and Gibraltar on the left and Morocco on the right.

The Mediterranean Sea is connected to the Atlantic Ocean by the Strait of Gibraltar in the west and to the Sea of Marmara and the Black Sea, by the Dardanelles and the Bosporus respectively, in the east.

64(D). The innermost layer of the Earth is mainly made up of Nickel and Iron.

The Earth is divided into four main layers: the solid crust on the outside, the mantle, the outer core, and the inner core. The outer core is in a liquid state while the inner core is in the solid-state.

The core is the innermost layer of the earth with density 5.1 to 13.00. It composed of heaviest minerals. This central mass is mainly made of nickel and iron and therefore is known as NIFE. The materials of this part may be liquid, plastic or even solid state due to tremendous pressure from above.

65(B). Asteroids are found between the orbits of Mars and Jupiter.

Apart from the stars, planets, and satellites, numerous tiny bodies also move around the sun. These bodies are called asteroids. They are found between the orbits of Mars and Jupiter. Scientists are of the view that asteroids are parts of a planet that exploded many years back. Asteroid Belt is a circumstellar disc in the Solar System.

66(B). The Battle of Chausa was fought in 1539.

The Battle of Chausa was fought between Humayun and Sher Shah Suri. The Battle of Chausa was a notable military engagement between the Mughal emperor, Humayun, and the Afghan, Sher Shah Suri. It was fought on 26 June 1539 at Chausa. Sher Shah defeated Humayun at Chausa (1539) and Kanauj (1540), forcing him to flee to Iran.

67(C). Amritsar was not related with Revolt of 1 8 5 7 .

- Indian Mutiny, also called Sepoy Mutiny or First War of Independence, widespread but unsuccessful rebellion against British rule in India in 1 8 5 7 − 5 9 .
- Begun in Meerut by Indian troops in the service of the British East India Company, it spread to Delhi, Agra, Kanpur, and Lucknow. In India, it is often called the First War of Independence.

68(C). The rebellion in Bihar was led by Babu Kunwar Singh.

- He was nearly 8 0 when he took charge of the sepoys who were placed at Danapur on 2 5 July 1 8 5 7 .
- Singh and his troops laid an attack on the district headquarters at Arrah.
- He held the fort for 7 days when British officer Major Vincent Eyre took Arrah back.
- Eyre's troops also raided Jagdispur.

69(B). Aravalli is the oldest mountain range of India.

Aravali Range:

- Aravalis is one of the world's oldest fold mountains running in the north-east to southeast direction from Delhi to Palampur in Gujarat.
- It expands in 3 states (Rajasthan, Haryana, Gujarat) and 1 union territory (New-Delhi).
- It is an example of a fold mountain.
- Guru Shikhar is the highest peak of Aravali.

70(B). The Chenab River is the largest tributary of the river Indus. It has a total length of about 605 miles (974 km), and it also feeds irrigation canals. The Chenab empties into the River Sutlej.

The major left bank tributaries of the Indus river are Jhelum, Chenab, Beas, Sutlej, and Zanskar.

71(B). Jawaharlal Nehru created the phrase 'unity in diversity'.

- This word perfectly describes India, which, despite its diversity of languages, faiths, castes, and creeds, has a strong sense of unity among its citizens.
- Jawaharlal Nehru used the phrase in his book 'Discovery of India.

72(B). A system of government in which power is divided between a central authority and various constituent units is called a Federal state.

- A federation has two levels of government. Both these levels of governments enjoy their power independent of the other.
- Federal state is a political entity characterized by a union of partially self-governing provinces, states, or other regions under a central federal government (federalism).

73(C). Article 22 provides protection to persons who have been arrested or detained. Article 22 has two parts—the first part deals with matters of common law and the second part deals with matters of preventive detention law. Right to information at the time of arrest of the offense for which the person is being arrested.

A person can be arrested by the state under 'preventive detention' only on the following four grounds-

(i) Security of the State.

(ii) Maintenance of public order.

(iii) Supply and maintenance of essential services and defence.

(iv) Foreign affairs or security of India.

74(C). When a community is forced to live on the fringes of social and economic development, this is known as marginalisation .

- A social process of being confined to lower social standing is known as marginalisation .
- It involves people being denied their fundamental rights that results in lowering their social and economical status.
- It is a situation when a particular social group or community is forced to live on the fringes rather than in the mainstream.
- A marginalised section of the society does not get proper opportunity of socio-economic development.
- Economic, social, cultural and political factors work together to make certain groups in society feel marginalised.

75(A). The statement "Regional and fragmented approach to healthcare delivery" is not true with respect to Ayushman Bharat scheme.

- Ayushman Bharat Programme is an umbrella health scheme of the Government of India.
- It was launched in 2018 by Prime Minister Narendra Modi.
- It is to address health issues at all levels – primary, secondary, and tertiary.

It has two components:

- Pradhan Mantri Jan Arogya Yojana (PM-JAY), earlier known as the National Health Protection Scheme (NHPS).
- Health and Wellness Centres (HWCs).

76(B). The Human trafficking and forced labour are prohibited under Right against Exploitation.
The Right against exploitation enshrined in Article 23 and 24 of the Indian Constitution guarantees human dignity and protect people from any such exploitation. Thus, upholding the principles of human dignity and liberty upon which the Indian Constitution is based.

77(C). Question Hour is an important method of controlling the executive in Parliament.
- The question hour is an important mechanism through which MPs can elicit information about the working of the government.
- This is a very important way through which Parliament controls the executive.
- By asking questions the government is alerted to its shortcomings, and also comes to know the opinion of the people through their representatives in the Parliament, i.e. the MPs.
- Asking questions of the government is a crucial task for every MP.
- The Opposition parties play a critical role in the healthy functioning of a democracy.
- They highlight drawbacks in various policies and programs of the government and mobilize popular support for their own policies.

78(A). Social sciences are the sciences that study human beings in relation to their social system and institutions. Social sciences include the disciplines like history, geography, political science, economics, sociology, psychology, anthropology, culture studies, public administration, etc.
- Social sciences differ from physical sciences with respect to their focus, contents, methods of study and analysis, etc.
- While physical sciences are concerned with studying physical matters/ materials like mass, volume, area, length, light, distance, pressure, density, chemicals, life, tissues, etc.
- Social Sciences are concerned with studying social issues like community living, state, administration, government, culture, tradition, ritual, social wellbeing, and welfare, economic system, religious systems, etc.
- Thus, social sciences possess distinct nature, which is different from the nature of physical sciences and many other sciences.

So, it can be concluded that, Both (A) and (R) are true and (R) is the correct explanation of (A).

79(D). Equally important are the expectations of social studies from teaching-learning and the 'content' it conveys.
- The teacher of social studies has different roles to play, e.g., developing personality values, and attitudes and civic responsibility to live together in a democracy.
- So, the teacher should be equipped with cognitive, affective, technical, professional and human competencies.

Thus from the above-mentioned points, it is clear that both A and B are true.

80(A). Being knowledgeable, having a prescriptive mind and inquisitiveness is an essential quality of a teacher of social studies.
- These qualities emphasize the teacher, his training and in-service training as an essential component of an effective teacher of social studies.
- The teacher should be knowledgeable, have a prescriptive mind and should continue to develop their competencies through cognitive skills. Also, he must possess impressive skills and functional skills to deal with the subject matter with a proper approach methodology and techniques that include, depicting, describing the various processes of inquiry through leadership of operations, decision making, etc. To do, to depict, to interpret, to collect, to demonstrate, to discuss, to evaluate, to analyze.

81(C). Models represent real things in all respects except size and shape. Larger objects are scaled down to smaller sizes so that they can be viewed with greater accuracy by the students.
- Model is a recognizable imitation of the real thing (eyes) or abstract thing (magnetic). Usually, a model is similar to the original object in every aspect except the size. The size of an object may be reduced or enlarged.
- When the size is reduced, the object is simplified to show only the essential parts. For example, the globe is a model of earth simplified to show the earth's essential parts only.
- On the other hand, when size is enlarged, it shows the details of the object. For example, the model of the eye is enlarged to allow all the details to be seen easily and clearly.

82(B). Methods is related to the activity of the class.
The teaching method refers to the general principles, pedagogy, and management strategies used for classroom instruction. Your choice of teaching method depends on what fits you- your educational philosophy, classroom demographic, subject area(s),

and school mission statement. It can be organized into four categories based on two major parameters: a teacher-centred approach versus a student-centred approach, and high-tech material use versus low-tech material use.

83(C). Prejudice, discrimination and prejudices can be avoided in the classroom by discussing various dimensions.
- Biases: It refers to a tendency of differentiating learners on the basis of their ability and skills.
- Prejudice: It refers to an unreasonable opinion or negative attitude for a specific group of learners.
- Discrimination: It refers to the process of treating learners unfairly on the basis of their characteristics.

84(B). Social studies helps learners to think globally and act locally.
- The term, originally used to mean "think globally and act locally", was coined by Scottish sociologist and Scottish town planner and social worker Patrick Geddes. It emphasizes on the health concerns of the entire nation and encourages the society to work for grassroots improvement.
- Social studies help learners to think globally and act locally because the aim of social studies is to develop a view of the sociological development of the world so as to encourage them to act well for their local environment.
- This means thinking open-mindedly about learning issues, cultures and events around the world and using this knowledge to improve your local area, hometown or country.

85(B). A social science teacher may relate literature in a language to social science in the classroom teaching-learning process such as literature-based tasks such as writing poetry on social science-based content.
- When the concept or issue of a subject is learned in relation to other subjects, the concept or issue is learned in a meaningful way. The social science curriculum at the school level is not a separate entity. It has meaningful connections with other disciplines.
- Social science deals with human beings and their social activities. Language deals with the communication and expression of men/women through symbols and sound; And literature is the expression of the imagination of the feelings of men/women through language.

86(A). Analyze the paragraph with students and discuss the assumptions made in the reference book, the most responsible approach for the history teacher.
While teaching history, a History teacher comes across a particular paragraph that

paints a famous historical figure in a bad light.

The responsible approach for the history teacher is to analyze the paragraph and discuss the issue with the students so they came to know about it.

As a history teacher, you need to formulate and implement creative and innovative strategies that are practical and meet the needs of students.

History teacher needs to have:
- Thorough Knowledge of the Subject.
- Knowledge of child Psychology
- Faith in Subject.
- Knowledge of Different Methods of Teaching
- Knowledge of Regional and Provincial History.

87(B). Visiting the community to collect data, the activity uses an inquiry/ investigation-based approach.

Here, going to the community to collect data uses an approach of inquiry-based learning, because:
- Students engage with their own experiences by asking questions and making decisions in search of new understanding.
- Students become active by engaging in practical investigations.
- Students gain information by visiting the community and asking questions to collect data.

88(B). Social studies emphasize the functional part of knowledge.
- The field of social studies differs from other areas of learning in the fact that its content, as well as objectives, emphasize the functional part of knowledge i.e. human and their various relationships rather than the theoretical part and the advanced study of human affairs and human relationship. but its content does not include humans and their relationships.
- In the social sciences, its fields of study have a social purpose and utility. They are an important part of the curriculum as they meet the needs of human beings.
- While understanding from social studies, the emphasis is on relationships rather than individuals, on social activities rather than individual performance, it is emphasized that society makes up individuals and that it is not made up of individuals alone.

89(D). None of the above is correct.
The objective of discussing 'gender' in a social science classroom is to
- Reduce gender disparity i.e., male superiority over women. For example- books at the school level address the role of men and women in society. The pattern of roles addressed in school text is due to the socialization process. The role reversal needs to be included in the

school curriculum and should be given to the learners.
- Challenge some stereotypical notions. Example- The existing notion is that women are soft and caring. So, they handle small children better than male primary education teachers. This notion needs to be reversed. There is no gender component with regard to caring for children.
- Start socially relevant courses, employability courses in a comprehensive manner for all genders to improve the number of students getting higher education especially women.
- Civil society should also join hands with the government to advance women in higher education.

90(D). The teacher of social studies is expected to take into account all the given facts.

The teacher of social studies is expected to keep in mind the following facts:
- Stating the objectives of the course for each student.
- Clear vision in the relation of specific facts and things of social studies.
- Selecting the content that will be appropriate to the level of the students.
- Concept of general facts and qualities of social studies.
- Establishment of facts, rules, definitions, knowledge and methods used in social studies.
- The teacher should have an appeal to the student's interests, needs, thinking and imagination and pose pleasant challenges to them.
- To select the learning activities or experiences that are most likely to be effective in developing and attaining the goals.

91(B). The field trip method is best suited for teaching history and geography at the primary level.
The teaching method is a way to put theory into practice . It generally describes the pedagogy of children, general principles, and management strategies that are to be used through the whole teaching-learning process.
- History and Geography are narrative accounts of the past, present, and future. It is the story of changing human cultures, beliefs, and lifestyles and helps to build up a sense of what could happen in the future.
- The main purpose of teaching history at the primary level is to make children aware o f historical events and to provide knowledge of how our present evolved from the past.
- There are different kinds of teaching-learning methods that make learning a fruitful process and ' Storytelling ' is one of them.

92(D). Tarachand Committee provided recommendations for Secondary education.
- Tara Chand Committee, 1948, suggested the multipurpose type of secondary schools without discouraging the uni-purpose schools.
- The Tara Chand Committee made the following two important recommendations:
- Secondary schools should be made multilateral,
- Appointment of a commission to examine the entire secondary education structure.
- The Committee, in view of the local conditions and time also recommended that indifference should not be shown towards unilateral schools.

93(C). The Government of India set up the Secondary Education Commission in 1952, under the Chairmanship of Dr. A. Lakshmanaswami Mudaliar. Therefore, this commission is also known as Mudaliar Commission (1952-53).
The major recommendations of the Commission were:
- Installation of higher secondary system;
- Diversified courses;
- Three language formula;
- Emphasis on education and vocational guidance;
- Improvement in methods of teaching, textbooks, and system of examination; and
- Improvement in building and equipment.
- The Commission introduced the policy of developing a three-year national system of secondary education (after eight years of elementary education)

94(B). Option I, II, III, IV and V are correct.
Types of Charts:
- Narration: This chart narrates the story through pictures and figures. These charts portray historical developments or depict steps in a procedure, such as how a bill becomes law.
- Tabulation charts present data in the form of a table in order to facilitate making comparisons.
- Relationship charts show cause-and-effect relationships such as factors related to pollution of the environment, resources and population, etc.
- Pedigree charts show development that has a single origin such as the lineage of a family.
- Classification charts point out various kinds of relations such as those for agriculture, industries, modes of transportation, etc.
- Organization charts show the internal structure of organizations such as a corporation or governmental bodies.
- Flow charts show stemming a process such as the manufacture of steel. Information charts are developed by the

teacher and students throughout a unit of study as a means of developing standards or summaries of materials related to the ongoing study.

95(B). Map preservation is not included in the map study.
- Some maps focus on specific information such as showing the distribution of temperature, rainfall, forests, minerals, industries, population, transportation, etc.
- These are known as thematic maps.
- Maps provide more information than a globe.
- Maps are a useful pedagogical tool.
- They help students learn concepts, synthesise and integrate ideas, and draw reasonable inferences and observations.

96(A). **Summative evaluation:-** To understand the ability, interest, and capabilities of learners, the teacher uses summative evaluation.
- Is the assessment of learning performance that is conducted at the end of a course or a unit of a course. Generally is taken by students at the end of a course or academic year to demonstrate the "sum" of what they have learned.
- Utilizes the most traditional assessment methods of evaluating students' work.
- The results are used for ranking or grading the students which are required in planning any large-scale academic intervention, inter and intra school comparison in terms of achievement.
- Grades are the basis for determining the readiness of the student to take statewide tests and in evaluating his overall academic performance.

97(B). The type of evaluation which gives feed-back to students as well as teachers is Formative evaluation.
The formative evaluation provides the teacher feedback regarding the efficiency of the teaching methods so that the teaching can be improved.
The main purpose of formative evaluation is improvement in learning.
Formative evaluation is done continuously throughout the course period.
It can be done by means of unit tests which can be given after teaching each unit, informal class tests, assignments, and other classroom activities.
Unlike summative evaluation which is formal in nature, formative evaluation is informal and can be undertaken by using multiple techniques like observation, oral tests, written tests, etc.

98(B). Democracy is a form of government in which the people have the right to choose their governing legislators.
- In the fifty years of democracy and dictatorship between 1950 and 2000, the rate of economic growth has been slightly higher in dictatorships.
- Economic growth depends on several factors: the size of a country's population and the global situation.
- On the whole we cannot say that democracy is a guarantee of economic development. Hence statement 1 is not correct.
- Non-democratic regimes often turn a blind eye to or suppress internal social differences.
- Democracy usually develops procedures to accommodate various social divisions thereby increasing the chances of building a harmonious social life. So, statement 2 is correct.

99(A). Koldihwa and Mehrgarh: It is situated to the south of Allahabad (Prayagraj). The site provides evidence of handmade raw pottery as well as circular huts. Hence pair 1 is correctly matched. There is also evidence of rice, which is the oldest evidence of rice not only in India but anywhere in the world.
- Mehrgarh: It is located in Balochistan, Pakistan. The earliest Neolithic sites, where people lived in houses made of mud bricks and cultivated crops such as cotton and wheat. Hence pair 2 is correctly matched.
- Gufkral: It is located in Kashmir. This Neolithic site is famous for the graves, stone tools and graveyards.

100(B). Individual Satyagraha: This was a direct result of the August Resolution. Hence statement 1 is not correct.
- The August resolution was brought by the British in 1940 during the critical period of the war. Both the Congress and the Muslim League rejected the August offer.
- The Congress wanted to start a civil disobedience movement, but Gandhi, seeing an atmosphere against such a movement, did not want to hinder the war effort. However, the Congress Socialist leaders and the All India Kisan Sabha were in favor of an immediate struggle.
- Gandhi was convinced that the British would not change their policy towards India. He decided to start Individual Satyagraha.
- Vinobha Bhave was the first and Nehru was the second to offer Satyagraha, by May 1941, 25,000 people were convicted for the Satyagraha. Hence statement 2 is correct.
- Though the objective of the Satyagraha was limited, it was successful in showing unity and patience among the people of India. So, statement 3 is correct.

101(D). British India Association: It was formed in 1851 as a result of the merger of the Landholders Society and the Bengal British India Society, with Raja Radhakanta Deva and Debendranath Tagore as its President and Secretary respectively. The organization also included many other members like Ram Gopal Ghosh, Piri Chand Mitra and Krishnadas Pal. Its membership was opened to Indians only.
- Bengal British India Society: It was founded in 1843 by the joint efforts of George Thompson, Dwarkanath Tagore, Chandra Mohan Chatterjee and Parmanand Maitra.
- It was founded on the advice of George Thompson. He was brought to India from England by Dwarkanath Tagore. George Thomas was the secretary of the British Indian Society. It mainly represented the elite class. The main goal of the organization was to collect and disseminate information about the health and welfare of the people.
- Servants of People Society: Lala Lajpat Rai established the Servants of People Society to work for the welfare of the people. He also opened several orphanages and hospitals in this regard.
- Therefore, 1, 2 and 3 are correct.

102(D).

Major energy Pipelines	Countries involved
1. Keystone Pipeline	USA-Canada
2. Power of Siberia	Russia-China
3. Nordstream-I	Germany-Russia

- Keystone is an Oil pipeline between the US and Canada which delivers crude oil to the midwestern region of the USA. It is operational since 2010. Hence pair 1 is incorrectly matched.
- It has been in news lately because of the public uproar over the Keystone XL pipeline. the pipeline has been opposed by environmental activists and its permit has been revoked by President Biden in 2021.
- The Power of Siberia project is a gas transmission system invaolving the development of a 4,000km-long gas pipeline to transfer natural gas from Yakutia and Irkutsk gas production centers in Eastern Russia to the Far East and China. Hence pair 2 is correctly matched
- The project is being developed by Russia's state-owned Gazprom, the world's biggest natural gas producer.
- Nordstream 1 is an underwater Natural gas pipeline running from Vyborg near St Petersburg in Russia to Lubmin in northeastern Germany. It started the flow of gas from Siberia to Europe through the 1,200 kilometres pipe in 2011. So, pair 3 is incorrectly matched.

103(B). The 'Mission Antyodaya' project was launched by the Government of India in 2017-18.
- The Ministry of Panchayati Raj and the

Ministry of Rural Development act as nodal agents to take the mission forward. Hence, statement 1 is not correct.
- The main objective of 'Mission Antyodaya' is to ensure optimum utilization of resources through convergence of various schemes that address multiple deprivations of poverty, making Gram Panchayat the center of development planning. Hence, statement 2 is correct.
- This planning process is supported by an annual survey that helps assess various development gaps at the village panchayat level, by collecting data on 29 subjects assigned to panchayats by the Eleventh Schedule of the Constitution.

104(C). India has the fifth largest coal reserves in the world. Hence, statement 1 is correct.
- A commercial coal-mining industry has been running since 1774, started by the East India Company on the banks of the Damodar River in West Bengal.
- 70% of India's coal supply comes from the states of Jharkhand, Chhattisgarh, Odisha, West Bengal and Madhya Pradesh. Hence, statement 2 is not correct.
- State-owned Coal India Limited has a virtual monopoly on coal mines in India, which produce about 75% of the coal in India's coal-fired power stations.
- Coal is expected to account for at least 21 per cent of India's electricity requirement by 2050 as well.
- Coal can help the country to meet its energy needs without having to depend on imports as it is available in abundance domestically. So, statement 3 is correct.

105(C). India currently ranks fifth in terms of installed solar power capacity, behind China, the US, Japan and Germany.
- As of December 2021, India's cumulative solar installed capacity is 55GW, which is almost half of the renewable energy (RE) capacity (excluding large hydro) and 14% of India's total electricity generation capacity.
- Within 55GW, grid-connected utility-scale projects account for 77% and the remainder comes from grid-connected rooftop and off-grid projects.
- In its early years, India's rooftop solar market stru ggled to grow due to lack of consumer awareness, inconsistent policy framework and funding of central/state governments.

106(A). Sacred groves are parts of a forest of varying sizes. They are communally protected and have an important religious meaning to protect the community. Hence statement 1 is correct.
- Generally, hunting and logging are strictly prohibited within these patches.
- It is a traditional way of conserving green resources where sacred groves are dedicated to the local deity.
- Examples: The sacred groves in the hills of Garhwal and Kumaon, the largest sacred groves in the greenery of Chamoli district, the Khasi hills of Meghalaya, etc.
- The Ganges shark is listed as 'Critically Endangered' in the IUCN Red List of Endangered Species. So, statement 2 is wrong.

107(B). Only 1 and 2 are correct.
Oceanic Trenches:
- Ocean trenches are topographic depressions of the ocean floor, relatively narrow in width and very long.
- These oceanographic features are the deepest parts of the ocean floor.
- Oceanic trenches are a distinctive morphological feature of convergent plate boundaries, along which lithospheric plates move toward each other by shifting from a few millimeters to tens of centimeters per year.
- A trench marks the position at which a flexed, subducting slab begins to descend under another lithospheric slab.
- The trenches are usually parallel to the volcanic island arc, and are approximately 200 km (120 mi) away from the volcanic arc.
- They occur along the base and island arcs of continental slopes and are associated with active volcanoes and strong earthquakes.
- The deepest area in the world is located in the Pacific Ocean in the Mariana Trench called Challenger Deep, which is about 11,033 m. Hence pair 1 is correctly matched.
- The Puerto Rico Trench is the deepest point in the Atlantic Ocean (8.65 km). Hence pair 2 is correctly matched.
- The Java Trench (7.72 km) is in the Indian Ocean. Hence pair 4 is wrongly matched.
- The Eurasia Basin (5.45 km) is the deepest part of the Arctic Ocean. So, pair 3 is wrongly matched.

108(C). Stagflation
- This is a period of rising inflation but falling production and rising unemployment.
- Stagflation is characterized by slow economic growth and relatively high unemployment.
- Stagflation was first recognized during the 1970s when many developed economies experienced rapid inflation and high unemployment as a result of the oil crisis.

Causes of stagflation:
- Stagflation occurs when governments or central banks expand the money supply at the same time they are constrained.
- This can also happen when the monetary policies of the central bank create credit. It is a combination of three undesirable economic conditions:
1. high level of inflation
2. high unemployment
3. very slow growth

109(D). A contractionary monetary policy:
- It is implemented by increasing the prime interest rates thereby reducing the liquidity (money supply) of the market.
- Low market liquidity usually negatively affects production and consumption. It can also have a negative impact on economic development.
- When RBI adopts a contractionary monetary policy, the central bank
- Increase in policy rates (interest rates) like Repo, Reverse Repo, MSF, Bank Rate etc.
- Increase in reserve ratios like Cash Reserve Ratio (CRR) and Statutory Liquidity Ratio (SLR)
- Sells government securities from the market as part of an open market operation (OMO) - extracts liquidity from the market. Hence statement 3 is correct.
- By increasing the SLR, banks invest more money in government securities and reduce the level of liquidity in the economy. Doing the opposite helps maintain cash flow in the economy. Hence statement 1 is correct.
- With an increase in the MSF rate, the cost of borrowing for banks increases resulting in less resources available for lending. So, statement 2 is correct.

110(B). Faizpur Session (1936): The fiftieth (50th) session of the Indian National Congress was held on 27 and 28 December 1936 at Faizpur, on the outskirts of Yaval taluka of Jalgaon district of Bombay Presidency (Maharashtra).
It was here that for the first time the annual session of the Congress was held in a backward rural environment. Hence, pair 1 is wrong.
Haripura Congress Session, 1938: The Indian National Congress met from 19 to 22 February 1938 at Haripura under the chairmanship of Subhas Chandra Bose. In 1938, he was elected president of the Haripura Congress session. Sardar Vallabhbhai Patel had chosen Haripura for the convention. The National Planning Committee was formed under the leadership of Jawaharlal Nehru. Hence, pair 2 is wrong.
Karachi Session (1931): The Karachi Congress session, held from March 26 to 31, 1931, was presided over by Sardar Vallabhbhai Patel. Pandit Jawaharlal Nehru has drafted the proposal for Fundamental Rights and National Economic Program. So,

pair 3 is correct.

111(A). Chuar uprisings (1766-1772):
- Chuar Rebellion occurred in the Bankura/Midnapore districts of modern West Bengal.
- The term "Chuar" was used for local tribals in Bengal and it was a derogatory word (meaning pig).

The Kol rebellion (1829-1839):
- It also known in British records as the Kol mutiny was a revolt of the Adivasi Kol people of Chhota Nagpur during 1829-1839 as a reaction to economic exploitation brought on by the systems of land tenure and administration that had been introduced by East India Company.
- The rebel kols were under the leadership of Buddho Bhagat, Madara Mahato, Joa Bhagat, and others.

Santhal rebellion (1855-56):
- The Santhal rebellion (also known as the Santhal rebellion or the Santhal Hul), was a rebellion against both the British East India Company and the zamindari system by the Santhal.
- Occurred in the regions of present-day Jharkhand, Odisha and West Bengal

Munda uprisings (1899-1900):
- Munda Rebellion is one of the prominent 19th century tribal rebellions in the subcontinent.
- The Mundas inhabited the Chotanagpur area.
- Birsa Munda led this movement in the region south of Ranchi in 1899-1900.

112(B). The Indian Constitution guarantees fundamental rights which are based on these secular principles. The Fundamental Rights of Article 25-28 ensure the protection of secularism. The Preamble of 26 January 1950 defined India as a sovereign, democratic and republican nation. Hence statement 1 is wrong.

Unlike the strict separation between religion and the state in western secularism, in Indian secularism the state can intervene in religious matters. In Indian secularism, although the state is not strictly separate from religion, it maintains a doctrinal distance with religion. Hence statement 2 is correct.

Government schools cannot propagate any one religion through their morning prayers or religious festivals. This rule does not apply to private schools. Hence statement 3 is wrong.

The Indian state recognizes that wearing the turban is central to Sikh religious practice and allows exceptions to the law not to interfere with it. So, statement 4 is correct.

113(C). The city is divided into various wards and ward councilors are elected.
- Complex decisions affecting the entire city are taken by groups of councillors who form committees to decide and debate issues. Hence statement 1 is correct.
- For example, if the bus stand needs improvement, or a crowded market needs to clean its garbage more regularly, or there is a drain that runs through the city that needs cleaning, etc.
- When there is a problem in any ward, the people living in the ward can contact their councillors.
- While councilors make decisions on committees and councilors, the commissioners and administrative staff implement them.
- Commissioner and administrative staff are appointed. So, statement 2 is correct.

114(A). Oligarchy: Oligarchies are governments in which a collection of individuals rules over a nation.
- A specific set of qualities, such as wealth, heredity, and race, are used to give a small group of people power.
- Oligarchies often have authoritative rulers and an absence of democratic practices or individual rights.

115(B). 'Government' refers to the political system by which a country or community is administered and regulated. It is responsible for enforcing and enforcing the laws. The government can change with elections.
- State on the other hand refers to a political institution that represents a sovereign people occupying a certain territory. Hence statement 1 is wrong.
- State refers to more than just government and cannot be used interchangeably. In India the head of state is the nominal executive while the head of government is the real executive as we follow the parliamentary form of government. So, statement 2 is correct.

116(A). Patwari is a village officer who is responsible for measuring the land and keeping the land records of the villages. Hence statement 1 is correct.
- Patwari is known by different names in different states - in some villages such officers are called Lekhpal, in others Kanungo or Karamchari or Village Officer etc.
- Each Patwari is responsible for a group of villages.
- Patwari is also responsible for organizing the collection of land revenue from farmers and providing information to the government about the crops grown in the region.
- This is done from the records that are kept, and that is why it is important for the patwari to update these regularly.
- Farmers change the crops grown in their fields or dig a well somewhere and it is the job of the revenue department of the government to keep an eye on all these.

So, statement 2 is wrong.

117(C). Hyderabad State was founded by Nizam-ul-Mulk Asaf Jah in 1724. Hence, statement 1 is correct, he was one of the prominent nobles of the post Aurangzeb era.
- He played a major role in overthrowing the Sayyid brothers and was rewarded with the Viceroy of the Deccan.
- From 1720 to 1722 he consolidated his hold on the Deccan by suppressing all the opposition of his Viceroy and organizing the administration on efficient lines.
- He never openly declared his independence from the central government, but in practice, he served as an independent ruler. So, statement 2 is correct.

118(D). Amuktamalyada is an epic in Telugu by Krishnadevaraya of the Vijayanagara dynasty. Hence pair 1 is correct.
- Regarded as a masterpiece, Amuktamalyada Srirangam narrates the story of the marriage of the Hindu god Vishnu and the daughter of the Andal (or Goda Devithe) Tamil Alvar poet and Periyalvar.
- Madhura Vijayam, meaning "Victory of Madurai", is a 14th century C.E Sanskrit poem written by the poet Gangadevi. Thus, pair 2 is correct.
- Manuritramu, or The Story of Manu, was written by the early sixteenth-century poet Allasani Peddana. So, pair 3 is correct.

119(D). Only 1, 2 and 5 are matched.
- Vishishtadvaita: Ramanuja's famous system of philosophy is known as Vishishtadvaita or qualified monism. Hence pair 1 is correct.
- Advaita: Adi Shankara (circa 788-820 CE) was a prominent exponent and propagator of Advaita Vedanta or complete monism. Hence pair 2 is correct.
- Dvaita, (Sanskrit: "dualism") is an important school of Vedanta, one of the six philosophical systems (darshanas) of Indian philosophy. Its founder was Madhava, also known as Anandatirtha (1199–1278 AD), who hailed from the area of modern Karnataka state, where he still has many followers. Hence pair 3 is wrong.
- Dvaitadvaita: Nimbarka is the founder of Dvaitadvaita which is dualistic monism. So, pair 4 is wrong.
- Suddadvaita is a "purely Advaita" philosophy propounded by Vallabhacharya (1479-1531 AD). So, pair 5 is correct.

120(A). Only 1 and 3 are correct.
- Shah Jahan's main concern was to recover the lost territories of the Deccan.

- He believed that the independence of Ahmednagar stood in the way of Mughal control in the Deccan.
- He decided to isolate Ahmednagar and conquer Bijapur and the Marathas. He was successful.
- Malik Ambar's son Fatah Khan also made peace with the Mughals. Now Mahabat Khan was appointed governor of Deccan. But the conflict with the Deccan states continued.
- Finally in 1636 treaties were signed with Bijapur and Golconda.

Child Development and Pedagogy

1. "A child may utter a sound which is common for every object and person s/he sees in the environment, like 'inna', but later on s/he starts pronouncing words denoting objects or persons, like maa, pa, and so on." This is the principle of
   - (a) Continuity
   - (b) Generalization to Specialization
   - (c) Differentiation
   - (d) Integration

2. A child is crying on seeing his mother who is busy in working on the laptop. The socialization of child is affected by which agent of socialization?
   - (a) Secondary Agent
   - (b) Primary Agent
   - (c) Anticipatory Agent
   - (d) Both Primary and Secondary Agent

3. Nupur is studying in class V. She can classify types of triangles in different categories but has difficulty in understanding the abstract proof for the exterior angle is equal to sum of opposite interior angles.
   According to Piaget, Nupur lies in
   - (a) Sensory Motor Stage
   - (b) Pre-operational Stage
   - (c) Concrete-operational Stage
   - (d) Formal-Operational Stage

4. In a classroom, students are experiencing and interacting with the curriculum, and all students are availing the opportunity to take part in their own learning. They are relating the information to prior experiences, thus deepening the connection with new knowledge. The above-mentioned phenomenon could be attributed to which kind of education?
   - (a) Special education
   - (b) Progressive Education
   - (c) Inclusive Education
   - (d) Integrated Education

5. Which of the following is not an effective practice adopted by a teacher in the classroom to address gender stereotypes?
   - (a) Counter gender bias.
   - (b) Separate seating arrangement for boys and girls in the class.
   - (c) Discussions on gender discrimination.
   - (d) Use of examples which show boys and girls in non-conformist roles.

6. Kritika is ready to solve the problem given by the teacher, most of the time she also finds a solution to the problem. Kritika belongs to a poor background. Despite that, which of the following motivation is strong in him?
   - (a) Approval motivator
   - (b) Power motivator
   - (c) Achievement motivator
   - (d) Relationship Motivator

7. When the teacher of Shivani explains the topic like mountain, rivers, planets. She tries to think how these things are looking, what does Shivani do-
   - (a) Concept Mapping
   - (b) Imagination
   - (c) Investigation
   - (d) Reflection

8. Which of the following is NOT a characteristic of a teacher-centered approach?
   A. The students are writing down the dictation given by the teacher.
   B. The students are developing different models using clay and paper in groups.
   - (a) only A
   - (b) only B
   - (c) neither A nor B
   - (d) A and B both

9. Authoritative teaching strategies are associated with what students identify as "good teachers." Identify which one of the following educators is demonstrating authoritative techniques in the classroom.
   - (a) When Rashmi failed to take her seat upon entering the room, her teacher reminded her of the class rules and consequences.
   - (b) Pooja, a shy new student to the class, was forced by the teacher on her first day in her new school to give a speech about her past experiences in school
   - (c) Disha was allowed by her teacher to skip recess and play inside by herself because she did not have any friends.
   - (d) Mr. Tapesh allowed the students to have two free days at the beginning of the year in which to become acquainted with their peers in the classroom.

10. When a child with a disability first comes to school the teacher should?
    - (a) Refer the child to a special school according to the disability
    - (b) Seclude him from other students
    - (c) Discuss with the child's parents to evolve collaborative plans
    - (d) Conduct an admission test

11. Learners who are very sensitive to sounds and have difficulty in filtering out background noises have the disability called
    - (a) ADHD
    - (b) APD
    - (c) Autism
    - (d) None of these

12. Many schools are working to become "child-friendly", why the concept of being child-friendly is such important?
    - (a) To improve every child's participation and learning in school
    - (b) To make children skilled
    - (c) To motivate children on multiple aspects
    - (d) To create a friendly situation in school

13. 'Dysgraphia' means
    - (a) difficulty in reading
    - (b) difficulty in writing
    - (c) difficulty in grasping spoken language
    - (d) None of the above

14. The term 'inclusive-education' refers to:
    - (a) Education of Children belong to Scheduled Caste and Schedules Tribes
    - (b) Education of children with disabilities along with normal ones
    - (c) Education in multigrade setting
    - (d) Education of children from minority groups

15. In an inclusive classroom with diverse learners, cooperative learning and peer-tutoring
    - (a) should not be practised and students should be segregated based on their abilities
    - (b) should be used only sometimes

since it promotes comparison with classmates

(c) should be actively discouraged and competition should be promoted

(d) should be actively promoted to facilitate peer-acceptance

16. **Which of the following statement is incorrect about the principles of child development?**

(a) Development follows a definite and predictable pattern.

(b) All individuals are similar in their development.

(c) Development is a product of hereditary and the environment.

(d) Development works on the principle of integration.

17. **Which of the following is not the element of emotion?**

(a) Behavioral   (b) Physical

(c) Cognitive   (d) Sensory

18. **The most useful term for describing the linguistic input to the language learning child is _____.**

(a) motherese

(b) infant-directed speech

(c) child-directed speech

(d) caregiver speech

19. **Assertion (A): A child's development progress can be accurately measured by comparing her rate of development with the other children of some age.**
Reason (R): Pattern and the rate of development of children is uniform and remains some for all children across cultures.
Choose the correct option.

(a) Both (A) and (R) are true and (R) is the correct explanation of (A).

(b) Both (A) and (R) are true but (R) is not the correct explanation of (A).

(c) (A) is true but (R) is false

(d) Both (A) and (R) are false

20. **A child learns to hop and jump before learning to play football. Which principal of development does this illustrate?**

(a) Cephalocaudal

(b) Pronimodistal

(c) Reversibility

(d) Equilibration

21. **Which of the following statements about development is NOT correct?**

(a) Development is a product of heredity and environment.

(b) Development is somewhat

predictable.

(c) Rate of development is uniform and universal.

(d) Development proceeds from general to specific.

22. **Assertion (A): Children pick up ways of behaving appropriately as per their culture from their friends media and various other source.**
Reason (R): Socialization is a complex process that takes place through various formal and informal means.
Choose the correct option.

(a) Both (A) and (R) are true and (R) is the correct explanation of (A).

(b) Both (A) and (R) are true but (R) is not the correct explanation of (A).

(c) (A) is true but (R) is false.

(d) Both (A) and (R) are false.

23. **For children who are in concrete operational stage teachers should-**

(a) Gave a lot of practice to deal with abstract concepts

(b) Provide opportunities to classify objects and ideas on increasingly complex levels

(c) Present problems that require higher order abstract thinking

(d) Give problems that require logical and scientific thinking

24. **According to Jean Piaget , at which stage of cognitive development does the child understand that symbols can be used to represent objects - 'bicycle' will generate an image even when absent?**

(a) Pre-conventional stage

(b) Pre-operational Stage

(c) Concrete operational Stage

(d) Formal operational Stage

25. **Aanav struggles with addition of three-digit numbers on his own but is able to do so with support from the teacher. In Lev Vygotsky's theory, this highlights-**

(a) Zone of proximal development

(b) Reinforcement

(c) Maturation

(d) Symbolism

26. **According to Lev Vygotsky learning is-**

(a) An active process of constructing knowledge

(b) A passive process of reception of knowledge

(c) A function of drill and practice

(d) A function of stimulus-response

associations

27. **Which of the following tools should a teacher use to assess children's learning?**
(i) Classroom interaction
(ii) Projects
(iii) Portfolios
(iv) self-assessment

(a) (ii) and (iii)

(b) (ii), (iii) and (iv)

(c) (i), (ii), (iii) and (iv)

(d) (i), (ii) and (iii)

28. **By encouraging students to reflect on their cognitive abilities to reach a specified goal, a teacher is facilitating the development of:**

(a) Declarative knowledge

(b) Procedural knowledge

(c) Meta-cognition

(d) Rote-memorisation

29. **To scaffold students in solving a problem, a teacher should-**

(a) confuse students by highlighting extraneous information.

(b) directly tell the answer to students and ask them to copy it.

(c) give cues that activities the relevant schemas.

(d) split the information in disconnected chunks.

30. **Assertion (A): During teaching-learning process, a teacher should give opportunities to students for sharing their misconceptions and alternative conceptions.**
Reason (R): Misconceptions and alternative conceptions are always baseless and are insignificant in process of learning.
Choose the correct option.

(a) Both (A) and (R) are true and (R) is the correct explanation of (A).

(b) Both (A) and (R) are true but (R) is not the correct explanation of (A).

(c) (A) is true but (R) is false.

(d) Both (A) and (R) are false.

Ques (31-39): Direction : Read the passage given below and answer the questions/complete the statements that follow by choosing the best options from the given ones.

(1) The Public distribution system, which provides food at low prices, is a subject of vital concern. There is a growing realization that though India has enough food to feed its masses two square meals a day, the monster of starvation and food insecurity continues to haunt the poor in

our country.

(2) Increasing the purchasing power of the poor through providing productive employment leads to rise in income, and thus good standard of living is the ultimate objective of public policy. However, till then, there is a need to provide assured supply of food through a restructured, more efficient and decentralized Public Distribution System (PDS)

(3) Although the PDS is extensive- it is one of the largest systems in the world-it has yet to reach the rural poor and the far-off places. It remains an urban phenomenon, with the majority of the rural poor still out of its reach due to lack of economic and physical access. The poorest in the cities and the migrants are left out, for they generally do not possess ration cards. The allocation of PDS supplies in big cities is larger than in rural areas.

(4) In view of such deficiencies in the system, the PDS urgently needs to be streamlined. Also considering the large stock of food grains combined with food subsidy on one hand and the continuing slow starvation and dismal poverty of the rural population on the other, there is a strong case for making PDS target-group oriented.

31. Read the following statements:
(a) India is a poor country and lacks resources to feed every citizen
(b) Food insecurity is one of the main concerns for the poor in the country
(a) (a) is true and (b) is false.
(b) (a) is false and (b) is true.
(c) Both (a) and (b) are true.
(d) Both (a) and (b) are false.

32. What should now be the objective of public policy on PDS?
(a) to improve the food production.
(b) to provide better fertilisers to the poor.
(c) to reduce administrative cost.
(d) to let the rural poor enjoy the food subsidy.

33. Read the following statements.
(a) The public distribution system is a system which is very popular in India only.
(b) It enables the government to provide food to the people in remote areas of the country successfully.
(c) People have to procure ration card to avail of this facility.
(a) (a) is true and (b) and (c) are false.
(b) (a) and (b) are true (c) is false.
(c) (a) and (b) are false and (c) is true.

(d) (a) and (c) are true and (b) is false.

34. What would be the purpose of making PDS target-group oriented?
(a) To remove the inequality between the rich and poor.
(b) To provide food to poor rural population.
(c) To improve the purchasing power of the people.
(d) To improve the standard of living of the people.

35. Study the following statements:
(a) There is less production of food grains in India.
(b) The poor do not have enough purchasing power.
(c) Cities get more food supplies than rural areas.
(a) (a) is right but (b) and (c) are wrong.
(b) (b) is right but (a) and (c) are wrong.
(c) (c) is right but (a) and (b) are wrong
(d) (a) is wrong but (b) and (c) are right.

36. 'In growing realization' in para 1, growing is used as a/an
(a) Verb   (b) Adverb
(c) Adjective   (d) Noun

37. In 'purchasing power' (para-2), the underlined word means the same as
(a) authority   (b) capacity
(c) energy   (d) will power

38. The word 'system' in 'public distribution system' stands for
(a) procedure
(b) outlook
(c) thought process
(d) routine

39. 'Streamlined' in para 4 is used as a/an
(a) noun   (b) verb
(c) adverb   (d) adjective

40. Which of the following is defined as regional dialect?
(a) Speech characteristics of a language in a region.
(b) Language of a state or country.
(c) Language with a script of a region.
(d) The written language and literature of a region.

41. Which of the following is true of Sign Language?

(a) Sign Language does not have a grammar.
(b) Sign Language has a grammar.
(c) Sign Language is set of gestures.
(d) Only one Sign language used across the world.

42. Language learning is
(a) natural and subconscious
(b) deliberate and conscious
(c) both natural and deliberate
(d) innate and involuntary

43. What does it mean to use 'multilingualism as a strategy' in the classroom?
(a) Using the common language of learners for translating the content in an English medium classroom.
(b) Making use of the languages of learners to teach-learn languages and content subjects.
(c) Not letting the learners to use their languages except the medium of instruction in the classroom.
(d) Learning of many languages in school to become multilingual speaker.

44. Which of the following you would not accept as authentic materials?
(a) A cartoon from a magazine.
(b) An advertisement in a newspaper.
(c) An essay on the COVID 19 written by textbook writer.
(d) A short story by the well-known writer Premchand.

45. A teacher asks her learners of class VIII as a follow up task of the reading lesson to list the events and ideas of the story in a sequence. What does she do?
(a) Asking her students to create a sub-text.
(b) Asking her students to read the story again.
(c) Reinforcing their writing skills.
(d) Promoting their skill to recall.

46. Which of the following statement is NOT true teaching of literary texts in language classroom?
(a) Literary texts should be used to teach grammar.
(b) Literary texts are for appreciation, pleasure and enjoyment.
(c) Literary texts are inputs for language learning.
(d) Literary texts develop critical

thinking.

47. **Ravi reads an article from a newspaper so as to present the overall idea of the text to his group the next day. What is his reading known as?**
(a) Reading between the lines.
(b) Reading beyond the lines.
(c) Scanning
(d) Skimming

48. **Words one recognizes while reading but is not able to use on her own. What is this vocabulary known as?**
(a) Active vocabulary
(b) Passive vocabulary
(c) Listening vocabulary
(d) Reading vocabulary

49. **Basic Interpersonal Communication skills are _____.**
(a) using language for here-and-now and on familiar topics
(b) using language for higher order thinking
(c) using language to convey abstract ideas and concepts
(d) using language for reporting scientific research on a topic

50. **Which approach to writing gives scope for learners to undergo different stage of writing in order to learn to write?**
(a) Product Approach
(b) Process Approach
(c) Communicative Approach
(d) Lexical Approach

51. **Arul Rahul, a teacher in his grammar class introduces rules of the grammar item, voice and tenses first and makes them understand how the form behaves and how to use it contexts. He then gives lots of tasks for learners to practice the language item. What is this process of teaching-learning grammar known as?**
(a) Content knowledge
(b) Procedural knowledge
(c) Process knowledge
(d) Declarative knowledge

52. **Which of the following is an input based task for language learning?**
(a) Learner read a story in groups of five.
(b) Learners write a dialogue for skit to be enacted in an event.
(c) Learners enact a role play on the issue of climate change.

(d) Learners asks questions to understand the ideas of the talk they listened to.

53. **Which of the following is NOT a concept from language education?**
(a) grammar translation method
(b) wavelength of sound
(c) first language interference
(d) error correction

Ques (54-59): Direction: Read the following stanzas and answer the questions/complete the statements by choosing the best options from those given below

In friction land there is a family
With some confusions as you will see.
There is Raghu aged fifteen and others all grown,
'Please will someone let me ever be on my own!' - 4
Rejection, refusal, Raghu saw red.
'Am I the prefect at school? or the baby at home?'
Crazy! What adventures! Bah teenagers!
Papa saw the threat
They think they can manage everything on their own - 8
'Look at your clothes, looks like you haven't bathed in years,
Cut your hair, you look like a scream!'
Raghu was in tears.
'Why can't I live like I wanna be?
I won't change! My friends love it and the girls-look at me.' - 12
Days passed by, things looked better, sometimes worse.
'Papa, there is a band, that wants me to sing a verse.'
"Join a band! yelled flabbergasted papa
'you've surely gone mad'.
Think of a career, for things gonna be sad. - 16

54. **'friction land' here stands for**
(a) a mysterious island
(b) a confused family
(c) a desert
(d) wonderland

55. **saw red' in line 5 means**
(a) was angry
(b) was in danger
(c) was excited
(d) was nervous

56. **Which of the following is not a point of clash between Raghu and his father?**
(a) different lifestyle
(b) different interests
(c) different food habits
(d) age difference

57. **Which line shows the dilemma faced by Raghu?**

(a) Line 2   (b) Line 4
(c) Line 6   (d) Line 6

58. **What is the rhyme in 1st stanza?**
(a) abab   (b) abcd
(c) acbd   (d) abcc

59. **In 'flabbergasted papa' flabbergasted is used as a/an**
(a) verb   (b) adverb
(c) adjective   (d) noun

60. **Which one of the following would you adopt in your language classroom to enhance critical thinking among the learners?**
(a) Read aloud the textbook in the classroom.
(b) Write the answers to the questions on the blackboard.
(c) Giving situations and asking them to discuss and solve them among the group.
(d) Organising a handwriting competition.

Social Studies

61. **Consider the following statements about Cholas.**
A. The inscriptions of the Cholas who ruled in Tamil Nadu refer to more than 400 terms for different kinds of taxes.
B. The most frequently mentioned tax is vetti, taken not in cash but in the form of forced labour, and kadamai, or land revenue.
C. Rajaraja I, considered the most powerful Chola ruler, became king in 985.
The correct statements are:
(a) A and B   (b) B and C
(c) A, B and C   (d) A and C

62. **In the sixth century B.C. Suktimati was the capital of:**
(a) Avanti   (b) Chedi
(c) Kuru   (d) Panchala

63. **With which of the following centres of learning, Chanakya the famous teacher of Chandragupta Maurya, was associated?**
(a) Taxila   (b) Nalanda
(c) Vikramshila   (d) Vaishali

64. **Direction: Answer the following questions by selecting the correct / most appropriate options.**
Statement A): Dantidurga, a Rashtrakuta chief, overthrew his Chalukya overlord and performed a ritual called Hiranya-Garbha
Statement B): As Samantas gained power and wealth, they declared

themselves to be Maha-Mandaleshvara.

(a) Both A) and B) are true and B) was ensured because of A)

(b) Both A) and B) are true, but A) has no relationship with B)

(c) A) is true, but B) is false

(d) A) is false, but B) is true

65. Consider the following statements and select the correct option regarding Sufis:
A. Sufis were Muslim mystics.
B. They rejected outward religiosity and emphasized love and devotion to God and compassion towards all fellow human beings.
C. Great Sufis of Central Asia were Ghazzali, Rumi and Sadi.

(a) Only A and C   (b) A, B and C

(c) Only A and B   (d) Only B and C

66. Direction: Answer the following question by choosing the correct / most appropriate option:
Statement A) The Mughals were descendants of two lineages.
Statement B) From their mother's side, they were successors of Timur and from their father's side, they were descendants of Genghiz Khan.

(a) Both A) and B) are true and B) is the correct explanation of A)

(b) Both A) and B) are true but B) is not the correct explanation of A)

(c) A) is true, but B) is false

(d) A) is false, but B) is true

67. Which of the following social reformers supported widow remarriage?
A. Ishwarchandra Vidyasagar
B. Swami Dayanand Saraswati
C. Veerasalingam Pantulu
D. Raja Rammohun Roy

(a) A, B and C   (b) Only A

(c) Only B and D (d) A, B, C and D

68. ____________ reformers founded "Arya Samaj".

(a) Raja Ram Mohan Roy

(b) Swami Dayananda Saraswati

(c) Atmaram Pandurang

(d) Ishwarachandra Vidysagar

69. Shifting cultivation has different names in different paces, choose the correct pair.
1. Roca - Indonesia,
2. Ladang - Brazil
3. Milpa - Central America & Mexico,
4. Jhumming - India

(a) 1 and 2 is true

(b) 2 and 3 is true

(c) 3 and 4 is true

(d) 1 and 4 is true

70. Read the following and choose the correct sentence/sentences about the Hydel Power.
A) Norway was the first country in the world to develop hydroelectricity.
B) The leading producers of hydel power in the world are Paraguay, Norway, Brazil, and China.
C) India has two major hydel power stations.
D) One-fourth of the world's electricity is produced by hydel power.

(a) Only (A) and (B) are correct

(b) Only (C) and (D) are correct

(c) Only (A), (B) and (C) are correct

(d) Only (A), (B) and (D) are correct

71. Consider the statement A and B about 'Tropical Evergreen Forest' and choose the correct answer.
A) The tropical evergreen forest in Brazil is so enormous that it is like the lungs of the earth.
B) The tropical evergreen forest generally draws in carbon dioxide and breathes out oxygen.

(a) A is true, B is false.

(b) A is false, B is true.

(c) Both A and B are true.

(d) Both A and B are false.

72. __________ place is known as the Grape capital of India.

(a) Nasik

(b) Muzaffarnagar

(c) Mumbai

(d) Faridabad

73. The maximum depth of Lithosphere is found in the which of the following?

(a) Pacific Ocean

(b) Siberian Plain

(c) Patagonian Desert

(d) Himalayan Mountains

74. _______ is the world's northernmost capital of a sovereign state.

(a) Reykjavík   (b) Helsinki

(c) Stockholm   (d) Akranes

75. __________ waves caused by the earthquakes cause maximum damage and destruction on earth's surface.

(a) P waves

(b) S waves

(c) Distortional waves

(d) Surface waves

76. Consider the following terms:
A. Lightning
B. Landslide
C. Thundering
D. Tsunami
E. Floods
Earthquakes can cause:

(a) B, D and E   (b) A, B and C

(c) B only   (d) B and E

77. Consider the statement about ocean currents and choose the correct answer.
A. Ocean currents are the continuous, predictable, directional movement of seawater.
B. Brazil Current and Labrador Current are Cold currents.
C. Gulf Stream and Alaska Current are warm currents.

(a) A and B are true C is false

(b) B and C are true and A is false

(c) C and A are true and B is false

(d) A, B, and C are true

78. Who among the following was popularly known as Napoleon of ancient India?

(a) Samudragupta

(b) Chandragupta Vikramaditya

(c) Srigupta

(d) Kumaragupta

79. Presently the Speaker of Uttar Pradesh Legislative Assembly is:

(a) Hriday Narayan Dikshit

(b) Mata Prasad Pandey

(c) Sukhdev Rajbhar

(d) Purushottam Das Tandon

80. What is the tenure of the members of the Uttar Pradesh Legislative Council?

(a) 3 years   (b) 4 years

(c) 5 years   (d) 6 years

81. Read the following about Article 21 and choose the correct answer.
A. Right to safe drinking water
B. Right to privacy
C. Right to education
D. Right against untouchability

(a) All A, B, C and D is true

(b) A, B and C is true

(c) B , C and D is true

(d) A, C and D is true

82. Read the following and choose the correct statement(s) which violate child rights.
Statement A: Child marriage arranged by parents
Statement B: Child who worked in

motels above 16 age
Statement C: Child forced to go to school by parents
Statement D: Abortion of female fetus, separate from legal methods
(a) Only A and D is true
(b) Only B and D is true
(c) Only C and A is true
(d) Only A and B is true

83. ____________ system was abolished first from the point of view of land reform.
(a) Tenancy
(b) Zamindari
(c) Agriculture for wages
(d) All of the above

84. Which of the following are the practices and ceremonies followed by the rural society?
(a) Tradition
(b) Folkways
(c) Rituals
(d) None of the above

85. What did the Supreme court add to Fundamental rights in the case of Subhash Kumar vs State of Bihar (1991)?
A. Right to life includes the right to the enjoyment of pollution-free water
B. Right to equality includes the right to the enjoyment of pollution-free water
C. Right to freedom includes the right to the enjoyment of pollution-free water
(a) Only A is true
(b) Only C is true
(c) None of these
(d) Only B is true

86. To provide opportunities for education to the child or as the case may be, ward between the age of six and fourteen years is a:
(a) Fundamental Right under Indian Constitution
(b) Fundamental Duty under Indian Constitution
(c) Directive Principles of state Policy Under Indian Constitution
(d) Legal Right under Indian Constitution

87. Which Article provides that, 'The State shall not discriminate against any citizen on grounds only of religion, race, caste, sex, place of birth or any of them'.
(a) Article 13   (b) Article 14
(c) Article 15   (d) Article 16

88. Article _____ of the Constitution of India deals with the 'protection of life and personal liberty'.
(a) 19   (b) 23
(c) 16   (d) 21

89. Which one among the following is not a Fundamental Right under the Constitution of India?
(a) Right to equality
(b) Right to freedom
(c) Right to citizenship
(d) Right against exploitation

90. Given below are two statements labelled as Assertion (A) and Reason (R). In the context of the two statements, which of the following is correct ?
Assertion (A) : The Indian Constitution closely follows the British Parliamentary model.
Reason (R) : In India, the Upper House of the Parliament has judicial powers.
(a) (A) is true, but (R) is false.
(b) (A) is false, but (R) is true.
(c) Both (A) and (R) are true and (R) is the correct explanation of (A).
(d) Both (A) and (R) are true, but (R) is not the correct explanation of (A).

91. In the context of social development ________ stages is characterized by 'Intense self Awareness'.
(a) Infancy   (b) Childhood
(c) Adolescence (d) Adulthood

92. What is the sequence of preparing a project ?
(a) Selection, Recording, Evaluation, Planning, Execution, Follow-up
(b) Planning, Evaluation, Selection, Recording, Execution, Follow-up
(c) Selection, Planning, Execution, Follow-up, Evaluation, Recording
(d) Selection, Evaluation, Recording, Planning, Execution, Follow-up

93. When a teacher evaluates students unit-wise periodically and conducts at the end of the course a comprehensive test, then it is called as
(a) comprehensive process
(b) continuous process
(c) formative process
(d) None of the above

94. Failure to provide for systematic organisation and expression of thought is one of the disadvantages of

(a) short answer type test
(b) very short answer type test
(c) essay type test
(d) objective type test

95. Which is the best method of teaching Sociology ?
(a) Book reading method
(b) Deduction method
(c) Question-answer method
(d) Field visit method

96. The most useful teaching material for Geography is
(a) calendar   (b) map
(c) flash card   (d) barometer

97. As a teacher, you need to engage your children in active engagement during curriculum transaction through
(a) inquiry
(b) exploration
(c) questioning
(d) all of the above

98. A day before Diwali holiday, a teacher tells his student "Go to your locality /village. Find out the people belonging to the different cultural, caste and religious groups who people live there.". The reason to give such project to students is
I. To let them know about people from diverse background
II. To judge if they listen to teacher
III. To teach them unity in diversity
(a) Only I   (b) I and II
(c) II and III   (d) I and III

99. Consider the following teaching methods:
(i) Heuristic
(ii) Dogmatic
(iii) Induction
(iv) Analysis
Which of the above method should be used for teaching gifted children?
(a) (i), (ii) and (iii)
(b) (ii), (iii) and (iv)
(c) (i), (iii) and (iv)
(d) (i), (ii) and (iv)

100. What adaptations in the teaching-learning process should a social science teacher make while engaging with learners who are visually challenged?
A. Speak clearly and loudly with appropriate pauses and reiterations.
B. Use a variety of visually appealing worksheets.
C. Give verbal clues to create opportunities to imagine.

D. **Introduce tactile materials during class room discussions.**
Choose the correct option.
(a) A and B only
(b) A, C and D only
(c) B only
(d) B, C and D only

101. Which one of the following methods would be most appropriate for a constructivist discussion on historical monuments?
(a) a question-answer chart on monuments.
(b) photographs of a social picnic to a monument.
(c) identifying a local monument and narration of stories around it.
(d) a collage of monuments with labels.

102. Which of the following is/are feature(s) of a learner-centred social science class?
I. Creating space for exploration into social issues.
II. Respect for multiple views.
III. Use of multilingualism.
(a) Only I   (b) Both I and II
(c) I, II and III   (d) Only II

103. The models/replicas of physical features are most suitable for teaching—
(a) History
(b) Economics
(c) Geography
(d) Political Science

104. Why is the study of Social Science 'scientific'?
(a) It comprises Systematically acquired verified knowledge.
(b) It helps its reader to study the Scientific society.
(c) It uses scientific terms in its content.
(d) It fulfills the demand for calling Social Studies as science.

105. Which of the following statements is correct about Social Science?
(a) Social Science is not concerned with diverse concerns of society.
(b) Social Science emphasises homogeneity and rituals.
(c) Social Science is a subjectivist discipline.
(d) Social Science lays the foundation for an analytical and creative mindset.

106. Empirical studies include :
(a) observation
(b) formal interviews
(c) mass media analysis
(d) all of the above

107. A good geographical enquiry usually involves
(a) worksheets
(b) textbook
(c) maps
(d) all of the above

108. Which of the following classroom activities symbolises development of critical thinking among students?
A. Encourage students to answer each other for questions related to textbook topics
B. Provide more than one explanation for the same phenomena or event
C. Teacher takes almost all the time to talk than students in each class
D. Attempt to answer questions which are expected in examination.
Choose the correct option.
(a) A, B and C only
(b) A and C only
(c) A and B only
(d) A and D only

109. Why should students learn to be critical?
(a) To print out flaws and being cynical about everything.
(b) To maintain the status quo in society.
(c) To understand how issues are related to their own lives.
(d) To appreciate uniform, homogeneous perspective.

110. During group projects the role of the teacher is to :
A. assign topics and leave the rest to groups.
B. take presentation and mark students.
C. evaluate the groups' progress.
D. facilitate the groups throughout the process.
Choose the appropriate option.
(a) A and B   (b) A and C
(c) B and D   (d) C and D

111. Which of the following statement is true regarding Panini?
Statement A: Panini was a scholar who prepared a grammar for Sanskrit
Statement B: He arranged the vowels and the consonants in a special order, and then used these to create formulae like those found in Algebra.
Statement C: Panini used these to write down the rules of the language in short formulae.
(a) A and B   (b) A, B, and C
(c) B and C   (d) A and C

112. The ultimate goal of education in Jainism is :
(a) Charity
(b) Pity and renunciation
(c) Moksha
(d) Non-violence

113. Consider the statements A, B, C regarding Bengal Partition and choose the correct answer:
A. In 1905 Viceroy Curzon partitioned Bengal.
B. The British argued for dividing Bengal for reasons of administrative convenience.
C. Among the Congress only Radicals opposed it.
(a) B and C are true, A is false
(b) A, B, C all are false
(c) A and B are true, C is false
(d) A and C are true, B is false

114. Consider statements A, B, C regarding Mughal Architecture and choose correct answer.
A) Mostly, red sandstone and white marble were used.
B) Mughal period marked a striking revival of Islamic architecture in northern India.
C) Pishtaq became an important aspect of Mughal architecture
(a) Only A   (b) Only C
(c) A, B and C   (d) Only B

115. Who was the finance minister during the 1991 economic reforms?
(a) Manmohan Singh
(b) PV Narasimha Rao
(c) R. K. Shanmukham Chetty
(d) R. Venkataraman

116. Which of the following is not a part of new economic reforms?
(a) Liberalization
(b) Globalization
(c) Privatization
(d) Centralization

117. Which among the following schemes fulfill the goal of 'Suposhit Rajasthan Vision-2022'?
(a) Indira Gandhi Matritva Poshan Yojana
(b) Nand Ghar Yojana

   (c) Utsav Bhoj

   (d) Indira Gandhi Matritva Sahyog Yojana (IGMSY)

118. **Which of the following departments has launched the scheme "SMILE: Support for Marginalised Individuals for Livelihood and Enterprise" on 12 Feberuary 2022?**

   (a) Department of Space

   (b) Department of Social Justice and Empowerment

   (c) Department of Commerce

   (d) Department of Pharmaceuticals

119. **Consider the statement A, B, and C about the population density and choose the correct answer.**
(A) Average density of population in India is 400 persons per square km.
(B) The average density of population in the whole world is 51 persons per square km.
(C) South-Central Asia has the highest density of population followed by East and South East Asia.

   (a) A and B is true and C is false

   (b) A, B and C are true

   (c) B and C is true and A is false

   (d) A and C is true and B is false

120. **Consider the following statement about Islam during Medieval tie and choose the correct answer.**
A. Merchants and migrants first brought the teachings of the holy Quran to India in the seventh century.
B. Ulama – learned theologians and jurists.
C. Sunni Muslims who accepted the authority of the early leaders Caliph(Khalifas) of the community.

   (a) B and C is true and A is false

   (b) A and C is true and B is false

   (c) A and B is true and C is false

   (d) A, B and C is true

// Hints and Solutions //

1(B). Principle of Continuity: Development follows the principle of continuity which starts with conception and ends with death. It is a never-ending process in life.

Principle of Generality to Specificity: The development process starts with general responses shown by the child as s/he passes through the later stages s/ he starts exhibiting specific behaviours. For example, a child may utter a sound which is common for every object and person s/he sees in the environment, like 'inna', but later on s/he starts pronouncing specific words denoting specific objects or persons, like maa, pa, and so on.

Principle of Interaction: The principle of interaction suggests that an individual is the product of heredity and environment. In other words, the interaction takes place within and outside forces of the child.

Principle of Differentiation in Rate: Differentiation in rate indicates that individuals differ in the rate of development. There is a difference in the rate of development in girls and boys like girls grow faster than the boys at the early stage of development.

Principle of Integration: Principle of Integration refers to the integration of various aspects of development like physical, mental, emotional, social and moral.

2(B). Primary socialization was implicitly understood as taking place in the family and during the first part of childhood. In this perspective, the socializing agents in the primary process are the parents, especially the mother.

Parents along with the family are the most important agents of socialization. Within the family, it is the mother who first begins to socialize the child. Socialization in basic values such as love and affection, manners, and etiquette are first taught in the family.

The situation within the family whether affectionate or disturbed will affect the growth of a child accordingly.

For example:- A child is crying on seeing his mother who is busy in working on the laptop. A child wants love and affection from his mother.

Thus, it is concluded that The socialization of child is affected by primary agent of socialization.

3(C). He made a systematic study of cognitive development in his theory.

He believed that children are the little scientist and they actively and gradually construct their understanding of the world through Cognitive transformation.

In this stage, Children gain the abilities of conservation of number, area, volume, and orientation.

Children can conserve numbers (age 6), mass (age 7), and weight (age 9). Conservation is the understanding that something stays the same in quantity even when its appearance changes.

Children enjoy the company of friends in this stage so, this stage is also referred to as gang age, where the feeling of class inclusion dominates in a child.

Unable to understand abstract thinking.

Reversibility, seriation, transitivity also developed in this stage

The ability to conserve is one of the major accomplishments of the concrete operational stage.

4(B). Dewey has proposed the concept of 'Progressive Education' which emphasizes that learning takes place through 'hands-on' approach so the students must interact with their environment to adapt and learn.

Dewey had a specific idea regarding how education should take place within the classroom. He criticized the undue importance given to the curriculum, which leads to the inactivity of the student in the entire process of learning.

Progressive Education:

In Progressive Education, students thrive in an environment where they are allowed to experience and interact with the curriculum, and all students avail the opportunity to take part in their own learning.

Content is presented in a way that allows the student to relate the information to prior experiences, thus deepening the connection with this new knowledge. Dewey advocated for an

the educational structure that strikes a balance between delivering knowledge while also taking into account the interests and experiences of the student.

Progressive Education is a continuous process of adjustment, having as its aim at every stage an added capacity of growth.' He advocated the importance of education not only as a place to gain content knowledge, but also as a place to learn how to live.

The experience of the child occupies the central place in this method of learning; 'all learning must come as a by-product of actions' child learns through participation in various activities.

Hence, it could be concluded that the above-mentioned phenomenon could be attributed to progressive education.

5(B). Effective practices that should be adopted by a teacher in the classroom to address gender stereotypes

Setting tasks which have to be done together by both girls and boys.

Use of examples that show boys and girls in non-conformist roles.

Providing equal opportunities in the classroom related to asking questions, responding in the class.

Developing the habit of respecting each other's gender in students and assigning equal opportunities to every student in the class.

Involving students in discussing gender issues and countering gender bias by engaging them in solving gender-related issues in society.

Hence, it could be concluded that separate seating arrangements for boys and girls in the class is not an effective practice adopted by a teacher in the classroom to address gender stereotypes.

6(C). Mastery of needs: An individual prefers jobs that are challenging, intellectually demanding, and thought-oriented. He or she enjoys playing a leadership role in groups and is able to complete tasks already started.

Work orientation: An individual takes a proactive attitude toward work and loves what he or she does. He or she obtains a sense of satisfaction from work and pursues self-realization and growth.

Competition: An individual hopes for victory and has the desire to win over others.

Personal unconcern: An individual does not consider success or stellar performance to be the cause of being rejected by others. In other words, there is no fear of success.

Hence, from the above points, we can conclude that the motivation present is the Achievement Motivator.

7(B). Imagination develops the thought process of the students, their thoughts became divergent.

It improves the cognition of the student by using their knowledge, and analogies, in different conditions.

Children become fully active during imagination, it covers all the possible aspects of the problem for image formation. So we can say that when the teacher explains about rivers, mountains, etc. Shivani tries to form an image in her mind, this is an example of imagination.

8(B). It focuses on the discipline of students.

The emphasis is given to the right answer by students.

The teacher gives instructions while students only listen to teacher not give any responses.

Courses prescribed for a class can be completed in a time because all activities are controlled by the teacher.

Power is primarily with teachers and the teacher is the only person who will give instructions and students will follow the instructions.

Acquisition of knowledge is focused.

So, in a teacher-centered approach, the student will not develop the ability to develop the ability to create different models using clay and paper in the group. because the teacher-centered approach focuses on imparting the knowledge and students passively grasp the knowledge.

9(C). Good teachers have positive interpersonal relationships.

They care about their students.

They keep the classroom organized and maintain authority without being rigid or "mean."

They are good motivators, they can make learning fun by being creative and innovative so students learn something.

Thus, it is concluded that Disha was allowed by her teacher to skip recess and play inside by herself because she did not have any friends-educator is demonstrating authoritative techniques in the classroom.

10(C). Disabled Child: A child with a disability is unable to perform certain functions properly than other children. The disability may be physical, it may involve senses like hearing or seeing, it may involve mental health.

To deal with the disabled child in teaching, the teacher should discuss with the child's parents to evolve collaborative plans, to know exactly about the problem and the possible ways to teach the child with other students. And the child can enjoy the presence of other students and feel free to sit with them and it will also motivate the child.

Hence, it becomes clear that when a child with a disability first comes to school the teacher should discuss with the child's parents to evolve collaborative plans.

11(B). It is also known as Central Auditory Processing Disorder, which affects how sound travels unimpeded through the ear is processed and interpreted by children's brain. Children with this disorder cannot recognize subtle differences between sounds in words, even when the sounds are loud and clear enough to be heard. Children suffering from this disorder are unable to block out background noise or to tell where the sound is coming from.

- A student with APD may also have Language Processing Disorder (LPD), which is a specific type of APD in which students find it difficult to attach meaning to sound groups that form words, sentences and stories. These disorders can, in turn, affect expressive (what someone says) and receptive (understanding what was said) language as well.

Disability	Key Points
APD (Auditory Processing Disorder)	• very sensitive to sounds and have difficulty in filtering out background noises. • hearing disorder • easily distracted
ADHD (Attention Deficit Hyperactivity Disorder)	• difficulty staying focused and paying attention. • the tendency to get distracted easily, difficulty controlling behaviour and hyperactivity.
Autism	• challenges with social skills, repetitive behaviours, speech and nonverbal communication.

12(A). Many schools are working to become child-friendly, where children have the right to learn to their fullest potential within a safe and welcoming environment. The aim is to improve every child's participation and learning in school, rather than concentrating on the subject matter and examinations. Being "child-friendly" is very important, but it is not complete.

13(B). Dysgraphia refers to a learning disability which:

affects learners' ability to write coherently.

hinders in organizing letters, numbers, or words on papers.

leads to problems with poor spelling, impaired handwriting, etc.

Remedies useful for treating students with Dysgraphia:

giving extra time for writing assessment, will reduce the copying activity and will emphasize the importance of writing original answers.

dividing tasks into small steps will enable the learners to assimilate the idea easily and will help them in putting their thoughts on paper.

providing low-stress opportunities will allow the learners to learn and write at their own pace and to foster their own strategy of learning and writing.

Hence, it could be concluded that 'Dysgraphia' means difficulty in writing.

14(B). Inclusive-education values the diversity, each child brings to the classroom and facilitates all with equal opportunities to learn and grow.

Inclusive education improves the quality and makes provisions of education for all. It welcomes and celebrates diversity.

It provides a provision to include disabled children along with normal children in a regular classroom environment.

It refers to an education system that accommodates all children regardless of their physical, intellectual, social, emotional, linguistic, or other conditions.

15(D). It refers to an education system that accommodates all children regardless of their physical, intellectual, social, emotional, linguistic, or other conditions.

It provides a provision to include disabled children along with normal children in a regular classroom environment.

Inclusive classroom refers to an education system that includes children regardless of physical, intellectual, social, linguistic, or other differently-abled conditions.

In an inclusive classroom with diverse learners, cooperative learning and peer-tutoring should be actively promoted to facilitate peer-acceptance.

Cooperative learning: It refers to a heterogeneous group where students work collaboratively to achieve learning outcomes. It develops critical thinking, brainstorming, communication, and life long learning skills.

Peer tutoring: It refers to the learning process where fellow students teach each other. In this strategy, a higher-performing student is paired with a lower performing student to teach specific skills.

An inclusive classroom is not limited to children with a disability but also gifted children, economically disadvantaged children, children from remote populations, children belonging to ethnic, linguistic, or cultural minorities or children from other marginalized groups.

Therefore, in an inclusive classroom with diverse learners, cooperative learning, and peer-tutoring should be actively promoted to facilitate peer-acceptance.

16(B). Development refers to an increase in structure for better and enhanced functioning of organs. It is a complex and continuous process, thus there are some principles that need to be followed for a better understanding of the concept.

- Principle of integration: By proceeding from general responses to specific responses again, these specific responses are integrated from the whole it means there is a movement from whole to parts and again from parts to whole.
- Principle of individual difference: With respect to development, the rate and quality of development in various dimensions differ from person to person. There is a difference in the growth rate between boys and girls. Girls mature earlier in comparison to boys.
- Development follows a pattern: Prenatal (before birth) and postnatal (after birth) development of human beings follow a pattern or a predictable sequence. Physical development, motor or language development and intellectual development take place in definite sequences.
- Product of hereditary and environment: Hereditary and environment play a vital role in determining the development of an individual.

So, it could be concluded that the statement 'All individuals are similar in their development' is incorrect about the principles of child development.

17(D). Emotion is a mental state associated with fear, anger, love, etc. The emotional states of an individual are the combination of cognitive experience, physiological change, and behavioral changes. Together, these are known as the elements of emotion.

Three elements of emotion are as follows:

- Cognitive experience: Emotions also involve cognitive processes such as memorials, perceptions, expectations, and interpretations. Our appraisal of an event plays an especially significant role in the meaning it has for us. Thinking of life events can produce emotions.
- Physical changes: Emotions involve the brain, nervous system, and hormones so that when you're emotionally aroused the hormone secretion is more to give us instant energy. Each emotion has a specific characteristic of physiological aspects. Fear may cause blood pressure to rise, pupils to dilate, etc.
- Behavioral changes: Emotions also involve behavioral reactions, both expressive and instrumental. Facial expressions such as smiles and frowns, as well as gestures and Lories of voice, all serve to communicate our feelings that may enhance our chances for survival. Overt expressions such as smiles, or frowns to reveal emotions.

So, we can conclude that Sensory is not an element of emotion, rather it refers to the use of senses to understand the physical world.

18(C). The most useful term for describing the linguistic input to the language learning child is child-directed speech.

19(D). Development involves the processes that are genetically programmed as well as those that are influenced by the environment.

- Development takes place in all aspects such as physical, cognitive, language, social, emotional, and others.
- Let us understand the assertion and reason statement:- Differences in the rate of development can be seen in many areas-the acquisitions of teeth, the age at which the child sits stands walks, becomes pubescent, etc.
- Development occurs at different rates for different parts of the body neither the growth of different parts of the body nor the mental growth takes place at the same rate. The different aspects of physical or mental growth take place at different rates and reach maturity at different times. In some areas, the body growth may be rapid, while in others relatively slow.
- A child's development progress can not be accurately measured by comparing her rate of development with the other children of some age a s patterns and rate of development are not the same or uniform for everyone.

Hence, it can be concluded that Both (A) and (R) are false .

20(A). Development is a process that creates growth, progress, positive change, or the addition of physical, economic, environmental, and social. and demographic components.

- Human development refers to the physical, cognitive, and psychosocial development of humans
- Principle of Sequential development- The principle of sequential states that every individual although exhibiting the difference in the change follows the same sequence of change. Cephalocaudal and Proximodistal tendencies are found to be followed in maintaining sequence and direction of development.

- The cephalocaudal tendency exhibits that the development proceeds in the longitudinal direction that is from head to foot. That is the reason why the child first gains control over head before he/she starts walking.
- Infancy develops control of the head and face movements in the first two months. In the next few months, they are able to lift themselves up by using their arms and then gain control over the toe and be able to crawl, walk, jump, and climb, day by day.
- For example:- Child learns to hop and jump before playing football.

Thus, it is concluded that when a child learns to hop and jump before learning to play football, this illustrates the Cephalocaudal principle of development.

21(C). Development involves the processes that are genetically programmed as well as those that are influenced by the environment.

- Development takes place in all aspects such as physical, cognitive, language, social, emotional, and others.
- Although all individuals grow and develop in their own unique way and in their own contexts, there are some basic principles which underlie the process of development and can be observed in all human beings. These are called the principles of development .
  - Development is a product of heredity and environment:- Heredity and the environment plays an important role in the development of the individual. From the earliest moments of life, the interaction of heredity and the environment works to shape who children are and who they will become.
  - Development proceeds from general to specific : In all the phases of pre-natal (before birth) development and post-natal (after birth) life, the child's responses are from general to specific. General activity proceeds to a specific activity. For example, when Sufi was less than 3 months of age and was shown a rattle, she would get excited and move her arms and kick her legs. This is a general response. At 5 months of age, she would reach out to hold it in her hand. This is a specific response.
  - Development is predictable - The rate of development is fairly constant for each child. This shows that it is possible to predict the future level of development of the child and to what

degree he will exhibit particularly so for height, weight, cognitive ability, etc.

- Principle of differentiation of rate - Differences in the rate of development can be seen in many areas-the acquisition of teeth, the age at which the child sits, stands, walks, becomes pubescent, etc.
  - Development occurs at different rates for different parts of the body, neither the growth of different parts of the body, nor the mental growth takes place at the same rate. The different aspects of physical or mental growth take place at different rates and reach maturity at different times. In some areas, the body growth may be rapid, while in others relatively slow.

Therefore, it can be concluded that Rate of development is uniform and universal is not correct statements about development.

22(A). Socialization is also considered as the passing of culture from one generation to the next.

- During the process of socialization, children learn about their family traditions from their elders and preserve them and pass them on to the next generation as they grow older.
- Socialization helps children to learn and perform the different roles and responsibilities which they have learnt from their elders.
- Children pick up ways of behaving appropriately as per their culture from their friends, media, and various other sources:- It is secondary socialization. **Secondary socialization is a type of socialization that refers to the growing child who learns a very important lesson in social conduct from his peers. Friends, media, and peer groups are the agents of secondary socialization which take place throughout one's life.**
- It helps children to learn appropriate social attitudes such as how to like and enjoy social life and group activities.
- Socialization is a process that continues throughout life from birth till adulthood. However, there are different phases in which the process takes place. These phases are usually spread across different age groups and have been categorized as the different types of socialization.
- It includes formal and informal means. Socialization is done by parents, teachers, peers, neighbors, and educational and religious institutions.

Thus, it is concluded that Both (A) and (R) are true and (R) is the correct explanation of (A).

23(B). Jean Piaget's stage theory describes the cognitive development in children.

- Cognitive development involves changes in cognitive processes and abilities. In Piaget's view, early cognitive development involves processes based upon actions and later progresses into changes in mental operations
- Concrete Operational Stage:
  - 'Concrete Operational Stage' lasts around 7 to 11 years of age which refers to the late childhood stage of child development.
  - In this stage, children can classify objects into groups and subgroups and gain the abilities of conservation of number, area and volume.
  - Children show attainment of the concept of reversibility, seriation, transitivity as a cognitive capacity.
  - Children can conserve numbers (age 6), mass (age 7), and weight (age 9). Conservation is the understanding that something stays the same in quantity even when its appearance changes.

Thus, it infers that according to Jean Piaget, for children who are in the concrete operational stage teachers should provide opportunities to classify objects and ideas on increasingly complex levels

24(B). Piaget's stage theory describes the cognitive development in children.

- Cognitive development involves changes in cognitive processes and abilities. In Piaget's view, early cognitive development involves processes based upon actions and later progresses into changes in mental operations
- 'Preoperational period' lasts around 2 to 6 or 7 years of age .
- In this stage, the child assumes that other people feel, see, and hear exactly the same as the child does.
- It refers to the child's inability to infer the perspective of other people or to see a situation from other's points of view.
- The child has mental representations and are also able to understand things symbolically (playing house, having a tea party).
- The child during this stage engages in what is called a symbolic play that is, the wooden box is considered as a car, a rounding, the steering wheel and the stick, a gun. That is during play an object takes the place of or represents something else in the child's mind.
- Piaget noted that children are unable to take the point of view of other people, which he termed egocentrism. Egocentrism is when children experience difficulty in experiencing another person's perspectives.

Thus, it infers that according to Jean Piaget, at the Pre-operational Stage of cognitive development the child understand that symbols can be used to represent objects - 'bicycle' will generate an image even when absent.

25(A). Lev Vygotsky, a Russian psychologist, proposed a theory of cognitive development known as 'Socio-Cultural Theory'. He believed that children gain knowledge through social and cultural experiences.

- When the child is having interactions with peers and adults, they learn the values, beliefs, customs, and language of their culture. As per his socio-cultural theory, development takes place due to the intermingling of culture, social interaction, and language.
- According to Vygotsky, ' zone of proximal development ' or ' ZPD ' refers to the:
  - the gap between what the child can do independently and with assistance.
  - difference between what a learner can do on his/her own and what he/she can do with someone's help.
  - range of tasks too difficult for the child to do alone, but possible with the help of adults and more skilled peer.
  - distance between learners' actual development level and his/her level of development under someone's guidance.

Therefore, it is concluded that Aanav struggles with addition of three digit numbers on his own but is able to do so with support with teacher, In Lev Vygotsky's theory, this highlights Zone of proximal development.

26(A). Lev Vygotsky was a Russian psychologist who believed that social interactions play a key role in development.

- According to him, learning occurs when children interact with people and the environment.
- Lev Vygotsky, a Russian psychologist, proposed a theory of cognitive development known as 'Socio-Cultural Theory'. He believed that children gain knowledge through social and cultural experiences.
  - When the child is having interactions with peers and adults, they learn the values, beliefs, customs, and language of their culture. As per his socio-cultural theory, development takes place due to the intermingling of culture, social interaction, and language.

Therefore, It infers that according to Lev Vygotsky learning is an active process of constructing knowledge.

27(C). Assessment is a process of collecting, receiving, and using data for the purpose of improvement in the learning process.

- Assessment is a systematic way of collecting information to make a judgment about student learning.
- It is integral to the teaching-learning process which helps in facilitating student learning and improving instruction.
- The assessment provides feedback on the performance of the student specifying his/her strengths and areas for improvement which provides insights for taking appropriate steps for improving the learning.
- Following are the tools a teacher uses to assess children's learning:-
  - Classroom interaction:- The students, in a group, share their experiences and learn better from each other. The students sharing each other's experiences and assessments can be more objective when the assessment is based on a shared set of assessment schedules. This assessment can further develop cooperative learning and team skills. The learners can overcome their difficulties easily and do better in their studies.
  - Projects:- It is a method that emphasizes the active participation of students by working in a group to complete a specific project. It encourages students to think creatively and assesses their intelligence and their representation.
  - Portfolio assessment Portfolio is a collection of students' work representing a selection of performance. It often documents a student's best work. It may also include information such as drafts of his/her work, his/herself assessment of work, and parents' assessment.
  - Self-assessment:- It is the ability of a person to accurately evaluate or assess his/her performance, and his/her strengths and weaknesses.

Thus, it is concluded that all the given options are the tools should a teacher use to assess children's learning.

- Following are the tools a teacher uses to assess children's learning:-
  - Classroom interaction:- The students, in a group, share their experiences and learn better from each other. The students sharing each other's experiences and assessments can be more objective when the assessment is based on a shared set of assessment schedules. This assessment can further develop cooperative learning and team skills. The learners can overcome their difficulties easily and do better in their studies.
  - Projects:- It is a method that emphasizes the active participation

of students by working in a group to complete a specific project. It encourages students to think creatively and assesses their intelligence and their representation.

  - Portfolio assessment Portfolio is a collection of students' work representing a selection of performance. It often documents a student's best work. It may also include information such as drafts of his/her work, his/herself assessment of work, and parents' assessment.
  - Self-assessment:- It is the ability of a person to accurately evaluate or assess his/her performance, and his/her strengths and weaknesses.

Thus, it is concluded that all the given options are the tools should a teacher use to assess children's learning.

28(C). Knowledge: knowledge is a complex one because the range of what constitutes knowing or knowledge is very wide.

- Knowledge can be used to mean a variety of things, such as familiarity with people, places, persons, skills, and competencies of performing various tasks, beliefs, faiths, and everyday experiences.
- Meta-cognition: A learner needs to be aware of the processes he/she is engaged in during the course of learning. This helps him/her to learn the new learning task effectively. This awareness of one's processes of learning a new learning task is understood as metacognition.

Thus, by encouraging students to reflect on their cognitive abilities to reach a specified goal, a teacher is facilitating the development of metacognition.

29(C). Vygotsky is known as the proposer of social constructivism . Social Constructivism approach talks of the importance of social interaction and context in learning.

- He believes that learning is social in nature. Through interactions, children shared their views and make their own meaning. It does not focus much on individual learning rather it emphasized social context; knowledge is mutually built and constructed.
- Scaffolding: A technique to provide the right kind of support in the right amount at right time to increase a child's competence.
  - Scaffolding can be defined in simpler terms as "a technique to provide the right kind of support in the right amount at right time to increase child's competence."
  - scaffolding is not only a technique to support learners to achieve their goals but it also helps in filling the 'learning gaps' i.e. what a learner has

learned and what was expected to learn.

  - It helps a learner to move from a Zone of Actual Development to a Zone of Proximal Development and finally reach to Zone of Desired Development, with the help of a more experienced person like peers, elders in the family, or teachers.
  - When a teacher starts supporting the learner initially for learning, and gradually reduces the support till the learner reaches a situation, where s/he can develop his/ her own meaning and understanding independently. The teacher is scaffolding the learner.

Thus, to scaffold students in solving a problem, a teacher should give cues that activities the relevant schemas

30(C). Learning does not stop with acquiring and integrating knowledge. Learners develop an in-depth understanding through the process of extending and refining their knowledge (e.g. by making new distinctions, clearing up misconceptions, and reaching conclusions).

- In knowledge creation, one cannot be free from one's own context. The social, cultural, and historical contexts are important for individuals because such contexts give the basis to individuals to give meaning to them.
- That is why limited interaction with the environment and externalization of personal knowledge can lead to misconceptions.
- The teacher needs to explain the difficulties and resolve the misconceptions among learners. After many such settings, learners may be assigned some challenging problems also to find out the solution.
- Inquire into the learner's understanding of concepts, exploring misconceptions and untrue ideas'
- Misconceptions are not always baseless and are insignificant in process of learning. It plays a significant role in the teaching-learning process.
- For example , there is often a belief that seasons change based on the earth's proximity to the sun. In reality, seasons change as the earth tilts toward or away from the sun at different times of the year.
- To counter this misconception, a teacher can implement a Think-Pair-Share activity. Where, first, she asks learners what causes the seasons, in order to assess their prior knowledge and potential misconceptions. Learners then pair with a partner to discuss answers and share as a class. The teacher then presents a well-organized lesson on this topic directly addressing the misconception. Learners again pair and explain the seasons. Learners harboring

the misconception may experience cognitive dissonance during the activity as they learn. Further activities continue to restructure and confirm their knowledge.

Thus, (A) is true but (R) is false.

31(B). Refer to the following lines from the passage:

1. "There is a growing realization that though India has enough food to feed its masses two square meals a day, the monster of starvation and food insecurity continues to haunt the poor in our country"

2. "The Public distribution system, which provides food at low prices, is a subject of vital concern. There is a growing realization that though India has enough food to feed its masses two square meals a day, the monster of starvation and food insecurity continues to haunt the poor in our country".

From the above sentences, it is clear that statement (A) is false as there is no mention in the passage whether India is a poor country or not and it also doesn't lack resources to feed every citizen.

Statement (B) is true as inspite of having enough food to feed our citizens, our country doesn't have a streamlined PDS due to which the poor is not getting required amount of food timely.

32(D). Refer to the following line from the passage:

1. "Also considering the large stock of food grains combined with food subsidy on one hand and the continuing slow starvation and dismal poverty of the rural population on the other, there is a strong case for making PDS target-group oriented".

From the above sentence, it is clear that the objective of public policy on PDS should now be to let the rural poor enjoy the food subsidy.

33(C). Refer to the following lines from the passage:

1. " The Public distribution system, which provides food at low prices, is a subject of vital concern".

2. "Although the PDS is extensive- it is one of the largest systems in the world-it has yet to reach the rural poor and the far-off places. It remains an urban phenomenon, with the majority of the rural poor still out of its reach due to lack of economic and physical access".

3."The poorest in the cities and the migrants are left out, for they generally do not possess ration cards".

From the above sentences, it is clear that statement (A) is false as there is no mention in the passage whether the public distribution system is very popular in India only or not.

Statement (B) is also false as it is mentioned in the passage that PDS is an urban phenomenon, it has yet to reach the rural poor and the far-off places.

Statement (C) is true as it is mentioned in the passage that those people who have ration cards can only avail of the PDS facility.

34(B). Refer to the following line from the passage:

1. "In view of such deficiencies in the system, the PDS urgently needs to be streamlined. Also considering the large stock of food grains combined with food subsidy on one hand and the continuing slow starvation and dismal poverty of the rural population on the other, there is a strong case for making PDS target-group oriented".

From the above sentence, it is clear that the purpose of making PDS target-group oriented is to provide food to poor rural population.

35(D). Refer to the following lines from the passage:

1. "There is a growing realization that though India has enough food to feed its masses two square meals a day, the monster of starvation and food insecurity continues to haunt the poor in our country".

2. "Increasing the purchasing power of the poor through providing productive employment leads to rise in income, and thus good standard of living is the ultimate objective of public policy".

3." The allocation of PDS supplies in big cities is larger than in rural areas".

From the first line mentioned above, it is clear that statement (A) is false as it is mentioned in the passage that India has enough food to feed its citizens two square meals a day.

From the second line mentioned above, it is clear that statement (B) is true as it is mentioned in the passage that if we increase the purchasing power of the poor people by providing productive employment to them, then the ultimate objective of PDS will be obtained.

From the third line mentioned above, it is clear that statement (C) is true as it is mentioned in the passage that allocation of PDS supplies is more in big cities than in rural areas or remote areas.

36(C). Here the underlined word 'growing' is an adjective i.e a word naming an attribute of a noun, such as sweet, red, or technical.

Growing means becoming greater over a period of time; increasing.

For example:- She added yet another item to the growing queue.

Realization is a noun and growing is modifying the same.

Thus, the part of speech is adjective here.

37(B). Power means the ability or capacity to do something or act in a particular way.

For example:-Alex was doing everything in his power to provide her with all the experiences of a natural mother.

Capacity means the ability or power to do or understand something.

For example:- He attended in his official capacity as mayor.

Hence, capacity is similar in meaning to the word power.

38(A). System means a set of principles or procedures according to which something is done; an organized scheme or method.

For example:-This system imposes additional financial burdens on many people.

Procedure means an established or official way of doing something.

For example:- New employees are taught the proper safety procedures.

Hence, procedure is similar in meaning to the word system.

39(D). Here the underlined word 'streamlined' is an adjective i.e a word naming an attribute of a noun, such as sweet, red, or technical.

Streamlined means having been made simpler and more efficient or effective.

For example:- The manufacturer has streamlined the car's design.

40(A). Language is not static but is subject to variation, this variation could be due to social factors such as geographical location, socioeconomic status, caste, ethnic group, and so on. This variation in language is termed as Dialect .

Regional dialect:

- When we travel from one place to another in a particular direction, we will notice linguistic differences, from one village to another. When the areas are close to each other, the differences will be relatively small.

- However, the further we get from our starting point, the larger the differences will become from that point. These differences are known as regional dialects.

- In other words, a regional dialect is the speech characteristics of a language in a region. More particularly, we can say that dialect is regional and it comes from a region.

- Linguistically, it refers to far greater differences than mere pronunciation which pertains to accents. For instance , take the case of Hindi spoken in different parts of India. We can find differences at the level of sounds, as well as vocabulary and grammar.

From the above points, we can conclude that regional dialect is the speech characteristics of a language in a region.

41(B). Sign Language is a visual language that uses hand shapes (the shape of the hand for different words or letters of the alphabet), movements, facial expressions, and body language to convey meaning.

- Every sign language has a

comprehensive vocabulary and its own grammatical rules. These grammatical rules are different from that of spoken languages. Sign language is used by people with different degrees of hearing loss. Some people learn it as young children, while others choose to learn it later in life.
- Main features of sign language include:
  - A sign language has its own grammar , just as Hindi has its own grammar which is quite different from the grammar of Bengali or English.
  - So when a young child is being taught Hindi, he will learn the vocabulary and grammar of Hindi; and when he is taught sign language he will learn the vocabulary and grammar of sign language.
  - Sign language is a natural language as just as a child acquires spoken language by listening to it from the time he is born, sign language is acquired by the young hearing impaired child, by 'seeing' it being used by people around him.

From the above points, we can conclude that ' Sign language has a grammar' is true of Sign Language.

42(B). development takes place through language acquisition and language learning .

Language learning :
- It refers to the result of deliberate and conscious effort in a formal environment, for a better understanding of foundational skills of language learning.
- In language learning, children should move from simple to complex rules to be proficient in all aspects of language skills.
- It is effectively done by providing comprehensible inputs to make the learners actively involved in real communication.
- It refers to have a basic knowledge of grammatical rules and their use in communication.

Hence, it could be concluded that Language learning is deliberate and conscious.

43(B). Multilingualism refers to speaking more than one language competently. The term multilingualism is derived from two Latin words namely "multi" which means many and "lingua" which means language.
- Multilingualism is constitutive of the identity of a child and a typical feature of the Indian linguistic landscape must be used as a tool, resource, and classroom strategy by a creative language teacher.
- Multilingualism as a strategy means using the languages of learners for teaching and learning languages and content subjects. It ensures the inclusion of all students irrespective of their linguistic background.

- In an environment of multilingualism, students get the opportunity to not only master their primary language but also get the opportunity to efficiently learn multiple languages at the same time.
- The multilingual students make rules across languages in a stimulating environment which helps them to sharpen their skills like observing, deducting, and reasoning thus leading to greater linguistic and cognitive flexibility.

Thus, it is concluded that 'Multilingualism as a strategy' in the classroom means making use of the languages of learners to teach-learn languages and content subjects .

44(C). The learning process is aimed to bring out the permanent desirable changes in the behavior of an individual. The teaching-learning process respects the diversity among students and the teacher follows different paths to achieve the goals of learning.
- Authentic materials refer to any text, audio, video, or object developed or written in natural language and contexts. These are the reading texts that were written by native speakers and published in newspapers or magazine contexts.
- '
- Authenticity means that nothing of the original text or material is changed and also its presentation and layout are retained.
- Authentic Material gives authentic and cultural information as it includes authentic resources such as newspaper advertisements , short stories of well-known writers, cartoons from magazines , hoardings, brochures, etc.
- Authentic materials are mostly drawn from periodicals that are constantly being updated. These materials relate more closely to learners' needs and provide them with a source of relevant materials for learning.

Therefore, it is concluded that " An essay on the COVID 19 written by the textbook writer " would not be accepted as authentic material.

45(A). Reading has been defined as a process whereby one looks at and understands what has been written, the reader does not necessarily need to look at everything in a given piece of writing. The reader actively works on the text and is able to arrive at understanding it without looking at every letter and word.
- The subtext is the meaning which is hidden in the text. It provides the reader with a piece of short information about the text regarding its characters and the plot of the story.
- The subtext is any content of a creative work that is not announced explicitly by

the characters or author. It is implicit or becomes something understood by the observer of the work.
- It refers to listing the events and ideas of the story in a sequence . It creates the interest of the reader as subtext provides bits and pieces of information and helps the reader to read between the lines.

From the above points, it is clear that the teacher is asking her students to create a sub-text.

46(A). Language occupies a key position in the School curriculum. The all-round development of the learner is the ultimate aim of education. Therefore, the curriculum should be designed and developed so that this ultimate objective could be achieved.
- Literature is considered to be a group of works of art made up of words in written or sometimes spoken forms.
- Literature for children is considered as an authentic source of reading as it is genuine material covering various genres. Travelogues, one-act plays, memoirs, etc. are the forms of literature.
- A literary text is one that is written for infotainment purposes, that it is for appreciation, pleasure, and enjoyment as well as it might contain some information that is useful to the learners.
- The literary text should be authorized and approved. Literary texts are of many types such as poetry, fictional & nonfictional stories, etc. "Harry Potter" is an example of a literary text.
- Literary texts are perceived as a resource and relevant input to stimulate language activities and they can be used in a language class for the teaching and learning of language functions.
- Literary texts develop critical thinking as by reading the text, the students get information about other cultural matters, and they are encouraged to read the text and form a personal opinion.
- Using literary texts in the language classroom can make the students more aware of the language they are learning, and help them in developing skills and strategies.

Thus, it is concluded that 'Literary texts should be used to teach grammar.' is NOT true teaching of literary texts in a language classroom.

47(D). Reading sub-skill refers to the well-planned reading approach which helps the learners to comprehend and perceive the meaning of the text effectively. There are different kinds of reading sub-skill and 'Skimming' is one of them.
- Skimming is one of the reading techniques which focuses on reading rapidly to get the overall idea or the gist of the text.

- It looks at the keywords of the text for a general overview. It ignores or skips unnecessary information to get the main idea.
- It involves one going through the text to get the central idea. All the insignificant words are avoided and the focus is on the meaning-bearing elements.
- For example, a reader reads an article from a newspaper to present the overall idea of the text to his group the next day.

Hence, it is clear that the above-mentioned type of reading is known as Skimming .

- Scanning involves quickly glancing through the text to find out a specific piece of information. It is used when looking into a dictionary, invoices, catalogs, etc. It involves going through a text in search of a specific piece of information; such as searching for a specific name, date, word, phrase, figures, or percentage.
- Reading between the lines refers to the phenomenon where the answers are not explicitly stated but only suggested in the text. It helps to infer literal meanings from the author's figurative language.

48(B). Vocabulary refers to the set of words an individual uses as a tool for communication. It is a collection of familiar words used or understood by an individual or group of people. There are mainly two types of vocabulary which include Active and Passive vocabulary.

- Passive vocabulary refers to the set of words that we recognize when we listen to them and read them as these words can't be recalled and used easily and frequently.
- One can recognize these words in a text or when spoken by others and can guess the meaning of these words but cannot use them confidently.
- Our active vocabulary is more limited (smaller) than our passive vocabulary. Students try their best to increase the repertoire of both active and passive vocabulary and gradually try to convert their passive into their active vocabulary.

Hence, it could be concluded that the above-mentioned types of words are known as Passive Vocabulary.

49(A). There are two major aspects of language proficiency that must be acquired by second language learners. Jim Cummins has identified these as Basic Interpersonal Communication Skills (BICS), or conversational proficiency, and Cognitive Academic Language Proficiency (CALP), or academic proficiency.

BICS:

- BICS stands for Basic Interpersonal Communication Skills. These language skills are needed in social situations.
- It is a cognitively undemanding language, i.e. it is easy to understand,

deals with everyday language and occurrences, and uses a simple language structure.

- It refers to using language for here-and-now and on familiar topics, for day-to-day living, including conversations with friends on day-to-day routines, and informal interactions.
- It is context embedded. Context embedded means that the conversation is often face-to-face, and offers many cues to the listener such as facial expressions, gestures, and concrete objects of reference.

Hence, it is clear that Basic Interpersonal Communication skills are using language for here-and-now and on familiar topics .

50(B). Writing is one of the language skills which refers to the graphical representation of speech sounds. There are different approaches to writing and the 'Process Approach' is one of them.

- Process approach to writing models the writing process rather than the written product. It involves the active participation of learners.
- It enables learners to learn how to write as it is a writing approach in which learners undergo different stages of writing fo r developing a good write-up .
- It focuses on the steps involved in creating a unique/creative piece of writing and emphasizes revising, editing, and producing a text before coming up with the final text.
- Stages involved in the process approach to writing are Brainstorming, Outlining, Drafting, Revising, Proof-reading, and Writing the final draft.

Hence, it could be concluded that the P rocess Approach to writing gives scope for learners to undergo different stages of writing in order to learn to write.

51(D). Knowledge is often considered synonymous with terms like familiarity, understanding, wisdom, education, awareness, etc. Knowledge can be expressed in the form of data, scientific formulae, product specifications, manuals, universal principles, and so forth. Knowledge may be declarative or procedural.

- Declarative knowledge comprises a number of knowledge consisting of known facts and active goals.
- Declarative encoding in learning grammar means that the information, i.e. an explicit grammar rule, is provided usually through instruction.
- The aim is for a learner to develop the language structure. It enables a student to describe a rule of grammar and apply it in structured and pattern practice drills.
- It means establishing knowledge of grammar rules or patterns in the learners' minds. In other words, here,

students learn how the form behaves and how to use it in contexts.

Hence, it could be concluded that the above-mentioned process of teaching-learning of grammar is known as declarative knowledge .

52(A). Task-Based Language Learning is an approach that implies the idea that language learning takes place by using language meaningfully and contextually. It is an approach in which students use language to complete a task. There are different types of language tasks such as input-based tasks, output-based tasks, etc.

- Input-based language tasks are typically designed to engage learners in input comprehension and attract their attention to specific linguistic features in a meaningful context.
- Input-based tasks could successfully facilitate vocabulary acquisition receptively as well as productively. Input-based tasks have been typically operationalized as read-and-comprehend tasks and listen-and-do tasks.
- These tasks don't require the production of language. They focus on an individual's ability of understanding and comprehending language. For example, reading a story, listening to a story, etc.

From the above points, we can conclude that 'learners read a story in groups of five' is an input-based task for language learning.

53(B). Language education/teaching refers to a process whereby a child gains communicative comprehension or fluency over a language. It involves practice by learners where facilitation is provided by a teacher.

Concepts related to language education:

Grammar translation method:

- Grammar translation is a traditional method through which language is taught with a detailed study of grammar. Learners apply the rule of grammar in translating sentences from their mother tongue to the target language.
- It explains grammatical rules therefore it gives correct and accurate knowledge of English. This method tries to establish a strong link between new ideas and old ideas and focuses on reading and writing skills.

Error correction:

- Error correction refers to understanding the error patterns of children so that they can be provided with better learning experiences which will help them in developing a contextual understanding of language learning processes.
- The teacher has to identify and assess these errors of children to identify the patterns of errors or mistakes that students make in their work so that

these can be minimized or removed.
First language interference:

- The positive influence of the first language could be seen in the classroom, but sometimes, it manifests in the form of incorrect pronunciation, and the importance of pronunciation in communication can't be denied.
- It is necessary to minimize the interference/influence of the first language by using it as a support in the English classroom, and it can be done by giving inputs from the target language in a simple & graded manner and using the languages of learners.

Hence, it is clear that the wavelength of sound is NOT a concept from language education.

54(B). In this poem 'friction land' stands for a confused family.

It has been used for Raghu and his father as they always have differences and their views don't match.

Friction Land means disagreement between people or groups.

55(A). saw red: means to be or become extremely angry.

The poem refers that Raghu took advice from his father to go mountain climbing.

When his father refused him to go there, Raghu got **saw red** at this rejection.

Means Raghu become extremely angry with his father.

56(C). Different food habits is not a point of clash between Raghu and his father.

Raghu's father used to ask him to change his lifestyle.

He wanted him to be quiet. His father wanted him to change himself.

The interests of Raghu and his father were different.

Raghu loved mountain climbing, but his father forbade him to do it.

Raghu wanted to sing poetry for the band, but even his father did not like it. He wanted him to think about his career.

It was their age difference that they could not understand each other's feelings.

Thus, we can say is that the food differences between Raghu and his father were not the subject of conflict.

57(D). Line 6 "Am I the prefect at school? or the baby at home?' shows the dilemma faced by Raghu.

He doesn't know whether he is prefect at school or at home as a kid.

Because he feels that he is liked by everyone in the school for who he is.

But at home her father wants to change him.

He want him to stay clean by wearing good clothes, washing his hair and getting his hair cut.

58(D). We look at the lines:
abcc is the rhyme in 1st stanza.

In friction land there is a family, family - a
With some confusions as you will see. see - b
There is Raghu aged fifteen and others all grown, grown - c
'Please will someone let me ever be on my own!' own - c

59(C). Here, flabbergasted is used as an adjective.

flabbergasted means overwhelm with shock, surprise, or wonder.

Flabbergasted is used for Raghu's father when Raghu asked his father to join a band to sing poetry, his father went to flabbergasted.

Adjective: a class of words that modify nouns and pronouns, primarily by describing a particular quality of the word.

Here, flabbergasted tells more about Raghu's father.

60(C). While teaching, a teacher usually conducts such type of activity that compels the children to think, analyze, observe, experiment, etc.

Critical thinking can be developed by giving activities that involve brainstorming sessions by them, assigning a problem-solving task, and observing how they perform in it.

To enhance critical thinking among the learners the teacher should give situations and ask learners to discuss and solve them among the group.

This activity will compel the children to use their existing knowledge and previous experiences to critically think, compare and analyze the situations to solve them effectively.

Hence, it could be concluded that to enhance critical thinking among the learners the teacher should give situations and ask learners to discuss and solve them among the group.

61(C). The Cholas formed one of the three ruling families in Tamil- speaking South India during the first two centuries CE.

- The Cholas ruled for more than 1500 years, making them one of the longest-ruling families in human history.
- Rajaraja I is considered the most powerful Chola ruler who reigned from 985 CE to 1014 CE.
- The inscriptions of the Cholas who ruled in Tamil Nadu refer to more than 400 terms for different kinds of taxes.
- The most frequently mentioned tax is:
- vetti, and
- Kadamai
- Vetti was taken in the form of forced labour and not in cash.

Thus, we can say that the above statements are correct.

62(B). In the sixth century B.C. Suktimati was the capital of Chedi.

Chedi kingdom was one among the many kingdoms ruled during early periods by Paurava kings in the central and western India. Suktimati was the capital city of the Yaduvanshi Chedi Kingdom in India. It lay on the banks of the river Shuktimati flowing through Chedi. It was built by a Chedi king known as Uparichara vasu.

63(A). Taxila had great influence on Hindu culture and the Sanskrit language. It is perhaps best known for its association with Chanakya, also known as Kautilya, the strategist who guided Chandragupta Maurya and assisted in the founding of the Mauryan empire.

64(B). By the seventh century, there were big landlords or warrior chiefs in different regions of the subcontinent.

- Existing kings often acknowledged them as their subordinates or Samantas .
- They were expected to bring gifts for their kings or overlords, be present at their courts and provide them with military support.
- As Samantas gained power and wealth, they declared themselves to be Maha-Samanta, Maha-Mandaleshvara (the great lord of a "circle" or region), and so on.
- Sometimes they asserted their independence from their overlords.
- One such instance was that of the Rashtrakutas in the Deccan. Initially, they were subordinate to the Chalukyas of Karnataka.
- In the mid-eighth century, Dantidurga, a Rashtrakuta chief, overthrew his Chalukya overlord and performed a ritual called Hiranya-Garbha (literally, the golden womb).
- When this ritual was performed with the help of Brahmanas, it was thought to lead to the "rebirth" of the sacrificer as a Kshatriya, even if he was not one by birth.

Thus, we can say that both statements A) and B) are true, but A) has no relationship with B).

65(B). Sufism:

- The Sants had much in common with the Sufis, so much so that it is believed that they adopted many ideas of each other.
- Sufis were Muslim mystics .
- They rejected outward religiosity and emphasized love and devotion to God and compassion towards all fellow human beings.
- The Sufis often rejected the elaborate rituals and codes of behavior demanded by Muslim religious scholars.
- They sought union with God much as a lover seeks his beloved with a disregard for the world.
- Like the saint-poets, the Sufis too composed poems expressing their feelings, and a rich literature in prose, including anecdotes and fables, developed around them.

- Among the great Sufis of Central Asia were Ghazzali, Rumi, and Sadi .
- Like the Nathpanthis, Siddhas, and Yogis, the Sufis too believed that the heart can be trained to look at the world in a different way.
- They developed elaborate methods of training using zikr (chanting of a name or sacred formula), contemplation, sama (singing), raqs (dancing), discussion of parables, breath control, etc. under the guidance of a master or Pir.
- Thus emerged the Silsilas, a genealogy of Sufi teachers, each following a slightly different method (tariqa) of instruction and ritual practice.

Thus, we can say that statements A, B, and C are true regarding Sufis.

66(C). The Mughals were descendants of two lineages:

- From their mother's side, they were descendants of Genghiz Khan, the Mongol ruler.
- From their father's side, they were successors of Timur, the ruler of Iran, Iraq, and modern-day Turkey.
- The Mughals did not like to be called Mughal or Mongols as Genghiz Khan was associated with the massacre of people.
- However, they were proud of their Timurid ancestry because Delhi was captured by their ancestor in 1398.

Hence, A) is true, but B) is false.

67(A). From the early nineteenth century, we find debates and discussions about social customs and practices taking on a new character.

- One important reason for this was the development of new forms of communication.
- For the first time, books, newspapers, magazines, leaflets, and pamphlets were printed.
- Therefore ordinary people could read these, and many of them could also write and express their ideas in their own languages.
- By the second half of the nineteenth century, the movement in favor of widow remarriage spread to other parts of the country. Social reformers supported widow remarriage are as follows:
  ◦ Famous reformers, Ishwar Chandra Vidyasagar , used the ancient texts to suggest that widows could remarry .
    ▪ His suggestion was adopted by British officials, and a law was passed in 1856 permitting widow remarriage.
    ▪ Those who were against the remarriage of widows opposed Vidyasagar and even boycotted him.
  ◦ In the Telugu-speaking areas of the Madras Presidency, Veerasalingam Pantulu formed an association for widow remarriage.
  ◦ Around the same time, young intellectuals and reformers in Bombay pledged themselves to work for the same cause.
  ◦ In the north, Swami Dayanand Saraswati , who founded the reform association called Arya Samaj, also supported widow remarriage .

Thus, we can conclude that Ishwar Chandra Vidyasagar, Veerasalingam Pantulu, and Swami Dayanand Saraswati were social reformers who supported widow remarriage.

68(B). Arya Samaj is a monotheistic Indian Hindu reform movement that promotes values and practices based on the belief in the infallible authority of the Vedas. Arya Samaj was founded by Swami Dayananda Saraswati in 1875 in Bombay. There are 10 principles related to Arya Samaj. The famous freedom fighter Lala Lajpat Rai was his disciple. Swami Dayananda Saraswati is known as the 'Grandfather of Indian Nation'.

69(C). Shifting cultivation is practiced in the thickly forested areas of Amazon basin, tropical Africa, parts of Southeast Asia and Northeastern India.

THese are the areas of heavy rainfall and quick regeneration of vegetation.

A plot of land is cleared by felling the trees and burning them.

The ashes are then mixed with the soil and crops like maize, yam, potatoes, and cassava is grown.

After soil loses its fertility, it is abandoned and the cultivator moves to a new plot.

It is also known as 'slash and burn' agriculture.

It is called by different names in different areas:

- Milpa in Central America and Mexico
- Jhumming in India
- Roca in Brazil
- Ladang in Malaysia

Thus, we can say that shifting cultivation is called Milpa in Central America and Mexico and Jhumming in India.

70(D). Hydroelectric energy is also called hydroelectric power or hydroelectricity.

- It is a form of energy that harnesses the power of water in motion—such as water flowing over a waterfall—to generate electricity.
- People have used this force for millennia.
- Norway was the first country to develop hydroelectricity. Hydroelectricity is the process of production of electricity using hydropower.
- China produces the most electricity from hydroelectric power, some 856.4 billion kilowatt-hours a year – more than double the amount produced by Brazil, i n second place.

- One-fourth of the world's electricity is produced by hydel power.

Hence, we can conclude that statements A, B, and D are correct.

71(C). Tropical Evergreen Forest is also called tropical rainforests.

- These thick forests occur in the regions near the equator and close to the tropics.
- These regions are hot and receive heavy rainfall throughout the year.
- As there is no particular dry season, the trees do not shed their leaves altogether. This is the reason they are called evergreen.
- The thick canopies of the closely spaced trees do not allow the sunlight to penetrate inside the forest even during the daytime.
- Hardwood trees like rosewood, ebony, and mahogany are common here.
- Tropical rainforests are often called the "lungs of the planet" because they generally draw in carbon dioxide and breathe out oxygen .
- But the amount of carbon dioxide they absorb or produce varies hugely with year-to-year variations in the climate.

Thus, we can conclude that both statements A and B are true .

72(A). Nashik district, Maharashtra is known as the Grape Capital of India as it contributes more than half of the total grape export in the country.

- Grape is grown from temperate to warm regions; however, a hot and dry climate is ideal. Indian grapes come in varied characteristics namely colored, white, seeded, unseeded, large, and small berries.
- Maharashtra ranks first in terms of production accounting for more than 81.22 % of total production and the highest productivity in the country.
- Nashik district is the 3rd largest district in Maharashtra in terms of population of 61,09,052 and area occupying an area of 15,582 square kilometers in the north Maharashtra region.

73(A). The maximum depth of Lithosphere is found in the Pacific Ocean. The Mariana Trench is the deepest part of the ocean and the deepest location on Earth about 11,035 meters (36,201 feet) deep. The deepest point of Mariana Trench is Challenger Deep. It is located in the South Pacific Ocean and so the maximum depth of Lithosphere is found in the Pacific Ocean.

74(A). Iceland's capital, Reykjavík, is the world's northernmost capital city of any sovereign state. According to tradition, Reykjavík ("Bay of Smokes") was founded in 874 by the Norseman Ingolfur Arnarson.

75(D). During an earthquake, surface waves cause the most damage. Unlike other seismic waves that move deep inside the

Earth, surface waves move along just under the surface of the Earth like waves in water. Surface waves are the slowest seismic waves and are the final waves to hit an area after an earthquake.

Surface waves move in last. Their slow roll just under the surface provides the greatest risk for damage to man-made structures and changes to natural landforms.

76(A). Earthquakes can cause Landslide, Tsunami and Floods.

- Earthquakes are able to initiate landslides over mountainous regions or wet regions.
- If the earthquakes are under the sea bed, this sudden shake can create extreme pressure outwards and might take a shape of a Tsunami.
- Sometimes the earthquakes can break the dams and overflows of water can create the situation of floods.

77(C). Ocean currents are streams of water flowing constantly on the ocean surface in definite directions.

Ocean currents are the continuous, predictable, directional movement of seawater.

It is a massive movement of ocean water that is caused and influenced by various forces.

They are like river flows in oceans.

Ocean currents are influenced by two types of forces namely:

primary forces that initiate the movement of water

secondary forces that influence the currents to flow.

Ocean currents can be classified based on temperature as cold currents and warm currents.

Cold currents:

Cold currents bring cold water into warm water areas.

These currents are usually found on the west coast of the continents in the low and middle latitudes (true in both hemispheres) and on the east coast in the higher latitudes in the Northern Hemisphere.

Examples: Labrador Current

Warm currents:

Warm currents bring warm water into cold water areas and are usually observed on the east coast of continents in the low and middle latitudes (true in both hemispheres).

In the northern hemisphere, they are found on the west coasts of continents in high latitudes.

Examples: Brazil Current, Gulf Stream, and Alaska Current

78(A). Samudragupta (335-375 AD) of the Gupta dynasty is known as the Napoleon of India. Historian A V Smith called him so because of his great military conquests known from the 'Prayag Prashati' written by his courtier and poet

Harisena, who also describes him as the hero of a hundred battles.

79(A). Hon'ble Shri Hriday Narayan Dixit is the Speaker of the Legislative Assembly since 30 March 2017. He is presently representing Bhagwantnagar in the Unnao district. He is a sophisticated writer and columnist for various newspapers and magazines.

80(D). The tenure of the members of the Uttar Pradesh Legislative Council is 6 years. In some states of India, there is an Upper House of Representatives i.e. Legislative Council. Till now 6 states have had Legislative Council. The minimum age to become a member of the Legislative Council is 30 years.

In the Indian Constitution, the states have been allowed to establish a Legislative Council (optional) in the form of an upper house under the state legislature, keeping in mind the geographical location, population, and other aspects of the state. While the parties of the Legislative Council consider it important to keep control over the proceedings of the Legislative Assembly and the autocracy of the ruling party, at times questions arise on its role and necessity by telling this House of the State Legislature the reason for the misuse of time and money. The functioning of the State Legislative Assembly is similar to that of the Rajya Sabha in many respects and the tenure of its members is of 6 years like that of the Rajya Sabha members.

81(B). The Right to Life and Personal Liberty is assured by the Indian Constitution under Article 21.

According to Article 21 - "Protection of Life and Personal Liberty: No person shall be deprived of his life or personal liberty except according to procedure established by law".

This fundamental right is available to every person, citizens and foreigners alike.

Article 21 provides two rights:

Right to life

Right to personal liberty

The fundamental right provided by Article 21 is one of the most important rights that the Constitution guarantees.

The Supreme Court of India has described this right as the 'heart of fundamental rights'.

The Court gave a list of rights that Article 21 covers based on earlier judgments. Some of them are:

82(A). Children's rights are economic, social and cultural rights, such as the right to education, the right to a decent standard of living, the right to health, etc. There are many instances in our country when the rights of children are violated.

Statement A : Child marriage arranged by parents.

Child marriage arranged by parents is a

violation of human rights as well as child rights.

The Prohibition of Child Marriage Act, 2006, presently sets the marriageable age to be 21 and 18 for boys and girls respectively.

Prohibition of Child Marriage (Amendment) Bill, 2021

The bill to raise the age of marriage from 18 to 21 years for women, was introduced by the Union Minister for Women and Child Development (MWCD), Smriti Irani, and was sent to the parliamentary standing committee for detailed scrutiny. This bill will override all the existing laws if passed.

83(B). The Zamindari system was first abolished from the point of view of land reform. The Zamindari system was a politico-social system prevalent in India during the Mughal period and the British period, in which the land was owned by someone else (zamindar) who collected taxes from the cultivators and not the workers on it. This practice ended after India became independent.

84(C). Rituals are the practices and ceremonies followed by the rural society. Rituals are a feature of all known human societies. They include not only the worship rites and sacraments of organized religions and cults, but also rites of passage, atonement and purification rites, oaths of allegiance, dedication ceremonies, coronations and presidential inaugurations, marriages, funerals and more.

85(A). In Subhash Kumar vs the State of Bihar, the Supreme Court held that the right to life is a fundamental right under Article 21.

It includes the right to the enjoyment of a pollution-free environment for full enjoyment of life.

Article 21 of the constitution guarantees the life and personal liberty of all persons.

It guarantees the right of persons to live with human dignity.

In this case, the petitioner filed public interest litigation against two iron and steel companies because they created health risks to the public by dumping waste from their factories into nearby Bokaro river.

The petitioner also claimed that the State Pollution Control Board had failed to take appropriate measures for preventing this pollution.

86(B). To provide opportunities for education to the child or as the case may be, ward between the age of six and fourteen years is a fundamental Duty under Indian Constitution.

Eleven Fundamental duties of the citizens towards the state have emerged in Article 51–A in Part-IV A of the Indian Constitution. It shall be a duty of every citizen of India who is a parent or guardian to provide education opportunities to his child or ward between the age of 6 and 14 years added by the 86th Constitution Amendment Act. Fundamental duties are mentioned in Part IV-A of the constitution.

87(C). Article 15 provides that the State shall not discriminate against any citizen on grounds only of religion, race, caste, sex, or place of birth.

The second provision of Article 15 says that no citizen shall be subjected to any disability, liability, restriction, or condition on grounds only of religion, race, caste, sex, or place of birth with regard to

(a) access to shops, public restaurants, hotels and places of public entertainment or

(b) the use of wells, tanks, bathing ghats, road and places of public resort maintained wholly or partly by State funds or dedicated to the use of the general public.

88(D). According to Article 21 of the constitution, No person shall be deprived of his life or personal liberty except according to the procedure established by law. This right is available for citizens as well as aliens. This Article includes the right to live with human dignity. It covers the protection against the arbitrary executive and legislative action. It is the part of the basic feature of the Constitution. It can be taken away according to the procedure which is established by law.

89(C). Citizenship in India is not a fundamental right and is the Part II of the Constitution (Article 5–11).

- Part III deals with the fundamental rights in the Indian Constitution.
- Right to Freedom comes under Article 19 of the Indian Constitution.
- Right against Exploitation comes under Article 23–24 of the Indian Constitution.
- Right to Equality comes under Article 14–18 of the Indian Constitution.

90(A). Our Indian Constitution has adopted the constitutional procedure of the United Kingdom (UK).

The system of Prime Minister, Parliament, Cabinet and its house, Council of Ministers were copied from the United Kingdom's Constitution by changing a bit in their selection procedure and tenure.

Hence assertion (A) is true.

The Upper House is often called the House of Review as it scrutinizes the actions and decisions of the Executive Government, holding them to account.

The Lower House initiates and approves money bills.

The Lower House don't have any judicial power.

Hence Reason (R) is not true.

91(C). In the context of social development Adolescence stages is characterized by 'Intense self Awareness'.

Adolescence:

- Adolescence is the transitional stage from childhood to adulthood that occurs between ages 13 and 19.
- The physical and psychological changes that take place in adolescence often start earlier, during the preteen or "tween" years: between ages 9 and 12.
- Self-awareness especially during the teenage phase has the power to help prepare young minds to face life ahead.
- Friendships, cliques, and crowds become increasingly central contexts for adolescent socialization.
- As adolescents work to form their identities, they pull away from their parents, and the peer group becomes very important. Despite spending less time with their parents, most teens report positive feelings toward them.

92(C). A project is a whole-hearted purposeful activity proceeding in a social environment. In the project method, teaching and learning are considered from the child's point of view and in this method knowledge and skills are learned by pupils through practical handling of problems in their natural setting.

Steps in a Project:-

1. Choosing:- The students need to choose the project themselves to satisfy their definite needs or purposes. There should not be any kind of hurry in selecting a project by the students. Sufficient time should be spent on the discussion of alternative situations selected by the students.

2. Planning:- Planning is concerned with working out detailed procedures for doing the project. Planning should be done by the students under the guidance of a teacher. The teacher can provide the guidelines to the students. The plan proposed by the students needs to be presented, discussed, and finalized in the classroom.

3. Execution:- This is a very important and interesting step of project teaching as it provides opportunities for the students to do the activities in which they are interested and capable and learn various usefull experiences.

4. Follow up: - It is very important to take a follow-up of the project.

5. Evaluation:- Evaluation of the whole project work experience needs to be done against present standards. The standards should be worked out by the teacher along with the students.

6. Recording: -It is very important and essential to maintaining a complete record of project work from its proposal to completion.

93(B). Evaluation is used for important purposes in society. Therefore, it must be valid and reliable. For this, the social studies teacher must know the various aspects of evaluation. Such knowledge will enable him to decide what to evaluate, when to evaluate and how to evaluate students' performance in social studies.

- Evaluation has become an integral part of the educational process in which social studies is an important aspect at the school stage.

Comprehensive process: The term 'comprehensive' implies that evaluation of learners' performance is carried out in both scholastic and co-scholastic areas.

Formative process:- When the purpose of the evaluation is to direct both the student and the teacher for specific learning to form or develop concepts, it is called formative evaluation. It is always for covering small content, maybe a concept, a small portion of a unit, or a unit.

Summative process:- The goal of summative assessment or process is to evaluate student learning at the end of an instructional unit by comparing it against some standard or benchmark.

Hence, we can conclude that when a teacher evaluates students unit-wise periodically and conducts at the end of the course a comprehensive test, then it is called a continuous process.

94(D). Evaluation is the process of collecting information and then to make a decision. It is nothing but gathering data and evidences of students' progress and achievements. Not only it is the formal examination, but also it involves analyzing, characterizing students' learning. Evaluation can be done in the following ways:

- Essay Type Test: In this, the answers are usually more than 100 words. It lets students think broadly and independently. Students are asked to write answers in detail. Students are required analytical skills for writing such questions.
- Objective Type Test: In this, along with questions, multiple choices are given to choose from. But in this, one does not have the freedom to provide for systematic organisation and expression of thought .
- Short Answer Type Test: It requires thinking skills though, yet students are not required to think broadly.
- Very Short Answer Type Test: Since its length is the shortest, it requires only facts related to the question.

Hence, we conclude that the above drawback is of Objective Type Test.

95(D). Sociology is the study of human social relationships and institutions. Sociologists emphasize the careful gathering and analysis of evidence about social life to develop and enrich our understanding of key social processes. Hence, the best method of teaching Sociology is Field visit method.

Co-curricular activities in Social Science are usually organized outside the classroom to provide opportunities for students to develop their special talents and to creatively express themselves through various forms. For example, participation in social science activities, field visits , involvement in science dramas, social welfare activities, etc.

Field visits for students are like an educational experience that they never could have had in the classroom. Field visits are considered fun, but the children learn as well, whether they realize it or not because they require significant planning and coordination for teachers and administrators to make a great combination of learning and fun together.

96(B). Geography concerns the study of people and places. It involves the study of humans and how they adjust to their environment. Thus, this subject deals with an in-depth study of the way human beings relate to their environment as well as how they make use of it. At the school level, therefore, students learn about the man and his environment of which encompasses a mass of information.

It is difficult to make understand the geographical concepts with the help of mere verbal description but it is easier to understand than through the media of teaching materials.

Some of the teaching materials are as follows:

* Maps:
  * Maps are useful tools in the teaching and learning of Geography.
  * They are required in the study of most topics including position, relief, climate, natural vegetation, minerals, population distribution, towns, industries, and communications.
* Flashcards: These are often used as a learning drill to aid memorization. Moreover, it appeals to visual learners and can be used to stimulate kinaesthetic learners too. They are a great way to introduce learners to new vocabulary. Teachers can use them in the classroom to practice and revise vocabulary. These are a set of cards on which are items are written to be studied.
* Calendar: It shows the dates, days, and months of one year. This can be used for primary school learners. It is used to teach time.
* Barometer: It is an instrument used to measure air pressure. Hence, it can be used to teach the concept of air pressure.

Therefore, Maps are the most useful teaching material for Geography.

97(D). You, as a teacher, need to bring changes in pedagogical practices by giving primacy to the children, by enabling them to express their voices, by nurturing their curiosity, by providing them opportunity to pursue investigations, and by sharing and integrating their experiences with school knowledge- rather than emphasizing on their ability to reproduce textual knowledge.

* You must note that children learn social sciences in varieties of ways through experience, making and doing things, experimentation, reading, discussion, asking questions, listening, thinking, reflecting and expressing their voices.
* They require opportunities of all these kinds in the course of classroom transaction. You must allow children to ask questions that require them to relate what they are learning in social science classrooms to things happening outside.
* You need to encourage children to answer to the questions in social sciences in their own words and from their own experiences, make an attempt to develop multiple perspectives upon the social science concepts and issues. This will foster creative and critical thinking among them.
* You need to engage your children in active engagement during curriculum transaction through inquiry, exploration, questioning, debate, application and reflection, leading to theory building and the creation of new ideas/ propositions.

Thus from the above-mentioned points it is clear that all of the above is true.

98(D). A project is an educational method where students working individually or in small groups analyze and develop "real-life" problem or tackle a present-day theme within a preset time limit, working independently and with the division of tasks clearly defined.

* The project method is based on the principles of active learning. The student gets totally involved in the activity which helps in enhancing his/her knowledge, understanding and skills in real-life situation and ultimately in developing a holistic personality. For example, to tell them to find out the people belonging to different cultural, caste, and religious groups who live there.
* The student gets acquainted with the types of work which he/she is expected to perform in future. Thus, the project method helps the student in his/her preparation for a future life.
* The student gets the scope to imbibe several social qualities like cooperation, and team-work, group affinity, and sacrifice through project work.

Hence, we conclude that both statements are correct about project method of teaching.

99(C). Different teaching methods have been propounded by educational thinkers to understand and practice the art of teaching. Teaching method changes with context, subject, and children . Gifted children are often driven by curiosity. They may show characteristics to analyze their own thought process and practice metacognition . Therefore, teaching methods must be in accordance with the thought process of gifted children.

To teach gifted children teachers should employ the method which:

* Brings forth children as the discoverer of the knowledge and develops a heuristic or scientific attitude .
* Help children reach well thought out a solution by analysis of the problem.
* Allow learners to collect, interpret and assess information using abstraction .
* Motivate learners to think openly and non-dogmatically i.e., children should be able to recognize their own presuppositions and consequences.

Hence, it could be concluded that teaching gifted children heuristic, Inductive and analytical method is more appropriate.

100(B). In the teaching-learning process, visually challenged learners suffer from an issue with sight or vision but when they are facilitated with the right training and tools , they develop a good literacy ability.

Adaptions that a social science teacher should make while engaging with visually challenged learners include:

* providing learning with the help of the auditory system.
* giving verbal clues to create opportunities to imagine.
* introducing tactile materials during classroom discussions.
* speaking clearly and loudly with appropriate pauses and reiterations.
* using the braille system as it's raised dots help in studying words through the pattern.

Hence, from the above-mentioned points, it becomes clear that use a variety of visually appealing worksheets is not appropriate for learners who are visually challenged.

101(C). Constructivist teaching, the process of gaining knowledge is viewed as being just as important as the product. Thus, assessment is based not only on tests, but also on observation of the student, the student's work, and the student's points of view. Some assessment strategies include-

* Oral discussions- The teacher presents students with a "focus" question and allows an open discussion on the topic.
* Mind Mapping - In this activity, students list and categorize the concepts and ideas relating to a topic.
* Hands-on activities -These encourage students to manipulate their environments or a particular learning tool. Teachers can use a checklist and observation to assess student success with a particular material.
  * When in a constructivist discussion

on historical monuments, a teacher asked students to identify a local monument and narration of stories around it. It will help the learners to construct their own knowledge through observation and discussion. Thus from the above-mentioned points, it is clear that most appropriate for a constructivist discussion on historical monuments is to tell students identifying a local monument and narration of stories around it.

102(C). A teacher teaching Social Sciences has the responsibility of making the class interesting. This is possible when the learners participate actively in the teaching-learning process. General features which are expected to be in a social sciences class are discussed below:

- Creating space for exploration into social issues: One of the objectives of teaching social sciences is to make the children sensitive to the problems and challenges of the society. Unless the teacher relates the lesson to local issues, children may not understand the issues of their society.
- Use of multilingualism: In an ordinary sense, using more than two languages is known as multilingualism. In a school system, in a country like ours, where we have thousands of dialects, there are chances of mother tongue of the child being different from the language used for instruction
- Respect for multiple views: India is a democratic country and citizens have the freedom to express their views. It becomes the duty of the listeners to respect their views
- Using Audio-Visual Materials: All of us know that what we see and experience remains for a longer time in our memory than what we hear. This holds good to learning too.

103(C). Social Science as a discipline has the unique capability of being able to look at both developmental and normative issues of the society. It includes disciplines of History, Geography, Political Science, Economics, and Sociology.

Teaching and Learning Resources in Geography:

According to NCF-2005, "Teaching should utilize greater resources of audio-visual materials, including photographs, charts and maps and replicas of archaeological materials."

- In the teaching-learning process of geography, we tend to use various objects, materials, people, and buildings to transact the contents. Common learning resources such as maps, globes, blackboard (chalkboard), charts, models, video film, radio, etc.
- Maps/Replicas help students learn faster, remember for a longer time, and

gain more accurate information.
- Learning resources help learners achieve learning objectives more effectively and efficiently.
- A good geographical inquiry usually involves the use and analysis of a rich variety of resources including worksheets, textbooks, maps, models, computer software, interactive games, internet, newspaper resources, weather instruments, specific items (rock samples and tools), and many others.
- Learning resources help in clarifying, interpreting, and appreciating concepts; establishing and correlating accuracy.
- They provide clarity, precision, and accuracy in processing information.

Therefore, the models/replicas of physical features are most suitable for teaching Geography .

104(A). Social sciences are the body of knowledge that is concerned with human affairs in the spectrum of broad socio-cultural system. Social sciences constitute an important component of the high school/higher education curriculum. The different social science subjects like history, political science, anthropology, philosophy, economics, etc. have independent status in high school/university education.

Nature of Social Sciences:

- Social sciences deal with different aspects of human society and interpersonal relationships among people in society. This happens because social sciences deal with society and social issues like marriage, Caste, family etc . of which most people are aware.
- Social science studies are well planned, systematic and based on specialized knowledge of its different components.
- Study of Social Science said to be ' scientific ' because we need to understand that while scientific facts are universal i.e., they remain applicable in different societies and in different periods of time , social facts are relevant within specific social contexts i.e., they often vary from one society to another.
- Social science is defined as a body of comprises systematically acquired and verified knowledge of facts and truths of all systematised knowledge (subjects, disciplines) that show the operations of general laws and others appropriate to them.

Thus from above-mentioned points, it is clear that the study of Social Science is 'scientific' because it comprises Systematically acquired verified knowledge.

105(D). The social sciences are academic disciplines concerned with the study of the social life of human groups and individuals including anthropology, economics, geography, history, political science, psychology, social studies, and sociology

- Social Studies is the study of relations and interrelations, historical, geographical, and social.
- It establishes the relationship between present and past, local and distant, and personal and national lives, and also with the lives and cultures of other men and women in different parts of the world.
- Social science helps to initiate the learner into a study of her/ his own region, state, and country in the global context.
- Social Science lays the foundation for an analytical and creative mindset.
- Social Science as a discipline has the unique capability of being able to look at both developmental and normative issues of the society.
- Social Science is concerned with the diverse concerns of society.
- Social science is concerned with both objective and subjective knowledge.
- Social Science is characterized by heterogeneity, mobility, and diversity in activities and values.

Hence, we can conclude that Social Science lays the foundation for an analytical and creative mindset is true about Social Science.

106(D). Empirical Enquiry: Empirical scientific research is essentially a way of looking at things. It can be thought of as a method of approaching the empirical world. Science consists of theory and facts. A fact is an empirically verifiable observation and a theory tries to find the relationship between facts. The facts of science are the product of observations.

Empirical studies include the whole gamut of research tools:

- observation – both participant and non-participant
- formal interviews with random samples
- semistructured and unstructured and in-depth interviewing
- key informant testimonies
- analysis of personal and institutional documents
- mass media analysis
- archive searching
- examination of official statistics; and reviews of published literature

Furthermore, empirical social research also uses a wide variety of analytical techniques, ethnographic interpretation, historical reconstruction, action research, multivariate analysis, structuralist deconstruction and semiological analysis.

Thus from the above-mentioned points, it is clear that empirical studies include all of the above.

107(D). The resources may be used by teachers, students or both during instruction so as to maximise the attainment of learning objectives . In this section, we will be acquainting you with some specific learning resources for geography. We will also facilitate you with their conceptual understanding, how to use these learning resources and why to use these learning resources.

A good geographical enquiry usually involves the use and analysis of a rich variety of resources including worksheets, textbooks, maps, models, computer software, interactive games, internet, newspaper resources, weather instruments, specific items (rock samples and tools) and many others.

Thus from the above-mentioned points, it is clear that all of the above is true.

108(C). Critical Thinking is the ability to apply reasoning and logic to new or unfamiliar situations, ideas, and opinions. It refers to the process of judging or analyzing facts, events, etc.
- Encourage students to answer each other for questions related to textbook topics.
- Provide more than one explanation for the same phenomena or event.
- These activities symbolize critical thinking among students as while doing these activities students try to think in multiple ways and provide the solution by analyzing it.

Thus, it is concluded that A and B only is the correct answer.

109(C). To be critical means to be able to perceive and understand any issues effectively to come up with the best possible inference.

Students should Learn to be Critical:-
- to approach an issue with an open-ended mind.
- to look at any issues from different points of view.
- to understand how issues are related to their own lives.
- to make logical connections between ideas by thinking rationally.
- to increase their own insight into the functioning of several things.
- to assess information and draw conclusions from the given raw data.

Hence, from the above-mentioned points, it becomes clear that students should learn to be critical to understanding how issues are related to their own lives.

110(D). Efficient teaching methods are the essential tools that can help teachers to make the students achieve success in the classroom. The methods used by a teacher will depend on the skills or information which the teacher wants to convey to the students.
- A project refers to a series of task that needs to be done by a group of students in order to achieve a particular goal.

During group projects the role of the teacher is to:-
- The teacher does not dictate or command rather the role of the teacher is that of a guide and a philosopher.
- The teacher encourages the students to work cooperatively and evaluates the group's progress.
- The teacher facilitates the groups throughout the process.
- The teacher creates a democratic atmosphere where the students can express themselves freely without fear.

Thus, it is concluded that Only C and D options are correct.

111(B). Panini was a legendary Indian grammarian and scholar who prepared a grammar for Sanskrit.

He was an expert in language and grammar and authored one of the greatest works on grammar called Ashtadhyayi.

He was a revered scholar in ancient India who was considered as the "Father of Linguistics" who gave a detailed scientific theory of phonetics, morphology and phonology.

He arranged the vowels and the consonants in a special order, and then used these to create formulae like those found in Algebra. He used these to write down the rules of the language in short formulae (around 3000 of them).

112(C). In Jainism, moksha is the highest and the noblest objective that a soul should strive to achieve. In fact, it is the only objective that a person should have; other objectives are contrary to the true nature of soul. With the right view, knowledge and efforts all souls can attain this state. That is why Jainism is also known as " attainment of salvation".

113(C). Bengal Partition:
- In 1905 Viceroy Curzon partitioned Bengal .
- At that time Bengal was the biggest province of British India and included Bihar and parts of Orissa.
- The British argued for dividing Bengal for reasons of administrative convenience .
  ◦ But what did "administrative convenience" mean? Whose "convenience" did it represent? Clearly, it was closely tied to the interests of British officials and businessmen .
  ◦ Even so, instead of removing the non-Bengali areas from the province, the government separated East Bengal and merged it with Assam.
- Perhaps the main British motives were to curtail the influence of Bengali politicians and to split the Bengali people.
- The partition of Bengal infuriated people all over India .
- All sections of the Congress – the Moderates and the Radicals , as they may be called – opposed it .

- Large public meetings and demonstrations were organized and novel methods of mass protest developed.
- The struggle that unfolded came to be known as the Swadeshi movement, strongest in Bengal but with echoes elsewhere too – in deltaic Andhra for instance, it was known as the Vandemataram Movement.

From the above, we can say that the statement statements A and B are true, but C is false.

114(C). Mughal architecture flourished in northern and central India under the patronage of the Mughal emperors from the mid-16th to the late 17th century.
- The Mughal period marked a striking revival of Islamic architecture in northern India.
- Under the patronage of the Mughal emperors, Persian, Indian, and various provincial styles were fused to produce works of unusual quality and refinement.
- Under the Mughals, architecture became more complex.
- Babur, Humayun, Akbar, Jahangir, and especially Shah Jahan were personally interested in literature, art and architecture.
- The buildings were mostly constructed with red sandstone and white marble.
- There were several important architectural innovations during Akbar's reign.
- The central towering dome and the tall gateway (pishtaq) became important aspects of Mughal architecture, first visible in Humayun's tomb.
- It was during Shah Jahan's reign that the different elements of Mughal architecture were fused together in a grand harmonious synthesis.
- His reign witnessed a huge amount of construction activity especially in Agra and Delhi.

115(A). Manmohan Singh served as the finance minister during the 1991 economic reforms.
- He was the finance minister in the PV Narasimha Rao government.
- Manmohan Singh is the 13th Prime Minister of India (2004 to 2014).
- He is the first Prime Minister from the Sikh community.
- First Prime Minister from the minority community.
- Only governor of RBI who became the prime minister of India.
- He was the deputy chairman of the planning commission during the period 1985 to 1987.
- He is the first prime minister to visit the Siachin glacier.
- Notable works: Changing India, The Quest for Equity in Development.

116(D). Indian economy experienced an economic crisis in 1991.
- The foreign currency assets declined to such an extent that it was barely enough to finance two weeks of imports.
- The annual rate of inflation reached 16.7% in August 1991.
- The government expenditure was greater than its revenue due to defence expenditure, subsidies, interest on loans, etc.
- The positive effects of the socialistic pattern of society were on the verge of decline.

On this ground, it was necessary to bring new changes to the economy. Hence, the Government of India adopted a New Economic Policy (NEP) in 1991.

It is also known as LPG i.e. Liberalization, Privatization and Globalization.

The process of new economic policy which started in 1985 got momentum in 1991.

117(D). Indira Gandhi Matritva Sahyog Yojana (IGMSY) was started on 19 November 2020 in Udaipur, Pratapgath, Banswara, and Dungarpur and Sahariya dominated Baran district.

This scheme fulfills the goal of 'Suposhit Rajasthan Vision-2022'. In this scheme, beneficiaries will receive Rs.6000 in a phased manner on the birth of the second child in these districts. The main objective of this scheme is to reduce the incidence of low birth weight and debility at birth.

118(B). The Department of Social Justice and Empowerment had launched the scheme "SMILE: Support for Marginalised Individuals for Livelihood and Enterprise" on 12 February 2022.

There are 2 sub-schemes under this - 'Central Sector Scheme for Comprehensive Rehabilitation for Welfare of Transgender Persons' and 'Central Sector Scheme for Comprehensive Rehabilitation of persons engaged in the act of Begging'. This umbrella scheme is designed to provide welfare measures to the Transgender community and the people engaged in the act of begging.

119(C). The population is a dynamic phenomenon.

Population density is the number of people living in a unit area of the earth's surface.

It is normally expressed as per square km.

The average density of population in India is 382 persons per square km.

The average density of population in the whole world is 51 persons per square km.

South-Central Asia has the highest density of population followed by East and South East Asia.

Thus, we can say that the average density of population in India is 382 persons per square km.

120(D). Merchants and migrants first brought the teachings of the holy Quran to India in the seventh century.
- Muslims regard Quran as their holy book and accept the sovereignty of one god, Allah.
- Ulama were the learned tehologians and jurists.
- Ulama are literally the "learned ones".
- They are the guardians, transmitters, interpreters of religious knowledge in Islam, including Islamic doctrine and law.

Sunni Muslim is the largest branch of Islam.
- Sunni Muslims who accepted the authority of the early leaders (Khalifas) of the community.

Thus, we can say that the above statements are correct.

Child Development and Pedagogy

1. **By motor development we mean the development of in the use of arms and legs' by:**
   (a) Mind and Spirit
   (b) Learning and Education
   (c) Training and Learning
   (d) Strength and speed

2. **Which of the principles of development is defined by the below given example?**
   Sufi has appropriate weight and height for her age. She also has a well-developed language ability that enables her to communicate with everyone. She is loved by all and has positive self-esteem.
   (a) Development involves change.
   (b) Development follows a fixed pattern/sequence.
   (c) Development proceeds from general to specific.
   (d) Development is correlated.

3. **Which of the following is not true regarding heredity and environment?**
   (a) Influence personality
   (b) Influence physical and intellectual development
   (c) Influence health
   (d) Influence the economy

4. **Schools teach new behaviours and rules to children and expect them to act accordingly. The school is acting as an agency of _____ socialisation.**
   (a) primary   (b) constructive
   (c) secondary   (d) analytic

5. **"At a particular stage children begin to use primitive reasoning and want to know the answer to all sorts of questions." Piaget called this "intuitive". As per Piaget, which of the following stage, he means?**
   (a) Concrete operation
   (b) Pre-operation
   (c) Formal operation
   (d) None of these

6. **Lawrence Kohlberg's theory of moral reasoning has been criticized on several counts. Which of the following statements is correct in the context of this criticism?**
   (a) Kohlberg has based his study primarily on a male sample.
   (b) Kohlberg has not given typical responses to each stage of moral reasoning.
   (c) Kohlberg has duplicated Piaget's methods of arriving at his theoretical framework.
   (d) Kohlberg's theory does not focus on children's responses.

7. **Curricular goals in progressive education emphasize:**
   (a) Rote-memorisation
   (b) Conformity to authority
   (c) Critical thinking
   (d) Recall and drill

8. **Howard Gardner's multiple intelligences theory impacts classroom today in the schools based upon its reflection of which current classroom strategy?**
   (a) Differentiated instruction
   (b) Inclusive Education
   (c) Socialization
   (d) Discovery Learning

9. **A child has ability to understand and effectively interact with others. He is showing which type of intelligence?**
   (a) Verbal
   (b) Mathematical
   (c) Interpersonal
   (d) Intrapersonal

10. **In _____ thinking, a child do simplification/ generalization on the one hand and truth and accuracy on the other.**
    (a) Reflective   (b) Critical
    (c) Aesthetic   (d) Creative

11. **Children acquire gender roles through all of the following, except:**
    (a) Media   (b) Socialization
    (c) Culture   (d) Tutoring

12. **A teacher should _______ if learners display individual differences.**
    (a) Enforce strict discipline in the class
    (b) Increase the number of tests / examinations
    (c) Provide a variety of learning experience
    (d) Provide a variety of learning materials

13. **Which one of the following would be the most effective way of conducting an assessment?**
    (a) Assessment is an inbuilt process in teaching-learning
    (b) Assessment should be done twice in an academic session at the beginning and at the end
    (c) Assessment should be done by an external agency and not by the teacher
    (d) Assessment should be at the end of the session

14. **A teacher asks his/her students to draw a concept map to reflect their comprehension of a topic. He/She is:**
    (a) Jogging the memory of the students
    (b) Conducting formative assessment
    (c) Testing the ability of the students to summarise the main points
    (d) Trying to develop rubrics to evaluate the achievement of the students

15. **In progressive-education children are seen as:**
    (a) Passive imitators
    (b) Active explorers
    (c) Blank slates
    (d) Miniature adults

16. **What instructional adaptations should a teacher make while working with students that are 'Visually Challenged'?**
    (a) Use a variety of visual presentations.
    (b) Orient herself so that the students can watch her closely.
    (c) Focus on a variety of written tasks especially worksheets.
    (d) Speak clearly and use a lot of touches and feel materials.

17. **Which of the following enrichment programmes is suitable for gifted children in the school?**
    (a) Mathematics or Science Olympiad
    (b) Challenging home assignments
    (c) Map work during studies
    (d) All of the above

18. **Which of the following is the best example of creativity?**
    (a) Writing a script for role play in class
    (b) Preparing an origami structure
    (c) Making a Rangoli
    (d) Making a painting

19. Which of the following is a method to teach Autistic children?
- (a) PECS
- (b) Braille
- (c) Taylor Frame
- (d) None of these

20. In order to address learners from diverse backgrounds, a teacher should:
- (a) Draw examples from diverse settings.
- (b) Use standardized assessment for all
- (c) Use statements that strengthen negative stereotypes
- (d) Avoid talking about aspects related to diversity.

21. As a teacher, what will you do if students do not attend your class?
- (a) Blame students for their absence from the class.
- (b) Ponder over the present attitude of students in a calm manner.
- (c) Think about using some interesting techniques for teaching.
- (d) Try to understand the reasons and try to eliminate them.

22. Alternate conceptions and misconceptions hold by children represent:
- (a) Inability to learn
- (b) Intuitive ideas about particular concept
- (c) Baseless assertions
- (d) Permanent conceptional stagnation

23. Which of the following statements about students' errors is correct?
- (a) Errors help the teachers in labelling students as 'weak' or 'bright'.
- (b) On the basis of their errors, the teacher can fail students and save her time.
- (c) Errors offer an opportunity for the teachers to understand students' thinking.
- (d) Errors should be immediately rectified by asking the students to repeatedly rewrite the 'correct answers'.

24. Which of the following is correct regarding emotion ?
- (a) Emotion is subjective in nature
- (b) Emotion is both subjective and objective
- (c) Physiological changes in emotions may not be noticed
- (d) Emotions are basically an affective process that is simple in nature

25. Which of the following example shows that intrinsic motivation is better than extrinsic motivation for learning?
- (a) A student want to participate in a sport because it's fun and she enjoys it.
- (b) A student did homework because he did not want to get scolded by teacher.
- (c) A teacher in a private school is taking more responsibility at work in order to receive a raise or promotion.
- (d) A child is speaking wrong English in the school to avoid fine.

26. Which of the following factors influence learning?
(i) emotional
(ii) cultural content
(iii) maturation
(iv) interest
- (a) (iii), (iv)
- (b) (ii), (iii), (iv)
- (c) (i), (ii), (iii), (iv)
- (d) (ii), (iv)

27. Which one of these factors plays a very important role in learning?
- (a) Genetic make-up alone
- (b) Physical infrastructure
- (c) Social context and emotions
- (d) Maturation and physical appearance

28. Which of the following is not correct regarding teaching-learning process?
- (a) Processes of learning move from the simple to the complex
- (b) Readiness and motivation to learn are the important to designing instructional activities
- (c) Skills of problem solving are integral parts of the internal conditions of learning
- (d) None of these

29. Which of the following is a property of "Deductive method"?
- (a) In this method, there is no opportunity to develop powers like logic, thinking and investigation.
- (b) In this method, children work mechanically because they do not know why they are doing such a thing.
- (c) By this method all the children of the class can be taught at the same time.
- (d) All of the above

30. Characteristics of thinking are:
- (a) It depends on both - perception and memory
- (b) Thinking is a mental process that starts with a problem and concludes with its solution
- (c) It is a symbolic behavior
- (d) All of the above

Language - I: English

Ques (31-39): Direction : Read the given passage and answer the questions that follow.

The move by the government to demonetize Rs.500 and Rs.1000 notes by replacing them with new Rs.500 and Rs.2000 notes has taken the country by surprise. The move by the government is to tackle the menace of black money, corruption, terror funding, and fake currency. From a market perspective, we think that this is a very welcome move by the government and which has taken the black money hoarders by surprise. The total value of old Rs.500 and Rs.1000 notes in circulation is to the tune of Rs.14.2 trillion, which is about 85% of the total value of the currency in circulation. This means that the total cash has to now pass through the formal banking channels to get legitimacy. The World Bank in July 2010 estimated the size of the shadow economy for India at 20.7% of the Gross Domestic Product (GDP) in 1999 and rose to 23.2% in 2007. Assuming that this figure has not risen since then (quite unlikely though) and that the cash component of the shadow economy is also proportional (it could be higher), the estimated unaccounted value of the currency could be to the tune of Rs.3.3 trillion. Now, post the announcement of demonetization by the government this money would have to either account for by paying the relevant tax and penalties or would get extinguished. There are higher chances of a larger proportion of this unaccounted currency getting extinguished as the tax rate and subsequent legal issues could be prohibitively high for such money.

This move by the government is likely to have long-term benefits for the economy. The extinguishing of the major proportion of unaccounted currency would reduce the liabilities of the government and would add to its finances. This move is likely to lead to better tax compliance, raise the Tax to GDP ratio and improved tax collection. The move is also likely to have a habit-changing impact on the Indian populous and there could be an increased belief in keeping cash in the banks rather than stashed at home and using formal banking channels for their spending needs. It will improve the medium to long-term Current Account and Savings Account (CASA) ratio of the banks. Another element of the demonetization would be a reduction in cash transactions in real estate which has been acting like a cash cow for the corrupt. This is likely to reduce real estate prices and make it affordable to some extent. This may be visible more in the rural belt, where many non-farming entities purchase fertile farmland, not for farming but for money parking purposes. The demonetization and consequent reduction in the shadow economy would bring the demand for such farmlands down.

31. How will the demand for fertile farmlands be brought down by demonetization?
(a) Lack of cash flow in the shadow economy
(b) Higher investments in real estate
(c) Cash hoarding
(d) Low agricultural output

32. What percentage of the total value of currency in circulation is made up by the old Rs.500 and Rs.1000 notes?
(a) 80%   (b) 85%
(c) 75%   (d) 60%

33. What does cash cow mean?
(a) Cash that buys cows
(b) People with low income from land
(c) Approximate estimate of cost of land
(d) A product or service that is a regular source of income for someone

34. Why will the demonetization move have a habit-changing impact on the Indian population?
(a) Indians will stop using black money for their daily needs and rely more on white money for day to day transactions.
(b) The Indian population generally uses mostly UPI for transactions and is not in the habit of saving. Demonetisation will make them wary of the future and grow their expanding habits altering their lifestyles.
(c) Demonetisation will affect the spending habits of the foreigners.
(d) The demonetization has affected all Indians and in the future, the scheme would make them wary

and help to create an atmosphere where banks and other legalized avenues will make their savings secure and easily accessible.

35. What is the main idea discussed in the passage?
(a) How black money is hid in the economy.
(b) The effects of demonetization on the Indian economy.
(c) Demonetization and its effect on the next elections.
(d) Demonetization and common man's woe.

36. Choose the correct synonym of the word 'formal'.
(a) Official   (b) Ceremonial
(c) Informal   (d) Traditional

37. What is the full form of CASA?
(a) Current action and Savings Action
(b) Current Affirmation and Savings Affirmation
(c) Current Account and Savings Account
(d) Current Act and Savings Account

38. According to World Bank estimates what percentage of the GDP did the shadow economy have in 2007?
(a) 20.7%   (b) 21.4%
(c) 22.6%   (d) 23.2%

39. Choose the correct antonym of the word 'compliance'.
(a) Agreement   (b) Assent
(c) Defiance   (d) Consensus

Ques (40-45): Direction : Read the poem given below and answer the questions that follow.

I was angry with my friend;
I told my wrath, my wrath did end.
I was angry with my foe:
I told it not, my wrath did grow.
And I waterd it in fears,
Night & morning with my tears:
And I sunned it with smiles,
And with soft deceitful wiles.
And it grew both day and night.
Till it bore an apple bright.
And my foe beheld it shine,
And he knew that it was mine.
And into my garden stole,
When the night had veild the pole;
In the morning glad I see;
My foe outstretched beneath the tree.

40. What did the poet water with his fears?
(a) Tree   (b) Plant
(c) Poison   (d) Anger

41. Which device is used in the

following lines?
And I sunned it with smiles,
And with soft deceitful wiles.
And it grew both day and night.
(a) Consonance
(b) Anaphora
(c) Satire
(d) Personification

42. What does the poet mean when he says 'My foe outstretched beneath the tree.'?
(a) Poet's enemy was using the tree
(b) Poet's enemy was trying to steal the fruits from the tree
(c) The enemy was relaxing under poet's tree
(d) The enemy was lying dead under the tree

43. 'night had veild the pole' means:
(a) Tree covered the pole
(b) The dark night covered the pole
(c) Night had covered the pole
(d) The dark night was all around the tree

44. Which literary device is used throughout the poem?
(a) Personification
(b) Simile
(c) Extended Metaphor
(d) Assonance

45. What does the garden refer to in the poem?
(a) Anger   (b) Kindness
(c) Forgiveness   (d) Apology

46. Consider the correct statements regarding language learning.
I. Input-rich communicational environments are a prerequisite for language learning.
II. It helps in bridging the gap between the burden of incomprehension and language learning.
(a) Only I
(b) Only II
(c) Both I & II
(d) None of these

47. The 'acquired system' or 'acquisition' of a language is the:
(a) Formal skills development
(b) Subconscious process of learning
(c) Input output process
(d) Self monitoring of learning

48. One of the principles of materials preparation for language learning is that:

(a) Complex materials should be chosen for each age group

(b) Materials need to be graded appropriately.

(c) Any kind of materials can be selected.

(d) Materials should be short and limited.

49. Principles of sequencing in teaching a foreign language, does not include:

(a) Grammatical sequence

(b) Lexical sequence

(c) Semantic sequence

(d) Phonetic sequence

50. Grammatical rules are_________ for learning a language.

(a) important

(b) compulsory

(c) not important

(d) mandatory

51. Given below are two statements, one leveled as Assertion (A) and the other leveled as Reason (R).

Assertion (A): Grammar is the backbone of any language, it is the womb that gives birth to sentences.

Reasoning (R): Grammar rules are made easier if the teacher teaches grammar using a standard textbook.

(a) Both (A) and (R) are correct and (R) is the correct explanation of (A).

(b) Both (A) and (R) are correct, but (R) is not the correct explanation of (A).

(c) (A) is correct, but (R) is not correct.

(d) (A) is not correct, but (R) is correct.

52. When child has difficulties in understanding or expressing language that is called:

(a) Grammatical language problem

(b) Delayed Language

(c) Language Disability

(d) All of the Above

53. The order advocated for learning the language skills is:

(a) writing, reading, speaking, listening

(b) reading, writing, listening, speaking

(c) listening, speaking, reading, writing

(d) speaking, listening, reading, writing

54. Through which of the following language skills should be taught?

(a) Through imitation

(b) In isolation

(c) Through detailed explanation

(d) In an integrated manner

55. Rohit, a English teacher, is planning to evaluate the speaking skills of his students. What should be the main focus for evaluating speaking skill?

(a) Accuracy of pronounciation

(b) Adequacy of fluency

(c) Communicative competence

(d) Accuracy of pronounciation and adequacy of fluency

56. Decoding in evaluating language proficiency refers to:

(a) The ability to enhance reading error.

(b) The ability to hear sounds to build and write words.

(c) The ability to read individual words and to sound out unfamiliar words accurately.

(d) The ability to provide remedial classes.

57. _________ is of great utility in teaching English pronunciation, accent and intonation.

(a) Epidiascope (b) Films

(c) Linguaphone (d) Radio

58. The objective of remedial teaching in English language is/are:

(a) Provides learning activities and practical experiences to pupils according to their abilities and requirements.

(b) Designs individualized teaching with intensive remedial support

(c) Help the pupils to get rid of their common or specific weaknesses.

(d) All of the above

59. The main purpose of using oral drill is:

(a) To assess the comprehension skills of learners

(b) To improve pronunciation and accuracy

(c) To enhance the speaking skills of learners

(d) To improve retention capacity of learners

60. A smartboard is a:

(a) A visual aid

(b) An audio aid

(c) An audio-visual aid

(d) None of these

61. During the Mughal rule, the police duties in the districts were entrusted to the officials known as:

(a) Faujdar (b) Mansabdar

(c) Kotwal (d) Amin

62. What was the capital of the French colony in India?

(a) Pondicherry (b) Calicut

(c) Cochin (d) Goa

63. _________established the "Atmiya Sabha" a precursor in the socio-religious reforms in Bengal?

(a) Vivekanand

(b) Dayanand Saraswati

(c) Raja Ram Mohan Roy

(d) Aurobindo

64. Direction : With reference to the Freedom Struggle of India, which of the following is / are correct observations?

1. Purna Swarajya Resolution was adopted by INC in Lahore Session.

2. Gopal Krishna Gokhle was founder of Servants of India Society.

3. The Chittagong Armory raid and temporary capture of port town were organized under Surya Sen.

Select the correct option from the codes given below:

(a) Only 1 and 2 (b) Only 2 and 3

(c) Only 1 and 3 (d) 1, 2 and 3

65. The concept of fraternity mentioned in the Preamble to the Indian constitution assures:

(a) The basic philosophy of the constitution.

(b) The absence of special privileges to any sections of the society.

(c) The dignity of the individual and the unity and integrity of the nation.

(d) The equal treatments of all citizens.

66. In India the First Municipal Corporation was set up in _________.

(a) Calcutta (b) Madras

(c) Bombay (d) Delhi

67. Who is the Chief Executive of the District Administration?

(a) District Magistrate (Consolidated)

(b) District Judge

(c) Deputy Commissioner

(d)   Superintendent of Police

68. What is contained in the Tenth Schedule of the Constitution?
(a)   Provisions regarding validation of certain Acts and Regulations
(b)   Provisions regarding disqualification on ground of defection
(c)   Provisions regarding the Administration and Control of Scheduled Areas and Scheduled Tribes
(d)   Provisions regarding the Administration of Tribal Areas in the States of Assam, Meghalaya, Tripura, and Mizoram

69. _______country is India's federal system related to.
(a)   Canada
(b)   United Kingdom
(c)   United State of America
(d)   Ireland

70. The original copies of the Indian Constitution was written in _______ language?
(a)   Hindi
(b)   English
(c)   Sanskrit
(d)   Both Hindi and English

71. _______was the Constituent Assembly of India formed.
(a)   By indirect elections by the members of the Provincial Legislative Assemblies established in 1935.
(b)   Through Nomination by the Viceroy.
(c)   By direct election by the members of Provincial Legislative Assemblies established in 1935.
(d)   By direct elections in Provinces.

72. The Central Government can give directions to the State Governments with regard to subjects in_______.
(a)   The Concurrent List
(b)   The Unionist
(c)   The State List
(d)   All of the above

73. The Marine cliffs are formed mainly due to_______.
(a)   Ocean Currents
(b)   Structure of Shall
(c)   Coast of Sea
(d)   Depth of The Ocean

74. In which of the following the Bum La is a border pass located?

(a)   Sikkim
(b)   Arunachal Pradesh
(c)   Himachal Pradesh
(d)   Nagaland

75. The Tropic of Cancer does not pass through ____________state.
(a)   Mizoram
(b)   Tripura
(c)   Orissa
(d)   Madhya Pradesh

76. ____________country is the leading producer of Uranium.
(a)   Australia   (b)   Canada
(c)   Kazakhstan   (d)   Russia

77. Where was the Busan Harbour situated?
(a)   North Korea   (b)   South Korea
(c)   China   (d)   Japan

78. Who defeated Humayun in the battle of Chausa in 1539?
(a)   Sher Shah
(b)   Bahadur Shah
(c)   Rana Sanga
(d)   None of these

79. Patanjali is well known for the compilation of:
(a)   Yoga sutra
(b)   Panchatantra
(c)   Brahma Sutra
(d)   Ayurveda

80. Kartarpur Sahib corridor connects Kartarpur Gurudwara in Pakistan to Dera Baba Nanak Shrine in India's ____ district.
(a)   Amritsar   (b)   Gurdaspur
(c)   Sangrur   (d)   Ludhiana

81. The two volcanic islands in the Indian territory are:
(a)   Kavaratti and New Moor
(b)   Bitra and Kavaratti
(c)   Pamban and Barren
(d)   Narcondam and Barren

82. Fiscal policy refers to:
(a)   Agricultural fertilizer policy
(b)   Rural credit policy
(c)   Interest policy
(d)   Related to revenue and expenditure policy of the government

83. ____ is the total value of goods and services produced in a country and is measured over a specific time frame.
(a)   Non-tax revenue
(b)   Gross fiscal deficit

(c)   Gross budgetary support
(d)   Gross domestic product

84. The Saubhagya Scheme aims at universal ______.
(a)   LPG connection
(b)   household electrification
(c)   primary school education
(d)   primary school education

85. 'Per Drop More Crop' is the goal for which Government of India scheme?
(a)   Pradhan Mantri MUDRA Yojana (PMMY)
(b)   Pradhan Mantri Awaas Yojana Gramin (PMAY-G)
(c)   Pradhan Mantri Jan-Dhan Yojana (PMJDY)
(d)   Pradhan Mantri Krishi Sinchayee Yojana (PMKSY)

86. Which of the following characterize the nature of social sciences?
(a)   Concern for value attainment is an important tenet of social sciences.
(b)   Social sciences are primarily interdisciplinary in nature.
(c)   Social sciences facilitate plurality in thinking in understanding an issue.
(d)   All of the above

87. Which of the following points may characterize the nature of social sciences?
A. Direct bearing on human activity
B. Advance studies of human society
C. Find out truths about human relationships
(a)   A is true but B and C is not true
(b)   Only C is true
(c)   All of the above is true
(d)   Only B is true

88. Which of the following is true about Social Studies?
A. Social studies is concerned with the practical aspects of the society.
B. Social studies helps to develop the competencies relating to healthy social living.
(a)   Only A
(b)   Only B
(c)   Both A and B
(d)   Neither A nor B

89. Read the following statements related to the problems in teaching social science and choose the correct option.
Assertion (A): Changing nature of interpretation of historical events

makes the teaching of social science a more challenging subject. Reasoning (R): There is lack of sufficient number of teachers to teach social science.

(a) Both (A) and (R) are true and (R) is the correct explanation of (A).
(b) Both (A) and (R) are true but (R) is not the correct explanation of (A).
(c) (A) is true but (R) is false
(d) Both (A) and (R) are false.

90. Which of the following should the teaching of History focus upon?
A. Concept of plural representations and building a sense of historical diversity.
B. Encouraging students to imagine living in the past and relate to their experiences.

(a) Only B
(b) Both A and B
(c) Neither A and B
(d) Only A

91. "Language of the textbook is often difficult for students to comprehend and readability of the text is affected." How can a teacher overcome this limitation of textbooks?
(i) The teacher may provide students a lot of supplementary information
(ii) Involve students in problem solving activities.

(a) Only (i) is ture
(b) Only (ii) is true
(c) Both (i) and (ii) are true
(d) Neither (i) nor (ii)

92. A social science teacher willing to enquire with a constructivist perspective would view the learners as:
A. Curious to explore on social processes
B. Imaginative on the basis of sources
C. Trying to suggest solutions to problems
D. Postponing discussions on controversial issues for higher education level
Choose the correct option.

(a) A and B only
(b) A, B and C only
(c) A, B and D only
(d) B, C and D only

93. In the context of student assessment or evaluation tool, which of the following is meant by portfolio?

(a) Autonomic and extraordinary work of the student
(b) An effective method of self-evaluation
(c) Assessment of particular part and department of work
(d) All of the above

94. What evaluation tool will the teacher use for recording teacher's observations about the personal and social qualities of students?
(a) Progress report card
(b) Anecdotal record card
(c) Cumulative report card
(d) Check list

95. In social science class, if the local health worker is invited to address the children, then the teacher is using which type of resource in teaching?
(a) Textbook
(b) Multimedia
(c) Community resource
(d) Both (A) and (B)

96. A social science teacher takes students to visit the Panchayat office for the learning about Panchayat. In this situation, which learning strategy is adopted by the teacher?
(a) Story telling   (b) Project work
(c) Field trip   (d) All the above

97. Assertion (A) : Social science textbooks based on NCF 2005 contains lots of graphics, pictures and cartoons.
Reasoning(R): Use of graphics, cartoons and pictures as learning resource brings visual relief and fun.
(a) Both (A) and (R) are true and (R) is the correct explanation of (A).
(b) Both (A) and (R) are true and (R) is NOT the correct explanation of (A).
(c) (A) is true but (R) is false.
(d) (A) is false but (R) is true.

98. Which teaching material may not be useful while teaching the topic "Transport" to class VI students?
I. Tourist map of a city
II. Pictures of means of transportation
III. Beaker
IV. Picture of telephone booth
(a) I and II   (b) II and III
(c) III and IV   (d) I and IV

99. Which of the following is primary source?

(a) SST Textbook
(b) River Ganga
(c) The Times of India
(d) TIME Magazine

100. Which of the following questions provide opportunities to assess critical thinking skills?
A. Why did Mahatma Gandhi want to teach children handicrafts?
B. Name two essential features of democracy.
C. Why do you think we need the government to find solutions to many disputes or conflicts?
D. What was the role of zamindar in Mughal administration?
Choose the correct option.
(a) A, B and C only
(b) A and C only
(c) A and B only
(d) A and D only

101. Surekha, a teacher of class VIII, conducts a discussion on the topic 'Global warming'. She does it because:
(a) For retention of facts related to global warming
(b) Memorizing information which leads to conceptual development
(c) To make learning process participative
(d) None of these

102. How many stages are in the development of critical thinking?
(a) 2   (b) 4
(c) 5   (d) 6

103. Which misperception does a social science teacher face while teaching?
(a) Students consider it redundant as it does not teach daily life skills
(b) Some consider it is merely encyclopedia
(c) Subjects like history is emphasize on retention of information
(d) All of the above

104. Which of the following is not the principle of project method?
(a) The Priniciple of Experience
(b) The Principle of Purpose
(c) The Priniciple of Social Experience
(d) Principle of Preparation

105. Which of the following is not an advantage of project based instruction?

(a) Increases student motivation by allowing choice

(b) Improves rote learning

(c) Connects school based instruction to real life

(d) All of the above

106. **Which of the following statement is/are incorrect ?**
(A) The Indian government works at different levels: at the local level, at state level and at the national level.
(B) The local level means in your village, town.
(C) The state level mean neighbor state
(D) The national level relates to the entire country

(a) Only (A) and (D)

(b) Only (B) and (C)

(c) Only (A) and (B)

(d) Only (C)

107. **Assertion (A): Democratic governments in our times are usually referred to as representative democracies.**
Reasoning (R): In representative democracies people do not participate directly but, instead, choose their representatives through an election process.
Choose the correct options.

(a) Both (A) and (R) is true, but (R) is not correct explanation of (A).

(b) Both (A) and (R) is true, (R) is correct explanation of (A).

(c) (A) is true and (R) is false

(d) (A) is false and (R) is true

108. **Assertion (A): The equator represents the zero degree latitude.**
Reasoning (R): Since the distance from the equator to either of the poles is one-fourth of a circle round the earth, it will measure ¼th of 360 degrees, i.e. 90°.
Choose the correct option.

(a) (A) is true but (R) is false.

(b) (A) is false but (R) is true.

(c) Both (A) and (R) is true but (R) does not support (A).

(d) Both (A) and (R) is true and (R) supports (A).

109. **Assertion (A): For centuries, rulers belonging to the Gurjara-Pratihara, Rashtrakuta and Pala dynasties fought for control over Kanauj.**
Reasoning (R): There were three "parties" in this long drawn conflict, historians often describe

it as the "tripartite struggle".
Choose the correct option.

(a) A is true but R is false.

(b) A is false but R is true

(c) Both A and R is true but R does not support A.

(d) Both A and R is true and R support A.

110. **Which of the following statements is/are incorrect regarding Mongol attack?**
Statement (A): Mongols attacked Delhi twice during the reign of Alauddin Khalji.
Statement (B): Muhammad Tughluq constructed a new garrison town named Siri for his soldiers.
Statement (C): Muhammad Tughluq's administrative measures were quite successful and chroniclers praised his reign for its cheap prices and efficient supplies of goods in the market.

(a) (A) and (B)

(b) (B) and (C)

(c) (A) and (C)

(d) (A), (B) and (C)

111. **Which of the following statement is/are incorrect?**
(A) In India, we have governments at the state level and at the centre.
(B) Panchayati Raj is the second tier of government.

(a) Only (A) is true

(b) Only (B) is true

(c) Both (A) and (B) is false

(d) Only (B) is false

112. **Which of the following statement is/are correct?**
Statement (A): Indian Constitution guarantees Fundamental Duty to every citizen of India.
Statement (B): Indian Constitution guarantees Fundamental rights to every citizen of India.

(a) Only (A)

(b) Only (B)

(c) Both (A) and (B)

(d) None of these

113. **Match List 1 with List 2 and choose the correct answer from the code given below:**

List 1 (Historic Period)	List 2 (Duration)
(a) Mughal	1. 600 BC to Ad 500
(b) Pre-	2. AD 1526 to
Historic	1800
(c) Early Historical	3. 2350 to 1800 BC
(d) Medieval	4. AD 600 to 1800

(a) (a) - 4, (b) - 1, (c) - 3, (d) - 2

(b) (a) - 3, (b) - 2, (c) - 4, (d) - 1

(c) (a) - 1, (b) - 4, (c) - 2, (d) - 3

(d) (a) - 2, (b) - 3, (c) - 1, (d) - 4

114. **With reference to the scholars/litterateurs of ancient India, consider the following statements.**
1. Banabhatta is associated with Harshavardhana.
2. Asvaghosa is associated with Kanishka.
3. Bharavi is associated with Samudragupta.
Which of the statements given above is/are correct?

(a) 1 and 3   (b) 1 and 2

(c) 2 only   (d) 1, 2 and 3

115. **Consider the following statements.**
1. The Harappans probably got copper from present-day Rajasthan, and even from Oman in West Asia.
2. Tin, which was mixed with copper to produce bronze, may have been brought from present-day Afghanistan and Iran.
3. Gold could have come all the way from present-day Karnataka.
Which of the above statements are correct?

(a) 1 and 2 only   (b) 2 and 3 only

(c) 1 and 3 only   (d) 1, 2 and 3

116. **Consider the following pairs.**

Hills	State
1. Lushai Hills	Mizoram
2. Erramalla Hills	Kerala
3. Javadi Hills	Tamil Nadu
4. Satmala Hills	Madhya Pradesh

Which of the pairs given above are correctly matched?

(a) 1 and 2   (b) 3 and 4

(c) 1 and 3   (d) 2 and 4

117. **Consider the following pairs.**

Mineral	Largest Producer state
1. Limestone	Karnataka
2. Gypsum	Rajasthan
3. Dolomite	Andhra Pradesh

Which of the pairs given above is/

are correctly matched?

(a) 1 only   (b) 2 and 3 only
(c) 3 only   (d) 1, 2 and 3

118. Consider the following pairs.

Place	Well known for
1. Bagor	Domestication of animals
2. Bhimbetka	Rock-cut shrines
3. Mehrgarh	Mud-brick houses

Which of the pairs given above is/ are correctly matched?

(a) 1 Only   (b) 1 and 2
(c) 1 and 3   (d) 2 and 3

119. Consider the following pairs.

Indus Vally Site	Well known for
1. Surkotada	Fortified lower town
2. Chanhudaro	Absence of fortified citadel
3. Banawali	Fortified township

Which of the pairs given above is/ are correctly matched?

(a) 2 only   (b) 2 and 3 only
(c) 1 and 3 only (d) 1, 2 and 3

120. With reference to the religious history of India, consider the following pairs:

List-I	List-II
1. Ajivikas	Theory of atoms
2. Charvaka	Focused on the upper-class people
3. Ajnanas	Radical scepticism

Which of the pairs given above are correctly matched?

(a) 1 and 3 only (b) 2 and 3 only
(c) 1 and 2 only (d) 1, 2 and 3

// Hints and Solutions //

1(D). Motor development refers to the development of motor skills that makes children able to explore and manipulate their immediate environment.

Motor development is divided into two groups:

- Gross motor development: Development of gross motor skills is concerned with strength and speed as it refers to the development of larger muscles like arms and legs for bigger movements such as walking, jumping, etc.
- Fine motor development: Development of fine motor skills is concerned with flexibility and dexterity as it refers to the development of small muscles like wrists and fingers fir smaller movements such as writing, grasping small objects, etc.

So, it becomes clear that by motor development we mean the development of in the use of arms and legs strength and speed.

2(D). Development is correlated: All types of developments, i.e. physical, mental, social, and emotional, are related to each other e.g. a physically healthy child is likely to have superior sociability and emotional stability. The child develops as a unified whole. Each area of development is dependent on the other and thus influences the other developments. Sufi has appropriate weight and height for her age. She also has a well-developed language ability that enables her to communicate with everyone. She is loved by all and has positive self-esteem.

So, we can conclude that Development is correlated is the correct answer.

3(D). The growth and development of the child influenced by heredity and environment. Heredity is discussed as an internal factor and environment as an external factor.

Heredity:

- Heredity is the sum total of the traits potentially present in the fertilized ovum. All the qualities that a child has inherited from the parents are called heredity.
- Heredity consists of all the structures, physical characteristics, functions or capacities derived from parents and other ancestors

Environment:

- Environment means the totality of the stimuli that impinge on the organism from without whatever found around the individual may be called by the term environment.
- The environment consists of various types of forces like physical, social, moral, economic, political cultural and emotional forces.

Thus from the above-mentioned points, it is clear that influence the economy is not true regarding heredity and environment.

4(C). Secondary Socialization:

- It occurs once the infant passes into the childhood phase and continues into maturity. It refers to the process that begins in the later years through agencies such as schools and peer groups.
- During this phase more than the family, some other agents of socialization like the school and peers' group begin to play a role in socializing the child.
- For example, Schools help children in learning the importance of social cohesion and unity and inculcating the informal cues about social roles through interaction. Schools teach new behaviors and rules to children and expect them to act accordingly.

So, it could be concluded that the school acts as an agency of secondary socialization.

5(B). Piaget's Pre-operational stage is from 2 - 7 years. In this stage, the child faces problems with the concept of conservation and struggles with the idea of centration and irreversibility.

Preoperational stage (2-7 yrs): It is categorized into two parts:

- Pre-conceptual stage (2-4 yrs): In this, they began to pretend play; egocentrism and animism are controlled.
- Intuitive (4-7 yrs): In this, the child begins to be curious, wants to use primitive reasoning to know the things work.

So, we conclude that by the intuitive stage, Piaget refers to the pre-operational stage.

6(A). Criticisms of Kohlberg's Theory of Moral Development:

- Carol Gilligan has suggested that Kohlberg's theory was gender-biased since all of the subjects in his sample were male.
- Kohlberg has based his study primarily on a male sample.
- Critics have pointed out that Kohlberg's theory of moral development overemphasizes the concept of justice when making moral choices.

So, the statement 'Kohlberg has based his study primarily on a male sample', is correct in the context of this criticism.

7(C). Curricular goals in progressive education emphasize critical thinking as progressive education focused on developing critical thinking and problem-solving skills among the learners by enabling them to think or analyze the concepts beyond traditional ways.

Critical thinking is a skill that focuses on the analysis, evaluation and synthesizing of various available facts through experience, reflection, reasoning, communication, and arguments that allow us to make the best decision that could be possible.

So, it is clear that curricular goals in progressive education emphasize critical thinking.

8(A). Howard Gardner's multiple intelligences theory:

- The theory of multiple intelligences offers support for instructional approaches that incorporate a variety of connections for teaching and learning that validate the unique experiences, interests, and cultures of all students.
- Given that individuals gravitate to the areas in which they have strengths and can incorporate these areas into their learning, the concept of multiple

intelligences is uniquely suited to support and enhance a differentiated classroom.

- This theory of multiple intelligence given by Gardner is useful in giving differentiated instruction to the students as they all are different in their capabilities so they are required to be instructed differently.
- Gardner initially formulated a list of seven types of intelligence and visual-Spatial Intelligence is one of them. Later, two more types of intelligence are added by Gardner.

So, it is concluded that Howard Gardner's multiple intelligences theory impacts classrooms today in schools in terms of differentiated instruction.

9(C). Interpersonal skills: The ability to understand and effectively interact with others. It is an ability to notice and make distinctions among the moods, temperaments, motivations, and intentions of other people and potential to act on this knowledge (teachers, mental health professionals, parents, religious and political leaders)

So, we can conclude that a child has the ability to understand and effectively interact with others. The child is showing interpersonal intelligence.

10(B). Critical thinking aims at simplification/ generalization on the one hand and truth and accuracy on the other. It adheres to establish canons of logic. Logic is the science of thinking. It offers general rules for thinking.

Critical thinking is described in psychology as convergent thinking because anyone and everyone who wants to arrive at truth must conform to the canons of logic.

11(D). Children acquire gender roles through media, socialization, culture and not by tutoring.

Acquiring Gender Roles:
- Socialization: Through socialization, the child learns that men are supposed to go and work, while women are supposed to take care of household work and other responsibilities regarding home.
- Media: It highly influences gender role because when a girl or a boy admires someone as their role model, they try to adapt their style which they observe in the movie, advertisement and news and they mould up their lifestyle by following them.
- Culture: It influences gender in several ways such as one's education, skill, thinking, language, emotions and behaviour.

12(C). Individual difference refers to the difference which distinguishes an individual from another on the basis of psychological characteristics. Individual differences could be seen in all domains of

development such as physical, emotional, mental, etc.

A teacher should provide a variety of learning experience if learners display individual differences as it will help in:
- selecting relevant prompts to be suitable for their ability level.
- combining different types of prompts to make them inculcate skills.
- catering to the range of learning needs and requirements of diverse learners.
- making learning effective for students who learn differently either visually, auditory, etc.

So, it could be concluded that a teacher should provide a variety of learning experience if learners display individual differences.

13(A). In order to know what children understand and are able to know, assessment is done. It is a systematic process of using data to measure skills and knowledge. By assessment, a teacher documents the improvements by a student and his endeavors towards learning.

With assessments as an inbuilt process in teaching-learning, teachers can understand the needs of the learners better and accordingly change or adjust the quality of their instruction during the process of teaching the unit itself.

14(B). From the above-mentioned situation, it could be interpreted that the teacher is assessing the students by conducting the formative assessment as it refers to monitor the child's progress throughout the teaching-learning process. In this case, it will help the teacher to know the children's learning needs regarding that topic and then meet the needs by remedial teaching.

Assessment for Learning (Formative Assessment):
- It is also referred to as internal evaluation.
- In this form of assessment, a teacher embeds various forms of assessment all through the teaching and learning process. Therefore, it is an ongoing assessment that allows teachers to monitor students on a day-to-day basis and modify their teaching based on what the students need to be successful.

So, we can conclude that a teacher asks his/ her students to draw a concept map to reflect their comprehension of a topic. He/ She is conducting the formative assessment.

15(B). In progressive-education children are seen as active explorers as progressive education:
- emphasizes to enhance skills and understanding of the learners by engaging with the contents and experiences.
- promotes 'learning by doing' to make

children self-reliant and productive to use their knowledge and talents effectively.
- ensures the active participation of students by working in a group and applying practical knowledge to complete an activity.

So, it could be concluded that in progressive-education children are seen as active explorers.

16(D). A visually challenged child is the one who has a problem seeing with the naked eyes or is not able to see completely. Instruction adaptations that a teacher can follow while working with students who are 'visually challenged' are:
- Should speak clearly and audibly to help them learn through listening or auditory learning
- Use a lot of touches and feel materials.
- Make use of material adaptations according to the individual needs, the actual degree of functional vision, presence of any other disabilities
- Using a variety of tactile materials like rough or smooth, cold or hot, wet or dry, vibrate or stationary helps the students to touch, feel, and understand the differences between the materials

So, we can conclude that a teacher should speak clearly and use a lot of touches and feel materials while working with students who are 'Visually Challenged'.

17(D). A gifted child is the one who displays consistently remarkable performance in various physical or cognitive aspects and exhibits superiority in general intelligence levels.

Map work during studies, Challenging home assignments, and Mathematics or Science Olympiad are the enrichment programs that are suitable for gifted children in the school as these programs:
- can satisfy and utilize their intelligence.
- can give enriched learning experiences to them.
- Can develop the ability to visualize the spatial relationship.
- Can allow students to express their interests in the subject.
- Can give students the opportunity to try new things and explore.

So, it could be concluded that all of these are true in the context of the question.

18(A). Creativity is a mental and social process involving the generation of new ideas or concepts , or new associations of the creative mind between existing ideas or concepts. An alternative conception of creativeness is that it is simply the act of making something new.
- From a scientific point of view, the products of creative thought (sometimes referred to as divergent thought) are usually considered to have both originality and appropriateness.

- Creativity is defined as the tendency to generate or recognize ideas, alternatives, or possibilities that may be useful in solving problems, communicating with others, and entertaining ourselves and others. Ability to generate, create, or discover new ideas, solutions, and possibilities. divergent thinking: the opposite of convergent thinking, the capacity for exploring multiple potential answers or solutions to a given question or problem (e.g., coming up with many different uses for a common object)

So, it is concluded that writing a script for role play in class is the best example of creativity.

19(A). PECS is a method to teach Autistic children.
- It is a type of augmentative and alternative communication technique where individuals with little or no verbal ability learn to communicate using picture cards.
- Children use the pictures to "vocalize" a desire, observation, or feeling.
- Many children with autism learn visually, and therefore, this type of communication technique has been shown to be effective in improving independent communication skills.

Thus from above-mentioned points, it is clear that PECS is a method to teach Autistic children.

20(A). Effective strategies to address learners from disadvantaged and deprived backgrounds:
- Inclusive education is a movement to empower the vulnerable and marginalized groups to overcome the disadvantages of unequalized socialization and give them examples from diverse settings.
- The curriculum should to be specific and related to the needs and real-life experiences. Emphasis should be on learning manual skills, life skills and technical efficiency.
- Sometime the teacher should talk to the learners to understand their needs and challenges faced by them.
- Interest in learning has to be, created by the teacher, effort should be towards developing self-confidence, self-respect and a sense of cultural identity.
- Form collaborative groups to work on activities and encourage students to support each other.
- Motivate the students to set moderately challenging goals and provide appropriate instructional support.

Thus from above-mentioned points, it is clear that in order to address learners from diverse backgrounds, a teacher should draw examples from diverse settings.

21(C). Effective teaching occurs when a teacher is successful in keeping the students actively involved in learning. A few of the effective teaching practices include:
- Delivering lessons in an interesting manner by connecting the content being taught with real-life situations
- Using appropriate teaching techniques such as brainstorming, group learning, activity method, role plays, etc. that allows students to actively participate in the learning process
- Making use of audio/visual aids to cater to all the different senses
- Motivating students to learn more effectively through inquiry, experimentation, questioning, application, and reflection, leading to the creation of ideas.
- Providing opportunities to question, enquire, debate, reflect, and arrive at concepts or create new ideas.
- Employing flexibility and creativity while imparting knowledge rather than being rigid.

So, students can be encouraged to attend regular classes if teachers ensure to make use of interesting techniques.

22(B). Alternative conceptions are generated as a concept is understood from different aspects, while the misconception is a thought process that goes in the wrong direction due to a lack of complete information or just ignorance.
- Alternative conceptions and misconceptions are not always baseless rather they represent children's intuitive ideas about particular concepts and the world around them as it shows their thinking and they can think and put forward their views.
- The formation of alternative conceptions and misconceptions is very natural among children as well as adults because it is a natural thought process and no two minds can think alike exactly.
- A teacher should definitely attend to these alternative conceptions and misconceptions as they are significant in process of teaching-learning because they are very helpful; in developing critical thinking. Without this, a child would not be able to put forward one's own views and would end up mugging things.

Thus, it is concluded that alternate conceptions and misconceptions hold by children represent intuitive ideas about particular concepts.

23(C). All learners make mistakes. As someone has said: "You can't learn without goofing". Whether you are learning how to ride a bicycle, how to fly a kite or learn a language, everyone does make mistakes.
- An error is an incorrect form and a sure indication that the learner has not mastered the core of the selective topic in a learning process.
- Errors offer an opportunity for the teachers to understand students' thinking or thought processes since they are a window to children's thinking.
- Errors are necessary for the learning process to give insight into children's thinking. It helps the teacher to be aware of learners' learning styles and to cater to them according to their needs.
- Making an error cannot be just due to negligence and carelessness. It may be so that students are thinking about it in a different manner other than what is the right process.
- To understand this, a teacher should analyze what mistake the students are doing, how the mistake is generated, and where exactly they tend to make mistakes.

So, it is clear that errors offer an opportunity for the teachers to understand students' thinking.

24(B). Characteristics of emotions
- Emotions are comparatively more complex in nature.
- Any emotional experience is preceded and accompanied by feelings. For example, the feeling of pleasure will lead or will be accompanied by the emotion of happiness/ joy.
- Emotion is an effective process that is much more active.
- Emotion is both subjective and objective.
- Emotions are of different types, for example, anger, joy, jealousy, and so forth.
- Physiological changes are experienced.

So, we can conclude that emotion is both subjective and objective statement is correct regarding emotion.

25(A). Learning is most effective when there is intrinsic motivation - a desire to learn from within, which finds satisfaction in the achievement itself and does not bother about other factors.
- Intrinsic Motivation refers to motivation that is driven by an interest or enjoyment in the task itself, and exists within the individual rather than relying on any external pressure. Intrinsic Motivation is based on taking pleasure in an activity rather working towards an external reward. Intrinsic motivation results in high-quality learning and creativity For example; preparing any project in science/ mathematics, participating in a sport may give pleasure to the pupil as a result of which he/she is motivated to undertake similar activities on his/her own.

Thus, it is concluded that student wants to participate in a sport because it's fun and she enjoys it is an example that shows Intrinsic motivation is better than extrinsic motivation for learning.

26(C). Factors influencing learning includes:

- Cultural content: Cultural content and its value are significant influencers in the process of learning. A child who is aware of his culture and is motivated to preserve the cultural integrity of the society develops an interest in learning more about the society and thinks about the ways towards the betterment of the society.
- Maturation: Maturation is the process by which we change, grow, and develop throughout life. The maturation of the learner affects learning because maturation is related to the structure and potential capacity.
- Interest: Interest refers to a feeling that keeps learners involved and attentive while learning or doing a specific task. Subjects in which a learner is interested reflect his motivation, attraction, and attentiveness in favor of that subject. If a learner is disinterested in learning a particular subject it shows that he/she has a feeling of demotivation against that subject.
- Emotional factor/Emotions: Emotion impacts our levels of motivation. Positive emotions can help a student engage with learning longer because they stay motivated. Emotions during learning also impact our feelings toward education. If we have positive experiences, we are more likely to enjoy our schooling and develop a love for learning.

So, it is clear that all (i), (ii), (iii) and (iv) factors influence learning.

27(C). Characteristics of Social-emotional Development

- The social context involves the interpersonal relationships of an individual, her acquired social skills, values, and how an individual adjusts to society. learning such qualities as sharing, cooperation, waiting for one's turn, respecting other people and things, and so on, forms a part of learning through social context.
- Emotions are the feelings or affect of an individual towards a person, object, or situation, which may generate physiological arousal, conscious experience, and/or behavioral expressions.
- Learning involves the acquisition of new knowledge, skills, values, and dispositions and as it takes shape in the young child's life it is more than intellectual in nature. It is a process located in and influenced by the social and emotional experiences and characteristics of the environment.
- The nature and quality of emotional experiences and the sense of security and belongingness at home and in the immediate surroundings at the early

stages in life and attachments developed are crucial for the learning to take place. Thus from the above-mentioned points, it is clear that social context and emotions play a very important role in learning.

28(D). The teaching-learning process is the heart of extension education, and the fulfillment of the aims and objectives of development depends on it.

- Prerequisite behavior: Gagne advocated that processes of learning move from the simple to the complex. The learner has to develop, prerequisite capabilities before s/he acquires new terminal behavior. Thus the use of a hierarchy of learning and task analysis are integral parts of instructional transactions.
- Learners' characteristics: Learners' individual differences, readiness, and motivation to learn are the important issues to be considered before designing instructional activities.
- Cognitive process and instruction: The transfer of learning, the self-management skills of the learner, and teaching learners the skills of problem-solving are integral parts of the internal conditions of learning, applicable to instruction. The skill of learning 'how to learn' should be developed in the learner and the emphasis should be on the learner's individuality.

So, we can conclude that none of the above is incorrect regarding teaching-learning process.

29(D). Deductive learning is a more teacher-centered approach to education. Introduction of Generalizations and concepts is firstly given to learners, and to support the learning examples and activities are suggested. Minimum interaction is there between teacher and student, and the teaching method which is generally used is the lecture method.

Features of the Deductive method are:

- General to particular or abstract to concrete.
- Facts are given to the child and the principle of growth is not considered.
- The formula is decided and children are made to memorize it without applying logic to it.
- Children are made to learn and a lot of emphasis is given to the rote learning process.
- It starts with a rule and the application part is more in it, does not appreciate or follow the principle of learning by doing.
- It requires individual learning and in this process, the child is inactive and is a one-way process.
- Less interaction between teacher and student, the student only listens but does not know why we are doing this or following this.

From the above points, we can conclude that all the above-mentioned properties are

of the deductive method.

30(D). Thinking is a pattern of behaviour in which we make use of internal representations (symbols, signs, etc.) of things and events for the solution of some specific, purposeful problem.

Characteristics of thinking are:

- It is one of the most important aspects of one's cognitive behaviour.
- It depends on both – perception and memory.
- It involves trial and error; analysis and synthesis; foresight and hindsight.
- It is a symbolic behaviour.
- It is always directed to achieve some purpose.
- Thinking is a symbolic activity. (e.g.: engineers use mental symbols to design the plan for buildings).
- Thinking is a mental process that starts with a problem and concludes with its solution.
- There is mental exploration instead of motor exploration.

So, we can conclude that all of the above is true.

31(A). According to the passage, "This may be visible more in the rural belt, where many non-farming entities purchase fertile farmland, not for farming but for money parking purposes. The demonetization and consequent reduction in the shadow economy would bring the demand for such farmlands down."

The paragraph clearly states that most black money hoarders utilize their hoarded cash to buy fertile agricultural land as means of turning the black to white, which is a part of the shadow economy.

32(B). According to passage, "The total value of old Rs.500 and Rs.1000 notes in the circulation is to the tune of Rs.14.2 trillion, which is about 85% of the total value of the currency in circulation."

So, it is concluded that 85% of the total value of currency in circulation is made up by the old Rs.500 and Rs.1000 notes.

33(D). The idiom 'cash cow' refers to any products or services that yield a profit or income on a regular basis.

34(D). According to the passage, "The move is also likely to have a habit-changing impact on the Indian populous and there could be an increased belief in keeping cash in the banks rather than stashed at home and using formal banking channels for their spending needs."

As per the paragraph, Indians are well-known for not availing of proper banking services and since people have been mightily inconvenienced because of this move, the future may change the lackadaisical habits.

35(B). The passage deals with the act of demonetization taken up by the Indian government and its effect on the economy.

36(A). The meaning of the given words:
- Formal: Officially sanctioned or recognized
- Official: relating to an authority or public body and its activities and responsibilities
- Ceremonial: relating to or used for formal religious or public events
- Informal: 'unorthodox' or 'unofficial'
- Traditional: existing in or as part of a tradition; long-established

So, from the meaning of the given word we can say that official is the correct synonym of the word 'formal'.

37(C). According to passage, "It will improve the medium to long-term "Current Account and Savings Account (CASA)" ratio of the banks."
The full form of CASA is Current Account and Savings Account.

38(D). According to passage, "The World Bank in July 2010 estimated the size of the shadow economy for India at 20.7% of the Gross Domestic Product (GDP) in 1999 and rising to 23.2% in 2007."

39(C). The meaning of the given words:
- Compliance: the state or fact of according with or meeting rules or standards
- Defiance: open resistance; bold disobedience
- Agreement: harmony or accordance in opinion or feeling
- Assent: the expression of approval or agreement
- Consensus: a general agreement

So, from the meaning of the given word we can say that defiance is the correct antonym of the word 'compliance'.

40(D). According to the given lines,
"And I waterd it in fears"
Here the 'it' refers to wrath which means anger. The poet is comparing suppressed anger to a tree that kept growing over years into a garden.
Therefore, the poet watered 'anger' with his fears.
Hence, the correct option is (D)

41(B). The poet is representing two scenarios in his poem.
- First, when he confessed his anger to his friend and it subsides.
- Second, when he suppressed his anger and how it kept growing over years and became poisonous.
- If we read both the lines carefully, we will easily notice the repetition of (And I).
- Such repetition of the same phrase at the beginning of multiple consecutive lines is called Anaphora.

42(D). The meaning of difficult words in the line:

- Foe: Enemy
- Outstretched: It means that something is stretched to its capacity.

When a person is outstretched it means they are lying on the floor.
But in the last stanza of the poem, the poet is narrating how his enemy sneaked into his garden.
Since the tree and its fruit were poisonous, the enemy died and that's why he was outstretched under the tree.
Therefore, from all the points given above, we can infer that the last line of the poem means 'The enemy was lying dead under the tree.'

43(D). The line given in the question is from the last stanza of the poem.
- Velid is an archaic use of the word veiled which means to cover.
- The word pole refers to the tree of wrath that the poet has cultivated.
- So, through this line, the poet is describing the nighttime.

Therefore, the expression When the night had veild the pole means 'The dark night was all around the tree.'

44(C). The poem uses simple language to present its readers with a powerful message.
- The poet believes that anger that stays with an individual for a long time is dangerous.
- A metaphor is when two things are compared directly.
- An extended metaphor is simply a metaphor that extends over lines, paragraphs or stanzas.
- In this poem, the extended metaphor is a tree and it is used for anger.

Therefore, from all the points given above, we can infer that the literary device used throughout the poem is 'Extended Metaphor'.

45(A). In the whole poem, the poet is actively cultivating his anger with fears, tears and smiles:
- And I waterd it in fears,
- Night & morning with my tears:
- And I sunned it with smiles

Eventually, his tree turned into a garden as he expressed in the last stanza "And into my garden stole"
Therefore, from all the points given above, we can infer that the garden in the poem refers to anger.

46(C). Language teaching is the process in which a child gains communicative comprehension or fluency over a language. It involves practice by learners where facilitation is provided by a teacher.
Language learning:
- It is a result of deliberate and conscious effort for a better understanding of the foundational skills of a specific language. It refers to have a basic knowledge of grammatical rules and their use in communication.
- Input-rich communicational environments are a prerequisite for language learning. It arouses the interest and curiosity of learners to learn a specific language.
- Inputs include textbooks, learner-chosen texts, and class libraries allowing for a variety of genres. For example, Big Books for young learners, parallel books and materials in more than one language, radio/audio cassettes, and "authentic" materials.
- Also, these inputs and the environment that is enriched with these types of resources can help to minimize the gap between incomprehension and language learning i.e., the disability to interpret and comprehend a language and the ability to comprehend and use a language practically.

So, both statements regarding language learning are true.

47(B). Language is a symbolic, rule-governed system, shared by a group of people to express their thoughts and feelings. In a child, language development takes place through language acquisition and language learning.
Language acquisition:
- It refers to the subconscious process of learning a native or second language because of the innate capacity of the human brain.
- It is a natural process whereby children acquire language by observing and repeating what they hear in their native environment.
- Language acquisition does not require any formal instruction, children acquire the language without being taught.
- Language acquisition is a natural process so, one does not forget one's native language.

Language learning:
- It refers to the result of deliberate and conscious effort for a better understanding of foundational skills of language learning.
- It refers to have a basic knowledge of grammatical rules and their use in communication.

So, it could be concluded that the 'acquired system' or 'acquisition' of a language is the subconscious process of learning.

48(B). Language teaching is less about the school and more about the process of learning English. The modern approach to all language learning and teaching is the scientific one and is based on sound linguistic principles.
- Principle of Graded Patterns is one of the principles of materials preparation for language learning that emphasizes that materials need to be graded appropriately.
- "To teach a language is to impart a new

system of complex habits, and habits are acquired slowly." So, language patterns should be taught gradually, in cumulative graded steps.

- This means the teacher should go on adding each new element or pattern to previous ones. New patterns of language should be introduced and practiced with vocabulary that students already know.

So, we can conclude that one of the principles of materials preparation for language learning is that materials need to be graded appropriately.

49(D). Language teaching is the process whereby a child gains communicative comprehension or fluency over a language. It involves practice by learners where facilitation is provided by a teacher. Some of the Principles of Language Teaching are the Principle of Graded Patterns, the Principle of Selection and graduation, etc.

Principle of Selection and Gradation:

Selection of the language material is considered as the first requisite of good teaching. It should be done in respect of grammatical items and vocabulary and structures.

Gradation of the language material means placing the language items in order. It involves grouping and sequence.

- Grouping the system of language means what sounds, words, phrases, and meanings are to be taught. Thus we have Phonetic grouping, Lexical grouping, Grammatical grouping, Semantic grouping, and Structure grouping.
- Sequence means what comes after what. In teaching a foreign language, the sequence should be there in the arrangement of phrases (grammatical sequence) words (lexical sequence), and meaning (semantic sequence).

So, we can conclude that the principles of sequencing in teaching a foreign language, do not include phonetic sequence.

50(C). Grammar is defined as a theory of language. We consider language as rule-governed behavior, relating to sounds, word formation, and structure. Here grammar constitutes a subset of rules relating to morphology and syntax.

- It takes time to learn a language, even if it is by acquisition. It requires context to learn a language, for example, children speak the language when they have previous knowledge or experience.
- Grammatical Rules instruct a language user that how language should be used correctly and clearly. But it is widely known that effective language learning takes place from practicing it in real context rather than following the accurate rule.

So. it could be concluded that grammatical rules are not important for learning a language.

51(C). Grammar is the backbone of any language. It is the womb that gives birth to sentences. These sentences are fertilized using grammar to form correct and appropriate speech.

- Grammar is defined as a theory of language. We consider language as rule-governed behavior, relating to sounds, word formation, and structure. Here grammar constitutes a subset of rules relating to morphology and syntax.
- Grammar rules are made easier if they are given in a context using examples and teaching grammar in context provides accuracy in the target language.
- Learning grammar in context using examples will allow learners to see how rules can be used in sentences.
- Providing the chance to practice grammar in context will allow learners to understand how language works and this will improve their communication skills.

Thus, it is concluded that (A) is correct, but (R) is not correct.

52(C). Language is the rule-based use of speech sounds to communicate. Language disorders or language disabilities involve the processing of linguistic information.

- Problems that may be experienced can involve grammar (syntax and/or morphology), semantics (meaning), understanding or expressing language, or other aspects of language.
- Disordered language may be due to a receptive problem, that is, a difficulty in understanding speech sounds (involving impaired language comprehension).
- It can also be due to an expressive problem, i.e., a difficulty in producing the speech sounds (involving language production), that follow the arbitrary rules of a specific language.
- The disorders that come under language disorders/disabilities include Stuttering, Specific Language Impairment, Developmental Phonological Disorders, Aphasia, Dyspraxia, etc.

Thus, it is concluded that when a child has difficulties in understanding or expressing language that is called language disability.

53(C). Language skills are necessary for effective communication in any environment and to interact with others. It allows an individual to comprehend and produce language for proper and effective interpersonal communication.

The four basic language skills and their natural order are listening-speaking-reading-writing. These foundational skills of language are divided into two categories which are receptive and productive skills.

Productive skills:

- The productive skills of language are speaking and writing because these

skills can measure learner's ability to produce language.

- Both skills are concerned with language product or output through speech or written tests.

Receptive skills:

- The receptive skills of language are listening and reading because these skills don't require the production of language.
- These skills focus on an individual's ability of understanding and comprehending language.

So, from the above-mentioned points, it becomes clear that the order advocated for learning the language skills is listening, speaking, reading, writing.

54(D). Language is a purely human and non-instinctive method of communicating ideas, emotions, and desires by means of voluntarily produced symbols.

- Language skills should be taught in an integrated manner. In order to provide more focused and significant learning situations, teachers must integrate the four language skills while teaching and practicing the language.
- When we speak, we also listen simultaneously. When we write we are also reading. This engagement with language enables us to internalize the underlying grammaticality of the language.

Thus, it is concluded that language skills should be taught in an integrated manner.

55(C). Communicative competence refers to a learner's ability to use language to communicate successfully. This competence can be oral, written, or even nonverbal.

- It is an inclusive term that refers to possessing the knowledge of the language as well as the skill to use the language in real-life situations for fulfilling communicative needs.
- It includes the ability to use grammatical structures in different situations to convey and interpret messages and to negotiate meanings.
- Teachers can use information gap and role-play activities to evaluate learners' competence for speaking. It includes accuracy, fluency, complexity, appropriateness, and capacity.

Thus, it is concluded that communicative competence should be the main focus for the evaluation of speaking skills.

56(C). Decoding: This refers to the ability to read individual words and to sound out unfamiliar words accurately and automatically. Most reading problems are related to difficulty with decoding.

Decoding should be evaluated in three ways:

- Decoding of word lists to eliminate context clues for the reader,

- Reading of nonsense words to eliminate memorization of words,
- Reading in context.

So, we can conclude that decoding in evaluating language proficiency refers to the ability to read individual words and to sound out unfamiliar words accurately.

57(C). Linguaphone: Speaking a language is an active skill, something you learn by doing, not just studying. This is the practical approach taken by Linguaphone to language learning. Linguaphone enables understanding of the language and is able to converse with and understand real people speaking the language. It helps in teaching pronunciation, accent and intonation.

So, it becomes clear that Linguaphone is a utility in teaching English pronunciation, accent and intonation.

58(D). Remedial Teaching is an integral part of the teaching-learning program, also known as compensatory or corrective teaching.

Objectives of Remedial Teaching in the English language:
- To eliminate ineffective habits
- To make learners learn better by giving additional help
- To provide learning activities and practical experiences to pupils according to their abilities and requirements.
- To teach again the language items not properly learned
- To arise learners' interest in learning with stimulating approaches
- Help the pupils to get rid of their common or specific weaknesses.
- To transmit practical experiences to learners according to their diverse needs
- To provide individualized teaching with intensive remedial support.

So, we can conclude that all of the above are the objectives of remedial teaching in the English language.

59(B). The main purpose of using oral drill is that they help students gain confidence, and they help the teacher draw learners' attention to phonological features (i.e., accuracy and pronunciation) of the target language.

60(C). A smartboard is an audio-visual aid that maximizes learning with the help of the auditory and visual systems.
- Smartboards in classrooms allow teachers and students to access a wide range of educational resources that are available online, from videos to texts to animations and apps.
- Audio-visual aids activate the sense of both hearing and vision to enrich learner's knowledge by providing information about different subjects and boost their self-confidence and

independence.
- Being an audio-visual learning aid video is used to present the lesson effectively involving both sound and pictures for heightening learner's intellectual abilities to make learning meaningful.

So, from the above-mentioned points, it becomes clear that smartboard is an audio-visual aid.

61(A). During the Mughal rule, Faujdar was responsible for maintaining law and order, functioning the police duties, executed the royal decrees and regulations at the district level.

62(A). Pondicherry is a union territory in India,
- Pondicherry was the capital of the French colony in India.
- Pondicherry is also called 'India's Little France'.
- The French laid their supremacy on Pondicherry in the year 1673.
- French East India Company set up a trading center at Pondicherry in 1674.
- The name Pondicherry was renamed Puducherry in 2006.

63(C). Raja Ram Mohan Roy established the "Atmiya Sabha" a precursor organization in the socio-religious reforms in Bengal in the year 1814 in Kolkata.
It was a philosophical discussion circle where debates and discussions were held leading to the ideas for social reforms.

64(D). The Indian National Congress passed the Purna Swaraj resolution (Complete independence) on 19th December 1929 during the Lahore session. Jawaharlal Nehru was the president of the session. It was decided to celebrate Independence day on 26th January 1930.
Gopal Krishna Gokhale left the Deccan Education Society and formed the Servants of India Society on June 12, 1905 in Pune, Maharashtra.
Chittagong armoury raid was conducted on 18 April 1930. The operation was led by Surya Sen. The mission was conducted by the members of the Indian Republican Army.

65(C). The concept of fraternity mentioned in the Preamble to the Indian constitution assures the dignity of the individual and the unity and integrity of the nation.
- The Preamble of the Constitution of India presents the principles of the Constitution and indicates the sources of its authority. It was adopted on 26 November 1949 by the Constituent Assembly and came into effect on 26 January 1950, celebrated as the Republic day of India.
- Fraternity refers to a feeling of brotherhood and sisterhood and a sense of belonging with the country among its

people.
- The Preamble declares that fraternity has to assure two things—the dignity of the individual and the unity and integrity of the nation.
- The word 'integrity' has been added to the Preamble by the 42nd Constitutional Amendment (1976).

66(B). In India, the First Municipal Corporation was set up in Madras.
- In 1687, the first municipal corporation in India was set up at Madras.
- The Chennai Municipal Corporation (officially the Corporation of Chennai), formerly known as the Corporation of Madras, is the civic body that governs the city of Chennai (formerly Madras), India.
- Inaugurated on September 29, 1688, under a Royal Charter issued by King James II on December 30, 1687, as the Corporation of Madras, it is the oldest municipal body of the Commonwealth of Nations outside Great Britain.
- It is headed by a mayor, who presides over 200 councillors, each of whom represents one of the 200 wards of the city.
- It is also the second oldest corporation in the world.

67(A). The District Collector is the chief executive officer of the district. A District Collector is an Indian Administrative Service officer (IAS). He is the in charge of revenue collection and administration of a district.

68(B). 'Provisions regarding disqualification on ground of defection' is contained in the Tenth Schedule of the Constitution.
The 52nd Amendment Act of 1985 provided for the disqualification of the members of Parliament and the state legislatures on the ground of defection from one political party to another. The Tenth schedule added under the 52nd amendment act.

69(A). The Federal System of India is governed in terms of the Constitution of India.
- The country of India is also referred to as the Sovereign, Secular, Democratic Republic and has a Parliamentary form of government.
- The nation is basically working according to the Indian Constitution, which was adopted on the 26th of November 1949.
- The federal nature of the Indian constitution was adopted from the Constitution of Canada.

70(D). The original copies of the Indian Constitution was written in Hindi and English.
- The original Constitution of India was

handwritten by Prem Behari Narain Raizada in a flowing italic style with beautiful calligraphy.

- Each page was beautified and decorated by artists from Shantiniketan.
- The original constitution had two copies each written in Hindi and English, are kept in special helium-filled cases in the Library of the Parliament of India.
- With 25 parts containing 448 articles and 12 schedules, the Indian Constitution is the longest written constitution of any sovereign country in the world.

71(A). By indirect elections by the members of the Provincial Legislative Assemblies established in 1935 was the Constituent Assembly of India formed.
The members of this assembly were elected indirectly, that is by the members of the provincial assemblies by the method of a single transferable vote of proportional representation.

72(D). The Central Government can give directions to the State Governments with regard to subjects in The Concurrent List, The Unionist and The State List.
The Center may give such directions to the State as may be necessary in this regard. Article 257 talks of central control over the state in certain cases. State executive power should be exercised in such a way that it does not conflict with the union executive.

73(A). The Marine cliffs are formed mainly due to Ocean Currents. Moving water works as degradational agent (erosional). As oceanic currents move constantly in their definite path. They erode away rock against which they strike.

74(B). Bum La or Bum Pass is a mountain pass in the Himalayas between the Indian state of Arunachal Pradesh and the Lhokha Department of Tibet (China-controlled). It is situated at a distance of 37 km from Tawang city of Arunachal Pradesh at an altitude of 15,200 feet above sea level.

75(C). The Tropic of Cancer does not pass through Orissa state.
Tropic of Cancer is an imaginary line, at an angle of 23.50 degrees North from the Equator, that passes through the middle of India.
Tropic of Cancer passes through 16 countries, 3 continents, and 6 water bodies.
The Tropic of Cancer passes through eight states in India: Gujarat (Jasdan), Rajasthan (Kalinjarh), Madhya Pradesh (Shajapur), Chhattisgarh (Sonhat), Jharkhand (Lohardaga), West Bengal (Krishnanagar), Tripura (Udaipur) and Mizoram (Champhai).

76(C). Kazakhstan produces the largest share of uranium from mines (42% of world supply from mines in 2019), followed by Canada (13%) and Australia (12%).

Over two-thirds of the world's production of uranium from mines is from Kazakhstan, Canada, and Australia. An increasing amount of uranium, now over 50%, is produced by in situ leachings.

77(B). The Busan Harbour is situated in South Korea.
Busan Harbour-
It is the fifth busiest container port in the world and the largest transshipment port in northeast Asia.
Apart from Jeju City, the Port of Busan was the only city that was not occupied by North Korea during the Korean War (1950-1953). The city has become home to major industries including shipbuilding, automobiles, steel, electronics, chemicals, ceramics, and paper.
It is developed, managed, and operated by the Busan Port Authority (BPA) which was established in January 2004.
The Port uses state-of-the-art facilities to enable it to handle active exchange with 500 ports in 100 countries, including the latest generation high-speed container cranes.

78(A). Sher Shah defeated Humayun in the battle of Chausa in 1539.
- The Battle of Chausa was a notable military engagement between the Mughal emperor, Humayun, and the Afghan, Sher Shah Suri.
- It was fought on 26 June 1539 at Chausa.
- Sher Shah was victorious and crowned himself Farid al-Din Sher Shah.

79(A). Yoga Sutra of Patanjali is a collection of 195 Sanskrit sutras (aphorisms) on the theory and practice of yoga.
Yoga Sutra was compiled sometime between 500 BCE and 400 CE by the sage Patanjali in India who synthesized and organized knowledge about yoga from much older traditions.

80(B). Kartarpur Sahib corridor connects Kartarpur Gurudwara in Pakistan to Dera Baba Nanak shrine in India's Gurdaspur district.
- Prime Minister Narendra Modi inaugurated the Kartarpur Corridor from India and from Pakistan by his counterpart, Imran khan.
- It is a 4.5 km long highway that connects Dera Baba Nanak shrine in India with Shri Darbar Sahib Kartarpur in Pakistan.
- Sikh devotees can access the Holy shrine in Pakistan without a visa through this corridor.
- **Kartarpur Sahib was founded by the first Sikh guru in 1504.**
- Sikhs could informally access the site till 1965 only.
- In the aftermath of the Indo-Pak war of 1965, the border regulations were made strict.
- The idea of establishing such a corridor

was mooted during the tenure of Prime Minister Atal Bihari Vajpayee.
- It was finally inaugurated on the 550th birth anniversary of Guru Nanak Dev in November 2019.
- Mr. Modi also compared this inauguration with the Fall of Berlin Wall.

81(D). The two volcanic islands in the Indian territory are Narcondam and Barren.
- Narcondam: It is a small volcanic island located in the Andaman Sea. The island's peak rises to 710 m above mean sea level, and it is formed of andesite.
- Barren Island: It is an island located in the Andaman Sea, dominated by Barren Volcano, the only confirmed active volcano in South Asia, and the only active volcano along a chain of volcanoes from Sumatra to Myanmar.

82(D). Fiscal policy refers to related to revenue and expenditure policy of the government.
- Fiscal policy is the means by which a government adjusts its spending levels and tax rates to monitor and influence a nation's economy. It is the sister strategy to monetary policy through which a central bank influences a nation's money supply.
- Fiscal policy deals with the taxation and expenditure decisions of the government. Some of the major instruments of fiscal policy are as follows: Budget, Taxation, Public Expenditure, public revenue, Public Debt, and Fiscal Deficit in the economy.

83(D). Gross domestic product (GDP) is the total monetary or market value of all the finished goods and services produced within a country's borders in a specific time period.
As a broad measure of overall domestic production, it functions as a comprehensive scorecard of a given country's economic health.

84(B). The Saubhagya Scheme aims at universal household electrification.
- The scheme was launched in September 2017 with an aim to achieve universal household electrification by providing last-mile connectivity and electricity connections to all households in rural areas and all poor households in urban areas across the country.
- The scheme was started with an outlay of 16,320 crore rupees.

85(D). Per Drop More Crop is a key component of 'Pradhan Mantri Krishi Sinchayee Yojana (PMKSY).
- To enhance the adoption of precision irrigation and other water-saving technologies, Per Drop More Crop, has been adopted.
- PMKSY is a Centrally Sponsored Scheme on Micro Irrigation (CSS), first launched

in January 2006.

- Centre- States funding ratio will be 75:25 percent and in the case of the north-eastern region and hilly states, it will be 90:10.
- The scheme is being implemented by the Department of Agriculture, Cooperation & Farmers Welfare (DAC&FW) under the Ministry of Agriculture and Farmers' Welfare.

86(D). The following points characterize the nature of social sciences:

- Concern for value attainment is an important tenet of social sciences. Therefore, social scientists bother always for the goodness or value of something that they attain or deal with.
- Social sciences are primarily interdisciplinary in nature. A concept or issue of social sciences may not be confined to one discipline of social sciences, rather the concept or the issue may be understood taking into account the perspectives of all disciplines of social sciences.
- Social sciences facilitate plurality in thinking in understanding an issue. Since in a social situation, a single effect has numerous causes and a single cause has numerous effects, so, social sciences facilitate multiple thinking referring to a single issue.

Thus from the above-mentioned points, it is clear that all of the above characterize the nature of social sciences.

87(C). The following points may characterize the nature of social sciences:

- Direct bearing on human activity is: Social sciences are those aspects of knowledge that have a direct bearing on man's activities in different sociocultural fields.
- Advance studies of human society: Social sciences are advanced level studies of human society, and they are generally taught at the higher education level.
- Find out truths about human relationships: Social sciences seek to find out truths about human relationships which ultimately contribute to the social utility and advancement of knowledge.
- Social studies are considered now as a core subject at the school level for developing necessary competencies relating to healthy social living.
- Social studies aim at enabling students to adjust to their socio-cultural environment which includes family, community, state, nation and at large the entire humanity.

Thus from the above-mentioned points, it is clear that all of the above is true.

88(C). Concept of Social Studies:

- Social studies aim at enabling students to adjust to their socio-cultural environment which includes family, community, state, nation, and at large the entire humanity.
- Social studies are a realistic course or deal with practical aspects of society.
- Social studies are now at the growing and developing stage. It is trying to make its scope broader and wider.
- Social studies are considered now as a core subject at the school level for developing necessary competencies relating to healthy social living.

So, both the statements are true regarding social studies.

89(C). Social Science is a dynamic discipline that is completely influenced by the social and cultural changes that take place with time. History keeps on changing with time as everything that takes place today becomes a part of history after some time.

- Since history keeps on changing. Hence, it is appropriate to say that the "Changing nature of interpretation of historical events makes the teaching of social science a more challenging subject ".
- It is true and related to the problem of teaching science.
- It is not true that there is a lack of a sufficient number of teachers to teach social science.
- It is not the reason for the changing nature of interpretation of historical events makes the teaching of social science a more challenging subject.

So, it is concluded that (A) is true but (R) is false.

90(B). The teaching of History should focus upon:

- inculcating a spirit of inquiry and discovery in students
- helping learners to build up a sense about what could happen in the future.
- the concept of plural representations and building a sense of historical diversity.
- encouraging students to imagine living in the past and relate to their experiences.
- making learners understand historical diversity and continuous process of development.
- providing learners an opportunity to better understand the world by comparing it with the past.
- making learners understand how the modern world has appeared over long centuries of development.
- enabling students to compare and contrast different time periods and how changes take place with time.

Hence, it could be concluded that the teaching of History focuses upon the concept of plural representations and building a sense of historical diversity and encouraging students to imagine living in the past and relate to their experiences.

91(A). The language of the textbook is often difficult for students to comprehend and the readability of the text is affected. This will result that the students cannot read or understand important concepts.

- A teacher may provide students with a lot of supplementary information, which are easily comprehensible, by using materials like websites, dictionaries, atlas, encyclopedias, etc.
- Always use the textbook sparingly or supplement it with other learning resources.
- The teacher needs to assess what students know about the topic prior to the instructional process and design the learning experiences based on student's existing knowledge.
- As a teacher, you may provide a lot of information by using supplementary materials like websites, dictionaries, atlas, encyclopedias, etc.

Thus from the above-mentioned points, it is clear that only (i) is true.

92(B). A social science teacher willing to enquire with a constructivist perspective would view the learners as c urious to explore on social processes, Imaginative on the basis of sources and trying to suggest solutions to problems.

Social Science teacher willing to enquire with a constructive perspective would view the learner as imaginative, curious and problem solver because it is an experience based teaching method. It keeps the learners active and interactive by providing them some work to make him learn by doing.

93(D). The portfolio is the systematic and organized collection of student work that covers a specific period of time. Alternative assessments can include essays, performance assessments, oral presentations, demonstrations, and portfolios.

A portfolio can contain the following items:

- Completed Assignments and Evaluation
- Journal Writings.
- Photos, sketches and other visuals.
- Self--assessment statements.
- A summary statement made at different points what has been learned.
- Reflections on discussions that have been held out of class.

Thus, it can be concluded that all the above-mentioned points are correct.

94(B). Anecdotal record card: An anecdotal record is a record of some significant item of conduct, a record of an episode in the life of students, a word picture of the student in action, a word snapshot at the moment of the incident, any narration of events in which may be significant about his personality.

- This is an Informal device used by the teacher to record the behaviour of students as observed by him from time to time.
- It provides a lasting record of behaviour which may be useful later in contributing to a judgment about a student.

95(C). Community resources can be used as a resource of teaching learning process to make students understand the concept more clearly.

- It is always suggested to invite a real farmer to the classroom to explain the various processes involved in cropping rather than teacher himself explaining it through lecture method.
- Here the students get a chance to understand the concepts through the narrations given by experience of real life people.
- Similarly in the above example a local health worker is invited to address the children regarding some topic. Here the local health worker shares all his experience with students which results in construction of true and authentic knowledge.
- Moreover here the children do not remain passive but they will be asking a lot of interesting questions to the people who are invited in the classroom.

So, In social science class, if the local health worker is invited to address the children, then the teacher is using Community resource in teaching.

96(C). Field trips are trips that school districts offer to enhance or supplement the educational experience of students. Field trips include events or activities where students leave the school grounds for the purposes of curriculum-related study or outdoor education.

Advantages of field trips

- Field trips offer a unique opportunity for students to create connections, which will help them gain understanding and develop an enjoyment of learning.
- Students on field trips sharpen their skills of observation and perception by utilizing all their senses.
- Students get hands-on experience when they visit any place.
- Field trips allow students to touch, feel and listen to what they're learning about, which helps them build on classroom instruction, gain a better understanding of topics, build cultural understanding and tolerance, and expose them to worlds outside their own.
- A social science teacher takes students to visit the Panchayat office the learn about Panchayat. This is also an example of a field trip where the teacher gives a real experience of learning to the students.

So, A social science teacher takes students to visit the Panchayat office for the learning about Panchayat. In this situation, Field trip learning strategy is adopted by the teacher.

97(A). Textbooks are considered to be the first and foremost tools of the teaching-learning process for both students and teachers. Text book acts as a guide for students and teachers to proceed through different chapters and lessons of the curriculum in a particular sequence which leads to the true construction of knowledge.

- Social science textbooks based on NCF 2005 contain a lot of graphics, pictures, and cartoons.
- As many social science topics are related to real-life only, pictures and cartoons can clearly explain the situations of social life.
- Pictures and cartoons make students understand better each and every concept of social science as a picture speaks 1000 words.
- The use of graphics, cartoons and pictures as learning resources brings visual relief and fun.
- As students like fun learning, they get more interest and curiosity in learning if pictures and cartoons are used.
- Including pictures and cartoons in the textbook acts as a big advantage in curriculum transactions.

So, Both (A) and (R) are true and (R) is the correct explanation of (A).

98(C). Teaching-learning materials (TLMs) also known as instructional aids, facilitate a teacher in achieving the learning objectives formulated by her/him prior to teaching-learning activities start. The materials should be chosen on the following considerations besides ensuring their characteristics:

- Since, at the primary grades, the learning activities are totally related to the real-life experiences of the learners , the materials need to be chosen from their world of real-life activities.
- The materials need to be relevant to the learning of a particular concept(s) dealt in the learning activity. For example, to teach about 'Transport', a teacher may require tourist map of a city, pictures of means of transportation, human settlements, terrain, landslides, road blockage.

So, we conclude that beaker and picture of telephonic booth may not be necessary for teaching transport.

99(B). Social Science is a branch of science that deals with human behaviour and social relationships, which rely primarily on empirical approaches. A source in a social science can be referred as something which tells the origin of an object or an event. For example, Taj Mahal says a lot about Shahjahan. There are two types of sources in social science:

- Primary Source: These are the sources created when the event had taken place. For example, coins, rivers , forts, etc.
- Secondary Source: These are sources which are derived from the primary source after some analysis. For example, biographies, dissertation, indexes, etc.

So, we conclude that biographies, dissertation, indexes are examples of primary source.

100(B). Critical Thinking is the ability to apply reasoning and logic to new or unfamiliar situations, ideas, and opinions. It refers to the process of judging or analyzing facts, events, etc.

Critical thinking in children can be promoted by asking questions in which children start divergent thinking and try to find different answers and assess positive and negative aspects.

- Here, Why did Mahatma Gandhi want to teach children handicrafts? and Why do you think we need the government to find solutions to many disputes or conflicts ? questions provide opportunities to assess critical thinking skills.
- As, in these questions, students think in multiple ways and analyze the facts.

Thus, it is concluded that A and C only is the correct answer.

101(C). Discussion method: Discussion takes place whenever there is a difference of opinion concerning the situation. It involves an interchange of questions and ideas among the students/peers . The purpose of the discussion is to encourage an exchange of ideas and viewpoints. Discussion methods may be superior to lectures or reading for the retention of information. This method has been found to be superior in building attitudes that are important in shaping behaviour patterns.

Note that:

- Develops the ability to discuss in students by active participation .
- Increases self-confidence of students.
- Inspires individuals to act to improve their own situations.
- Brings out past experiences and known facts that may help in the present situation.
- Helps in knowing the viewpoints of others, hence makes it an interactive session.
- Improves analytical and communication skills.

So, the teacher does the above-mentioned activity to make learning process participative.

102(D). The 6 stages involved in the development of critical thinking are as follows:

- Stage One: The Unreflective Thinker (Individual is unaware of significant

problems in thinking)
- Stage Two: The Challenged Thinker (Individual is aware of problems in thinking)
- Stage Three: The Beginning Thinker (Individual try to improve but without regular practice)
- Stage Four: The Practicing Thinker (Individual recognize the necessity of regular practice)
- Stage Five: The Advanced Thinker (Individual advance in accordance with practice)
- Stage Six: The Master Thinker (skilled & insightful thinking becomes second nature)

Thus from the above-mentioned points, it is clear that there are 6 stages involved in the development of critical thinking.

103(D). Some of the popular perceptions about social sciences are that social science is nothing but an encyclopedia of events and places.
- Students also feel that social sciences transmit textbook information which require only to be memorized.
- There is a general perception that since the subject does not inculcate any specialized skill required of the job market, students of social sciences are generally deprived of jobs in the market. Therefore, people sometimes consider social science as a redundant subject.
- There is a common perception among people that social sciences emphasize on retention of information without comprehension.
- Since textbooks in social sciences very often do not include local content and realities, students, teachers and community lack interest and relevance in the social science textbooks due to absence of local content and realities.

So, we conclude that all the above points are misconceptions about social science.

104(D). Main Principles of Project Method:
- The Principle of Purpose: Knowledge of purpose is a great stimulus which motivates the child to realize his/her goal. The student must have a purpose. Purpose motivates learning. Interest cannot be aroused by aimless and meaningless activities.
- The Principle of Activity: Opportunities should be provided to students that make them active and learn things by doing. Physical as well as mental activities are to be provided to them. They are to be allowed to 'do' and to 'live through doing'.
- The Principle of Experience: Experience is the best teacher. What is learnt must be experienced. The children learn new facts and information through experience
- The Principle of Social Experience: The

child is a social being and we have to prepare the student for social life. Training for a corporate life must be given to him. In the project method, the students work in groups.

So, we conclude that the principle of preparation does not come under the project method.

105(B). Project-based instruction: It is a dynamic approach to teaching in which students explore real-world problems and challenges, simultaneously developing cross-curriculum skills while working in small collaborative groups.
- There is already a tendency for students to focus only on their projects, neglecting, therefore, the rest of the courses in the semester.
- In the process of instructing a PBL, some instructors do not prepare all the necessary material and milestones necessary to carry out the project successfully. This occurs mostly as a result of the instructor being new to the PBL process.
- The teacher's unpreparedness and ready for the process affect the students' attitude greatly. The instructors are responsible for making tools available for the project and the necessary technology or software to be used.

So, we conclude that 'Improves rote learning' is not the advantage of project-based instructions.

106(D). Indian government works at three levels:
- the union government;
- the state government; and
- the local level i.e., Panchayats and Municipalities

The local levels include the villages and towns over a certain population. These are called Panchayati System or the Municipalities. The government at the state level relates to the issues of that particular state. The Union government relates to the issues of the entire country.

Thus, we can say that statement (C) is incorrect.

107(B). Democratic governments in our times are referred to as Representative democracies. In representative democracies, people do not participate directly but choose heir representatives through an election process.

MLAs meet and make decision for the entire population. These days, a government cannot call itself democratic unless it allows what is known as Universal Adult Franchise. This means that all adult citizens of the country have the right to vote.

Thus, b oth (A) and (R) is true, (R) is correct explanation of (A).

108(D). Equator is an imaginary line that divides the globe into two equal halves. The Equator represents the zero degree

latitude. Since the distance form the equator to either of the pole is one-fourth of a circle round the Earth, it will measure one-fourth of 360 degrees, i.e. 90°. Thus, 90 degree north latitude marks the North Pole. 90 degrees south latitude marks the South Pole.

Thus, we can say that both (A) and (R) is true and (R) supports (A).

109(D). The parties involved in the "tripartite struggle" were Gurjara-Pratihara, Rashtrakuta and Pala dynasties. They fought for centuries for control over Kanauj. As these three parties were in a long drawn conflict, historians often describe it as the "tripartite struggle". Rulers also tried to demonstrate their powers and resources by building large temples. When they attacked one's kingdoms, they often chose to target temples, which were sometimes extremely rich.

Thus, we can say that b oth A and R is true and R support A.

110(B). The Mongols attacked Delhi twice during the reign of Allaudin Khilji. The first was in the year 1299 and then in 1302-03. Allaudin Khilji constructed a new garrison town called Siri for his soldiers.
Muhammad Tghlaq's administrative measures were a failure. His campaign into Kashmir was a disaster.

Thus, we can say that statements (B) and (C) are incorrect.

111(C). In India, we have governments at the centre, state and local levels.
The Union Government is the first tier of government and the state, is the second tier. Panchayati Raj is the third tier of government in India. The Union government manages the issues of the country. The State government manages the issues of the state. Panchayats and Municipalities manage the issues at the district level.

Thus, we can say that b oth (A) and (B) is false.

112(B). The Indian Constitution guarantees Fundamental Rights to every citizen of India.
There are six fundamental rights in all. Fundamental duties were incorporated into the Indian constitution by the 42nd Amendment. Fundamental Duties cannot be enforced by the courts.
The Indian Constitution also enlists certain core duties that every citizen is expected to perform. These duties are educative in nature and direct the citizens to behave in a virtuous and honourable manner. Fundamental Duties imply the moral obligations of all the citizens of the country. There are 11 fundamental duties in all.

Thus, we can say that only fundamental rights is guarantees by Indian constitution.

113(D). The correct answer from the code is:

(Historic Period)	(Duration)
Mughal (AD 1526 to 1800)	• The Mughal dynasty is Turkish-Mongol Muslim origin dynasty that ruled most of Northern India from the early 16th to mid-18th century
Pre-Historic (2350 to 1800 BC)	• Prehistory, the vast period of time before written records or human documentation, includes the Neolithic Revolution, Neanderthals and Denisovans, Stonehenge, the Ice Age, and more.
Early Historical (600 BC to Ad 5000)	• Early Historical is between 600 BC to AD 5000
Medieval (AD 600 to 1800)	• The medieval period starts from AD 600 to 1800

114(B). Statements 1 and 2 are correct.
Banabhatta: Banabhatta was the court poet of King Harshavardhana of the Vardhana dynasty. Banabhatta has written the biography of 'Harshavaradhana' and called it 'Harshacharita'. So, statement 1 is correct.
Asvaghosa: The scholarship that followed, surmised that "Ashu Ghosa" is possibly the famous Buddhist scholar Asvaghosa, who lived around the 2nd century CE. It is widely known that Ashwagosh was the philosopher guide of king Kanishka. So, statement 2 is correct.
Bharavi: Bharavi, a Sanskrit poet who was the author of Kiratarjuniya, one of the classical Sanskrit epics classified as a maha kavya. So, statement 3 is incorrect.

115(D). While some of the raw materials that the Harappans used were available locally, many items such as copper, tin, gold, silver, and precious stones had to be brought from distant places.
• The Harappans probably got copper from present-day Rajasthan, and even from Oman in West Asia. So, Statement 1 is correct.
• Tin, which was mixed with copper to produce bronze, may have been brought from present-day Afghanistan and Iran. So, Statement 2 is correct.
• Gold could have come from present-day Karnataka, and precious stones from present-day Gujarat, Iran, and Afghanistan. So, Statement 3 is correct.

116(C). Lushai Hills:
• The Lushai Hills are a mountain range in Mizoram and Manipur, India. Hence, 1st pair is correct.
• The range is part of the Patkai range system and its highest point is 2,157 m high Phawngpui, also known as 'Blue Mountain '.
Erramalla Hills:
• It is a range of hills in western Andhra Pradesh state. Hence, 2nd pair is incorrect.
• The hills, which trend northeast to southwest, are situated on the eastern edge of the Deccan plateau, between the basins of the Krishna River (north) and the Penneru River (south).
Javadi Hills:
• They are an extension of the Eastern Ghats spread in the northern part of the state of Tamil Nadu. Hence, 3rd pair is correct.
• Javadi Hills is home to spectacular waterfalls .
Satmala Hills:
• Satmala is a mountain range which runs across Nashik District, Maharashtra. Hence, 4th pair is incorrect.
• They are an integral part of the Sahyadris range within Nashik.

117(B). Rajasthan is the largest producer of Limestone and Karnataka has largest reserves of Limestone.
Limestone:
• Limestone is a sedimentary rock composed mainly of calcium carbonate ($CaCO_3$) in the form of the mineral calcite.
• Madhya Pradesh is the largest producer of limestone and accounts for over 16 per cent of the total limestone production of India.
Gypsum:
• Gypsum is a minor mineral.
• By States, Rajasthan alone accounts for 81% resources, Jammu & Kashmir 14% and Tamil Nadu 2% resources.
• Rajasthan is also the leading producer.
Dolomite:
• Dolomite ($CaCO_3.MgCO_3$) theoretically contains $CaCO_3$ (54.35%) and $MgCO_3$ (45.65%).
• Andhra Pradesh is the leading producer of Dolomite.

118(C). 1 and 3 pairs are correctly matched.
• Bagor:-Mesolithic sites are found in good numbers in Rajasthan. Of them, the Bagor site is very well excavated. Adamgarh in Madhya Pradesh and Bagor in Rajasthan provide the earliest evidence for the domestication of animals; this could be around 5000 B.C. So, pair 1 is correct.
• Bhimbetka in Madhya Pradesh is a striking site belonging to primarily the Paleolithic age. It is situated in the Vidhyan range, 45km south of Bhopal and has more than 50 painted rock shelters. It does not have rock shrines. So, pair 2 is incorrect.
• Mehrgarh: The neolithic people of Mehrgarh were more advanced. They produced wheat, cotton, and lived in mud-brick houses. So, pair 3 is correct.

119(D). 1, 2 and 3 are correct.
• Surkotada follows a different expression for the layout of the settlement. Here, a common periphery wall encloses both the citadel and the lower town. So, pair 1 is correct.
• Chanhudaro is a site located 130 kilometres (81 mi) south of Mohenjodaro, in Sindh, Pakistan. Chanhudaro is the only Harappan city that does not have a fortified citadel. So, pair 2 is correct.
• Banawali is an archaeological site belonging to Indus Valley Civilization period in Fatehabad district, Haryana, India. It is marked by the presence of a well-planned fortified township laid in a radial pattern. So, pair 3 is correct.

120(A). Ajivikas: It was founded by Makkhali Gosala (also called Gosala Makkhaliputta), a friend of Mahavira, the 24th Tirthankara of Jainism. The Ajivikas' central belief was that absolutely everything is predetermined by fate, or niyati, and hence human action has no consequence one way or the other. It is based on the theory of atoms and believes that everything is composed of atoms and various qualities emerge from the aggregates of atoms which is predetermined. So, pair 1 is correct.
Ajnanas: This sect believed in radical scepticism. So, pair 3 is correct.
Charvakas: Philosophical Indian school of materialists who rejected the notion of an afterworld, karma, liberation (moksha), the authority of the sacred scriptures, the Vedas, and the immortality of the self. Of the recognized means of knowledge (pramana), the Charvaka recognized only direct perception (anubhava). The school was main propounded of materialistic view to achieve salvation. It was geared towards the common people, hence, the school was soon referred to as Lokayata or something derived from the common people. So, pair 2 is incorrect.

Practice Test 06

1. While playing, a group of children enact scenes from a recent popular movie. This situation highlights that _______ is an important agency of socialization.
   (a) Family
   (b) Media
   (c) Peers
   (d) Religion

2. According to Kohlberg, which level of moral development of a child shows no internalization of moral values and the moral reasoning of the child is controlled by external rewards and punishment?
   (a) Preconventional
   (b) Conventional
   (c) Postconventional
   (d) Universal ethical principle

3. Children in _____ stage have symbolic thinking but do not realize that actions can be reversed and their judgments are based on the immediate appearance of things.
   (a) Sensori-motor
   (b) Pre-operational
   (c) Concrete operational
   (d) Formal operational

4. Which of the following statement is not correct about development?
   (a) Each phase of the development has hazards
   (b) Development is not aided by stimulation
   (c) Development is affected by cultural changes
   (d) Each phase of the development has characteristics behaviour

5. When a child watches a nature documentary the child may discover new animals and add them to the existing group of animals in his memory. This is called:
   (a) Schema
   (b) Accommodation
   (c) Assimilation
   (d) Equilibration

6. During classroom discussions, the teacher pay attention to boys only rather than girls. This is an example of:
   (a) Gender bias
   (b) Gender identity
   (c) Gender equity
   (d) Gender constancy

7. Which kind of assessment 'Sums-up' how much a student has learned over a period of time?
   (a) Assessment as learning
   (b) Assessment for Learning
   (c) Assessment of learning
   (d) Assessment in Learning

8. Which of the following activities defines cephalocaudal principle?
   (a) Development of spinal cord after other parts of the body
   (b) Development of spinal cord before other parts of the body
   (c) Development in behavior
   (d) Infants waving hands and arms randomly

9. According to Vygotsky, the upper limit of tasks that a learner can successfully perform with the assistance of a more competent individual is termed as:
   (a) Level of Potential Development
   (b) Actual Developmental Level
   (c) Zone of Proximal Development
   (d) All options are correct

10. Which of the following statement are best suited to cater to individual differences of students?
    (i) The curriculum should be organized and made flexible.
    (ii) A separate arrangement should be made for the education of exceptional children.
    (iii) The methods of teaching should be in keeping with the needs of the individuals.
    (iv) The division in classes should be in heterogenous groupings.
    (a) (i), (ii) and (iii)
    (b) (i), (ii) and (iv)
    (c) (ii), (iii) and (iv)
    (d) (i), (iii) and (iv)

11. What is egocentrism according to Piaget?
    (a) Environment is the center of knowledge.
    (b) School is the center of knowledge.
    (c) The child is the center of the world and everything revolves around him.
    (d) None of the above

12. Which of the following is likely to motivate students towards mastery learning?
    (a) Urge for competence
    (b) Urge for fame
    (c) Urge for money
    (d) Urge for power

13. Inclusive Education implies:
    (a) Ensuring learning outcome of every child to be the same
    (b) Including the disabled in the mainstream
    (c) Provides compulsory education for children below 14 years
    (d) Ensuring that no child is left behind in education

14. Which of the following best describes the extent of the effect of heredity upon development?
    (a) Heredity determines how far we will go
    (b) Heredity is the primary determinant of how far we can go
    (c) Heredity is the primary determinant of how far we will go
    (d) Heredity determines how far we can go

15. When the elder brother hides the toy, Karan looks for the toy and finds it. Karan's age according to Piaget is _________.
    (a) 2 year
    (b) 2 month
    (c) 8 to 12 month
    (d) 7 year

16. The young child learns to speak single, discrete words in the beginning. Later, he can join together these sentences in the form of language. Which principle of development is this?
    (a) Development follows a pattern
    (b) Development proceeds from general to specific
    (c) Development is continuous
    (d) Development leads to integration

17. In which stage, does the tendency of children to explore new and move around greatly increase?
    (a) Post Childhood
    (b) Infancy
    (c) Pre-childhood
    (d) None of these

18. Bani doesn't speak much at home, but speaks a lot in school. It shows:
    (a) She does not like her home

much.

(b) Her thoughts and ideas get importance in her school.

(c) Students get a lot of chance to speak in school.

(d) The teachers pay almost no attention to the discipline of classroom.

19. Which of the following does not determine problem solving:

(a) Insight

(b) Mental sets

(c) Entrenchment

(d) Fixation

20. Which of the following statements should not be considered a characteristic of the learning process?

(a) Educational institution is the only place where learning takes place.

(b) Learning is a comprehensive process.

(c) Learning is goal oriented.

(d) Un-learning is also a process of learning.

21. According to the principles of motivation, a teacher promotes learning through?

(a) As a teacher, care should be taken that children behave ethically

(b) Do not expect any kind from the students

(c) Having real expectations from students

(d) Forcing students for their knowledge

22. Which of the following is an instance of formal learning?

(a) Children learning through correspondence lessons

(b) Children learning to draw from their art teacher

(c) Children learning to cook from their parents

(d) Children learning a new game from friends

23. Which characteristic is a student with Attention Deficit Hyperactive Disorder (ADHD) likely to have?

(a) Tendency to sit and do work quietly

(b) Tendency to get distracted easily

(c) Tendency to listen to others carefully for long

(d) Ability to read long passages without breaks

24. Reena always thinks of varied solutions for any problem given in the class. This is a characteristic of-

(a) Mental impairment

(b) Low comprehension

(c) Convergent thinking

(d) Divergent thinking

25. The 'fear of failure' needs to be discouraged in children within a classroom because:

(a) Children's fears cannot be handled within a classroom by a teacher

(b) School cannot take responsibility for emotional lives of children

(c) Failure and errors are a natural part of children's learning

(d) Children who experiences fear are developmental failures

26. The best way to motivate a child to learn is:

(a) To appeal to his/her sense of pride and self respect

(b) To rechannel the motives he/she already has

(c) To threaten him/her with failure and punishment

(d) To tempt him/her with praise

27. A child belonging to a high-class family generally has a pool of information about new technologies but a mediocre child probably has a gist of the information. Which factor affecting learning showed by the statement?

(a) Heredity factor

(b) Personal factor

(c) Environmental factor

(d) Educational Factors

28. Teachers need to create a good classroom environment to facilitate children's learning. To create such a learning environment, which one of the given statements is not true?

(a) Compliance with teachers

(b) Acceptance of the child

(c) Positive tone of the teacher

(d) Approval of the child's efforts

29. Teachers blame learning problems in students based on:

(a) Lack of Motivation

(b) Very low intelligence

(c) Casual parental attitude

(d) None of the above

30. Special needs education is the type of education:

(a) Given to very special people

(b) Given to persons with disabilities

(c) Provided to intelligent people

(d) Established by colonial masters

Ques (31-39): Direction: Read the passage given below and answer the questions that follow by choosing the correct/most appropriate options:

Wimbledon is a tournament apart. It is delightfully anachronistic in that it is played on pristine grass courts, a throwback to the era when the sport was still called 'lawn tennis'. Star players, who otherwise resemble walking billboards, are required to be reticent and don spotless white attire, resonating with the tournament's strict policy of keeping the site relatively free of commercial sponsorships. Until 2021, the tournament even had a 'Middle Sunday' holiday, an out-of-place idea in the era of mega television deals and ambush marketing. And such is the event's magnetic pull that even the biggest crisis to hit tennis in recent times — of Wimbledon barring Russian and Belarusian players against the backdrop of the Russia-Ukraine war and the ATP and WTA retaliating by removing ranking points — did not turn into a smoky inferno. Rafael Nadal, who three weeks ago won his 14th French Open and a record-extending 22nd Grand Slam title literally on one leg, is set to feature after undergoing radiofrequency treatment. Seven-time singles champion Serena Williams has come out of a year-long semi-retirement. Roger Federer's grass-court majesty will be missed — for the first time since 1998 — but such is sport's uncanny knack to replenish itself that there will be enough verdant pomp and splendor as the iconic Centre Court celebrates its centenary year.

Nadal and three-time defending champion Novak Djokovic will be the biggest men's drawcards, along with eighth seed Matteo Berrettini who is seemingly back to his best after recovering from a hand injury. The absence of the top-two ranked men in Daniil Medvedev (barred) and Alexander Zverev (injured) are unfortunate, but the farthest they had progressed at SW19 was the fourth round. Nadal, who is halfway towards an improbable Grand Slam (winning all four Majors in a single year), can be a handful if he survives the first week when the grass is still lush and the bounce low and skiddy. Djokovic will be desperate to add to his 20 Slam titles and avoid the rare scenario where he would not be the reigning champion at any of the four Majors. Berrettini comes in with a grass-court win-loss record of 20-1 since Wimbledon 2019, including two titles at Queen's Club, one at Stuttgart, and a final at Wimbledon 2021. Among women, after the retirement of defending champion Ash Barty, Iga Swiatek has established herself as the numerouno. Grass is admittedly the Pole's weaker surface and there is a closely bunched group with established credentials comprising Serena, Petra Kvitova, Garbine Muguruza, Simona Halep, and Angelique Kerber. But Swiatek's splendid recent form — six titles including Roland-Garros and 35 consecutive match-wins on hard and clay — means she will not be short on confidence even without the specific skillsets demanded by grass courts.

31. Who among the following has a win loss record of 20-1?
(a) Matteo Berrettini
(b) Novak Djokovic
(c) Daniil Medvedev
(d) Alexander Zverev

32. According to the passage, why did Wimbledon bar Russian and Belarusian players?
(a) Due to doping issues
(b) Due to financial crisis
(c) As a part of COVID-19 protocols
(d) Due to the Russia-Ukraine war

33. In this question, a sentence (in bold) from the passage has been divided into five parts (A), (B), (C), (D), and (E). Read the sentence to find out whether there is any grammatical error in it. The error if any, will be in one part of the sentence. If there is no error, the answer is 'No error'. Ignore the error of punctuation if any.
The absence of the top-two ranked men (A)/ in Daniil Medvedev (barred) and Alexander Zverev (injured) are (B)/ unfortunate, but the farthest they (C)/ had progressed at SW19 was the fourth round. (D)/ No error (E)
(a) A (b) B
(c) C (d) D

34. Choose the synonym of the word 'Reticent'.
(a) Reserved (b) Loquacious
(c) Gabby (d) Expansive

35. Which of the following is/are correct according to the given passage?
A. Rafael Nadal will not participate at Wimbledon as he is undergoing radiofrequency treatment.
B. Serena Williams has made a return to the court after a semi-retirement.
C. Roger Federer is the defending Wimbledon men's champion.
(a) Only A (b) Both A and B

(c) Only B (d) Both B and C

36. Why is Rafael Nadal not able to participate at Wimbledon?
(a) Due to doping issues
(b) Due to retirement
(c) As he needs to undergo radiofrequency treatment
(d) All are false

37. Identify the part of speech of the underlined word:
Nadal and three-time defending champion Novak Djokovic will be the biggest men's drawcards.
(a) Adjective (b) Adverb
(c) Noun (d) Pronoun

38. Which of the following women players has established herself better?
(a) Ash Barty
(b) Iga Swiatek
(c) Garbine Muguruza
(d) Simona Halep

39. Choose the antonym of the word 'Pristine'.
(a) Blemished (b) Virgin
(c) Immaculate (d) Flawless

Ques (40-45): Direction: Read the following poem and answer the questions by choosing the correct/most appropriate options:
When the humid shadows hover
Over all the starry spheres
And the melancholy darkness
Gently weeps in rainy tears,
What a bliss to press the pillow
Of a cottage-chamber bed
And lie listening to the patter
Of the soft rain overhead!
Every tinkle on the shingles
Has an echo in the heart;
And a thousand dreamy fancies
Into busy being start,
And a thousand recollections
Weave their air-threads into woof,
As I listen to the patter
Of the rain upon the roof.
Now in memory comes my mother,
As she used in years agone,
To regard the darling dreamers
Ere she left them till the dawn:
O! I feel her fond look on me
As I list to this refrain
Which is played upon the shingles
By the patter of the rain.

40. What is the meaning of the word 'melancholy'?
(a) Happiness (b) Thoughtful
(c) Mysterious (d) Sadness

41. What are the raindrops compared to in the poem?

(a) Drops (b) Tears
(c) Pain (d) Roof

42. Which figure of speech has been used in the line?
And the melancholy darkness
(a) Personification
(b) Anaphora
(c) Alliteration
(d) Repetition

43. The overall tone of the poem is:
(a) Gloomy (b) Optimistic
(c) Challenging (d) Bitter

44. Which figure of speech has been used in the line?
Now in memory comes my mother
(a) Onomatopoeia
(b) Personification
(c) Alliteration
(d) Metaphor

45. What is the central idea of the poem?
(a) Aggravate rain
(b) Rain on the roof
(c) Power of weather
(d) Healing power of rain

46. While learning vocabulary, learners connect one word with its related words and the words which can occur before and after it. What is this technique called?
(a) Dictation
(b) Note making
(c) Collocation
(d) Conversation

47. The 'natural order' in the process of learning English suggests that children:
(a) Are able to speak first then listen
(b) Learn to read and write simultaneously
(c) Are slow at learning to speak when not in school
(d) Acquire some language structures earlier than others

48. The conduction of debate in a language classroom is useful for:
(i) Acquisition of new words
(ii) Fluency practice
(iii) Acquisition of grammatical rules
(iv) Developing the ability to express one's ideas
(a) (i) and (ii) (b) (ii) and (iii)
(c) (ii) and (iv) (d) (i) and (iii)

49. Which of the following is not the advantage of teaching by story telling students?

(a) Enhances a child's vocabulary

(b) Enhances speaking skills of children

(c) Encourage development of emotions and feeling in a child

(d) Makes learning easier

50. **A child is not able to pay attention in a language classroom and shows irrelevant and inappropriate behavior. Which of the following can be considered as the possible reason for this type of behavior of child?**

(a) Dyspraxia (b) Autism

(c) Aphasia (d) ADHD

51. **Authentic material can be used in the classroom:**

(a) to expose students to real language

(b) to make the language learning experience more meaningful

(c) to make language learning enjoyable

(d) All of the above

52. **The teacher prepares questions to see the language ability of the students. In this question, she omits every fifth word in a paragraph and asks students to search for that word. This method of test contrivance is called ______.**

(a) Cognitive test

(b) Vocabulary test

(c) Fill in the blanks test

(d) Bound question test

53. **In language teaching, creative expressions develop the ability to assimilate the concept efficiently by building creative thinking skills. Which is the best method to develop creative expression among students?**

(a) Write summary of the story that has read

(b) Write your experiences about the earthquake

(c) Write a letter for leave for two days

(d) Write an essay on - My Ideal School (in 100 words)

54. **Direction : Answer the following question by selecting the most appropriate option.**
Teachers can remediate for the student with language learning difficulty by:

(a) focusing on individual progress with individualized instruction

(b) providing notes that are summarized and simplified

(c) initially, giving information as reading only, no writing

(d) conduct extra classes for the student to 'catch up' with others

55. **Collection and organisation of ideas, sequencing, cohesion and use of vocabulary are subskills of ______.**

(a) listening (b) speaking

(c) reading (d) writing

56. **A teacher of class VII asks her learners to bring at least two or three objects from home and she asks them exchange the objects among themselves. She now asks them to describe the objects in their hands In at least ten sentences. What are the objects known as in language teaching-learning materials?**

(a) Teachers materials

(b) Inputs for language learning

(c) Realia

(d) Home objects

57. **A child studying in Class V says, 'I drinked water.'**
It indicates that the child ____

(a) has not learnt grammar rules properly.

(b) should memorize the correct sentence.

(c) has over generated the rules for making past tense verbs showing that his learning is taking place.

(d) is careless and should be taught to be conscious of its errors.

58. **Which of the following defines "Innateness Hypothesis" of language acquisition?**

(a) Humans already possess the knowledge of language by birth.

(b) Humans have a natural tendency to acquire language.

(c) Humans are born to learn language.

(d) All of the above

59. **The textbooks included in the curriculum should have which of the following characteristics?**

(a) The introduction at the beginning and conclusion at the end of the chapter should be given in the textbook

(b) It should be content-oriented

(c) A standardized language should be used

(d) A speech on a particular topic should be organized among the students

60. **Which of the following is an**
example of active listening?

(a) Comprehensive Listening

(b) Critical Listening

(c) Therapeutic Listening

(d) All of the above

Social Studies

61. **Who discovered the ruins of Harappa?**

(a) Charles Masson

(b) Dr. Sahni

(c) M. Wheeler

(d) M.S. Vats

62. **Which part of Madhya Pradesh is associated with the Mahajanapada of Avanti?**

(a) Malwa

(b) None of these

(c) Baghelkhand

(d) Bundelkhand

63. **Was the Round Table Conference in London successful for Gandhi?**

(a) Yes, the demands were agreed to

(b) Partial agreements were made

(c) No, the negotiations broke down and Gandhi returned disappointed

(d) Gandhi was treated disrespectfully

64. **In which year Portuguese Pedro Alvares Cabral arrived in India?**

(a) 1485 CE (b) 1455 CE

(c) 1500 CE (d) 1454 CE

65. **The Shuddhi Movement, involving the conversion of non-Hindus to Hinduism, was started by:**

(a) Swami Vivekanand

(b) Swami Vivekanand

(c) Swami Dayanand Saraswati

(d) Aurobindo Ghosh

66. **Whose reign was called the Golden Age of Mughal Architecture?**

(a) Akbar (b) Jahangir

(c) Shahjahan (d) Humayun

67. **The Tropic of Cancer does not pass through which of the following state?**

(a) Mizoram

(b) Tripura

(c) Odisha

(d) Madhya Pradesh

68. **Consider the following statements:**
(A) Rivers existing before the upheaval of the Himalayas and forming valleys in the mountains and cutting towards the south are

known as superimposed rivers.

(B) The Rivers which follow the general direction of the slope are known as the consequent rivers.

Which of the statements given above is/are correct.

(a) Only (A)

(b) Only (B)

(c) Both (A) and (B)

(d) Neither (A) nor (B)

69. The maximum depth of Lithosphere is found in the:

(a) Pacific Ocean

(b) Siberian Plain

(c) Patagonian Desert

(d) Himalayan Mountains

70. In which one of the following countries is intensive subsistence agriculture not predominantly practiced?

(a) India   (b) Japan

(c) Canada   (d) Indonesia

71. Who among the following developed the concept of agrarian society?

(a) Pradipta Rai

(b) Gilet

(c) M N Srinivas

(d) Robert Redfield

72. Which among the following is a Multinational Trade Negotiation Body?

(a) IDA   (b) WTO

(c) IMF   (d) SAARC

73. In July 2022, CRISIL lowered its real GDP growth forecast for India to what percent in FY23?

(a) 7.0 %   (b) 7.1 %

(c) 7.3 %   (d) 7.6 %

74. 'Rubber Board of India' is located at which place?

(a) kozhikode   (b) Kasaragod

(c) Kottayam   (d) Transgender

75. Indira Col forms the triangular border of which 3 countries?

(a) India, Nepal and China

(b) India, Pakistan and China

(c) India, Myanmar and China

(d) India, Bhutan and China

76. What is the name of the Mental Health Rehabilitation Helpline, to be launched by the Social Justice Ministry?

(a) Man Ki Baat   (b) Kiran

(c) Empower   (d) Mind Tree

77. Which Indian state is to launch a direct benefit transfer scheme named "Arunodoi (Orunodoi)"?

(a) Assam   (b) Sikkim

(c) Maharashtra   (d) Gujarat

78. Who appoints the Secretary of Gram Panchayat?

(a) Government

(b) Ordinary person

(c) Election Commissioner

(d) Landlord of village

79. Which of the following is an example of appreciating diversity?

(a) Treating women fairly

(b) Respecting and enjoying cultural and individual differences

(c) Treating people from other ethnic groups fairly

(d) Tolerating people from different racial groups

80. Which of the following belong to the State level government?

(a) The decision of the Indian government to maintain peaceful relations with Russia.

(b) Introduction of a new 1000 Rupee note.

(c) Introduction of two new train connections between Jammu and Bhubaneswar.

(d) The decision of the West Bengal Government on whether to have Board exam in Class VIII for all government schools.

81. Why peoples' lives in India are highly unequal?

(a) Religion and Resources

(b) Deficiency of Efforts

(c) Deficiency of Time

(d) Poverty and Lack of Resources

82. Which of the following statements about Media is/are correct?

A) It helps the citizens to understand how government works.

B) Writing a balanced report depends on the media being censored.

C) Citizens take action on the basis of the information provided by the media.

Select the correct answer using the codes given below:

(a) Only A and B

(b) Only B and C

(c) Only A and C

(d) All of the above

83. Who among the following was not one of the nine gems of the Mughal Emperor Akbar?

(a) Raja Todar Mal

(b) Abdul Rahim Khan-I-Khana

(c) Osman Ali Khan

(d) Raja Birbal

84. Which of the following Maratha ruler defeated the Mughal forces in the Battle of Salher in 1672?

(a) Balaji Vishwanath

(b) Shivaji Maharaj

(c) Balaji Baji Rao

(d) Baji Rao

85. A social science textbooks provide you with several advantages in the classroom one of them are:

(a) Good textbooks are excellent learning resources for both teachers and students.

(b) It encourage the child to use local knowledge and their experiences as pedagogical practices.

(c) Both A and B

(d) Neither A nor B

86. Direction : Select the appropriate option after reading the Assertion and Reason.

Assertion (A): Activity based questions make Social Science lessons debatable.

Reason (R): Social Science is branch of Science that deals with human behavior and social relationships, which rely primarily on empirical approaches and includes disciplines of History, Geography, Political Science. Economics and Sociology.

(a) Both (A) and (R) are correct

(b) Both (A) and (R) are incorrect

(c) (A) is correct and (R) is incorrect

(d) (A) is incorrect and (R) is correct

87. Which of the following is an aspect of progressive education in a Social Science classroom?

(a) Segregation of learners

(b) Functional intelligence

(c) Emphasis on scoring in examination

(d) Respect for plurality and multiplicity

88. A Social Science teacher often takes an objective type formative assessment but she has a doubt about the reliability of the test developed by her. What should be done to increase the reliability of these assessments?

(a) Use standardised test

(b) Use questions given in the booklet of exemplars published by NCERT

   (c) Try to find out what other teachers do

   (d) Increase the number of questions

89. The teaching of social and political life should focus on:
A. Study of Political Institutions.
B. Study of Basic Principles.
(a) Only B
(b) Both A and B
(c) Neither A nor B
(d) Only A

90. Following activities may be included in constructivist approach of teaching:
(a) Drama
(b) Individual assignments
(c) Group work
(d) All options are correct

91. Suppose a teacher has to teach the Chapter, 'The Cold Desert—Ladakh' in Class VII. Which one of the following methods would be most appropriate?
(a) Workshop method
(b) Survey method
(c) Case study method
(d) Regional method

92. Read the given statements A and B and select the correct answer :
A. Critical thinking promotes the building of concepts, applications, and the expansion of ideas.
B. It does not help in understanding and evaluating the arguments and beliefs of others.
(a) A is true and B is false
(b) A is false and B is true
(c) Both A and B are false
(d) Both A and B are true

93. According to the National Focus Group (2006) the teaching of Social Science is losing popularity as:
(a) It presents several situations of conflict in human values
(b) It lays too much emphasis upon scientific temperament
(c) It is considered as a non-utilitarian subject
(d) It encourages many subjects of study

94. Which of these can be considered thinking critically?
(a) Thinking emotionally
(b) Thinking logically
(c) Think actively
(d) None of the above

95. Why would you use narratives in Social Science teaching? Choose the most appropriate reason from the given options.
(a) To ensure completed that syllabus is
(b) To sensitize students so that they can find appropriate role models
(c) To entertain and enliven a class
(d) To link concepts to live realities

96. A student has graduated from a university. He wants help in making the choice of stream of education. The type of guidance to be put in place for such a case will be called ____.
(a) Personal guidance
(b) Educational guidance
(c) Vocational guidance
(d) Social guidance

97. The main problem of social science teaching is:
(a) Traditional teaching methods
(b) Lack of library facilities
(c) Untrained teacher
(d) All of the above

98. Social Science curriculum at the upper primary stage focuses on:
A. Understanding earth as the habitat of life forms
B. Studying own region, state and country
C. Studying India's past and current development
Choose the correct option:
(a) A, B and C
(b) Only A and C
(c) Only A
(d) Only A and B

99. Free and compulsory education is laid down by:
(a) Article 21
(b) Article 21 a
(c) Article 45
(d) Article 42

100. The institution responsible for framing the National Curriculum Framework is:
(a) CBSE
(b) SCERT
(c) NCERT
(d) NUEPA

101. To teach the Partition of India through an inquiry method, which one of the following methods would be most suitable?
1. Collecting eyewitness accounts through interviews/discussions.
2. Holding a lecture on the freedom struggle.
3. Drawing a timeline of India's struggle for independence.
4. Narrating the role of political leaders.
(a) 1 and 2
(b) 1 and 3
(c) only 1
(d) only 4

102. Which one of the following is the most suitable teaching aid to show proportionate size and shape of continents?
(a) Physical map of the World
(b) Poster of the Earth
(c) Globe
(d) Political map of the World

103. A recent education reform proposed by the UGC that seeks to promote uniformity in the evaluation system at higher education is ____.
(a) CBCS
(b) CGPA
(c) SGPA
(d) SSCA

104. ____ evaluation is usually done during the development or modification of a program or product.
(a) Summative assessment
(b) Formative assessment
(c) Term end assessment
(d) Diagnostic assessment

105. In the context of the "Challenge of Expansion", which of the following ideas is correct?
(i) Ensuring greater power to local government.
(ii) Establishing a sovereign and functional state.
(iii) Extension of federal principles to all the units of federation.
(iv) Inclusion of women and minority groups.
(a) (i), (ii), (iii)
(b) (ii), (iii), (iv)
(c) (i), (iii), (iv)
(d) (i), (ii), (iv)

106. Consider the following statements:
1. Gypsum is the residual mass of weathered material.
2. Bauxite is formed as a result of evaporation.
3. Zinc is obtained from the veins and layers of igneous and metamorphic rocks.
Which of the above statements is/are correct?
(a) Only 1
(b) Only 3
(c) 1 and 2 only
(d) 2 and 3 only

107. Consider the following statements:
1. Rooftop rainwater harvesting was usually done to store drinking water, especially in Rajasthan.
2. The concept of rainwater harvesting involves excellent costly technology.
3. Rajasthan is the first state in India to make rooftop rainwater harvesting structures mandatory

for all houses across the state.
Which of the above statements are correct?
(a) 1 and 2 only
(b) Only 1
(c) Only 2
(d) 1, 2 and 3 only

108. **Consider the following statements:**
1. This type of vegetation is found in the north-western part of the country
2. Acacia, palms and euphorbia are the main plant species.
3. Trees are scattered and long roots penetrate deep into the soil to obtain moisture.
4. The leaves are mostly thick and small while the stems are juicy.
The above statements describe which of the following plant types?
(a) Tropical moist deciduous
(b) Tropical dry deciduous
(c) Mountain forest
(d) Tropical thorns and shrubs

109. **Consider the following statements:**
1. The western current brings about a western cyclonic disturbance that affects the weather over the north and north-west regions of India.
2. The eastward flow causes tropical cyclones that occur in October-November along with the monsoon in India.
Which of the above statements is/are correct?
(a) only 1
(b) only 2
(c) both 1 and 2
(d) Neither 1 nor 2

110. **With reference to the Sangam age in Indian history, consider the following statements:**
1. During the Sangam era, Tamilakam was divided into 4 ecozones.
2. The megalithic practice of offering the dead was stopped in the Sangam age.
Which of the above statements is/are not correct?
(a) Only 1
(b) Only 2
(c) Both 1 and 2
(d) Neither 1 nor 2

111. **Consider the following statements:**
1. The Harappans probably got copper from present-day Rajasthan and even Oman in West Asia.
2. Tin, which was mixed with copper to produce bronze, may have been brought from present-day Afghanistan and Iran.
3. Gold could have come from present day Karnataka.
Which of the above statements are correct?
(a) 1 and 2 only   (b) 2 and 3 only
(c) 1 and 3 only   (d) 1, 2 and 3

112. **With reference to the history of India, consider the following pairs:**

Terms	Description
1. Sangrihitri	Tax collecting officer
2. Vrihi	Iron metal
3. Ashramas	Stages of life

Which of the above pairs is/are correctly matched?
(a) 1 and 3 only   (b) 2 and 3 only
(c) 1 and 2 only   (d) 1, 2 and 3

113. **Which of the following statements about the Mughal painting style is correct?**
1. Royal court scenes, battlefield scenes were mostly used as subjects in Mughal paintings.
2. Akbar established the Department of Painting and patronized the use of calligraphy in paintings.
3. The paintings made during the reign of Jahangir lacked vibrancy due to excessive use of gold and bright colours.
Select the correct answer from the options given below.
(a) 1 and 2 only   (b) Only 3
(c) 2 and 3 only   (d) 1,2 and 3

114. **Consider the following statements.**
1. The policy of ring-fencing was followed by Warren Hastings to create a buffer zone to protect the company's borders.
2. It was a policy of protecting the borders of its neighbors to protect its own territories.
3. Warren Hastings used this policy in the war against the Marathas and Mysore.
Which of the given statements is/are correct?
(a) 1 and 2 only   (b) 2 and 3 only
(c) 1 and 3 only   (d) 1, 2 and 3

115. **With reference to the parallel governments formed in provinces as part of the Quit India movement, which among the following pairs are correct:**

1. Ballia	Chittu Pandey
2. Tamluk	Prati Sarkar
3. Satara	Jatiya Sarkar
4. Talcher	Lakshman Nayak

Select the correct answer using the codes given below:
(a) 1 and 4 only
(b) 2 and 3 only
(c) 1, 3 and 4 only
(d) 2, 3 and 4 only

116. **Consider the following pairs:**

Case	Popular for
1. Kesavanandha Bharati case	Basic Structure doctrine
2. Kihoto Hollohan case	Defection
3. M. Nagraj case	Curative petition
4. Rupa Ashok Hurra case	Reservations in promotions

Which of the pairs given above is/are correctly matched?
(a) 1, 3 and 4 only
(b) 1, 2 and 4 only
(c) 1 and 2 only
(d) 2 and 3 only

117. **In which of the following can special provisions for Scheduled Tribes be found?**
1. Fundamental Rights
2. Directive Principles of State Policy
3. Fundamental Duties
4. Legal Rights
Select the correct answer using the code given below.
(a) 1 and 2 only
(b) 1, 2 and 3 only
(c) 1, 2 and 4 only
(d) 1, 2, 3 and 4

118. **With reference to the retired judges of the High Court, consider the following statements:**
1. Ad hoc judges in the Supreme Court can be appointed by the Chief Justice of India only with the prior concurrence of the President and the Chief Justice of the High Court concerned.
2. A retired judge of the High Court can be appointed to act as a judge of the Supreme Court for a temporary period.
Which of the following statement(s) given above is/are correct?
(a) 1 and 2

(b) only 2
(c) only 1
(d) None of the statements are true

119. **With reference to the Directive Principles of State Policy (DPSP), which of the following statements is/are correct?**
1. **They assist the courts in examining and determining the constitutional validity of laws.**
2. **They are not legally enforceable by the courts for their violation.**
3. **They are classified by the constitution into three broad categories, namely socialist, Gandhian and liberal-intellectual. Select the correct answer using the code given below.**
(a) 1 and 2 only (b) 2 and 3 only
(c) only 2 (d) 1, 2 and 3

120. **Consider the following statements:**
1. **The Representation of the People Act, 1951 lays down the guidelines for the registration of a political party.**
2. **The Election Commission of India does not have the power to cancel the registration of parties on the ground of violation of the Constitution.**
Which of the above statements is/ are correct?
(a) Only 1
(b) Only 2
(c) 1 and 2
(d) None of the statements are true

// Hints and Solutions //

1(B). While playing, a group of children enact scenes from a recent popular movie. This situation highlights that media is an important agency of socialization.
The process of learning to internalize the values and norms into itself or the mode of learning to live in society is called the process of socialization. There are many sources of socialization such as School, College, Friends, Society, Neighbourhood, Religion, Caste, Media, newspapers, Meetings, Events, etc.
Media is the source in which observational skills are considered, media such as Television, magazines, Mobile phone, reality shows, newspapers, etc.

2(A). According to Kohlberg the pre-conventional level of moral development of a child shows no internalization of moral values. In this level, the moral reasoning of the child is controlled by external rewards and punishment.
Pre-conventional Level:
• Obedience and Punishment: Based on avoiding punishment, a focus on the consequences of actions, rather than intentions; intrinsic deference to authority
• Individualism and Exchange: The "right" behaviours are those that are in the best interest of oneself, tit for tat mentality.

3(B). Children in Pre-operational stage have symbolic thinking but do not realize that actions can be reversed and their judgments are based on the immediate appearance of things.
Cognitive development involves cognitive processes such as knowing, thinking, remembering, recognizing, categorizing, imagining, reasoning, decision-making, and so forth. Cognitive development proceeds as children mature. Piaget divided cognitive development into four stages.
• Sensorimotor (Birth – 2 years) & Preoperational (2-7 years)
• Concrete Operational (7-11 years) & Formal Operational (11 years and above)
The Pre-operational Stage: This is the second stage of cognitive development which is basically a pre-logical stage as logic has not yet fully developed. It extends from two to seven years of age. They begin to think symbolically. During the Symbolic play, children can create mental images of objects and store them in their minds for later use. For example, such a child can draw a picture of or pretend to play with a puppy that is no longer present there.

4(B). 'Development is not aided by stimulation' statement is not correct about development.
Development is aided by stimulation: While most development occurs as a result of maturation and environmental experiences, much can be done to aid development so that it will reach its full potential. Stimulation is especially effective at the time when the ability is normally developing, though it is important at all times.

5(C). Two basic processes are involved in adaptation: assimilation and accommodation.
• Assimilation takes place when people try to understand something new by fitting it into what they already know.
• For example, When a child watches a nature documentary the child may discover new animals and add them to the existing group of animals in his memory. The fitting of new experience into the already existing scheme is called Assimilation.
• The modification of existing schemes (and the development of new ones) in order to make sense of new experiences is called accommodation.
• For example, the child will keep calling a cat a "dog" until someone corrects him and made him understand the difference between a cat and a dog. He will now have a different scheme for understanding cats.

6(A). During classroom discussions, the teacher pay attention to boys only rather than girls. This is an example of Gender bias.
Gender Bias is behavior that shows favoritism toward one gender over another. Gender bias occurs when we make assumptions regarding the behaviors, abilities, or preferences of students based upon their gender. Therefore, During classroom discussions, when the teacher pays attention to boys only rather than girls. This shows the scenario of gender biaseness.

7(C). Assessment of learning evaluates student learning by comparing it against some standard or level. It 'Sums-up' how much a student has learned over a period of time. The main objective is to rank, grade, classify and compare students periodically that indicate their level of performance. It is considered a Formal method of Assessment as it is conducted at a specific time.

8(B). Cephalocaudal Principle: It states that growth and development follow a pattern that starts with the head then proceeds to the rest of the body (head to foot).
The cephalocaudal principle refers to the general pattern of physical and motoric development followed from infancy into toddlerhood and even early childhood whereby development follows a head-to-toe progression.

9(A). According to Vygotsky, the upper limit of tasks that a learner can successfully perform with the assistance of a more competent individual is termed as level of Potential Development.
The zone of potential development is the upper limit of tasks that a learner can successfully perform with the assistance of a more competent individual. It can be understood as the difference/gap between the actual developmental level and potential developmental level (the upper limit of tasks that a learner can successfully perform with the assistance of a more competent individual) that can be identified while a child is working on a problem.

10(D). (i), (iii) and (iv) statement are best suited to cater to individual differences of students.
By individual differences, we mean physical and behavioural variations, seen in all species including human beings. Some of us are tall, some short, some bright and some are dull. Some of the instructional strategies are discussed below-
• The methods of teaching should be in

keeping with the needs of the individuals.

- The curriculum should be organized and made flexible as per the needs and requirements of the individual.
- Instruction should aim at the development of the student's cognitive process beyond the attainment of information alone.
- In a heterogeneous classroom situation, you can organize instruction based on ability grouping where students are grouped according to the level of their ability, and instruction is modified as stated above to suit the level of their ability.
- The methods of teaching should be in keeping with the needs of the individuals.

11(C). Egocentrism can be defined as the child being the center of the world and everything revolves around him.

Egocentrism in early childhood refers to the tendency of young children to think that everyone sees things in the same way as the child.

12(A). Urge for competence is likely to motivate students towards mastery learning. "Mastery" is a key characteristic of "competency-based learning" that allows learners to keep learning until they feel that they can demonstrate skills mastery.

13(D). Inclusive Education implies ensuring that no child is left behind in education.

Inclusive Education: It is concerned with the learning and participation of all students vulnerable to exclusionary pressures not only those with impairments or those who are categorised 'having special educational needs'. Inclusion is all about embracing all.

14(B). Heredity is the primary determinant of how far we can go this describes the extent of the effect of heredity upon development best.

Heredity provides a basis or potential for the development of any personality trait. Heredity influences physique, motor-sensory equipment and level of intelligence, certain diseases, and temperamental characteristics.

- Heredity is the primary determinant of how far we can go to develop the basis or potential of a child
- The bad environment can suppress good inheritance but the good environment is not a substitute for bad heredity
- Heredity sets the limit of the maximum development of a characteristic, which cannot be crossed by providing the best environment.
- Heredity is represented by 'genes' and the environment is represented by any stimulation minus genes. Thus we find that our body size, the color of skin and

the ceiling of our intellectual capacities are all genetically determined but the final shape of our personalities emerges through our interactions with varied physical, geographical, social, and cultural environments that envelope us. Thus the development of personality is a dynamic process.

15(C). When the elder brother hides the toy, Karan looks for the toy and finds it. Karan's age according to Piaget is 8 to 12 months.

Knowing that objects and people exist even when you can't see or hear them is an important part of object permanence. Jean Piaget, a child psychologist, was the first to uncover this notion, and it is a critical milestone in a baby's brain development.

The capacity of a youngster to perceive that items remain even after they are no longer visible or audible is referred to as object permanence. When an object is concealed from view, infants under a particular age are frequently distressed that it has disappeared.

16(D). The young child learns to speak single, discrete words in the beginning. Later, he can join together these sentences in the form of language. This is Development leads to the integration principle of development.

Development leads to integration: Once the child learns specific or differentiated responses, then, as development continues, she can synthesise or integrate these specific responses to form a whole. For example, the young child learns to speak single, discrete words in the beginning. Later, he can join together these sentences in the form of language. Similarly, a young child may have a specific concept of a car. Later, as she grows, her concept expands as she is able to synthesise new aspects into it.

17(C). In pre-childhood, the tendency of children to explore new and move around greatly increases.

Pre-childhood covers the period from 2 to 6 years. It is also known as the preschool stage. The characteristics of pre-childhood are:

- Some parents feel that behavioral problems of the childhood period are more troublesome than physical care of infants.
- Some behavioral problems occur during this period such as obstinacy, stubbornness, disobedience, and antagonistic.
- It is a toy age because most of the time children are engaged with their toys. These toys are also helpful to educate the children. Toys are an important element of their play activities.
- The tendency of children to explore new and move around greatly increases.
- This is a period when a child is

considered physically and mentally independent. This is also a school-going age.

- Children become more self-sufficient, and independent, and develop self-esteem.
- This is the age of foundations of social behavior. They are a more organized social life they will be required to adjust to when they enter first grade.
- Develop physical, cognitive, emotional, and social development.

18(B). Bani doesn't speak much at home, but speaks a lot in school. It shows her thoughts and ideas get importance in her school.

Selective Mutism is a complex childhood anxiety disorder characterized by a child's inability to speak and communicate effectively in select social settings. These children are able to speak and communicate in settings where they are comfortable, secure, and relaxed. This applies to Bani in the given example, she talks a lot in school because she feels comfortable, secure, and relaxed as her thoughts get acknowledged at school.

19(D). Fixation does not determine problem solving.

Problem-solving is thinking that is goal-directed. In problem-solving, there is an initial state (i.e. the problem) and there is an end state (the goal). These two anchors are connected using several steps or mental operations.

Fixation, or hyper-focusing on a specific interest, is a recognized feature of autism. Fixations, along with other features or symptoms of autism like repetitive behaviors and cognitive inflexibility, may appear from the outside to be symptoms of obsessive-compulsive disorder (OCD).

Insight: Developing Insight is synthesizing the available information and facts to derive a new solution. Insight is preceded by a gradual process whereby relevant parts of the problem are identified.

Mental sets: A mental set is a tendency of a person to solve problems by following already tried mental operations or steps. However, this tendency also creates a mental rigidity that obstructs the problem solver to think of any new rules or strategies. Thus, while in some situations mental set can enhance the quality and speed of problem-solving, in other situations it hinders problem-solving.

Entrenchment- In this a person's not moving beyond how he or she has seen problems in the past. Thus it also determines problem-solving.

20(A). Educational institution is the only place where learning takes place statement should not be considered a characteristic of the learning process.

Learning is the process of being modified,

more or less permanently, by what happens in the world around us, by what we do, or by what we observe.

The characteristics of the learning process are:

- Learning is a continuous process
- Learning is comprehensive
- Learning is goal-directed
- Learning is intentional
- Learning is an active process
- Learning is the outcome of the interaction of the individual with the environment
- Learning is individualistic
- Un-learning is also a process of learning
- Learning is transferable

21(A). According to the principles of motivation, a teacher promotes learning through as a teacher, care should be taken that children behave ethically.

Principle of the motivation in learning:

- Motivation is controlled both intrinsically and extrinsically.
- Motivation should encourage curiosity in the students.
- The motivation should be blended with both praise and encouragement to develop self-reliance among the students.
- The teacher promotes learning through motivation by taking care of the students so that the students behave ethically. The role of the teacher is to guide in the learning process so they take part in the process actively instead of feeling that learning is a burden, the students should feel learning is fun and interesting.
- When students start behaving ethically it will help to develop their character, they will be able to judge which is good or bad, which help them to understand the world.
- The teacher should motivate the students by guiding them, not by forcing and punishment because the child may learn in fear of punishment, but he will never understand the knowledge because he studies in fear of punishment.

22(B). Children learning to draw from their art teacher is an instance of formal learning.

Formal learning is also called structured learning or synchronous learning. Examples of formal learning include classroom instruction, web-based training, remote labs, e-learning courses, workshops, seminars, webinars, etc.

23(B). A student with Attention Deficit Hyperactive Disorder (ADHD) is likely to have the tendency to get distracted easily.

Developmental disorder refers to the severe, chronic disability of an individual which is likely to continue indefinitely. There are different kinds of developmental disorders and ADHD is one of them.

24(D). Reena always thinks of varied solutions for any problem given in the class. This is a characteristic of Divergent thinking.

Divergent Thinking: It is the ability of a student which create something new and present novel ideas. Divergent thinking students have the ability to use imagination and critical reasoning to create new and meaningful ideas.

25(C). Fear is an emotion that creates high levels of anxiety in a person and causes the loss of courage in a person.

- Fear of failure makes a person scared of failing. It commonly happens to the students. The reason for such fear is due to peer pressure, focusing on the outcome rather than concentrating on the learning.
- It even damages the mental and emotional state. Sometimes the fear overpowers the students in such a manner that they even commit drastic measures.
- Children should be counseled and should be made to understand that failure and errors are natural in the process of learning and they should not focus on failure or success, rather they should put effort into developing their concepts.
- Understanding of errors is necessary in the learning process to give insight into children's thinking. It helps the teacher to be aware of learners' learning styles, to cater to them according to their needs.

Thus, it is concluded that the 'fear of failure' needs to be discouraged in children within a classroom because failure and errors are a natural part of children's learning.

26(A). The best way to motivate a child to learn is to appeal to his/her sense of pride and self respect.

Learning is the acquisition of new behavior or the strengthening or weakening of old behavior as a result of experience. It represents progressive changes in behavior. It also involves the acquisition of knowledge, habits, and attitude.

Motivation refers to the process that guides an individual to achieve a goal. Motivation plays important role in the learning process. The teacher is an important person inside the classroom to motivate the child and provide rewards to induce interest in the learner.

27(B). A child belonging to a high-class family generally has a pool of information about new technologies but a mediocre child probably has a gist of the information. Personal factor affecting learning showed by the statement.

Any one of several internal, external, or unknown factors can influence learning. In this section, a classification of the factors influencing learning has been made under the broad headings physiological, personal, socio-emotional, and educational factors.

28(A). Teachers need to create a good classroom environment to facilitate children's learning. To create such a learning environment, compliance with teachers of the given statements is not true. The environment in which learning takes place may be described as a composite of natural conditions, circumstances and influences, and sociocultural contexts in which an individual is situated. Therefore, you can say that the learning environment is the sum total of the surroundings in which individuals interact to enrich experiences and thus leading to learning.

29(A). Teachers blame learning problems in students based on lack of Motivation.

Learning may be defined as "any relatively permanent change in behavior or behavioral potential produced by experience".

- One must remember that some behavioral changes occur due to the use of drugs, or fatigue.
- Such changes are temporary. They are not considered learning.
- Changes due to practice and experience, which are relatively permanent, are illustrative of learning.

30(B). Special needs education is the type of education given to persons with disabilities.

Special education is individualized education for children with special needs. Special education means, Specially designed instruction, to meet the unique needs of a child with special needs including instructions conducted in the classrooms, in the home, in hospital, and institutions and in other settings and instruction in physical education.

31(A). As we can see in the second paragraph of the passage, it is clearly mentioned that " Berrettini comes in with a grass-court win-loss record of 20-1 since Wimbledon 2019, including two titles at Queen's Club, one at Stuttgart, and a final at Wimbledon 2021".

Thus, it can be concluded that Matteo Berrettini has a win loss record of 20-1.

32(D). The fifth sentence of the first paragraph says "And such is the event's magnetic pull that even the biggest crisis to hit tennis in recent times — of Wimbledon barring Russian and Belarusian players against the backdrop of the Russia-Ukraine war and the ATP and WTA retaliating by removing ranking points — did not turn into a smoky inferno."

From the above sentence, we can say that according to the passage, Wimbledon barred Russian and Belarusian players due to the Russia-Ukraine war.

33(B). In the second part of the given sentence, the plural form of the verb 'are' is incorrect.

In the given sentence, the subject 'absence' is a singular subject.

We know that a singular subject always takes a singular verb.

The singular form of the verb 'is' should be used with the singular subject 'absence'.

Therefore, the singular form of the verb 'is' should be used in place of the plural form of the verb 'are'.

Correct sentence: The absence of the top-two ranked men in Daniil Medvedev (barred) and Alexander Zverev (injured) is unfortunate, but the farthest they had progressed at SW19 was the fourth round.

34(A). The word 'Reticent' means Not revealing one's thoughts or feelings readily; not wanting to tell people about things.

Example: She is so reticent about her achievements.

Reserved: slow to reveal emotion or opinions.

35(C). The sixth sentence of the first paragraph says "Rafael Nadal, who three weeks ago won his 14th French Open and a record-extending 22nd Grand Slam title literally on one leg, is set to feature after undergoing radiofrequency treatment" and the first sentence of the second paragraph says "Nadal and three-time defending champion Novak Djokovic will be the biggest men's drawcards, along with eighth seed Matteo Berrettini who is seemingly back to his best after recovering from a hand injury".

From the above sentence, we can say that statements A and C are incorrect according to the given passage.

The seventh sentence of the first paragraph says "Seven-time singles champion Serena Williams has come out of a year-long semi-retirement."

From the above sentence, we can say that statement B is correct according to the given passage.

36(C). The sixth sentence of the first paragraph says "Rafael Nadal, who three weeks ago won his 14th French Open and a record-extending 22nd Grand Slam title literally on one leg, is set to feature after undergoing radiofrequency treatment".

Thus, it can be concluded that Rafael Nadal will not be able to participate at Wimbledon as he needs to undergo radiofrequency treatment.

37(A). Here the underlined word 'biggest' is an adjective i.e a word naming an attribute of a noun, such as sweet, red, or technical.

Biggest means of considerable size or extent; of considerable importance or seriousness.

For example:- I think her biggest fear was that she'd lose him.

38(B). Among women, after the retirement of defending champion Ash Barty, Iga Swiatek has established herself as the numerouno.

Grass is admittedly the Pole's weaker surface and there is a closely bunched group with established credentials comprising Serena, Petra Kvitova, Garbine Muguruza, Simona Halep, and Angelique Kerber.

Thus, it can be deduced that Iga Swiatek has established herself better.

Numerouno means better, more important, or more popular than anything else or anyone else of its kind.

39(A). The word 'Pristine' means Clean and fresh as if new; spotless.

Example: He wasn't about to blemish that pristine record.

40(D). The meaning of the word 'melancholy' is Sadness.

The poet calls darkness as melancholy as it makes him sad.

The rain on the roof take the poet back to the sad memories of his mother when he was a child.

He gets lost in the feeling of being a child, of better days and togetherness of mothers and siblings and becomes sad or gloomy.

41(B). The drops of rain to the tears falling from the eyes on dark gloomy nights.

It represents the poet's sorrowful mood.

It is a representation of the bittersweet feelings that the rainy weather brings.

It shows the duality of enjoying the sound of rain yet thinking of sadness for which the clouds weep.

42(A). Here, personifies darkness who is presented to be in a melancholy mood and sheds tears in the form of raindrops.

It is shown as something with human attributes which is capable of feeling sad.

Personification: a figure of speech in which an idea or thing is given human attributes and/or feelings or is spoken of as if it were human.

Ex: In the poem: recollection is personified when he says that they weave dreams.

43(A). From reading the poem we can clearly see that the tone of this poem is full of sadness.

The poet is sad and thoughtful, and the rain also seems to mirror his emotions as it looks like tears falling softly from human eyes.

After some time the sound of raindrops helps him recover from his melancholic mood.

The poet remembers his mother and the poet takes on a nostalgic tone.

44(C). Alliteration: a literary device that reflects repetition in two or more nearby words of initial consonant sounds.

Alliteration does not refer to the repetition of consonant letters that begin words, but rather the repetition of the consonant sound at the beginning of words.

Ex: 'Darling dreamers' – 'd' sound is repeating

Thus, Alteration figure of speech has been used in these word in the above line: memory my mother

'Now in memory comes my mother' – 'm' sound is repeating

45(D). The central idea of the poem is the healing power of rain.

The musical sound of raindrops falling on the rooftop at night has the ability to revive sweet memories and rouse fancies in an otherwise busy mind.

It represents controlling idea.

The rain has power of healing the mind and the heart of humans as it heals the earth.

46(C). Vocabulary learning includes knowing a word in the language. This means knowing several aspects of words, namely word form, word meaning, and word use. The aspect of word form alludes to the language, either speaking or written as well as the word parts in the language.

Collocation Technique: A collocation is described as a pair or group of words that are connected to one word with its related words and frequently used together. Collocation is a pervasive feature of language and one which is considered very difficult for language learners, even at an advanced level.

47(D). Natural Approach theory is based on the radical notion that we all learn the language in the same way. And that way can be seen in how we acquire our first languages as children. The Natural Approach is a language learning theory developed by Stephen Krashen and Tracy Terrell.

Stephen Krashen, a linguist, propounded the "Theory of Second Language Acquisition", in which he proposed the five main hypotheses, natural order hypothesis is one of them.

The Natural Order Hypothesis in the Process of Learning English Suggests that:
- children acquire their first language in a predictable order.
- children acquire some language structures earlier than others.
- children's age, deliberate teaching, etc don't influence the natural order of acquisition.

The first stage in the natural approach is essentially a silent phase, where nothing seems to be happening.

In this approach, students are given plenty of comprehensible input by the teacher, which facilitates the acquisition of language.

Hence, it becomes clear that the 'Natural Order' in the process of learning English suggests that, children acquire some language structures earlier than others.

48(C). Language learning is the process of learning to speak and understand a foreign language. It helps children to acquire practical commands of language. It is a result of deliberate and conscious effort for a better understanding of foundational skills of language learning.

When a teacher uses the debate as a framework for language learning, s/he hopes to get students to look at any issues from different angles, gather supporting evidence, engage in collaborative learning, delegate tasks, improve communication skills, and develop leadership and team skills - all at one go.

49(B). Storytelling refers to the art of narrating a story. It is used as a strategy in language teaching which broadens children reading choices.

Storytelling is the best teaching method to develop morals, values, and cultural norms among children at the primary level.

To develop morals, values, and cultural norms among children at the primary level Storytelling is the best teaching method, Because:

- Stories are universal in that they can bridge cultural, linguistic, and age-related divides.
- Storytelling can be used as a method to teach ethics, values and cultural norms, and differences.
- Stories function as a tool to pass on knowledge in a social context.
- Stories are effective educational tools because listeners become engaged and therefore remember which also makes learning easier.
- Storytelling is used as a tool to teach children the importance of respect through the practice of listening.
- As well as connecting children with their environment, through the theme of the stories, and giving them more autonomy by using repetitive statements, which improve their learning to learn competence.
- It is also used to teach children to have respect for all life, value inter-connectedness, and always work to overcome adversity which also encourages the development of emotions and feelings in a child.
- Children in indigenous communities can also learn from the underlying message of a story.
- It increases the child's vocabulary as they learn so many new words from the stories in different contexts.

50(D). Learning disabilities refer to certain kinds of disorders in the basic psychological processes of an individual. These disorders are mainly caused by nervous system dysfunction (brain or neurological damage impending one's motor or learning abilities) and also by genetic factor.

Attention Deficit Hyperactivity Disorder (ADHD):

- It is a complex neurodevelopmental disorder that leads to hyperactivity in a child's behavior.
- The child who is suffering from ADHD will show irrelevant and inappropriate behavior i.e., he will be constantly in motion, tapping fingers, poking others for no apparent reason, talking out of turn, and fidgeting is often called hyperactive.
- These children also have difficulty in concentrating i.e., they would not be able to pay attention in class for long. So, they may not be able to complete the task on time and shy away from taking independent charge of doing tasks.
- ADHD leaves a negative impact on language learning as children can be easily distracted. Due to this, they are unable to learn and comprehend the language.
- They will continuously face problems like restlessness and impulsiveness. Their activities and movements seem haphazard which can be observable through their behavior in the classroom.

51(D). The learning process is aimed to bring out the permanent desirable changes in the behavior of an individual. The teaching-learning process respects the diversity among students and the teacher follows different paths to achieve the goals of learning.

The teachers use different materials such as charts, models, film-strips, video clips, etc. to arouse the interest of students in learning and to keep them indulging actively in the teaching-learning process. These materials are known as "TLM" or "teaching-learning materials".

52(B). A test is a kind of assessment to measure the knowledge, skills, and aptitude in a specified field. A test is used to analyze the performance of the students and also to know the reliability of the teaching-learning process.

There are generally oral and written types of tests. The written tests can be short answer type, objective type, long answer type, and essay type tests.

The teacher usually takes the written test in a classroom and may or may not inform the students about the content, date, and duration of the test.

53(A). Creativity is the recombination or reconstruction of ideas that leads to a new thought, a new output, or a new product. Everyone has a need to express him/herself in a way that is unique to him or her and any such expression is creative.

- Creative thinking can be developed while promoting the acquisition of content knowledge through approaches that encourage exploration and discovery rather than rote learning and automation.
- While designing learning experiences, teachers can plan and frame the curriculum and provide tools that give students options, voice, and choice in order to enable them to be creative.

54(A). Remedial Teaching is an integral part of the teaching-learning program, also known as compensatory or corrective teaching.

The objective of remedial teaching is to give additional help to learners who have fallen behind the rest of the class in any topic or subject.

It is the process of identifying slow learners and providing them with the necessary help and guidance to overcome their problems.

Objectives of Remedial Teaching in the English language:

- To provide individualized teaching with intensive remedial support.
- To eliminate ineffective habits.
- To make learners learn better by giving additional help.
- To provide learning activities and practical experiences to pupils according to their abilities and requirements.
- To teach again the language items not properly learned.
- To arise learners' interest in learning with stimulating approaches.
- Help the pupils to get rid of their common or specific weaknesses.
- To transmit practical experiences to learners according to their diverse needs.

Hence, teachers can remediate for the student with language learning difficulty by focusing on individual progress with individualized instruction.

55(D). Collection and organisation of ideas, sequencing, cohesion and use of vocabulary are subskills of writing.

Sub-skill- A skill that makes up a part of a larger skill. The language skills of speaking, listening, writing, and reading is often divided into sub-skills, which are specific behaviors that language users do to be effective in each of the skills.

56(C). Teaching Learning Material (TLM), also known as instructional aids, facilitate a teacher in achieving the learning objectives formulated by her/him before starting teaching-learning activities. These are used by teachers to help learners to learn concept with ease and efficiency.

Realia refers to the objects associated with everyday life to be used in the classroom. Using realia in the language class means bringing real objects as teaching aids. It includes coin, newspaper, map, tickets, fruits, vegetables, etc.

57(C). Grammar has been succinctly defined as a study of the morphology and syntax of a language. In simple words, grammar has to do with the form and function of words and the way they are combined to form sentences. In essence, grammar is the study of how language functions.

A child studying in Class V says, 'I drinked water.'

- It indicates that the child knows the rule of the past tense but couldn't make clear sentences.
- It also shows that his learning is taking place.
- The child is aware of the rule that we use the '-ed' form of the verb in the past tense, but he/she isn't aware of how to frame sentences.

From the above, we can say that the child has over-generated the rules for making past tense verbs showing that his learning is taking place.

58(B). The "Innateness Hypothesis" of language acquisition is also known as "Language Acquisition Device". It was proposed by Noam Chomsky. Language Acquisition Device or LAD is a hypothetical module of the human mind through which an infant or child is enabled to acquire or produce language. In simple words, the theory proposes that humans have a natural tendency to acquire language.

59(A). The textbook is the area in which the language material presented is prescribed for teaching and learning. A good textbook not only teaches but it also tests. The content of the book should be very clear, a proper beginning is required to prepare the learners for the upcoming content and a perfect conclusion is required to assemble the entire learning.

60(D). All the given types of listening in the options are active form of listening. They require analysis and deep understanding of what is being said by the speaker. Active listening involves responding to the speaker so that she understands that the listeners are getting the message she wants to deliver. It is focused listening, where our aim is to gain something from the speaker. The qualities like empathy, attention and practice are very important for active listening. These qualities help the listener to understand the speaker and her message.

61(A). Charles Masson 1800-1853 was the pseudonym of James Lewis, a British East India Company soldier and explorer. He was the first person to discover the ruins of Harappa near Sahiwal in Punjab, now in Pakistan.

62(A). The correct answer is **Malwa** . Avanti was an ancient Indian Mahajanapada, roughly corresponded to the present-day Malwa region.

- Avanti was an ancient Indian Mahajanapada, roughly corresponded to the present-day Malwa region.
- According to the Buddhist text, the Anguttara Nikaya, Avanti was one of the solace Mahajanapada (sixteen great realms) of the 6th century BCE.
- The Janapada was divided into two parts by the Vindhyas, the northern part had its capital at Ujjayini and the southern part had its centre at Mahishmati.

63(C). No, Gandhiji was disgusted at the Second Round Table Conference because nobody paid any attention to his demands for immediate and full responsible Government for India.

The Second Round Table conference was held in London from September to December 1931. Gandhiji was the sole representative of the Congress. Nothing could be achieved from the Second Round Table Conference. Gandhiji was disappointed, he came back and started the Civil Disobedience Movement.

64(C). In c. 1500 CE, another Portuguese Pedro Alvares Cabral arrived in India and Vasco da Gama also made a second trip in c. 1502 CE.

Pedro lvares Cabral was a European Portuguese. Whose birth is believed to be around 1467 or 68 in Belmonte, Portugal. Pedro was a sailor and explorer. But after the discovery of Brazil, he also came to be known as Brazil explorer.

65(C). The Shuddhi Movement, involving the conversion of non-Hindus to Hinduism, was started by Swami Dayanand Saraswati. The socio-political movement, derived from ancient rite of shuddhikaran, or purification was started by the Arya Samaj, and its founder Swami Dayanand Saraswati and his followers like Swami Shraddhanand, who also worked on the Sangathan consolidation aspect of Hinduism, in North India, especially Punjab in early 1900s, though it gradually spread across India. Shuddhi had a social reform agenda behind its belligerent rationale and was aimed at abolishing the practise of untouchability by converting outcasts from other religions to Hinduism and integrating them into the mainstream community by elevating their position, and instilling self-confidence and self-determination in them.

66(C). Shahjahan's reign (1628 - 1658) is known as the golden age of Mughal architecture.

Reasons:-

- He erected several large monuments like the Taj Mahal, the Red fort etc.
- There was peace during his reign.
- There were no foreign threats.
- He also did a lot of welfare work like constructing roads, canals.
- Trade and commerce flourished.

Shah Jahan (1628 - 1658)

- Shah Jahan transferred his capital from Agra to Delhi in 1638.
- He created Shahjahanabad.
- He constructed the Jama Masjid and the Moti Masjid.
- He also built the famous Peacock throne.
- Aurangzeb imprisoned him in 1658.

67(C). The Tropic of Cancer does not pass through Odisha state.

- Tropic of Cancer is an imaginary line, at an angle of 23.50 degrees North from the Equator, that passes through the middle of India.
- Tropic of Cancer passes through 16 countries, 3 continents, and 6 water bodies.
- The Tropic of Cancer passes through eight states in India: Gujarat (Jasdan), Rajasthan (Kalinjarh), Madhya Pradesh (Shajapur), Chhattisgarh (Sonhat), Jharkhand (Lohardaga), West Bengal (Krishnanagar), Tripura (Udaipur) and Mizoram (Champhai).

68(B). The Rivers which follow the general direction of slope are known as the consequent rivers. Most of the rivers of peninsular India are consequent rivers. For example, rivers like the Godavari, Krishna and Kaveri, descending from the Western Ghats and flowing into the Bay of Bengal, are some of the consequent rivers of Peninsular India. Therefore, statement (B) is correct.

The Rivers that existed before the upheaval of the Himalayas and cut their courses southward by making gorges in the mountains are known as the antecedent rivers. The Indus, Satluj, Ganga, Sarju (Kali), Arun (a tributary of Kosi), Tista and Brahmaputra are some of the important antecedent rivers, originating from beyond the Greater Himalayas. Therefore, statement (A) is not correct.

69(A). The maximum depth of Lithosphere is found in the Pacific Ocean. The Mariana Trench is the deepest part of the ocean and the deepest location on Earth about 11,035 meters (36,201 feet) deep. The deepest point of Mariana Trench is Challenger Deep. It is located in the South Pacific Ocean and so the maximum depth of Lithosphere is found in the Pacific Ocean.

70(C). Intensive subsistence agriculture not predominantly practiced in Canada.

- Intensive farming is the kind of farming in which farmers grow their crops, fruits, and vegetables on a small piece of land using simple tools.
- These farmers usually grow food for personal use, or they sell it to local groceries.
- This type of agriculture can be found in China, Japan, Korea, India, Pakistan, Indonesia and Sri Lanka.

71(D). Robert Redfield developed the concept of an agrarian society.

According to Robert Redfield, "the rural people who control and cultivate their land for a living and whose agriculture is a part of the traditional way of life and who look to the elite or urban people and are influenced by them." Those whose way of life is somewhat more civilized than them are called agrarian society.

72(B). WTO is a Multinational Trade Negotiation Body.

The World Trade Organization (WTO) is an intergovernmental organization that is aimed to promote and regulate the regulation of international trade between nations. It commenced its operations on 1 January 1995 under the Marrakesh Agreement.

73(C). Domestic rating agency CRISIL lowered its real GDP growth forecast for India to 7.3 percent in FY23 from 7.8 percent estimated earlier.

- It attributed the downward revision to higher oil prices, slowing of export demand, and high inflation.
- This is in line with the RBI's estimate of 7.2 real GDP growth for this fiscal year.
- There is a slew of negatives like high commodity prices, elevated freight prices, drag on exports as global growth projections get lowered, and the largest demand-side driver of private consumption remains weak.
- Inflation, which has been pegged to average at 6.8 percent in FY23 as against 5.5 percent in FY22, reduces purchasing power and would weigh on the revival of consumption the largest component of GDP.
- The current account will be impacted and estimated the current account deficit to widen to 3 percent of GDP in FY23 from 1.2 percent in FY22.
- The agency expects global crude to average between USD 105-110 per barrel in FY23, which is higher by 35 percent when compared to the last fiscal year and will be the highest price since 2013.

74(C). Rubber Board was established by the Rubber Act, 1947, the headquarter of this board is located at Kottayam, Kerala.

- The Rubber Board works for the development of the rubber industry in the country by supporting and promoting related research, development, extension and training activities.
- Rubber Research Institute is under Rubber Board.
- The British established the first rubber plantation in India in the year 1902 on the banks of the Periyar River in Kerala.
- India is currently the fifth largest producer of this natural material with the highest productivity.
- Top rubber producing states: Kerala > Tamil Nadu > Karnataka.
- Recently, there were protests by farmers and various organizations due to the price of Natural Rubber-NR hitting a 16-month low in the Indian market.

75(B). Indira Kol is situated at an altitude of 5,764 meters in the Siachen Glacier, the place bordering India, Pakistan and China. India's northernmost point Indira Col is located at Siachen Muztagh in the Karakoram Range at an altitude of 5,764 meters (18,911 ft). This is the point where the borders of India, Pakistan and China are adjacent.

Indira Kol is not related to the former Prime Minister of India, Indira Gandhi. Eastern Indira Kol Bindu was named after one of the names of Goddess Lakshmi by the "Bulk Workman" in 1912.

76(B). The Union Minister for Social Justice and Empowerment Thaawarchand Gehlot launched the mental health rehabilitation helpline "Kiran".

To provide relief and assistance to persons suffering from mental illness, a 24x7 toll-free Mental Health Rehabilitation Helpline, "Kiran" was launched by the Ministry of Social Justice & Empowerment, virtually through webcast.

77(A). The state of Assam has proposed to launch a Direct Benefit Transfer (DBT) scheme named "Arunodoi".

This scheme will be launched in lines with the flagship DBT scheme Jan Dhan Yojana. This is claimed as the largest DBT scheme of Assam till date. The scheme also called as Orunodoi, seeks to transfer Rs 830 per month to around 19.7 lakh families. The main beneficiaries of the scheme will be women.

78(A). The Gram Panchayat Secretary is appointed by the government.

Gram Panchayat is the lowest level of governing institute of villages. Gram Panchayat is constituted of 5 members- the Sarpanch, the Upsarpanch, and Three Panch.

- The Secretary of the Gram Panchayat is a non elected representative selected by the State Government.
- He is responsible for conducting the meetings and also keeps a record of the proceedings.
- The Secretary ensures that the meetings are conducted smoothly without any disputes. He also ensures that all members attend the meetings and presents the Action Taken Report on resolutions of previous Gram Sabha meetings.
- The Secretary overviews all the Panchayat Activities . So, the correct answer is the Government .

79(B). The true meaning of diversity is to respect and enjoy a wide range of cultural and individual differences.

- To appreciate diversity, a person must go beyond tolerating and treating people from different racial and ethnic groups.
- To be diverse is to differ in some measurable way, even if the difference is not apparent on the surface.
- The diversity umbrella should cover everyone in an organization.
- To value diversity is to appreciate individual differences among people.
- The goal of a diverse organization is for individuals of all cultural backgrounds to achieve their full potential, not restricted by group identities such as gender, nationality, or race.

80(D). "Decision of the Government of West Bengal on whether there is a board examination in class VIII for all government schools" This statement pertains to the state level government.

- A state government is the government of a country subdivision in a federal form of government , which shares political power with the federal or national government .
- A state government may have some level of political autonomy , or be subject to the direct control of the federal government .
- This relationship may be defined by a constitution .

81(D). The life of the people in India is due to extreme unequal poverty and lack of resources.

Poverty:

- It is a function not only of income but also of income distribution.
- Importantly, the relationship between development and poverty is mediated by inequality.
- It is caused by lack of food, resources, government aid, income, infrastructure, high costs and social injustice.

Lack of resources:

- This can lead to inter-state disparities like in Maharashtra, Andhra Pradesh and Karnataka due to excess water logging in Maharashtra from Koyna dam.
- In an area due to paucity of resources, people may try to use maximum from minimum resource which can lead to over-exploitation.

82(C). Some facts about Media:

- The media provides information to the public by its reporting of and commentary upon the proceedings within the Parliament, the operations of the Government, and the views and alternate policies of the Opposition.
- It helps the citizens to understand how the government works .
- But the reality is that the media is far from independent . The government has control over the media.
- A balanced report is one that discusses

all points of view of a particular story and then leaves it to the readers to make up their minds.

- Citizens take action on the basis of the information provided by the media.
- Writing a balanced report, however, depends on the media being independent.

So, the correct statements are Only A and C.

83(C). Osman Ali Khan was not one of the nine gems of the Mughal emperor Akbar.

He was the last Nizam of the Princely State of Hyderabad, the largest princely state in British India.

He ascended the throne on 29 August 1911, at the age of 25, and ruled the Kingdom of Hyderabad between 1911 and 1948, until India annexed it.

84(B). Shivaji Maharaj defeated the Mughal forces in the Battle of Salher in 1672. He was the second son of Shahaji, was the creator of the Maratha nation.

He united the Maratha Chiefs from Malwa, Konkan, and Desh regions to carve out a small kingdom. He took control of the hereditary Jagir after the death of his guardian Konadev in 1647. He was born in the hill fort of Shivner in 1627. He began his military career at a young age. He captured the fort of Toran in 1656. From 1656, he started capturing many other forts from the local officers of Bijapur. After some time, Shivaji raided the Bijapur.

85(A). Textbooks provide you with several advantages in the classroom:

- They provide organized units of work; they provide you with ideas for planning your instructional process.
- They provide a balanced, chronological presentation of information.
- They provide administrators and teachers with a complete programme.
- Good textbooks are excellent learning resources for both teachers and students .
- They are very helpful for beginner teachers as they contain course to be dealt with in the class, and each lesson's design is carefully elaborated.

Thus from the above-mentioned points, it is clear that good textbooks are excellent learning resources for both teachers and students.

86(D). Activity-based questions that make Social Science lessons debatable is incorrect statement.

- Activity-based questions indulge students in activities by stimulating their senses such as sight, smell, the vision of feeling, and getting them involved in the subject.
- Activity-Based Questions do not make social science more debatable but it makes social science more enjoyable, interesting, enjoyable and also gives freedom to students for self-learning,

self-guiding.

- Through these questions, students are involved more in learning activities rather than listening and less emphasis is placed on transmitting information and more on developing students' skills.

So, it can be concluded that given Assertion(A) is incorrect but Reason (R) is correct.

87(B). Functional intelligence is one aspect of progressive learning in a social science classroom.

- Progressive learning, with an emphasis on learning by doing (actionable intelligence), is based on three main ideas: autonomous student work, living and learning in a community, and the involvement of students and parents in school life.
- In the curriculum based on progressive learning, the emphasis will be on enabling the learner to understand the world in his/her own terms through the enquiry below.
- The course will therefore focus on the processes that enable the learner to build a higher understanding of the world.
- In the social science classroom, there is an emphasis on the child's problem-solving and critical thinking.
- Group work, cooperative learning, and development of social skills, development of democracy.

88(A). Standardized testing should be used to increase the reliability of these estimates.

- **Standardized tests:** They are concerned with the whole field of knowledge or ability tested. These tests are made by experts to compare the achievement of individual groups. If a teacher wants to increase the reliability of the test developed by her so should use a standardized test.
- **Non-standardized tests (Teacher-made tests):** They are concerned with limited and specific fields of knowledge or ability of performance. These are for local use for some particular institutions on small scale.

89(B). Teaching of social sciences requires the use of non-textual sources like diagrams, maps etc. It studies human behavior and elucidates vision or attitude about society.

- Political Science is a social science discipline that deals with the study of state, nation, government and politics and policies of government.
- The teaching of social and political life should focus on both political institutions and basic principles.
- Teaching of social and political life requires an interactive and experimental situation, therefore both

require creativity, critical comprehension and problem-solving ability of the learners.

- It helps to learn socialization and become a gem for the society.

Thus, it becomes clear that the teaching of social and political life should focus on the study of political institutions and the study of fundamentals.

90(D). Acting, individual work and group work are activities that are included in the constructivist teaching approach.

Some activities encouraged in constructivist classrooms:

- Experimentation - Students individually perform an experiment and then come together to discuss the results in the group.
- Project Work - Students choose a topic as a project and complete the project and present their findings to the class.
- Field Trips - This allows students to put the concepts and ideas discussed in class in a real-world context. Field trips are followed by classroom discussions.
- Visuals - These provide visual context and thus bring another sense into the learning experience
- Classroom discussions - This technique is used in all of the methods described above. It is one of the most important aspects of constructivist teaching methods.

91(C). Case study method is the best method for the above situation.

Types of case study:

- Illustrative Case Studies: These are primarily descriptive studies. They typically utilise one or two instances of an event to show what a situation is like. Illustrative case studies serve primarily to make the unfamiliar familiar and to give readers a common language about the topic in question.
- Exploratory (or pilot) Case Studies: This type of case studies performed before implementing a large scale investigation. Their basic function is to help identify questions and select types of measurement before the main investigation. The primary pitfall of this type of study is that initial findings may seem convincing enough to be released prematurely as conclusions.
- Cumulative Case Studies: These serve to aggregate information from several sites collected at different times. The idea behind these studies is the collection of past studies will allow for greater generalisation without additional cost or time being expended on new, possibly repetitive studies.

92(A). Critical Thinking: The ability to apply reasoning and logic to new or unfamiliar situations, ideas, and opinions. It refers to the process of judging or analyzing facts, events, etc. It requires proper analysis, evaluation, inference, and explanation.

- Thinking critically involves seeing and observing things in an open-minded way and examining an idea or concept in a way to form as many angles as possible.
- Critical thinking promotes the building of concepts, applications, and the expansion of ideas.
- It helps in understanding and evaluating the arguments and beliefs of others.

So, from the above-mentioned points, it becomes clear that statements A is true, and statements B is false.

93(C). According to the National Center Group (2006), teaching of the social sciences is declining in popularity, considering it a non-utilitarian discipline.

- According to the National Focus Group (2006) report, the popular belief of social science is that it is a non-utility subject.
- As a result, low self-esteem controls the classroom-transactional process, given that both teacher and student are uninterested in understanding its content.
- In the early stages of schooling, it is often suggested to students that the natural sciences are superior to the social sciences, and that they are the domain of 'bright' students.
- Therefore, there is a need to emphasize that the social sciences are essential to provide the social, cultural and analytical skills needed to adjust to an increasingly interdependent world, and to deal with political and economic realities.

94(C). "Think actively and be aware of potential problems in the information you encounter." can be considered thinking critically.

Critical thinking is the analysis of available facts, evidence, observations, and arguments to form a judgement. The subject is complex; several different definitions exist, which generally include the rational, skeptical, and unbiased analysis or evaluation of factual evidence.

95(D). Narration is important to link concepts to live realities.

Narration/Storytelling: It is a skill wherein the narrator communicates to the listeners through oral and non-verbal gestures. This withholds the attention of the listeners. In fact it is an art in itself which aims at presenting to the students through the medium of speech which is clear, vivid and interesting, with an ordered sequence of events in such a way that the students are able to reconstruct these happenings and they live in their imagination through experiences recounted.

96(B). If a student has graduated from a university and he wants help in making the choice of the stream of education, then educational guidance will be required.

Educational Guidance: Educational guidance is concerned with the assistance given to students in their choice and adjustment in relation to school, curriculum, courses and school life. It is primarily concerned with the problems related to courses, curriculum and study.

Objectives of Educational Guidance:

- To monitor the academic progress of the students.
- To acquaint the students with the prescribed curriculum.
- To identify the academically gifted, backward, creative, and another category of special learners.
- To assist students in getting information about further education.
- To diagnose the learning difficulties of students and help them overcome the same.

97(D). Social sciences occupy an important place in the school curriculum, however, social science teaching faces a number of problems which include:

- Untrained teacher.
- Lack of library facilities.
- Less use of audio-visual aids.
- Traditional examination system.
- Traditional teaching methods.
- Lack of inadequate training facilities.

So, it can be interpreted that all the problems mentioned are related to social science teaching.

98(A). **The remarks of National Focus Group on Teaching Social Sciences (2006) on the teaching of Social Sciences at the Upper Primary Stage:**

The objectives of teaching the social sciences at the upper primary stage are:

- To develop an understanding of the earth as the habitat of humankind and other forms of life.
- To initiate the learner into a study of her/ his own region, state, and country in the global context.
- To initiate the learner into a study of India's past, with references to contemporary development in other parts of the world.

99(B). The Constitution (Eighty-sixth Amendment) Act, 2002 inserted Article 21-A in the Constitution of India to provide free and compulsory education of all children in the age group of six to fourteen years as a Fundamental Right in such a manner as the State may, by law, determine.

100(C). The institution responsible for framing the National Curriculum Framework is NCERT.

The National Education Policy 2020 (NEP 2020) aims to devise four National Curriculum Frameworks (NCFs), for which a comprehensive strategy has been worked out jointly by the Ministry of Education (MoE) and National Council of Educational Research and Training (NCERT).

101(C). The most appropriate strategy is to teach the partition of India through an investigative method to collect eyewitness views through interviews/discussions. So, only statement 1 is correct.

- Inquiry-Based Learning: The inquiry-based instructional method treats learning as an experience, a process, and not as a passive set of facts. Therefore, rather than the product (amount of accumulated knowledge), the path (learning process) is important.
- It is suitable for learning concepts and propositions in science as well as other subject areas.
- Its levels are affirmed, structured, directed and free. The level of inquiry is determined by the guidance/ information provided by the teachers to the students to find out the solution to the problem.
- Artifacts are representative of cultures, historical eras and geographic location. They make history learning meaningful because children have opportunities to understand and build knowledge.

102(C). Globe is the most suitable teaching aid to show the proportionate size and shape of continents.

- Globes are the exact figure or model of the earth.
- It illustrates the correct shape, size, and location of various Continents, Countries, Oceans, Seas, and Cities on the earth.
- The rotation and revolution of the earth can be very clearly shown by it along with the continents and oceans.

103(A). A recent education reform proposed by the UGC that seeks to promote uniformity in the evaluation system in higher education is the CBCS.

- A choice-Based Credit System (CBS) is one of the steps of UGC to bring equity, efficiency, and academic excellence to the National Higher Education System.
- The majority of Indian higher education institutions have been following marks or percentage-based evaluation system, which obstructs the flexibility for the students to study the subjects/courses of their choice and their mobility to different institutions.
- There is a need to allow flexibility in the education system so that students depending upon their interests and aims can choose interdisciplinary, intra-disciplinary, and skill-based courses.
- This can only be possible when a choice-based credit system (CBCS), an internationally acknowledged system, is adopted.

104(B). Formative evaluation is usually

done during the development or modification of a program or product.

- Formative evaluation ensures that a program or program activity is feasible, appropriate and acceptable before it is fully implemented.
- It is usually conducted when a new program or activity is being developed or when an existing one is being adapted or modified.

105(C). The correct options are (i), (iii), (iv).

Most of the established democracies face the challenge of expansion. This involves applying the basic principle of democratic government across all the regions, different social groups, and various institutions. Ensuring greater power to local governments, extension of the federal principle to all the units of the federation, inclusion of women and minority groups, etc., fall under this challenge. This also means that less and fewer decisions should remain outside the arena of democratic control. Most countries including India and other democracies like the US face this challenge.

106(B). Minerals are commonly found in the following forms:

Minerals in igneous and metamorphic rocks can occur in cracks, vents, faults or joints. The smaller presence is called a vein and the larger one is called a vein deposit. Major metallic minerals like tin, copper, zinc and lead are obtained from veins and lodes. Hence statement 3 is correct.

Many minerals in sedimentary rocks are found in beds or layers. They are formed as a result of deposition, accumulation and concentration in horizontal strata. Some forms of coal and iron ore have been concentrated as a result of prolonged extreme heat and pressure. Another group of sedimentary minerals includes gypsum, potash salts and sodium salts. These are formed as a result of evaporation especially in arid regions. Hence statement 1 is wrong

Another method of formation involves the decomposition of surface rocks and the removal of soluble components, leaving the residual mass of weathered material containing the ore. This is how bauxite is formed. Thus, statement 2 is wrong.

107(B). Statement 1 is correct.

Rainwater Harvesting: It is a technique to collect runoff from a structure or other impervious surface to store it for later use. Traditionally, this involves the harvesting of rain from the roof. The rain will collect in the drain that drains the water into the drainpipe and then into some sort of storage vessel.

- Rainwater harvesting systems can be as simple as collecting rain in a rain barrel or collecting rainwater in large pools to meet your entire household demand.

- The practice of 'rooftop rainwater harvesting' (rooftop rainwater harvesting) to store drinking water was prevalent especially in Rajasthan.
- Tamil Nadu is the first state in India to make rooftop rainwater harvesting structure mandatory in all houses across the state. Hence statement 3 is wrong.
- Amendments to section 215(a) of the Tamil Nadu District Municipalities Act, 1920 and Building Rules 1973 have made it mandatory for all new buildings to provide RWHS structures
- It is a simple, low-cost technology that requires minimal specialized expertise or knowledge and offers many benefits. Thus, statement 2 is wrong.

108(D). The statements given in the question describe tropical thorny and shrubby vegetation.

Thorny Forests and Shrubs:

- Thorny forests and shrubs are found in areas where rainfall is less than 70 cm.
- Natural vegetation consists of thorny trees and shrubs.
- This type of vegetation is found in the north-western part of the country including the semi-arid regions of Gujarat, Rajasthan, Madhya Pradesh, Chhattisgarh, Uttar Pradesh and Haryana.
- Acacia, palm tree, euphorbia and hawthorn are the main plant species.
- The trees are scattered and the long roots penetrate deep into the soil to obtain moisture.
- The stems are juicy to conserve water.
- The leaves are mostly thick and small to reduce evaporation.
- Common animals in these forests are rats, mice, rabbits, foxes, wolves, tigers, lions, wild donkeys, horses and camels.

109(C). Western Cyclonic Disturbance:

It is a seasonal phenomenon of the winter months brought about by westerly currents from the Mediterranean. They usually affect the weather in the north and north-western regions of India. Hence statement 1 is correct.

Tropical cyclone:

They occur during the monsoon as well as in October–November, and are part of the eastern flow. Hence statement 2 is correct. These disturbances affect the coastal areas of the country. These cyclones usually cross the eastern coasts of India, causing heavy and widespread rainfall.

110(C). Sangam literature is primarily secular, and because of their diverse themes and authorship, the Sangam poems offer a rich, varied history of Tamilakam.

During this period Tamilakam was divided into five tinis or eco-zones on the basis of their economic resources. Hence statement 1 is not correct.

The Sangam poems show the emergence of

new grounds of royal prestige and legitimacy through Brahmanical sacrifices. The megalithic practice of providing for the dead continued even into the Sangam age, as people offered rice to the dead. Thus, statement 2 is not correct.

111(D). Few of the raw materials used by the Harappans were locally available, many items like copper, tin, gold, silver and precious stones had to be brought from distant places. The Harappans probably got copper from present-day Rajasthan and even Oman in West Asia. Hence, statement 1 is correct.

Tin, which was mixed with copper to produce bronze, may have been brought from present-day Afghanistan and Iran. Hence statement 2 is correct.

Gold could have come from present-day Karnataka, and precious stones could have been brought from present-day Gujarat, Iran and Afghanistan. Thus, statement 3 is correct.

112(A). Sangrihitri: It refers to the officers with whom taxes were deposited. Hence pair 1 is correct.

- In the later Vedic age, taxes and collection of taxes seem to have become common. The epics tell us that at the time of great sacrifices there was mass distribution by the princes and all sections of the people were given plenty of food.
- Vrihi: The Vedic people first got acquainted with rice in the Doab. It is called Vrihi in Vedic texts, and its remains from Hastinapura date back to the 8th century BCE, so pair 2 is incorrect.
- Ashrams refer to the four stages of life. Thus, pair 3 is correct.

113(A). Mughal paintings reflect a combination of Indian, Persian and Islamic styles. It originated in 1560 AD during the reign of Akbar. The Mughal style miniatures mostly depict romantic scenes, Mughal royal courts, battlefields using gold and stone colors. Hence, statement 1 is correct.

Development of Mughal Paintings:

- The use of 3D drawing, foresight in paintings and calligraphy began during the reign of Akbar.
- Paintings were made on themes based on fairs, festivals, hunting etc.
- Famous artists during the reign of Akbar were Daswant, Basavan etc.
- Akbar established the Department of Painting and Factory and gave regular awards to the painters. Thus, statement 2 is correct.

114(D). Of the given statements 1, 2 and 3 are correct.

Ring-fence policy:

- Warren Hastings took over as Governor-General during a crucial period of British rule when the British faced a powerful combination of the Marathas, Mysore and Hyderabad.

- He followed a policy of ring-fence which aimed to create a buffer zone to protect the company's borders. Hence statement 1 is correct.
- Broadly speaking, it was a policy to protect the borders around them and treat them as buffer zones to protect their territories. Hence statement 2 is correct.
- This policy of Warren Hastings was reflected in the areas for his war against the Marathas and Mysore. Thus, statement 3 is correct.

115(A). The Quit India Movement, or India August Movement, was a movement launched by Mahatma Gandhi at the Bombay session of the All India Congress Committee on 8 August 1942, during World War II, demanding an end to British rule of India . Parallel governments were established at several places:

- Ballia (for a week in August 1942) under Chittu Pandey. He got many Congress leaders released. Hence, pair 1 is correct.
- Tamluk (Midnapore, December 1942 to September 1944) under the Jatiya government. Hence, pair 2 is wrong.
- Satara (mid 1943 to 1945) nicknamed "Prati Sarkar", organized by Y.B. Chavan, Nana Patil etc. Hence, pair 3 is wrong.
- In Talcher, the Orissa parallel government was established under Lakshmana Nayaka. Thus, pair 4 is correct.

116(C). In the Kesavananda Bharati case (1973), the Supreme Court laid down a new doctrine of the 'basic structure' (or 'basic features') of the constitution. Hence pair 1 is correct. It ruled that the constituent power of Parliament under Article 368 does not enable it to change the 'basic structure' of the Constitution.

In Kihoto Holohan v. Zachilhu et al. (1992) case, a constitutional challenge to the Tenth Schedule (Defection Law) was decided by the Apex Court. The court upheld the wide discretion available to the Speaker in deciding the cases of disqualification of MLAs. Hence this case is popularly known as the defection case. Hence pair 2 is correct.

In M. Nagaraj v. Union of India (2006), the Court upheld the decision of the Parliament to extend the reservation for SC/ST to include promotion (reservation in promotion). Hence pair 3 is wrong.

Rupa Ashok Hurra case: The Supreme Court of India developed the concept of curative petition in the landmark case Rupa Ashok Hurra v. Ashok Hurra et al (2002). Thus, pair 4 is wrong.

117(C). Only 1, 2 and 4 are correct.
A brief description of the provisions is as follows:

Fundamental Rights:
Reservation in educational institutions is provided in Article 15(4) while reservation in posts and services is provided in Article 16(4), 16(4A) and 16(4B) of the Constitution.

Directive Principles of State Policy:
Article 46 of the Constitution of India clearly provides that the State shall promote with special care the educational and economic upliftment of the weaker sections of the society, in particular the Scheduled Castes and the Scheduled Tribes, and shall protect them from injustice and all forms of exploitation.

Other Constitutional Rights:
Article 335 relating to claims to the services and posts of Scheduled Castes and Scheduled Tribes.

According to Article 338-A of the Constitution of India, the National Commission for Scheduled Tribes was established, inter alia, for the protections provided for the Scheduled Tribes under the Constitution or under any other law or under any order of the Government. To investigate and monitor all matters relating to the measures and to evaluate the working of such safeguards; and to inquire into specific complaints regarding denial of rights and safeguards to the Scheduled Tribes.

Legal Rights:
In order to uphold the constitutional mandate and protect the interests of this section of the society, special social acts have come into force from time to time, which include privileges in the form of reservation for them.

118(A). According to Article 127 of the Constitution of India, when there is a lack of quorum of permanent judges for holding or continuance of any session of the Supreme Court, the Chief Justice of India shall appoint a High Court Judge as ad-hoc to the Supreme Court for a temporary period. can be appointed as a judge.

He can do so only in consultation with the Chief Justice of the High Court concerned and with the prior concurrence of the President. Hence statement 1 is correct.

The Chief Justice of India may request a retired Judge of the Supreme Court or a retired Judge of a High Court (who is duly qualified for appointment as a Judge of the Supreme Court) to act as a Judge of the Supreme Court for a temporary period. can. Hence statement 2 is correct.

119(A). Features of Directive Principles of State Policy (DPSP):

- It reflects the ideals that the state should keep in mind while making policies and making laws.
- It constitutes a very broad economic, social and political program for a modern democratic state.
- They are not legally enforceable by the courts for their violations. Hence, the second statement is correct.
- The Directive Principles, though non-judicial in nature, assist the courts in examining and determining the constitutional validity of laws. Hence, the first statement is correct.
- There is no classification of Directive Principles in the Constitution. Hence, the third statement is false.
- However, on the basis of their content and direction, they can be classified into three broad categories, namely, socialist, Gandhian and liberal-intellectual.

120(C). The Representation of the People Act, 1951, Section 29A lays down certain conditions for a political party to be formed and registered by the Election Commission of India (ECI). Hence statement 1 is correct.

- It should be Indian citizens only. It should call itself a political party established for the purpose of contesting elections to Parliament and State Assemblies and not for any other purpose. It should have at least 100 registered voters as its members.
- The Election Commission of India does not have the power to cancel the registration of parties on the ground of violation of the constitution or breach of an undertaking given at the time of registration. Thus, statement 2 is correct.

Child Development and Pedagogy

1. Which of the following statement is correct about the process of development of an individual?
(a) It is uni-dimensional in nature.
(b) It is influenced only by heredity of an individual.
(c) There is cultural diversity in the process of development.
(d) Development is only based on environmental factors.

2. The belief that children's behaviour can be modified by reinforcers and punishers is based on the idea that development is primarily influenced by:
(a) Heredity only
(b) Both heredity and environment
(c) Environment only
(d) Neither heredity nor environment

3. Most classrooms in India are multilingual and this needs to be seen as _____ by the teacher.
(a) a problem   (b) a resource
(c) an obstacle   (d) a bother

4. Individuals who have the ability to understand the motives, feelings and behaviours of others to bond with them are high on_____intelligence in Howard Gardner's theory.
(a) naturalistic
(b) interpersonal
(c) intrapersonal
(d) spatial

5. Monozygotic is to ____ twins as dizygotic is to ____ twins.
(a) Male, female
(b) Female, male
(c) Fraternal, identical
(d) Identical, fraternal

6. Who used the word IQ first?
(a) Thorndike
(b) William stern
(c) Alfred Binet
(d) Terman

7. Vygotsky's social development theory laid the foundations for:
(a) Behaviourism
(b) Humanism
(c) Constructivism
(d) Operant Conditioning Theory

8. Kohlberg's idea of moral development has levels.
(a) Three   (b) Four
(c) Two   (d) Eight

9. On the basis of child psychology which statement is appropriate?
(a) Every child is same.
(b) Every child is special.
(c) Some children are special.
(d) Some children are same.

10. A teacher wants her students to know about government schemes through primary sources. Which one of the following schemes is inappropriate ?
(a) A review of a book on government schemes
(b) An interview with a Block Development Officer
(c) A survey of schemes in the students' neighbourhood
(d) A report on expenditure incurred, on various schemes in the student's neighbourhood.

11. For which group of learners, sign-language method is the most appropriate?
(a) Visually impaired
(b) Hearing impaired
(c) Mentally retareded
(d) Physically disabled

12. The hyperactive children need:
(a) Special attention in the classroom
(b) A separate classroom
(c) Special teachers
(d) Special curriculum

13. The term used to describe 'reading disability' is:
(a) Dyslexia   (b) Dysgraphia
(c) Dyscalculia (d) Dysparaxia

14. The stage of creative problem solving in which the individuals do not give attention to the problem is:
(a) Translation (b) Illumination
(c) Incubation   (d) Preparation

15. Which IQ range is called trainable IQ level of mentally retarded children?
(a) 70 - 79
(b) 50 - 69
(c) 35 - 50
(d) 35 and below

16. Which of the following is not considered as a factor of cognition?
(a) Anger   (b) Hunger
(c) Retreat   (d) Fear

17. 'Choice of challenge' is a characteristic of which of the following?
(a) Values
(b) Motivation
(c) Discipline
(d) Inclusive education

18. When a child gets bored while doing a task, it is a sign that:
(a) the task may have become mechanically repetitive.
(b) the child is not intelligent.
(c) the child is not capable of learning.
(d) the child needs to be disciplined.

19. Which of the following factors affect learning?
A. Motivation of the learner
B. Maturation of the learner
C. Teaching strategies
D. Physical and emotional health of the learner
(a) A, B and C   (b) A, B C and D
(c) A and D   (d) A and C

20. _____ exhibits a basic level of order, but the teacher still struggles to maintain it.
(a) Adequate classroom environment
(b) Orderly restrictive learning environment
(c) Orderly enabling learning environment
(d) Dysfunctional classroom environment

21. Primary objective of analysing errors in student's work is:
(a) to rank students and segregate them in ability-based groups.
(b) to understand children's thinking.
(c) to reprimand students for making any kind of mistakes.
(d) to compare the efficiency of teachers at the school.

22. Which one of the following is not one of the stages of learning?
(a) Acquisition
(b) Maintenance
(c) Generalization
(d) Adoptation

**23. If a previously learned task

impedes a new task, which is being learnt. This transfer of learning will be:

(a) Positive Transfer

(b) Negative Transfer

(c) Zero Transfer

(d) Primary

24. Several research studies show that teachers have more overall interacting with boys than girls. What is the correct explanation for this?

(a) Boys need more attention than girls.

(b) This is an example of gender bias in teaching.

(c) Boys are easier to manage than girls in the classroom.

(d) Boys have much more academic capabilities than girls.

25. 'Gender' has primarily been viewed ____.

I. as concerning only girls and women (a biological category)

II. as an isolated category, not related to other issues

III. in terms of provision of equal facilities

(a) Only I   (b) I, II and III

(c) I and III   (d) II and III

26. The knowledge of individual differences helps teachers in:

(a) understanding the futility of working hard with backward students as they can never be at par with the class

(b) accepting and attributing the failure of students to their individual differences

(c) making their presentation style uniform to benefit all students equally

(d) assessing the individual needs of all students and teaching them accordingly

27. School-based assessment was introduced to:

(a) decentralize the power of Boards of school education in the country

(b) ensure the holistic development of all the students

(c) motivate teachers to punctiliously record all the activities of students for better interpretation of their progress

(d) encourage schools to excel by competing with the other schools in their area

28. The evaluation in which the evaluation is done by the one who

teaches students is:

(a) Internal   (b) External

(c) Diagnostic   (d) Placement

29. Which of the following are examples of secondary socializing agency?

(a) Family and neighbourhood

(b) Family and media

(c) School and media

(d) Media and neighbourhood

30. One of the basic principles of socializing individuals is:

(a) Religion   (b) Caste

(c) Education   (d) Imitation

Language-I: English

Ques (31-36): Direction: Read the poem given below and answer the questions that follow by selecting the most appropriate options:

Do not go gentle into that good night,
Old age should burn and rave at close of day;
Rage, rage against the dying of the light.
Though wise men at their end know dark is right,
Because their words had forked no lightning they
Do not go gentle into that good night.
Good men, the last wave by, crying how bright
Their frail deeds might have danced in a green bay,
Rage, rage against the dying of the light.
Wild men who caught and sang the sun in flight,
And learn, too late, they grieved it on its way,
Do not go gentle into that good night.
Grave men, near death, who see with blinding sight.
Blind eyes could blaze like meteors and be gay,
Rage, rage against the dying of the light.

31. What does light symbolize in the following expression:
"Rage, rage against the dying of the light".

(a) Life   (b) Heaven

(c) Inspiration   (d) Morning

32. What does this expression "Because their words had forked no lightning" mean?

(a) They haven't seen the lightning yet

(b) They haven't said anything about the lightning yet

(c) They were not smart enough to say anything

(d) They haven't said anything revolutionary to make a mark

33. Which literary device is used in the following line:
"Blind eyes could blaze like meteors and be gay"

(a) Elegy

(b) Assonance

(c) Consonance

(d) None of the above

34. Which of the following statements is not true?
A) Men dislike the dark
B) One should not accept death gently
C) Even small actions could have had a great effect
D) One should rage against death

(a) A   (b) B

(c) C   (d) D

35. Name the literary device used in: Dying of the light

(a) Simile   (b) Metaphor

(c) Imagery   (d) Alliteration

36. The word 'frail' in the line 'Good men, the last wave by, crying how bright/Their frail deeds might have danced in a green bay,' means:

(a) Good   (b) Cry

(c) Weak   (d) Lonely

Ques (37-45): Direction: After reading the passage given below, choose the best answer to each question that follows.

What advice would I give to new entrepreneurs who need funding? Forget about your business plan and buy a lottery ticket — your chances are better. My point is that when you need venture funding no one will give any money until you already have a marketable product. In other words, funding comes just when you do not need it. A myth is that the way to start a venture is to create a great business plan, perfect your pitch, and then present this to investors, starting with venture capitalists. If that does not work, you knock on the door of angel investors. But ask any entrepreneur who has called on venture capitalists and they will probably tell you that it is almost impossible to even get calls returned. If venture capitalists do respond and you are invited to present your idea, the process will drag on for many months while you borrow more and survive on hope. If you do hit the jackpot, you are required to let the investors make many of the business decisions in exchange for an investment. To be fair, most business plans do not deserve funding. Venture capitalists receive hundreds of plans every week, and few are worth the paper they are printed on. Everyone jumps on the same new trend, or the ideas are so far out that they have no chance of success. And great ideas are not enough: it takes experienced management, excellent execution, and a receptive market. It is hard for even the best venture capitals to identify the potential successes. So what should an entrepreneur do? What all new entrepreneurs should understand is that, even if you have a realistic business plan for a great idea that can change the world, you need to develop it yourself until you can prove it. Focus on validating your idea and building it up. Raise money to get started by begging and borrowing from family and friends. And be prepared to dip into your savings and credit cards, obtain second mortgages, and perhaps look for consulting work or customer advances. There is no single recipe for developing your business idea yourself, but there are some essential ingredients. Here are some pointers: Consult widely. Share your ideas with those who have done it before. You can learn a lot from the experience of seasoned entrepreneurs, and they are much more approachable than you think. If you cannot find anyone who is excited about your idea, the chances are it is not worth being excited about. This may be time to reflect deeply and come up with another. Identify markets. Speak to anyone who can help you understand your target customers. If you can sell your concept, some customers may help you find it or agree to be a test site or a valuable reference. Customers do not usually know what they want, but they always know what they do not need. Make sure that there is a real need for your product. Start small. Your idea may be grand and have the potential to change the world, but you are only going to do this one step at a time. Look for simple solutions, test them and learn from the feedback. If you are starting a restaurant, work for someone else first. If you are creating a software product, learn by doing some consulting assignments or create some utilities. You do not have to start with the ultimate product. Watch every penny. Focus on revenue and profitability from the start. Find creative ways to earn cash by selling tactical products, prepaid licenses, or royalties. Pay employees partially in stock. Look for access to free hardware or premises. And sweep the floors yourself. In short, use any methods to avoid costs. Prepare for the worst. It is going to take longer than you think. There will likely be product problems, unhappy customers, employee turnover, and lots of financial challenges. You may even fail a number of times before you achieve your goals. By learning from each success and failure alike, you increase the odds that you eventually make it. Keep your integrity. Never forget the importance of business ethics and your own values. Ethics need to be carefully sewn into the fabric of any start-up. And the only way to reach long-

term success is by achieving outstanding customer satisfaction. With a lot of luck and hard work, you may build a successful company that markets products customers really want. It is very likely that by this stage, you receive phone calls from venture capitalists. This is the time to think of exit strategies and decide if you want to own a small piece of a big pie or a large piece of a small pie. (The passage taken from Book/News/Open source)

37. **Which of the following statements is true as per the given passage?**

(a) Investors always respond promptly to funding applications

(b) Venture Capitalist is a sure source of funding for new businesses

(c) Ethics need to be carefully sewn into the fabric of any start-up

(d) The process of obtaining funding will proceed at a fast pace

38. **Which of the following advices are given by the writer in this passage?**

(a) Make sure that you have enough money before you start your business

(b) Make sure you have secured an educational degree before you start your business

(c) Make sure that there is a real need for your product. Start small

(d) Make sure that you have approached an angel investor before you start your business

39. **What are the two business ideas that are shared in the passage as examples?**

(a) Starting a school and creating a web portal for selling grocery

(b) Starting a clothing store and creating a web portal for house hold services

(c) Starting a hospital and manufacturing a product

(d) Starting a restaurant and creating a software product

40. **A. It is hard for even the best venture capitals to identify the potential successes.**
B. Focus on validating your idea and building it up.

(a) According to the above passage, both A and B are true

(b) According to the above passage, both A and B are false

(c) According to the above passage A is true and is false

(d) According to the above passage is false and B is true

41. **According to the given passage which of the following is NOT a correct statement?**

(a) Ethics need to be carefully sewn into the fabric of any start-up

(b) Share your ideas with those who have done it before

(c) It also shows that the phenomenon is heterogeneous

(d) In other words, funding comes just when you do not need it

42. **According to the passage which are the essential ingredients for developing a business idea?**

(a) Identify market but hide the idea from others

(b) Consult widely. Share your ideas with entrepreneurs. Identify markets

(c) Always share your ideas and go for joint ventures

(d) Always speak to your investors first even before you develop your idea

43. **"Exit strategies", as mentioned in the passage, signifies:**

(a) An entrepreneur's strategic plan to sell his or her ownership in a company to investors or another company

(b) An entrepreneur's strategic plan to execute the daily plan for his/her business

(c) An entrepreneur's strategic plan to conduct exit interviews for employees who plan to leave

(d) An entrepreneur's strategic plan to analyse market and exit from one product to another

44. **The phrase "and few are worth the paper they are printed on" as exists in the above passage means:**

(a) The ideas are good

(b) Hardly any idea is good

(c) Some ideas are good

(d) The few ideas that are good can get others to invest in it

45. **"a marketable product" as mentioned in the passage signifies:**

(a) A product that appeals to buyers and sell at a certain price range to generate profit

(b) A product that appeals to investors and help them get their money back

(c) A product whose market value is increasing continuously and becoming difficult for buyers to buy the same

(d) A product that is appreciated by the media houses and earn revenue from advertisements

46. **Pick the option that includes the correct matches of column A with column B.**

Column 'A'	Column 'B'
a. The Structural Approach	(i) patterns or structures of the language
b. The Humanistic Approach	(ii) oral/aural work and pronunciation taught through drills
c. Communicational Teaching	(iii) emphasized the importance of creating environments
d. The Audio Lingual Method	(iv) a five-year project of exploratory teaching of English as a second language

(a) a-(ii), b-(iii), c-(iv), d-(i)

(b) a-(iv), b-(ii), c-(i), d-(iii)

(c) a-(i), b-(iii), c-(iv), d-(ii)

(d) a-(i), b-(ii), c-(iii), d-(iv)

47. **According to National Curriculum Framework 2005, which one of the following is NOT an objective of language teaching-learning?**

(a) The competence to understand what one hears.

(b) Ability to read with comprehension.

(c) Effortless expression.

(d) To know the history of languages.

48. **Anshu is teaching English to class VI students and her class seems to be noisy. She is probably:**

(a) teaching a crowded class.

(b) not able to manage a class.

(c) not bothered about the noise.

(d) having group work.

49. **When a test item expects the learners to use tense forms, voice, connectors, prepositions, and articles accurately, such an approach can be called:**

(a) integrated grammar testing

(b) asserted grammar practice

(c) mixed grammar task

(d) improper grammar testing

50. **Students learning a language often lack confidence when speaking due to the language's unique pronunciation rules. One way to overcome this problem is:**

(a) children reading aloud in class

(b) using game-like activities which

require verbal interactions in the classroom

(c) conducting special speech therapy with a counsellor

(d) correcting errors whenever they happen

51. **Children substitute sounds made in the back of the mouth (g, k) for sounds made in the front of the mouth (d, t) so that tab becomes cab and dot becomes got. This type of error is known as:**

(a) Reading error

(b) Phonological error

(c) Both (A) and (B)

(d) None of the above

52. **In________approach a teacher working with a small group of students who demonstrate similar reading behaviors and can read similar levels of texts.**

(a) Guided reading

(b) Read aloud

(c) Free reading

(d) Formal reading

53. **Teaching aids are used for making a lesson**
A. interesting
B. effective
C. stimulating
D. exciting

(a) A, B and C   (b) A, B, C and D

(c) B and C   (d) A and D

54. **Directions: In the question below is given a statement you have to decide which of them logically follows beyond a reasonable doubt from the information given in the statement. Give the answer.**
(a) Thorough diagnosis with a pretest.
(b) Frequent planned remedial lessons.
(c) Co-operation with the parents.
Which of the above are general principles of remedial teaching?

(a) (a) and (b)

(b) (a) and (c)

(c) (b) and (c)

(d) All of the above

55. **"Children deserve most of the credit for the language that they acquire." This observation implies that in modern classrooms:**

(a) students pursue their own lines of inquiry.

(b) students need not attend L2 classes.

(c) students may choose L2 on their own.

(d) the teacher established the task support or facilitates learning.

56. **Which is not a correct parameter of reading skill assessment?**

(a) Recognition of words in a text

(b) Reading aloud

(c) Comprehension questions

(d) Enriched vocabulary

57. **Which of the following is least important to you as a language teacher?**

(a) Development of the abilities to use a language

(b) Knowledge of grammatical rules

(c) Knowledge of language skills

(d) Knowledge of constitutional values

58. **Which of the following is important for the selection of teaching learning material for students?**

(a) It should be easily available in nearby market

(b) It should not be very expensive

(c) The student should make them themselves

(d) It should be contextualised and fit to be used in an integrated manner

59. **The intonation of question-tags is often quoted as a case of a difference in meaning being falling and rising tone. Thus the question tag 'aren't they' in "They are coming on Tuesday, aren't they" means:**

(a) The speaker is comparatively certain that the information is correct

(b) The speaker is not certain that the information is correct

(c) Both of the above are correct

(d) None of the above is correct

60. **What could be the reason to ask questions from listeners in story-based lessons?**
I. To check pupil's understanding and learning.
II. To encourage pupil's to think about and express their reactions to a story or character.

(a) Only I

(b) Only II

(c) Neither I nor II

(d) Both I and II

61. **Direction: Consider the statements A, B, C on Vedas and choose the correct answer:**

A. There are many prayers in Rigveda for cattle, children (especially sons), and horses.
B. Some of the hymns in the Rigveda are in the form of dialogues.
C. The oldest Veda is the Samaveda, composed about 3500 years ago.
(a) B and C are correct but A is incorrect
(b) A and B are correct but C is incorrect
(c) A, B, C all are correct
(d) A and C are correct but B is incorrect

62. **Direction:** Consider the following statements and find out which one is/are correct?
A. Millets have been found at Hallur.
B. People in Burzahom lived in Rectangular houses.
C. Chirand is a site in Kashmir.
D. Jadeite, found in Daojali Hading, may have been brought from China.
(a) B and C
(b) A and D
(c) A, B and C
(d) All of the above

63. Which of the following is not the characteristic feature of the Harappan settlement?
1. Houses were either one or two storeys high.
2. Houses generally had separate bathing areas and toilets.
3. The citadel was smaller but higher, the lower towns was larger but lower.
4. Many of these cities had uncovered drains.
(a) Only 1
(b) 1 and 3 both
(c) Only 2
(d) Only 4

64. Which of the statement(s) is/are correct regarding the revolt of 1857?
1. The company had recaptured the Delhi from the rebel forces in October 1857.
2. Bahadur Shah Zafar and his wife were sentenced to life imprisonment and were sent to Kala Pani.
(a) Only 1
(b) Only 2
(c) Both 1 and 2
(d) None of the above

65. Which of the following statements is/are applicable to Jaina Doctrine?
A. The surest way of annihilating Karma is to particle penance.
B. Every object, even the smallest practice has a soul.
C. Karma is the bane of the soul and

must be ended.
Select the correct answer using the codes given below:
(a) Only A
(b) A and B
(c) A and C
(d) A, B and C

66. **Direction:** Consider the following statements about the Tripartite Struggle of the 8th century AD:
A. It was a struggle between Palas in the East, Gurjar-Pratihara in the North and Rashtrakutas in the Deccan.
B. The main cause for this struggle was the desire to possess the city of Kannauj (UP) which was a symbol of sovereignty at that time.
Which of the statement(s) given above is/are correct?
(a) Only A
(b) Only B
(c) Both A and B
(d) Neither A nor B

67. **Direction:** Which of the following is/are the teachings of Buddha?
1. The Buddha taught that life is full of happiness and people have to search for it.
2. The Buddha taught people to be kind, and to respect the lives of others, including animals.
3. The Buddha taught that the constant craving could be removed by meditation.
(a) Only 1
(b) Only 2
(c) Only 3
(d) 1 and 2 both

68. Which Delhi Sultan introduced 'token' currency somewhat like present day paper currency?
(a) Alauddin Khiliji
(b) Ghiyasuddin Tughlaq
(c) Muhammad bin Tughlaq
(d) Bahlul Lodi

69. Which of the following tribes is associated with the "Tana Bhagat" movement?
(a) Oraon
(b) Munda
(c) Santhal
(d) Konadora

70. **Direction:** In the following questions, the Assertions (A) and Reason(s) (R) have been put forward. Read both the statements carefully and choose the correct alternative from the following.
Assertion (A): Aurangzeb succeeded Shah Jahan to the Mughal throne.
Reason (R): The law of primogeniture was followed.
(a) Both (A) and (R) are true and (R) is the correct explanation of (A)

(b) Both (A) and (R) are true, but (R) is not the correct explanation of (A)
(c) (A) is true, but (R) is false
(d) (A) is false, but (R) is true

71. In which of the following Battles Rana Amar Singh defeated Mughal prince Mohammed Parvez?
(a) Battle of Dewair
(b) Battle of Haldighati
(c) Battle of Merta
(d) Battle of Ajmer

72. The term 'Kammakaras' used during ancient India, refers to:
(a) Artisans
(b) Landless agricultural labourers
(c) Perfume makers
(d) Tax collecting officers

73. Who was the first Tirthankara of the Jains?
(a) Aristhenemi   (b) Parshwnath
(c) Ajitnath   (d) Rishabhdev

74. **Direction:** Consider the following pairs:

Temple	State
A. Bhitargaon	Uttar Pradesh
B. Monolithic temples	Mahabalipuram
C. Durga temple	Aihole

Which of the pairs given above is/ are correctly matched?
(a) A and C only   (b) A only
(c) B only   (d) A, B and C

75. Aconcagua is the highest peak of which of the below mountains?
(a) Alps Mountains
(b) Ural Mountains
(c) Andes Mountains
(d) None of them

76. **Direction:** Identify which of the following latitudes are correctly matching:
1. Indian Standard Meridian ⇒82°30'E
2. Frigid Zone ⇒ 66°30'N & S to Pole
3. Antarctic circle ⇒ 66°30'N
4. Roaring Forties ⇒ 40°S and 50°S
(a) 1, 2 and 3 only
(b) 1, 2 and 4 only
(c) 2, 3 and 4 only
(d) 1, 3 and 4 only

77. Which of the following Straits and its Location is not correctly matched?
(a) Florida Strait - Cuba and USA

(b) Bering Strait - Russia and USA

(c) Strait of Gibraltar - Spain and Morocco

(d) Malacca Strait - India and Sri Lanka

78. **Direction: Identify the source of energy from the given features A and B:**
   A. More than 50% of this energy used by the villagers in our country.
   B. It has widespread use in cooking and heating purposes.
   (a) Coal
   (b) Fire wood
   (c) Bio gas
   (d) Natural gas

79. **Direction: Identify the type of agriculture from the given features A and B:**
   A. Practiced in dense rainforest regions.
   B. After the soil loses its fertility, the land is abandoned and the cultivator moves to a new plot.
   (a) Shifting cultivation
   (b) Subsistence farming
   (c) Intensive farming
   (d) Commercial farming

80. **Direction: Match the following:**

Mineral	Use
a. Aluminum	i. Computer chips
b. Copper	ii. Used in automobiles industry and airp lanes
c. Silicon	iii. Use to make coins and pipes
d. Hard minerals	iv. Jewellery making

   Choose the correct option from the following:
   (a) a - ii, b - iii, c - i, d - iv
   (b) a - iii, b - ii, c - i, d - iv
   (c) a - iv, b - iii, c - i, d - ii
   (d) a - iv, b - ii, c - ii, d - iii

81. **In India, Cyclone is tracked through which satellite?**
   (a) SCATSAT-1
   (b) SCATSAT-2
   (c) Ocean SAT
   (d) None of the above

82. **Direction: Consider the statements A, B, C on dolphin and choose the correct answer:**
   A. One-horned rhinoceroses are the largest of the rhino species.
   B. They live in swampy and marshy lands of the northern plain of India.
   C. Project Rhino was launched by Assam.
   (a) A, B, C all are correct
   (b) B and C are correct but A is incorrect
   (c) A and C are correct but B is incorrect
   (d) B and C are incorrect but A is correct

83. **Which is the second most abundant metal in the earth's crust?**
   (a) Zinc
   (b) Iron
   (c) Aluminium
   (d) Copper

84. **Direction: Consider the following points about the major domains of the earth.**
   1. The earth's surface is composed of three major spheres and the life-supporting zone is the biosphere.
   2. The highest point of the earth is located in the landmass.
   3. The lowest point is located under the sea.
   Choose the correct answer from the codes given below:
   (a) 1 and 2 are correct
   (b) 2 and 3 are correct
   (c) 1 and 3 are correct
   (d) All are correct

85. **Which one of the following is characteristic of a village community?**
   (a) Jajmani system
   (b) Uncomplicated lifestyle
   (c) Faith in religion
   (d) All of above

86. **Which of the following constitutional amendments provided for the Right to Education?**
   (a) 88th amendment
   (b) 89th amendment
   (c) 87th amendment
   (d) 86th amendment

87. **Which among the following States does not come under the Sixth Schedule of Indian Constitution?**
   (a) Tripura
   (b) Mizoram
   (c) Assam
   (d) Sikkim

88. **In India, some people feel that there should be a partyless parliamentary democracy. If this advice is accepted and implemented its effect on the working of the Government would be that:**
   (a) It would be free from corruption
   (b) It would not have to face an organised opposition
   (c) It would work on clear-cut policy lines in the interests of all people
   (d) It would be most conscious of its obligations

89. **Simla Accord Signed on 1914 is related to:**
   (a) Status of Tibet
   (b) Liberation of Bangladesh
   (c) Both (A) and (B)
   (d) None of these

90. **Direction: Match the following:**

A. Executive Head of the state government	I. Ruling party
B. Head of the government (state level)	II. Governor
C. Party with a majority	III. Opposition
D. Party in minority	IV. Chief Minister

   (a) A-II, B-IV, C-I, D-III
   (b) A-III, B-IV, C-I, D-II
   (c) A-I, B-II, C-III, D-IV
   (d) A-IV, B-I, C-II, D-III

91. **Direction: In the following questions, the Assertion (A) and Reason (R) have been put forward. Read both the statements carefully and choose the correct alternative from the following.**
   Assertion (A): Our constitution does not provide safeguards to religious and linguistic minorities.
   Reason (R): Minorities encompasses issues of power, access to resources and has social and cultural dimensions
   (a) Both (A) and (R) are true and (R) is the correct explanation of (A)
   (b) Both (A) and (R) are true but (R) is not the correct explanation of (A)
   (c) (A) is true, but (R) is false
   (d) (A) is false, but (B) is true

92. **Which one of the following statements about the Rajya Sabha is correct?**
   (a) It selects the executive.
   (b) It represents the states of India in the Parliament.
   (c) It consists of 245 nominated members.
   (d) It is led by the Prime Minister.

93. **The Parliament in our system has immense power because:**
   (a) it has the power to make laws
   (b) it has the power to overrule

judiciary

(c) it is the representative of the people

(d) all power are vested with the Parliament

94. Who among the following is the communication channel between the Council of Ministers and the President of India?

(a) Speaker of the Lok Sabha

(b) The Vice-President

(c) The Prime Minister

(d) Chairman of the Rajya Sabha

95. Which one of the following statements with regard to Panchayats is not correct?

(a) Members of Panchayats are elected directly by the Gram Sabha.

(b) The elections to Panchayats are conducted by the State Election Commission.

(c) The Central Government may by law authorize a Panchayat to levy taxes.

(d) Every Panchayat continues for five years from the date of convening of its first meeting.

96. Under what can the agrarian relations in rural society in India be understood?

(a) Under class structure

(b) Under ecological differences

(c) Agriculture and division of labor

(d) All of the above

97. In August 2022, the Bank of England (BoE) raised the U.K.'s bank rate by half a percentage point to _______ marking the biggest interest rate increase since 1995.

(a) 1.50   (b) 1.75

(c) 2.00   (d) 2.25

98. In August 2022, SBI Research Ecowrap revised India's current account deficit (CAD) estimates from 3.2 percent of GDP to _______ percent of GDP in the current financial year.

(a) 3.3   (b) 3.5

(c) 3.7   (d) 3.9

99. Which ministry in June 2022 launched Policy & Portal of the e–auction for Commercial earning & Non-Fare Revenue (NFR) contracts?

(a) Ministry of Commerce & Industry

(b) Ministry of Railways

(c) Ministry of Agriculture & Farmers Welfare

(d) Ministry of Road Transport & Highways

100. Which state government has launched 'Aama Yojana' & 'Vatsalya Yojana' for the welfare of women of the state in August 2022?

(a) Manipur   (b) Sikkim

(c) West Bengal (d) Assam

101. Direction: In the following questions, the Assertion (A) and Reason (R) have been put forward. Read both the statements carefully and choose the correct alternative from the following.

Assertion (A): Social Science teachers should only focus on textual knowledge.

Reason (R): It will promote higher-level thinking among the student.

(a) Both (A) and (R) are correct

(b) Both (A) and (R) are incorrect

(c) (A) is correct and (R) is incorrect

(d) (A) is incorrect and (R) is correct

102. Which of the following statement(s) is/are correct regarding the nature of social science?

I. Social science are the advanced level study of human society.

II. Social Science contributes to the social utility and advancement of knowledge.

III. Social Sciences are those aspects of knowledge that have a direct bearing on man's activities in different socio-cultural fields.

(a) Only III   (b) Both I and II

(c) I, II, and III (d) Both I and III

103. The study of Social Science is necessary for:

(a) The understanding of the socio-cultural structure and its relation with the environment

(b) The development of infrastructure facilities

(c) The understanding of educational problems

(d) None of these

104. Which of the following is not the merit of the lecture method?

(a) Development of speech-related skills

(b) Convenient for teacher

(c) Development of hearing skills

(d) Child-centered method

105. Direction: In the following questions, the Assertions (A) and Reason(s) (R) have been put forward. Read both the statements carefully and choose the correct alternative from the following.

Assertion (A): Activity based questions make Social Science lessons debatable.

Reason (R): Social Science is branch of Science that deals with human behavior and social relationships, which rely primarily on empirical approaches and includes disciplines of History, Geography, Political Science. Economics and Sociology.

(a) Both (A) and (R) are correct

(b) Both (A) and (R) are incorrect

(c) (A) is correct and (R) is incorrect

(d) (A) is incorrect and (R) is correct

106. Field trips are useful in Social Science for the:

(a) Evaluation

(b) Empirical evidence

(c) Entertainment

(d) All of these

107. Which of the following social science questions provides opportunity to develop students' critical thinking?

A. Explain your views on installing solar power panels on a building.

B. Do you think that electric vehicles can help in reducing air pollution? Discuss.

C. How did the conflict between Russia and Ukraine start?

Choose the correct option:

(a) A, B, and C   (b) A and B

(c) B and C   (d) A and C

108. While discussing the functions of the State Government, issues related to health, water, transport, etc. may be discussed to:

(a) make students aware of how their State is doing on these accounts

(b) make students remember the role of the Government in these areas

(c) allow learners to understand these issues and express their critical views

(d) enlighten students to organize movements for better facilities for all

109. When a teacher is providing

students items like research articles, books, photographs, audio and video recordings, materials, websites, etc; for an upper primary school, the objective would be towards _____.

(a) facilitating the school projects scientifically.

(b) providing background information as a key component of enquiry process.

(c) participate on National level seminars, workshops, and conferences.

(d) teaching review of the literature.

110. A student interviews Tsunami survivors for a project in Geography. This can be considered a project based on which one of the following sources?

(a) Secondary source

(b) Hearsay

(c) Both primary and secondary sources

(d) Primary source

111. Effective teaching of social science would require:
A. Perpetuating all cultural practices of the past.
B. Critical analysis of literary texts, howsoever old they may be.
C. Discarding all sources which are non-textual.
D. Giving primacy to triangulation of sources.
Choose the correct option.

(a) A and C only (b) B and C only

(c) B and D only (d) C and D only

112. The most effective important method of teaching history at the elementary level is:

(a) Lecture method

(b) Project method

(c) Storytelling method

(d) Discussion method

113. Direction: In the following questions, the Assertion (A) and Reason (R) have been put forward. Read both the statements carefully and choose the correct alternative from the following.
Assertion (A): The textbooks, instead of being treated as the 'only source', should be seen as 'one of the sources' for developing one's understanding.
Reason (R): There are various supplementary materials like websites, dictionaries, atlas, encyclopedias, activities (debate, projects, discussions, experience)

to develop a better understanding of the subject.

(a) Both (A) and (R) are true and (R) is the correct explanation of (A).

(b) Both (A) and (R) are true and (R) is the incorrect explanation of (A).

(c) (A) is true but (R) is false.

(d) (A) is false but (R) is true.

114. Projects in Social Science are useful:
a. in theme-based tasks
b. if they do not involve collection and analysis
c. if based on contexts from within the text
d. for the group work in class or at home
Which two alternatives from amongst the forms given above are correct?

(a) b and d (b) a and b

(c) a and d (d) c and d

115. "Open a water tap. Adjust the flow so that it forms a thin stream. Charge a refill. Bring it near the water stream. Observe what happens. Write a short report on the activity." The skills(s) developed in the students through this activity is/are:

(a) experimentation only

(b) observation, experimentation, and communication

(c) observation, experimentation, and creativity

(d) observation only

116. In formative evaluation:

(a) the examination is held after the end of an academic session

(b) the learners are evaluated through external examination

(c) Both (A) and (B)

(d) None of the above

117. As per continuous and comprehensive evaluation, which of the following objectives is most appropriate regarding assessment?

(a) To motivate students by giving marks

(b) To encourage students to give responses

(c) To check student's recall of subject content

(d) To compare and rank students

118. What is a secondary source?

(a) A source that is someone's second choice to use for

research

(b) A source created after an event has happened by someone not present at the event

(c) The second piece of information written about an event

(d) A source created at the time of an event

119. What is a primary source?

(a) A source used often

(b) A source found in an important book like an encyclopedia

(c) A source created at the time of an event by an individual who was there

(d) A source created after an event has happened

120. Which among the following is a secondary source of data?

(a) Archival data

(b) Participant's diary

(c) National Sample Survey Organization data

(d) Oral narratives

// Hints and Solutions //

1(C). Development refers to qualitative changes in an individual such as a change in personality or other mental and emotional aspects.

- The term individual development is the process of maturation of a child up to a stage where he\she can independently make their own decisions about their life.

- Individual development caters to the overall development of the child in terms of its physical, mental, emotional, and psychological growth.

As we live in a society, we come across persons who are followers of different cultures which allows us the opportunity to understand and expose our minds to the different customs and cultures of the society.

When individual experiences and interacts with different persons he is influenced by them and this influence plays an important role in the psychological development of a person.

It not only affects psychological development, but it also affects the other factors of development as the kind of society we grow up in, makes an impact on our lifestyle.

Such as if a person grows up in a family of sportspersons he is also going to be affected and influenced to participate in sports which will impact his physical and mental development.

Thus, it is concluded that there is cultural diversity in the process of development is correct for the process of development of an individual.

2(C). Development refers to an increase in structure for better and enhanced functioning of organs. It is a product of the interaction of hereditary and the environment.

Development takes place when environmental forces interact with the hereditary forces in an organism as they are the elements that play a vital role in determining the development of an individual.

The belief that children's behavior can be modified by reinforcers and punishers is based on the idea that development is primarily influenced by the environment only.

A reinforcer increases the probability of a behavior it is contingent on; a punisher decreases the probability.

Behavior modification involves assessing and modifying the current environmental events that are functionally related to the behavior.

Human behavior is controlled by events in the immediate environment, and the goal of behavior modification is to identify those events.

Environment refers to the circumstances in which an individual lives. Child's immediate environment strongly influenced their behavior, development, personality, and intelligence.

All mental and social traits depend on the environment. Environment determines the numeric position of IQ within these limits.

So, it could be concluded that the belief that children's behaviour can be modified by reinforcers and punishers is based on the idea that development is primarily influenced by environment only.

3(B). Multilingualism is the ability to use more than two languages. Multilingualism is constitutive of the identity of a child and a typical feature of the Indian linguistic landscape, must be used as a resource, classroom strategy, and a goal by a teacher.

Benefits of Multilingual Classroom:
- It emphasizes on the significance of a smooth transition between the home and school language.
- Multilingualism encourages children to believe in themselves.
- It shows a greater number of independent cognitive strategies at their disposal and exhibits greater flexibility in the use of these strategies to solve problems.
- It is also a way of ensuring that every child feels secure and accepted and that no one is left behind on account of his / her linguistic background.
- Multilingual children are capable of greater cognitive flexibility and creativity and perform better academically than monolinguals.

Thus, it could be concluded that most classrooms in India are multilingual and this needs to be seen as a resource by the teacher.

4(B). Individuals who have the ability to understand the motives, feelings and behaviours of others to bond with them are high on interpersonal Intelligence in Howard Gardner's theory.

Interpersonal intelligence: In this type of intelligence people have the ability to understand others' feelings, wishes, expectations, and needs & others' behavior. These people have better social communication skills and have the ability to relate well with others and manage relationships.

Thus, people having interpersonal intelligence have the ability to interact with others in society.

5(D). Monozygotic is to Identical twins as dizygotic is to fraternal twins.

Twins refer to two children produced by the same pregnancy. There are two types of twins including identical and fraternal twins.

Monozygotic twins are also known as identical twins. They are reproduced from one fertilized egg(ovum) that splits, resulting in the birth of two babies with the same genetic conditions.

On the other hand, reproduction of dizygotic twins which are also known as fraternal twins occurs during the fertilization of two eggs (ova) by two sperm resulting in the production of two genetically unique babies.

Thus, we conclude that Monozygotic is to identical twins as dizygotic is to fraternal twins.

6(B). William stern used the word IQ first.

Assessment of Intelligence:
- In 1905, Alfred Binet and Theodore Simon made the first successful attempt to formally measure intelligence.
- In 1908, when the scale was revised, they gave the concept of Mental Age (MA), which is a measure of a person's intellectual development relative to people of her/his age group.

7(C). Vygotsky's social development theory laid the foundations for Constructivism.

Constructivism: It is the theory which backs the idea that child construct their knowledge by themselves when they explore. Lev Vygotsky, who idealized the fact that children learn whey they collaborate with others, derived sociocultural theory which says that development takes place due to the intermingling of culture, social interaction (which has three components explained below), and language.

Zone of Proximal Development (ZPD): It is the zone a child wants to master in. For example, if he wants to learn chess, it would be ZPD for him.

More knowledgable other (MKO): To learn chess, when he needs a person who is good at chess, that person is more knowledgable other.

Scaffolding: It is the help or motivation that is provided by MKO to that child.

Thus, it can be concluded that Vygotsky's social development theory laid the foundations for Constructivism.

8(A). Kohlberg's idea of moral development has three levels.
- Lawrence Kohlberg, an American psychologist, has propounded the 'Theory of Moral Development'.
- He has made a systematic study of moral development in his theory that is categorized in three levels and six stages.
- He has studied moral development by posing moral dilemmas to groups of children as well as adolescents and adults.

9(B). The basis of child psychology, 'Every child is special' is an appropriate statement. The study of child psychology helps the teacher to teach students in the most appropriate manner as it helps to be familiar with children's progressive developmental stages.

On the basis of child psychology, 'Every child is special' is an appropriate statement as the study of psychology helps:
- To know the child's views about the world.
- To understand how a child's brain functions.
- To know and meet children's diverse needs.
- To be aware of individual differences of children.
- To be familiar with children's progressive developmental stages, etc.
- To observe how a child interacts with their parents, themselves, and the world.

10(A). A review of a book on government schemes is not appropriate to take knowledge of primary sources.

Primary Sources: A source will be considered as a primary source in case it carries newly generated information, original work of research, or a new interpretation of already known facts. The document is the first and often the only published record of original research. The information contained in primary sources is generally scattered and unorganized.

11(B). Hearing impaired learners, sign language is the most appropriate.

A hearing-impaired person is the one who has difficulty in hearing. For such people, sign languages are used to show them what one is saying. The first person credited with the creation of a formal sign language for the hearing impaired was Pedro Ponce de

León, a 16th-century Spanish Benedictine monk.

- A language that employs signs made with the hands and other movements, including facial expressions and postures of the body is called sign language.
- But people with disabilities including Autism, Apraxia of speech, Cerebral Palsy, and Down Syndrome may also find sign language beneficial for communicating.
- Sign language may be as coarsely expressed as mere grimaces, shrugs, or pointings; or it may employ a delicately nuanced combination of coded manual signals reinforced by facial expression and perhaps augmented by words spelt out in a manual alphabet.

12(A). The hyperactive children need special attention in the classroom.

Attention Deficit Hyperactivity Disorder (ADHD) belongs to the group of externalising disorders of childhood. The term hyperactive is familiar to most people, especially parents and teachers. The child who is constantly in motion, tapping fingers, jiggling legs, poking others for no apparent reason, talking out of turn, and fidgeting is often called hyperactive. These children also have difficulty concentrating on the task at hand for an appropriate period of time.

- Children with ADHD seem to have particular difficulty controlling their activity in situations that call for sitting still, such as in the classroom or at mealtimes. When required to be quiet, they appear unable to stop moving or talking.
- They have poor attention to details and distractibility. Their activities are often disorganised. They are often forgetful and leave many activities incomplete, make many silly mistakes in school work.
- Due to poor attention, they fail to comprehend long instructions, even avoid activities that require sustained attention. Thus, they require special attention in the classroom.

13(A). The term used to describe 'reading disability' is dyslexia.

Dyslexia is the most common learning disability(Reading disorder) which makes learners:

- Confuse with the same shapes and sounds of the alphabet.
- Unable to read, interpret, and understand letters and words.
- Bewilder in identifying and relating speech sounds with letters and words.

14(C). The stage of creative problem solving in which the individuals do not give attention to the problem is incubation.

Graham Wallas (1926) outlined the creative thinking process into four stages:

- Preparation: It involves collecting information regarding a problem in order to solve it through trial and error, recalling personal experiences, and investigating in all possible directions.
- Incubation: It is a slow process in which the individual sinks into the unconscious and reflects on the problem. In this stage, individuals forget irrelevant information or unsuccessful attempts and engage with the task effectively.
- Illumination: It is the stage the individual is most active and conscious. It is in this stage that an insight to the problem is experienced suddenly and a new idea or solution emerges.
- Verification: This stage might involve modifications to the solution reached in the previous stage by adding or subtracting, or making new connections. The final solution achieved is tested in reality. If the solution does not apply to the problem then the whole process is repeated.

15(C). The 35 – 50 IQ range is called a trainable IQ level of mentally retarded children.

Mental retardation, as a developmental disability, has attracted considerable public attention. Its general debilitating character has made it a distinct category of disability. Individuals with mental retardation, face considerable difficulty in their lives in adapting to the demands of day-to-day life. Based On IQ: There are mainly three methods of classification of mental retardation. They are medical, psychological, and educational. The psychological and educational classifications are more commonly and widely used than medical classifications.

16(C). Retreat is not considered as a factor of cognition.

Cognitive factors refer to characteristics of the person that affect performance and learning. These factors serve to modulate performance such that it may improve or decline. These factors involve cognitive functions like attention, memory, and reasoning.

- Most psychologists today believe that our cognitions, i.e. our perceptions, memories, interpretations are essential ingredients of emotions.
- Stanley Schachter and Jerome Singer have proposed a two-factor theory in which emotions have two ingredients: physical arousal and a cognitive label.
- They presumed that our experience of emotion grows from our awareness of our present arousal. They also believed that emotions are physiologically similar.
- Therefore, Anger, Hunger, and fear are factors of cognition.

17(B). 'Choice of challenge' is a characteristic of motivation.

Motivation is the drive to achieve something in life that satisfies one's needs. There are two primary types of motivation namely, intrinsic motivation and extrinsic motivation. A number of behavioural characteristics are indicators of high motivation. Here are some of the important factors and some ways to help a child develop these characteristics:

- Persistence is the ability to stay with a task for a reasonably long period of time. While very young children cannot concentrate on one activity for an hour, there are still measurable differences in the length of time that young children will engage in an activity. A highly motivated child will stay involved for a long period of time, whereas an unmotivated child will give up very easily when not instantly successful. Children learn persistence when they are successful at a challenging task.
- Choice of challenge is another characteristic of motivation. Children who experience success in meeting one challenge will become motivated, welcoming another. These motivated learners will choose an activity that is slightly difficult for them but provides an appropriate challenge. Unmotivated children (those who have not experienced early success) will pick something that is very easy and ensures instant success.
- The amount of dependency on adults is another indicator of motivation. Children with strong intrinsic motivation do not need an adult constantly watching and helping with activities. Children who have a lower level of motivation or are extrinsically motivated need constant attention from adults and cannot function independently.
- The last indicator of motivational level is emotion. Children who are clearly motivated will have a positive display of emotion. They are satisfied with their work and show more enjoyment in the activity. Children without appropriate motivation will appear quiet, sullen and bored.

18(A). When a child gets bored while doing a task, it is a sign that the task may have become mechanically repetitive.

These activities have the following characteristics to avoid boredom in the classroom:

- It allows vigorous physical activity as children are energetic. Keeping this in mind, plan play activities involving running, jumping, climbing, catching and throwing.
- During the day there should be some indoor and some outdoor play activities. Outdoor play is generally vigorous and

indoor activities are usually quieter.
- There must be a balance between structured activities initiated by you and free play initiated by the children. For example, taking the children out on a trip or organizing activities around a particular theme are structured activities.
- During the day you must organize both group and individual activities. The group activities will foster a spirit of cooperation and social skills, while the individual activities will give the child a chance to be alone and do something on her own, hence children are intelligent enough to do things by their own, and are capable of learning.
- The schedule of activities should be at a reasonable pace throughout the day. This means that you should allow enough time to children. But it should not be too slow that children begin to repeat it after completing it, else it will make children bored.

19(B). Learning is the acquisition of new behaviour or the strengthening or weakening of old behaviour as a result of experience. It represents progressive changes in behaviour. It also involves the acquisition of knowledge, habits, and attitude.

Factors Affect Learning:
The main factors affecting learning are Motivation of the learner, Maturation of the learner, Teaching strategies, and Physical and emotional health of the learner.
- The Interest of the Student - The factor of interest is very closely related in nature to that of symbolic drive and reward. A favourable mental attitude facilitates learning.
- Teaching Strategies - The strategies or steps taken by the teacher to make the class environment interactive and that also engrave interest among students regarding the topic.
- Physical and Emotional Health of the Learner: Concentration needs emotional and mental poise and absence of mental conflict or complexity. Some children find it difficult to prepare for the examinations, simply because of fear of the examination and anxiety neurosis.
- Giving motivation to the learner can increase their interest in learning.
- Maturation of the learner affects learning because maturation is related to the structure and potential capacity. Maturation is the process by which we change, grow, and develop throughout life.

So, from the above-mentioned points, it becomes clear that all the given factors affect learning.

20(A). Adequate classroom environment exhibits a basic level of order, but the teacher still struggles to maintain it.

There are four categories of classroom environment including dysfunctional, adequate, orderly restrictive and orderly enabling/flexible environment, in which adequate classroom environment exhibits the basic level of order for meaningful learning, but the teacher still struggles to maintain it.

21(B). Primary objective of analysing errors in student's work is to understand children's thinking.
All learners make mistakes. As someone has said: "You can't learn without goofing". Whether you are learning how to ride a bicycle, how to fly a kite or learn a language, everyone does make mistakes.
- An error is an incorrect form and a sure indication that the learner has not mastered the core of the selective topic in a learning process.
- The primary objective of analyzing errors in students' work is to understand children's thinking or thought processes since they are a window to children's thinking.
- Errors are necessary for the learning process to give insight into children's thinking. It helps the teacher to be aware of learners' learning styles and to cater to them according to their needs.
- Making an error cannot be just due to negligence and carelessness. It may be so that students are thinking about it in a different manner other than what is the right process.
- To understand this, a teacher should analyze what mistake the students are doing, how the mistake is generated, and where exactly they tend to make mistakes.

22(D). Adoptation is not the stage of learning.
'Learning' means a relatively permanent change in behavior that occurs as a result of experience with the environment.
- For example, a child touches a hot pan placed near the gas stove in the kitchen because he is unaware that it can burn his fingers.
- Once he has had such an experience, he becomes careful in the future. He has 'learned' that hot objects can burn his fingers.

23(B). If a previously learned task impedes a new task, which is being learnt. This transfer of learning will be negative transfer.
Transfer of learning is the process of applying or carrying over the knowledge, skills, habits, attitudes or other responses from one learning situation, in which they were initially acquired, to a different learning situation.
Negative Transfer-
- There are cases in which the previous learning interferes with subsequent learning.
- In such cases, the carryover of knowledge or experience in one task interferes with further learning.
- As a result of negative transfer, performance on one task may block performance on the subsequent task.
- For example, a child's experience in learning the plural of 'house' may inhibit his/her learning the plural of the word 'mouse'. He/She may spell the plural of the word 'mouse' as 'mouses', instead of 'mice'.

24(B). Teachers interacting more with boys than girls is an example of gender bias in teaching.
Gender refers to the socially and culturally constructed system that attributes meaning to what it means to be a male or a female in a particular society.
Gender bias in teaching leads to differential learning experiences, even though the girls and boys of a class sit in the same classroom and attended by the same teacher.
- It refers to the belief when someone prioritize one gender more than the other one.
- The result of the research studies about teachers interacting more with boys than girls is an example of gender bias in teaching.

25(B). Gender:
- Gender is what we make of boys and girls.
- It is about the opportunities we give them to develop.
- It has got to do with their upbringing, socialization, culture and the role models we present for them.
- Gender is what a society and culture make of boys and girls.

Sex:
- Sex of a person indicates a boy or girl, a male or female, a man or woman.
- This distinction is based on the natural differences that exist in the body of males and females.
- These differences are biological and do not generally change.

However, if we talk about it in the Indian context, For three decades gender has been accepted as a category in the formulation of policy and curricula frameworks in India. "Gender", "Equality" and "Empowerment" of girls have also been used as keywords in educational documents for a long as it is evident from the policy review section.
"Gender" has primarily been viewed:
- As concerning only girls and women (a biological category) where
- As an isolated category, not related to other issues
- In terms of provision of equal facilities

So, we conclude that all the above-mentioned statements are correct.

26(D). The knowledge of individual

differences helps teachers in assessing the individual needs of all students and teaching them accordingly.

Individual differences, as the term suggests, refer to how individuals differ from each other.

- Different people have different interests; and their behavior is influenced by these interests, likings, dislikings, values and beliefs, etc.
- Understanding of individual differences helps in planning course material and training programmes.
- Understanding of individual differences of the teachers and the taught can help in matching teaching and learning styles for better- academic results.
- To take care of individual differences you should design your instructional activities to suit the mental level of each student.

27(B). School-based assessment was introduced to ensure the holistic development of all the students.

In order to overcome the maladies and shortcomings that had crept in during the implementation of CCE causing serious malfunctioning, school-based assessment has been proposed as next-generation assessment.

It may be fourth in the sequence of one-time external (board) examination to a combination of external and internal examination to CCE and now SBA.

School-Based Assessment (SBA) may be defined as-

- Assessment that facilitates the attainment of competencies specified in terms of learning outcomes in a holistic manner during the teaching-learning process.
- Assessment embedded in the teaching and learning process within the broader educational philosophy of 'assessment for learning'.
- Assessment of school students by school teachers in the schools.

28(A). The evaluation in which the evaluation is done by the one who teaches students is internal.

An internal evaluation is done by someone who knows the subject taught. It is usually the class teacher. The criterion is that the evaluator knows what has been taught and how it has been taught. All other types of evaluation are external evaluations.

29(C). School and media are secondary socializing agencies.

Socialization is the process where the child learns to associate and relate with others. It refers to the process which transforms a quite helpless human infant into a self-aware, knowledgeable person who is skilled in the ways of their society's culture.

30(C). One of the basic principles of socializing individuals is education.

Socialization is a process by which an individual becomes a member of society through a mechanism of interaction. Its purpose is to prepare individuals for future roles.

Principles of Socialization:

- To make new members of society familiar with social traditions, manners, customs, etc.
- To prepare the members of the society to adapt to the constantly changing environment
- To lead to education through a process of social interaction
- To study the various types of social relationships and their impact on individual development.
- To control the teaching-learning process to achieve the personality development of every single child.

31(A). The correct answer is 'Life'.

Symbols in literature are a 'stand-in' for bigger ideas.

It can be a motif, location, character, image or so on.

Poet Dylan Thomas dedicated this poem to his ailing father.

The poem encourages the dying people to bravely and valiantly fight the death.

Death and life are in contrast in the poem.

If life is light then death is night or dying of light.

Therefore, in the given expression, light refers to life.

32(D). The correct answer is 'They haven't said anything revolutionary to make a mark'.

This poem was written by Dylan Thomas and was published in 1951.

Given line is in the second stanza of the poem,

Because their words had forked no lightning they

Do not go gentle into that good night.

Poet expresses that wise people are aware that death is inevitable.

However, their words were not like lighting i.e revolutionary or startling to leave a mark.

That's why they resist and refuse to accept death peacefully.

So, the given expression means They haven't said anything revolutionary to make a mark.

33(B). The correct answer is Assonance.

Assonance is a literary device where the same vowel sound is repeated in a phrase or sentence.

It only occurs when sounds and not letters get repeated.

For example:

She seems to beam rays of sunshine.

In the given line, the sound "i" is getting repeated.

Blind eyes could blaze like meteors and be gay.

Therefore, from all the points given above, we can infer that the literary device used is Assonance.

34(A). The correct answer is Men dislike the dark.

The whole poem is about the brave resistance to death by smart and wise men.

The poet in every stanza describes a different type of person who wants to live more or do more in life.

He explains how these men know about death and its inevitability but at the same time, they don't want to die and are fighting death bravely.

It is mentioned in the first line of the second stanza:

Though wise men at their end know dark is right.

Thus, the men know that dark i.e. death is right.

Therefore, the incorrect statement will be men dislike the dark.

35(B). The poem is about the brave efforts of people to resist death even when it's inevitable.

Poet wrote this for his ailing father who was also fighting for his life.

Metaphors are figures of speech that create comparisons between different notions or entities.

For example, day and light in the poem refer to life.

Thus, dying of the light stands for the end of life i.e. death.

These phrases appear in the following lines:

Rage, rage against the dying of the light.

Therefore, the literary device used in the given phrases is a 'metaphor'.

36(C). This line is given in the third stanza and describes when good people resist death.

Frail in the given lines means weak.

Thus, the line describes the emotions of men when they realise even a small deed could have meant something.

So, the word 'frail' means weak.

37(C). The given passage is about different aspects that should be considered while opting for Entrepreneurship or starting a new business:

Let's refer to the passage: Never forget the importance of business ethics and your own values. Ethics need to be carefully sewn into the fabric of any start-up. And the only way to reach long-term success is by achieving outstanding customer satisfaction.

On perusal of the above statement, we can state that ethics should be integrated into the core of star up.

38(C). The given passage is about different aspects that should be considered while opting for Entrepreneurship or starting a new business:

Let's refer to the passage: "Customers do

not usually know what they want, but they always know what they do not need. Make sure that there is a real need for your product. Start small. Your idea may be grand and have the potential to change the world, but you are only going to do this one step at a time."

On perusal of the above statement, we can state that entrepreneurs should go for products that are useful for the customers and appeals to them.

Option (B), is nowhere stated in the passage.

Option (A) and Option (D) are incorrect as it is clearly mentioned that in the passage go for borrowing for money from family and friends instead of going for investors and waiting for their response.

39(D). The given passage is about different aspects that should be considered while opting for Entrepreneurship or starting a new business:

Let's refer to the passage: If you are starting a restaurant, work for someone else first. If you are creating a software product, learn by doing some consulting assignments or create some utilities.

By stating the above examples the author is stating that before going for a bigger step, we need to consider the product from the ground up and understand its usability from users' point of view.

Seeking advice from the experienced entrepreneur and understanding it from the users' point of view are the basic aspects that need to be considered.

40(A). The given passage is about different aspects that should be considered while opting for Entrepreneurship or starting a new business:

Let's refer to the passage:

- Everyone jumps on the same new trend, or the ideas are so far out that they have no chance of success. And great ideas are not enough: it takes experienced management, excellent execution, and a receptive market. It is hard for even the best venture capitals to identify the potential successes.
- The above statement means that having ideas is not enough for a business to be successful. It needs management with great experience, proper execution, and market with users that accept the product that is being sold out.
- What all new entrepreneurs should understand is that, even if you have a realistic business plan for a great idea that can change the world, you need to develop it yourself until you can prove it. Focus on validating your idea and building it up.
- The above statement means that, for a business to be successful it requires the ideas to be properly substantiated with usability. Without proper planning and proof for your ideas, it becomes difficult

to determine their success in the future.

41(C). Let's check each of the given options:

- Ethics need to be carefully sewn into the fabric of any start-up.
- Never forget the importance of business ethics and your own values. Ethics need to be carefully sewn into the fabric of any start-up. And the only way to reach long-term success is by achieving outstanding customer satisfaction.
- Share your ideas with those who have done it before.
- Share your ideas with those who have done it before. You can learn a lot from the experience of seasoned entrepreneurs, and they are much more approachable than you think.
- In other words, funding comes just when you do not need it
- My point is that when you need venture funding no one will give any money until you already have a marketable product. In other words, funding comes just when you do not need it.

Option (C) is nowhere postulated in the passage. Thus, it not the correct statement.

42(B). The given passage is about different aspects that should be considered while opting for Entrepreneurship or starting a new business

Let's refer to the passage: "There is no single recipe for developing your business idea yourself, but there are some essential ingredients. Here are some pointers: Consult widely. Share your ideas with those who have done it before. You can learn a lot from the experience of seasoned entrepreneurs, and they are much more approachable than you think. If you cannot find anyone who is excited about your idea, the chances are it is not worth being excited about. This may be time to reflect deeply and come up with another. Identify markets. Speak to anyone who can help you understand your target customers. "

On the perusal of the above statement, we can understand sharing ideas with experienced entrepreneurs, taking advice and understanding the market and buyers' needs are some of the points that need to be considered while going for entrepreneurship.

43(A). "Exit strategies", as mentioned in the passage, signifies an entrepreneur's strategic plan to sell his or her ownership in a company to investors or another company.

The given passage is about different aspects that should be considered while opting for Entrepreneurship or starting a new business:

Let's refer to the passage: " With a lot of luck and hard work, you may build a successful company that markets products customers really want. It is very likely that

by this stage, you receive phone calls from venture capitalists. This is the time to think of exit strategies and decide if you want to own a small piece of a big pie or a large piece of a small pie."

On the perusal of the above statement, we can say the author is asking for contriving a plan in such manner that is useful to customers and that lures the investors to put their investment in the company.

44(B). The phrase "and few are worth the paper they are printed on" as exists in the above passage means hardly any idea is good.

On perusal of the following statement given in the passage: "Venture capitalists receive hundreds of plans every week, and few are worth the paper they are printed on. Everyone jumps on the same new trend, or the ideas are so far out that they have no chance of success"

Investors receive hundreds of propositions and there are rarely any in which investors like to invest their money.

'Hardly any idea' means 'rarely any idea'.

45(A). "a marketable product" as mentioned in the passage signifies a product that appeals to buyers and sell at a certain price range to generate profit.

Across the passage, the author presents certain constraints/ aspects that need to be considered when one opts for entrepreneurship.

Let us inspect the individual options:

According to the lines given in the passage:

- You do not have to start with the ultimate product. Watch every penny. Focus on revenue and profitability from the start.
- Customers do not usually know what they want, but they always know what they do not need. Make sure that there is a real need for your product.

Thus, option (A) is correct as the production that generates profit and pleases the buyers will be considered as a marketable product.

Option (B) is incorrect. From the lines given in the passage:

- "If you do hit the jackpot, you are required to let the investors make many of the business decisions in exchange for an investment. To be fair, most business plans do not deserve funding."
- "Raise money to get started by begging and borrowing from family and friends."

Upon the perusal of the given statements, we can clearly say the author is against getting funds from investors.

Option (C) and Option (D) are incorrect as nothing is mentioned about 'market value' and 'media houses' in the given passage.

46(C). Language educators have sought to solve the problem of language teaching by focusing attention almost exclusively on method'.In other words, they have assumed that if a teacher teaches using the right method, learning will automatically take place.

Teaching method: Different teaching methods are used by teachers as per the requirements of students. For choosing the one, the teacher may classify students based on their abilities (ability grouping) or he can choose it based on the compatibility of the topic.

Following are the methods of language teaching:-

Structural Approach: A structural approach is a language tool that helps the learner to master the structure or pattern of sentences. It is the descriptive approach that gives more importance to speech only without reference to meaning.

Humanistic Approach: The Humanistic movement in language teaching emerged, as did some of the other approaches, from developments that occurred in education and psychology. This approach argued even more strongly against the authoritarian teacher-centered classroom and emphasized the importance of creating environments that minimized anxiety, enhanced personal security, and promoted genuine interest through a deeper engagement of the learner's whole self.

Communicational Teaching: Communicational teaching refers to a five-year project of exploratory teaching of English as a second language which was 'planned, carried out and reviewed regularly by a group of interested teacher trainers and teachers of English as a part-time activity but with institutional support from the Regional Institute of English, Bangalore and the British Council in Madras.

Audio-Lingual Method: This method focused on oral/aural work and pronunciation taught through drills as well as dialogue practice in small groups of motivated learners and native language teachers. Dialogues were the main aspect of the audio-lingual approach as they provided the learners an opportunity to mimic/imitate, practice, and memorize bits of language considered to be relevant to their situations.

Thus, from the above-mentioned points, it is clear that option (C) is correct.

47(D). NCF (National Curriculum Framework) 2005 is one of the four NCFs published in India by NCERT. It seeks to provide a framework for the betterment of educational purposes and experiences.

Language is a medium through which human beings tend to communicate with each other by using various attributes of a language that are symbols, gestures, words, etc.

The main purpose of teaching a language is to enable the children to use it practically while communicating with others.

48(D). One of the main advantages of the group-learning approach is that it can be used to achieve an extremely wide range of educational objectives, especially higher-cognitive objectives of all types like problem-solving, decision-making and other complex life skills. It is also an approach for developing creative thinking and other divergent thought processes. Some general features of group learning are:

- Several learners can provide more time/effort/resources available than one;
- A wider range of knowledge/skills/experience can be acquired through sharing knowledge and experience;
- More and a variety of ideas can be generated through brainstorming in the groups, hence class can be noisy sometimes.
- Errors can be identified and corrected more easily;
- Participation increases the commitment of the students to the activity

So, in the above situation, the teacher may have group work.

49(A). When a test item expects the learners to use tense forms, voice, connectors, prepositions, and articles accurately, such an approach can be called integrated grammar testing.

Grammar teaching:

- It should be done in an integrated manner, that is, learners should use tense forms, voice, connectors, prepositions and articles accurately, such an approach can be called integrated grammar testing.
- The teaching rules at the initial stage do not lend much to language learning. Grammar teaching should move from meaning to form.
- While teaching grammar, the activities should be designed in a way that requires the Inductive and creative reasoning of the child.
- Inductive approach, rules learners discover for themselves are more likely to fit their existing mental structures than rules they have been presented with.
- By teaching grammar, we not only give our students the means to express themselves, but we also fulfill their expectations of what learning a foreign language involves.

So, we conclude that when a test item expects the learners to use tense forms, voice, connectors, prepositions and articles accurately, such an approach can be called integrated grammar testing.

50(B). Students learning a language often lack confidence when speaking due to the language's unique pronunciation rules. One way to overcome this problem is using game-like activities which require verbal interactions in the classroom.

- Using game-like activities which require verbal interactions in the classroom is the way to overcome the above-mentioned problem.
- A language game is a system of manipulating spoken words to render them incomprehensible to the untrained ear. Language games are effective in learning a language because they:
- allow students to practice language skills.
- encourage them to interact and communicate in a meaningful context.
- provide a stress-free and natural environment for all learners to enhance the usage of language.

So, it could be concluded that using game-like activities which require verbal interactions in the classroom is the way to overcome the above-mentioned problem.

51(B). Children substitute sounds made in the back of the mouth (g, k) for sounds made in the front of the mouth (d, t) so that tab becomes cab and dot becomes got. This type of error is known as Phonological error.

Phonological error: Children with phonological process disorders have difficulty learning the sound systems of the language, and may not understand that changing sounds can change meanings. They produce consistent error patterns (called phonological processes).

- These patterns may be normal in early childhood, but should not occur past a certain age.
- An example of a phonological process is substituting sounds made in the back of the mouth (g, k) for sounds made in the front of the mouth (d, t) so that tab becomes cab and dot becomes got.
- Children may simplify consonant clusters (i.e., consecutive consonants in a word) so that string becomes sting or even sing.
- Another pattern is replacing sounds made without the voice (e.g., p, t, k) with voiced sounds (e.g., b, d, g), such that pie becomes bye and cat becomes gat.

52(A). In_Guided reading approach a teacher working with a small group of students who demonstrate similar reading behaviors and can read similar levels of texts.

Guided reading is an instructional approach that involves a teacher working with a small group of students who demonstrate similar reading behaviors and can read similar levels of texts.

- The text is easy enough for students to read with your skillful support.
- it offers challenges and opportunities for problem-solving but is easy enough for students to read with some fluency. You choose selections that help students expand their strategies.

53(B). Teaching aids are used for making a lesson interesting, effective, stimulating, and exciting.

Teaching Aids:
- These are sensory devices, they provide a sensory experience to the learner, and i.e. the learners can see and hear simultaneously using their senses.
- Teaching Aids are an integral part of teaching which are used by the teachers to teach in a classroom
- These are instructional devices that are used to communicate messages more effectively through sound and visuals.
- For example, LCD project, Film projector, TV, Computer, VCD player, Multimedia, etc.
- Teaching aids are used for making a lesson interesting, effective, stimulating, and exciting.
- They provide more clarity and detail to the teaching process.
- Motivate the learners to learn by providing the learning content in an attractive and interesting way rather than monotonous lectures by the teachers.
- Through the inclusion of audio and visual effects, teaching aids can and stimulate the learners and transform a learning process or environment
- Since it provides more detail and enhances learning through sensory perceptions, teaching outcomes can be more effective.
- Teaching aids include audio-visual aids like slideshows, charts, flashcards, animations, pictures, models, television, radio, online sources, etc.

54(A). In remedial teaching, the teacher manages students' records in a timely and appropriate way. A teacher works with the students who have difficulty in learning and retaining the information. Before preparing for their lessons, teachers should identify pupils' diverse learning needs as soon as possible so that they may design appropriate teaching plans to facilitate pupils' effective learning.

55(A). "Children deserve most of the credit for the language that they acquire." 'This observation implies that in modern classrooms students pursue their own lines of inquiry.

Acquiring a language refers to learning the basics of a language through the natural process of observation of the language.
- A child learns the language through his parents. A person living outside the hometown learns the local language by observing his/her colleagues.
- Children deserve most of the credit for the language that they acquire means that the students deserve all the appreciation for the efforts they have put together to acquire their language.
- It is not so easy to acquire a language

other than one's mother tongue. It takes constant observation of the peer group, consistent efforts to grasp the accent, and parallelly understand and comprehend each and every word.

So, it should be noted that efforts pursued by the students deserve the credits for the language acquired.

Thus, it is concluded that "Children deserve most of the credit for the language that they acquire." 'This observation implies that in modern classrooms students pursue their own lines of inquiry.

56(D). Enriched vocabulary is not a correct parameter of reading skill assessment.

Parameters of reading skill assessment:-
- Reading assessment has to be done on the basis of recognition of words in a text because if the reader cannot read the words, it will be a failure of the reading exercise.
- Reading aloud has to be assessed during reading as while reading, a person has to be clear in his pronunciation so that listeners can listen well to what reader is trying to inform them.
- Comprehension directly means how much a person can comprehend or understand what they are reading. If they fail in this criteria, the purpose of reading will be zero because the person will not be able to understand the information.

57(D). Knowledge of constitutional values is least important to you as a language teacher.

A good language teacher has fluency in the language, is enthusiastic about it, and is someone who can deliver well and in an interesting manner.

Knowledge of constitutional values does not require for a language teacher because these values are inculcated through teaching social studies by a social science teacher.

58(D). Important thing for the selection of teaching-learning material for students is that the teaching-learning material should be contextualized and fit to be used in an integrated manner.

The learning process is aimed to bring out the permanent desirable changes in the behavior of an individual. The teaching-learning process respects the diversity among students and the teacher follows different paths to achieve the goals of learning.

The teachers use different materials such as charts, models, film-strips, video clips, etc. to arouse the interest of students in learning and to keep them indulging actively in the teaching-learning process. These materials are known as "TLM" or "teaching-learning materials".

59(A). The intonation of question-tags is

often quoted as a case of a difference in meaning being falling and rising tone. Thus the question tag 'aren't they' in "They are coming on Tuesday, aren't they" means the speaker is comparatively certain that the information is correct.

Intonation:-, Intonation is the use of changing vocal pitch to convey grammatical information or personal attitude. It describes how the voice rises and falls.
- When the speaker is adding a question-tag he/she might increase or decrease the volume tone at the end.
- If the volume is increasing, it is called rising intonation.
- If the volume is decreasing, it is called falling intonation.

60(D). Listening and telling stories helps children in learning language in primary classes. Listening to stories is of interest to children and also enhances their creativity. Often it is seen that children mould the stories they have heard as per their wishes while telling it to their friends. Through this children not only learn the meaning of the words but also develop an understanding of various incidents and this facilitates in enhancing their imagination. Another way in which stories are beneficial is that it enhances the ability of children to estimate. For example, whenever children are listening to a story, they are curious to know about what happens next.
- Discussing a story after listening to it, is a little difficult task but if the teacher is prepared with its objective then it can become a useful medium.
- Most of the teachers feel that after telling the story, it is their right to ask the children, about the lesson they have learnt from it.
- Telling stories to children is as important as listening to stories from them.
- This helps the children in developing their ability to express themselves, makes them curious, and motivates them to learn.
- Instead of asking the children to repeat the story told by the teacher, it is more beneficial to ask them questions so as to check their understanding and learning and encourage them to think about and express their reactions to a story or character.
- While responding to the personality and the character of the story, the child includes her experiences in it.
- Every child in the classroom should be given the freedom that she can talk about anything regarding the story, can even exaggerate it through her imagination.

So, we conclude that both the points could be the reason to ask questions from listeners in story-based lessons.

61(B). There are four Vedas – the Rigveda,

Samaveda, Yajurveda and Atharvaveda.
- The oldest Veda is the Rigveda, composed about 3500 years ago.
- The Rigveda includes more than a thousand hymns, called Sukta or "well-said". These hymns are in praise of various gods and goddesses.

About Vedas:

Some of the hymns in the Rigveda are in the form of dialogues.
- This is part of one such hymn, a dialogue between a sage named Vishvamitra, and two rivers, (Beas and Sutlej) that were worshipped as goddesses.

There are many prayers in the Rigveda for cattle, children (especially sons), and horses.
- Horses were yoked to chariots that were used in battles, which were fought to capture cattle.
- Battles were also fought for land, which was important for pasture, and for growing hardy crops that ripened quickly, such as barley.
- Some battles were fought for water, and to capture people.

Thus, we can say that the statements A and B are correct and C is incorrect.

62(B). Millets:
- Millets are basically the cereal crops that are vastly used in African and Asian nations.
- Hallur in present time is in Karnataka.
- Here, traces of Millets have been found.

Jadeite:
- Daojali Hading is located on the hills near the Brahmaputra valley.
- It is very close to the routes to nations like China and Myanmar. Stone tools were found here.
- Stone Jadeite has been brought from China. Its deep significance in Chinese culture became a symbol of ancient Chinese morality and ideology and representative of the progress of Chinese culture. There are many cultures that provide evidence of Jade in China.

So, the correct answer is A and D.

63(D). Harappa was one of the oldest cities in the subcontinent, which archaeologists found 80 years ago.

Harappan Cities:
- The first settlement was smaller but located at the higher ground. It was called Citadel. Its buildings were constructed on mud-brick platforms. It was walled and separated from the other settlements of the town.
- The second settlement was called lower town. It was larger but lower.

Houses, Drains and Streets:
- Even smaller towns and villages had impressive drainage systems. This indicates that people had a great civic sense of sanitation and care for health and hygiene.
- Generally, houses were either one or two storeys high, with rooms built around a courtyard.
- Most houses had a separate bathing area and some had wells to supply water.
- Many cities had covered drains.

So, the correct answer is Many of these cities had uncovered drains.

64(D). The Indian Rebellion of 1857 was a major, but ultimately unsuccessful, uprising in India in 1857–58 against the rule of the British East India Company, which functioned as a sovereign power on behalf of the British Crown. The rebellion began on 10 May 1857 in the form of a mutiny of sepoys of the Company's army in the garrison town of Meerut.
- The Company did not get nervous to see the strength of the rebel forces.
- Instead, it decided to suppress the revolt with all its might.
- It brought reinforcements from England, passed new laws so that the rebels could be convicted with ease, and then moved into the storm centres of the revolt.
- Delhi was recaptured from the rebel forces in September 1857.
- The last Mughal emperor, Bahadur Shah Zafar was tried in court and sentenced to life imprisonment.
- He and his wife were sent to prison in Rangoon in October 1858.

So, the correct answer is None of the above.

65(D). Jainism is an ancient religion that is rooted in the philosophy that teaches the way to liberation and a path to spiritual purity and enlightenment through disciplined nonviolence to all living creatures. It came into prominence in the 6th century B.C., when Lord Mahavira propagated the religion.

Doctrines of Jain:
- The fundamental tenet of Jain doctrine is that all phenomena are linked in a universal chain of cause and effect. Every event has a definite cause.
- The annihilation (nirjara) of karma comes about through penance. The surest way of annihilating Karma is to practice penance.
- Souls are not only the property of animal and plant life, but also of entities such as stones, rocks, running water, and many other natural objects not looked upon as living by other sects.
- Every object, even the smallest particle has a soul.
- Jaina holds that every living and non-living being is gifted with a soul. By removing the karmas, a soul can remove bondage and regain its natural perfections.
- Karma is the bane of the soul and it must be ended.
- Acquired karmas can be annihilated through a process called Nirjara ("wearing away"), which includes

fasting, restricting diet, controlling taste, retreating to lonely places, along with mortifications of the body, atonement, and expiation for sins, modesty, service, study, meditation, and renunciation of the ego.

So, the correct answer is A, B, and C.

66(C). The Tripartite Struggle for control of northern India took place in the ninth century. The struggle was between the Pratihara Empire, the Pala Empire, and the Rashtrakuta Empire.

Beginning of the Tripartite Struggle:
- The Pratihara ruler named Vatsaraja was very ambitious about Kannauj. Similarly Dharmapala, the Pala ruler also wanted to rule over Kannauj.
- And thus these two rulers were in conflict.
- Vatsaraja defeated Dharmapala in a battle at Gangetic Doab.
- And at the same time, Vatsaraja was defeated by Rashtrakuta king Dhruva.
- Dhruva also defeated Dharmapala.
- Finally, this pronounced enmity led to Tripartite Struggle between Palas, Rashtrakutas, and Pratiharas.

Causes of the Tripartite Struggle:
- Kannauj was the erstwhile capital of the Harshavardhana Empire in North India.
- Kannauj was the symbol of prestige and power during the early medieval period and this provoked the struggle.
- Control of Kannauj also implied control of Central Gangetic valley which had plenty of resources and thus it was both strategically and commercially important.

So, the correct answer is both A and B.

67(B). Teachings of Buddha:
- The Buddha taught that life is full of suffering and unhappiness. This is caused because we have cravings and desires (which often cannot be fulfilled).
- Sometimes, even if we get what we want, we are not satisfied, and want even more (or want other things). The Buddha described this as thirst or tanha.
- He taught that this constant craving could be removed by following moderation in everything.
- He also taught people to be kind and to respect the lives of others, including animals.
- He believed that the results of our actions (called karma), whether good or bad, affect us both in this life and the next.
- The Buddha taught in the language of the ordinary people, Prakrit, so that everybody could understand his message.

Thus, we can conclude that the statement 'The Buddha taught people to be kind and to respect the lives of others, including animals' is the teaching of Buddha.

68(C). Muhammad bin Tughluq was the Sultan of Delhi. He is also known as the wisest fool. He ruled the Tughlaq dynasty from 1325 to 1351. He moved his capital from Delhi to Daulatabad in 1327. After two years he shifted the capital back to Delhi due to lack of water supplies and many other issues. He introduced the 'token' currency in 1330. The coins introduced by Muhammad bin Tughlaq were made of brass and copper. The values of the coins were equal to that of gold and silver coins. The use of token currency has stopped in 1333 due to the issues in trade and commerce.

69(A). Tana Bhagat movement was associated with Oraon.
Tana Bhagat Movement (1914-1920) was a movement in Chota Nagpur area of British India against the policies of the local British authorities and exploitative business practices of local zamindars, mostly by Oraon people.
It is a tribal community in India. They opposed British government for the unfair taxes imposed on them. They were the followers of Mahatma Gandhi and believed in Ahinsa (Non-Violence).

70(C). The law of primogeniture implies that the firstborn child inherits the throne and the property of the father.
Shah Jahan, a Mughal ruler ruled from 1628 to 1658CE.
- During his reign, Shah Jahan led some of the successful military campaigns against Mewar, Kangra, and the Deccan.
- Shah Jahan had four sons, Dara Shikoh, Shuja, Murad, and Aurangzeb, who battled among each other to inherit the throne and property of their father.
Aurangzeb succeeded in the battle of inheritance, seized the Agra Fort, and ruled from 1658 to 1707CE.
Further, he imprisoned his father, Shah Jahan, who died in 1666CE in the jail.
Mughals followed their own custom of inheritance of the throne and property where the brothers fight for the succession and the powerful ones win.
We can conclude that Aurangzeb succeeded Shah Jahan but in their own Mughal law and not by the law of primogeniture.
So, the correct answer is (A) is true, but (R) is false.

71(A). The battle of Dewair was held in 1606. It was fought in a valley 40 km from Kumbalgarh. Rana Amar Singh defeated and killed Sultan Khan. The Mughal prince Muhammad Parviz fled from the battlefield with his commander Asaf Khan.

72(B). Kammakaras: It refers to landless agricultural labourers who worked on other's land. In the later Vedic age Kammakaras along with women and dasas (slaves) were not allowed to participate in the assemblies.

Vajji:
- The capital at Vaishali (Bihar) was one of the sixteen Mahajanapas. It was under a different form of government, known as Gana or Sangha.
- In a gana or a sangha there were not one, but many rulers. Sometimes, even when thousands of men ruled together, each one was known as a raja.
- These rajas performed rituals together. They also met in assemblies, and decided what had to be done and how, through discussion and debate.
- However, women, dasas, and kammakaras could not participate in these assemblies.
- Both the Buddha and Mahavira belonged to ganas or sanghas.
- Some of the most vivid descriptions of life in the sangha's can be found in Buddhist books. Kammakaras were also referred to in Buddhist texts in Pali.

73(D). Rishabhdev was the first Tirthankara of the Jains. He was born to King Nabhi Raja and Queen Marudevi at Ayodhya in the Ikshvaku clan. Mahavira (6th-century BCE) was the last Tirthankara to appear.

Jain Tirthankaras	Description
Aristhenemi	22 nd Tirthankara of J ain.
Parshwnath	23 rd Tirthankara of J ain.
Ajitnath	2 nd Tirthankara of Jai n.
Rishabhdev	1 st Tirthankara of Jai n.

74(D). An early temple at Bhitargaon, Uttar Pradesh was built about 1500 years ago, and was made of baked brick and stone.
Monolithic temples at Mahabalipuram. Each of these was carved out of a huge, single piece of stone (that is why they are known as monoliths). While brick structures are built up by adding layers of bricks from the bottom upwards, in this case, the stone cutters had to work from the top downwards.
The Durga temple at Aihole, built about 1400 years ago. Originally dedicated to Surya, it has the most embellished and largest relief panels in Aihole depicting the artwork of Shaivism, Vaishnavism, Shaktism, and Vedic deities.

75(C). Situated along the border of Argentina and Chile, Aconcagua is the highest peak of Andes Mountains. It is a snow-capped extinct volcano rising to a height of 6960 m (22,834 ft.) above the sea level. It was first climbed by Edward A. Fitzgerald in 1897. It has vertical zones in its natural vegetation ranging from the deciduous forests at the foothills, pine and

fir above 2000 m, and alpine pastures at higher altitudes.

76(B). Indian Standard Meridian:
- In India, the longitude of 82½° E (82° 30'E) is treated as the standard meridian.
- The local time at this meridian is taken as the standard time for the whole country.
- It is known as the Indian Standard Time (IST).
Frigid Zone:
- The frigid Zone is the uppermost and the lowermost zone of the Earth which includes the Northern and the Southern Pole.
- It is located between 66°30'N & S to the Pole
- As the Rays of the sun fall slant on it with the shorter reach of light the area gets cold.
- Thus, Frigid Zone is the coldest zone of Earth.
Antarctic circle:
- Antarctic Circle, parallel, or line of latitude around the Earth, at 66°30' S.
- It referred to as a polar circle, is one of the five latitude circles that are used to divide maps of Earth.
Roaring Forties:
- The Roaring Forties are strong westerly winds found in the Southern Hemisphere, generally between the latitudes of 40°S and 50°S.
- The strong west-to-east air currents are caused by the combination of air being displaced from the Equator towards the South Pole.
- The Earth's rotation, and the scarcity of landmasses to serve as windbreaks at those latitudes.
So, it is clear that statements 1, 2 and 4 are correct statements here.

77(D). Malacca Strait - India and Sri Lanka is not correctly matched.
Malacca Strait, which flows between Indonesia, Malaysia, and Singapore, connects the Indian Ocean with the Pacific Ocean through the South China Sea. It is the shortest sea route between Persian Gulf suppliers and key Asian markets.

78(B). The above statements are defining the characteristics of firewood.
Firewood:
- It is widely used for cooking and heating.
- In our country, more than fifty percent of the energy used by villagers comes from firewood.
- Wood is considered humankind's very first source of energy.
- Today it is still the most important single source of renewable energy providing about 6% of the global total primary energy supply.
- Wood fuel is a fuel, such as firewood, charcoal, chips, sheets, pellets, and

sawdust.
- Today, the burning of wood is the largest use of energy derived from solid fuel biomass.

79(A). The above feature is found in the case of Shifting cultivation.
Shifting cultivation:
- Shifting cultivation is practiced in the thickly forested areas of the Amazon basin, tropical Africa, parts of Southeast Asia, and Northeast India.
- These are the areas of heavy rainfall and quick regeneration of vegetation.
- A plot of land is cleared by felling the trees and burning them.
- The ashes are then mixed with the soil and crops like maize, yam, potatoes, and cassava are grown.
- After the soil loses its fertility, the land is abandoned and the cultivator moves to a new plot.
- Shifting cultivation is also known as 'slash and burn agriculture.

80(A).

Mineral	Characteristics
Aluminium	• Aluminum obtained from its ore b auxite • It is used in automobiles and airp lanes, bottling industry, buildings, and even in kitchen cookware
Copper	• Copper is another metal used in ev erything from coins to pipes. • Most copper is used in electrical e quipment such as wiring and moto rs. • This is because it conducts both h eat and electricity very well, and c an be drawn into wires.
Silicon	• Silicon, used in the computer indu stry is obtained from quartz. • The same way silicon is used to m ake glass, it is also used to make p ottery.
Hard minerals	• Precious metals gold, platinum, et c are used for making jewelry. • Minerals that are used for gems ar e usually hard. • These are then set in various style s for jewelry.

So, the correct matching is a - ii, b - iii, c - i, d - iv.

81(A). In India, Cyclone is tracked through SCATSAT-1 satellite.

SCATSAT-1 satellite is formed by the ISRO Satellite Centre, Bangalore. This satellite is used for making predictions about a cyclone and weather forecasts. However, due to TWTA instrument failure, SCATSAT-1 satellite has been disabled in India from 28 February 2021.

82(A). One-horned rhinoceroses:
- The greater one-horned rhino (or "Indian rhino") is the largest of the rhino species.
- One-horned rhinoceroses are the other animals, which live in swampy and marshy lands of Assam and West Bengal.
- The one-horned rhinoceros inhabits the riverine grasslands of the Terai and Brahmaputra basins.
- The species prefers alluvial plain grasslands but is also found in adjacent swamps and forests.
- Project Rhino was launched in 2005.
- Indian Rhino Vision 2020 is an ambitious effort to attain a wild population of at least 3,000 greater one-horned rhinos spread over seven protected areas in the Indian state of Assam by the year 2020.

So, all the statements given are correct.

83(B). The second most abundant metal in the earth's crust is Iron.
- Iron is the second most abundant metal in the earth's crust 5.0%.
- Aluminium is the most abundant metal found in the earth's crust 8.1%.
- Oxygen comprises of 46.6% of the total weight of the earth's crust.

84(D). Statement 1: The earth's surface is composed of three major spheres and the life-supporting zone is the biosphere.
- The surface of the earth is a complex zone in which three main components of the environment meet, overlap, and interact.
- The solid portion of the earth on which we live is called the Lithosphere.
- The gaseous layer that surrounds the earth, is the Atmosphere, where oxygen, nitrogen, carbon dioxide, and other gases are found.
- Water covers a very big area of the earth's surface and this area is called the Hydrosphere.
- The Hydrosphere comprises water in all its forms, that is, ice, water, and water vapor.
- The Biosphere is the narrow zone where we find land, water, and air together, which contains all forms of life.

So, the statement 1 is correct.
Statement 2: The highest point of the earth is located in the landmass
- The highest point on Earth's surface measured from sea level is the summit of Mount Everest, on the border of Nepal and China.
- Its elevation of 8,848.86 m was most

recently established in 2020 by the Chinese and Nepali authorities.
- It is completely located in a landlocked position.

So, statement 2 is also correct.
Statement 3: The lowest point is located under the sea
- The lowest point on Earth's surface is Challenger Deep, at the bottom of the Mariana Trench, 11,034 m (36,201 ft) below sea level.
- The Mariana Trench or Marianas Trench is located in the western Pacific Ocean about 200 kilometers east of the Mariana Islands
- It is the deepest oceanic trench on Earth.
- It is crescent-shaped and measures about 2,550 km in length and 69 km in width.

So, statement 3 is also correct.
Therefore, all are correct.

85(D). Characteristics of a village community:
- Jajmani system
- Uncomplicated lifestyle
- Faith in religion
- Specific locality
- Smaller size
- Significance of neighborhood
- Community sentiment
- Joint family system
- Agricultural economy

86(D). The 86th amendment to the Constitution of India in 2002, provided the Right to Education as a Fundamental Right in Part-III of the Constitution.
The amendment inserted Article 21A which made the Right to Education a fundamental right for children between 6-14 years.
The 86th amendment provided for follow-up legislation for the Right to Education Bill 2008 and finally the Right to Education Act, 2009.

87(D). The Sixth Schedule of the Indian Constitution consists of provisions for the administration of Tribal Area in Assam, Meghalaya, Tripura, and Mizoram. It seeks to safeguard the rights of the tribal population through the formation of Autonomous District Councils (ADC).

88(C). If the advice of party-less parliamentary democracy is adopted in India, it would have a positive effect on the working of the government as it would work on clear-cut policy lines in the interests of all people. Instead of party-less democracy, the representatives of people should only form the Government which would be more stable and will make decisions that will benefit the citizens of the country, hence promoting every aspect of development. This avoids the growing corruption and other ill-practices employed by the various party leaders.

89(A). Simla Accord (1914), signed in

1914, to purported to settle a dispute over the boundary line between inner and outer Tibet.

The Simla Convention provided that Tibet would be divided into "Outer Tibet" and "Inner Tibet". Outer Tibet, which roughly corresponded to U-Tsang and western Kham, would "remain in the hands of the Tibetan Government at Lhasa under Chinese suzerainty", but China would not interfere in its administration.

90(A). A political party whose MLAs have won more than half the number of constituencies in a state can be said to be in a majority.

The political party that has the majority is called the ruling party and all other members are called the opposition.

Governor is the executive head of the state.

- He plays an important part in the state executive where he acts as the chief executive head.
- The governor is nominated by the Central Government for each state.

As a real executive authority, the Chief Minister is called the head of the government.

- He is assisted by his council of ministers who are a part of the state executive along with Governor and Advocate-General of State.
- Similar to the Prime Minister who is the head of the government at the centre, the Chief Minister is the head of the government at the state level.

Thus, the correct matching is A-II, B-IV, C-I, D-III.

91(D). Our constitution provides safeguards to religious and linguistic minorities as part of our Fundamental Rights.

- The term minority is most commonly used to refer to communities that are numerically small in relation to the rest of the population.
- However, it is a concept that goes well beyond numbers.
- It encompasses issues of power, access to resources and has social and cultural dimensions.
- The Indian Constitution recognized that the culture of the majority influences the way in which society and government might express themselves.
- In such cases, size can be a disadvantage and lead to the marginalization of the relatively smaller communities.
- Thus, safeguards are needed to protect minority communities against the possibility of being culturally dominated by the majority.
- They also protect them against any discrimination and disadvantage that they may face.

Thus, we can conclude that (A) is false, but (R) is true.

92(B). Indian Parliament is bicameral in nature i.e. that it has two houses. Rajya Sabha is one of those two houses, i.e. the upper house of the Parliament. The other house is the Lok Sabha (Lower House of Parliament). Rajya Sabha is the second chamber of the parliament and represents the states and union territories of the nation. It is empowered to protect the interests of the states and union territories if there is interference by the centre in their work.

- The Rajya Sabha functions primarily as the representative of the states of India in the Parliament.
- The Rajya Sabha can also initiate legislation and a bill is required to pass through the Rajya Sabha in order to become a law.
- It, therefore, has an important role in reviewing and altering (if alterations are needed) the laws initiated by the Lok Sabha.
- The members of the Rajya Sabha are elected by the elected members of the Legislative Assemblies of various states.
- The Rajya Sabha should consist of not more than 250 members - 238 members representing the States and Union Territories, and 12 members nominated by the President.
- The Vice President of India is the ex-officio Chairman of Rajya Sabha.
- The House also elects a Deputy Chairman from among its members.
- Besides, there is also a panel of "Vice Chairmen" in the Rajya Sabha.
- The senior-most minister, who is a member of Rajya Sabha, is appointed by the Prime Minister as Leader of the House.

From the above, it is clear that the statement 'It represents the states of India in the Parliament.' is correct about the Rajya Sabha.

93(C). The Parliament of India (Sansad) is the supreme law-making institution. It has two Houses, the Rajya Sabha and the Lok Sabha.

Created after 1947, the Indian Parliament is an expression of the faith that the people of India have in principles of democracy.

- These are participation by people in the decision-making process and government by consent.
- The Parliament in our system has immense powers because it is the representative of the people.
- Elections to the Parliament are held in a similar manner as they are for the state legislature.

94(C). The Prime Minister is the real executive authority and the Head of the Government.

Article 75 - The Prime Minister is appointed by the President. The Prime Minister is the ex-officio Chairman of NITI Aayog, National Integration Council, and Inter-State Council. The tenure of the Prime Minister is not fixed and he holds office during the pleasure of the President for 5 years. The oath of office to the Prime Minister is administered by the President.

95(C). The elections to Panchayats are conducted by the State Election Commission by way of superintendence, direction, and control of the preparation of electoral rolls and the conduct of all elections.

- All the members of panchayats at the village, intermediate, and district levels shall be elected directly by the people of Gram Sabha.
- The act provides for a five-year term of office to the panchayat at every level from the date of convening its first meeting.

The State Government may by law authorize a Panchayat to levy, collect, and appropriate - taxes, duties, tolls, and fees. So, statement (C) is NOT correct.

96(B). Agricultural relations in rural society in India can be understood under ecological differences. Agriculture and allied sectors are important from the point of view of employment and livelihood for small and marginal farmers who dominate the agricultural ecosystem in India.

97(B). Bank of England (BoE) raised the U.K.'s bank rate by half a percentage point to 1.75%, marking the biggest interest rate increase since 1995. The U.K. economy is projected to go into recession from the fourth quarter of 2022, the BoE warned. This is due to the near doubling of wholesale gas prices since May, owing to Russia's restriction of gas supplies to Europe and the risk of further curbs.

98(C). SBI Research Ecowrap released a report that said India's fiscal deficit in the current financial year is expected to come around 6.5 percent, as against the budget estimate of 6.4 percent. Furthermore, higher nominal GDP will provide a cushion. The report has also revised current account deficit (CAD) estimates from 3.2 percent of GDP to 3.7 percent of GDP in the current financial year.

99(B). Union Minister Ashwini Vaishnaw, Ministry of Railways launched e-auction for commercial earning, and Non-Fare Revenue (NFR) contracts, in Rail Bhavan, New Delhi (Delhi). This launch was made to bring Commercial Earning and NFR contracts under the ambit of electronic auction through Indian Railway e-Procurement System (IREPS), in line with the prevailing e-auction of scrap sale. The e-auction for commercial earning will increase railway earnings, and also enhance the ease of doing business.

100(B). Sikkim Chief Minister P S Tamang

on 15 August 2022 launched 2 schemes, 'Aama Yojana' & 'Vatsalya Yojana' for the welfare of women of the state.

Under Aama Yojana all unemployed mothers in the state will receive Rs 20,000 annually which will be deposited in their bank accounts.

Under Vatsalya Yojana an aid of Rs 3 lakh will be provided to childless women for in vitro fertilization treatment.

101(B). Social Science is a branch of science that deals with human behavior and social relationships, which rely primarily on empirical approaches.

- The textbook provides a balanced, chronological presentation of information but Students visualize only a limited perspective on a concept or issue and it does not promote higher-level thinking among students. From a pedagogic point of view, teachers should not rely on a single textbook for their instructional planning.
- In order to incorporate local knowledge, traditional skills, diversity among the learners, and learning environments, there is a need for a plurality of textbooks and other learning resources as well.
- It is necessary to give primacy to the children, by enabling them to express their voices, by nurturing their curiosity, by providing the opportunity to pursue investigations, and by sharing and integrating their experiences with school knowledge- rather than emphasizing their ability to reproduce textual knowledge.
- It is necessary to engage children in active engagement during curriculum transaction through inquiry, exploration, questioning, debate, application, and reflection, leading to theory building and the creation of new ideas/propositions in order to promote higher-order thinking which can not be only gained by the textual leaning.

So, it can be concluded that both Assertion (A) and Reason (R) are incorrect.

102(C). Charles Beard: Social sciences are the body of knowledge and thought pertaining to human affairs as distinguished from sticks, stones, stars, and physical objects. (S. K. Kochhar, The Teaching of Social Studies, 1984-First Edition)

James High: Social sciences are those bodies of learning and study which recognize the simultaneous and mutual action of physical and non-physical stimuli which produce social reactions (Dr. Y.K. Singh, Teaching of Social Studies,2008).

The following points may characterize the nature of social sciences

- Direct bearing on human activity: Social sciences are those aspects of knowledge that have a direct bearing on man's activities in different sociocultural fields.
- Advance studies of human society: Social sciences are advanced-level studies of human society, and they are generally taught at higher education levels.
- Find out truths about human relationships: Social sciences seek to find out truths about human relationships which ultimately contribute to the social utility and advancement of knowledge.

So, we conclude that all the above points are correct regarding the nature of social science.

103(A). Social Science is a branch of science that deals with human behaviour and social relationships, which rely primarily on empirical approaches. The study of Social Science is necessary for the understanding of the socio-cultural structure and its relation with the environment as this understanding will make students:

- respect diversity in cultural practices.
- understand the society in which they live.
- grow up better to become responsible citizens.
- knowledgeable about civilization and social behaviour.
- assimilate norms, beliefs, cultures, and values of society.

So, we conclude that the study of Social Science is necessary for the understanding of the socio-cultural structure and its relation with the environment.

104(D). Lecture Method: It is a teaching strategy in which the teacher makes an effort to clarify concepts for the benefit of the students. While the students are passive listeners, the teacher is an active participant. The teacher speaks to the class in a very constant manner. The students take notes as they listen, write, and write down ideas and data to remember and reflect on afterward. The majority of the time, students keep their conversations with the teacher during lectures. It only works one way. The students might ask a few questions to further clarify a concept, but there is typically no discussion.

Merits of Lecture Method:

- It is cost-effective because one teacher can educate many students at once, something that is impossible with other techniques. It saves a lot of time and makes it simple to finish the syllabus in a short amount of time.
- It makes the teachers convenient. Less effort is required on the part of the instructor to prepare her lessons, and she is free to develop the presentation as she sees fit. She doesn't need to bother about showing how to do something.
- It helps in developing students' hearing skills and speech-related skills.
- It is helpful for conveying factual information and highlighting its essential components.
- The teacher feels more secure as a result.
- There are no interruptions or distractions.

So, we can conclude that the child-centered method is not merited the lecture method.

105(D). Social Science is a branch of science that deals with human behavior and social relationships, which rely primarily on empirical approaches and includes disciplines of History, Geography, Political Science. Economics and Sociology.

Activity-based questions that make Social Science lessons debatable is incorrect statement.

- Activity-based questions indulge students in activities by stimulating their senses such as sight, smell, the vision of feeling, and getting them involved in the subject.
- Activity-Based Questions do not make social science more debatable but it makes social science more enjoyable, interesting, enjoyable and also gives freedom to students for self-learning, self-guiding.
- Through these questions, students are involved more in learning activities rather than listening and less emphasis is placed on transmitting information and more on developing students' skills.

So, it can be concluded that given Assertion (A) is incorrect but Reason (R) is correct.

106(B). A field trip refers to a learning approach that ensures the active involvement of learners in the learning process by taking them to a certain place where they can earn knowledge by engaging with real situations.

- Field trips are useful in Social Science for empirical evidence (information obtained through observation and experimentation) as in it:
- reinforces experiential and contextual learning.
- provides an active learning experience to learners.
- involves learners in both group and self-directed activities.
- links classroom learning to life outside school or with the real world.
- gives students a lot of opportunities for observation and exploration.

So, we conclude that Field trips are useful in Social Science for Empirical evidence.

107(A). Social science is a collection of academic disciplines that study human behavior, specifically how people interact with one another, act, evolve as a culture, and influence things. This wide and diverse field of science includes disciplines like anthropology, economics, political science, psychology, and sociology.

Critical thinking is a process that challenges an individual to use reflective, reasonable, rational thinking to gather, interpret, and evaluate information in order to derive a judgment. According to John Dewey , critical thinking is a process of "active, persistent, and deliberate analysis" of the credibility and conclusions of assumed knowledge or information.

- Critical thinking includes interpreting and analyzing many difficulties and situations that one encounters on a daily basis.
- Following are the various intellectual abilities that are required for critical thinking:
  ○ Creating well-reasoned, convincing arguments, as well as evaluating and responding to objections.
  ○ Examining ideas or events from several angles, including diverse cultural viewpoints.
  ○ In order to obtain innovative findings, data and assumptions must be challenged.
  ○ Generating creative solutions to issues, especially those that are unexpected or complex.
  ○ Generating and expressing insightful, perceptive queries.
  ○ Finding themes or patterns, and drawing connections between disparate subjects in an abstract way.
- Explain your views on installing solar power panels on a building . Here, in this question, the student will do analyses, evaluations, and innovative findings and then will give a creative solution. This provides an opportunity to develop students' critical thinking.
- Do you think that electric vehicles can help in reducing air pollution? Discuss. Here, in this question, the student will do critical thinking in finding an innovative and creative solution. This provides an opportunity to develop students' critical thinking.
- How did the conflict between Russia and Ukraine start? Here, in this question, the student will do an analysis and evaluation. This provides an opportunity to develop students' critical thinking.

So, we can conclude that A, B, and C are correct.

108(C). To teach different topics in social sciences and to achieve learning objectives associated with these topics, you use a number of teaching-learning methods or techniques which constitute various teaching-learning strategies.

Teaching through Discussion-

- Discussion is one of the widely used group-centred learning techniques. It can be used in a variety of situations in the secondary school context.
- It is a process of thinking together that breaks down if one member or group

dominates it.

- It is the responsibility of the teacher to encourage the more relevant students to participate.
- For example, situations like "functions of the State Government, issues related to health, water, transport, etc", helps to understand the issue, clarifying the doubts of students in discussion, generating alternative solutions to a classroom problem, and give feedback on student's view and misconceptions are some of the situations in which the discussion technique could be used.
- Through discussion, students-
  ○ become open-minded, respect and accept the contributions of others, but think independently.
  ○ assume responsibility for the discussion and be able to support ideas with factual evidence.
  ○ recognise the problem of semantics in arriving at group decisions or in discussing a controversial issue.

Thus, from the above-mentioned points, it is clear that while discussing the functions of the State Government, issues related to health, water, transport, etc. may be discussed to allow learners to understand these issues and express their critical views.

109(B). Items such as research articles, books, photographs, audio and video recordings, materials, websites, etc. are a source of information. They help the child in gathering some knowledge.

- Knowledge is gathered for a purpose and this is a key component of the Enquiry process.
- An inquiry is a question, an investigation, a request for information, or the process of seeking information.
- The teacher here is trying to emphasize the inquiry learning process by providing their background knowledge through sources such as research articles, books, photographs, audio and video recordings, materials, websites, etc.

Thus, it is concluded that option (B) is the correct answer.

110(D). Today, the use of statistical methods in the analysis, presentation, and drawing of conclusions plays a significant role in almost all disciplines, including geography, which uses the data. It may, therefore, be inferred that the concentration of a phenomenon, e.g., population, forest, or network of transportation, or communication not only varies over space and time but may also be conveniently explained using the data.

The data are collected in the following ways. These are:

Primary Sources:

- The data which are collected for the first time by an individual or a group of

individuals, institutions/organizations are called Primary sources of the data.

- It refers to the collection of information by an individual or group of individuals through direct observations in the field.
- Through a field survey, information about the relief features, drainage patterns, types of soil and natural vegetation, as well as, population structure, sex ratio, literacy, means of transport and communication, urban and rural settlements, etc., is collected.

Secondary Sources:

- On the other hand, data collected from any published or unpublished sources are called Secondary sources.
- The publications of the various ministries and the departments of the Government of India, state governments, and the District Bulletins are one of the most important sources of secondary information.
- These include the Census of India published by the Office of the Registrar General of India, reports of the National Sample Survey, Weather Reports of the Indian Meteorological Department and Statistical Abstracts published by state governments, and the periodical reports published by different Commissions.

Thus, from the above-mentioned points, it is clear that a student interviews Tsunami survivors for a project in Geography. This can be considered a project based on primary sources.

111(C). Social Science is a branch of science that deals with human behaviour and social relationships, which rely primarily on empirical approaches. The teacher of social science has different roles to play. For example, developing personality values, and attitudes, and civic responsibility to live together in a democracy.

Effective Teaching of Social Science would Require:

- Use of non-textual sources like diagrams, maps, etc.
- Giving primacy to the triangulation of sources.
- Critical analysis of literary texts, howsoever old they may be.
- Addressing social issues and making plans to bring improvements.
- Studying human behaviour and enhancing vision or perspective about society.

Triangulation of sources implies the idea of collecting data from multiple sources to ensure authentic learning.

So, from the above-mentioned points, it becomes clear that effective teaching of social science would require critical analysis of literary texts and giving primacy to the triangulation of sources.

112(C). A teacher has to make use of various kinds of methods, devices, and techniques of teaching. A teacher has to make use of a suitable method for making his teaching meaningful, purposeful, interesting, and effective.

Lecture method	• The lecture method simply means teaching through lecture. • Makes students inactive. • There is very little scope for pupil activity. • May include irrelevant material.
Project method	• A project is a problematic act carried to completion in its natural setting. • It gives freedom to children. • It takes too much time to complete.
Storytelling method	• By nature, children are fond of stories. • Children have a genuine interest in listening to stories. • History was originally presented in stories and it is felt that students, particularly at the early school stage, should be taught history through a series of stories. • Stories can give them immense pleasure, extend their imagination and develop their creative powers.
Discussion method	• Discussion methods are a variety of forums for the open-ended, collaborative exchange of ideas among a teacher and students. • Among students for the purpose of furthering students thinking, learning, problem-solving, understanding, or literary appreciation.

Thus, the most effective important method of teaching history at the elementary level is by telling stories about the event of history, which will make them interested in history.

113(A). The basic purpose of teaching social sciences at the school level is to make students informed and rational citizens.
- The textbooks, instead of being treated as the 'only source', should be seen as 'one of the sources' for developing one's understanding.
- There is no textbook that is totally perfect and complete in all respects. As textbook needs to address the requirements of diverse learners, it may have certain limitations also.
- A teacher may provide students with a lot of supplementary information, which is easily comprehensible, by using materials like websites, dictionaries, atlas, encyclopedias, other important reference books, etc.
- Sometimes textbooks might have failed to arouse students' interest and students reject textbooks simply because of what they are – compendiums of a large chunk of information for students and they may

find it difficult to understand the relevance of a lot of information to their personal lives.
- Activities like debate, discussions, question-answer sessions, projects will help to make learning enjoyable and interesting.

So, it can be concluded that Both (A) and (R) are true and (R) is the correct explanation of (A).

114(C). A project refers to a series of task that needs to be done by a group of students in order to achieve a particular goal.

Projects in Social Science are useful in purposeful theme-based tasks and for group work in class or at home because the project promotes:
- voluntary participation of students by working in a group.
- personal experiences of students as the basis of knowledge.
- applying practical knowledge to complete a thematic project.
- imparting practical knowledge to the students for quality experiences.
- active learning by association and mutual co-operation of a group of peers.

So, it could be concluded that projects in Social Science are useful in theme-based tasks and for group work in class or at home.

115(C). Science is a powerful way of investigating and understanding the world. Therefore, the teaching-learning of science must enable children to examine and analyze their everyday experiences.

The skills developed in the students through the above activity are:
- Children raise questions, form hypothesis and test them, record observations, collect, organize and record data, manipulate materials, and examine their innovative ideas.
- Children get the opportunity to share their ideas and findings with their peers and adults.
- Students develop the ability to inquire, explain, analyze, and interpret scientific processes and phenomena more than their ability to recall specific facts.
- For example, by experimenting with objects to see how the water flow and how the refill deviates the path of water, etc. the learners are engaged in finding out how the world around them works.
- They learn through observation and interaction with the environment around them, nature, things, and people both through action and languages.
- This will promote challenge and allow independent thinking, and multiple ways of being solved encourage independence, creativity, and self-discipline in learners.
- It will promote experimentation, the ability to think logically and rationally, and maybe her attitude of inquiry and

interest in science.

Thus, from the above-mentioned points, it is clear that the skills developed in the students through this activity are observation, experimentation and creativity.

116(D). Evaluation refers to a process of making value judgments based on both qualitative and quantitative data collected over a period of time.
- CCE describes two different types of evaluation which include 'formative' and 'summative' evaluation.
- 'Formative evaluation' is a type of evaluation that refers to monitor the child's progress throughout the teaching-learning process.
- Oral testing, anecdotal records, portfolios, class test, etc are the tools of formative evaluation.

Characteristics of Formative Evaluation:
- It is used to monitor the learning progress of students during the period of instruction.
- For a teacher, formative evaluation provides information for making instructions and remedies more effective.
- It gives the opportunity for students participation, improves their academic achievements, and encourages motivation level.
- Feedback to the teacher provides information for max living instruction and for prescribing group and individual remedial work.
- It is a process-oriented evaluation as feedback to students reinforces successful learning and identifies the specific learning errors that need correction.
- This evaluation provides the student with feedback regarding his or her success or failure in attaining the instructional objectives.
- It provides continuous & effective feedback to both teacher and student concerning learning successes and failures while instruction is in process.

So, it could be concluded that none of the above is correct in the context of formative evaluation.

117(B). Evaluation is a systematic process of collecting, analyzing, and interpreting evidence of student's progress and achievement. Continuous evaluation is required in teaching for successful learning. It needs to be integrated with the process of teaching and learning.

Continuous and Comprehensive Evaluation (CCE) has been introduced as a school-based system of evaluation by the CBSE in 2009 with the enactment of the 'Right to Education Act'.
- CCE refers to all-around development including both scholastic and co-scholastic aspects of a child's growth.

- It never assesses students according to their economic status rather it emphasizes the continuity of assessment.
- Objectives are most appropriate regarding assessment is to encourage students to give responses.
- The continuous assessment facilitates mapping different dimensions of a child's development holistically to provide a more authentic picture to help the child, teacher, and hence the system.

So, it becomes clear that as per the continuous and comprehensive evaluation, encouraging students to give responses is most appropriate regarding assessment.

118(B). Secondary sources offer an analysis, interpretation, or a restatement of primary sources and are considered to be persuasive. They often involve generalisation, synthesis, interpretation, commentary, or evaluation in an attempt to convince the reader of the creator's argument. They often attempt to describe or explain primary sources.
Examples of secondary sources include:

- journal articles that comment on or analyse research
- textbooks
- dictionaries and encyclopaedias
- books that interpret, analyse
- political commentary
- biographies
- dissertations
- newspaper editorial/opinion pieces
- criticism of literature, art works or music

119(C). Primary sources provide a first-hand account of an event or time period and are considered to be authoritative. They represent original thinking, report on discoveries or events, or can share new information. Often these sources are created at the time the events occurred but they can also include sources that are created later. They are usually the first formal appearance of original research.
Examples of primary resources include:

- diaries, correspondence, ships' logs
- original documents e.g. birth certificates, trial transcripts
- biographies, autobiographies, manuscripts
- interviews, speeches, oral histories
- case law, legislation, regulations, constitutions
- government documents, statistical data, research reports
- a journal article reporting NEW research or findings
- creative artworks, literature
- newspaper advertisements and reportage and editorial/opinion pieces

120(C).
Secondary data: It refers to data that is collected by someone other than the primary user. It is basically Past data.
Common sources of secondary data are-

- Census data
- tax records data
- Information collected by government departments, like National Sample Survey Organization data or Election commission of India
- Organizational records and data that were originally collected for other research purposes.

Child Development and Pedagogy

1. Which of these is an external factor influencing the growth and development of a child?
(a) Physical environment
(b) Intelligence
(c) Biological factors
(d) Hereditary factors

2. Which statement about a creative child is not true?
(a) A creative child is curious
(b) A creative child is not adventurous
(c) A creative child is extrovert
(d) A creative child is ambitious

3. Which is an example of intrinsic motivation?
(a) Aspiration
(b) Praise
(c) Encouragement
(d) Prize

4. According to Kohlberg's theory of moral development, the period of pre moral state is:
(a) From birth to 5 years of age
(b) From birth to 2 years of age
(c) From the 3 years to 6 years of age
(d) From the 7 years to the early teenage

5. According to Jean Piaget, the adolescence stage of cognitive development is termed as :
(a) Pre-operational stage
(b) Concrete operational stage
(c) Formal operational stage
(d) Sensory-motor stage

6. Which among the following is correct regarding Curriculum?
i) Everything that goes on within the school, including extra-class activities, guidance, and interpersonal relationships.
ii) Everything that is planned by school personnel.
iii) A course of study
iv) A program of studies
(a) i, ii
(b) iii, iv
(c) i, ii, iv
(d) All of the above

7. Which among the following is considered as the teacher's guide for running a particular lesson?
(a) Unit plan
(b) Lesson plan
(c) Simulated plan
(d) None of the above

8. What is/are the functions of the School Management Committee as per the Right to Education Act, 2009?
i) To monitor the working of the school
ii) To monitor the utilization of grants
iii) To prepare the school development plan
(a) Only (i)
(b) Both (ii) and (iii)
(c) (i), (ii) and (iii)
(d) Both (i) and (ii)

9. Which of the following statements does not represent an attribute of growth?
(a) This is a quantitative aspect.
(b) It is not measurable.
(c) It's not lifelong.
(d) It only shows physical development.

10. The sequence in which a child develops, follows two trends:
(a) Constant and correlation
(b) Learning and maturation
(c) Growth and development
(d) Cephalocaudal and proximodistal

11. In a diverse classroom, a teacher responsibility is:
(a) To teach all students together with an appropriate teaching method
(b) To provide varieties of learning experiences
(c) To make a lesson plan before starting teaching
(d) To evaluate learner's academic performance

12. Which of the following is/are the factors affecting language learning?
(a) Age   (b) Motivation
(c) Aptitude   (d) All of these

13. Child development emphasis on:
(a) Role of environment
(b) Role of experience
(c) Role of intelligence
(d) All of the above

14. Which of the following is not correct regarding the growth of an individual?
(a) Growth is quantitative changes in an individual
(b) Growth does not continue throughout the life
(c) Growth always brings development
(d) Changes produced by growth are subject to measure

15. On the basis of which of the following principles does the child learn the language?
(a) On the principle of multi-faceted effort
(b) On the principle of simulation
(c) On the principle of entertainment
(d) On the principle of practice

16. The causes of learning disabilities are________.
(a) Genetic factors
(b) Organic and environmental factors
(c) Both (A) and (B)
(d) None of the above

17. In order to address the needs of students who are facing learning difficulties, a teacher should NOT________.
(a) Using a creative pedagogical approach
(b) Implementation of individual educational plan
(c) Practice of Rigid Structures for Teaching and Assessment
(d) Use of multiple audio-visual aids

18. A child with Learning Disability________.
(a) Needs to be put in a separate institution and not in mainstream schools
(b) Has a right to study in the regular school where there are special provisions for him
(c) Should be given vocational education, but should not be taught science and writing skill
(d) Needs to be dealt with severely and punished harshly for these mistakes

19. How would you identify a child with a learning disability?
(a) By administering intelligence tests
(b) By seeing their physical appearance
(c) By looking at their notebooks for

writing

(d) By observing how much they fight with other children

20. What is inclusive education?

(a) Increases diversity in the classroom

(b) Encourages strict admissions procedures

(c) It involves the inclusion of facts

(d) This includes teachers from marginalized groups

21. At the age of 6 - 9, children start taking interest in:

(a) Religion   (b) Human body

(c) Intimacy   (d) School

22. Who called infancy the ideal time to learn?

(a) Rousseau   (b) Strang

(c) Stanley hall   (d) Valentine

23. Very young infants can either look at an object or grasp it when it comes in contract with their hands. They cannot coordinate looking and grasping at the same time. As per Piaget, the characteristics reflects the tendency of:

(a) Adaptation

(b) Assimilation

(c) Organization

(d) Accommodation

24. IQ level of extraordinary students lies between:

(a) 80-90   (b) 110-120

(c) 50-60   (d) 130-144

25. If a student frequently remains inattentive in class, he or she should be:

(a) Punished hard

(b) Expelled from school

(c) Advised to stop reading in school

(d) None of the above

26. A child falling in love with a parent of other sex is the characteristic behavior of:

(a) Anal stage

(b) Phallic stage

(c) Latency stage

(d) Genital stage

27. ______takes place when a child strikes balance between the two processes while trying to internalise the perceived object.

(a) Equilibration

(b) Adaptation

(c) Assimilation

(d) Accommodation

28. A child watches a classmate get in trouble for hitting another child. They learn from observing this interaction that they should not hit others. This is a classic example of learning by ______.

(a) doing

(b) imitation

(c) trial and error

(d) observation

29. Baby Bhavya starts to look for her toys which was hidden by her mother. In which stage of development does Bhavya lies?

(a) Sensory-motor Stage

(b) Pre-operational Stage

(c) Concrete-operational Stage

(d) Formal-operational Stage

30. At the age of 4 - 5 years, a male child develops a more profound attachment towards his mother as compared to his father. What was the term coined by Freud for this change of behaviour of child?

(a) Oedipus complex

(b) Electra complex

(c) Super ego

(d) Narcissism

Language - I: English

Ques (31-36): Direction : Read the poem given below and answer the questions that follow by selecting the correct/most appropriate options.

The cardboard shows me how it was
When the two girl cousins went paddling
Each one holding one of my mother's hands,
And she the big girl – some twelve years or so.
All three stood still to smile through their hair
At the uncle with the camera, a sweet face
My mother's that was before I was born
And the sea, which appears to have changed less
Washed their terribly transient feet.
Some twenty-thirty years later
She'd laugh at the snapshot. "See Betty
And Dolly," she'd say, "and look how they
Dressed us for the beach." The sea holiday
Was her past, mine is her laughter. Both wry
With the laboured ease of loss
Now she has been dead nearly as many years
As that girl lived. And of this circumstance
There is nothing to say at all,
Its silence silences.

31. Explain the feelings of the poet in "Both wry with the laboured ease of loss."

(a) Sad and nostalgic

(b) Mixed sentiments

(c) Happy and nostalgic

(d) Sad and Ironic

32. The phrase "Its silence silences." means:

(a) Pain of her mother's loss

(b) Tranquility of the ocean

(c) Standing still for the picture

(d) All of the above

33. Which of the following is the synonym of the word 'transient'?

(a) Permanent   (b) Short-lived

(c) Ceaseless   (d) Dull

34. What is the figure of speech used in the following line of the poem? "All three stood still to smile through their hair"

(a) Repetition

(b) Alliteration

(c) Metaphor

(d) Personification

35. How old was the poet's mother when the photograph was taken?

(a) Eleven years old

(b) Twelve years old

(c) Thirteen years old

(d) Fourteen years old

36. Complete the line: __________ later She'd laugh at the snapshot.

(a) Twenty-thirty year

(b) Twenty four year

(c) Forty- fifty year

(d) Twenty five year

37. Ravi, a English teacher, is planning remedial teaching for his student who faces problems in expressing his view while talking with someone. Remedial work for spoken English involves:

(a) Drill and studying

(b) Revision, drill, situation communicative practice and reviewing

(c) Going through situational practice

(d) Revision and practice

38. A teacher divides the class in small groups and asks them to discuss and present their views on "Save Environment".
Students are free to plan and present their choice and creativity. The teacher is facilitating them as and when required. Which approach/method is followed in

the class?

(a) Structural approach

(b) Natural approach

(c) Deductive approach

(d) Constructivist approach

39. A language teacher, while teaching grammar, writes some examples on the blackboard and with the help of students tries to point out some of the rules. She tries to stimulate the power of thinking and reasoning. Which method of teaching grammar is she adopting?

(a) Direct method

(b) Inductive method

(c) Inductive deductive method

(d) Translation method

40. Teaching grammar should focus on ______.

(a) rules of language

(b) forms and structures of language

(c) communicative functions of language

(d) both structures and rules of language

41. Direction : Answer the following questions by selecting the most appropriate option.

Students of Class IV can recognize flawed usage or sentence construction when the teacher

(a) Tells them something is wrong

(b) Gives alternatives as possible corrections

(c) Lets them find the corrections

(d) Focuses on certain surface errors

42. Given below are two statements, one leveled as Assertion (A) and the other leveled as Reason (R) :

Assertion (A) - At first, the child starts listening to the sounds then observes how people speak, and then later development of reading and writing skills takes place.

Reasoning (R) - The four basic language skills and their natural order are reading-writing-listening-speaking.

(a) A is correct and R is incorrect

(b) A is incorrect and R is correct

(c) Both A and R are correct

(d) Both A and R are incorrect

43. At upper primary level, the language/languages used by children in a multilingual classroom is/are:

(a) Resource

(b) Puzzle

(c) Complex challenge

(d) Difficult problem

44. A teacher found an advertisement pamphlet for sale of biscuits. She uses it for reading and speaking activities in her class. What do you call the pamphlet?

(a) Realia

(b) An authentic text

(c) Extra materials

(d) Newspaper clipping

45. A Hindi - speaking teacher gets posted in a primary school which is situated in a remote area of Rajasthan. Since she doesn't known the local language, she faces lots of problems. She should:

(a) Focus on the textbook as a source of standard Hindi.

(b) Use the child's language as a resource while teaching

(c) Encourage the community to learn standard Hindi

(d) Try to get a positing to a Hindi speaking area.

46. Fluency in English can be developed through:

(a) Creating opportunities to use the language for communication among learners

(b) The teacher talking for most of the time

(c) The teacher being alert to spot the errors and correcting them

(d) Allowing students who are not confident to have the freedom to be quiet

47. Continuous comprehensive evaluation emphasises ______ evaluation.

(a) process   (b) product

(c) term end   (d) formation

48. In which method of teaching language, the learning is based on repetition of dialogues and phrases about every day situations?

(a) Direct method

(b) Grammar-translation method

(c) Audio-Lingual Method

(d) Task based language teaching

49. Reading longer texts usually for one's 'own pleasure is known as:

(a) Skimming

(b) Scanning

(c) Extensive Reading

(d) Intensive Reading

50. Which language is a part of the

personal, social and cultural identity of a child?

(a) First language

(b) Second language

(c) School language

(d) Foreign language

51. Which one of the following is an essential characteristic of a good textbook in English?

(a) Every lesson should have a proper introduction at the beginning and a conclusion at the end.

(b) It should be based on the guiding principles of curriculum and syllabus.

(c) No difficult words should be given in the textbook at primary level.

(d) The maximum number of textual exercises should be given to practise at the end of the lesson.

Ques (52-60): Direction : Read the passage carefully and answer the questions given below.

As NASA works toward its long-term goal of establishing a human settlement on Mars, SpaceX is fleshing out its plans to help NASA make that dream a reality.

The private spaceflight company, which regularly launches cargo to the International Space Station with the Falcon 9 rocket and will soon launch astronauts up there, is currently building an interplanetary spacecraft for Mars. Known as Starship, the rocket-spacecraft combo will be able to launch 100 passengers and large amounts of cargo to and from the Red Planet.

Before Starship can launch to Mars, it will start off launching commercial satellites as early as 2021, followed by a manned flight around the moon in 2023. Although SpaceX has not given a timeline for its first missions to Mars, SpaceX founder Elon Musk has said that the first Mars base could be up and running in 2028. And while Musk shared some eye-catching artist illustrations depicting what he called "Mars Base Alpha" as an intricate network of buildings and infrastructure, SpaceX's plans for the Red Planet are not quite that extensive.

"SpaceX very much is a transportation company," Paul Wooster, the principal Mars development engineer at SpaceX, said during a speech at the Humans to Mars Summit in Washington in May. He explained that SpaceX plans to build whatever infrastructure is necessary to support the company's Starship flights to and from Mars; that could include landing pads and refueling stations for the reusable rockets.

For its very first Mars missions, SpaceX

will land at least two unmanned cargo ships on the Red Planet before sending any humans there, Wooster said. Those cargo missions would bring supplies, such as life- support systems and power generators that the first astronauts on Mars will need when they set up camp.

The first unmanned Mars missions will also be tasked with confirming the presence of natural resources that can provide fuel for future two-way missions to the Red Planet, Wooster said. SpaceX wants to use water ice from the planet's surface and carbon dioxide from the Martian atmosphere to refuel Starships on Mars, enabling the rockets to return to Earth.

After those first two cargo missions, SpaceX will launch two manned missions alongside two additional cargo-only flights to begin setting up a propellant production plant. At that plant, water and carbon dioxide will be converted into liquid methane and liquid oxygen, which fuel the rocket's engines.

So, while SpaceX intends to set up a transportation system for humans and cargo traveling to the Red Planet, the company won't be building an entire Mars base on its own. Musk has laid out his vision to create a million-person colony on Mars, but to establish that colony SpaceX will have to work together with NASA and the agency's international partners and other commercial space companies. Several companies have already begun designing concepts for Mars habitats and have proposed orbital outposts similar to NASA's Lunar Gateway, which could serve as a waypoint for Starship and reduce the amount of fuel needed for return trips to Earth.

52. What is the name of the spacecraft that SpaceX is building that will carry passenger Falcon 9and cargo to mars?
(a) Falcon 9
(b) Starship
(c) Mars Base Alpha
(d) Lunar Gateway

53. As per the passage, what fuel will be used to power the Starship rocket while returning from Mars?
(a) Liquid hydrogen
(b) Liquid oxygen
(c) Liquid methane
(d) Both B and C

54. Which of the following statements is/are true with respect to the passage?
(a) In the first Mars mission, SpaceX will land one unmanned cargo ship on the Red Planet.
(b) A propellant production plant will be set up on Mars in the first unmanned mission with the help of robots and A.I.
(c) SpaceX is expected to conduct a manned flight around moon in 2023.
(d) SpaceX is collaborating with Jaxa and ISRO for its Mars missions.

55. Which of the following statements is/are not true with respect to the passage?
(a) Starship is expected to start off launching commercial satellites by 2021.
(b) Only SpaceX and NASA are designing concepts for Mars habitats.
(c) In spite of primarily being a transportation company, SpaceX has quite extensive plans for Mars.
(d) Both B and C are not true

56. As per the passage, which rocket is used by SpaceX to send cargo to the International Space Station?
I. Falcon 9
II. Falcon Heavy
III. Starship
(a) Only I   (b) Only II
(c) Only III   (d) Both I and II

57. According to Elon Musk, when could the first Mars base be operational?
(a) By 2021   (b) By 2023
(c) By 2028   (d) By 2030

58. What is the vision of Elon Musk, as mentioned in the passage?
(a) Elon Musk wants to see the human race as an interstellar species.
(b) Elon Musk wants to build a lunar base so that launch costs can be dramatically reduced.
(c) Elon Musk wants to harness the power of the sun to meet the energy needs of the human species.
(d) Elon Musk wants to build a colony of 10 lakh people on Mars.

59. What is the name of the proposed Mars base as put forward by SpaceX?
(a) Mars Base Alpha
(b) Mars Base Beta
(c) Martian Gateway
(d) Starship

60. Which of the following statements is/are correct as per the passage?
I. SpaceX is currently building an interstellar spacecraft.
II. SpaceX wants to use water ice from the Martian surface and carbon dioxide from the Martian atmosphere to power the Starship rockets.
III. NASA has a long term goal of establishing human settlement on Mars.
(a) Only I and III
(b) Only II and III
(c) Only III
(d) Only I

Social Studies

61. Select the correct statement(s).
(A) Ibrahim Lodi was the first ruler of the Lodi Dynasty.
(B) Babur fought the first Panipat battle with Sikandar Lodi.
(C) Mughal empire was established after Lodi Dynasty.
(a) Only A and C   (b) Only A and B
(c) Only B   (d) Only C

62. Who composed 'Bijak'?
(a) Mirabai   (b) Kabir
(c) Ravidas   (d) Guru Nanak

63. Which Governor General was called as the Father of Local Self-Government in India?
(a) Lord Wellesley
(b) Lord Canning
(c) Lord William Bentick
(d) Lord Ripon

64. The rule of which of the following dynasties is popularly known as 'the Golden Period of Indian History'?
(a) Lodhi Dynasty
(b) Sena Dynasty
(c) Gupta Dynasty
(d) Pratihara Dynasty

65. Direction: Answer the following questions by selecting the correct / most appropriate options.
Statement A): Under the Delhi Sultans and the Mughals, the hierarchy between social classes decreased.
Statement B): The tribal societies were not divided into numerous unequal classes.
(a) Both A and B are true and B is the correct explanation of A
(b) Both A and B are true, but B is not the correct explanation of A
(c) A is true, but B is false
(d) A is false, but B is true

66. Consider the following events:

1. Jallianwala Bagh Massacre
2. Chauri-Chaura incident
3. Formation of Swaraj Party
4. Gandhi-Irwin Pact
The correct chronological order of these events is:
(a) 1 - 2 - 3 - 4   (b) 4 - 3 - 2 - 1
(c) 2 - 3 - 4 - 1   (d) 3 - 4 - 2 - 1

67. Vinoba Bhave was the first to offer the Individual Satyagraha. Who among the following was the second person for the same?
(a) Jawaharlal Nehru
(b) C. Rajagopalachari
(c) K. Kelappan
(d) P. Krishna Pillai

68. Who was the ruler of Gujarat when Mahmud invaded the Somanath temple ?
(a) Sukhpal
(b) Aqueen
(c) Gand Chandel
(d) Bhimdev

69. Consider the following statements regarding the Mughals' policy towards other rulers.
1. Mughals had matrimonial alliances with Rajputs for cordiality.
2. Rajputs were defeated if they did not accept the Mughals but were not humiliated, instead they were given back their possessions and restored their dignity.
Select the correct answer using the code given.
(a) Only 1
(b) Only 2
(c) Both 1 and 2
(d) None of these

70. During whose reign did the Moroccan traveller Ibn Battuta visit India in the 14th century?
(a) Alauddin Khalji
(b) Jalaluddin Khalji
(c) Mohammad Bin Tughlaq
(d) Feroz Shah Tughlaq

71. How many Carnatic Wars were fought between the British and French?
(a) 1   (b) 2
(c) 3   (d) 4

72. Read the following statements (A) (B) (C), and select the true statement(s) regarding minerals.
(A) Non-metallic minerals contain 50% metals.
(B) Limestone, mica, and gypsum are examples of such metals minerals.
(C) The mineral fuels like coal and petroleum are also non-metallic minerals.
(a) Only A and B (b) Only B
(c) Only C   (d) All of these

73. Read the following statements and select which option is false.
(A) Heat energy obtained from the earth is called bio energy.
(B) The temperature in the interior of the earth rises steadily as we go deeper.
(C) This Bioenergy can be used to generate power.
(a) Only A and B (b) Only B and C
(c) Only A   (d) Only A and C

74. Which among the following is wrong paired?
(A) Sericulture - Cultivation of grapes.
(B) Pisciculture - Breeding of fish in specially constructed tanks and ponds.
(C) Viticulture - Commercial rearing of silkworms.
(D) Horticulture - Growing vegetables, flowers, and fruits for commercial use.
(a) Only B and D (b) Only A and C
(c) Only A and D (d) Only C and B

75. In which one of the following soils, the Soils are rich in iron oxides but poor in nitrogen and lime and are unsuitable for agriculture due to high content of acidity?
(a) Arid Soils   (b) Laterite soils
(c) Alluvial Soils (d) Regur Soils

76. Who appoints the acting Chief Justice of India?
(a) Chief Justice of India
(b) Chief Justice of India with previous consent of the President
(c) President of India
(d) President in consultation with the Chief Justice of India

77. Which of the following statement is correct?
1. The first meeting of the constituent assembly was held on 9 December 1947.
2. The constitution was signed by the member of the constituent assembly on 24th January 1950.
(a) Only 1
(b) Only 2
(c) Both 1 and 2
(d) Neither 1 nor 2

78. Which of the following is NOT mentioned in the Preamble to the Constitution of India?
(a) Social Justice
(b) Economic Justice
(c) Political Justice
(d) Religious Justice

79. Which of the following is not a fundamental duty?
(a) Preserve composite culture
(b) Develop scientific temper
(c) Strive for excellence
(d) To pay tax to the government

80. As per Article _____ of the Constitution of India, English is the official language for all the high courts in the country.
(a) 329 (1)   (b) 348 (1)
(c) 315 (1)   (d) 336 (1)

81. Which of the Article deals with the grants in aid by the Union Government to the States ?
(a) Article 275   (b) Article 265
(c) Article 270   (d) Article 280

82. The 74th amendment added municipalities in which part of Indian Constitution?
(a) IXA   (b) X
(c) XIA   (d) XII

83. The Federal system with strong Central Government has been borrowed from.
(a) France   (b) England
(c) Canada   (d) USA

84. Which of the following tax gives maximum revenue to the government of India?
(a) Corporate tax
(b) Excise duty
(c) Income tax
(d) Customs duty

85. Which of the following is the largest Government body in India?
(a) Indian Railway
(b) National Thermal Power Corporation Limited
(c) Indian Metro Rail Corporation
(d) Bharat Heavy Electricals Limited

86. Pradhan Mantri Ujjwala Yojana is being implemented by which Ministry?
(a) Ministry of Power
(b) Ministry of Petroleum
(c) Ministry of Rural Development
(d) Ministry of New and Renewable Energy

87. Which statement/s is/are incorrect about Majhi Kanya Bhagyashree

Scheme.
1. **This Scheme was launched on National Women's Day.**
2. **The aim of this scheme is to control sex ratio in the state.**
3. **Bollywood film actress Bhagyashree is the Brand Ambassador of this scheme.**
Seleect the correct answer by using code given below.
(a) 1 Only
(b) 1 and 2 Only
(c) 3 Only
(d) None of the above

88. **Social science teaching needs to be revitalized towards:**
(a) Giving information related to subject
(b) Preparing students for exams
(c) Helping the teacher acquire skills in teaching-learning process
(d) Helping the learner acquire knowledge and skills in an interactive environment

89. **Which of the following should not be a method in Social Science teaching?**
(a) Teacher should always give answers to the questions herself/himself
(b) Teacher should adopt collaborative learning
(c) Teacher should encourage students to suggest answer
(d) Teacher should relate the topic with real life examples

90. **Which of the following is not a component of instructional process in a social science classroom?**
(a) Planning
(b) Execution
(c) Implementation
(d) Normalization

91. **Peer teaching is a very good and effective system or process of engaging learner in ______.**
(a) active atmosphere
(b) silent atmosphere
(c) noisy atmosphere
(d) open atmosphere

92. **Which of the following teaching methods would be most effective in Social Science, that teachers must use?**
(a) Ensure that learners have learnt the content by taking repetitive tests.
(b) Assign grades liberally.
(c) Engage learners in critical and thought provoking activities.
(d) Assign home assignments.

93. **Which of the following is most appropriate method to develop understanding of social problems?**
(a) Picture Essay
(b) Screen Play
(c) Role Play
(d) Case Study

94. **The abilities that underlie critical thinking is/are:**
A. Recognise problems
B. Interpret data
C. Recognize logical connections
D. Draw the topic at the centre
(a) A, B, C   (b) A, B, D
(c) A, C, D   (d) B, C

95. **Meaningful social studies instruction is geared at promoting gender equality which enhances full participation of ______.**
(a) women in resolving societal problems
(b) men in resolving societal problems and preferring of sustainable solutions
(c) women and men in resolving societal problems and preferring of sustainable solutions
(d) none of the above

96. **At the upper primary stage, Social Science includes content from which of the following subjects?**
(a) History, Political Science, Geography and Psychology.
(b) Geography, Political Science, Anthropology and Psychology.
(c) History, Geography, Economics and Political Science.
(d) History, Geography, Political Science and Philosophy.

97. **In learning approach, PBL represents:**
(a) Project-based learning
(b) Program-based learning
(c) Problem-based learning
(d) Process-based learning

98. **Which one of the following activities is most appropriate for developing an understanding of the Indian Parliament's role and functions ?**
(a) Flow diagram of functions and responsibilities.
(b) Discussion on newspaper report on Parliament disruption.
(c) Holding a youth Parliament.
(d) Reading from the text.

99. **How will teacher try to make teaching social studies in effective and interesting manner?**
(a) By using Audio Visual Aids
(b) By giving home work
(c) By illustrating answer
(d) By Telling Jokes

100. **Which is the most useful step for studying relationships among pupils ______.**
(a) anecdotal record
(b) sociogram
(c) rorschach test
(d) kuder programme test

101. **In science teaching, which of the following is a useful strategy to understand learning gaps in learners ?**
(a) Using achievement test
(b) Using Diagnosis teaching
(c) Conducting assessment
(d) Doing action research

102. **Assertion (A): The sun sets in Gujarat after about two hours from Arunachal Pradesh.**
Reasoning (R): Arunachal Pradesh is located at a higher latitude than Gujarat.
Choose the correct option.
(a) (A) is true (R) is false
(b) (A) is false (R) is true
(c) Both (A) and (R) are true, (R) is not the correct explanation of (A)
(d) Both (A) and (R) are true, (R) is the correct explanation of (A)

103. **Statement (A) When air is heated, it expands, becomes lighter and goes up.**
Statement (B) Cold air is denser and heavy. That is why it tends to sink down.
Statement (C) When cold air rises, hot air from the surrounding area rushes there to fill in the gap.
Which statement is/are true regarding air?
(a) Only A and C (b) Only B and C
(c) Only A and B (d) All of these

104. **(A) The first English factory was set up on the banks of the river Hugli in 1651.**
(B) Two years later it bribed Mughal officials into giving the Company zamindari rights over three villages.
(C) It also persuaded the Mughal emperor Akbar to issue a farman granting the Company the right to trade duty free.
Which statement is/are true ?

(a) Only A and B (b) Only B and C

(c) Only A and C (d) All of these

105. **Select right option regarding ocean.**
(A) Ocean currents also move in the same pattern as winds.
(B) Ocean current move anit-clockwise in the northern hemisphere and clockwise in the southern hemisphere.

(a) Only A is true

(b) Only B is true

(c) Both A and B are true

(d) None of these

106. **Panchayati Raj is based on :**
(A) Democratic Decentralization
(B) People's Participation
(C) Increasing Political awareness in a rural areas

(a) Only A and C (b) Only A and B

(c) Only A   (d) Only B

107. **Consider the following statements:**
A) A democracy is a rule by the people.
B) In representative democracies people rule themselves.
C) In representative democracies, people participate directly in the making of the rules.
Select the correct answer using the codes given below:

(a) Only A and C

(b) Only B and C

(c) Only A and B

(d) All of the above

108. **The chronological order of the pre-historic period is:**
I. Chalcolithic Age
II. Paleolithic Age
III. Iron Age
IV. Neolithic Age

(a) I, II, III, IV   (b) II, IV, III, I

(c) I, III, II, IV   (d) II, IV, I, III

109. **Choose the correct statement.**
(A) Persian court chronicals described Sultan as the 'Shadow of God'.
(B) An inscripation in Qawwat-al-islam mosque explained that God choosen Balban as a king.

(a) Only A

(b) Only B

(c) Both A and B

(d) None of these

110. **Read statements A and B about social science approach and choose the correct answer.**
Statement A: The organization of the social studies curriculum is not done by any fixed approach.
Statement B: The approach is always contextual and relevant to the needs of the individual society and nation in addition to teachers' potentialities.

(a) A is true and B is false.

(b) A is false and B is true.

(c) Both A and B are true.

(d) Both A and B are false.

111. **What are the general objectives and aims of social studies?**
A)The teaching of social studies is aimed at helping learners to develop greater awareness of themselves, to clarify and examine their values, and establish a sense of self-identity.
B) The teaching of social studies helps promote learners' concern for the development of an understanding and acceptance of others with different values and lifestyles.
C) Social studies teaching helps provide learners with a knowledge of human systems in areas of economics, government, and culture.
D) Social studies teaching aims at providing learners with an awareness of possible situations and their possible roles in shaping the future.

(a) A, B and C   (b) A, B and D

(c) B, C and D   (d) A, B, C and D

112. **Statement A: Models are three-dimensional visual aids. They represent real things in all respects except size and shape.**
Statement B: Models are learning resource for teaching social science.
Choose the correct option from the given alternatives.

(a) Both A and B are true.

(b) A is true but B is false.

(c) Both A and B are false.

(d) A is false but B is true.

113. **Consider the following statements.**
Statement A: In an inclusive social science classroom there is the enrolment of all children.
Statement B :- It is the duty of school management and teacher to undertake functional assessments of children about what they can do and what they cannot do..
Choose the correct option.

(a) Both (A) and (B) are true.

(b) Both (A) and (B) are false.

(c) (A) is true and (B) is false.

(d) (A) is false and (B) is true.

114. **Objective: The teaching of social studies should aim at inculcating among children the spirit of peace and mutual understanding.**
Keeping in view the.above objective choose the correct statements that the teacher may identify and organise content and its sequence for instruction.
(i) Prevention of war is mankind's number one task.
(ii) Formation of peace-loving forces through formulating a policy of peace, disarmament and international cooperation.
(iii) Schools have a responsibility to promote peace.
(iv) Social studies has a responsibility to promote the spirit of peace.

(a) (i), (ii), (iv)

(b) (i), (iii), (iv)

(c) (ii), (iii), (iv)

(d) (i), (ii), (iii), (iv)

115. **There are many other concerns that social sciences education has to incorporate in its curriculum and pedagogical practices. Which of the following are concerns that social science education should address?**
I. Giving the learner the prime place in the teaching-learning process, i.e. learner-centered.
II. Creating a strong bond between school knowledge and knowledge available in the community.
III. The role of the textbook should be directive and instructive for the learner.

(a) Only I and III (b) Only II

(c) Only I and II (d) I, II, III

116. **Assertion (A)- Most of the rain in India is brought by monsoon winds.**
Reason (R) - India is located in tropical region.
Choose the correct alternative from the given options.

(a) (A) is true, but (R) is false.

(b) (A) is false, but (R) is true.

(c) Both (A) and (R) are true and (R) is the correct explanation of (A).

(d) Both (A) and (R) are true, but (R) is not the correct explanation of (A)

117. **Match the following and select the correct option.**

A.	Fixing people i	(i)	Prejudi

	nto one image		ce.
B.	Judging other people negativ ely	(i i)	Untouc hability
C.	Treating some one less fairly than others	(ii i)	Stereot ype
D.	Practicing pur ity and polluti on	(i v)	Discri minati on

(a) (A) - (iii), (B) - (i), (C) - (iv), (D) - (ii)

(b) (A) - (i), (B) - (iv), (C) - (ii), (D) - (iii)

(c) (A) - (iv), (B) - (iii), (C) - (ii), (D) - (i)

(d) (A) - (ii), (B) - (iii), (C) - (i), (D) - (iv)

118. Match the following and choose the correct option.

	Level s of g over nme nt		Types of Decision s
a.	Cent ral g over nme nt	(i)	Decision to open a park in Vellore, a small town in T amil Nadu
b.	State gove rnm ent	(i i)	Introduction of n ew 2000 rupee n ote
c.	Local gove rnm ent	(ii i)	Decision to set up a regional transp ort office

(a) a - (ii), b - (i), c - (iii)

(b) a - (iii), b - (ii), c - (i)

(c) a - (ii), b - (iii), c - (i)

(d) a - (iii), b - (i), c - (ii)

119. Identify the peak in India based on the following statements:
1. The range associated with this peak has 14 protected areas for the conservation of wildlife and nature.
2. It is delimited in the west by the Tamur River, in the north by the Lhonak Chu and Jongsang La, and in the east by the Teesta River.
3. The peak lies in the Sikkim-Nepal border and is one of the highest peaks in India.
Select the correct answer from the codes given below
(a) Kabru
(b) Kanchenjunga
(c) Santoro Kangri
(d) Kangtoh

120. Consider the following statements regarding the international borders of India with its neighbouring nations:
1. Six Indian states share a boundary with India's north-west neighbour Nepal.
2. The state of West Bengal does not share its border with the country of Bhutan.
3. Arunachal Pradesh, Nagaland, Manipur and Mizoram share a boundary with Myanmar.
Which of the above statements is/ are correct?
(a) 1 and 2 only   (b) 3 only
(c) 2 and 3 only   (d) 1 and 3 only

// Hints and Solutions //

1(A). The physical environment is an external factor that affects the growth and development of a child.

The development of a child is primarily determined by two factors: heredity and environment. Heredity refers to the inborn traits and capacities. These inborn capacities are transmitted from parents to the child. The birth of a child is also considered to be a social phenomenon.

The family, particularly the socialization practices and parent-child-relationship (i.e. the physical environment) has a great impact on cognitive, language, social, and personality development.

- A group of theorists, known as Behaviourists, believe that human development is controlled by these external factors and they totally ignore the significance of hereditary factors.
- Both heredity and environment interact (multiply) to influence various aspects of development.
- The effect of the two is not simple addition (heredity + environment), rather it is multiplication (heredity x environment).
- It is not easy to separate the effects of the two since dynamic interaction between them is continuous and complex.
- Therefore, we conclude that the Physical environment is an external factor influencing the growth and development of a child.

2(B). "A creative child is not an adventurer" The statement about the creative child is not correct.
Creative children express opinions and constantly ask many questions. So curiosity is the main aspect of creativity. Creative children are ambitious, courageous, and persistent and extrovert, but the level of creativity differs from person to person.

3(A). Aspiration is an example of intrinsic motivation.

Intrinsic Motivation:
An intrinsically motivated activity will always be rewarded due to the direct relationship between the activity and the goal. This secures a continuous motivation to do the activity.
Intrinsic motivation is internal. It occurs when people are compelled to do something out of pleasure, importance, or aspiration.
So, it does not require an external push, unlike extrinsic motivation which requires an external motivating factor. So intrinsic motivation is more beneficial.
Extrinsic Motivation:
- When an activity is performed to accomplish the goal of an external reward, the person is said to be extrinsically motivated.
- Extrinsic motivation occurs when external factors compel the person to do something.
- This is motivation based on external rewards and has nothing to do with the activity directly. The Behaviourists' approach to motivation mainly focuses on the external rewards of reinforcement and punishment.
- Thus from the above-mentioned points, it is clear that aspiration is an example of intrinsic motivation.

4(B). According to Kohlberg's theory of moral development, the period of prior moral state is from birth to 2 years of age. At this age, children think about their needs. The relationship of moral work is socially and culturally related to what is right and what is wrong.

5(C). The adolescence stage of cognitive development is termed the formal operational stage; in this stage, an individual has the ability to think and reason from concrete visible events to an ability to think hypothetically. An individual can solve problems through abstract concepts and utilize them hypothetically.

6(D). The curriculum is that which is taught in schools, a set of subjects, Content, a program of studies, A set of mater, a sequence of courses, a set of performance objective, a course of study, everything that goes on within the school (including extra-class activities, guidance, and interpersonal relationships), everything that is planned by school personnel, a series of experiences undergone by learners in a school, it is that which an individual learner experience as a result of schooling.

7(B). A lesson plan is the teacher's guide for running a particular lesson. A lesson plan is a teacher's detailed description of the course of instruction or "learning trajectory" for a lesson. A daily lesson plan is developed by a teacher to guide class learning. Details will vary depending on the preference of the teacher, the subject being covered, and the needs of the students. There may be requirements mandated by the school system regarding the plan. A lesson plan is the teacher's guide for running a particular lesson, and it includes the goal, how the goal will be reached, and a way of measuring how well the goal was reached.

8(C). According to the Right to Education Act 2009, the school management committee is prepared. This committee monitors the utilization of grants, prepares the school development plan, and monitors the working of schools. School management committees have 50% women members from the disadvantaged groups of the community.

9(B). The terms growth and development are often used interchangeably. They are conceptually different. Neither growth nor development takes place all by itself.
- Growth refers to quantitative changes in size which include physical changes in height, weight, size, internal organs, etc (which are measurable). As an individual develops, old features like baby fat, hair, teeth, etc., disappear, and new features like facial hair, etc. are acquired.
- When maturity comes, the second set of teeth, primary and secondary sex characteristics, etc., appear. Similar changes occur in all aspects of the personality. During infancy and childhood, the body steadily becomes larger, taller, and heavier. To designate this change the term growth is used.
- Growth involves changes in body proportions as well as in overall stature and weight. The term growth thus indicates an increase in bodily dimensions. But the rate of growth differs from one part of the body to the other. Development, by contrast, refers to qualitative changes taking place simultaneously with quantitative changes of growth.

10(D). Every individual has a different rate of development. The development of all human beings follows a similar direction or sequence. Two types of sequential patterns are the cephalocaudal sequence and proximodistal sequence.

11(B). In a diverse classroom, a teacher's responsibility is to provide varieties of learning experiences. In a child-centered approach, a child learns better from experiences. So, providing varieties of learning experiences will result in active learning in which students take initiative to learn new things.

12(D). Language learning is affected by motivation, interest, age, gender, aptitude, etc. Learning a language is affected by all these factors, if a child is motivated and reinforced for his learning then he/she takes more interest. Proper guidance and reinforcement should be given to the learner for better learning.

13(D). Child development involves the study of the patterns of growth, change and stability that occurs from conception through adolescence and therefore its emphasis on internal and external factors for its growth. The role of environment, experience and intelligence play a major role in the development of a child.

14(C). All the options given in the question about growth are correct except option C. i.e. it is not necessary that growth always bring development for example if a child becomes fat may not bring any qualitative improvement.

15(B). The child learns language on the basis of the principle of imitation.
Psychologists such as Chapini, Shirley, and Valentine have studied language learning through simulation. They had opinion that children learn by following the language of their family and peers, that is, children learn the language in the same society or family in which the language is spoken.

16(C). The causes of learning disabilities are genetic factors, biological and environmental factors.
Learning disabilities can also cause problems in coordinating movements, making the child seem (and feel) awkward. Learning disabilities are disorders that affect a person's ability to understand or respond to new information, or they are disorders that affect the ability to remember information that appears to have been taken in. Learning disabilities tend to cause problems with listening skills, language skills (including speaking, reading, or writing), and mathematical operations.

17(C). To meet the needs of students experiencing learning difficulties, a teacher should not practice rigid structures for teaching and evaluation.
- Learning difficulties can be defined as imperfect ability to listen, think, speak, read, write, spell, or do mathematical calculations.
- Learning disability is believed to be present if there is a substantial difference between expected and actual performance based on intelligence, ruling out other contributing factors such as poor learning-teaching environment, second language etc.

18(B). A child with Learning Disability has a right to study in the regular school where there are special provisions for him. Learning disability is a syndrome found in children of normal or above intelligence characterized by specific difficulties in learning to read (dyslexia), to write (dysgraphia), and to do grade-appropriate mathematics (dyscalculia).

19(A). Identify a child with a learning disability by conducting an IQ test.
- Learning Disability is an umbrella term that encompasses a variety of specific kinds of learning problems.
- Children with learning disabilities experience difficulty in learning and using certain skills namely reading, writing, listening reasoning, and mathematics.

20(A). A classroom/institution that welcomes diversity of categories, abilities, cultures, disabilities, etc. is an inclusive education.
The principles of inclusive education include:
- No discrimination among students
- Equal educational opportunity for all
- Adapting to the needs of students, for example, making institutions disabled-friendly
- Equal educational benefits to all students
- Individual difference is promoted among students
- The needs of the students are taken seriously.

21(D). At the age of 6-9 years, children start taking interest in school.
Developmental psychology studies the development of human emotional, intellectual, cognitive and social abilities. It studies the actions of man from infancy to old age.
The following are the stages of human development:
Infancy and Toddlerhood
- Early childhood
- Middle Childhood
- Adolescence
- Early Adulthood

22(D). Valentine called infancy the ideal time to learn.
- Human development is divided into different stages infancy, childhood (early and middle childhood), adolescence and adulthood.
- It refers to the first year or early period of a baby's development in which the baby grows rapidly after birth.
- This is a critical period of development in which the child learns to sit, crawl, stand etc.

23(C). The situation given in the above question shows the trend of the organization
- Two Basic Inclinations and Tendencies in Thinking: According to Piaget's research on biology, humans have two basic tendencies. The first is inclined towards organization which deals with the arrangement, recombination and rearrangement of behavior and thought

into a coherent system.

- Organization: This concept assumes that people have a tendency to organize their thinking processes into psychological structures. For example, very young children can either look at an object or hold it when their hands contract.
- Adaptation: As the term suggests this concept refers to the adjustment of man to the new environment. It can be defined as "changing one's cognitive structure or one's environment (or to some extent both) in order to better understand one's environment".

24(D). Exceptional students have an IQ level between 130-144

- Intelligence Quotient is commonly known as IQ refers to the score of a standardized test that assesses and measures human intelligence.
- The first test to measure intelligence was developed by Binet and Simon in 1905.
- Terman in 1916 revised the test and devised the concept of Intelligence Quotient.

25(D). If the teacher comes to know that a student is absent in the class, in such a case, instead of expelling/punishing/preventing him/her from attending the class, the teacher should know the reason for his/her negligence and find out the appropriate remedy.

Improving Teacher Preparation in Classroom Management

- Provide teacher candidates with instructional approaches for classroom management through coursework and guided practice with feedback, and
- Address the challenges facing teacher candidates and new teachers in creating a positive classroom context

26(B). If a child expresses affection for a parent of the opposite sex, it will be characterized by the phalic stage.

Freud's Psychological Stages of Development: Freud proposed a five-stage model of personality development. According to him, the main aspects of a person's personality develop by the age of five and remain unchanged throughout time. Furthermore, he said that in order to move from one stage to another, a child needs to successfully resolve the conflicts of each stage.

27(A). Equilibration takes place when a child strikes balance between the two processes while trying to internalise the perceived object.

Equilibration: The process of striking a balance between accommodation and assimilation. On the other hand, When the child strikes a balance between the two processes while trying to internalize the perceived object, adaptation (a relatively stable structure) takes place.

28(D). A child sees that a classmate has gotten into trouble by hitting another child. They learn by observing this interaction that they should not kill others. This is a classic example of learning by observation.

Learning style refers to a range of principles that aim to take into account differences in individuals' learning. Many theories share the proposition that humans can be classified according to their 'style' of learning, but differ in how the proposed styles should be defined, classified and assessed. A general concept is that individuals differ in the way they learn.

29(A). In this question, Baby Bhavya starts looking for her toys that her mother had hidden because Bhavya is aware of her toys even when they are not in front of her, that is, she has developed object permanence, Hence it is in pre-operational stage or pre-operational stage.

Object permanence means that an object still exists, even if it is hidden. It requires the ability to create a mental representation of the object (i.e. a schema).

30(A). At 4 – 5 years of age, a male child develops a deeper attachment to his mother, known as the Oedipus complex, than to his father.

Psychological stages of development:

- Stage I: Oral Stage (birth to 18 months)
- Stage II: Anal Stage (18 months to three years)
- Stage III: Phallic Stage (three to five years)
- Stage IV: Latency Stage (six to twelve years)
- Stage V: Genital Stage (thirteen years to adulthood)

31(A). The line " Both wry with the laboured ease of loss" implies that the poet and her mother both are saddened by the loss that they have experienced over time.

Thus, it is clear that the feeling hidden in this line is 'Sad and nostalgic.'

Nostalgic means feeling happy and also slightly sad when you think about things that happened in the past.

32(A). In the above-given poem, the poet is nostalgic after seeing a photograph of her mother's childhood.

- The phrase "Its silence silences" indicates the constant pain experienced by the poet on account of her mother's loss which makes her speechless.
- The silence is prevalent in the situation and it also silences everything else at that moment.

Thus, it can be inferred that the phrase "Its silence silences" indicates her her mother's loss.

33(B). The word ' transient' means temporary. It stands for something that doesn't last forever.

The phrase 'terribly transient feet,' from the

above-given poem, implies that human life is not eternal.

Thus, we can conclude that the correct answer is Option B.

34(B). Alliteration is a figure of speech that repeats a speech sound in a sequence of words that are close to each other. For example, "Clean your cluttered closet."

Let's look at the line:

"All three stood still to smile through their hair"

- In this line, stood, still and smile – all are beginning with the similar sound of speech -'s'.

Thus, it is clear that the figure of speech used here is 'Alliteration.'

35(B). Let's look at the line:

"And she the big girl – twelve years or so"

- It clearly indicates that the poet's mother was around twelve years old when the photograph was taken.

Thus, the most appropriate answer is 'twelve years old.'

36(A). Twenty-thirty years later She'd laugh at the snapshot.

From the given lines: "Some twenty-thirty years later,

She'd laugh at the snapshot. "See Betty"

37(B). Remedial teaching:

- During learning, a child makes mistakes. It is the job of a teacher to help students to correct those mistakes after diagnosing them.
- The method is known as remedial teaching. It helps the teacher to provide learners with the necessary help and guidance to overcome the problems.

The following are its characteristics:

- It can be used for improving language skills by revision, drill, situation communicative practice, and reviewing.
- For example, a student is confused about the pronunciation of 'no' and 'know', he can be taught the concept of silent letters.
- It also helps teachers to know which areas are left during regular teaching. It is used by teachers to remove the weakness of the learner.
- It is carried out after the identification of problems and challenges faced by students. It is a systematic process as the teacher first diagnoses the problem of students and then applies appropriate remedial methods.

Thus, it is concluded that remedial work for spoken English involves revision, drill, situation communicative practice, and reviewing.

38(D). Constructive approach: One of the most important principles in the constructivist approach to language teaching is action orientedness. Another principle of constructive approach refers to content-oriented language teaching and usually takes place in bilingual classes. A constructive approach to language teaching is based on the foundation that knowledge is constructed. Students are given the freedom to plan their choice and to be creative.

- Structural Approaches: Structural approach is a scientific study of the fundamental structures of the English language, their analysis and logical arrangement. Every structure expresses an important grammatical point. A sentence needs a grammatical background. The different arrangements or patterns of words are called structures.
- Natural approaches: It is the theory that is based on the notion that we learn the language in the same way as we acquire our first language. It doesn't force to utter words or phrases, much less pronounce them correctly. There are no endless drills on correct usage and no mentions of grammar rules or long lists of vocabulary to wrap the head around.
- Deductive approaches refer to developing a Hypothesis. It is testing of Existing theory.

Thus, we conclude that the above situation

39(C). Advantages of the Inductive Deductive Method

- This method is considered to be the best method for teaching grammar because it follows some sound educational principles
- Rules discovered by the pupils themselves are easily remembered. So there is no need for memorizing rules.
- It develops thinking ability among the pupils.
- It makes learning grammar interesting.
- It keeps the pupils active.

Thus, we can conclude that the inductive-deductive method is used to teach grammar.

40(C). Communicative competence should be the goal in language learning. This concept takes into account both the linguistic aspect of the target language and the importance of context in language acquisition.

- Communicative competence is the ability not only to apply the grammatical rules of a language in order to form grammatically correct sentences but also to know when and where to use these sentences and to whom.
- It includes the ability to use grammatical structures in different situations to convey and interpret messages and to negotiate meanings.
- Teachers can use information gap and role-play activities to evaluate learners' competence for speaking. It includes accuracy, fluency, complexity, appropriateness, and capacity.
- Communicative tasks are important

because they allow learners to practice the target grammar feature under 'real operating conditions.

Thus,it is concluded that Teaching grammar should focus on communicative functions of language.

41(B). For the students of class IV learning English, their learning outcomes include, reciting poems correctly, being responsive to simple announcements, they having a simple knowledge of correct punctuations in writing.

The teacher can provide possible alternative corrections for the sentence as the students can get better insight about the words, their usage and also learn about the flaws in the wrong sentence.

Thus, it is concluded that Students of Class IV can recognize flawed usage or sentence construction when the teacher gives alternatives as possible corrections.

42(A). The four basic language skills and their natural order are listening-speaking-reading-writing. These foundational skills of language are divided into two categories which are receptive and productive skills.

For example, at first, the child starts listening to the sounds of people around him and then observes how they speak and started speaking, then later development of reading and writing skills takes place.

Let's understand it briefly:

	Skills	Description
Receptive	Listening	Receiving information through the ears.
	Reading	Process of looking at a series of written words/symbols and getting meaning from them.
Productive	Speaking	Delivery of information through the mouth.
	Writing	Process of using symbols (letters of the alphabet, punctuation, and spaces) to communicate thoughts in a readable form.

Thus, from the above-mentioned points, it becomes clear that **A is correct and R is incorrect**.

43(A). Multilingualism is the ability to use more than two languages, it refers to using the language of learners as a strategy in school.

- Multilingualism is constitutive of the identity of a child and a typical feature of the Indian linguistic landscape must be used as a resource, classroom strategy, and a goal by a creative language teacher.
- Multilingualism as a resource means using the languages of learners as a strategy in school.
- It is used as a resource to teach a new language to the child with the help of a mother tongue or other known language.

Benefits of Multilingualism (NCF - 2005):

- It emphasizes on the significance of a smooth transition between the home and school language.
- Multilingualism encourages children to believe in themselves.
- It improves cognitive flexibilities to express thought in multiple ways.

Thus, from the above points, we can conclude that at the upper primary level, the language/languages used by children in a multilingual classroom is a resource.

44(B). A teacher found an advertisement pamphlet for the sale of biscuits. She uses it for reading and speaking activities in her class.

He is using an authentic text as the advertisement pamphlet is the authentic pamphlet that a shopkeeper is using to increase his sale of biscuits.

Whereas Realia refers to the objects associated with everyday life to be used in the classroom. Using realia in the language class means bringing real objects as teaching aids.

The advertisement pamphlet is a type of realia but if we have to say it more accurately, we will say it is an authentic text. The newspaper clipping and extra materials can be a type of realia also. But here as per the given question, the authentic text is best suited.

45(B). A teacher should overcome the language barrier to go through the process of teaching-learning.

- The basis of the communication of ideas and information to the learners is the responsibility of the teacher.
- A teacher should use the child's language as a resource and start teaching.
- As mentioned in the question above, a teacher should not apply for transfer since it shows that he wants to run away from his duty.
- Communicating in English is not the correct choice in such situations because not all students may be able to understand English.

Thus from the above-mentioned points, it is clear that a teacher should use the child's language as a resource while teaching.

46(A). Fluency in English means that the child can use the basic skills of langauge that are listening, speaking, reading, and writing.

- One who can perform these basic skills properly and collectively with full accuracy and speed is said to be fluent in English.
- The goal of language learning is communication competence and the child who learns the basic skills of a language is able to develop real communication in a natural setting environment.
- The teacher must create opportunities to use the language for communication among learners to develop their fluency in English.
- This can be done by conducting several language-based activities such as discussions, drama, dialogues, conversations, debates, questionnaires, etc.

Thus, we can conclude that fluency in English can be developed through creating opportunities to use the language for communication among learners.

47(A). Continuous comprehensive evaluation emphasises **process** evaluation.

- Continuous Comprehensive Evaluation treats evaluation as a developmental process.
- The term 'continuous' refers to regularity in the assessment.
- The development of a child is a continuous process.
- Therefore, students' development should be assessed continuously.
- The Evaluation has to be completely integrated with the teaching and learning process.
- The term 'comprehensive' implies that evaluation of learners' performance is carried out in both scholastic and co-scholastic areas.
- CCE is comprehensive in nature as it takes care of the achievement of learners in various school subjects from science, mathematics, languages, social science, work education, and physical health activities as well as includes the assessment of co-scholastic abilities like attitude, values, life skills, interests, habits, etc.

48(C). **The Audio-Lingual Method:** This self-teaching method is also known as the Aural-Oral method. The learning is based on the repetition of dialogues and phrases about everyday situations. These phrases are imitated, repeated, and drilled to make the response automatic. Reading and writing are both reinforcements of what the learner practices.

- More emphasis is given to the listening and speaking part of dialogues, not the written part. In this students are more focused on dialogues delivering.
- In this method, students develop correct language habits through the drilling of patterns.
- The theory behind this method is that the students can form new habits by basing them on habits of their native language.
- The Audio Lingual method is the method that focuses on the repetition of some words to memorize.
- In the execution of the learning process, the Audio Lingual method gives more practice, drill, memorize vocabularies, and the students memorize and practice some vocabulary unconsciously.

So, we can conclude that in the audio-lingual method of teaching language, the learning is based on the repetition of dialogues and phrases about everyday situations.

49(C). Reading longer texts usually for one's 'own pleasure is known as extensive Reading.

Types of reading skills:

Exte nsiv e rea ding	Extensive is a reading strategy tha t focuses on: • **Reading for pl** easure and over all understanding of the text. • Helping learners to build readi ng speed and reading fluency to understand language faster and better. • **Reading novels, discussion a bout stories, etc.**
Inte nsiv e rea ding	Intensive is a reading strategy that focuses on: • Gaining a deeper and better un derstanding of the text. • Enhancing reading comprehens ion and critical thinking skills. • Reading materials such as label s, reports, contracts, articles, et c.

Thus, we can conclude that reading longer texts usually for one's 'own pleasure is known as extensive reading.

50(A). The **first language** of a child is part of the personal, social and cultural identity.

- A first language (L1) is the language or are the languages a person has been exposed to from birth or within the critical period, or that a person speaks the best and so is often the basis for sociolinguistic identity.
- Language is fundamental to cultural identity.
- First Language is intrinsic to the expression of culture.
- As a means of communicating values, beliefs, and customs, it has an important social function and fosters feelings of group identity and solidarity.
- People are also categorized by other people according to the language they speak.
- People belong to many social groups and have many social identities.
- Speaking that language/variety/jargon gives a sense of belonging to the group.

51(B). Qualities of a good textbook of English:

- Comprehensible inputs
- Age-appropriate materials
- Adequate subject matter
- Use of suitable language
- Interesting and attractive
- Use of appropriate vocabulary
- Proper introduction & Conclusion

Thus from the above-mentioned points, it is clear that **an essential characteristic of a good textbook in English is it should be based on the guiding principles of curriculum and syllabus.**

52(B). The private spaceflight company, which regularly launches cargo to the International Space Station with the Falcon 9 rocket and will soon launch astronauts up there, is currently building an interplanetary spacecraft for mars. Known as Starship, the rocket-spacecraft combo will be able to launch 100 passengers and large amounts of cargo to and from the Red Planet.

From the highlighted part, it is clear that SpaceX is building a spacecraft named 'Starship' to carry passenger and cargo to mars.

53(D). After those first two cargo missions, SpaceX will launch two manned missions alongside two additional cargo-only flights to begin setting up a propellant production plant. At that plant, water and carbon dioxide will be converted into liquid methane and liquid oxygen, which fuel the rocket's engines.

From the highlighted part, it is obvious that both liquid methane and liquid oxygen will be used to power the Starship rocket while returning from Mars. Liquid hydrogen is nowhere mentioned in the passage.

54(C). For its very first Mars missions, SpaceX will land at least two unmanned cargo ships on the Red Planet before sending any humans there, Wooster said.

The highlighted part confirms that the statement given in option A is false.

After those first two cargo missions, SpaceX will launch two manned missions alongside two additional cargo-only flights to begin setting up a propellant production plant. Robots and A.I. were not mentioned in the passage. Besides, the highlighted part confirms that the the statement given in option B is false.

As NASA works toward its long-term goal of establishing a human settlement on Mars, SpaceX is fleshing out its plans to help NASA make that dream a reality.

Jaxa and ISRO are nowhere mentioned in the passage, and the highlighted part confirms that SpaceX tied up with NASA.

So, the statement given in option D is clearly false.

Before Starship can launch to Mars, it will start off launching commercial satellites as early as 2021, followed by a manned flight around the moon in 2023.

Starship is being developed by SpeceX and the highlighted part confirms that the statement given in option C is true.

55(D). Before Starship can launch to Mars, it will start off launching commercial satellites as early as 2021, followed by a manned flight around the moon in 2023.

- The highlighted part confirms that the statement given in option A is correct.
- Several companies have already begun designing concepts for Mars habitats and have proposed orbital outposts similar to NASA's Lunar Gateway, which could serve as a waypoint for Starship and reduce the amount of fuel needed for return trips to Earth.
- The highlighted part confirms that the statement given in option B is not true.
- And while Musk shared some eye-catching artist illustrations depicting what he called "Mars Base Alpha" as an intricate network of buildings and infrastructure, SpaceX's plans for the Red Planet are not quite that extensive.
- The highlighted part confirms that SpaceX's plans for Mars are not quite extensive. It clearly proves that the statement given in option C is not true.
- Both the statements given in options B and C are not true.

56(A). The private spaceflight company, which regularly launches cargo to the International Space Station with the Falcon 9 rocket and will soon launch astronauts up there, is currently building an interplanetary spacecraft for Mars. Known as Starship, the rocket-spacecraft combo will be able to launch 100 passengers and large amounts of cargo to and from the Red Planet.

The second highlight part confirms that Starship is being designed to send passenger and cargo to the Mars, not the International Space Station. There is no mention of Falcon Heavy in the passage.

The first highlighted part confirms that option A is correct.

57(C). Although SpaceX has not given a timeline for its first missions to Mars, SpaceX founder Elon Musk has said that the first Mars base could be up and running in 2028.

The highlighted part validates that option C is correct.

58(D). "SpaceX very much is a transportation company," Paul Wooster, the principal Mars development engineer at SpaceX, said during a speech at the Humans to Mars Summit in Washington in May.

Nothing related to harnessing the power of the sun, creating a lunar base or 'human race as an interstellar species' is anywhere mentioned in the passage. So, option A, option B and Option C are false.

59(A). And while Musk shared some eye-catching artist illustrations depicting what he called "Mars Base Alpha" as an intricate network of buildings and infrastructure, SpaceX's plans for the Red Planet are not quite that extensive.

The highlighted part confirms that option A is correct.

60(B). The private spaceflight company, which regularly launches cargo to the International Space Station with the Falcon 9 rocket and will soon launch astronauts up there, is currently building an interplanetary spacecraft for Mars.

The highlighted part clearly shows that statement I is incorrect.

Statement II: SpaceX wants to use water ice from the Martian surface and carbon dioxide from the Martian atmosphere to power Starship rockets.

SpaceX wants to use water ice from the planet's surface and carbon dioxide from the Martian atmosphere to refuel Starships on Mars, enabling the rockets to return to Earth.

The highlighted part confirms that statement II is correct.

Statement III: NASA has a long term goal of establishing human settlement on Mars.

As NASA works toward its long-term goal of establishing a human settlement on Mars, SpaceX is fleshing out its plans to help NASA make that dream a reality.

The highlighted part clearly shows that statement III is correct.

61(D). Bahlul Khan Lodi was the first ruler of the Lodi dynasty. Hence statement (A) is false.

- Ibrahim Lodi was the last ruler of the Lodi dynasty.
- The first battle of Panipat was fought between Babur and Ibrahim Lodi on 21 April 1526. Hence statement (B) is false.
- The Lodi dynasty was the fifth and the last dynasty of the Delhi Sultanate.
- Mughal Empire was established after the Lodi dynasty. Hence Statement (C) is true.

62(B). Bijak is written by Kabir and it is a holy scripture of Kabirpanthis.

It is one of the earliest of the major texts in modern Hindi. The main commentary on the Bijak is by Mahatma Puran Saheb.

Kabir's ideas were collected in verses called Sakhis and pads which were composed by him and sung by wandering bhajan singers. Both Hindus and Muslims were his followers.

63(D). Lord Ripon, British Governor-General was called the Father of Local Self-Government in India.

- Lord Ripon was a British viceroy who gave wider rights and powers to local bodies in 1882. He started the local self-government and laid the foundations of representative institutions in India.
- Lord Ripon was appointed as Viceroy of India in 1880.

64(C). The Gupta Empire initiated a period known as the Golden Age of India, marked by extensive inventions and discoveries in science, technology, engineering, art, dialectic, literature, logic, mathematics, astronomy, religion, and philosophy. Chandragupta II promoted the synthesis of science, art, philosophy, and religion, in part because his court contained the Navartna, or the Nine Jewels, a group of nine scholars who produced advancements in many academic fields.

Sri Gupta founded the Gupta Empire and was succeeded by his son, Ghatotkacha, followed by Ghatotkacha's son, Chandragupta.

65(D). In large parts of the subcontinent, society was already divided according to the rules of varna.

Many societies in the subcontinent did not follow the social rules and rituals prescribed by the Brahmanas nor were they divided into numerous unequal classes. Such societies are often called tribes.

These rules, as prescribed by the Brahmanas, were accepted by the rulers of large kingdoms.

- The difference between the high and low, and between the rich and poor, increased.
- Under the Delhi Sultans and the Mughals, this hierarchy between social classes grew further.

66(A). The correct chronological order of these events is 1 - 2 - 3 - 4.

In 1920, after Jalianwala Bagh Massacre he called for a campaign of non-cooperation with British Rule and joined hands with the Khilafat movement.

He was of the opinion that coupling the non-cooperation with the Khilafat would result in Hindu-Muslim unity to end the colonial rule.

The British Raj was shaken to its foundations for the first time since the Revolt of 1857.

The non-cooperation movement was suspended in 1922 after the Chauri-Chaura incident where 22 policemen were killed by a violent crowd.

In 1928, Gandhiji began to think of re-entering politics. After the failure of the Simon Commission, in its annual session at Lahore Congress demanded Purna Swaraj and decided to observe 26th January 1930 as Independence Day.

In the Lahore Session of Congress held in December 1929, it was decided that now the struggle will be for complete independence and 26 Jan 1930 will be observed as independence day nationwide. In 1931, the 'Gandhi-Irwin Pact' was signed by the terms of which civil disobedience was called off and all prisoners were released. This pact drew many criticisms because Gandhiji was unable to obtain a commitment to political independence for Indians from the Viceroy, he could obtain merely an assurance of talks.

67(A). Vinoba Bhave was the first to offer the satyagraha and Jawaharlal Nehru was the second.

Towards the end of 1940, Gandhiji decided to launch Individual Satyagraha.

The aims of launching individual satyagraha were—
- to show that nationalist patience was not due to weakness;
- to express people's feeling that they were not interested in the war; and
- to give another opportunity to the government to accept Congress' demands peacefully.

68(D). In 1024, during the reign of Bhimdev, the prominent Turkic Muslim ruler Mahmud of Ghazni raided Gujarat, plundering the Somnath temple and breaking its jyotirlinga.
- He took away a booty of 20 million dinars.
- Historians expect the damage to the temple by Mahmud to have been minimal because there are records of pilgrimages to the temple in 1038, which make no mention of any damage to the temple.
- However, powerful legends with intricate detail developed in the Turko-Persian literature regarding Mahmud's raid, which "electrified" the Muslim world.
- They later boasted that Mahmud had killed 50,000 devotees who tried to defend the temple, a formulaic figure.
- The temple at the time of Mahmud's attack appears to have been a wooden structure, which is said to have decayed in time.
- Kumarapala (r. 1143–72) rebuilt it in "excellent stone and studded it with jewels," according to an inscription in 1169.
- During its 1299 invasion of Gujarat, Alauddin Khalji's army, led by Ulugh Khan, defeated the Vaghela king Karna and sacked the Somnath temple.

69(C). The Mughals treated other rulers as their vassals if those rulers submitted voluntarily to Mughal sovereignty.

Mughals had matrimonial alliances with Rajputs for cordiality.

The Mughal rulers campaigned constantly against rulers who refused to accept their authority. Hence statement 1 is correct.

But as the Mughals became powerful many other rulers also joined them voluntarily.

The Rajputs are a good example of this. Many of them married their daughters into Mughal families and received high positions.

The careful balance between defeating but not humiliating their opponents enabled the Mughals to extend their influence over many kings and chieftains.

Thus, we can say that the Mughals had matrimonial alliances with Rajputs for cordiality.

70(C). Ibn Battuta visited India during the rule of Mohammed Bin Tughlaq.
- Ibn Battuta was a Moroccan traveller.
- Rihla was a book written by Ibn Batuta.
- Rihla is a travelogue based upon the experiences of the travellers.

71(C). 3 Carnatic wars were fought between the British and the French.
- The Carnatic wars were fought between the British and the French.
- Through the British and the French came to India for trading purposes, they were ultimately drawn into the politics of India.
- The Anglo-French rivalry in India reflected the traditional rivalry of England and France throughout their histories.
- The Carnatic wars decided once for all that the English were to overpower French ambition in India.

72(C). Minerals are naturally occurring substances that have a definite chemical composition.

On the basis of composition, minerals can be classified as:
- metallic minerals
- non-metallic minerals

Metallic minerals contain metals in raw form. Examples are bauxite, iron ore etc.

Non-metallic minerals do not contain metals. Hence statement (A) is wrong.

Limestone, mica and gypsum are examples of non-metal minerals. hence statement (B) is wrong.

The mineral fuels like coal and petroleum are also non-metallic minerals. Hence statement (C) is right.

73(D). Heat energy obtained from the earth is called geothermal energy. Hence statement (A) is false.
- The word geothermal comes from the word 'geo' meaning earth and 'therme' meaning heat. It is a renewable resource that can be harvested for human use.
- The temperature in the interior of the earth rises steadily as we go deeper. Temperature increases due to the gas and pressure present inside the surface of the earth. The temperature increases because we go near to the core of the earth which is metallic and hotter.
- Hence statement (B) is true.
- This geothermal energy can be used to generate power. Hence statement (C) is false.

74(B). Sericulture is the process of cultivating silkworms and extracting silk from them.

Pisciculture is the breeding of fish in specially constructed tanks and ponds.

Viticulture is the term used for encompassing the cultivation, protection and harvest of grapes.

Horticulture is growing vegetables, flowers, and fruits for commercial use.

75(B). Laterite Soils:
- The word Laterite is derived from the Latin word 'later' which means 'brick'.
- Laterite is a soil and rock type rich in iron and aluminium and is commonly considered to have formed in hot and wet tropical areas.
- Nearly all laterites are of rusty-red colouration, because of their high iron oxide content.
- They develop by intensive and long-lasting weathering of the underlying parent rock.
- Laterite soil is reddish to yellow in colour with a lower content of potassium, phosphorus, nitrogen, lime, and magnesia with 90 to 100% of aluminium, iron, titanium, & manganese oxides.

76(C). The appointment of acting Chief Justice is to be made by the President under Article 126 of the Constitution. Vacancy in the office of the Chief Justice must be filled whatever the period of vacancy. Article 126 – Appointment of acting Chief justice. As of August 2022, Justice Uday Umesh Lalit is the 49th Chief Justice of India.

77(B). The first meeting of the constituent assembly was held on the 9th of December, 1946. There were a total of 389 members in the constituent assembly. It took 2 years, 11 months, and 18 days to make the constitution. It was adopted on 26th November 1949 and it came into effect 26 January 1950.

78(D). The term 'justice' in the Preamble embraces three distinct forms– social, economic, and political, secured through various provisions of Fundamental Rights and Directive Principles.
- Social justice denotes the equal treatment of all citizens without any social distinction based on caste, color, race, religion, sex, and so on. It means the absence of privileges being extended to any particular section of the society, and improvement in the conditions of backward classes (SCs, STs, and OBCs) and women.
- Economic justice denotes the non-discrimination between people on the basis of economic factors. It involves the elimination of glaring inequalities in

wealth, income, and property.
- A combination of social justice and economic justice denotes what is known as 'distributive justice'.
- Political justice implies that all citizens should have equal political rights, equal access to all political offices, and an equal voice in the government.
- The ideal of justice–social, economic, and political–has been taken from the Russian Revolution (1917).

Therefore, Religious Justice is NOT mentioned in the Preamble to the Constitution of India.

79(D). To pay tax to the government is not a fundamental duty. To pay tax is a legal duty.

Important information about Fundamental Duties:
- Article-51A
- Part-IVA
- Total Fundamental duties-11
- Added by Amendment-42nd,1976
- Borrowed from Russia
- Recommended by-Swaran Singh Committee

80(B). As per Article 348 (1) of the Constitution of India, English is the official language for all the high courts in the country.
- Article 348(1) stipulates the use of English in the Supreme Court and High Courts as well as for drafting Bills, Acts and Orders.
- Article 348(2) read with Section (7) of the Official Languages Act 1963 provides for Hindi or other official languages to be used in High Courts "in addition to English".

81(A). Article 275 deals with the grants in aid by the Union Government to the States.
- Article 265 - No tax shall be levied or collected except by the authority of law.
- Article 270 - Taxes levied and collected by the Union and distributed between the Union and the States.
- Article 280 - Finance commission.

82(A). Part IXA in the Constitution, which deals with Municipalities in an article 243 P to 243 ZG, has been introduced under the 74th Amendment Act.

74th Amendment Act:
- The act provides for a five-year term of office for every municipality from the date of its first meeting.
- The elections to constitute a municipality shall be completed before the expiry of its duration of five years.
- However, it can be dissolved before the completion of its term.

83(C). The federal government system of India has been taken from the Canadian Constitution.
- Only the Parliament has the power to make laws on the subjects of the Union List.
- Article 245 to 255 of the Constitution discusses the Centre-State legislative relations in Part-XI.
- In the Constitution of India, three types of lists are present in the Seventh Schedule as the legislative powers between the Center and the States.
- The 'Union List' mentions important subjects, which include defence, communication, foreign policy, etc., and where only the laws of the Center are effective.

84(A). Corporate tax is the single largest source of income to the government of India.

According to the Budget for 2019-20 presented in Parliament by Finance Minister Nirmala Sitharaman, Goods and Services Tax collections will contribute 19 paise in every rupee revenue.

Corporation tax is the single largest source of income, contributing 21 paise to each rupee earned.

85(A). Indian Railways is a government agency under the ownership of the Ministry of Railways.
- The government of India operates India's national railway system.
- It manages the fourth-largest railway network in the world by size.
- With a route length of 67,956 km as of 31 March 2020.

86(B). Pradhan Mantri Ujjwala Yojana (PMUY) was launched in 2016 and is implemented by the Ministry of Petroleum and Natural Gas through its Oil Marketing Companies.

Through PMUY, initially, 5 crores below poverty line (BPL) households were targeted for providing deposit-free LPG connections to BPL households by 31st March 2019. This target has been achieved. PMUY aims at providing clean-cooking fuel to poor households and bringing in qualitative charges in the living standards.

The scheme provides financial support of Rs 1600 for each LPG connection to the BPL households.

PMUY beneficiaries are identified through Socio-Economic Caste Census List-2011 and in such cases where names are not covered under the SECC list, beneficiaries are identified from seven categories:
- All SC/STs households beneficiaries of Pradhan Mantri Awas Yojana(PMAY) (Gramin)
- Antyoday Anna Yojana (AAY)
- Forest dwellers
- Most Backward Classes (MBC)
- Tea & Ex-Tea Garden Tribes
- People residing in Islands
- People residing in river islands.

87(A). The Maharashtra government approved a revised policy of the 'Majhi Kanya Bhagyashree' scheme, according to which families who have a yearly income of upto Rs 7.5 lakh will be benefited.

The new Scheme was launched on International Women's Day, hence statement 1 is incorrect.

The aim of the Majhi Kanya Bhagyashree Scheme is to control sex ratio in the state, hence statement 2 is correct.

The scheme, launched by the state government on April 1, 2016 in place of 'Sukanya' scheme.

The scheme is named after Bollywood film actress Bhagyashree as she is the Brand Ambassador of this scheme, hence statement 3 is correct,therefore the correct answer is option 1.

This scheme is aimed at improving the skewed girl child ratio, prevent sex determination and female foeticide, and support female education.

This scheme aims to enhance the quality of life of the women in Maharashtra.

88(D). Social science teaching needs to be revitalized towards helping the learner acquire knowledge and skills in an interactive environment.
- Problem-solving, dramatization and role play are some hitherto underexplored strategies that could be employed.
- Teaching should utilize greater resources of audio-visual materials, including photographs, charts and maps, and replicas of archaeological and material cultures.
- In order to make the process of learning participative, there is a need to shift from mere imparting of information to debate and discussion. This approach to learning will keep both the learner and teacher alive to social realities.
- Concepts should be clarified to the students through the lived experiences of individuals and communities. It has often been observed that cultural, social and class differences generate their own biases, prejudices and attitudes in classroom contexts. The approach to teaching, therefore, needs to be open-ended.

89(A). The teacher givinng answers to the questions himself should not be a method in social science teaching.

Social Science is the study of relations of humans with society and their social life. It includes a number of disciplines (history, political science, economics, psychology, science, etc.) that deal with human society.
- It is a part of social studies that is slender than social studies.
- It aims at enabling students to adjust to their socio-cultural environment which includes family, community, state, nation, and at large the entire humanity.

90(D). Normalization is not a component of instructional process in a social science classroom.

The processes in the classroom are designed by the teacher to achieve the objectives of teaching social studies. The teacher deals with instructional processes in dealing with content. When you, as a teacher, try to develop the instructional process, you may think what the change in learners' behaviour will be through the pre-designed learning environment consisting of content, media, activity, resources, learning styles, etc. Hence, the instructional process in social studies may be considered as providing a learning environment consisting of relevant components with which an individual interacts and gains experience, leading to the attainment of certain prespecified/preplanned learning outcomes. The instructional process provides a systematised teaching-learning procedure in any school setting. To create a genuine instructional environment, one has to develop an understanding of various components of the instructional process, namely:

- Planning
- Execution or implementation
- Managing and monitoring
- Feedback mechanisms

91(A). Peer teaching is a very good and effective system or process of engaging learner in active atmosphere.

- In peer teaching, the teacher taught a particular lesson to the bright students who in turn would teach the same lesson to other students. Sometimes, the teacher assigned the task of teaching young children to the students of senior classes.
- It being individualized instruction is effective for all teaching situations, especially for skill learning.
- It develops a sense of responsibility and accountability among students.
- Peer teaching is a very good and effective system or process of engaging learners in active atmosphere.
- In active atmosphere, the learner is actively engaged in the learning.
- Active Learning Environments provide cooperative learning spaces that encourage student collaboration and peer teaching.

92(C). Engage learners in critical and thought provoking activities teaching methods would be most effective in Social Science, that teachers must use.
Social science teaching should aim at generating in students critical, moral, and mental energy, making them alert to social forces that threaten these values.

93(C). Roleplay is very helpful in sensitizing the students to certain issues and making them understand the difficulties involved by placing them in the given roles. It develops confidence, communication skills, etc. which are also a part of life skills.

Steps in a Role Play includes-
- Fixing a theme or deciding on a theme that is related to the textual content.
- Deciding on the type of roles, the number of students required and developing the conversation in a flexible manner.
- A small rehearsal may be organized if the conversations are involved.
- Enacting the role play with or without simple costumes.
- Feedback by the teacher and the peers.

94(A). Critical thinking is a process that challenges an individual to use reflective, reasonable, rational thinking to gather, interpret, and evaluate information in order to derive a judgment. Critical thinking should be the ultimate goal of all education. John Dewey defines critical thinking as "reflective thought" rather than routine though; it's the process of "active, persistent, and careful consideration" of the credibility and conclusions of supposed knowledge or information.
Developing a habit of questioning is basic to critical thinking. According to Edward Glaser, there are a few abilities that underlie critical thinking. They are the ability to:
- Recognise problems
- Find workable means to meet those problems
- Gather and marshal pertinent information
- Recognise unstated assumptions and values
- Comprehend and use language with accuracy, clarity and discrimination
- Interpret data
- Appraise evidence and evaluate statements
- Recognize logical connections between statements
- Draw warranted conclusions and generalizations
- Test the conclusions and generalizations arrived at

95(C). Meaningful social studies instruction is geared at promoting gender equality which enhances full participation of women and men in resolving societal problems and preferring of sustainable solutions.
Meaningful social studies instruction is geared at promoting gender equality which enhances full participation of women and men in resolving societal problems and preferring sustainable solutions.

96(C). The upper primary stage, Social Science includes content from History, Geography, Economics and Political Science.
- At the upper primary stage, the subject-area of Social Science drawing its content from history, geography, political science, and economics will be introduced.
- Simultaneously, the child may be introduced to contemporary issues and problems.
- Contemporary issues may be looked at from multiple perspectives introducing the child to the social and economic problems of society.
- Emphasis needs to be given to issues like poverty, illiteracy, child and bonded labor, class, caste, gender, and environment.

97(C). In learning approach, PBL represents Problem-based learning.
- Problem-based learning (PBL) is a student-centered instructional strategy in which students collaboratively solve problems and reflect on their experiences.
- Problem-based learning (PBL) is typically organized with small groups of learners, accompanied by an instructor, faculty person, or facilitator
- It can be used to enhance content knowledge and foster the development of communication, problem-solving, and self-directed learning skill.
- During this process, a series of problems are provided to learners with guidance early in the PBL process (with introductory problems), and then later guidance is faded as learners gain expertise.

98(C). Holding a youth Parliament is most appropriate for developing an understanding of the Indian Parliament's role and functions.
Parliament makes laws for the whole country. It is the supreme law-making body in the country. For developing an understanding of the Indian Parliament's role and functions youth parliament activity will be appropriate.
YOUTH PARLIAMENT:
There are four techniques which are used to develop skills and attitudes to deal with problems of group life and which have received the attention of educationists:
- Group Discussion,
- Sociodrama and Role-playing,
- Use of Sociograms and other Devices of Sociometry, and
- Application of Action Research.

99(A). Aids are most effective and interesting to teaching social studies.
Audio-Visual Aids is the most effective of all teaching-learning methods as it is nearest to reality and thus generates interest and motivate learners. Televisions, Video, Multimedia programmes, interactive video are audio-visual teaching-learning methods used by Teachers.

100(B). The sociogram is the most useful step for studying relationships among pupils. It is a graphic representation of peer groups that a child has.

- It is used to analyse the choices or preferences each child makes within a peer group as they interact with each other.
- Sociogram could be constructed by asking each student to list any of their peers with whom he/she wants to do an activity. Their answers are tabulated in a chart or diagram to determine how many times each student is selected and by whom.
- Helps the teacher to assess the class's social relationships and identifying issues, social groups within the classroom, and make changes in group structures if there is any sign of isolation, gender bias and undisciplined groups affecting ambience of class.

101(B). Science refers to the study of the structure and behavior of physical and natural things through observation and experimentation. In other words, science is a classified knowledge gained from a systematic study of the behavior of nature.

The Purpose of Diagnostic Test:
- This test helps to know the gaps in children's understanding.
- It is specially conducted for removing the learning difficulties of learners.
- The diagnostic test enables the educator and students to recognize issues that they have with the subject.
- It is a comprehensive test that provides feedback to teachers and students on their strengths and weaknesses.
- This test provides a way to identify the part which makes the child slow down in the learning process and provide appropriate feedback to the child.

102(C). Arunachal Pradesh is located at a higher altitude than Gujarat. Arunachal Pradesh lies on the eastern tip of India while Gujarat lies on the western tip. There is a time lag of two hours from Gujarat to Arunachal Pradesh. The states are separated by a distance of 3300 km.

The longitudinal difference between the two points is 30 degrees and the sun crosses each longitude in 4 minutes. The sun sets in Gujarat after about two hours from Arunachal Pradesh.

Thus, we can say that both the statements are correct but the second statement is not the correct explanation of the first one.

103(C). When air is heated, it expands, becomes lighter and rises up. Hence, statement (A) is correct.

Hot air rises because it is less dense than cold air.

Cold air is denser and heavy. That is why it tends to sink down. Hence, statement (B) is correct.

When hot air rises, the cold air from the surroundings rushes in to fill in the gap. Hence, statement (C) is incorrect.

This is known as convection.

Thus, we can say that when air is heated it expands and becomes lighter and cold air is denser and heavy.

104(A). The first English factory was set up on the banks of the river Hugli in 1651. Hence, statement (A) is correct.

As the trade expanded, the Company persuaded merchants and traders to come and settle near the factory.

Two years later it bribed the Mughal officials into giving the Company zamindari rights over three villages. Hence, statement (B) is correct.

It also persuaded the Mughal emperor Aurangzeb to issue a farman granting the Company the right to trade duty-free. Hence, statement (C) is incorrect as Emperor Aurangzeb issued the farman and not king Akbar.

Thus, we can say that the Mughal Emperor Aurangzeb issued a farman granting the Company the right to trade duty-free.

105(A). Ocean currents are streams of water flowing constantly on the ocean surface in definite directions.

The ocean currents may be warm or cold.

Ocean currents are set in the motion of winds.

They also move in the same pattern as winds. Hence, statement (A) is correct.

Ocean currents move clockwise in the northern hemisphere and anit-clockwise in the southern hemisphere. Hence, statement (B) is incorrect.

Thus, we can say that the Ocean currents also move in the same pattern as winds.

106(B). The Panchayati Raj is the system of local self-government of villages in rural areas of india.

It consists of panchayat raj institutions through which the self-government of villages is realized.

It is based on democratic decentralization and people's participation.

Democratic decentralization is the concept of developing the powers from the lower level of government to the highest level. Hence statement (A) is true.

Panchayats were seen as instruments of decentralization and participatory democracy. Hence statement (B) is true.

Thus, we can say that Panchayati Raj is based on democratic decentralization and people's participation.

107(C). Democracy is the government by the people, a form of government in which the supreme power is vested in the people and exercised directly by them or by their elected members under a free electoral system.

Democracy is a form of government where power is held by the people.
- A democracy is a rule by the people.
- In representative democracies people do not participate directly but, instead, choose their representatives through an election process.
- In a representative democracy, people rule themself.
- Citizens in a democracy have not only rights but also the responsibility to participate in the political system.

108(D). Prehistory is the period of history between the use of the first stone tools by hominids and the beginning of recorded history.

The chronlogical order of the pre-historic period is:
- Palaeolithic Age (500,000 BCE- 10,000 BCE)
- Neolithic Age (6000 BCE- 1000 BCE)
- Chalcolithic Age (3000 BCE- 500 BCE)
- Iron Age (1500 BCE-200 BCE)

Paleolithic period is divided into Lower, Middle and Upper Palaeolithic.

Neolithic age was characterised by development of settled agriculture.

Chalcolithic period or the Copper Age is the transitional period between the Neolithic and Iron Age.

Iron age is the final epoch of pre-history.

109(A). The Persian court described Sultan as the 'Shadow of God'.

An inscription in Qawwat-al-Islam mosque explained that God chose Allaudin Khilji as the king.

It was because he had the qualities of Moses and Soloman, the great lawgivers of the past.

Allaudin Khilji was a Turco-Afghan emperor of the Khiji dynasty that ruled the Delhi Sultanate.

Thus, we can say that an inscription in Qawwat-al-Islam mosque explained that God chose Allaudin Khalji as a king.

110(C). Social science is one of the branches of science, devoted to the study of societies and the relationships among individuals within those societies.

There are some important points related to the Social science approach.
- Some methods of teaching Social science include stimulation, laboratory, inquiry, project, dramatizations, questions, and answers, field trips, discussion, lecture, problem-solving, etc.
- The understanding of social science is important both to the teachers and students for meaningful Social Studies instruction.
- The simulation method is a simplified model of the real world.
- A field visit is the best way of teaching social science.
- The organization of the social studies curriculum is not done by any fixed approach.
- Teaching is a process by which one interacts with another person with the intention.
- The approach of social science is always contextual to society and nation in

addition to teachers' potentialities.

111(D). Social Studies the part of a school or college curriculum concerned with the study of social relationships and the functioning of society.

There are some important points related to social studies given below:

- To develop the ability of learners to adapt to changing environments.
- To include national consciousness and national unity in students.
- To include the student's right type of attitude.
- The teaching of social studies is aimed at helping learners to develop greater awareness of themselves clarify and examine their values and establish a sense of self-identity.
- The teaching of social studies helps promote learners' concern for the development of an understanding and acceptance of others with different values and lifestyles.
- Social studies teaching helps provide learners with a knowledge of the human system in areas of economics, government, and culture.
- Social studies teaching aims at providing learners with an awareness of possible situations and their possible roles in shaping the future.
- To make students good citizens who are capable and willing to develop society.

112(A). Teaching aids are tools that facilitate the process of teaching and learning. There are various types of teaching aids, including traditional teaching aids.

There are some important points related to Teaching aids:

- Visual teaching aids - Teachers use these types of things to show something in the classroom.
- Audio Aids - Audio aids help to improve the listening and communication skills of students.
- Audio visual aids_Videos and animations are used in the classroom to explain concepts better.
- Models are three-dimensional visual aids. They present real things in all respects except for size and shape.
- Modals are learning resources for teaching social science.
- Teaching aids give the real environment.
- Teaching aids enhance the interest of students.

113(A). Inclusion in education refers to all students being able to access and gain equal opportunities for education and learning.

There are some important points related to inclusive social classrooms and functional assessment:

- Inclusive education aims to provide equal and quality education to all,

instead of these variations of caste, color, and creed.

- Every student is born with a different kind of talent so as a teacher we have to use different types of teaching methods.
- In the classroom we should include physically disabled students by this we make the meaning of inclusive education.
- Inclusive education is a process of bringing all children together.
- In an inclusive social science classroom there is the enrollment of all children this is the feature of inclusive education.
- The school management and teacher must undertake a functional assessment of children about what they can do and what they can't do.
- Inclusive education helps to reduce the inferiority complex within the children.

114(D). The teaching of social studies should aim at inculcating among children the spirit of peace and mutual understanding.

Keeping in view the above objective the teacher may identify and organize content and its sequence for instruction as follows:

- Prevention of war is mankind's number one task.
- Formation of peace-loving forces through formulating a policy of peace, disarmament and international cooperation.
- Schools have a responsibility to promote peace.
- Social studies have a responsibility to promote the spirit of peace.
- Social studies have the responsibility of promoting respect for and understanding among people.
- Social studies have the responsibility to create a commitment to international solidarity.

115(C). Social science is considered a non-utilitarian subject in our society. So, it is necessary that the in curriculum, In textbooks and in the classroom, the content, language, and images should be comprehensible, gender-sensitive, and critical of social hierarchies and inequalities of all kinds. It is necessary to revitalize social science teaching, to help the learner acquire knowledge and skills in an interactive environment. It should be learner-centered and textbooks should be directive and instructive then automatically a bond between knowledge and society will be created.

116(C). Monsoon is a major wind system that seasonally reverses its direction. It blows for approximately six months from the Northeast and six months from the Southwest.

They cause wet and dry seasons throughout much of the tropics. India is a tropical country.

Therefore, most of the rain in India is brought by monsoon winds. Thus, we can say that India is located in the tropical region and therefore, most of the rain in India is brought by monsoon winds.

117(A). Prejudice means to judge other people negatively.

Practicing purity and pollution is called untouchability.

Stereotyping is fixing people into one image.

A stereotype is a fixed, over generalized belief about a particular group or class of people.

Discrimination is termed as treating someone less fairly than others.

118(C). The Central Government regulates trade and trade affairs between states and foreign trade; the Introduction of the 2000 rupee note is the work of the Central government.

A state government is a government that controls a subdivision of a country in a federal form of government, which shares political power with the federal or national government. Setting up a regional transport office is the work of the State government.

Councilors work with local people and partners, such as local businesses and other organizations, to agree and deliver on local priorities. The decision to open a park comes under local government.

119(B). This lies on the Sikkim-Nepal border. It is the third highest peak in India after Mt.Everest and K2.

- This range has 14 protected areas for the conservation of wildlife and nature. It lies in the Himalayan Mountain Range.
- It stands tall with an elevation of 8,586 m in a section of the Himalayas called Kanchenjunga Himal delimited in the west by the Tamur River, in the north by the Lhonak Chu and Jongsang La, and in the east by the Teesta River.
- It lies between India and Nepal, with three of the five peaks, namely Main, Central and South, directly on the border, and the peaks West and Kangbachen in Nepal's Taplejung District.
- From the above features it can be seen that Kanchenjunga is the correct answer.

120(B). Indian States which shares international border with Pakistan (3,323 km):

- Gujarat, Rajasthan, Punjab, Jammu and Kashmir (4 states share their borders with Pakistan).
- Indian States which shares international border with China (3,488 km):
- Jammu and Kashmir, Himachal Pradesh, Uttarakhand, Sikkim and Arunachal Pradesh (5 states borders with China).
- Indian States which shares international border with Nepal (1,751 km):
- Uttarakhand, Uttar Pradesh, Bihar, West

Bengal, Sikkim (5 states share its border with Nepal). Hence Statement 1 is incorrect.

- Indian states which shares international border with Bhutan (699 km):
- Sikkim, West Bengal, Assam, Arunachal Pradesh (4 states shares border with Bhutan). Hence Statement 2 is incorrect.
- Indian states which shares international border with Bangladesh (4,096.7 km):
- West Bengal, Assam, Meghalaya, Tripura and Mizoram (5 states shares border with Bangladesh).
- Indian states which shares international border with Myanmar (1,643 km):
- Arunachal Pradesh, Nagaland, Manipur, Mizoram (4 states shares its border with Myanmar). Hence Statement 3 is correct.
- Length of border shared between India and Afghanistan – 106 Km (as per India's claim; the shared border with Afghanistan lies in Gilgit-Baltistan which is in Pakistan's control)

Child Development and Pedagogy

1. Training before normal maturation is generally:
(a) highly beneficial with respect to the performance of the common skills
(b) beneficial from the point of view of long term
(c) harmful from all points of view
(d) beneficial or harmful depending on the method used in training

2. Which of the sequence is appropriate when development proceeds from the centre to the peripheral areas of the body?
(a) Cephalo-Caudal Sequence
(b) Proximo distal Sequence
(c) Locomotion Sequence
(d) Bilateral Sequence

3. A 6-year-old girl shows exceptional sporting ability. Her parents are sportspersons, send her for coaching daily and train her on weekends. Her capabilities are most likely to be the result of an interaction between:
(a) Health and training
(b) Discipline and nutrition
(c) Heredity and environment
(d) Growth and development

4. Peer groups are the agent of ______.
(a) Secondary Socialization
(b) Anticipatory Socialization
(c) Primary Socialization
(d) Developmental Socialization

5. During a task, Saina is talking to herself about ways she could proceed on the task. According to Lev Vygotsky's ideas on language and thought; this kind of 'private speech' is a sign of:
(a) Self-regulation
(b) Ego-centricism
(c) Psychological disorder
(d) Cognitive immaturity

6. The teacher observed that Ravi is not able to solve a problem alone while he solves it easily when individualized support is provided to him by his teacher. In Vygotsky's view, this kind of support is called:
(a) Generalization
(b) Abstract thinking
(c) Peer tutoring
(d) Scaffolding

7. Which of the following is central to the concept of progressive education?
(a) Belief in the capability and potential of every child
(b) Standard instruction and assessment
(c) Extrinsic motivation and uniform assessment parameters
(d) Textbook centric learning

8. According to Howard Gardner, ______ is not a type of intelligence.
(a) Musical
(b) Skeptical
(c) Spatial
(d) Interpersonal

9. Theory of multiple intelligence emphasize that:
(a) Intelligence in one domain ensures intelligence in all other domains
(b) There are several forms of intelligence
(c) There are no individual differences in intelligence
(d) Intelligence Quotient (IQ) can b measured only by objective tests

10. Which of the following psychologists is associated with 'language development'?
(a) Binet
(b) Chomsky
(c) Pavlov
(d) Maslow

11. During classroom discussions, a teacher often pays more attention to boys than girls. This is an example of:
(a) Gender bias
(b) Gender identity
(c) Gender relevance
(d) Gender constancy

12. Which of the following may not be expected from a teacher to keep in mind while respecting individual differences?
(a) Ability grouping
(b) Adjusting the curriculum
(c) Leaving Children for self-study
(d) Adjusting the methods of teaching

13. Continuous and Comprehensive Evaluation mainly aims at promoting:
(a) Competition among children
(b) Competition among teachers
(c) Academic excellence among children
(d) Inclusive education

14. Continuous and comprehensive evaluation includes:
(a) only formative assessment
(b) only summative assessment
(c) neither formation nor summative assessment
(d) both formative and summative assessments using a wide variety of strategies

15. A self-guided, self-disciplined thinking which attempts to reason at the highest level of quality in a fair-minded way is called:
(a) critical thinking
(b) complex thinking
(c) intelligent thinking
(d) abstract thinking

16. A child 'who is in the middle of his school (about ten and half years) is unable to do the work of the class below that which is normal for his age" is known as which types of children?
(a) Mentally retarded
(b) Educationally retarded
(c) Moron
(d) Idiot

17. Which of the following is not a trait (ability) of a creative child?
(a) Originality
(b) Elaboration
(c) Novelty
(d) Accuracy

18. A child's notebook shows errors in writing like reverse images, mirror imaging, etc. Such a child is showing signs of:
(a) Learning disability
(b) Learning difficulty
(c) Learning problem
(d) Learning disadvantage

19. What effort will you make for bringing change in the behaviour of a problematic child?
(a) Make effort to bring change in the child's environment and attitude
(b) Try to improve by punishing the child
(c) Will not pay attention to him/her
(d) Will seat him in the front row in the class

20. What instructional adaptations should a teacher make while

working with students who are 'Visually Challenged'?

(a) Use a variety of visual presentations

(b) Orient herself so that the students can watch her closely

(c) Focus on a variety of written tasks, especially worksheets.

(d) Speak clearly and use a lot of touches and feel materials

21. Children's errors and misconceptions:

(a) Are a hindrance and obstacle to the teaching-learning process

(b) Should be ignored in the teaching-learning process

(c) Signify that children's capabilities are far inferior to that of adults

(d) Are a significant step in the teaching-learning process

22. Which of the following is not the curve of learning?

(a) Convex

(b) Combination type

(c) Concave

(d) Longitudinal

23. 'Learning is any change in behaviour, resulting from behaviour' who said it?

(a) Crow & Crow

(b) Guilford

(c) Woodworth

(d) Skinner

24. Which of the following statements about children are correct?
A. Children are passive recipients of knowledge.
B. Children are problem solvers.
C. Children are scientific investigators.
D. Children are active explorers of the environment.

(a) A, B, C, and D　(b) A, B, and C

(c) A, B, and D　(d) B, C, and D

25. Knowing the naive conceptions that students bring to the classroom:

(a) hampers the teacher's planning and teaching

(b) pulls down the teacher's morale since it increases his work

(c) does not serve any purpose of the teacher

(d) helps the teacher to plan teaching more meaningfully

26. Which of the following is a constructive approach for dealing with the 'misconceptions' carried by students?

(a) Assign a lot of content to memorize and remember

(b) Create circumstances where misconceptions are not allowed to be expressed

(c) Give opportunities for experimentation and observation to counter misconceptions

(d) Ignore prior beliefs and alternative conceptions of students

27. The relationship between cognition and emotions is:

(a) independent of each other

(b) uni-directional - emotions influence cognition

(c) uni-directional - cognition influences emotions

(d) bi-directional - a dynamic interplay between both

28. Ashok is very fond of playing cricket and is very good at it. He is the captain of his college team. He spends long hours playing or watching cricket and never gets tired or bored. Which personal factor is affecting learning in this example?

(a) Maturation

(b) Motivation

(c) Self-concept

(d) Levels of Aspiration

29. Which of the following is a teacher-related factor affecting learning?

(a) Maturation & Motivation

(b) The socio-emotional climate of the class

(c) Structure of the discipline

(d) Leadership style of teacher

30. Identify the factor that does not influence student difficulty in learning.

(a) Intellectual factor

(b) Social factor

(c) Economic factor

(d) All of the above

Ques (31-39): Direction: Read the passage given below and answer the questions by choosing the correct/most appropriate options.

1. Today when we pick up a daily newspaper, we invariably find an increased incidence of vandalism, fraud, theft, robbery, rape, child spouse, battered spouses, murders, hate crimes, genocide (now termed as "ethnic cleansing") along with a multitude of other senseless violent acts that have become disturbingly common. These are not the actions of people who like themselves.

2. The solution to a great many problems, whether personal, national or global, lies in improving our feelings about ourselves both as individuals and members of society. When the significance of good self-esteem is well understood and it achieves the prominence it deserves, a transformation will begin, for as the people will learn they are deserving of self-respect, their respect for others will automatically increase.

3. Most of our behaviour has been shaped by our parent's caregivers and authority figures who played an important part in our early springing and were responsible for crystallizing our ideas about ourselves and the world. While everyone has self-esteem, only a small percentage of us have high self-esteem. High self-esteem denotes that we accept ourselves unconditionally exactly as we are, we appreciate our value as a human being. When, on the other hand, we have low self-esteem, we believe that we have little intrinsic worth.

4. We believe our personal value is in direct proportion to the value of our accomplishments. If we cannot accomplish certain results, we tend to feel low about ourselves. Some of us try too hard and become workaholics and over-achievers. With a few genuine feelings of self-worth, we try to create some and prove that we are somebody by our successes and achievements. Because our desire for perfection is so great, we tend to set unrealistic goals and place unreasonable demands on ourselves. Failing, rather than encouraging us to have realistic aspirations, only leads to a mere punishing round of self-blame and a resolve to drive ourselves harder next time. If we do finally achieve our goals we are disappointed; despite everything we have done, we still feel empty inside.

5. Vulnerable to the opinions of others, we desperately try to gain their recognition and approval sometimes through risky and dangerous behaviour. Thus, we are at the mercy of our emotions, instead of controlling them, we permit them to control us. Since we allow circumstances to influence our feelings, we are inclined to be moody. The insecurity we feel as a result of devaluing ourselves makes us react with jealousy, envy and possessiveness. Fear makes us greedy and acquisitive, and feelings of self-hate alternate with those of futility, unhappiness, and depression.

31. Which of the following are the things the newspapers are full of these days?

(a) News about the development of the country

(b) News about politics

(c) News about acts of crime and violence

(d) News about educational matters and employment

32. Identify the parts of speech of the underlined segment in the given sentence.
When the <u>significance</u> of good self-esteem is well understood.

(a) Adverb   (b) Pronoun

(c) Noun   (d) Conjunction

33. Find the word from the passage which is the antonym of the word, 'futility' as used in the passage(para 5)?

(a) Pointlessness

(b) Vanity

(c) Usefulness

(d) Failure

34. Why is good self-esteem stressed?

(a) It is essential in solving many problems.

(b) It builds up self-confidence.

(c) It increases one's reputation.

(d) It helps one respect others.

35. Find the word from the passage which means the same as the word, 'vandalism' as used in the passage(para 1)?

(a) Construct   (b) Destruction

(c) Build   (d) Mend

36. Find the error in a part of the sentence:
The solution to a great many problems(A)/, whether personal, national, and global(B)/, lies in improving our feelings(C)/ No error. (D)

(a) (A)   (b) (B)

(c) (C)   (d) (D)

37. Which of the following statements is true?
A. We need to accept ourselves unconditionally exactly as we are.
B. We give permission to others to control our emotions.
C. All non-violent acts are the actions of those who like themselves.

(a) Only A

(b) Only B

(c) Both A and B

(d) All of the above

38. According to the passage, when does a person start feeling empty inside?

(a) When we get involved in crimes.

(b) When we push ourselves towards achieving goals and prove that we are somebody by our successes and achievements.

(c) When others start influencing our behaviour.

(d) None of the above

39. Identify the part of speech of the underlined word:
We tend to set <u>unrealistic</u> goals and place unreasonable demands.

(a) Noun   (b) Adverb

(c) Adjective   (d) Pronoun

Ques (40-45): Direction: Read the extract given below and answer the questions.

There is a Reaper, whose name is Death,
And, with his sickle keen,
He reaps the bearded grain at a breath,
And the flowers that grow between.
"Shall I have naught that is fair?" saith he;
"Have naught but the bearded grain?
Though the breath of these flowers is sweet to me,
I will give them all back again."
He gazed at the flowers with tearful eyes,
He kissed their drooping leaves;
It was for the Lord of Paradise
He bound them in his sheaves.
"My Lord has need of these flowerets gay,"
The Reaper said, and smiled;
"Dear tokens of the earth are they,
Where He was once a child.
"They shall all bloom in fields of light,
Transplanted by my care,
And saints, upon their garments white,
These sacred blossoms wear."
And the mother gave, in tears and pain,
The flowers she most did love;
She knew she should find them all again
In the fields of light above.
Oh, not in cruelty, not in wrath,
The Reaper came that day;
'T was an angel visited the green earth,
And took the flowers away.

40. The poem presents death in a:

(a) gloomy light

(b) positive light

(c) fearful light

(d) negative light

41. According to the poet, the mother will meet her flowers in ____.

(a) Garden   (b) Playground

(c) Home   (d) Paradise

42. Who were the flowers for?

(a) Death   (b) Satan

(c) God   (d) Mother

43. Identify the figure of speech in the line:
She knew she should find them all again

(a) Alliteration

(b) Personification

(c) Metaphor

(d) Simile

44. Who wears the flowers in the new world?

(a) Angels   (b) Cherubs

(c) Saints   (d) God

45. How did Death gaze at the flowers?

(a) Happy eyes   (b) Fearful eyes

(c) Angry eyes   (d) Tearful eyes

46. Ravi, an English teacher, is planning remedial teaching for his student who faces problems in expressing his view while talking with someone. Remedial work for spoken English involves

(a) Drill and studying

(b) Revision, drill, situation communicative practice, and reviewing

(c) Going through situational practice

(d) Revision and practice

47. A teacher divides the class in small groups and asks them to discuss and present their views on "Save Environment".
Students are free to plan and present their choice and creativity. The teacher is facilitating them as and when required. Which approach/method is followed in the class?

(a) Structural Approach

(b) Natural Approach

(c) Deductive Approach

(d) Constructivist Approach

48. A Hindi - speaking teacher gets posted in a primary school which is situated in a remote area of Rajasthan. Since she doesn't know the local language, she faces lots of problems. She should:

(a) focus on the textbook as a source of standard Hindi.

(b) use the child's language as a resource while teaching.

(c) encourage the community to learn standard Hindi.

(d) try to get a posting to a Hindi-speaking area.

49. Direction: Answer the following questions by selecting the most appropriate option.
Students of Class IV can recognize flawed usage or sentence construction when the teacher:

(a) tells them something is wrong

    (b) gives alternatives as possible corrections

    (c) lets them find the corrections

    (d) focuses on certain surface errors

50. **'Pedagogical Grammar' means that:**
    (a) Begin from form and move on to use
    (b) Teaching through immersion
    (c) All grammar teaching should be rule focussed
    (d) Teaching grammar in context

51. **A teacher found an advertisement pamphlet for the sale of biscuits. She uses it for reading and speaking activities in her class. What do you call the pamphlet?**
    (a) Realia
    (b) An authentic text
    (c) Extra materials
    (d) Newspaper clipping

52. **Choose the most appropriate option for the question given below:**
At the end of each semester, a teacher tests the students in listening, comprehension, speaking, reading, and writing.
The purpose of this approach is most likely to:
    (a) Measure the student's proficiency
    (b) Measure the student's aptitude for language learning
    (c) Help the teacher to define the curricular objective
    (d) Determine the student's attitudes toward language classes

53. **'The material should be according to the child's mental age, mental ability, grade, and level'.**
Which principle of teaching is involved in this statement?
    (a) Concreteness
    (b) Accuracy and correctness
    (c) Selection and Gradation
    (d) Proportion

54. **The multilingual nature of the Indian classroom must be used as a resource so that ______.**
    (a) every child feels secure and accepted
    (b) every child learns at the same pace
    (c) children can learn many languages
    (d) the teacher develops language proficiency

55. **Damage to this area in the brain** causes problems in speech production:
    (a) Frontal cortex
    (b) Occipital cortex
    (c) Broca's area
    (d) Wernicke's area

56. **Which of the following statements is correct?**
    (a) Receptive vocabulary are words we speak and productive vocabulary are words we hear.
    (b) Receptive vocabulary are words we recognize when we hear or see and productive vocabulary are words we speak or write.
    (c) Receptive vocabulary are words we discourse with people and productive vocabulary are words in written text.
    (d) Words from other languages are receptive vocabulary and words from native languages are productive vocabulary.

57. **According to the National Curriculum Framework 2005, which one of the following is NOT an objective of language teaching-learning?**
    (a) The competence to understand what one hears
    (b) Ability to read with comprehension
    (c) Effortless expression
    (d) To know the history of languages

58. **The term 'Comprehensible input' is associated with ____.**
    (a) Lev Vygotsky
    (b) Stephen Krashan
    (c) Noam Chomsky
    (d) James Asher

59. **While reading a text, which one among the following can help students understand the relations between the parts of a sentence?**
    (a) Adverbs   (b) Pronouns
    (c) Nouns   (d) Verbs

60. **Using 'realia' in the language class means bringing ____.**
    (a) real life situations to communicate
    (b) real objects as teaching aids
    (c) realistic objectives and targets for the learners
    (d) the real level of a child's learning to the knowledge of parents

Social Studies

61. **With reference to countervailing** duties, consider the following statements:
1. These are imposed in order to counter the negative impact of import subsidies to protect domestic producers.
2. These duties cannot be imposed under the specifications given by the WTO (World Trade Organization).
3. The Directorate General of Anti-Dumping & Allied Duties which comes under Ministry of Finance is responsible for carrying out investigations and recommending countervailing duty.

Which of the statements given above is/are correct?
    (a) 2 and 3 only   (b) 1 and 3 only
    (c) 1 only   (d) 1, 2 and 3

62. **Which one of the following pairs is correctly matched?**

Mahajanapada	Town
A. Gandhara	Mathura
B. Anga	Ujjain
C. Avanti	Sotthavati
D. Kamboja	Rajpur

    (a) A   (b) B
    (c) C   (d) D

63. **Which Nagaland Queen raised the banner of rebellion against foreign rule on the call given by Gandhiji and was imprisoned for life?**
    (a) Rani Gaidinliu
    (b) Rani Ambika
    (c) Rani Meitei Jagoi
    (d) Rani Rongmei

64. **The issue on which the Civil disobedience movement of 1930 was launched was:**
    (a) Equal employment opportunities for Indians
    (b) The proposed execution of Bhagat Singh
    (c) Salt monopoly exercised by the British Government
    (d) Complete freedom

65. **Fatehpur Sikri was founded as the capital of the Mughal Empire by ____.**
    (a) Babur   (b) Humayun
    (c) Jahangir   (d) Akbar

66. **Aaram Bagh was originally constructed by which among the following Mughal Emperor?**
    (a) Humayun   (b) Akbar
    (c) Jahaangir   (d) Babur

67. Which Indian state is surrounded by Bangladesh to the north, south and west?

(a) West Bengal (b) Assam

(c) Meghalaya (d) Tripura

68. In the region of the eastern shore of the Adriatic Sea, a cold and dry wind blowing down from the mountain is known as:

(a) Mistral (b) Bora

(c) Bise (d) Blizzard

69. Which one of the following mountains separates the Black Sea and the Caspian Sea?

(a) Urals

(b) Caucasus

(c) Carpathians

(d) Balkan mountains

70. Which among the following countries of South America does the Tropic of Capricorn not pass through?

(a) Chile (b) Bolivia

(c) Paraguay (d) Brazil

71. Which among the following markets has only one buyer for a particular goods or service?

(a) Monopoly (b) Monopolistic

(c) Monopsony (d) Oligopoly

72. Under which project, National Commission for Women (NCW) has organized a workshop on 'Gender Responsive Governance' for elected women representatives (MLAs) in June 2022?

(a) Salon-i

(b) SAKHI

(c) Swayam

(d) 'She Is A Changemaker'

73. Which scheme has been approved by central government for recruitment of youth in armed forces?

(a) Samay (b) Warrior

(c) Ajey yuva (d) Agnipath

74. To prevent cynicism among students about democratic institutions, which of the two given options would be most appropriate?
A. Emphasise Ideal functioning and principles
B. Indicate impossiblity of changing institutions
C. Emphasise that social inequality is inevitable
D. Indicate the role of the informed public

(a) Both A and B (b) Both A and D

(c) Both C and D (d) Both C and B

75. In order to promote cooperative learning in the classroom, a teacher should:

(a) engage students in debate and discussions

(b) give them individual projects

(c) divide the class in small groups for work

(d) provide them various sources to do the project

76. The following is not an example of gender stereotyping:

(a) Only boys being encouraged to participate in the football tournament.

(b) Only the girls in class are asked to decorate the class boards.

(c) While boys try to monopolise the class discussions, attention is given to both girls and boys to encourage participation.

(d) Boys and girls are made to sit in separate rows for ensuring discipline in class.

77. Project work is given in social science course mainly to _____.

(a) provide opportunities to students to utilize their time judiciously

(b) ensure that syllabus is competed

(c) develop student's listing and reading skills

(d) connect learning at school with social realities

78. The first step of project method is:

(a) Planning

(b) Selection of the project

(c) Creating the situation

(d) Executing

79. Which of the following statements is true?

(a) Social science scientists are the source and repository of social knowledge.

(b) Social science studies people as subject matter.

(c) Social science is the relationship of humans with their environment.

(d) Social science deals with the study of human relationships.

80. Which subject is not included in the Upper Primary Social Study Curriculum?

(a) History

(b) Civics

(c) Economics

(d) Political Science

81. When the students become failed, it can be understood that:

(a) the system has failed

(b) the teacher's personal failure

(c) the textbook's failure

(d) the individual student's failure

82. These are the ways of collaborative learning:

(a) Activity based learning and doing homework

(b) Activity based learning, discovery learning and learning through exploration

(c) Discovery learning and solitary play

(d) Learning through exploration and watching T.V

83. To avoid gender stereotyping in a class, a teacher should needs to _______.

(a) encourage boys to be strong

(b) discourage girls from taking part in wrestling

(c) appreciate students good work by saying good girl, good boy

(d) try to put both boys and girls in non-traditional roles

84. Which of the following statement is correct regarding Public Protest?

(a) Writing letters to the concerned minister,

(b) Starting a signature campaign,

(c) Asking the government to rethink its programme,

(d) All of the above

85. When the government prevents either the news item, or scenes from movie, or lyrics of the song from being shared with the larger public, this is referred as _____.

(a) Press Conference

(b) Censorship

(c) Communication

(d) Sensorship

86. What do you mean by factual information?

(a) Information about completed issues

(b) Information about issue that is often not complete

(c) Information about future topics

(d) Information about current topics

87. Which of the following are the aims of Mid day meal programme?
A. Increasing enrolment and

retention of children in schools.
B. Reinforcing caste prejudices among school children.
C. Reducing hunger and increased concentration in studies.
D. Decreasing the malnutrition levels prevailing among children.
Choose the appropriate option.

(a) A, B and C   (b) A, C and D
(c) B, C and D   (d) A, B and D

88. What are the D.K. Basu guidelines which were laid down by the Supreme Court of India?

(a) guidelines related to prevention of sexual harassment at workplace.

(b) guidelines related to protection of children from hazardous employment.

(c) guidelines related to protection of women from domestic violence.

(d) guidelines related to the procedures to be followed by police for arrest, detention, and interrogation.

89. The ability to break down information into smaller pieces and to establish relation among parts and the whole is:

(a) understanding
(b) applying
(c) analyzing
(d) remembering

90. Direction: Consider the two statements and choose the correct option:
Statement (A): Rulers of Harappa sent people to distant lands to get metal, precious stones, and other things that they wanted.
Statement (B): People of Harappa didn't knew how to write.

(a) Both (A) and (B) are true
(b) Both (A) and (B) are false
(c) (A) is false, but (B) is true
(d) (A) is true, but (B) is false

91. Direction: Consider the following statements and select the correct option regarding Aryabhata:
A. He wrote a book in Sanskrit known as the Aryabhatiyam.
B. He stated that day and night were caused by the rotation of the earth on its axis, even though it seems as if the sun is rising and setting every day.
C. He also found a way of calculating the circumference of a circle, which is nearly as accurate as of the formula we use today.

(a) Only A and C   (b) A, B and C
(c) Only A and B   (d) Only B and C

92. Direction: Answer the following questions by selecting the correct/ most appropriate options.
Statement (A): Rammohun Roy was particularly moved by the problems widows faced in their lives.
Statement (B): Rammohun Roy tried to show through his writings that the practice of widow burning had no sanction in ancient texts.

(a) Both (A) and (B) are true and (B) was ensured because of (A).
(b) Both (A) and (B) are true, but (A) has no relationship with (B).
(c) (A) is true, but (B) is false.
(d) (A) is false, but (B) is true.

93. Which of the following is/are correct about minerals and rocks
(A) Generally metallic minerals are found in igneous and metamorphic rocks.
(B) If a rock contains copper then the rock looks blue in color.
(C) Al ore minerals are not rocks.
(D) All rocks are not ore minerals.

(a) Only (A) and (B) are correct
(b) Only (C) and (D) are correct
(c) Only (A), (B) and (C) are correct
(d) Only (A), (B) and (D) are correct

94. Direction: Answer the following questions by selecting the correct/ most appropriate options.
Statement (A): Indian National Congress had promised that once the country won independence, each major linguistic group would have its own province.
Statement (B): Nehru went to campaign in Madras Presidency during the general elections of 1952, he was met with black flags.

(a) Both (A) and (B) are true and (B) is the correct explanation of (A)
(b) Both (A) and (B) are true, but (B) is not the correct explanation of (A)
(c) (A) is true, but (B) is false
(d) (A) is false, but (B) is true

95. Direction: Read the information and answer the question.
Statement (A): The sepoys of Meerut forced into the red fort and proclaimed Bahadur Shah Zafar as their leader.
Statement (B): The Mughal dynasty had ruled the country once.

(a) Both (A) and (B) are true and (B) is the correct explanation of (A).
(b) Both (A) and (B) are true, but (B) is not the correct explanation of (A).
(c) (A) is true but (B) is false.
(d) (A) is false but (B) is true.

96. Direction: Consider the statements A, B, C on sedimentary rocks and choose the correct answer:
A. The remains of the dead plants and animals trapped in sedimentary rock.
B. Loose sediments are compressed and hardened to form layers of rocks.
C. Imance heat and pressure transform metamorphic rocks into sedimentary rocks.

(a) B and C are correct and A is incorrect
(b) A and B are correct and C is incorrect
(c) A, B, C all are correct
(d) A and C are correct and B is incorrect

97. Direction: Identify the suitable natural condiitons for human settlement.
1. Favourable climate
2. Availability of water
3. Suitable land
4. Fertile soil
Choose the correct answer from the codes given below.

(a) 1, and 2 are correct only
(b) 1,2 and 3 are correct only
(c) 2 and 3 are correct only
(d) All are correct

98. Match the following types of vegetation with their characteristics.

A. Tropical Evergreen	I. Trees that alway s have leaves
B. Tropical Deciduous	II. Receive rainfall less than 50 cm
C. Tropical Thorn Forests	III. Salt-tolerant species of plants
D. Littoral Forests	IV. Most widespread forests in India

(a) A (III), B (IV), C (II), D (I)
(b) A (III), B (II), C (IV), D (I)
(c) A (I), B (IV), C (II), D (III)
(d) A (IV), B (II), C (III), D (I)

99. "Imagine that you have come across two old newspapers reporting on the Battle of Shrirangapattanam and the death of Tipu Sultan. One is a British paper and the other is from Mysore. Write the headline for each of the two newspapers."

What is the reason for including this activity in the history textbook of class VIII?

(a) Develop writing skills in students

(b) Develop the concept of diversity of views in students

(c) Create a record of annexation by the British

(d) Communicate British policies to the masses

100. **Direction: Consider the following statements and select the correct option regarding the representative democracies:**
A. People participate directly in the decision making.
B. People choose their representatives through an election process.
C. In representative democracy a king has absolute powers to rule the country.

(a) Only A and C   (b) A, B and C

(c) Only A   (d) Only B

101. **Direction: Consider statements A and B about the marginalisation of Adivasis and choose the correct answer:**
A. Adivasis are being increasingly marginalised.
B. Changes in forest laws have deprived the Adivasis of access to forest produce.

(a) Both A and B are true and B is the correct explanation of A.

(b) Both A and B are true but B is not the correct explanation of A.

(c) A is false, but B is true.

(d) A is true, but B is false.

102. **Direction: Consider the following statements:**
A. District collector is the head of the tehsil.
B. Revenue Officers come under the District collector and are also known as tehsildars.
C. District collector reviews the work of patwaris.
Which of the following statement(s) is/are correct?

(a) A and B are true, C is false

(b) A and C are true, B is false

(c) B and C are true, A is false

(d) A, B and C are true

103. **Which of the following statements about social science is not true?**

(a) Social science is related to diverse concerns of society.

(b) Social science is subjective

discipline.

(c) Social science lays foundation for analytic and creative mind.

(d) None of the above

104. **At the upper primary/elementary school level, which one of the following is not a common objective of social science learning?**

(a) To develop moral values, emotional qualities and sense of belonging in the students

(b) Helping students to participate in socio-economic institutions

(c) To develop the qualities of democratic citizenship in the students

(d) Lack of development of social competence and sense of social commitment in students

105. **Match the word to the correct meaning:**

a.	Stupa	i.	Tower
b.	Mandapa	ii.	Mound
c.	Shikhara	iii.	Hall

(a) a - ii, b - iii, c - i

(b) a - ii, b - i, c - iii

(c) a - iii, b - ii, c - i

(d) a - i, b - iii, c - ii

106. **The basis of democracy can be attributed to:**

(a) Periodic elections

(b) One-time election

(c) No elections

(d) Rule of law

107. **Direction: Read the information and answer the question.**
Statement (A): Panchayati Raj is the third tier of government.
Statement (B): It comes under the feature of federalism in India.
Choose the correct/appropriate option regarding federalism in India.

(a) Both (A) and (B) is True and (B) is correct explanation of (A).

(b) Both (A) and (B) is True but (B) is incorrect explanation of (A).

(c) (A) is true and (B) is false.

(d) (A) is false and (B) is true.

108. **Direction: Consider the following statement(s) in reference to Article 22 of the Constitution and criminal law and choose the correct/appropriate statement(s).**
1. **The Right to be informed at the time of arrest of the offence for which the person is being arrested.**

2. **The Right to be presented before a magistrate within 24 hours of arrest.**
3. **Confessions made in police custody can be used as evidence against the accused.**
4. **A boy under 15 years of age and women cannot be called to the police station only for questioning.**

(a) 1, 2 and 4   (b) 3, and 4

(c) 1, 2 and 3   (d) 1 and 2

109. **Which Act was framed in 1989 in response to demands made by Dalits and others that the government must take seriously the ill treatment and humiliation of Dalits and tribal groups?**

(a) Scheduled Tribes (Prevention of Atrocities) Act

(b) Protection of Civil Rights Act

(c) Hindu Succsession Act

(d) The Scheduled Castes and Scheduled Tribes Orders

110. **Direction: Raed the following statement(s) with respect to the Supreme Court, and choose the correct option.**
1. **Delhi has the seat of the Supreme Court.**
2. **Supreme court was established on 15th August 1947.**
3. **It is the guardian of our fundamental rights.**
Select the correct answer using the code given below.

(a) 1 and 2

(b) 2 and 3

(c) 1 and 3

(d) All of the above

111. **The challenging dimension of evaluation of school teaching is:**

(a) Preparation of examinations

(b) Adequate check on performance

(c) Measurement of growth

(d) Ranking

112. **Which of the following is measured by continuous comprehensive evaluation?**

(a) Holistic development

(b) Development of creativity

(c) Development of experience

(d) Development of divergent thinking

113. **Direction: Consider the following statements about Ain-i-Akbari and choose the correct option.**
(A) It was written by Abul Fazl.
(B) It has rich statistical details about crops, prices, revenues and

wages etc.

(C) It deals with details of Akbar's ancestors.

(a)   (A) and (B) are true.

(b)   (B) and (C) are true.

(c)   (A) and (C) are true.

(d)   (A), (B) and (C) are true.

114. **Direction: Which of the following statements is correct about iqtadar and jagirdar?**

A. These titles were given to military commanders of specific territories during Delhi Sultanate and Mughal Rule respectively.

B. They resided in and administered their lands called iqta and jagir respectively.

(a)   Only A

(b)   Only B

(c)   Both A and B

(d)   Neither A nor B

115. **Match the following and choose the correct options.**

a.	William Jones	(i)	Promotion of English
b.	Rabindra Nath Tagore	(ii)	Respect for ancient culture
c.	Mahatma Gandhi	(iii)	Critical of English Education
d.	Thomas Macaulay	(iv)	Learning in a natural environment

(a)   a - (ii), b - (iv), c - (iii), d - (i)

(b)   a - (iii), b - (ii), c - (iv), d - (i)

(c)   a - (iv), b - (ii), c - (iii), d - (i)

(d)   a - (i), b - (iv), c - (ii), d - (iii)

116. **Direction: Consider these following statements and choose the correct option.**

(A) A population pyramid that is broader at the base indicates an expanding labour force in the future.

(B) A country having a large number of younger children will have an economic advantage in the labour market.

(C) The bottom of the population pyramid reflects the level of deaths while the top reflects the number of births.

(a)   Only (A) and (B) are true.

(b)   Only (B) and (C) are true.

(c)   Only (A) is true.

(d)   Only (B) is true.

117. **Direction: Consider the following statements with respect to role of text books in the classroom processes.**

(A) Exercise given in the textbook helps a teacher to gauge the extent to which the student has understood what has been discussed in the chapter.

(B) They disturb the system of the lesson that is being taught.

(C) They help students to recall and make connections with what has been taught earlier.

(a)   Only (A) and (B)

(b)   Only (A) and (C)

(c)   Only (B) and (C)

(d)   (A), (B) and (C)

118. **When discussing the theme 'Adivasis,' a social science teacher is expected to ______.**

(a)   discuss only the textbook content with a sensitive approach.

(b)   highlight social status of adivasis as seen by dominant groups in society.

(c)   introduce a variety of local examples during class discussions.

(d)   present mainly issues of social marginalisation.

119. **'Hussain Sagar Lake' is located in which of the following state?**

(a)   Telangana

(b)   Maharashtra

(c)   Gujarat

(d)   Andhra Pradesh

120. **Direction: Match the following and choose the appropriate option.**

a.	Bikaner	(i)	Humid
b.	Mumbai	(ii)	Rainy
c.	Mawsynram	(iii)	Hot
d.	Drass	(iv)	Cold

(a)   a - (iv), b - (ii), c - (iii), d - (i)

(b)   a - (iii), b - (i), c - (ii), d - (iv)

(c)   a - (ii), b - (iv), (c) - (i), (d) - (iii)

(d)   a - (iv), b - (iii), c - (ii), d - (i)

// Hints and Solutions //

1(D). Every child has his own set of qualities. Also, there is the right time to learn a skill. The time at which a child becomes ready to learn is called maturation.

Maturation is interpreted as a relatively permanent change in an individual, such as cognitive, emotional, or physical, that occurs as a result of biological aging, regardless of personal experience.

Things to remember during training:

- A child can learn a new skill prematurely or late.
- Training of a child to learn a new skill is worth appreciating but it should be remembered that the child is mature enough to learn.
- Premature training may be both beneficial and harmful for the children based on the methodology used by the trainer in the training process.
- For example, for a primary school child to multiply 895 and 568 is rugged, explaining to him to multiply this may be troublesome and a burden for him. But there are instances when a child learns to multiply numbers of this extent using an abacus it becomes easy for him/her.

So, it could be concluded that training before normal maturation is generally beneficial or harmful depending on the method used in training.

2(B). The term development" is generally used to refer to the dynamic process by which an individual grows and changes throughout its lifespan. It is often thought of as the process of qualitative change taking place from conception to death. In this way, development is a broad term and deals with all areas including physical, motor, cognitive, physiological, social, emotional, and personality. It should be noted that developments in all these areas are interrelated.

- Cephalo - Caudal Sequence: The direction of development is from head to limbs i.e, in a longitudinal axis called 'cephalocaudal'.
- Proximo distal Sequence: The spinal cord develops before the outer parts of the body. The child's arms develop before the hands and the hands and feet develop before the fingers and toes. The development direction is from the center to the periphery called 'proximodistal'.
- Locomotion Sequence: Various kinds of motions such as walking, running, jumping, swimming, etc. by the body are known as locomotion. Movement is one of the characteristic features of all living organisms. Locomotion helps us to move from one place to another.
- Bilateral Sequence: The human body plan is bilateral with symmetrical sense organs, a fast responding brain, half the body weight in muscles, a powerful heart, miles of arteries and veins, and a brain that coordinates it all.

So, we can conclude that the Proximo distal Sequence is appropriate when development proceeds from the center to the peripheral areas of the body.

3(C). According to the question girl's parents are sportspersons and she obtained training from coaching. Both of her parents are sportspersons. So, we can say that her capabilities depend on heredity and the environment.

- The individual's personality is the product of both heredity and environment.

- Heredity determines a child's potential, while the Environment influences the extent to which that potential is achieved.

Role of Heredity and Environment:

Heredity	Environment
• Heredity or "Natu re" • Strong Influence on Physical Devel opment. • Physical Makeup, that a child Inheri ts from parents.	• Environment o r "Nature" • Everything sur rounds and infl uences a child. • Family, School, Neighbours, M edia, etc.

So, from the points, as mentioned above, it becomes clear that the girl's capabilities are most likely to be the result of an interaction between heredity and the environment.

4(A). Socialization is a process of internalizing the norms, culture, values, and customs of society to be socially acceptable. Peer groups are the agents of 'Secondary Socialization' throughout one's life.

Peer groups help children to be socialized by making them learn to behave in a way that is socially acceptable with age-peers. At this age, children learn appropriate social attitudes such as how to like and enjoy social life and group activities.

5 TYPES OF SOCIALIZATION	
1. P rim ary Soc iali zat ion	• It happens during infancy and c hildhood. It refers to the process where the child becomes socializ ed through the family in the earl y childhood years. • This highlights that the key agen t in the process of primary social ization is the family. • For example, a very young child i n a family has little knowledge o f his culture. Through the family, the child learns what is accepted and what is not in a particular so ciety.
2. S eco nd ary Soc iali zat ion	• It occurs once the infant passes i nto the childhood phase and con tinues into maturity. It refers to t he process that begins in the late r years through agencies such as neighborhoods, schools, and pee r groups. • During this phase more than the family, some other agents of soc ialization like the neighborhood, school, and peers' group begin to play a role in socializing the chil d. • For example, Schools help childr en in learning the importance of social cohesion and unity and inc ulcating the informal cues about social roles through interaction.
3.D eve	• It is the process of learning beha vior in a social institution or dev

lop me nt Soc iali zat ion	eloping social skills
4. Ant ici pat ory Soc iali zat ion	• It refers to the mental rehearsal s, concrete plans, and subtle cha nges in values and perceptions t hat a significant difference in soc ial roles is about to occur.
5. Re- soc iali zat ion	• It refers to the process of discard ing former behavior patterns an d accepting new ones as part of a transition in one's life. This occu rs throughout human life. • (Schaefer & Lamn, 1992)

5(A). Lev Vygotsky was a Russian psychologist and a social constructivist. He has propounded 'Socio-cultural Theory' which emphasizes the role of social interaction in cognitive development.

- Lev Vygotsky emphasized that the acquisition of speech is the major activity in cognitive development.
- Vygotsky embedded in this theory, the concept of 'private speech' which is a kind of speech directed to the self with no communicative function.
- Children use private speech to guide their actions by speaking to themselves.

Private Speech:

- It refers to the speech produced aloud by young children that seem to be addressed either to the self or others, which sometimes cannot be easily conceived by a listener.
- It has a significant role in the augmentation of the self and self-consciousness. It is the main aspect in the development of self and subjectivity.
- This phenomenon starts in the early years of life and proceeds to the end of adolescence and even later.

So, from the points, as mentioned above, it becomes clear that the above-mentioned kind of 'private speech' is a sign of Self-regulation.

6(D). 'Lev Vygotsky', a Soviet psychologist, has propounded the "Socio-cultural Theory". This theory implies the idea that social interaction plays a crucial role in the development of learners' cognitive ability.

In Vygotsky's view, the above-mentioned kind of support is called 'scaffolding' as it refers to a process through which:

- required assistance is given to children according to their individual needs.
- temporary support is imparted to the children to enhance their learning skills.
- individualized support is provided to

children to increase their learning boundaries.

So, it could be concluded that in Vygotsky's view, the above-mentioned kind of support is called 'scaffolding'.

- Abstract thinking is the ability to think about objects, principles, and ideas that are not physically present. It is a great way to generate new ideas and gain new insights during any problem-solving process.
- Peer tutoring refers to the learning process where fellow students teach each other. In this strategy, a higher-performing student is paired with a lower-performing student to teach specific skills.
- Generalization refers to the tendency to have conditioned responses caused by related stimuli.

7(A). John Dewey, an American philosopher has proposed the concept of 'P **rogressive Education' which emphasizes that learning takes place only through 'hands-on' approach so the students must interact with their environment to adapt and learn.**

Belief in the capability and potential of every child is central to the concept of progressive education as it promotes:

- emphasizes to enhance skills and understanding of the learners by engaging with the contents and experiences.
- promotes 'learning by doing' to make children self-reliant and productive to use their knowledge and talents effectively.
- ensures the active participation of students by working in a group and applying practical knowledge to complete an activity.

So, it could be concluded that belief in the capability and potential of every child is central to the concept of progressive education.

8(B). Intelligence refers to a set of different cognitive abilities to think rationally, act purposefully, resolve problems and deal with the demands of the environment.

The Theory of Multiple Intelligence:

Howard Gardner proposed this theory wherein he formulated eight categories of intelligence. He defined intelligence as "Intelligence is a bio-psychological potential to process information that can be activated in a cultural setting to solve problems or create products that are of value in a culture".

To define intelligence more broadly, Gardner established several criteria for defining intelligence:

- the potential for brain isolation by brain damage
- its place in evolutionary history
- the presence of core operations

- susceptibility to encoding
- a distinct developmental progression
- the existence of idiot-savants, prodigies and other exceptional people
- support from experimental psychology
- support from psychometric findings

From the criteria mentioned above he formulated the following types of intelligence:

Type of Intelligence	Description
Linguistic	ability to effectively use language to express oneself
Logical-mathematical	ability to analyse problems logically, perform mathematical operations and scientific investigation
Spatial	ability to recognise and manipulate wide spaces such as navigation
Musical	ability to recognise and compose musical patterns
Bodily-kinesthetic	ability to use mental abilities to coordinate bodily movements
Interpersonal	ability to understand the intentions, motivations & desires of people
Intrapersonal	ability to understand oneself, appreciate one's feelings, fears, and motivations
Naturalistic	nature, nurturing, and relating information to one's natural surroundings

From the above table, it becomes clear that 'skeptical' is not a type of intelligence formulated by Howard Gardner.

9(B). The 'Theory of Multiple Intelligence' or 'Multidimensional Intelligence Theory' was propounded by an American psychologist 'Howard Gardner' in his book 'Frames of Mind'.

This theory describes eight different kinds of intelligence and emphasizes that:
- intelligence is of several kinds.
- intelligence can't be tied to a single domain.
- each individual has his/her own unique abilities.
- intelligence is not dominated by a general factor.

So, it could be concluded that the Theory of multiple intelligence emphasize that there are several forms of intelligence.

10(B). Noam Chomsky, known as the father of modern linguistics, has made a crucial contribution in the field of linguistics.

Let's understand Chomsky's view about language in brief:
- Innate ability: He strongly believes that children are born with an innate knowledge of grammar that serves as the basis for all language acquisition.
- Generative grammar: According to Chomsky it refers to a finite set of rules to generate sentences and can be used to produce more sentences in that language.
- Universal grammar: Chomsky's universal grammar suggests that all children have an innate ability to acquire, understand and develop grammar.
- Language Acquisition Device: Chomsky proposed that humans are equipped with a language acquisition device that enables a child to acquire and produce language.

A brief description of other psychologists:

Alfred Binet	A French psychologist, is known for developing the first intelligence test and the concept of mental age.
Ivan Pavlov	The Russian Psychologist propounded 'The Theory of Classical Conditioning' which emphasizes that behaviour is learnt by a repetitive association between the response and the stimulus.
Abraham Maslow	An American psychologist, best known for creating "Maslow's Hierarchy of Needs", in which he proposed a series of needs.

So, Noam Chomsky is associated with 'language development'.

11(A). Classroom Discussions play a vital role in shaping or constructing the overall personality of a child. The discussions help the child to not only presents his or her point of view but to get an idea of other's perception as well and this helps in shaping the all-round thinking of a child.

Gender Bias:
- It refers to the belief that someone prioritizes one gender more than another.
- It is a form of unconscious bias, or implicit bias, which occurs when one individual attributes certain attitudes and stereotypes to another person or group of people.
- It is a preference or prejudice toward one gender over the other for example preferring boys over girls during an activity. Bias can be conscious or unconscious and may manifest in many ways, both subtle and obvious.

Examples of Gender Bias in Teaching and at school:
- Stereotypical expressions of male and female characters in textbook content.
- Assigning work differentially to boys and girls.
- Girls being given lesser opportunities to participate in school and classroom events.

Gender Constancy: The concept of gender constancy refers to a cognitive stage of development of children at which they come to understand that their gender (meaning their biological sex) is fixed and cannot change over time.

Gender Relevance: It is an important consideration in development. It is a way of looking at how social norms and power structures impact on the lives and opportunities available to different groups of men and women.

Gender Identity: It is a personal conception of oneself as male or female. This concept is intimately related to the concept of gender role, which is defined as the outward manifestations of personality that reflect gender identity.

So, during a classroom discussion if a teacher pays more attention to boys than girls then it will be regarded as an example of Gender Bias.

12(C). Individual difference: Every child is unique and different from others. It should be kept in mind that learners possess different abilities, and personalities, and belong to different backgrounds. The stimulus needs of every learner will be different. Teaching has to be done keeping in mind the individual differences and problems arising out of it.

The teacher should take care of the below points:
- As per the need of the students, the teaching method can vary.
- Generally confused with discrimination, ability grouping is a measure in which students of similar traits are grouped so that the teacher can choose a compatible teaching method.
- Keeping in mind the child-centered education as proposed by the NCF, adjusting the curriculum is no exception because it is the child who has the freedom to choose what he wants to learn.
- The pace of learning should not be a matter of concern for a teacher as every child has his pace and more than results, the attempt to learn is important.

It should be noted that, though self-study improves knowledge, it should not be done simultaneously when the teacher's responsibility is to teach children.

So, we conclude that for a teacher, leaving children for self-study is not recommended

13(D). Continuous and Comprehensive Evaluation, commonly known as 'CCE', was introduced as a school-based evaluation system by the CBSE in 2009 with the enactment of the Right to Education Act.

- Continuous and comprehensive Evaluation mainly aims at promoting Inclusive education.
- CCE can be incorporated in the inclusive classroom while engaging in teaching through a variety of activities.
- Incorporating strategies for attending to diverse needs in classrooms would be particularly useful in developing CCE processes for the classroom.

Aims of CCE:

- Emphasizing continuity and regularity of assessment.
- Assessing both scholastic and co-scholastic aspects of a child's growth.
- Emphasize the thought process and de-emphasize memorization as CCE includes all aspects of students' development.
- Recording the methods of learning to make the required improvements.
- Making evaluation an integral part of learning through diagnostic and remedial teaching.
- Evaluating children comprehensively rather than focus only on cognitive or intellectual functioning.
- Ensuring all-around development of students including cognitive, psychomotor, and affective domains.
- Evaluate every aspect of the child during their presence at the school.
- Developing a student's cognitive, psychomotor, and affective domains.
- Assessing both scholastic and co-scholastic aspects of a child's growth.
- Evaluation of the interest of the child during their presence at the school.
- Observing and recording the methods of learning to make improvements.

So, we can conclude that Continuous and Comprehensive Evaluation mainly aims at promoting Inclusive education.

14(D). Continuous and Comprehensive Evaluation (CCE) refers to a system of school-based evaluation of students that covers all aspects of students' development.

- CCE was introduced by the Central Board of Secondary Education (CBSE) in India to evaluate the student's development in all aspects throughout the academic year on a continuous basis.
- The objective of CCE is to make evaluation an integral part of learning through diagnostic and remedial teaching.
- CCE helps improve student's performance by identifying his/her learning difficulties at regular intervals right from the beginning of the academic session and employing suitable remedial measures for enhancing their learning performance.

CCE describes two different types of evaluations which include summative and formative assessment/evaluation.

- "Summative Evaluation", commonly known as "Assessment of Learning" is a type of evaluation which:
  - measures, certifies, and reports the level of students' learning by assessing them at the end of the term.
  - produces an accurate description of students' potential and achievement to promote them to the next grades.
- "Formative evaluation", commonly known as "Assessment for Learning" is a type of evaluation which:
  - monitor the child's progress throughout the teaching-learning process and improve students' academic achievements.
  - diagnoses and removes the learning difficulties of students with appropriate strategies.

So, it becomes clear that Continuous and Comprehensive Evaluation includes both formative and summative assessments using a wide variety of strategies.

15(A). According to Ross, "Thinking is a mental activity in its cognitive aspect of mental ability with regard to the psychological object."

According to Garrett, "Thinking is behaviour which is often implicit and hidden and in which symbols (images, ideas, and concepts) are ordinarily employed."

Critical Thinking: The ability to apply reasoning and logic to new or unfamiliar situations, ideas, and opinions. It refers to the process of judging or analyzing facts, events, etc. It requires proper analysis, evaluation, inference, and explanation.

- Critical thinking is self-guided, self-disciplined thinking which attempts to reason at the highest level of quality in a fair-minded way. People who think critically consistently attempt to live rationally, reasonably, and empathically.
- People use the intellectual tools that critical thinking offers – concepts and principles that enable them to analyze, assess, and improve their thinking.
- Thinking critically involves seeing and observing things in an open-minded way and examining an idea or concept in a way to form as many angles as possible.
- It can be enhanced by asking children to discuss among themselves in groups followed by sharing in a large group.

Abstract thinking is the ability to understand real concepts, such as freedom or vulnerability, but not directly tied to concrete physical objects and experiences.

So, self-guided, self-disciplined thinking which attempts to reason at the highest level of quality in a fair-minded way is called critical thinking.

16(B). Exceptional children are those who deviate from the normal population and need special education services to meet their needs. It includes children who are gifted, backward, creative, learning disabled, educationally retarded, etc.

The above-mentioned characteristic is related to 'Educationally retarded children' as a class consists of students with varying learning abilities as some learn fast and some learn slowly.

'Educationally retarded children':

- An educationally retarded child is not mentally retarded or physically disabled.
- He may have a neurological handicap or emotional disorder which hinders their abilities.
- Appropriate training is required to make educationally retarded children learn some self-care and communication skills.
- Educationally retarded children show the inability to do the work of the class below that which is normal for their age.

So, it could be concluded that if a child 'who is in the middle of his school (that is about ten and half years) is unable to do the work of the class below that which is normal for his age" is known as 'Educationally retarded children'.

Mental retardation: It refers to an intellectual disability characterized by low Intelligence Quotient (IQ) and impairments in adaptive daily life skills.

Moron: A child with mild intellectual disability and an IQ of (51-70).

Idiot: A child with the least intelligence on the IQ scale (0-25).

17(B). Creativity is a cognitive ability to produce something original by offering a fresh perspective. It is the ability possessed by people who are creative, persistent, and imaginative.

Creativity is related to divergent thinking which refers to a way of solving problems by more than one approach. It is goal-directed thinking which is unusual, novel, and useful and includes brainstorming and out-of-the-box thinking in it

- Creative children are those who show high-performance capability in several areas such as artistic and creative work, leadership quality, keen power of observation, etc.
- These children have divergent thinking and are very curious in nature that's why sometimes the classroom seems monotonous to them because they grab things fastly than of their age-peers.

Trait (ability) of a creative child:

- Elaboration
- Abstracting ability
- Fluency & Flexibility
- Originality & Novelty
- Sensitivity of problems

Characteristics of Creative Children:

- Perceive relation between impossible things.
- Curious, extrovert, and ambitious in nature.

- Think quickly and solve problems in a novel way.
- Convert imaginative and original ideas into reality.
- Use divergent and out-of-the-box thinking in different situations.
- Try new things and risk failure in executing innovative ideas.

Accuracy refers to the ability to do anything without making any mistakes. it is the state of being precise and accurate. It is not necessary that every time the creative child will be accurate as it is natural for them also to make mistakes.

So, it could be concluded that 'Accuracy' is not a trait (ability) of a creative child.

18(A). Learning disability includes distinguished from the things related to a logical arrangement like unable to write, read or sturring, etc. Children with learning disabilities experience difficulty in learning and using certain skills namely reading, writing, listening, and reasoning.

Errors in writing like reverse images, mirror imaging, etc represent learning disabilities. Dyslexia is the most common learning disability which results in reverse or mirror images of the alphabet.

Dyslexia is a learning disability that makes learners:

- unable to read and interpret letters and words.
- confuse with the same shapes and sounds of the alphabet.
- bewilder in identifying and relating speech sounds with letters and words.

Types of Learning Disability: It is categorized either by the type of information processing that is affected or by the specific difficulties caused by a processing deficit.

Learning Disabilities	Related to
Dysgraphia	Writing disability, inability to write properly, illegible handwriting
Dysphasia	Speech and language disorders
Dyscalculia	Mathematics disability, difficulty in learning mathematical concepts and organizing numbers besides, subtraction, multiplication, division
Dyspraxia	Difficulty with motor skills, non-verbal learning disability, motor clumsiness, and poor visual-spatial skills
Dysnomia	Inability to retrieve or recall appropriate words for oral or return language

Learning disability constitutes a condition that affects learning and intelligence across all areas of life.

A learning difficulty constitutes a condition that creates an obstacle to a specific form of learning but does not affect the overall IQ of an individual.

So, we can conclude that child is showing signs of a learning disability.

19(A). Children are divided into different categories based on their interests, behavior, nature, I.Q level, understanding, grasping abilities, etc. Children live through critical phases of development, which influence their behavior.

- Most children learn to adapt well to this changing nature of skill demand, but some of these children find it difficult to do so.
- Further, much problematic behaviour which goes unnoticed or even tolerated in a home setting becomes more conspicuous in the school environment due to competition and frequent evaluation.
- Common problematic behaviours are attention deficit hyperactivity disorder, learning disability, bullying, and delinquent behaviour.

Problematic children are particularly those who are difficult to teach, due to a lack of self-control and disruptive and antisocial behavior.

Making an effort to bring change in a child's environment and attitude will be the best way for bringing change in the behavior of a problematic child as:

- A good learning environment helps in building a culture of mutual trust and respect that engages the learners meaningfully in the task of learning.
- Besides that, it also supports a relationship between teaching and learning that helps in improving childhood mental health and academic performance.
- By bringing a change in attitude child's thinking, feeling and behavior could be influenced towards a place, people, or situation.

So, it could be concluded that making effort to bring change in a child's environment and attitude will be the best way for bringing change in the behavior of a problematic child.

20(D). In the teaching-learning process, visually challenged learners suffer from an issue with sight or vision but when they are facilitated with the right training and tools, they develop a good literacy ability.

Instructional adaptations that a teacher should make while working with visually challenged learners include:

- using a lot of touches and feel materials.
- giving verbal clues to create opportunities to imagine.
- introducing tactile materials during classroom discussions.
- speaking clearly and loudly with appropriate pauses and reiterations.
- providing learning with the help of auditory systems such as an audio CD of the textbook, radio, etc.
- using the braille system to make them read-write as its raised dots will help the child to study the words through the pattern.

A teacher should not use a variety of visual presentations and written tasks especially worksheets for visually challenged learners as it could lead to low self-esteem and feeling of failure in them.

So, it could be concluded that a teacher should speak clearly and use a lot of touches and feel materials while working with visually challenged learners.

Tactile materials: It refers to the inputs which children receive through the receptive sensors of their skins.

Braille system: It refers to a pattern of raised dots called "Braille" to represent letters, numbers, and punctuation marks, that can be felt with a finger.

21(D). Error: When a learner can't master a topic, he/she is vulnerable to make errors. Errors are nothing but incorrectness made by a child during learning.

Misconceptions: It takes place due to the mismatch in previously assimilated and newly accommodated knowledge.

Children's errors and misconceptions:

- are significant steps in the teaching-learning process.
- are necessary in the learning process to give insight into children's thinking.
- help the teacher to be aware of learners' learning styles, to cater them according to their needs.
- are considered as a part of the teaching-learning process as it helps to understand the child.

So, it could be concluded that children's errors and misconceptions are a significant step in the teaching-learning process.

22(D). A learning curve visualizes changes in pupil overall performance over time. The line graph displays opportunities across the x-axis, and a measure of student performance along the y-axis. A good learning curve which is also known as the 'experience curve', reveals improvement in pupils' performance as opportunity count (i.e., exercise practice with a given knowledge component) increases.

- Learning curve was first defined by Hermann Ebbinghaus in 1885.
- By learning curve, learners can relate his/her development through the method visually presented in the graph.
- There are 3 varieties of the curve of learning i.e. concave curve, convex curve, and concave and convex curve/ Combination type curve.

Let's Understand in Brief:

Concave curve	It is a slow initial improvement and learning increases with time. When the task is difficult we get such type of learning curve.
Convex curve	It depicts rapid initial improvement in learning that slows down with time. When the task is simple and the learner has previous practice on a similar task, we get this type of learning curve.
Combination type curve	It is the combination of the convex-concave curve that looks like the capital letter 'S'. The curve takes a concave or convex shape, in the beginning, depending upon the nature of the task.

So, it could be concluded that longitudinal is not the curve of learning.

23(B). Learning is a comprehensive process that refers to a change in behavior, knowledge, and skills as a result of practice and experience. It is difficult to give a precise definition of learning so every psychologist has different beliefs about the derivation of the word 'learning' and they have defined it in different ways.

Some well-known definitions of learning are as follows:

Psychologist	Definition of learning
J.P. Guilford	"Learning is any change in behaviour, resulting from behaviour."
Woodworth	"Learning is the process of acquiring new knowledge and new responses."
B.F. Skinner	"Learning is a process of progressive behaviour adaptation."
Crow & Crow	"Learning is the acquisition of knowledge, habits, and attitudes. It involves new ways of doing things and it operates in an individual's attempts to overcome obstacles or to readjust to new situations. It represents a progressive change in behaviour."

So, it could be concluded that the above-mentioned definition of learning is given by J.P. Guilford.

24(D). The active participation and involvement of children play a very vital role in learning and shaping the personality of a child.

A child-centered method is one that gives primacy to children's experiences and needs and provides ample opportunities for the children.

- While investigating the problems, it is often found that children break the problem into parts and analyze it, then they try solving the parts logically, this critical thinking shapes the child to be Scientific Investigators.
- When a child is encouraged to be self-dependent, it helps in developing thoughts and rationality in them and they try multiple ways to find a solution, and doing this multiple times helps them evolve as a Problem Solver.
- Children are Active Explorers of the environment as they are excited to learn about what is this, why it is here, how it is working, etc. They ask many questions about objects and situations in their surroundings.

So, the statements about children emphasizing to be Scientific Investigators, Problem Solver, and Active Explorers of the environment are correct.

25(D). Naive Conceptions (also referred to as commonsense theory or folk theory) is a coherent set of knowledge and beliefs about a specific content domain (such as physics or psychology), which entails ontological commitments, attention to domain-specific causal principles, and appeal to unobservable entities.

- Teaching and learning are complements of each other.
- Changes in teaching methods and techniques are required to make learning more effective.
- As a teacher, it is very important to understand children's needs, curiosities, and problems.

By knowing the naive conceptions, the teacher can plan to make his teaching work more meaningful.

For example, if the child is comfortable reading and learning in the mother tongue if his concept is taught, then teaching can be made more meaningful for the teacher.

So, knowing the naive conceptions that students bring to the classroom, helps the teacher to plan to teach more meaningfully.

26(C). The constructivist approach to learning is based on the idea that meaningful learning takes place when learners actively construct their own knowledge. It allows learners to foster their own strategies of learning to perform a task.

- In order to follow a constructivist approach to deal with the misconceptions carried by students, a teacher should give opportunities for experimentation and observation to counter misconceptions.
- It will help the student to search for the truth and they can test their misconceptions whether they are true or not.
- They will build their knowledge on the basis of experiments and experiences, which will clear the ambiguity related to their misconceptions.

Thus, it is concluded that Give opportunities for experimentation and observation to counter misconceptions is a constructive approach for dealing with the 'misconceptions' carried by students.

27(D). Emotion is a mental state associated with fear, anger, love, etc. Cognition is the process of acquiring knowledge through experiences and senses.

Cognition describes how mental processes i.e. learning, remembering, problem-solving, and thinking develop from birth until adulthood . Understanding cognitive development is useful in determining the kind of thinking children are capable of at different age levels.

- The relationship between cognition and emotion has fascinated important thinkers within the intellectual tradition. Physical, cognitive, emotional, and social development in a child is the development of an integrated and holistic fashion.
- Cognition is closely intertwined with emotions and language. Mind states are powerful determinants of one's current judgments and decision-making, which often effect once performance outcome in a task both in social and non-social contexts.
- Emotions or emotional approach is a psychological construct that involves the use of emotional processing and emotional expression in response to a different situation.
- The relationship between cognition and emotions is bi-directional - a dynamic interplay .
- Emotions are experienced as positive feelings, negative feelings, and undesired reactions to any stressful situation, these often impact decision making i.e. cognition.
- The Emotional Approach involves the conscious use of emotional expression and processing to better deal with stressful situations.

So, the relationship between cognition and emotions is bi-directional i.e. a dynamic interplay between both cognition and emotions.

28(B). Learning is a process by which the individual acquires various habits, knowledge, and attitude that are necessary to meet the demands of life in general. There are different factors that affect learning.

These include learner-centered factors like motivation, needs, self-concept, interests, goals, level of aspiration, etc., teacher and task-related factors such as teaching style, classroom ethos, transactional skills, and methodology, etc., and environmental factors such as the physical and psychological structures in which learning occurs.

Ashok is very fond of playing cricket and he is very good at it too. He is the captain of his college team. He spends long hours playing or watching cricket and never gets tired or bored. Motivation and personal factors is affecting learning in this example.

- Ashok is intrinsically motivated i.e. he derives internal satisfaction from the game. Intrinsic motivation is closely related to one's need for self-fulfillment, and achievement.
- These needs impel us to become better by learning more, interacting with our environment, and developing ourselves.
- Learning is most effective when there is intrinsic motivation - a desire to learn from within, which finds satisfaction in the achievement itself and does not bother about other factors.

Thus, it is concluded motivation is the personal factor that affects learning in the given an example.

Maturation: A one-year-old cannot be made to write and a three months old child cannot walk. Unless the learner has 'matured' optimally, he cannot learn. In order for learning to take place, physical, intellectual, and socio-emotional maturation is essential. Also, individual variations in the process of maturation should be acknowledged and appropriately dealt with.

Self-concept: Self-concept is very important in matters of learning because it influences individual differences in learners, in their learning orientations, cognitive styles, and the self-learning strategies which they use.

Level of aspiration: This refers to the extent to which an individual wish to strive to achieve. It emanates from the targets, goals, and ambitions that individuals construct for themselves.

29(D). Learning is a process by which behaviour is either modified or changed through experience or training. Learning is thus a relatively permanent change in response potentiality which occurs as a function of reinforced practice.

Teacher-related factors affecting learning:

- Teacher's Knowledge over the subject matter : Teachers who are firmly rooted in their subject knowledge make clearer presentations and recognize students' difficulties readily. He/she should be able to undertake application-oriented teaching as well.
- The leadership style adopted by the teacher in terms of whether it is authoritarian, democratic, benevolent, or indifferent greatly influences how the students will respond and involve themselves in the learning tasks.

- The relationship which teachers have with their students also sets the tone and climate of the classroom.
- The evaluative comments that teachers make either verbally or in writing also have a great bearing on students learning. They have the power to motivate and encourage or stifle and discourage.
- Apart from expectations, there are many other characteristics related to teachers that influence their learners and the teaching-learning process. The most significant among these are modeling, enthusiasm, caring, and positive expectations .
- Research indicates that teachers who present information enthusiastically , increase learners' self-efficacy, attributions of effort and ability, self-confidence, and achievement.
- The caring attitude of a teacher and how he/she communicates it is another important factor, Caring refers to a teacher's ability to emphasize and invest in the protection and development of her learners.

From the above, we can conclude that mastery over the subject matter is a teacher-related factor affecting learning.

30(D). Learning is an active process, transferable, measurable and goal-oriented. It is the desired change or modification of behaviour attained through experience and environment. It is both a formal and informal process, it is universal and continuous. From birth, every child should have access to high-quality learning opportunities for language, literacy and mathematics. These should be available in all early years settings, including the home, and facilitated by parents.

- Psychological Factors: Psychological factors are unique or specific to the individuals engaged in the process of learning. Thorough knowledge and understanding of these factors are very essential for the teachers and parents in providing and guiding learning among the children.
  ◦ Intelligence
  ◦ Motivation
  ◦ Maturation for Readiness to Learn
  ◦ Emotions
  ◦ Interests
  ◦ Attitudes
  ◦ Self-Concept
  ◦ Learning Styles
- Socio-Cultural (Environmental) Factors Influencing Learning: The socio-cultural environment, within which a child grows, has a significant impact on his/her learning. In fact, all learning occurs with special reference to the cultural context of an individual. The social constructivist view of psychology holds that all learning is culturally oriented and guided. For our own understanding,

we can subdivide socio-cultural factors into a) family, b) neighbourhood and community; and c) socio-cultural diversities like caste, class, ethnicity, religion, etc. Also, since, socio-culture factors are affecting learning, so does economic factor, because, suppose, a poor boy may not have access to online learning while a rich boy may have.

- School-Related Factors Influencing Learning: Learning is also assumed to be greatly influenced by the school and the school environment in which students are imparted with different types of learning experiences. The term 'school environment' encompasses the terms 'school culture' and 'school climate' that affect the behaviour of teachers and students.
- Teaching-Learning Processes Related Factors Influencing Learning: It includes methods of learning and the influence of media on learning.

So, we conclude that all the facts influence student difficulty in learning.

31(C). As we can see in the first paragraph of the passage, it is clearly mentioned that "when we pick up a daily newspaper, we invariably find an increased incidence of vandalism, fraud, theft, robbery, rape, child spouse, battered spouses, murders, hate crimes, genocide (now termed as "ethnic cleansing") along with a multitude of other senseless violent acts that have become disturbingly common".

Thus, it is concluded that newspapers are full of news about acts of crime and violence these days.

32(C). The underlined word significance is a noun that means a word (other than a pronoun) used to identify any of a class of people, places, or things (common noun), or to name a particular one of these (proper noun).

It can be defined as any member of a class of words that typically can be combined with determiners to serve as the subject of a verb, can be interpreted as singular or plural, can be replaced with a pronoun, and refer to an entity, quality, state, action, or concept.

Significance can be defined as the quality of being important.

33(C). Futility means the quality or state of being futile; uselessness.

Usefulness means the quality or fact of being useful.

From the above meanings, it is evident that usefulness is the correct antonym of the word futility.

The meaning of the other given words are as follows:

- Pointlessness - The fact of having no purpose or of being a waste of time.
- Vanity - excessive pride in or admiration of one's own appearance or

achievements.

- Failure - lack of success.

34(D). As we can see in the second paragraph of the passage, it is clearly mentioned that "when the significance of good self-esteem is well understood and it achieves the prominence it deserves, a transformation will begin, for as the people will learn they are deserving of self-respect, their respect for others will automatically increase".

Thus, it is concluded that good self-esteem is stressed because it helps one to respect others.

35(B). Vandalism means an action involving deliberate destruction of or damage to public or private property.

Destruction means the action or process of causing so much damage to something that it no longer exists or cannot be repaired.

From the above meanings, it is evident that destruction is the correct synonym of the word vandalism.

The meaning of the other given words are as follows:

- Construct - build or make (something, typically a building, road, or machine).
- Build - construct (something) by putting parts or materials together.
- Mend - repair (something that is broken or damaged).

36(B). The error is in part (B).

Whether- "or" is correlative conjunction.

Example: I didn't know whether you'd want the cheesecake or the chocolate cake, so I got both.

So, in part (B), and should be replaced by or.

Correct part: whether personal, national, or global

Correct sentence: The solution to a great many problems, whether personal, national, or global, lies in improving our feelings

37(C). Let's refer to the lines:

- High self-esteem denotes that we accept ourselves unconditionally exactly as we are , and we appreciate our value as human beings.
- Vulnerable to the opinions of others, we desperately try to gain their recognition and approval sometimes through risky and dangerous behaviour. Thus, we are at the mercy of our emotions, instead of controlling them, we permit them to control us.
- Today when we pick up a daily newspaper, we invariably find an increased incidence of vandalism, fraud, theft, robbery, rape, child spouse, battered spouses, murders, hate crimes, genocide (now termed as "ethnic cleansing") along with a multitude of other senseless violent acts that have become disturbingly common. These are not the actions of people who like themselves.

Upon the perusal of the above lines, it can be concluded that A and B are true, and (C) is false.

38(B). Refer to para 4:

- If we cannot accomplish certain results, we tend to feel low about ourselves. Some of us try too hard and become workaholics and over-achievers. With a few genuine feelings of self-worth, we try to create some and prove that we are somebody by our successes and achievements.
- If we do finally achieve our goals we are disappointed; despite everything we have done, we still feel empty inside.

Upon the perusal of the above lines, it can be concluded that a person starts feeling empty inside when he pushes himself towards achieving goals and proving that he is somebody by his successes and achievements.

39(C). Adjectives are words that are used to describe or modify nouns or pronouns.

Goals is a noun. Unrealistic is a word that is modifying the word 'goals'. Thus, unrealistic is an adjective.

So, the part of speech of the underlined word is an adjective, making option (C) the correct answer choice.

Adjective modifies a noun while an adverb modifies a verb, adjective, adverb, or phrase.

40(B). Look at the lines:

There is a Reaper, whose name is Death,

_And, with his sickle keen

- The poem subverts the meaning of death.
- Death is a character in the poem .
- Death may seem merciless on the surface but it takes loved ones to a new world .
- Therefore, death is not gloomy or fearful.
- Gloomy means dark or poorly lit, especially so as to appear depressing or frightening.
- Thus, death is shown in a positive light.

41(D). Let us take a look at the line, 'And the mother gave, in tears and pain,/_The flowers she most did love;/She knew she should find them all again/_In the fields of light above.'

- It says the mother will meet her flowers in fields of light .
- 'Fields of light' is an allegory for Paradise .
- Paradise is the garden of Eden .
- Thus the mother will meet her flower in Paradise.

42(C). Let us take a look at the line, 'It was for the Lord of Paradise'.

The lines state that the flowers are for the 'Lord of Paradise'.

'Lord of Paradise' refers to God.

Thus, the flowers are for God.

43(A). The figure of speech is 'Alliteration'.

'A figure of speech' is a word or phrase that is used in a non-literal way to create an effect.

'Alliteration' is a literary device that reflects repetition in two or more nearby words of initial consonant sounds.

For example:

- rocky road.
- big business.

Similarly in the expression 'She knew she should find them all again', the figure of speech 'Alliteration' is used as consonant sound 's' is being repeated in she, she, and should.

44(C). Let us take a look at the line, 'And saints, upon their garments white, _These sacred blossoms wear.'

It is stated that saints wear the blossoms.

Blossoms are a kind of flower.

Thus, saints wear flowers over their white garments.

45(D). Let us take a look at the line, 'He gazed at the flowers with tearful eyes'.

It is stated that Death gazed at the flowers with tearful eyes.

Thus, Death gazed at the flowers with tearful eyes.

46(B). A great teacher is warm, accessible, enthusiastic, and caring. This is the teacher to whom students know they can go with any problems or concerns.

- Effective teachers strive to motivate and engage all their students in learning rather than simply accepting that some students cannot be engaged and are destined to do poorly.
- They believe every student is capable of achieving success at school and they do all they can to find ways of making each student successful.

Remedial teaching:

- During learning, a child makes mistakes. It is the job of a teacher to help students to correct those mistakes after diagnosing them.
- The method is known as remedial teaching. It helps the teacher to provide learners with the necessary help and guidance to overcome the problems.

The following are its characteristics:

- It can be used for improving language skills by revision, drill, situation communicative practice, and reviewing.
- For example, if a student is confused about the pronunciation of 'no' and 'know', he can be taught the concept of silent letters.
- It also helps teachers to know which areas are left during regular teaching. It is used by teachers to remove the weakness of the learner.
- It is carried out after the identification of problems and challenges faced by students. It is a systematic process as the

teacher first diagnoses the problem of students and then applies appropriate remedial methods.

So, it is concluded that remedial work for spoken English involves revision, drill, situation communicative practice, and reviewing.

47(D). Approach: The practices in language teaching are based on theories concerning the nature of language and language learning. These theories together form the first component of a method.

- Constructive approach: One of the most essential principles in the constructivist approach to language teaching is action-orientedness. Another principle of constructive approach refers to content-oriented language teaching and usually takes place in bilingual classes. A constructive approach to language teaching is based on the foundation that knowledge is constructed. Students are given the freedom to plan their choice and to be creative.
- Structural Approaches: Structural approach is a scientific study of the fundamental structures of the English language, their analysis, and logical arrangement. Every structure expresses an important grammatical point. A sentence needs a grammatical background. The different formats or patterns of words are called structures.
- Natural approaches: The theory is based on the notion that we learn the language the same way as we acquire our first language. It doesn't force to utter words or phrases, much less pronounce them correctly. There are no endless drills on correct usage and no mentions of grammar rules or long lists of vocabulary to wrap the head around.
- Deductive approaches refer to developing a Hypothesis. It is a testing of the Existing theory.

So, we conclude that the above situation

48(B). Different teachers would face different challenges in their regular teaching– in terms of the curriculum, classroom transactions, time and resource management, as well as dealing with individual students. These may change from time to time.

- A teacher should overcome the language barrier to go through the process of teaching-learning.
- The basis of the communication of ideas and information to the learners is the responsibility of the teacher.
- A teacher should use the child's language as a resource and start teaching.
- As mentioned in the question above, a teacher should not apply for transfer since it shows that he wants to run away from his duty.
- Communicating in English is not the

correct choice in such situations because not all students may be able to understand English.

Thus from the above-mentioned points, it is clear that a teacher should use the child's language as a resource while teaching.

The Three-Language Formula as Stated in the 1968 Policy is:

- The First language: It has to be studied must be the mother tongue or the regional language.
- The Second language: In Hindi-speaking States, the second language will be English or some other modern Indian language.
- In non-Hindi-speaking States, the second language will be Hindi or English.
- The Third language: The third language is taught at a later stage in school, and that too for a shorter time, as it is needed only in a limited context i.e. in a social situation where neither first nor second language could help the child to communicate.

49(B). Children learn various lessons of learning the English language throughout their school life. At various stages/standards, children learn different difficulty levels of English. For the students of class IV learning English, their learning outcomes include, reciting poems correctly, being responsive to simple announcements, they having a simple knowledge of correct punctuations in writing. The teacher can provide possible alternative corrections for the sentence as the students can get better insight about the words, and their usage and also learn about the flaws in the wrong sentence.

- The teacher does not have to tell them something is wrong as it will not help them in learning the correct usage.
- The teacher has to guide a little to the students and cannot just let them find the corrections on their own as it is not their level yet, they need guidance.
- Students of Class IV cannot recognize flawed usage or sentence construction when the teacher focuses on certain surface errors such as grammatical errors as they are learning only to know the basics of sentences and their usage in daily life and thus do not have that knowledge.

Thus, it is concluded that Students of Class IV can recognize flawed usage or sentence construction when the teacher gives alternatives as possible corrections.

50(D). Pedagogical grammar means that teaching grammar in context.

Pedagogical Grammar:

- It is a grammatical analysis and instruction designed for language students.
- It is a description of how to use the grammar of a language to communicate,

for people wanting to learn the target language.

- Pedagogical grammar is grammar in context to connect grammar points with real-life context.
- It focuses on how grammatical items may be made more learnable and teachable for meaningful learning.
- It is the study of the grammatical problems of learners or a combination of approaches.
- Pedagogical grammar is the learning of grammar in context through use.
- Pedagogic grammars contain assumptions about how learners learn, follow certain linguistic theories in their descriptions, and are written for a specific target audience.

51(B). Teaching aids or teaching-learning material is used by teachers to help learners to learn concepts with ease and efficiency. It can be an artificial or real object which makes learning more effective.

- A teacher found an advertisement pamphlet for the sale of biscuits. She uses it for reading and speaking activities in her class.
- He is using authentic text as the advertisement pamphlet is the authentic pamphlet that a shopkeeper is using to increase his sale of biscuits.
- Whereas Realia refers to the objects associated with everyday life to be used in the classroom. Using realia in the language class means bringing real objects as teaching aids.
- The advertisement pamphlet is a type of realia but if we have to say it more accurately, we will say it is an authentic text.
- The newspaper clipping and extra materials can be a type of realia also. But here as per the given question, the authentic text is best suited.

52(A). The five parts of language learning are:

- Listening
- Comprehension
- Speaking
- Reading
- Writing

If the student is able to perform successfully in all these skills, it shows that: He or she is proficient in the language.

Thus the correct answer is: "Measure the students' proficiency".

53(C). English is a global language spoken by 700 hundred million people in the world. It is officially recognized all over the world. It is the link language in India.

- It is a language of the library, language of media, language of trade, internet, commerce, business, international negotiations, and higher education.
- Since English is a language of international communication, learning

the English Language is a common goal for many people.

T o achieve the desired goals in English language teaching, a teacher uses various principles. Each of them is listed below along with its characteristics:

Concreteness	This principle implies the idea that the language used by the speaker must be concrete, specific, definite, concise, and considerable for a better understanding of the listener.
Selection and gradation	It deals with selecting age-appropriate teaching materials and placing the language materials properly in order or sequence. The material should be according to the child's mental age, mental ability, grade, and level.
Accuracy and Correctness	This principle implies the idea that a language learner must be accurate and correct in spelling, pronunciation, structure, expression, etc.
Proportion	Equal attention should be paid to all the aspects and skills of language learning along with equal balance should be maintained among all the elements of language teaching.
Purpose Related	If the purpose is decided in the beginning it becomes a simple affair to design a course suitable for that purpose. In the absence of any specific purpose they simply dragon.
Habit formation	A habit of listening to the sounds of English words, speaking English with proper accent and intonation, and spelling.
Motivation	The ways of arousing interest are linguistic games, use of gramophone records, use of flashcards and other audiovisual aids, conversational approach, pictures, models, etc.
Multiple lines of Approach	The teacher has to proceed simultaneously from many different points of view toward the goals to be realized by him. He has to select and reject judiciously without favor or prejudice, the material to be presented and the method of its presentation.
Interest	Children learn easily and quickly things in which they are interested.
Linking with Life	The job of an English teacher should be to encourage his students to use the learned structures of the English language in their daily life situations.

So, we conclude that the above statement deals with the Principle of Selection and gradation.

54(A). A multilingual classroom refers to a classroom in which learners can interact in their own language and can be a mix of words from more than one language.

This multilingual nature of the Indian classroom must be used as a resource so that every child could:

- feel secure and accepted.
- learn various language skills.
- connect the classroom with real life.
- express their thought in multiple ways.

So, we conclude that the multilingual nature of the Indian classroom must be used as a resource so that every child feels secure and accepted.

55(C). Aphasia is an impairment of language functioning caused by damage to the left hemisphere of the brain. There are different types of aphasias, for example; Broca's aphasia and Wernicke's aphasia.

Broca's aphasia is caused by damage to the brain's left frontal lobe area, responsible, in part, for controlling motor commands used in speech production. A person suffering from Broca's aphasia exhibits speech containing excess pauses and 52 slips of the tongue, and he has trouble finding words when talking. The person also fails to make use of function words such as a, the, and, of. For this reason, Broca's aphasics also produce ungrammatical sentences. Furthermore, they have a problem using syntactic information when understanding sentences. For example, while a Broca's aphasic has no trouble understanding a sentence such as "The bicycle that the man is holding is blue", but he has trouble comprehending a sentence such as "the dog that the woman is biting is grey."

Wernicke's aphasia is caused by damage to the left temporal lobe of the brain. It is characterized by notable impairment in the understanding of spoken words and sentences. People with Wernicke's aphasia have generally fluent phonetic and syntactic but semantically coherent speech.

Some other notable terms:

- The occipital cortex is located at the back and base of each cerebral hemisphere. It is responsible for the processing of the visual information that is received from the eyes. Any damage to the occipital lobe leads to problems in vision when flashes of light are seen, a visual hallucination or visual agnosia.

- Frontal lobes(left and right) are present in front of the brain. They are responsible for motor movements and fine movements, such as moving of a finger at a point of time, etc. Since it is connected to the limbic system, it also controls emotions. They are also involved in language functions (in most cases, the left frontal lobe). If there is any damage or lesion to the Broca's area, then it causes difficulties in producing and fluency in speech and sound, also called Broca's aphasia.

So, we conclude that Damage to Broca's area in the brain causes problems in speech production.

56(B). Vocabulary: It is a collection of words a person knows. uses or want to learn.

Types of Vocabulary:

Receptive Vocabulary: It refers to a word which an individual:

- recognises when he/she hears or sees it.
- understands and comprehends when others use it.
- perceives and retrieves while listening and reading the word.

Productive Vocabulary: It refers to a word which an individual:

- uses when he/she speaks or writes.
- frequently uses while writing or speaking.
- regularly uses to express his/her thoughts appropriately.

So, we conclude that Receptive Vocabulary are words we recognize when we hear or see and Productive Vocabulary are words we speak or write.

57(D). NCF (National Curriculum Framework) 2005 is one of the four NCFs published in India by NCERT. It seeks to provide a framework for the betterment of educational purposes and experiences.

- Language is a medium through which human beings tend to communicate with each other by using various attributes of a language that are symbols, gestures, words, etc.
- The main purpose of teaching a language is to enable the children to use it practically while communicating with others.

The objectives defined by NCF 2005 regarding language teaching-learning include:

Ability to understand various verbal and non-verbal clues

- A child must be able to understand various verbal and non-verbal clues coming from the speaker for comprehending what has been said i.e., the competence to understand what one says and what one hears.
- Verbal clues can be one/two-word phrases, etc. and non-verbal clues can be silence, facial expressions, hand movements, etc.

Ability to read with comprehension, and not merely decode:

- The ultimate test of reading ability is a critical appreciation of an unseen text that is at least one stage above the cognitive level of the reader.
- The child must be able to construct meaning by drawing inferences and relating to the text with his previous knowledge.
- He must also develop confidence in reading the text by critically analyzing it.

Ability to express effortlessly in a variety of situations

- The child should be able to employ her communicative skills in a variety of situations.
- He must be capable of expressing his ideas and thoughts in different kinds of situations smoothly.
- He must be able to engage in a discussion in a logical, analytical and creative manner.

The ability to write coherently by a proper organization of thoughts

- Writing involves a rich control on grammar, vocabulary, content, and punctuation as well as abilities to organize thoughts coherently often using a variety of cohesive devices such as linkers.
- A child should develop the confidence to express her thoughts effortlessly and in an organized manner.

Use of creativity

- In a language classroom, a child should get ample space to develop her imagination and creativity.
- Classroom ethos and healthy teacher-student relationships build confidence to enable the children to use their creativity.

So, it is clear that knowing the history of language is not an objective of language teaching-learning as per the objectives given by NCF-2005.

58(B). Language Acquisition is the process in which a child acquires the capacity to comprehend language. Language acquisition is the process in which a child learns his mother tongue. When language is learned without any practice and with the help of surroundings, it is known as language acquisition.

Theory of Second Language Acquisition: Stephen Krashen proposed the five main hypotheses, the input hypothesis is one of them. According to the Input hypothesis, comprehensible input refers to the input slightly above the learner's current level. It helps learners in language learning by making them able to:

- communicate efficiently.
- acquire language naturally.
- understand the text effectively.

The other hypotheses are given below:

Psycholo Theory	Main Idea

gist		
Levy Vygotsky	Socio-cultural Theory	Three stages of language that a child progresses through while developing language functions are social, private, and silent inner speech.
Noam Chomsky	Theory of language acquisition	Children are borns with an innate knowledge of grammar that serves as the basis for all language acquisition.
James Asher	Total Physical Response	Coordination of speech and student's physical movement is a good tool to be used in language learning.

So, we conclude that the term 'Comprehensible input' is associated with Stephen Krashen.

59(D). Reading texts typically implies a wide range of structures and vocabulary, registers and styles, formats, and patterns of organization. The type of reading activity we, engage in with such 'real' reading texts is also very different from the traditional classroom approach to a specially written text.

Verbs determine the relations between the different words in the sentence according to the grammar of the language. It treats the structure of sentences and their structural relationships with one another.

- A verb is a word or a combination of words that indicate an action or a state of being or condition. A verb is the part of a sentence that tells us the relationship between different parts of sentences like an affirmative sentence, negative sentence, complex sentences, etc.
- That verb may be a single word or a word made up of more than one word.
  - Examples:
  - Jacob walks in the morning.
  - Mike is going to school.
  - Albert likes to walk.
  - Anna is a good girl.

Nouns	
	Nouns are used to identify people, places, and things. For eg: cat.

Pronouns	
	A **pronoun is a word that is used instead of a Noun. Example: This, He, She, etc.**
Adverbs	Adverbs are used to give us more information and are used to modify verbs, clauses, and other adverbs. Example: Quickly, Gently, etc.

So, we can conclude that While reading a text, a Verb can help students understand the relations between the parts of a sentence.

60(B). Realia refers to the objects associated with everyday life to be used in the classroom. Using realia in the language class means bringing real objects as teaching aids as it is a tangible teaching-learning aid that:

- includes coins, newspapers, maps, tickets, fruits, vegetables, etc.
- makes learning more interesting by bringing the class to real life.
- ensures the use of accurate and realistic teaching-learning materials.
- Encourages classroom interaction and helps in meeting individual differences.

Realia has also been included as part of CLT (communicative language technique), i.e. posters, advertisements, maps, train schedules, and graphs. The tasks set have a specific communicative purpose and train the learners to be fluent as well as accurate, although CLT has tended to emphasize fluency over accuracy.

So, we conclude that using 'realia' in the language class means bringing real objects as teaching aids.

61(C).

- Duties that are imposed in order to counter the negative impact of import subsidies to protect domestic producers are called countervailing duties.
- In cases foreign producers attempt to subsidize the goods being exported by them so that it causes domestic production to suffer because of a shift in domestic demand towards cheaper imported goods, the government makes mandatory the payment of a countervailing duty on the import of such goods to the domestic economy.
- This raises the price of these goods leading to domestic goods again being equally competitive and attractive. Thus, domestic businesses are cushioned. These duties can be imposed under the specifications given by the WTO (World Trade Organization) after the investigation finds that exporters are

engaged in dumping.

- The Directorate General of Anti-Dumping & Allied Duties was constituted in April 1998. It is a Commerce's Minister investigation arm and is responsible for carrying out investigations and recommending, where required, under the Customs Tariff Act, the amount of anti-dumping duty/countervailing duty on the identified articles as would be adequate to remove injury to the domestic industry.

62(D). According to the Buddhist text Anguttara Nikaya , Surasena was one of the solasa (sixteen) Mahajanapadas (powerful realms) in the 6th century BCE.

Mahajanapadas with their Important Towns:

Mahajanapadas	Towns
Surasena	Mathura
Gandhara	Taxila
Anga	Champa
Avanti	Ujjain
Kamboja	Rajpur

So, we can say that the capital of Kamboja is Rajpur . It was located around Hindukush mountains of Kashmir.

Hence, the correct option is (D).

63(A). Rani Gaidinliu raised the banner of rebellion against foreign rule on the call given by Gandhiji and was imprisoned for life.

Rani Gaidinliu:

- She was born on 26 January 1915 in the northeastern state of Manipur.
- Rani Gaidinliu was awarded the Padma Bhushan award in the year 1982.
- She was also conferred with the 'Tamrapatra Freedom Fighter Award' in 1972.
- She joined the freedom struggle at the age of 13.
- Jawaharlal Nehru gave her the title of 'Rani'.

64(C). The issue on which the Civil disobedience movement of 1930 was launched was Salt monopoly exercised by the British Government.

On March 12, 1930, Indian independence leader Mohandas Gandhi begins a defiant march to the sea in protest of the British monopoly on salt, his boldest act of civil disobedience yet against British rule in India.

65(D). Fatehpur Sikri town was built by the Mughal Emperor, Akbar.

- He had planned this city as his capital but the shortage of water compelled him to abandon the city.
- After this within 20 years, the capital of Mughals was shifted to Lahore.
- Fatehpur Sikri was built between 1571 and 1585.

66(D). Aaram Bagh was originally built by the Mughal Emperor Babur in 1528.

- The Aaram Bagh is the oldest Mughal Garden in India, located in Agra, five kilometres northeast of the Taj Mahal.
- Before being interred in Kabul, Babur was temporarily buried there.
- The garden is a Persian garden, where the garden is divided by paths and canals to represent the Islamic ideal of paradise, a plentiful garden through which rivers flow.
- Two viewing pavilions face the Jamuna river and include an underground 'tahkhana' that was used to provide visitors with relief during the hot summers. There are numerous watercourses and fountains in the garden.

67(D). Tripura is surrounded by Bangladesh on its north, west, and south. It is surrounded by the state Mizoram and Assam on the eastern side. Agartala is the capital of Tripura. It is bordered by Bangladesh, Mizoram, and Assam.

68(B). In the region of the eastern shore of the Adriatic Sea, a cold and dry wind blowing down from the mountain is known as Bora.

Bora : It is a cold and dry wind, that blows from Hungary to North Italy in the region of the eastern shore of the Adriatic Sea.

69(B). Caucasus mountains separate the Black Sea and the Caspian Sea.

It is the point of intersection between Asia and Europe. It stretches in between the Caspian Sea and the Black Sea. It is the home to Mount Elbrus which is the highest peak in Europe.

70(B). Tropic of Capricorn does not pass from Bolivia.

The Tropic of Capricorn passes through 10 countries, 3 continents and 3 waterbodies. It passes through South America, Africa, and Australia. In the South America continent, it passes through 4 countries which include Chile, Argentina, Paraguay, and Brazil. In the African continent, it passes through Namibia, Botswana, Mozambique, South Africa, and Madagascar.

The Tropic of Capricorn passes through 3 waterbodies which include the Indian ocean, Atlantic ocean, and Pacific ocean.

71(C). A monopsony occurs when a firm has market power in employing factors of production. It means there are one buyer and many sellers.

When the market is under a monopsony, the market is dominated by a single buyer while, in the case of monopoly, a single seller is seen in the market.

An example of a monopsony is a company coal town, where the coal company acts as the sole employer.

72(D). The National Commission for Women (NCW) organized a workshop on 'Gender Responsive Governance' for elected women representatives (MLAs) under the 'She Is A Changemaker' project.

The three-day workshop is being organised in Dharamshala, Himachal Pradesh from June 22 to 24, 2022.

The Governor of Uttar Pradesh Anandiben Patel participated as Chief Guest in the inaugural ceremony on 22 June 2022.

73(D). The Centre has cleared the AGNIPATH Scheme for recruitment of youth in the armed forces.

The youth selected under this scheme will be known as Agniveers. They will be getting an attractive monthly package with risk and hardship allowances as applicable in the three services. They will be also paid one-time Seva Nidhi Package upon completion of engagement period of four years.

74(C). "Democratic institution" refers to an institution where decisions are made by majority vote. For instance, legislative bodies, electoral boards, executive bodies, and institutions, etc.

To prevent cynicism among students about democratic institutions, the teacher can follow the following strategies:

By emphasizing that social inequality is inevitable. This will allow students to know:

- Social inequality describes a condition in which people have different amounts of wealth, prestige, and power.
- In every society, we can see some degree of inequality.
- Social inequality is present in our society due to gender differences, economic position, religion, ethnicity, etc.

By indicating the role of informed public Steps that will cause cynicism are:

- By emphasizing the Ideal functioning and principles of democratic institutions.
- By indicating the impossibility of changing institutions.

From the above, it's clear that all the above points are correct for the above situation.

75(A). In order to promote cooperative learning in the classroom, a teacher should engage students in debate and discussions.

Ways to Promote Cooperative Learning in the Classroom:

- Facilitate classrooms with diverse and flexible social structures.
- Asked them to work together, promotes dialogue, which is the key to learning.
- Be open to other students' ideas and encourage their participation and make sure no one is left out.
- Engage students in debates and discussions.
- Every day one student of each group is designated as a facilitator. The facilitator

is not in-charge of the group, but simply keeps the group organized on a particular day.

76(C). Gender refers to the socially constructed differences between men and women. It refers to the masculine and feminine qualities, behaviour, roles, and responsibilities that society upholds. Gender can be changed / re-oriented.

Examples of Gender Stereotyping:
- Only boys being encouraged to participate in the football tournament.
- Only the girls in the class are asked to decorate the class boards.
- Boys and girls are made to sit in separate rows for ensuring discipline in class.

So, the given example, "While boys try to monopolise the class discussions, attention is given to both girls and boys to encourage participation." is not an example of gender stereotyping.

77(D). Project work is given in social science course mainly to connect learning at school with social realities.

A project is an activity-based method that provides learners with real-life experiences. It is a problematic act carried out in a natural setting. This method provides an opportunity to integrate the features of many other methods like field visits, activity-based methods, cooperative learning, concept mapping, map-based learning, etc.
- A project is student-centered rather than teacher-directed.
- The students plan, execute and evaluate the entire undertaking.
- Projects may be driven by a certain issue based on realities.
- It connects learning at school with social realities. The learned knowledge must serve the immediate needs of the students in their present life.

78(C). The first step of project method is creating the situation.

The project method is a method that emphasizes the voluntary participation of students by working in a group to complete a specific project.

It is the first step of the project method where the teacher creates/provides the situation related to the real-life problems to the students. The teacher gives the knowledge about the project method procedures, steps, and uses to the students.

79(D). Social Sciences include a body of knowledge, which deals with social and cultural aspects of human life. Social Sciences have emerged as distinct disciplines in order to be taught at different levels of the education system (starting from school level to higher education level) across the globe because of their immense importance for achieving better social cohesion, solidarity, and development.
- Like many other countries of the world,

in India, social sciences constitute a compulsory aspect of the school curriculum, both at basic/ elementary school and secondary school levels, for promoting democratic and social values among students. Hence, teachers should possess basic knowledge on social sciences and their nature and importance of learning at the school level.
- Social Sciences constitute a broad field of knowledge and deal with human beings in relation to their social behavior. Social Sciences study the concepts or issues like culture, tradition, lifestyles, places, and environment, power and authority, governance, economy, civic sense, etc. which have social implications. Social sciences deal with human beings and their relation to each other in society at different places and times.

80(B). 'Social and political life (SPL)' is a new learning area of the social science curriculum at the upper primary stage replacing the earlier learning area of 'Civics'. NCF (2005) remarked that "Civics appeared in the Indian school curriculum in the colonial period against the background of increasing 'disloyalty' among Indians towards the Raj. Emphasis on obedience and loyalty were the key features of civics".
- At the upper primary stage, the subject area of Social Science drawing its content from history, geography, political science, and economics will be introduced.
- Simultaneously, the child may be introduced to contemporary issues and problems.
- Emphasis needs to be given to issues like poverty, illiteracy, child and bonded labour, class, caste, gender, and environment.
- The child will be introduced to the formation and functioning of governments at the local, state, and central level and the democratic processes of participation.

81(A). When the students become failed, it can be understood that the system has failed.

Failure is the state or condition of not meeting a desirable aim and may be viewed as the opposite of success. There are many cognitive, physical, intellectual, scholastical, emotional, and cultural causes for the failure of students.

82(B). Activity based learning, discovery learning and learning through exploration are methods where midsized groups can be made by the teacher and the teacher can give some task to the group rather than an individual.

Ways of Collaborative learning:
- Activity-based learning as the name

suggests actively involves learners in the construction and re-construction of knowledge based on his or her individual experiences. It is known as the learning by doing method. The activity approach takes you a little more time to prepare than a lecture or a demonstration. But the activity approach will not add to your burden. Rather, it will promote and support you by providing a range of appropriate educational material and ideas, and orientation on the creative use of the same. And the rewards for both you and your students will be significant and satisfying.
- Discovery learning is a method of inquiry-based instruction. It involves a method of instruction through which students interact with their environment by exploring and manipulating objects and performing experiments.
- Exploration-based learning is an active learning approach which helps children learn through curiosity and inquiry. Learning through exploration as a process changes the way one approaches a particular situation. Indeed, one can assert that it is the most effective way of learning.

83(D). To avoid gender stereotyping in a class, a teacher should needs to try to put both boys and girls in non-traditional roles. Gender stereotyping is an unfair idea which refers to a generalized view or characteristics that ought to be possessed by women and men.
- To avoid gender stereotyping in class, a teacher should try to put both boys and girls in non-traditional roles.
- This activity will remove the stereotype from the mind of students that certain activities are only meant to be done by the girls and not by the boys and vice versa.
- It will also promote the sense of gender equality among them.

84(D). Public protest and take action through writing letters to the concerned minister, organizing a public protest, starting a signature campaign, and asking the government to rethink its program.

Media plays a very important role in providing news and discussing events taking place in the country and the world.
- It is on the basis of this information that citizens can, for example, learn how government works.
- They can take action on the basis of these news stories. Some of the ways in which they can do this is by writing letters to the concerned minister, organizing a public protest, starting a signature campaign, and asking the government to rethink its program.
- A balanced report is one that discusses

all points of view of a particular story and then leaves it to the readers to make up their minds.

85(B). When the government prevents either the news item, or scenes from movie, or lyrics of the song from being shared with the larger public, this is referred as censorship.

Censorship is the changing or the suppression or prohibition of speech or writing that is deemed subversive of the common good. It occurs in all manifestations of authority to some degree.

86(A). Information is processed, organized, and structured data. It provides context for data and enables decision-making processes.

Factual information is information that solely deals with facts. It is short, non-explanatory, and rarely gives in-depth background on a topic.

87(B). Mid-day meal scheme is a school meal programme designed in India for better nutritional standing of school-age children nationwide.

The aims of the Mid-day meal programme are:

- Increasing enrolment and retention of children in schools.
- Reducing hunger and increased concentration in studies.
- Decreasing malnutrition levels prevailing among children.

Thus, we can say that the above statements about the mid-day meal programme is true.

88(D). The Supreme Court of India is the supreme judicial body of India and the highest court of India under the constitution.

D. K. Basu Guidelines:

Guidelines related to the procedures to be followed by police for arrest, detention, and interrogation laid down by the Supreme court in D.K. Basu Vs State of West Bengal Case.

- Clear Police identification
- Memos and Attesting
- Friends and Relatives to be told
- Law Assistance
- Communication to other Headquarters

Guidelines are related to the procedures to be used by various agencies for the arrest, detention, and interrogation of any person.

Guidelines are related to the prevention of sexual harassment at the workplace. (Vishaka Guideline in 1997, Prevention, Prohibition and Redressal Act, 2013)

Guidelines are related to the protection of children from hazardous employment. (The Child Labour Protection and Regulation Act 1986 under the recommendation of Gurupadswamy Committee)

Guidelines are related to the protection of women from domestic violence. (The Protection of Women from Domestic Violence Act 2005).

So, from the above points, it becomes clear that D.K. The Basu guidelines were related to the procedures to be followed by the police for arrest, detention and interrogation.

89(C). In order to solve the problems, there is a need to identify the nature of the problems, collection of information from different sources, analyse and interpret the information to arrive at a solution of the problems. Therefore the problem-solving method is a process that involves the collection, organise, analysis and interpret skills of information for arriving at the solution.

Analytic Method of Problem-Solving-

- In Analytic method, we break up the unknown problem into simpler parts and then see how these can be recombined to find the solution.
- So we start with what is to be found out and then think of further steps or possibilities that may connect the unknown built the known and find out the desired result.
- The nature of the analytic method is that-
- it leads from conclusion to hypothesis
- it proceeds from unknown to known
- Analytic statements are not considered as the statements of proofs for the problem. Rather analysis is considered as the means of discovering the proof.
- Solving problems effectively requires a controlled mixture of analytical and creative thinking.

Thus from above-mentioned points, it is clear that the ability to break down information into smaller pieces and to establish relationships among parts and the whole is analyzing.

90(D). A Harappan city was a very busy place.

- There were people who planned the construction of special buildings in the city. These were probably the rulers.
- It is likely that the rulers sent people to distant lands to get metal, precious stones, and other things that they wanted.
- They may have kept the most valuable objects, such as ornaments of gold and silver, or beautiful beads, for themselves.
- And there were scribes, people who knew how to write, who helped prepare the seals, and perhaps wrote on other materials that have not survived.

So, we can say that statement (A) is true, but statement (B) is false.

91(B). Aryabhatta was a fifth-century mathematician, astronomer, astrologer, and physicist. He was also a pioneer in the field of mathematics.

Aryabhata:

- Aryabhata, a mathematician, and astronomer wrote a book in Sanskrit

known as the Aryabhatiyam.

- He stated that day and night were caused by the rotation of the earth on its axis, even though it seems as if the sun is rising and setting every day.
- He developed a scientific explanation for eclipses as well.
- He also found a way of calculating the circumference of a circle, which is nearly as accurate as of the formula we use today.
- Varahamihira, Brahmagupta, and Bhaskaracharya were some other mathematicians and astronomers who made several discoveries.

Thus, we can say that statements A, B, and C are correct options regarding Aryabhata.

92(A). Rammohun Roy was particularly moved by the problems widows faced in their lives.

- He began a campaign against the practice of Sati.
- Rammohun Roy was well versed in Sanskrit, Persian and several other Indian and European languages.
- He tried to show through his writings that the practice of widow burning had no sanction in ancient texts.
- The strategy adopted by Rammohun was used by later reformers as well.
- Whenever they wished to challenge a practice that seemed harmful, they tried to find a verse or sentence in the ancient sacred texts that supported their point of view.
- They then suggested that the practise as it existed at present was against early tradition.

Thus, we can say that both statements (A) and (B) are true and (B) was ensured because of (A).

93(A). The correct statement is (A) and (B).

- Generally, metallic minerals are found in igneous and metamorphic rock formations.
- Sedimentary rock formations of plains and young fold mountains contain non-metallic minerals like limestone.
- Mineral fuels such as coal and petroleum are also found in the sedimentary strata.
- If a rock contains copper because then the rock looks blue in color.

94(A). Back in the 1920s, the Indian National Congress – the main party of the freedom struggle – had promised that once the country won independence, each major linguistic group would have its own province.

- However, after independence, Congress did not take any steps to honour this promise.
- For India had been divided on the basis of religion: despite the wishes and efforts of Mahatma Gandhi, freedom had come not to one nation but to two.

- As a result of the partition of India, more than a million people had been killed in riots between Hindus and Muslims.
- Both Prime Minister Nehru and Deputy Prime Minister Vallabhbhai Patel were against the creation of linguistic states.
- The Kannada speakers, Malayalam speakers, the Marathi speakers, had all looked forward to having their own state.
- The strongest protests, however, came from the Telugu-speaking districts of what was the Madras Presidency.
- When Nehru went to campaign there during the general elections of 1952, he was met with black flags and slogans demanding "We want Andhra".

Thus, we can say that both statements (A) and (B) are true and Statement (B) is the correct explanation of (A).

95(A). Bahadur Shah Zafar and The Revolt of 1857:

- He was the last Mughal emperor of India and is remembered for his role in the Indian uprising of 1857.
- By 1857, Bahadur Shah Zafar was reduced to just a nominal emperor who exercised few powers limited to the city boundaries of Delhi.
- The sepoys of Meerut forced into the red fort and proclaimed Bahadur Shah Zafar as their leader.
- He was reluctant at first as he had no means to maintain an army but agreed after convincing.
- Other leaders too accepted to fight under his banner.
- The revolt of 1857 started only when Bahadur Shah Zafar, the last ruler of the Mughals, gave his permission.
- He wrote letters to the various chiefs and rulers of the country to come forward and organize a confederacy of Indian states to fight the British.
- The Sepoy Mutiny broke out in 1857 and the sepoys rallied around the emperor. He was practically powerless, but the mutineers were fighting in the name of Bahadur Shah Zafar, the Emperor of India.
- Why Bahadur Shah Zafar was proclaimed as the leader of the revolt of 1857?
- Not so long ago, India was ruled by the Mughals only to be replaced by the British.
- When an army faction decided to revolt against the British regime, they needed a symbol under whom the revolt could be carried out.
- Since the Mughals were the earlier ruler, they decided to choose their descendent as their symbolic leader to bring multiple factions under one group.

From the above, it is clear that the Indian rebellion of 1857 spread, Sepoy regiments reached the Mughal Court at Delhi and proclaimed Bahadur Shah Zafar as their leader. They proclaimed him as their leader because the Mughals were the earlier ruler, they decided to choose their descendent as their symbolic leader.

96(B). Characteristics of sedimentary rock:

- Rocks roll down, crack, and hit each other and are broken down into small fragments.
- These smaller particles are called sediments.
- These sediments are transported and deposited by wind, water, etc.
- These loose sediments are compressed and hardened to form layers of rocks.
- These types of rocks are called sedimentary rocks.
- For example, sandstone is made from grains of sand.
- These rocks may also contain fossils of plants, animals, and other microorganisms that once lived on them.
- The remains of the dead plants and animals trapped in the layers of rocks are called fossils.
- Igneous and sedimentary rocks can change into metamorphic rocks under great heat and pressure.

So, options A and B are correct.

97(D). Suitable sites for the settlement:
The place where a building or a settlement develops is called its site.
The natural conditions for the selection of an ideal site are
Favorable climate:

- A favorable climate is an important factor in the development of permanent settlement
- Most of the population of the world found between the 20-40ºN latitude due to the temperate climate
- The arctic and antarctic regions do not have human settlement due to extreme cold climate

Availability of water: It is another important requirement of human civilization.
Suitable land: fertile land and uniform nature of the land surface are other favourable conditions for the development of the human settlement.
Fertile soil: fertile soil is very important for cultivation and cropping.
So, all of the above is correct as a factor of the development of human settlement.

98(C). Natural vegetation refers to a plant community, which has grown naturally without human aid and has been left undisturbed by humans for a long time.
The following major types of vegetation may be identified in our country:

- Tropical Evergreen Forests
- Tropical Deciduous Forests
- Tropical Thorn Forests and Scrubs
- Montane Forests
- Mangrove Forests

A. Tropical Evergreen	I. Trees that always have leaves
B. Tropical Deciduous	II. Most widespread forests in India
C. Tropical Thorn Forests	III. Receive rainfall less than 50 cm
D. Littoral Forests	IV. Salt-tolerant species of plants

99(B). The concept of diversity encloses acceptance and respect. The ability to see the world from the individual, social, religious, cultural, and other perspectives of others does not always happen naturally and, thus, must be taught to the students.
The reason for including this activity in the history textbook of class VIII is to develop the concept of diversity of views in students.
Diversity of views:

- Diversity means differences between people. It can be the physical differences like gender, race, and age, to cultural differences as well as how a person dresses, practices religion, and speaks.
- In later life, pupils need to understand these differences, respect them, and look for the opportunities they bring with them.
- This activity will give pupils an opportunity to learn different perspectives. It can also facilitate a more worldly view, which is important to have in a global world.
- Different perspectives can urge pupils to shove through their own biases and look at challenges anew.

From the above, it's clear that the reason for including this activity in the history textbook of class VIII is to develop the concept of diversity of views in students.

100(D). Democratic governments in our times are usually referred to as representative democracies.

- In representative democracies people do not participate directly but, instead, choose their representatives through an election process.
- These representatives meet and make decisions for the entire population.
- These days a government cannot call itself democratic unless it allows what is known as a universal adult franchise.
- This means that all adults in the country are allowed to vote.

Thus, we can say that only statement B is correct regarding the representative democracies.

101(A). Adivasis today as somewhat marginal and powerless communities.

- In the precolonial world, they were traditionally ranged hunter, gatherers and nomads and lived by shifting agriculture and also cultivating in one place.

- Although these remain, for the past 200 years Adivasis have been increasingly forced – through economic changes, forest policies and political force applied by the State and private industry – to migrate to lives as workers in plantations, at construction sites, in industries and as domestic workers.
- For the first time in history, they do not control or have much direct access to the forest territories.
- Adivasis have also lived in areas that are rich in minerals and other natural resources.
- These are taken over for mining and other large industrial projects.
- Powerful forces have often colluded to take over tribal land.
- Much of the time, the land is taken away forcefully and procedures are not followed.
- According to official figures, more than 50 per cent of persons displaced due to mines and mining projects are tribals.
- When Adivasis are displaced from their lands, they lose much more than a source of income.
- They lose their traditions and customs – a way of living and being.

From the above, we can conclude that Both A and B statements are true and Statement B is the correct explanation of A.

102(A). At the head of the tehsil is the District Collector.

Under her are the revenue officers, also known as tehsildars.
- They have to hear disputes.
- They also supervise the work of the Patwaris and ensure that records are properly kept and land revenue is collected.
- They make sure that the farmers can easily obtain a copy of their record, students can obtain their caste certificates etc.
- The Tehsildar's office is where land disputes are also heard.

From the above, it is clear that statements A and B are true, but statement C is false.

103(D). Characteristic of social sciences:
- Social science is concerned with human study in relation to the socio-cultural environment.
- Social science reveals subjective, objective, inter-subjective and structural aspects of society.
- The social sciences encompass diverse concerns of society and include a wide range of content drawn from the disciplines of history, geography, political science, economics, sociology, and anthropology.
- Social scientists have been evolved from social sciences as an instructional area in order to be taught at the school level for promoting healthy social/democratic living among learners.

- Significance of the social sciences by not only highlighting its increasing relevance for a job in the rapidly expanding service sector but by pointing to its indispensability in laying the foundations for an analytical and creative mindset.
- Social science stresses more on contemporary human life and its problems than the past history of man.
- Social science aims at enabling students to adjust to their socio-cultural environment which includes family, community, state, nation, and at large the entire humanity.
- Social science is a realistic course or deals with practical aspects of society.
- Social science is now at the growing and developing stage. It is trying to make its scope broader and wider.

So, from above it is clear that social science is all, a diverse field, a subjective discipline, and a foundation for the analytic and creative mind.

104(D). The objectives of teaching the social sciences at the upper primary level are:
- To develop moral values, emotional qualities and a sense of belonging in students.
- Helping students to participate in socio-economic institutions.
- To develop qualities of democratic citizenship in the students.
- To initiate a learner into the study of his/her own region, state, and country in the global context.
- To initiate a learner into the study of India's past
- To develop an understanding of the earth as the habitat of humankind and other forms of life.

Thus, we can say that the lack of development of social competence and sense of the social environment in students is not a common objective of social science learning at the Upper Primary stage.

105(D). Most of the art and architectural remains that survive from Ancient and Medieval India are religious in nature. The basic form of the Hindu temple comprises the following:

Garbhagriha is the room where the image of the temple deity is placed.

Stupa - An important small box placed at the center of the temple.

Mandapa - The entrance to the temple. It could be a portico or a colonnaded hall where worshippers stand.

Shikhara/Vimana - The structure built on top of the temple. In north India, it is called Shikhara and is curving in shape. In the south, it is like a pyramidal tower and is called Vimana.

106(A). The basis of democracy can be attributed to periodic elections.

The possibility of controlling leaders by requiring them to submit to regular and periodic elections helps to solve the problem of succession in leadership and thus contributes to the continuation of democracy. Moreover, where the electoral process is competitive and forces candidates or parties to expose their records and future intentions to popular scrutiny, elections serve as forums for the discussion of public issues and facilitate the expression of public opinion. Elections thus provide political education for citizens and ensure the responsiveness of democratic governments to the will of the people.

107(A). The Panchayati Raj is the third tier of government and it comes under the feature of federalism in India.
- Federalism is a system of government in which the power is divided between a central authority and various constituent units of the country.
- There are two or more levels of government in a federal system.
- Different tiers of government govern the same citizens, but each tier has its own jurisdiction in specific matters of legislation, taxation, and administration.
- The jurisdictions of the respective levels or tiers of government are specified in the constitution.

Levels of government in India are:
- Union government
- State government
- Panchayati Raj

Panchayati Raj is the third tier of the government. It comes under the feature of federalism in India.

108(A). The right to be informed at the time of arrest of the offence for which the person is being arrested and the right to be presented before a magistrate within 24 hours of arrest are correct regarding Article 22 of the Indian Constitution.
- Article 22 deals with the protection against arrest and detention in certain cases.
- The Right to be informed at the time of arrest of the offence for which the person is being arrested.
- The Right to be presented before a magistrate within 24 hours of arrest.
- A boy under 15 years of age and women cannot be called to the police station only for questioning.
- This article is applicable to citizens as well as non-citizens.

According to this article, every person has a Fundamental Right to be defended by a lawyer.

109(A). The Scheduled Tribes (Prevention of Atrocities) Act was framed in 1989 in response to demands made by Dalits and others that the government must take seriously the ill-treatment and humiliation of Dalits and tribal groups.

- The Scheduled Castes and the Scheduled Tribes (Prevention of Atrocities) Act was framed in 1989.
- It was framed in response to demands made by Dalits and others that the government must take seriously the ill-treatment and humiliation of Dalits and tribal groups.

110(C). The Supreme Court was established on 26 January 1950.
- The Supreme Court is the supreme judicial body of India and the highest court of the Republic of India.
- It was established on 26 January 1950.
- Delhi has the seat of the Supreme Court.
- The functions and responsibilities of Supreme Court are defined by the constitution.
- It is the guardian of our fundamental rights.
- The decisions of the Supreme Court are binding on all courts.
- It can transfer the judges of High courts.
- It has specific jurisdiction or scope of powers.

111(B). The challenging dimension of evaluation of school teaching is adequate check on performance.
- A teacher has multiple responsibilities in school teaching so it becomes very difficult for him to keep an adequate check on the performance of the students.
- The teacher has to check the performance of students under different kinds of circumstances i.e., while playing, experimenting, and learning in a classroom, etc.
- Also, the teacher has to plan the learning activities which makes it difficult for him to observe and analyze the behaviour of the students throughout the learning process.
- Teachers establish friendly relationships with students to observe them effectively to get realistic information regarding performance. They don't let them realize that they are under observation that's why students act naturally which leads to qualitative evaluation.

112(A). Holistic development is measured by continuous comprehensive evaluation.
Continuous and Comprehensive Evaluation (CCE) aims to measure the 'Holistic development' or 'All aspects of the development of the child' as it ensures all-around development of students including cognitive, psychomotor, and affective domains.

113(A). The above statements about Ain-i-Akbari are true.
- Ain-i-Akbari is third volume of Akbarnama.
- It was written by Abul Fazl in the 16th century.
- It has rich statistical details about crops, prices, revenues and wages etc.
- It also describes details about the traditions and cultures of the people of India.
- Ain-i-Akbari is divided into five books.

114(C). The above statements about iqtadars and jagirdars are correct.
- The Iqtadari system was used by the Delhi Sultans whereas the Jagirdari system was followed by Mughal Empire.
- The iqtadar and jagirdar were military commanders of the Delhi sultanate and Mughal Empire respectively.
- They used to reside in and administer their lands called iqtas and jagirs respectively.

115(A). The above statements are correct.
- William Jones had great respect for ancient cultures, both Indian and Western.
- He thought that it was important to discover sacred texts in order to understand India.
- Rabindranath Tagore initiated learning in a natural environment.
- Mahatma Gandhi was critical to English education.
- He thought that teaching English created a sense of inferiority among Indians.
- Thomas Macaulay laid emphasis on the promotion of English.
- He thought that Indians should be made familiar with the advances being made by the West.

116(A). A population pyramid is a graphical illustration of the distribution by age group and sex. The shape of the pyramid indicates the characteristics of the population. If the pyramid has a broad base, it indicates that a relatively high proportion of the population lies in the youngest age of 0 to 14 years. A broader base indicates an expanding labour force in the future. A country having a large number of young children will have an economic advantage in the labour market. The population pyramid of a country in which death rates and birth rates are both high is broad at the base and narrows towards the top.

117(B). Role of textbooks in the classroom processes:-
- Textbooks help the learning and teaching process. The educational philosophy of the textbook will influence the class and the learning process.
- Exercise given in the textbook helps a teacher to gauge the extent to which the student has understood what has been discussed in the chapter.
- They help students to recall and make connections with what has been taught earlier.
- Textbooks make it possible for students to review and prepare their lessons. They are efficient in terms of time and money.

Thus, it is concluded that Only (A) and (C) statements are correct.

118(C). When discussing the theme 'Adivasis,' a social science teacher is expected to introduce a variety of local examples during class discussions.
To teach different topics in social sciences and to achieve learning objectives associated with these topics, the teacher uses a number of teaching-learning methods or techniques which constitute various teaching-learning strategies.
- Here, while discussing the theme of Adivasis, a teacher is expected to introduce a variety of local examples.
- It is always a good idea to teach students using local examples, better if they are practical and related to real life. Students visualize things with the help of examples they relate things and think over them.
- It can be given orally which develops a pupil's thought, logic, and imagination.

119(A). 'Hussain Sagar Lake' is located in telangana state.
Hussain Sagar is a heart-shaped lake in Hyderabad, Telangana built by Ibrahim Quli Qutab Shah. The lake was built in the year 1563 and is fed by the River Musi.

120(B). The above statements are correct.
- The climate of a place is affected by its location, altitude, distance from the sea and relief.
- Jaisalmer in Rajasthan has a hot climate.
- Drass region of Jammu and Kashmir is extremely cold.
- Mawsynram receives the world's highest rainfall, therefore the climate there is rainy.
- Mumbai is neither very hot nor too cold and thus, has a humid climate.

Child Development and Pedagogy

1. Whom of the following has not propounded the learning theory?
(a) Thorndike   (b) Skinner
(c) Kohler   (d) B.S. Bloom

2. Meaning of stagnation in education is:
(a) Retention of a child in a same class for more than one year
(b) Not going to school by the child
(c) Taking not admission in school by the child
(d) Leave the school by the child

3. Learning of children will be most effective when:
(a) Teacher will lead the learning process and keep the children passive
(b) Development of cognitive, affective and psychomotor domain of children will take place
(c) Emphasis will be only on reading, writing and mathematical skills
(d) Teaching system will be autocratic

4. Human development starts from:
(a) Stage of infancy
(b) Pre-childhood stage
(c) Pre-natal stage
(d) Post-childhood stage

5. "Adolescence is the period of great stress, strain, storm and strike" is the statement of :
(a) Crow & Crow
(b) Stanley Hall
(c) Jersield
(d) Simpson

6. Which of the following stages of development is called as 'A unique stage of emotional development' by Cole and Bruce?
(a) Adolescence   (b) Childhood
(c) Infancy   (d) Adulthood

7. In cognitive development heredity establishes:
(a) The basic nature of physical structure such as the brain.
(b) The development of the physical structure.
(c) The existence of reflexes.
(d) All of these

8. According to Piaget's cognitive development theory, accommodation is referred to:
(a) A find of matching between the already existing cognitive structures and the environmental needs as they arise.
(b) Adjust to new ways of thinking and behaving by making modifications in one's existing cognitive structures.
(c) Disequilibrium between previous knowledge and new knowledge.
(d) Arrangement of perceptual and cognitive in formations in meaningful patterns.

9. Which of the following is not among the three domains of behaviour that are covered by evaluation?
(a) Cognitive domain
(b) Affective domain
(c) Conative domain
(d) Psychomotor domain

10. Which type of learning mainly influences personality of the child?
(a) Trial and Error learning
(b) Imitation learning
(c) Insightful learning
(d) Instructional learning

11. Which of the following is considered a sign being gifted?
(a) Curiosity
(b) Creative ideas
(c) Fighting with other
(d) (A) and (B) both

12. In which stage, the child responds to inferred reality?
(a) Sensori-motor stage
(b) Pre-operational stage
(c) Concrete operational stage
(d) Formal operational stage

13. Growth in adolescence is reverse of that in childhood because:
(a) All part of the body grow simultaneously.
(b) The torso grows first.
(c) Legs accelerate first.
(d) Hands, legs and feet accelerate first.

14. What is the adverse effect of insisting on the same answers from all children?
(a) It will discourage children from listening to the teacher.
(b) It will stop children from speaking in the classroom.
(c) It will hinder the growth of the child's own understanding and imagination.
(d) It will encourage children to copy from others.

15. What is the responsibility of a teacher for proper social development of adolescents?
(a) Information about HIV and other sex-related diseases should be provided on a scientific manner by the teachers to the young adolescents. If necessary. teachers and parents must take help of counselors.
(b) The adolescents are generally interested in experimentation and self-examinations of objects. Hence, it is suggested that importance should be given on using new dynamic methods of teaching.
(c) The adolescent has to face a large number of problems at this stage. As such, proper guidance and counseling should be provided by teachers.
(d) Group games, debates, seminars, conferences may be organised. These will help the adolescents to participate in social activities,

16. After occurrence of a desirable behaviour, the teacher says 'very good' to the child. She has used:
(a) Primary reinforcer
(b) Secondary reinforcer
(c) Negative reinforcement
(d) None of the above

17. Which one of the following is NOT a type of learning according to Gagne's Theory of Learning?
(a) Verbal association
(b) Signal learning
(c) Proper Prerequisites
(d) Concept learning

18. Which sequence depicts the correct hierarchical order of learning outcomes of affective domain in Bloom's taxonomy?
(a) Receiving, responding, valuing, organizing, characterizing,
(b) Responding, valuing, organizing, receiving, characterizing
(c) Organizing, receiving, valuing, characterizing, responding
(d) Valuing, receiving, responding, characterizing, organizing

19. Which one of the following is the key principles of inclusive education for children?

(a) Principle of Equality

(b) Principle of Participation

(c) Principle of acceptance

(d) All of above

20. Which one of the following statement is related to inclusive education?

(a) No discrimination among students

(b) Equal educational opportunity for all

(c) Adapting to the needs of students, for example, making institutions disabled-friendly

(d) All of above

21. At what stage was this task done in a three-minute run to read short sentences?

(a) Peace

(b) Childhood

(c) Adolescence

(d) None of these

22. To which of the following events does the child first start getting attracted?

(a) Light   (b) Mother

(c) Sound   (d) Meal

23. The socialization of a child is determined by which of the following techniques?

(a) Interview technique

(b) Sociometry Techniques

(c) Inspection techniques

(d) Biography study techniques

24. ______________ places the child at the centre of the learning, and can also be referred to as 'invisible pedagogy'.

(a) Constructivist pedagogy

(b) Social constructivism pedagogy

(c) Both (A) and (B)

(d) None of these

25. What should be the amendments in teacher preparation in classroom management?

(a) Teacher with instructional approach to classroom management To provide candidates with feedback through curriculum and guided exercises

(b) Addressing the challenges faced by teacher candidates and new teachers in creating a positive classroom context

(c) Both (A) and (B)

(d) None of the above

26. What role should parents play in a child's learning process?

(a) Forward-looking

(b) Sympathetic

(c) Neutral

(d) Negative

27. ________ aims to study a child's development, especially information processing, conceptual processing, perceptual skills, language learning and other aspects related to brain development.

(a) Cognitive development

(b) Psychodevelopment

(c) Both (A) and (B)

(d) None of the above

28. On the basis of which principle of learning can the feelings of fear, love and hate be easily generated in the child?

(a) Classical contract theory

(b) Psychology contract theory

(c) Educational contract theory

(d) All of the above

29. The theory of classical conditioning was propounded by I.V. Paulov in the year __________.

(a) 1904   (b) 1906

(c) 1930   (d) 1924

30. The ________ of learning in children, in which the learner perceives and responds to the whole situation, comes under Kohler's theory of understanding.

(a) field theory

(b) associative principle

(c) Both (A) and (B)

(d) none of the above

Language - I: English

Ques (31-39): Direction : Read the passage given below and answer the question that follow by selecting the most appropriate option.

One day in 1924, five men who were camping in the Cascade Mountains of Washington saw a group of huge apelike creatures coming out of the woods. They hurried back to their cabin and locked themselves inside. While they were in, the creatures attacked them by throwing rocks against the walls of the cabin. After several hours, these strange hairy giants went back into the woods. After this incident the men returned to the town and told the people of their adventure. However, only a few people accepted their story. These were the people who remembered hearing tales about footprints of an animal that walked like a human being. The five men, however, were not the first people to have seen these creatures called Bigfoot. Long before their experience, local Native Americans were certain that a race of apelike animals had been living in the **neighbouring** mountain for centuries. They called these creatures Sasquatch. In 1958, workmen, who were building a road through the jungles of Northern California often found huge footprints in the earth around their camp. Then in 1967, Roger Patterson, a man who was interested in finding Bigfoot went into the northern California jungles with a friend. While riding, they were suddenly thrown off from their horses. Patterson saw a tall apelike animal standing not far away. He managed to shoot seven rolls of film of the hairy creature before the animal disappeared in the hushes. When Patterson's film was shown to the public, not many people believed his story. In another incident, Richard Brown, a music teacher and also an experience hunter spotted a similar creature. He saw the animal clearly through the telescopic lens of his rifle. He said the creature looked more like a human than an animal. Later many other people also found deep footprints in the same area. In spite of regular reports of sightings and footprints, most experts still do not believe that Bigfoot really exists.

31. What did the five campers do when they saw a group of apelike creatures?

(a) They ran into the woods and hid there for several hours.

(b) They quickly ran back into their cabin and locked the cabin door.

(c) They threw rocks against the walls of their cabin to frighten the creatures away.

(d) They attacked the creatures by throwing rocks at them.

32. Did the town people believe the story of the five men about their meeting with Bigfoot ?

(a) No, not everyone believed their story.

(b) Only those who had heard the same tale the second time believed them.

(c) Some said the five men were making up their own story.

(d) All the people believed what they said..

33. Who were the first people to have seen these apelike creatures before the five campers?

(a) The workers who built the road in the jungles of Northern California.

(b) Roger Patterson and his friend.

(c) The local Native Americans

(d) Richard Brown, a music teacher and a hunter.

34. The word neighbouring would BEST be replaced with:

(a) Far-off   (b) Nearby

(c) Remote   (d) Far-away

35. Who gave the name 'Sasquatch' to the apelike creatures?

(a) The five campers

(b) Roger Patterson

(c) The local Native Americans

(d) Richard Brown

36. Which of the following pairs is INCORRECT ?

(a) Creatures -- animals

(b) Woods -- jungles

(c) Spotted -- saw

(d) Huge -- hairy

37. The BEST title for this passage would be

(a) The adventures of the five campers.

(b) The experts and the existence of Bigfoot.

(c) The creature called Bigfoot.

(d) The adventures of Bigfoot.

38. Who has seen the telescopic lens?

(a) Roger Patterson

(b) Richard Brown

(c) The five adventures men

(d) Robert Brown

39. How many photo shot had been taken by Roger Patterson of hairy creature?

(a) Four   (b) Five

(c) Six   (d) Seven

Ques (40-45): Direction : Read the given poetry and answer the question that follow by selecting the most appropriate option.

The sun descending in the west,
The evening star does shine,
The birds are silent in their nest.
And I must seek for mine.
The moon, like a flower
In heaven's high bower,
With silent delight
Sits and smiles on the night.
Farewell, green fields and happy grove,
Where flocks have took delight,
Where lambs have nibbled, silent move
The feet of angels bright;
Unseen they pour blessing
And joy without ceasing
On each bud and blossom,
And each sleeping bosom.
They look in every thoughtless nest
Where birds are covered warm;
They visit caves of every beast,
To keep them all from harm:
If they see any weeping
That should have been sleeping,
They pour sleep on their head,
And sit down by their bed.

40. The evening star rises when ____________.

(a) the birds leave their nests

(b) it is midnight

(c) it is dawn

(d) the sun descends in the west

41. Here, 'bower' represents:

(a) a potted plant

(b) a framework that supports climbing plants

(c) a bouquet of flowers

(d) a flower vase

42. The poet compares the moon to:

(a) a flower

(b) a bird in the nest

(c) an evening star

(d) an angel

43. The angels come down on earth to ____________.

(a) spread moonlight

(b) give blessing and joy

(c) make people, dance and have fun

(d) take blessing and joy

44. Birds' nest is described as 'thoughtless' because:

(a) the angels are blessing the birds to be happy

(b) the birds are covered in the warmth of their nest

(c) it is made without any thought

(d) the occupants are asleep without any care

45. The figure of speech used, in the line 'In heaven's high bower' is:

(a) Metaphor

(b) Personification

(c) Alliteration

(d) Simile

46. Which of the following should be the characteristic of the textbooks included in the curriculum?

(a) The introduction at the beginning and conclusion at the end of the chapter should be given in the textbook.

(b) It should be content oriented

(c) A standardized language should be used

(d) All of the above

47. Grammar-translation method of teaching English heavily relies on :

(a) Form-focussed teaching

(b) Meaning-focussed teaching

(c) Direct teaching as a strategy for learning

(d) Language use as the main focus

48. Which one of the following is not accepted in association with multimedia and its pedagogical strengths?

(a) It helps in problem solving by means of learning by doing.

(b) It facilitates individualized and cooperative learning.

(c) It proves to be time consuming and not so effective for slow learners.

(d) It facilitates mastering basic skills of a student by means of drill and practice.

49. Which of the following programme helps students to reinforce their knowledge and develop their communication and co-operation skill as well as good interpersonal relation?

(a) Reward scheme

(b) Handling pupils language acquisition problems

(c) Peer support programme

(d) None of these

50. What are the things that as a teacher should follow before, during or after the parent teacher meeting?

(a) Start the meeting by showing that you care and know something positive about their child.

(b) Do use materials from the student's work folder.

(c) Do use clear and descriptive terms.

(d) All of these

51. When a child learns a language naturally, without much practice, it is called:

(a) Language adaptation

(b) Language learning

(c) Language acquisition

(d) Language generalization

52. The study of 'chunks of language' which are bigger than a single sentence is :

(a) Discourse   (b) Morphology

(c) Syntax   (d) Semantics

53. A teacher asks the questions in the class to:
(a) Keep students busy
(b) Attract student's attention
(c) Maintain discipline
(d) For curriculum

54. Micro teaching focuses on the competency over:
(a) Methods
(b) Skills
(c) Contents
(d) None of these

55. Why oral composition is useful in development of child?
(a) It provides fluency in language
(b) It correct grammar
(c) It build self confidence
(d) All of the above

56. What is the importance of reading?
(a) It increase vocabulary
(b) It makes pupil knowledge
(c) It helps in getting information
(d) All of the above

57. Which one of the following is the usage of language laboratory?
(a) It makes education child centered
(b) It reduce the burdon on the teacher
(c) It provides mass education
(d) The student can hear his own mistake for himself

58. The material on opaque sheet is projected with the help of _____ hardware.
(a) Episcope
(b) Audio player
(c) Video cassette player
(d) Board, charts and graphs

59. Direction : Answer the following question by selecting the most appropriate option.
__ is the backbone of learning a language.
(a) Listening skill
(b) Speaking skill
(c) Reading skill
(d) Writing skill

60. Evaluation covers _____ domains of behavior.
(a) four   (b) three
(c) two   (d) five

Social Studies

61. An overhead absorption rate is used to:
(a) Share out common costs over benefiting cost centre
(b) Find the total overheads for a cost centre
(c) Charge overheads to products
(d) Control overheads

62. Consider the following statements regarding Labour code reforms, 2020:
1. All the previous codes were merged into 4 new codes.
2. A "Social Security Fund" will be created to implement schemes for the workers.
3. IT & Service sector workers are covered under this new code.
Which of the statements given below is/are correct?
(a) 1 and 2 only   (b) 2 and 3 only
(c) 1 only   (d) 1, 2 and 3

63. The Five E model is considered as one of the popular lesson plans used to develop lesson plans in different subjects including social sciences. Which of the following is the second step of this model?
(a) Evaluate   (b) Elaborate
(c) Explore   (d) Entertain

64. Consider the following statements A and B and choose the correct option.
A. A debate builds up in learners the ability to gather information, process it, and present it to the audience.
B. Debate is used in the classroom when the topic is based on facts.
(a) Only A is true.
(b) Only B is true.
(c) Both A and B are true.
(d) Both A and B are false.

65. The purpose of End-text Questions given in Social and Political Life textbooks is to:
(a) Rote memorize the concepts.
(b) Cover the main concepts raised by the chapter and ask learners to explain these in their own words.
(c) Assess the extent to which content has been assimilated.
(d) Provide all answers by the teacher.

66. In a Social Science class, which one of the following is a suitable method for underlining the phenomenon that spaces of rural areas are disappearing fast?
(a) Make presentation with the help of computers
(b) Discussion on the basis of text prescribed
(c) A survey project
(d) Group discussion over the topic

67. For undertaking a project of social studies what step would you follow first?
(a) Planning
(b) Choosing and purposing
(c) Providing a situation
(d) Executing

68. A Social Science teacher must employ which of the following methods for being effective?
(a) Increase engagement of students by thought provoking and interesting activities.
(b) Increase the knowledge of students by taking tests on every Monday.
(c) Award grades in a lax manner to boost the confidence of slow learners.
(d) Assign projects to be done at home so as to involve parents in the studies of their ward.

69. Which one of the following is not the nature of social science?
(a) Study of man's development through ages
(b) Study of human relationship
(c) Unrealistic course of study
(d) A unique combination of various subjects

70. In the teaching of Social Studies direct experiences can very well be supplemented with:
(a) Printed aids
(b) Visual aids
(c) Audio visual aids
(d) Audio aids

71. Problems of teaching social science in school includes:
(a) Study of all the discipline of social science
(b) Trust in students ability
(c) Lack of integration with life and other school subjects
(d) Equalities on weekly course hours

72. Which is not related with the comprehensive objective of social science?
(a) Determining the relation between economy and development of the country

(b) Showing the historical places in the map

(c) Showing the differences of different regions in the field of transport

(d) Showing the causes of the change of environment

73. The teaching of social and political life textbooks at the upper primary level focusses on which one of the following approaches?

(a) Learning through real life situations

(b) Learning through definitions

(c) Rote learning

(d) Learning through synthesis of concepts

74. When a teacher of Social Studies evaluates pupils' learning outcomes on tolerance of different religions, languages, regions, political ideologies, etc., and appreciation, desirable attitude, commitment, etc., then this evaluation is called as:

(a) Cognitive

(b) Non-cognitive

(c) Summative

(d) Formative

75. Consider the following statements-
1. Hinayana original teachings of Buddha and believe in idol worship
2. Mahayana believed in the heavenliness of Buddha
3. Maitreya future Buddha

(a) 1 only   (b) 1, 2 only

(c) 1, 3 only   (d) 2, 3 only

76. How have we come to know about the first farmers and herders?
A. We have written records of that time.
B. We have evidence of grains and animal bones.

(a) Only A

(b) Only B

(c) Both A and B

(d) Neither A nor B

77. Who among the following Governor- Generals decided that Bahadur Shah Zafar would be the last Mughal emperor and after his death none of the descendents would be recognized as a ruler?

(a) Lord Dalhousie

(b) William Bentinck

(c) Lord Canning

(d) Lord Cornwallis

78. Identify the vegetation by the features given below:
A) This vegetation can survive in saline water.
B) Sundari is a well-known species of trees of this vegetation.
C) It is located in the Andaman and Nicobar Islands.

(a) Tropical Rainforests

(b) Tropical Deciduous forests

(c) Mangrove forests

(d) Coniferous forests

79. What is the most basic outcome of democratic government?

(a) Significant decision making

(b) Powerful repressive governance

(c) Accountability to the citizens

(d) None of these

80. Name one branch or part of the government.

(a) State Government

(b) Parliament

(c) Administration

(d) Legislative

81. A particular area from which all the voters living there choose their representatives called _______.

(a) Constituency   (b) Block

(c) Confrenece   (d) Parliament

82. Consider the following statements related to the Indian Constitution and choose the correct option.
Statement (A): Indian state ensures non-interference in the religious practices and respects sentiments of all religions.
Statement (B): There is no provision to provide educational rights to cultural and linguistic minorities in the Indian Constitution.

(a) A is correct and B is incorrect

(b) A is incorrect and B is correct

(c) Both A and B are correct

(d) Both A and B are incorrect

83. The literacy rate among women in India is only _______.

(a) 45 percent

(b) 50 percent

(c) 65.46 percent

(d) 54 percent

84. What was the title of Rashsundari's autobiography?

(a) Discovery of India

(b) Amar Jiban

(c) Meri 21 Kavitayen

(d) None of these

85. Dispute Resolution is related to:

(a) Judicial system

(b) Parliament

(c) Legislative

(d) Executive

86. Who in the Constituent Assembly helped the Scheduled Castes get some safeguards in the draft constitution?

(a) Mahatma Gandhi

(b) B.R. Ambedkar

(c) Rajendra Prashad

(d) Jawahar Lal Neharu

87. India is the country of _____.

(a) Diversity

(b) Presidency

(c) Direct Democracy

(d) Religion

88. Which term is used when we fix people into one image?

(a) Inequality

(b) Discrimination

(c) Equality

(d) Stereotype

89. _______ is a form of government, where people participate in the decision-making process directly or indirectly.

(a) Monarchy   (b) Democracy

(c) Aristocracy   (d) Socialism

90. Which institution has approved 32 beneficiaries under the production-linked incentive (PLI) scheme for large-scale electronics manufacturing in September 2022?

(a) Ministry of Commerce

(b) Central Electricity Regulatory Commission (CERC)

(c) Central Electricity Authority (CEA)

(d) NITI Aayog

91. Which of the following questions provide opportunities to promote critical thinking skills?
A. What powers does the speaker of Lok Sabha holds?
B. Discuss the issues of Poverty in India.
C. What are the challenges faced by the students going to school in rural areas?
D. What is the difference between tropic of cancer and tropic of Capricorn?
Choose the correct option.

(a) A and B only

(b) A, B and C only

(c) A, B, C and D

(d) B and C only

92. Choose an appropriate and meaningful written assignment in

Social Science from the following:

(a) An original assignment that tests concepts

(b) A summary of the chapter

(c) Searching for an exact answer from the text book

(d) The previous year's assignments

93. History will help you to:
A. understand how the present evolved
B. understand the working of our physical and social world
C. compare the past with the present
Which of the above are correct?

(a) A and C   (b) A and B

(c) A, B and C   (d) B and C

94. Which of the following approaches have been considered while developing social and political life textbooks?
A. Learning through use of concrete examples and experiences.
B. Learning through retention based on facts and data.

(a) Only A

(b) Only B

(c) Both A and B

(d) Neither A nor B

95. The objective of discussing 'equality' in a social science classroom is to
A. address issues of dignity with the learners.
B. sensitize learners towards respecting everyone.
C. build upon values enshrined in the Constitution.
D. explain that all differences leads to inequality.
Choose the correct option:

(a) A, C, D are true

(b) B, C, D are true

(c) A, B, C are true

(d) A, B, D are true

96. What do you look for when you assess your children's learning of social sciences in upper primary school?
(A) Explain the methods of evaluation being followed for social science subjects at the upper primary level.
(B) Use only old methods of evaluation in social sciences that enhance students learning.
(C) Use grading system in the assessment of students learning, particularly in social science.

(a) A and B

(b) A and C

(c) B and C

(d) All of the above

97. Direction : Answer the following question by selecting the correct / most appropriate options.
Statement (A): Mahavira taught in the Prakrit language.
Reason (R): Ordinary people could understand the teachings of Mahavira.

(a) Both (A) and (R) are true and (R) was ensured because of (A)

(b) Both (A) and (R) are true, but (A) has no relationship with (R)

(c) (A) is true, but (R) is false

(d) (A) is false, but (R) is true

98. Consider the following statements:
A. All inscriptions contain only scripts.
B. Inscriptions are inscribed on hard surfaces.
Choose the correct option from the codes given below:

(a) Only A

(b) Only B

(c) Both A and B

(d) None of the above

99. Consider the following sentences:
A. People who composed hymns described themselves as Aryas. They also called their opponents dasas or dasyus.
B. People who composed the hymns called themselves as aryas. They termed their opponents as dasas or dasyus.
C. The terms 'dasa' and 'dasyus' were mentioned in the Vedas several times. They were later associated with the meaning 'slave'.
Which of the above statement is/ are correct?

(a) Only A and B   (b) Only C

(c) Only B   (d) Only B and C

100. Consider the following statements and select the correct option regarding the British:
A. The first English factory was set up on the banks of the river Hugli in 1651.
B. As trade expanded, the Company persuaded merchants and traders to come and settle near the factory.
C. They persuaded the Mughal emperor Aurangzeb to issue a Farman granting the Company the right to trade duty-free.

(a) Only A and C   (b) Only A

(c) Only A and B   (d) Only B and C

101. Direction : Answer the following question by selecting the correct /

most appropriate options.
Statement (A): Various forms that the Non-Cooperation Movement took in different parts of India.
Reason (R): At Kheda in Gujarat, Patidar peasants organized nonviolent campaigns against the high land revenue demand of the British.

(a) Both (A) and (R) are true and (R) is the correct explanation of (A)

(b) Both (A) and (R) are true, but (R) is not the correct explanation of (A)

(c) (A) is true, but (R) is false

(d) (A) is false, but (R) is true

102. Direction : Answer the following questions by selecting the correct / most appropriate options.
Statement (A): According to Gandhi, disruptions tendencies had come to the fore, and to check them, the nation had to be strong and united.
Reason (R): There was a reluctance to divide the country into linguistic lines.

(a) Both (A) and (R) are true and (R) is the correct explanation of (A)

(b) Both (A) and (R) are true, but (R) is not the correct explanation of (A)

(c) (A) is true, but (R) is false

(d) (A) is false, but (R) is true

103. Consider the statements A, B, C on construction in the medieval period and choose the correct answer:
A. Between the seventh and tenth centuries architects started adding more rooms, doors, and windows to buildings.
B. Between the eighth and thirteenth centuries the trabeate style was used in the construction.
C. "Arcuate" architectural form was not used in the twelfth century.

(a) B and C are correct but A is incorrect

(b) A and B are correct but C is incorrect

(c) A, B, C all are correct

(d) A and C are correct but B is incorrect

104. Consider the following statements:
A. Hiuen Tsang wrote 'Si-Yu-Ki' or 'The records of Western World'.
B. Al-Beruni wrote 'Tahqiq-i-Hind'.

Select the correct answer from the code below:
(a) Only A
(b) Only B
(c) Both A and B
(d) Neither A nor B

105. Below are the two statements regarding the Tribal lives:
Statement (A): Under British rule, the functions and powers of the tribal chiefs changed.
Reason (R): They lost their administrative power and were forced to follow laws made by British officials in India.
(a) Both (A) and (R) are correct and (R) is the correct interpretation of (A)
(b) Both (A) and (R) are correct but (R) is not the correct interpretation of (A)
(c) (A) is correct, but (R) is wrong
(d) (A) is wrong, but (R) is right

106. Direction: Answer the following questions by selecting the correct / most appropriate options.
Assertion (A) : Temples and mosques were beautifully constructed.
Reason (R) : Temples demonstrate the power, wealth and devotion of the patron.
(a) Both (A) and (R) are true and (R) is the correct explanation of (A)
(b) Both (A) and (R) are true but (R) is not the correct explanation of (A)
(c) (A) is true, but (R) is false
(d) (A) is false, but (R) is true

107. Consider the following statements:
A) The trade with South East Asia during post Gupta age registered a significant increase.
B) Saurastra (Gujarat) was famous for its bell metal industry during this period.
Select the correct answer using the code below:
(a) Only A
(b) Only B
(c) Both A and B
(d) Neither A nor B

108. Consider the following statements:
Assertion (A): Nuclear energy is a promising source of futuristic demand for energy supply in India.
Reason (R): Nuclear minerals are ubiquitously available in India.

Select the correct answer by using the codes given below:
(a) Both (A) and (R) are true and (R) is the correct explanation of (A)
(b) Both (A) and (R) are true. But (R) is not the correct explanation of (A)
(c) (A) is true, but (R) is false
(d) (A) is false, but (R) is true

109. Consider the following statements regarding the Mauna Kea:
A. It is in the Arctic Ocean.
B. It is an undersea mountain.
C. It is lower than Mount Everest being 10,205 metres high.
Which of the following statement(s) is/are FALSE?
(a) A, B and C
(b) Only B
(c) Only A
(d) Only C

110. Identify the continent from the given features:
A. It covers about one-third of the total land area of the earth.
B. It lies in the Eastern hemisphere.
C. The tropic of cancer passes through this continent.
(a) Africa
(b) Europe
(c) South America
(d) Asia

111. Consider the following statements:
A. All the oceans of the world are connected with one another.
B. The level of seawater remains the same everywhere.
C. Elevation of land is measured from the sea level of the sea, which is taken as zero.
Which of the following statement(s) is/are correct?
(a) Only A
(b) Only B
(c) Only C
(d) A, B and C

112. Statements A and B describe the features of which of the following forests?
A. This is located in the mid-latitudinal coastal region.
B. These are commonly found along the eastern margin of the continents like in south-east USA, South China and in South-East Brazil.
(a) Tropical Evergreen Forests
(b) Tropical Deciduous Forests
(c) Temperate Evergreen Forests
(d) Temperate Deciduous Forests

113. With reference to asteroids, consider the following statements.

A. Asteroids are small pieces of rocks that move around the sun.
B. They are found between the orbits of Earth and Saturn.
C. Ceres is the largest asteroid.
Which of the following statement(s) is/are correct?
(a) Only A and C (b) Only B
(c) Only C   (d) A, B and C

114. Consider the following statements regarding the interior of the earth:
A. Crust is the thinnest of all the layers.
B. It is about 38 km on the continental masses and 10 km on the ocean floors.
C. Continental crust includes Silica and Alumina, whereas, Oceanic crust includes Silica and magnesium.
Which of the following statement(s) is/are FALSE?
(a) Only A
(b) Only B
(c) Only A and B
(d) None of the above

115. Choose the correct matching from the given options.

1. Permanent winds	easterlies and westerlies
2. Precipitation	snow, sleet, hail
3. Local winds	monsoons
4. Pressure belts	3 low and 4 high- pressure belts

(a) 1, 2 and 3
(b) 2, 3, and 4
(c) 1, 2, and 4
(d) All of the above

116. Consider the following statements about the Winter season in India and choose the correct answer:
A. The northeast trade winds prevail over the Indian Subcontinent
B. The coastal area of Tamil Nadu receives rainfall
C. The weather is normally marked by clear sky, low temperatures and low humidity and feeble, variable winds.
(a) A and B are true, C is false
(b) B and C are true, A is false
(c) A, B and C all are correct
(d) A and C are true, B is false

117. Consider the statements in the nature of social science at upper primary level?

1. It is a study of the people in their environment.
2. It is not the study of people's relationships and their interdependence.
3. It is a study of the relationship with the past and the present.
(a) 2 & 3   (b) 1 & 3
(c) 1, 2 & 3   (d) 1 & 2

118. Which of the following statements regarding an inquiry approach to teaching science in the classroom is/are correct?
I. It is an extension of the discovery approach.
II. In this approach, cause and effect relationship is established and the teacher provides no cues to the students.
(a) Only I
(b) Only II
(c) Both I and II
(d) Neither I nor II

119. Which of the following acts as a learning resource in social science?
I. Movies
II. Internet
III. Books
IV. Newspaper Clippings
(a) I, III and IV
(b) I, II, III and IV
(c) I, II and III
(d) II, III and IV

120. With reference to the Production Linked Incentive(PLI) scheme, consider the following statements:
1. It was introduced with the objective to scale up domestic manufacturing capability.
2. The incentives, calculated on the basis of incremental sales.
3. It supports the labour-intensive sectors and aims to increase the employment ratio in India.
4. This scheme works to reduce import bills.
Which of the statements given above is/are correct?
(a) 1 and 2 only
(b) 2 and 3 only
(c) 1, 2, and 3 only
(d) 1, 2, 3 and 4

// Hints and Solutions //

1(D). There are many learning theories in psychology that are related to different schools of psychology such as cognitive, humanistic, behavioristic, etc. These theories are propounded by eminent psychologists to provide a framework to understand different aspects of human behavior.
Some of the famous learning theories include:

Theory	Propounder	Main Idea
Trial and Error Theory	Thorndike	The theory emphasizes that learning is the result of associations forming between stimulus and responses.
Instrumental Learning Theory/ Theory of Operant Conditioning	B. F. Skinner	Theory implies the idea that learning takes place through rewarding a certain behavior or withholding reward for undesirable behavior.
Insight Theory of Learning	Kohler	The theory emphasizes that a sudden solution to the problem as insight doesn't rely on behavior or observation.
Socio-cultural Theory	Lev Vygotsky	Theory implies the idea that interaction with society and environment plays a vital role in shaping the behaviour, action, and abilities of a child.
Classical Conditioning Theory	Ivan Pavlov	The theory emphasizes that behaviour is learnt by a repetitive association between the response and the stimulus.

B.S. Bloom has not propounded any learning theory rather he has proposed a taxonomy which is a set of three hierarchical models that refers to the classification of educational learning objectives.
Bloom's Taxonomy Identified Three Domains of Learning:
- Cognitive Domain: It involves knowledge and the development of intellectual skills. The six major categories of objectives which come under the cognitive domain are Knowledge, Comprehension, Application, Analysis, Synthesis, and Evaluation
- Affective Domain: It includes how we deal with things emotionally, such as feelings, values, appreciation, enthusiasms, motivations, and attitudes.
- Psychomotor Domain: It includes physical movement, coordination, and use of the motor-skill areas.

So, it could be concluded that B.S. Bloom has not propounded any learning theory.

2(A). Stagnation stands for the retention of a child in a class for a period of more than one year. Gradually when a student takes more than one year to pass a class it is considered a case of stagnation.
- Stagnation is one of the most acute problems of tribal education. Absenteeism leads to stagnation and both naturally lead to wastage.
- Formerly stagnation used to occur due to lower achievement in the examinations. It means those who fail to secure minimum marks in the class tests will not be sent for the terminal examination and such candidates will have to remain in the same standard for one more year.
- But this practice is now stopped, whether a student secures minimum marks in the class tests or not he/she is eligible to sit for terminal examinations. At present minimum attendance is prescribed for students for promotion.

So, it could be concluded that retention of a child in a same class for more than one year is the meaning of stagnation in education.

3(B). Learning refers to the modification of behavioral patterns. It is a comprehensive process which refers to a change in behavior, knowledge, and skill as a result of practice and experience.
- Learning of children will be most effective when development of cognitive, affective, and psychomotor domains of children will take place.
- These domains are proposed by Benjamin Bloom's in his taxonomy. It is a set of three hierarchical models that refers to the classification of educational learning objectives.

Let's Understand these domains in the context of child's learning:
- Cognitive domains: In this domain, a child deals with knowledge and hence, learns to create, evaluate, analyze, etc.
- Affective domains: This domain comes into play when child grows in emotional areas such as feelings, attitudes, etc.
- Psychomotor domains: It is concerned with acquiring skills that require the integration of mental and physical movements.

So, it could be concluded that the learning of children will be most effective when development of cognitive, affective, and psychomotor domains of children will take place.

4(C). Development refers to an increase in structure for better and enhanced functioning of organs. It is a wide and continuous process that starts from the pre-natal stage.

In the pre-natal stage, baby develops inside the mother's womb and becomes a mature one by passing through three different stages of prenatal development.

The three stages of pre-natal development include:

- Germinal period: First 2 weeks after conception.
- Embryonic period: 8 weeks from conception.
- Fetal Period: 9 weeks until birth or 38 to 40 weeks.

Hence it could be concluded that development starts from the pre-natal stage.

Additional Information

Stage of infancy	• It refers to the first year or the early period of a child's development in which the child grows rapidly after birth. • It is a crucial period of development in which the child learns to sit, crawl, stand, etc.
Pre-childhood stage	• It refers to the time period from the age of 'Two to Seven years'. It is a very crucial period for child's overall development. • It is also known as the toy age, pregang age, and exploratory age, etc.
Post-childhood stage	• It refers to the time period from the age of 'seven to twelve years'. The signs of puberty usually begin to appear in this stage. • It is also known as troublesome age, gang age, play age, etc.

5(B). Childhood refers to the period of the human lifespan, ranging from birth to puberty. It consists of many developmental stages and 'adolescence' is one of them.

'Adolescence' comes from the Latin word 'Adolescere' which means 'to grow to become mature'. It a stage which lies between the age of '12 to 19 years'.

According to Stanley Hall:

- Adolescence is a turbulent time charged with conflict and mood swings.
- The time period of transition from childhood and adolescence is of great stress.
- Adolescence fails to think clearly and it creates great frustration and stress in their lives.

So, it could be concluded that "Adolescence is the period of great stress, strain, storm and strike" is the statement of Stanley Hall.

6(B). Development: It is a broad term that includes a series of qualitative and progressive changes. These qualitative changes lead to the enhancement of various abilities and enable one to function effectively.

- Emotions: These are the feelings generated as an effect of experiences, or relationships of an individual with others. They are instinctive reactions that come naturally to all and contribute to personal and social adjustments of an individual.

According to Cole and Bruce, childhood is a unique stage of emotional development.

- Emotional development relies heavily on the process of socialization and proceeds in a stepwise manner.
- Basic emotions such as fear, disgust, happiness, sadness, surprise, anger, and interest, are present since birth.
- During childhood, mood tantrums are pretty common.
- Toddlers have a tendency to have fast temper swings. While their emotions may be very intense, these emotions additionally have a tendency to be pretty short-lived.
- One might be stunned at how an infant can go from screaming hysterically about a toy at one second to sitting in the front of the TV quietly looking at a favorite show simply moments later.
- Children at this age are very possessive and have difficulty in sharing.

So, it could be concluded that 'Childhood' is called as 'A unique stage of emotional development' by Cole and Bruce.

7(A). In cognitive development, heredity establishes the basic nature of physical structure such as the brain.

Cognitive development is a field of study in neuroscience and psychology focusing on a child's development in terms of information processing, conceptual resources, perceptual skill, language learning, and other aspects of brain development and cognitive psychology compared to an adult's point of view.

8(B). The Piaget theory of cognitive development has used the following two stages or activities, namely, organization and adaptation as described below:

Adaptation: According to Piaget, children have an innate tendency to adjust to their environment. This trend has been termed 'adaptation'. According to him, the child starts adapting to the environment from the beginning

Organization: When a child encounters an aggravating situation, their individual mental activities do not work separately, but they work together and collectively help them to acquire knowledge. At the mental level, this activity happens continuously. Adaptation to the environment is the result of the organization.

9(C). A conative domain is not among the three domains of behavior that are covered by the evaluation.

The cognitive domain is focused on intellectual skills such as critical thinking, problem solving, and creating a knowledge base. For evaluating cognitive development oral, written, essay type, objective type questions examinations are used.

The affective domain includes the manner in which we deal with things emotionally, such as feelings, values, appreciation, enthusiasms, motivations, and attitudes. For evaluating affective domain interest inventory, practical examinations, and observation techniques are used.

For evaluating psychomotor domain performance tests, practical examination, and observation techniques are used.

10(B). Imitation learning mainly influences the personality of the child. Imitation is an advanced behavior whereby an individual observes and replicates another's behavior. An imitation is also a form of social learning that leads to the "development of traditions, and ultimately our culture.

11(D). Curiosity and Creative ideas are considered a sign of being gifted. Fighting is a confrontation in which two or more people compete for dominance and respect to satisfy their own egos. Thus, it cannot be regarded as a sign of being gifted. Curiosity is a valuable agent in education when it is rightly valued and employed. Curiosity is highly important because it is a starting point of interest. Creative ideas are concerned with a holistic approach to education, focusing upon the learner becoming part of a professional community, involving the dimensions of knowledge, performance and identity formation.

12(C). In concrete operational stage, the child responds to inferred reality. Children are much less egocentric in the concrete operational stage. It falls between the ages of 7 to 11 years old and is marked by more logical and methodical manipulation of symbols. The main goal at this stage is for a child to start working things out inside their head.

13(D). In childhood, physiological development follows the cephalocaudal sequence. their growth occurs from head to extreme parts.

In adolescents, their body size will increase, with the feet, arms, legs, and hands sometimes growing "faster" than the rest of the body. it does not follow the cephalocaudal sequence.

So, growth in adolescents is reverse of that in childhood because in adolescents hands feet and legs accelerate first than other parts.

14(C). The adverse effect of insisting on

the same answers from all children will hinder the growth of the child's own understanding and imagination. Cognitive powers of a child, like imagination power, intelligence, ability to make a decision, etc. are related to the child's 'mental development' as mental development refers to the development of the ability to understand, learn, reason, think, perceive, and solve a problem.

Hence, the correct option is (C).

15(D). Teachers can identify children who take part in all school activities and those children who are always left out. so he should organize group games, debates, seminars, conferences, etc. so that students can take part in these activities.

Teachers can make use of sociometric devices to identify isolates and cliquish in a given group.

The disliked or rejected can be helped by making them aware of the reasons and also planning and implementing some remedial programmes such as making groups consisting of disliked or rejected ad popular children for various work, such as assignment during school day programmes, Child's hostility, tension, nervousness, rebellion. temper tantrums, withdrawal, indifference and other undesirable reactions. Hence. parents and teachers should try to understand the probable causes for their children's aggressive behaviour.

Teachers and parents should help the children to release their emotions by playing with dolls. Children need many opportunities at school and home to sing, play outdoor games, to tell a poem or painting to release their emotions.

16(B). Secondary or social rewards such as praise, smile, or money: A secondary reinforcer is a stimulus to which we have learned to respond because of past learning by the association of the stimulus with a primary reinforcer. An example is money, as it is associated with primary reinforcers like it is used to get food when we are hungry.

Hence, we can conclude that after the occurrence of desirable behavior, the teacher says 'very good to the child. She has used secondary reinforcers as she had praised the child.

17(C). Eight Intellectual Levels or Eight Conditions of Learning:

- Signal learning: The learner makes a general response to a signal.
- Stimulus-response learning: The learner makes a precise response to a signal.
- Chaining: The connection of a set of individual stimulus and responses in a sequence.
- Verbal association: The learner makes associations using verbal connections.
- Discrimination Learning: The learner

makes different responses to different stimuli that are somewhat alike.

- Concept learning: The learner develops the ability to make a generalized response based on a class of stimuli.
- Rule learning: A rule is a chain of concepts linked to demonstrated behaviour.
- Problem-solving: The learner discovers a combination of previously learned rules and applies them to solve a novel situation.

Thus from the above-mentioned points, it is clear that proper prerequisites are not a type of learning according to Gagne's Theory of Learning.

18(A). Bloom's Taxonomy: It is a hierarchical ordering of cognitive, affective, and psychomotor domains and each domain has some objectives that can help teachers teach and students learn. As per him, there are three Domains of Learning:

- Cognitive domains: In this domain, a child deals with knowledge and hence, learns to create, evaluate, analyze, apply, understand, remember.
- Affective domains: When it comes to growth in emotional areas, this domain comes into play.

1. Receiving: When a learner shows sensitivity to certain stimuli.
2. Responding: It is defined as the tendency to respond to an object or stimuli.
3. Valuing: It refers to the acceptance of a behaviour and commitment to it. One values certain behaviours not by desires but by commitment.
4. Organizing: It refers to organizing the value system which is attained when one develops one's code of conduct or standard of public life.
5. Characterizing: It deals with behaviour as per values or attitudes a child has imbibed; children show teamwork.

- Psychomotor domains: These domains are nothing but manual or physical skills. It deals with physical coordination, movements, and motor skills. It includes imitation, manipulation, precision, articulation, and naturalization.

Therefore, we conclude that the correct order is Receiving, Responding, Valuing, Organizing, Characterizing.

19(D). The key principles of inclusive education for children:

Principle of Equality: Everyone has the right to access knowledge skill and information. Indian constitution guarantees some educational rights for the children. In spite of these provisions there are some group of people who are deprived of education because of some special causes or factor. But inclusive education includes all those section of people and provides equality to all.

Principle of Participation: Inclusive education is based on the principle of participation. Inclusive education includes all the children in common educational settings where they can learn together without any discrimination. It provides opportunities for the students with disabilities for the active participation equally. Thus inclusive education promotes the participation for all children or adults in teaching learning process.

Principle of acceptance: It is another principle of inclusive education. Every parents wants to their child to lean or educate with all other students in a regular classroom and become able to lead their life independently. And it is base on this principle of acceptance of all children in education process irrespective of their disabilities.

Principle of Togetherness: Inclusive education provides such learning environment that promotes all round development of all learners together in the same educational setting. Irrespective of their caste, color and gender. So it is an approach which brings all children together in a common educational community.

20(D). A classroom/institution that welcomes diversity of categories, abilities, cultures, disabilities, etc. is an inclusive education.

The principles of inclusive education include:

- No discrimination among students
- Equal educational opportunity for all
- Adapting to the needs of students, for example, making institutions disabled-friendly
- Equal educational benefits to all students
- Individual difference is promoted among students
- The needs of the students are taken seriously.

21(A). Speaking short sentences and riding a three-wheeled bicycle, this work is done in infancy. From the birth of a child to the age of 6 years is called infancy or infancy. In this stage the child is completely dependent. Of course, he is completely dependent on the other. Parents and family member have to depend for his developmental care.

22(A). The child first starts getting attracted towards the light. Child development refers to the biological and intellectual changes that occur in humans from birth to the end of adolescence, when they gradually move from dependence to more autonomy. Since these developmental changes can be largely influenced by genetic factors and events during prenatal life, genetics and prenatal development are typically included as part of the study of child development.

23(B). The socialization of a child is determind by sociometry techniques. Sociometric techniques are methods that qualitatively measure aspects of social interactions, such as social acceptance (i.e., how well a person is liked by peers) and social status (i.e., a child's social status compared to peers).

24(A). Constructivist pedagogy places the child at the centre of the learning, and can also be referred to as 'invisible pedagogy'. It is an approach to learning in which learners are provided the opportunity to construct their own sense of what is being learned by building internal connection or relationship among the ideas and facts being taught."

25(C). If the teacher comes to know that a student is absent in the class, in such a case, instead of expelling/punishing/preventing him/her from attending the class, the teacher should know the reason for his/her negligence and find out the appropriate remedy.

Revision in Teacher Preparation in Classroom Management:
- Teacher with an instructional approach to classroom management, providing candidates with feedback through curriculum and guided exercises, and
- Addressing the challenges faced by teacher candidates and new teachers in creating a positive classroom context.

26(A). Parents should play a forward-looking role in the learning process of their children and encourage them to do better. As preschoolers grow into school-age children, parents become their children's learning coaches. Through guidance and reminders, parents help their children organize their time and support their desire to learn new things in and out of school.

27(A). Cognitive development aims to study a child's development, especially information processing, conceptual processing, perceptual skills, language learning, and other aspects related to brain development. The process of striking a balance between adjustment and assimilation. Whereas on the other hand adaptation (a relatively stable structure) occurs when the child strikes a balance between the two processes while trying to internalize the perceived processes.

28(A). On the basis of the classical contract theory of learning, feelings of fear, love and hatred can be easily generated in the child. In classical contract theory, an association is established between the stimulus response. Before understanding classical conditioning, it is necessary to know that there are other functions in human beings, some are innate like breathing, digestion etc and some are for psychological reasons like blinking, salivation etc.

29(A). The theory of classical conditioning was propounded by I.V. Paulov in 1904. According to this theory, a response to a natural stimulus that is similar to a natural stimulus is classical conditioning, that is, the establishment of an association between the stimulus and the response is conditioning. Before understanding classical conditioning, it is necessary to know that there are other functions in human beings, some are innate like breathing, digestion etc and some are for psychological reasons like blinking, salivation etc.

30(A). The field theory of learning in children, in which the learner perceives and responds to the whole situation, comes under Kohler's theory of understanding.
The associative theory of learning in children is described on the basis of stimulus response. In this, a relationship is established between the stimulus response. It is also called stimulus response or S-R principle.

31(B). According to the passage, five men who were camping in the Cascade Mountains of Washington saw a group of huge apelike creatures coming out of the woods. They hurried back to their cabin and locked themselves inside.

32(A). According to the passage, After the incident when five men saw the big foots they returned to the town and told the people of their adventure. However, only a few people accepted their story.

33(C). The local native Americans were the first people to have seen these apelike creatures before the five campers.
According to the passage, Then in 1967, Roger Patterson, a man who was interested in finding Bigfoot went into the northern California jungles with a friend. While riding, they were suddenly thrown off from their horses. Patterson saw a tall apelike animal standing not far away. Therefore the first people to have seen these apelike creatures before the five campers was Roger Patterson and his friend.

34(B). According to the passage, neighbouring means: a person or place which is adjacent with the given person of place. Therefore nearby will be correct option which can replace the word 'neighbouring.'

35(C). According to the passage, The local Native Americans were certain that a race of apelike animals had been living in the neighboring mountain for centuries. They called these creatures Sasquatch.

36(D). According to the passage, Animals are the creatures, woods are found in jungles and after seeing the objects are spotted. But there is no relation between huge and hairy.

Therefore Huge – hairy is not correct pair.

37(C). According to the passage, After carefully reading the passage the best title of the passage would be "The creature called Bigfoot."

38(B). According to the passage, Richard Brown, a music teacher and also an experience hunter spotted a similar creature. He saw the animal clearly through the telescopic lens of his rifle. He said the creature looked more like a human than an animal.

39(D). According to the passage, Roger Patterson managed to shoot seven rolls of film of the hairy creature before the animal disappeared in the hushes.

40(D). From the lines ' The sun descending in the west, The evening star does shine, The birds are silent in their nest. ' it is clear that t he evening star rises when the sun descends in the west.

41(C). From the lines 'The moon, like a flower, In heaven's high bower'. Here, 'bower' represents a bouquet of flowers.

42(A). From the lines, The moon, like a flower, In heaven's high bower. Then in the passage the poet compares the moon to an angel.

43(B). From the lines 'The feet of angels bright; Unseen they pour blessing, And joy without ceasing, On each bud and blossom,'. It is clear that the angels come down on earth to give blessing and joy.

44(D). From the lines 'They look in every thoughtless nest Where birds are covered warm; They visit caves of every beast, To keep them all from harm'. Therefore in the poem, birds' nest is described as 'thoughtless' because the occupants are asleep without any care.

45(A). The figure of speech used, in the line 'In heaven's high bower' is Metaphor. A metaphor is a figure of speech that, for rhetorical effect, directly refers to one thing by mentioning another.

46(A). Textbook is the area in which the language material presented prescribed for teaching and learning. A good textbook not only teaches but it also tests. The content of the book should be very clear, a proper beginning is required to prepare the learners for the upcoming content and a perfect conclusion is required to assemble the entire learning.

47(A). Grammar-translation method of teaching English heavily relies on form-focussed teaching. The grammar–translation method is a method of teaching foreign languages derived from the classical (sometimes called traditional) method of teaching Greek and Latin. In grammar–translation classes, students learn grammatical rules and then apply those rules by translating sentences between the target language and the native language.

Form-focused instruction (FFI) refers to any pedagogical practice aimed at drawing learners' attention to language form. The "form" may consist of phonological (sound), morphosyntactic (word form, word order), lexical, pragmatic, discourse, or orthographical aspects of language.

48(C). Multimedia provides a technology based constructivist learning environment where students are able to solve a problem by means of self exploration, collaboration and active participation. This approach provides various opportunities to the learners and provides a platform to the learners to be an avtive individual performer. It is helpful for each kind of learner.

49(C). In this type of programme teachers may teach and train students who perform better in a particular subject and also helps to maintain their teaching learning difficulties within group teaching and self study itself. This programme helps students to reinforce their knowledge and develop their communication and co-operation skill as well as good interpersonal relation.

50(D). Keeping in mind teachers has many children demanding their time and attention; a good conference can help a busy teacher to focus on what your child needs. Review reports and check your files from previous conferences to see if they remind you of important topics you may have missed. Be clear in your own mind about each child's strengths, weaknesses and appropriate goals.

51(C). When a child learns a language naturally, without much practice, it is called language acquisition. It is the process by which humans acquire the capacity to perceive and comprehend language, as well as to produce and use words and sentences to communicate. It is one of the quintessential human traits, because non-humans do not communicate by using language.

52(A). The study of 'chunks of language' which are bigger than a single sentence is Discourse. It denotes written and spoken communications. It is a conceptual generalization of conversation within each modality and context of communication.

53(B). Children need frequent changes of activity: they need activities which are exiting and stimulate the curiosity, they need to be involved in something active, and they need to be appreciated by the teacher, an important figure for them. Question answer activity is an example to attract student's attention. In this activity, teachers can give examples of question and answer. Teachers can start to train students by Yes/No question. Furthermore, teachers can give Wh-question. It is expected the students can give relevant and suitable answers based on real situation.

54(B). Interaction analysis based on practice teaching training in teaching skills using micro-teaching approach and simulated teaching exercise are some of innovative technologies through which effective training program can be transacted. The present mode also pointed out each one of these technologies, its major emphasis on the use of micro-teaching in Indian situation for developing the required skills of teaching at the mastery level.

55(D). Oral compositions have been very popular in English language teaching for some time. The idea is for the teacher and students working together to build up a narrative orally before writing it. The process of building up the composition with the whole class allows the teacher and students to focus in on a variety of language items from tense usage to cohesive elements, etc. Oral composition develop much influencing grammar, once a child communicate orally to other self confidence also develop on him. After making such practice he get fluency in language too.

56(D). Reading is important because it increases vocabulary, makes pupil to gain knowledge and helps them in getting information.

Reading affects our attitudes, beliefs, standards, morals, judgments, and general behavior. It shapes our thinking and our actions. The purpose of reading is to correlate the ideas on the text to what you have already known. The reader must understand about the subject that he/she read to connect the ideas. Learning to read is about listening and understanding as well as working out what's printed on the page. Through hearing stories, children are exposed to a wide range of words. This helps them build their own vocabulary and improve their understanding when they listen, which is vital as they start to read. Reading is important because it makes you more empathetic, knowledgeable and stimulates your imagination. Reading allows one to develop a better understanding of the subject and gain conceptual clarity. It is one of the simplest entertainment entities for humans.

57(D). Language laboratory is the place where the learners have to listen on headphone. It is an audio or audio-visual installation used as an aid in modern language teaching. Here, the student can hear his own mistake for himself and also the student's active speaking time is increased considerably.

58(A). The material on opaque sheet is projected with the help of episcope hardware. The opaque projector, epidioscope, epidiascope or episcope is a device which displays opaque materials by shining a bright lamp onto the object from above. A system of mirrors, prisms and/or imaging lenses is used to focus an image of the material onto a viewing screen.

59(A). In any language, attending to and interpreting the oral rendition is termed as listening. The student imitates and memorizes linguistic items, such as words, idioms, phrases, tone, etc. and thus learns speaking the language. Listening skill forms the backbone of learning a language, irrespective of the fact that it is a first language or a second language.

60(B). Evaluation encompasses more aspects than measurement, but proper evaluation is not possible without the process of measurement. Evaluation covers all the three domains of behavior which are; cognitive domain, affective domain and psychomotor domain.

61(C). An overhead absorption rate is used to charge overheads to products.

The overhead absorption rate is a rate charged to the cost unit intended to account for the overhead at a predetermined level of activity. On the basis of direct labor hours, direct labor cost, or machine hours, overhead is attributed to a product or service. It is used to charged overheads to products.

62(D). **Occupational Safety, Health & Working Conditions Code, 2020:**
- Free health checkup once a year by the employer.
- Providing appointment Letter to workers coming for the first time.
- Film Workers have been designated as Audio Visual Worker to ensure their rights.
- It can now over cover workers from the IT and Service Sector.
- So, statement 3 is correct.

Social Security Code, 2020:
- Provision of "Social Security Fund" for 40 Crore unorganized workers has been made.
- Registration of all workers of the unorganised sector would be done on an online portal to make a national database.
- The facility of ESIC would now be provided in all 740 districts.
- At present, this facility is being given in 566 districts only.
- Formulation of various schemes for providing social security to workers in the unorganised sector.
- A "Social Security Fund" will be created on the financial side in order to implement these schemes.
- So, statement 2 is correct.

- EPFO's coverage would be applicable to all establishments having 20 workers.
- Provision for Gratuity has been made for Fixed Term Employee.
- There would not be any condition for a minimum service period for taking gratuity.

Industrial Relations Code, 2020:
It includes:
- Making a national database of migrant workers.
- Provision for the accumulation of leave.
- 14 days prior notice for Strike so that in this period amicable solution comes out.
- Compulsory facility for Helpline for redressal of grievances of migrant workers.
- Equality for women in every sphere.
- The employer will be responsible for her safety & security.
- In case of the death of a worker or injury due to an accident at his workplace, at least a 50 % share of the penalty would be given.
- It would be in addition to Employees Compensation.

63(C). The Five E model is considered as one of the popular lesson plans used to develop lesson plans in different subjects including social sciences. Explore is the second step of this model.
- Through exploration experiences, students are given a common framework of tasks that allow for the identification of present concepts (i.e., misconceptions), procedures, and skills as well as the facilitation of conceptual change.
- Students can complete lab exercises that enable them to draw on existing knowledge to develop fresh concepts, ponder issues and options, and plan and carry out a pilot study.

64(A). A debate builds up in learners the ability to gather information, process it, and present it to the audience:
- Debating helps students develop these skills and be ready to tackle whatever challenges come their way.
- Debating provides the opportunity for students to develop important leadership skills such as public speaking, teamwork, communication, and being able to argue a point of view in a positive, calm, and logical manner.
- A debate is a formal discussion on a particular theme or topic.
- It is mostly conducted in a public setting in which people present their opposing arguments for or against a particular theme or topic.

65(B). The purpose of End-text Questions given in Social and Political Life textbooks is to cover the main concepts raised by the chapter and ask learners to explain these in their own words.

- In drafting the end-text questions, care has been taken to encourage the student to understand rather than to blindly memorize the contents of the book.
- These various types of questions will allow the teacher to evaluate whether the child has not only understood a concept but that this learning includes an ability to relate to the concept meaningfully.

66(C). In a Social Science class, a survey project is a suitable method for underlining the phenomenon that spaces of rural areas are disappearing fast.

"Survey project" is a suitable method for underlining the above-mentioned phenomenon as it helps in:
- enabling the learner to interact with the community.
- collecting accurate information by asking questions.
- drawing an authentic conclusion to make important decisions.
- making the learner being sensitized to different issues and people.
- taking students to the place of occurrence to make the right decisions.
- making learning meaningful by engaging learners with real-life situations.

67(C). Providing a situation is the first step of doing a project of Social Studies.

It is the first step of the project method where the teacher creates/provides the situation related to the real-life problems to the students. The teacher gives the knowledge about the project method procedures, steps, and uses to the students.

68(A). A Social Science teacher must employ a method of Increase the engagement of students by thought-provoking and interesting activities for being effective as it will create interest and awareness among the students.

It is necessary to revitalize social science teaching, to help the learner acquire knowledge and skills in an interactive environment.

69(C). Unrealistic course of study is not the nature of social science.
- Social sciences are basically concerned with human relationship. Study of the nature of human society is the ultimate goal of all social sciences.
- Social sciences aim at making a sensitive, reflective and informed human being.
- Different social sciences like history, economics, sociology, anthropology etc. constitute an area or field of knowledge. And, this area or field of knowledge is functionally different from other areas or fields of knowledge like languages, mathematics, general sciences, etc.

70(C). Social Science is a branch of Science that deals with human behaviour

and social relationships, which rely primarily on empirical approaches.

While teaching Social Science, a teacher must attempt to focus upon facts, values and patterns as teaching of Social Science focuses upon making student assimilate norms, beliefs, cultures and values of society.

71(C). Problems of teaching social science in school include lack of integration with life and other school subjects.

A social science teacher faces the challenges of not only helping students develop skills of observation, identification, classification, and interpretation of contemporary issues but also integrating them in teaching other subjects such as language and mathematics.

72(B). 'Showing the historical places in the map' is not a comprehensive objective of social science.

It should be noted that showing the historical places on the map is not falling under a comprehensive objective of social science as it is a limited activity. Other given activities has a comprehensive nature. These require a specific tool to comprehend the learning activity.

73(A). The teaching of social and political life textbooks at the upper primary level focuses on learning through real-life situations approach.

Used real-life situations in order to teach concepts since it acknowledged that children learn best through real experiences. It uses material that draws upon the experiential understanding of familial and social issues that middle school children bring to the classroom.

74(B). When a teacher of Social Studies evaluates pupils' learning outcomes on tolerance of different religions, languages, regions, political ideologies, etc., and appreciation, desirable attitude, commitment, etc., then this evaluation is called as non-cognitive.

The teacher of social studies has to evaluate certain non-cognitive learning outcomes. Such learning outcomes will include tolerance for different religions, languages, regions, political ideologies, etc., and appreciation, desirable attitudes, commitment, conduct, skills, habits, etc.

75(D).

Option 1 (incorrect)	Option 2 (correct)	Option 3 (correct)
The Hinayana sect of Buddhism believed in the original teachings of buddha and did not believe in id	The Mahayana sect of Buddhism believed in the heavenliness of Buddha and believed in idol worship. They favoured the Sanskrit lan	Maitreya is a future Buddha. He will be a bodhisattva. He is having the goal of achiev

ol worship. They favou red pali lan guage	guage.	ing absolu te enlighte nment an d spreadin g knowled ge of pure Dhamma.

76(B). We come to know about the first farmers and herders as we have evidence of grains and animal bones.

- The first farmers and herders were discovered by archaeologists in various regions such as Mehrgarh, Chirand, Hallur and many more.
- Grains and bones were also discovered in several locations around the globe.
- We have no written records of that time because the script wasn't developed during the period of early farmers and herders.
- Wheat, barley, rice were grown in Mehrgarh, lentil in Burzahom.

77(C). In 1856, Lord Canning decided that Bahadur Shah Zafar would be the last Mughal king and after his death, none of his descendants would be recognized as a ruler – they would just be called princes.

- This disrespectful behaviour towards the Mughal Emperor is also one of the political reasons for the revolt of 1857.
- Lord canning became the first Viceroy of India and served from year 1858 - 1862.
- He also served as the " Governor-General of India" from 1856 - 1862.
- He abolished the "Doctrine of Lapse" and established three universities in Bombay, Calcutta, and Madras.

78(C). Mangrove forests grow along the coasts in the salt marshes, tidal creeks, mudflats and estuaries.

- In India, Mangrove forests are spread over 6,740 sq. km.
- They are highly developed in the Andaman and Nicobar islands and the Sunderbans of West Bengal.
- This vegetation can survive in saline water.
- Sundari is a well-known species of trees of this vegetation.

79(C). Accountability to the citizens is the most basic outcome of a democratic government.

A parliamentary system or parliamentary democracy is a system of democratic governance of a state. In a parliamentary system, the head of state is usually a person distinct from the head of government.

80(D). There are three branches of government the executive, the legislative, and the judiciary.

- The three branches of the union government are charged with different responsibilities, but the constitution also provides a fair degree of interdependence.
- The executive branch consists of the president, vice president, and a Council of Ministers, led by the prime minister. Within the legislative branch are the two houses of parliament—the lower house, or Lok Sabha (House of the People), and the upper house, or Rajya Sabha (Council of States).
- The president of India is also considered part of the parliament.
- At the apex of the judicial branch is the Supreme Court, whose decisions are binding on the higher and lower courts of the state governments.

81(A). A particular area from which all the voters living there choose their representatives called Constituency.

- The elections are held by dividing the whole country or a State into several representative areas called constituencies.
- Thus, a constituency is a fixed area with a body of voters or residents with strong voting rights. There are separate constituencies each for Assembly elections and Parliamentary elections.
- The elected representatives are known as Members of the Legislative Assembly or Members of Parliament.

82(A). Indian state ensures non-interference in the religious practices and respects sentiments of all religions.

The state has no religion.The constitution of India does provide certain provisions for minority communities. Under Article 30, the Constitution of India provides provisions for minority communities to establish and manage educational institutions. Cultural and Educational Rights is a fundamental right too.

Thus, we can say that there are provisions to provide educational rights to cultural and linguistic minorities in the Indian Constitution.

83(C). The literacy rate among women in India is only 65.46 percent.

- Female literacy is particularly wanted in the country as a significant proportion of them are still illiterate with major ramifications for the Indian economy.
- Apart from the low female literacy, there is also a wide gender disparity in India's performance in literacy with a difference of around 20 percentage points between male and female literacy rates.

84(B). Rashsundari's autobiography is titled Amar Jiban.

- She was a housewife from a rich landlord's family. During her time, it was believed that if a woman learned to read and write, she would bring bad luck to her husband and become a widow.
- However, even after knowing this, she taught herself how to read and write in secret, well after her marriage.
- At the age of 60, she wrote her autobiography in Bangla. Her book titled 'Amar Jiban' is the first known autobiography written by an Indian woman.

85(A). Dispute Resolution is related to Judicial system.

According to the 'Dispute Resolution' function of the judicial system is to provide a mechanism for resolving disputes between citizens, between citizens and the government, between two state governments, and between the center and state governments.

86(B). B.R. Ambedkar in the Constituent Assembly helped the Scheduled Castes get some safeguards in the draft constitution.

- He was the leader of the depressed class and worked for the promotion of education among the Scheduled Castes.
- He fought for the upliftment of the Dalits and their rights in society.
- He founded the Scheduled Castes Federation in July 1942.
- He was awarded the Bharat Ratna posthumously in 1990.

87(A). India is the country of Diversity.

- We speak different languages, have various types of food, celebrate different festivals, practice different religions.
- India's national anthem, composed by Rabindranath Tagore, is another expression of the unity of India.
- India has adopted a Parliamentary form of government.
- It has indirect democracy where different castes, different religions, and different languages citizens participate in elections.

88(D). Stereotype, term is used when we fix people into one image.

- When people say that those who belong to a particular country, religion, sex, race or economic background are "stingy," "lazy," "criminal" or "dumb," they are using stereotypes.
- Stereotypes stop us from looking at each person as a unique individual with his or her own special qualities.
- They fit large numbers of people into only one pattern or type.
- Stereotypes affect all of us as they prevent us from doing certain things, that we might otherwise be good at.

89(B). Democracy is a form of government, where people participate in the decision-making process directly or indirectly.

In case of indirect participation, they select their representatives, who take decision on people's behalf. Democracy is used as a part of liberal democracy or representative democracy, which includes political pluralism, right to fight elections, equality before law, due process of law, human rights, civil rights, and so on.

90(D). NITI Aayog has approved 32 beneficiaries under the production-linked incentive (PLI) scheme for large-scale electronics manufacturing in September 2022.
- NITI Aayog on 9 September 2022 approved 32 beneficiaries under the production-linked incentive (PLI) scheme for large-scale electronics manufacturing.
- This is the first-ever disbursement under any PLI scheme.
- Padget Electronics Pvt Ltd, a domestic company, is the first beneficiary approved to receive incentive under mobile manufacturing.

91(D). Students who acquire critical thinking abilities can get higher grades, become less reliant on professors and textbooks, create knowledge, and assess, criticize, and change societal structures.
- Discuss the issues of Poverty in India. Here, in this question, the student will do reasoning, and innovative findings and then will give creative solutions. Thus, this will provide opportunities to promote critical thinking skills.
- What are the challenges faced by the students going to school in rural areas? Here, in this question, the student will do an analysis and evaluation of challenges faced by the students going to school in rural areas. Thus, this will provide opportunities to promote critical thinking skills.

92(A). An original assignment that tests concepts is an appropriate and meaningful written assignment in Social Science from the following as it will give the students an opportunity to critically examine, understand, and appreciate the concepts.
A summary of the chapter will help the learners to explain the chapter in his/her own words. It will develop their cognitive domain.

93(C). History is a narrative account of the past. It is the story of changing human cultures, beliefs, and lifestyles and helps to build up a sense of what could happen in the future. It is a journey across time and space. It leads us into another world, another age, in which people lived differently.
History helps us in the following:
- compare the past with the present.
- understand how the present evolved.
- build up a sense of what could happen in the future.
- imagine living in the past and relate to the experiences.
- understand the working of our physical and social world.
- trace continuity and change in the social processes in history.
- view events by situating them within socio-political context of a particular period.
- understand how the modern world has appeared over long centuries of development.

So, it could be concluded that all the above-mentioned statements are correct in the context of History.

94(A). Social and Political Life is a new subject area in middle school social science that has replaced the earlier subject of Civics. NCF 2005 strongly argues that Civics should be discontinued and its focus on government institutions and functioning should be tempered in the new subject that replaces it.
Social and Political Life, as its name suggests, focuses on topics related to social, political, and economic life in contemporary India. This subject recognizes that children learn best through concrete experiences.
Approaches like learning through use of concrete examples and experiences should have been considered while developing social and political life textbooks as Social and Political Life:
- focuses on real situations to teach concepts.
- develops learners' abilities of critical understanding.
- uses case studies and narratives to explain concepts.
- avoids the use of definitions to sum up a concept.
- uses material that draws upon experiential understanding.

Hence, it could be concluded that learning through use of concrete examples and experiences is the best approach in the context of the question.

95(C). Social sciences comprise a branch/field of knowledge which basically studies human society or human relationship. Social sciences study the social behaviour of human life. The different core-components of social behaviour of human life are- economic behaviour, political behaviour, cultural behaviour and tradition, customs and social institutions, religious faiths and ethics, value patterns followed in society, etc. Social sciences occupy a significant component of both university/higher education as well as school curriculum. The objective of discussing 'equality' in a social science classroom is to:
- address issues of dignity with the learners.
- sensitize learners towards respecting everyone.
- build upon values enshrined in the Constitution.

It should be noted that a teacher, in any way, should not promote inequality. In fact, he should promote the benefits of individual differences.
Hence, 'explaining all differences leads to inequality' is not the objective.

96(B). Assessment is integral to the teaching-learning process which helps in facilitating student learning and improving instruction. The methods of assessment can be either formal or informal. Assessment is a process of collecting, receiving, and using data for the purpose of improvement in the learning process. The primary purpose of assessment in social science is to give learners feedback and setting standards for them to strive towards so that better learning outcomes could be achieved.

97(A). The last and 24th Tirthankara of the Jainas, Vardhamana Mahavira, also spread his message around this time, i.e. 2500 years ago.
He was a Kshatriya prince of the Lichchhavis, a group that was part of the Vajji sangha. At the age of thirty, he left home and went to live in a forest. For twelve years he led a hard and lonely life, at the end of which he attained enlightenment.

98(B). Statement B is correct.
There are several ways of finding out about the past. One is to study inscriptions.
- These are writings on relatively hard surfaces such as stone or metal.
- Sometimes, kings got their orders inscribed so that people could see, read and obey them.
- There are other kinds of inscriptions as well, where men and women (including kings and queens) recorded what they did.
- For example, kings often kept records of victories in battle.
- All inscriptions contain both scripts and languages.
- Languages that were used, as well as scripts, have changed over time.
- Scholars understand through a process known as decipherment.

99(B). Statement C is correct.
There are several ways of describing people in terms of the work they do, the language they speak, the place they belong to, their family, their communities and cultural practices.
Sometimes, the people who composed the hymns described themselves as Aryas and called their opponents Dasas or Dasyus. These were people who did not perform sacrifices and probably spoke different languages. Later, the term Dasa (and the feminine Dasi) came to mean slave. Slaves were women and men who were often captured in war. They were treated as the property of their owners, who could make them do whatever work they wanted.

100(D). The first English factory was set up on the banks of the river Hugli in 1651.
This was the base from which the Company's traders, known at that time as "factors", operated.
The factory had a warehouse where goods for export were stored, and it had offices

where Company officials. As trade expanded, the Company persuaded merchants and traders to come and settle near the factory.

By 1696 it began building a fort around the settlement. Two years later it bribed Mughal officials into giving the Company zamindari rights over three villages. One of these was Kalikata, which later grew into the city of Calcutta or Kolkata as it is known today. It also persuaded the Mughal emperor Aurangzeb to issue a Farman granting the Company the right to trade duty-free. The Company tried continuously to press for more concessions and manipulate existing privileges. Aurangzeb's Farman, for instance, had granted only the Company the right to trade duty-free. But officials of the Company, who were carrying on private trade on the side, were expected to pay duty. This they refused to pay, causing an enormous loss of revenue for Bengal.

Thus, we can conclude that statements B and C are true regarding the British.

101(B). Both (A) and (R) are true, but (R) is not the correct explanation of (A)

Various forms that the Non-Cooperation Movement took in different parts of India.

Different places in the country showed different reactions, given below:

- At Kheda in Gujarat, Patidar peasants organised nonviolent campaigns against the high land revenue demand of the British.
- In coastal Andhra and interior Tamil Nadu, liquor shops were picketed.
- In the Guntur district of Andhra Pradesh, tribals and poor peasants staged a number of "forest satyagraha", sometimes sending their cattle into forests without paying grazing fee.
- In Sind (now in Pakistan), Muslim traders and peasants were very enthusiastic about the Khilafat call.
- In Bengal too, the Khilafat-Non-Cooperation alliance gave enormous communal unity and strength to the national movement.
- In Punjab, the Akali agitation of the Sikhs sought to remove corrupt mahants – supported by the British – from their gurdwaras.

Therefore, we can say that both statements (A) and (R) are true, but (R) is not the correct explanation of (A).

102(D). (A) is false, but (R) is true.

Back in the 1920s, the Indian National Congress – the main party of the freedom struggle – had promised that once the country won independence, each major linguistic group would have its own province.

However, after independence, Congress did not take any steps to honor this promise. For India had been divided on the basis of religion: despite the wishes and efforts of Mahatma Gandhi, freedom had come not to one nation but to two.

As a result of the partition of India, more than a million people had been killed in riots between Hindus and Muslims. There was a reluctance to divide the country into linguistic lines as millions of people were killed in riots during partition.

Both Prime Minister Nehru and Deputy Prime Minister Vallabhbhai Patel were against the creation of linguistic states. After the Partition, Nehru said, "disruptions tendencies had come to the fore"; to check them, the nation had to be strong and united.

Or, as Patel put it: " the first and last need of India at the present moment is that it should be made a nation ... Everything which helps the growth of nationalism has to go forward and everything which throws obstacles in its way has to be rejected ... We have applied this test to linguistic provinces also, and by this test, in our opinion [they] cannot be supported."

103(B). A and B are correct but C is incorrect.

Monuments provide an insight into the technologies used for construction.

Between the seventh and tenth centuries, architects started adding more rooms, doors, and windows to buildings. Roofs, doors, and windows were still made by placing a horizontal beam across two vertical columns, a style of architecture called "trabeate" or "corbelled". Between the eighth and thirteenth centuries, the trabeate style was used in the construction of temples, mosques, tombs, and in buildings attached to large stepped-wells (baolis).

104(C). The Indian Sub-continent is one of the earliest civilizations in the World.

Indian civilization attracted many travelers and scholars in ancient times. Huien Tsang and Al-Beruni were two Foreign Travellers who came to India in the Ancient and Medieval Period respectively.

Si-Yu-Ki was written by Chinese pilgrim, monk, and scholar Hiuen Tsang Xang. He resided in India for 17 years in search of Buddhist texts.

Abu Rayhan Beruni or Alberonius was a Persian Scholar, wrote this book Tahqiq-i-hind. He travelled to South Asia in 1017 and authored a study of Indian culture (Tahqiqma li-l-hind) after exploring the Brahmanical traditions and Hinduism practiced in India during those days.

105(B). The lives of tribal groups changed during British rule.

Before the arrival of the British, in many areas, the tribal chiefs were important people. They enjoyed a certain amount of economic power and had the right to administer and control their territories.

In some places, they had their own police and decided on the local rules of land and forest management. Under British rule, the functions and powers of the tribal chiefs changed considerably.

They were allowed to keep their land titles over a cluster of villages and rent outlands, but they lost much of their administrative power and were forced to follow laws made by British officials in India. They also had to pay tribute to the British, and discipline the tribal groups on behalf of the British. They lost the authority they had earlier enjoyed amongst their people and were unable to fulfil their traditional functions.

Thus, it is clear that both statements (A) and (R) are correct. But (R) is not the correct interpretation of (A) as statement (R) does not explain why their functions and powers were changed considerably.

106(A). Temples and mosques were beautifully constructed because they were places of worship.

- They were also meant to demonstrate the power, wealth and devotion of the patron. Take the example of the Rajarajeshvara temple.
- An inscription mentions that it was built by King Rajarajadeva for the worship of his god, Rajarajeshvaram.
- We will also notice that names of the ruler and the god are very similar. The king took the god's name because it was auspicious and he wanted to appear like a god.
- Through the rituals of worship in the temple one god (Rajarajadeva) honoured another (Rajarajeshvaram).

Thus, it is clear that both (A) and (R) are true and (R) is the correct explanation of (A).

107(C). Many important changes happened in Indian society in the post Gupta period. The economy in the post-Gupta era:

- During the post-Harsha period, the literary and inscriptional evidence shows the advanced state of agriculture, trade and economy.
- It is also mentioned that different kinds of fields were selected for different classes of crops.
- In the field of industry, the oldest one is that of textile.
- The profession of weavers, dyers, tailors etc. is mentioned by the contemporary literature.
- Working in metal was also very popular during that period.
- Some centres of the metal industry were famous.
- Saurashtra (Gujarat) was famous for its bell metal industry while Vanga (Bengal) was known for its tin industry.
- The trade with South East Asia during the post-Gupta age registered a significant increase.

Both A and B is correct.

108(C). (A) is true, but (R) is false.
Nuclear power is the fifth-largest source of electricity in India after coal, gas, hydroelectricity, and wind power.
As of November 2020, India has 22 nuclear reactors in operation in 7 nuclear power plants, with a total installed capacity of 6,780 MW. Nuclear power produced a total of 35 TWh and supplied 3.22% of Indian electricity in 2017. 7 more reactors are under construction with a combined generation capacity of 4,300 MW. India has a largely indigenous nuclear power program.
Ubiquitous resources are found everywhere are called ubiquitous resources, i.e. Air, land, water, etc. Nuclear minerals are available in India in a localized manner. They are not available everywhere.

109(A). A, B and C statement is false.
Mauna Kea is located in the Pacific Ocean. Mauna Kea mountain is extended both below and above sea level. Mauna Kea's summit is at 13,796 feet (4,205 meters) above sea level, but it extends about 19,700 feet (6000 meters) below the water's surface. Therefore, its total height is 33,500 feet (10,210 meters), nearly a mile taller than Mount Everest.

110(D). Asia is the largest continent. It covers about one-third of the total land area of the earth. The continent lies in the Eastern Hemisphere. The Tropic of Cancer passes through this continent. Asia is separated from Europe by the Ural mountains on the west. The combined landmass of Europe and Asia is called Eurasia (Europe + Asia).
It is clear that the mentioned statements are the features of Asia.

111(D). Oceans are a major part of the hydrosphere. They are all interconnected. The three chief movements of ocean waters are the waves, the tides and the ocean currents. The level of seawater remains the same everywhere. The elevation of the land is measured from the sea level of the sea, which is taken as zero.
From the above, we can conclude that all statements A, B and C are correct.

112(C). Temperate Evergreen Forests:These forests are located in the mid latitudinal coastal region.
Temperate evergreen forests are found predominantly in areas with warm summers and cool winters.
• Region: Eastern margin of the continents like in South-East USA, South China and South-East Brazil.
• Trees: Hard and softwood trees like oak, pine, eucalyptus.
Thus, the statement A and B describe the Temperate Evergreen Forests.

113(C). Ceres is the largest asteroid present between the orbit of Mars and Jupiter.
Ceres is also known as a dwarf planet. It is so much bigger and so different from the rocky neighbours that scientists classified it as a dwarf planet in 2006. Even though it comprises 25 per cent of the asteroid belt's total mass, tiny Pluto is still 14 times more massive. Ceres, Vesta, and Psyche are some famous asteroids of the solar system. Scientists are of the view that asteroids are parts of a planet, which exploded many years back.
From the above, it is clear that statement C is correct regarding asteroids.

114(B). The interior of the earth can be divided into 3 different layers – crust, mantle, and core. The crust is the outermost layer of the earth, and the core is the innermost layer of the earth, located at a depth of 2900 Km.
The crust is the outermost solid part of the earth. It is fragile. It is the thinnest of all the layers. The thickness of the crust varies under the oceanic and continental areas. Oceanic crust is thinner as compared to the continental crust. The continental crust is thicker in the areas of major mountain systems. It is about 35 km on the continental masses and only 5 km on the ocean floors.

115(C). Permanent winds: The winds that blow constantly throughout the year are called Permanent Winds. They also blow constantly in a particular direction. The trade winds, westerlies and easterlies.
Forms of precipitation: The most common types of precipitation are rain, snow, hail, and sleet. Rain is precipitation that falls to the surface of the Earth as water droplets.
Pressure belts: On the earth's surface, there are seven pressure belts (3 low and 4 high-pressure belts). They are the Equatorial Low, the two Subtropical highs, the two Subpolar lows, and the two Polar highs. Except for the Equatorial low, the others form matching pairs in the Northern and Southern Hemispheres.

116(C). Four main seasons can be identified in India – the cold-weather season, the hot weather season, the advancing monsoon, and the retreating monsoon with some regional variations.
The cold weather season begins from mid-November in northern India and stays till February. December and January are the coldest months in the northern part of India. The temperature decreases from the south to the north.
The average temperature of Chennai, on the eastern coast, is between 24° – 25° Celsius, while in the northern plains, it ranges between 10°C and 15° Celsius. Days are warm and nights are cold. Frost is common in the north and the higher slopes of the Himalayas experience snowfall.
During this season, the northeast trade winds prevail over the country. They blow from land to sea and hence, for the most part of the country, it is a dry season. Some amount of rainfall occurs on the Tamil Nadu coast from these winds as here they blow from sea to land.
In the northern part of the country, a feeble high-pressure region develops, with light winds moving outwards from this area. Influenced by the relief, these winds blow through the Ganga valley from the west and the northwest. The weather is normally marked by a clear sky, low temperatures, and low humidity, and feeble, variable winds.
Hence, all the statements given in the question comes true about the cols weather season or the winter season over the Indian subcontinent. Therefore, A, B, and C all are correct.

117(B). As per John V. Michaela's, social studies are concerned with man and his interaction with his social and physical environment; they deal with human relationships. The central function of social studies is identical to the central purpose of education – the development of democratic citizenship. (S. K. Kochhar, The Teaching of Social Studies, 1984-First Edition). The objectives of teaching the social sciences at the upper primary stage are:
• To develop an understanding of the earth as the habitat of humankind and other forms of life.
• To initiate the learner into a study of her/ his own region, state, and country in the global context.
• To initiate the learner into a study of India's past, with references to contemporary development in other parts of the world.
• To introduce the learner to the functioning and dynamics of social and political institution and processes of the country. At this stage, the subject areas of the social sciences – drawing their content from history, geography, political science, and economics – will be introduced.
• The child may be introduced simultaneously to contemporary issues and problems. Emphasis needs to be given to issues like poverty, illiteracy, child and bonded labour, class, caste, gender, and environment.

118(C). Both the above statements are true about inquiry approach.
In Inquiry Approach, the students are given a problem or a discrepant event. The students will ask the teacher questions to collect the data and they through interaction find out a satisfactory solution to a given problem or explanation to the given discrepant event. In this approach, the teaching-learning process is totally controlled by the students. The Inquiry Approach is the extension of the discovery

approach. In any inquiry discovery is always there but vice versa is not true. In this method cause and effect relationship is established and the teacher provides no cues to the students.

In Discovery Approach some cues in the form of a learning material is presented by the teacher to the students and using Inductive thinking, the students are expected to discover the concept or the generalization/rule. Therefore the teaching-learning process is partially controlled by the teacher and students also involved to a great extent.

In Expository Approach all the cues provided by the teacher while teaching, the deductive thinking wherein abstract content is differentiated by the teacher giving appropriate examples to the students. Teaching Learning process is totally controlled by the teacher.

119(B). Learning resources are texts, audio-video materials and digital aids that assist you in effective transaction of curricular content. The major learning resource is the textbook prepared by central and state governmental educational agencies while a number of other learning resources are also available. Learning Resources in Social Science:

Movies: Most of our schools may not be well equipped with infrastructural facilities like Television, Over Head Projector, Slide Projector, and Multimedia. Even if these facilities are been provided, teachers hardly use them due to one or the other reasons but movies can be a very good source for not only motivation and elaboration of points in the text but also for providing review and overview of the people, processes and phenomena.

Internet: a global computer network providing a variety of information and communication facilities, consisting of interconnected networks using standardized communication protocols.

Books: There are several types of books like textbook, reference books and manuals, periodicals, technical and professional magazines and journals, collections, and instructional materials.

Newspapers Clippings: Social science teacher should keep abreast of current events by reading a variety of newspapers. It is important to read newspapers which represent various points of view on current and controversial issues.

120(D). The PLI scheme was conceived to scale up domestic manufacturing capability, accompanied by higher import substitution and employment generation. Hence, statement 1 is correct.

The incentives, calculated on the basis of incremental sales, range from as low as 1% for electronics and technology products to as high as 20% for the manufacturing of critical key starting drugs and certain drug intermediaries. Hence, statement 2 is correct.

The Government introduced this scheme to reduce India's dependence on China and other foreign countries. It supports the labour-intensive sectors and aims to increase the employment ratio in India. Hence, statement 3 is correct.

This scheme works to reduce import bills and boost domestic production. Hence, statement 4 is correct.

However, PLI Yojana invites foreign companies to set up their units in India and encourages domestic enterprises to expand their production units.